THREE *by* THREE ILLUSTRATION DIRECTORY 2011

CURATED BY

Charles Hively
Design Director
3x3 Magazine

DESIGNED BY

Charles Hively

ART DIRECTOR

Sarah Munt

PRODUCTION ASSISTANT

Jessica Quiñones
Darci Bogdan

COVER ART

Serge Seidlitz

PRINTED BY

DiYa Corporation USA

PRINTED IN

Shanghai, China

THREE *by* THREE ILLUSTRATION DIRECTORY 2011

CURATED *by*

CHARLES HIVELY *Publisher*

3X3 THE MAGAZINE *of* CONTEMPORARY ILLUSTRATION

Richard M Abarno
Eleftheria Alexandri
A. Richard Allen
Toril Bækmark
Scott Bakal
Davor Bakara
Anna & Elena Balbusso
Barry Barnes
Beck
Naama Benziman
Kako Bergamini
Megan Berkheiser & Mike Caldwell
Guy Billout
Josée Bisaillon
Phil Bliss
Freddy Boo
Richard Borge
Jacqueline Kari Bos
Minako Saitoh Botsford
Shannon Robert Brady
Calef Brown
Nigel Buchanan
Marc Burckhardt
Chris Buzelli
Patricia Cantor
Steven Carroll
Q. Cassetti
Kat Chadwick
Joohong Chae
Lina Chen
Chie Chie
Marcos Chin
Cathy Choi
Nishant Choksi
Jamey Christoph
Julien Chung
Jim Cohen
Timothy Cook
David Copestakes
Christopher Corr
Martin Côté
Ned Culic
Peter Cusack
Margaret Cusack
Dave Cutler

Hugh D'Andrade
Andrea D'Aquino
Sylvie Daigneault
Paul Dallas
Lyman Dally
Toni Damkoehler
Sid Daniels
Sonja Danowski
Victoria Davis
Liam Derbyshire
Amy DeVoogd
Tim Dinter
Penelope Dullaghan
Jean-Manuel Duvivier
Mark Eberhardt
Elke Ehninger
Peter Ellis
Max Estes
Susan Farrington
João Fazenda
Brian Fitzgerald
Barry Fitzgerald
James Flames
Jessica Fortner
Jose Fragoso
Martin French
Chris French
Ryan (illworx) Friant
Sarajo Frieden
James Fryer
David Fullarton
Yoko Furusho
Tom Garrett
Beppe Giacobbe
Michael Gibbs
Eric Giriat
Michael Glenwood
Johanna Goodman
David Gothard
Aad Goudappel
Karen Greenberg
Molly Grundy
Constanze Guhr
Olaf Hajek
Antony Hare
Janne Harju
Takahisa Hashimoto

Lars Henkel
Kim Herbst
Denise Hilton-Campbell
Jakob Hinrichs
Agnieszka Hobbs
Mark Hoffmann
Sara Hofmann
David Hohn
Paul Hoppe
Mayumin Hosoya
Robin Hursthouse
IC4DESIGN
Hiromichi Ito
Lance Jackson
Marilyn Janovitz
Scott Jessop
Hayato Jome
Ross Jones
Kathi Kaeppel
Tibor Kárpáti
Terri Fry Kasuba
Hideki Kessoku
Don Kilpatrick III
Tatsuro Kiuchi
Jean-Christian Knaff
Urs J Knobel
Uli Knörzer
Katrina Kopeloff
Takashi Koshii
Jon Krause
Nora Krug
Thomas Kuhlenbeck
Anita Kunz
David Labrozzi
Anna Emilia Laitinen
Hugh Langis
Mathieu Lavoie
Catherine Lazure
Dongjun Lee
André Letria
Anson Liaw
Anders Lindholm
Caroline List
Brigitta Garcia Lopez
Amalia Low
Anne Lück
John MacConnell

Keith MacLelland

Jens Magnusson

Bruno Mallart

John Malloy

Christa Marquez

Tim Marrs

Jorge Mascarenhas

Bill Mayer

Melissa McGill

Jonathan McHugh

Josh McKible

Kagan McLeod

Luc Melanson

Solongo Mellecker

Aaron Meshon

Kate Miller

Peter Mitchell

Andrew Mitchell

Kelly Frederick Mizer

Gerald Moll

Christian Montenegro

Goni Montes

Leslie Moore

Joe Morse

Nick Mott

Shawn Murenbeeld

Chris B. Murray

Alex Nabaum

Toby Thane Neighbors

Gary Neill

Meredith Nelson

Robert Neubecker

Shaw Nielsen

Christopher Nielsen

Peg Nocciolino

Anja Nolte

James O'Brien

Tim O'Brien

Kate O'Leary

Donough O'Malley

Martin O'Neill

Jim Paillot

Cap Pannell

Papriko

Doug Panton

Soyoon Park

Nishan Patel

Valeria Petrone

Noah Patrick Pfarr

Leah Palmer Preiss

Elena Prette

Sean G. Qualls

Maurizio Quarello

Jason Raish

Claude Ramey

Steph Ransom

Maria Rendon

Marcela Restrepo

Marian Heibel Richardson

Carolyn Ridsdale

John Riordan

Lizzie Roberts

Paul Rogers

Kim Rosen

Matt Rota

Takayuki Ryujin

Joseph Salina

Shelley Savor

Jeremy Schilling

Florian Schmitt

Rick Sealock

Serge Seidlitz

Jason Seiler

Andrew Selby

Thom Sevalrud

Michael Sheehy

Steve Simpson

Laura Smith

Alenka Sottler

Carlo Stanga

Brian Stauffer

Judy Stead

Otto Steininger

Erika Steiskal

Daniel Stolle

Steven Streisguth

Squid

Steven Tabbutt

Binny Talib

Ai Tatebayashi

Dante Terzigni

Jacob Thomas

Davey Thompson

Angeline Thong

Sue Todd

Keiko Tokushima

Tim Tomkinson

Anthony Tremmaglia

Jim Tsinganos

Pol Turgeon

Richard Tuschman

Sara Tyson

Kurt Vargo

Riccardo Vecchio

Gary Venn

Marco Ventura

Goncalo Viana

Stefano Vitale

Sally Vitsky

Constanze Von Kitzing

Andrea Wan

Ellen Weinstein

Jakob Westman

Elyse Whittaker-Paek

Carl Wiens

Mick Wiggins

Jonathan Williams

Tania Willis

Katia Wish

Phil Wrigglesworth

Stephanie Wunderlich

Ayako Yamazaki

James Yang

Heidi Younger

Yeji Yun

Vincent Zawada

Drz (James) Zdaniewski

Tina Zellmer

Henning Ziegler

*Links to each artist's
site can be found at
www.3x3Directory.com*

CONTENTS

WHY NOT MORE ILLUSTRATION?
Page 10

HOW DO I FIND AN ILLUSTRATOR?
Page 12

HOW DO I WORK WITH ILLUSTRATORS?
Page 14

WHAT ABOUT PROBLEMS?
Page 16

CATEGORIES

CONCEPTUAL
Page 20

FIGURATIVE
Page 98

FASHION
Page 181

CHILDREN
Page 188

LANDSCAPE
Page 235

ANIMAL
Page 264

MEDICAL
Page 294

WHIMSICAL
Page 296

DECORATIVE
Page 354

LETTERING
Page 380

INDEX
Page 389

Why not more illustration?

I'm often asked why art directors don't use more illustration. And the truthful answer is far too few know anything about illustration.

They've never been taught about their choices. When I was coming up through the ranks I knew I had three tools in my toolbox: photography, typography *and* illustration. Today's educator's emphasize only two of those tools so young art directors have no clue that illustration exists and if they do they are fearful of engaging in finding and using an artist.

What will the client say? How do I know what I'm getting? What if I'm not pleased with the end result?

How do I find an illustrator?

Finding them is easy, you'll generally find them in the same locations as photographers: in annuals, juried shows, galleries and publications.

Hiring them is easy, too. It's really no different than hiring a photographer. With one exception. You have a concept that needs a visual—you may have come up with one yourself or the better plan is to work with the illustrator to develop the visual.

In my day I'd always show the client something in the layout but made it clear that I was asking for other ideas from the illustrator and it always worked. Good clients will respect a better idea

How do I work with illustrators?

Working with illustrators is fun, you're actually involved in the creative process as the idea develops.

Asking for ideas from someone whose sole job is visual imagery means you have an extra pair of hands and another brain on tap.

Working with a hesitant client can be a challenge but sharing that with the illustrator upfront means you're both invested in doing the best possible job.

What if there are problems?

Being a subjective world there will be times
when no one agrees and at that point every-
one is back to square one.

But take heart, illustrators will work with
you to make it right.

Showing a comp photo leaves little to the
imagination, making a leap of faith with an
illustrator can mean you'll end up with an
even better idea.

Working with an illustrator may be something
new for you but isn't that a gamble you're
willing to make?

THREE *by* THREE ILLUSTRATION DIRECTORY 2011

CURATED *by*

CHARLES HIVELY *Publisher*

3X3 THE MAGAZINE *of* CONTEMPORARY ILLUSTRATION

 Jakob Hinrichs JAKOBHINRICHS.COM

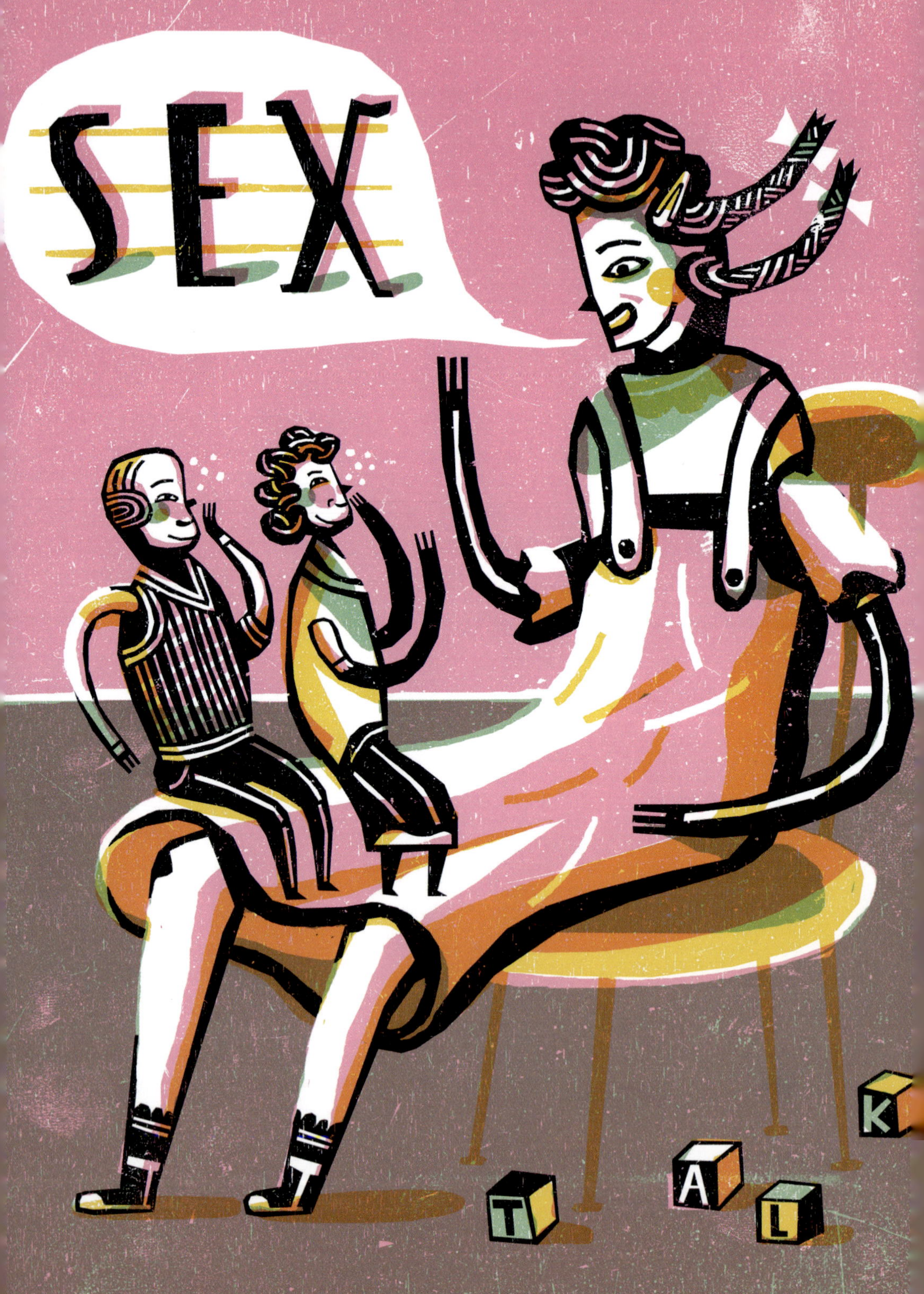

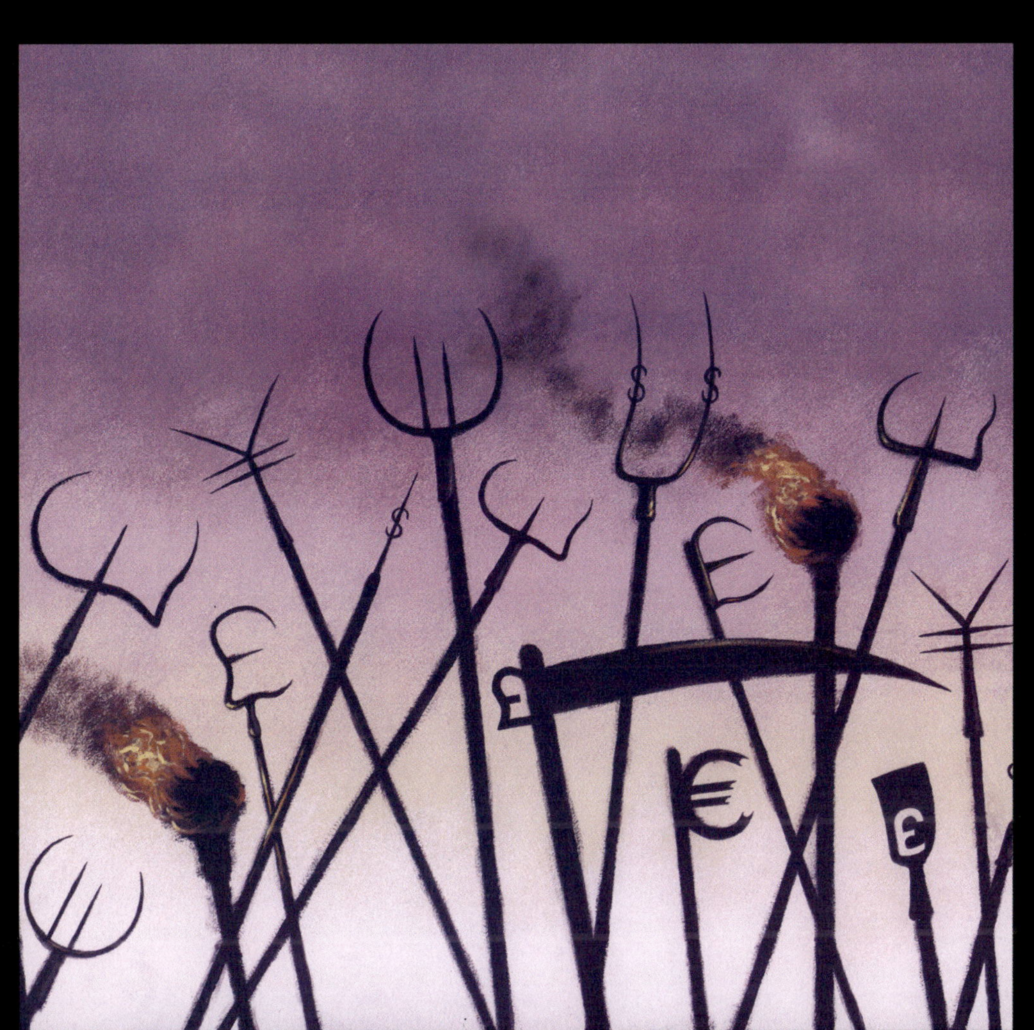

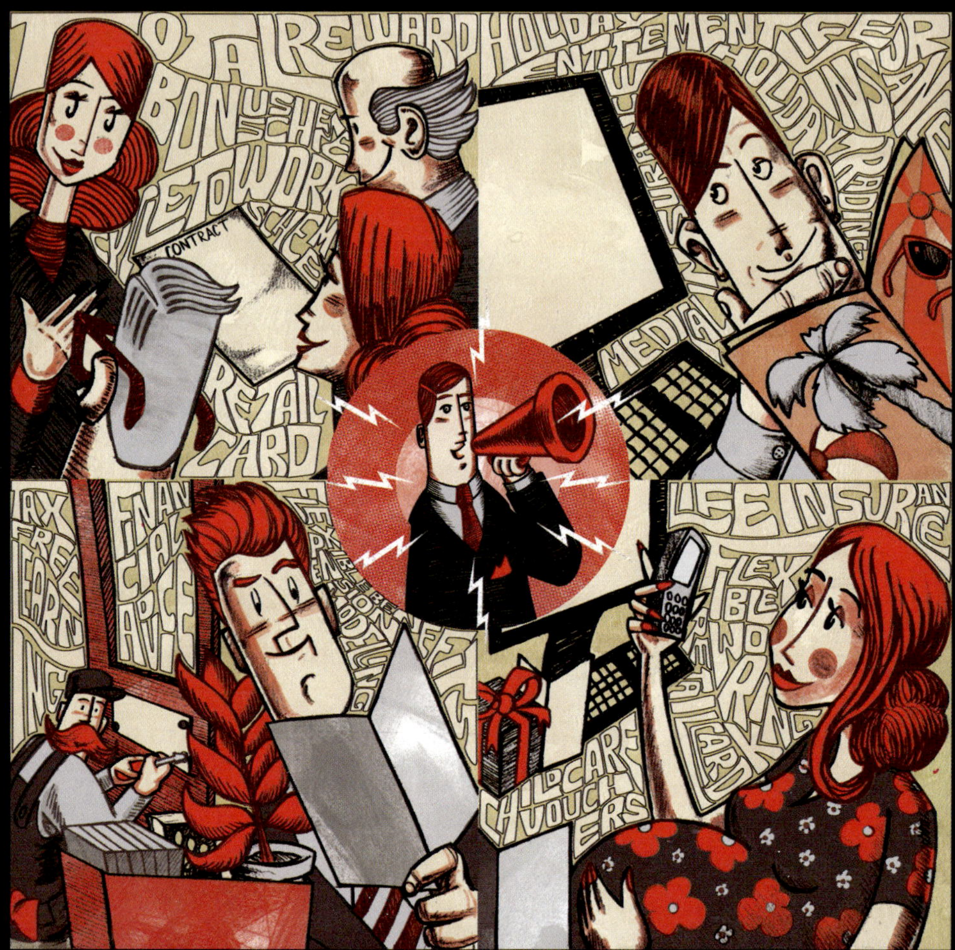
REWARD
HOLIDAY
ENTITLEMENT
BONUS
CYCLE TO WORK SCHEME
CONTRACT
RETAIL CARD
MEDICAL
TAX FREE LEARNING
FINANCIAL ADVICE
LIFE INSURANCE
FLEXIBLE WORKING
CHILDCARE VOUCHERS

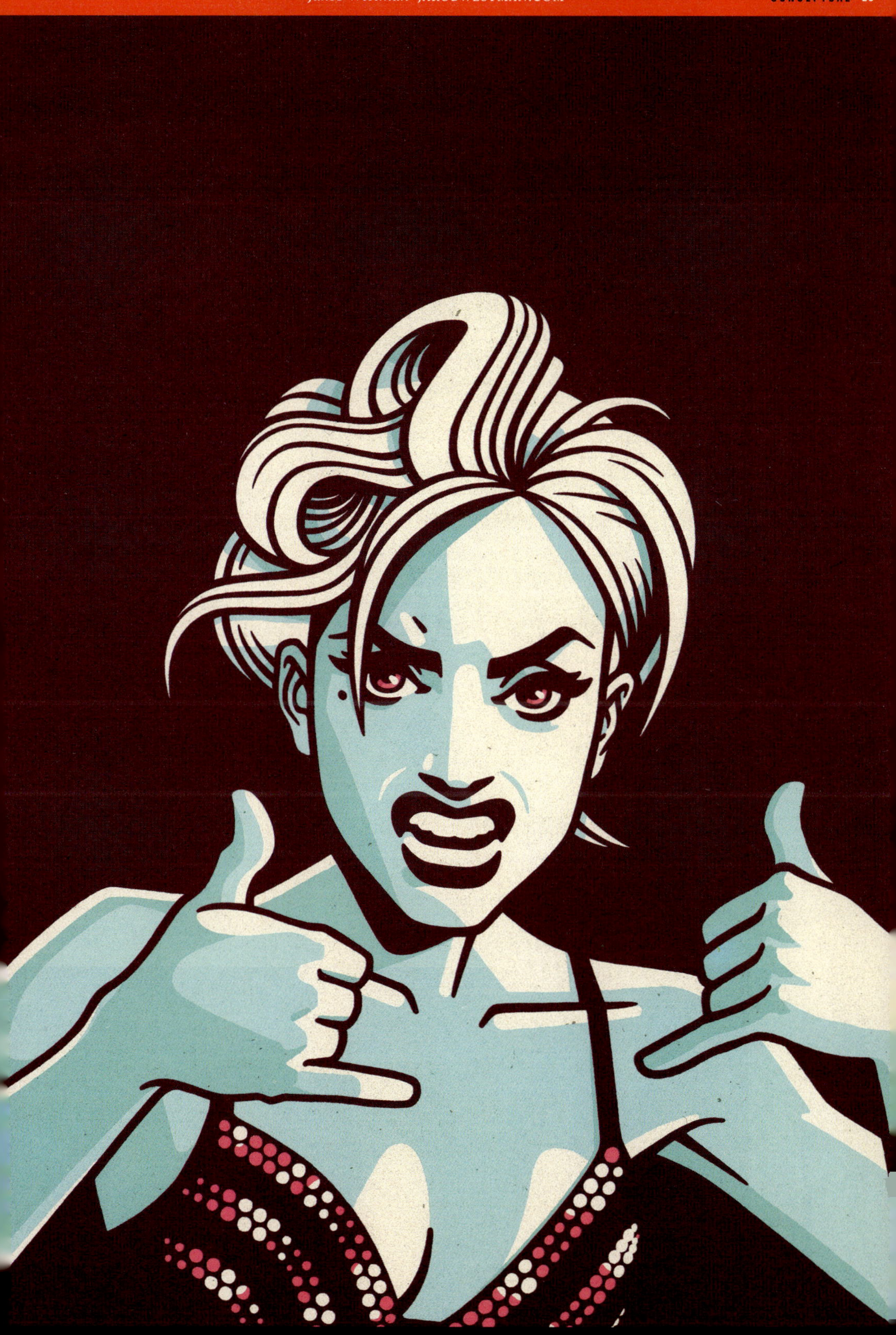

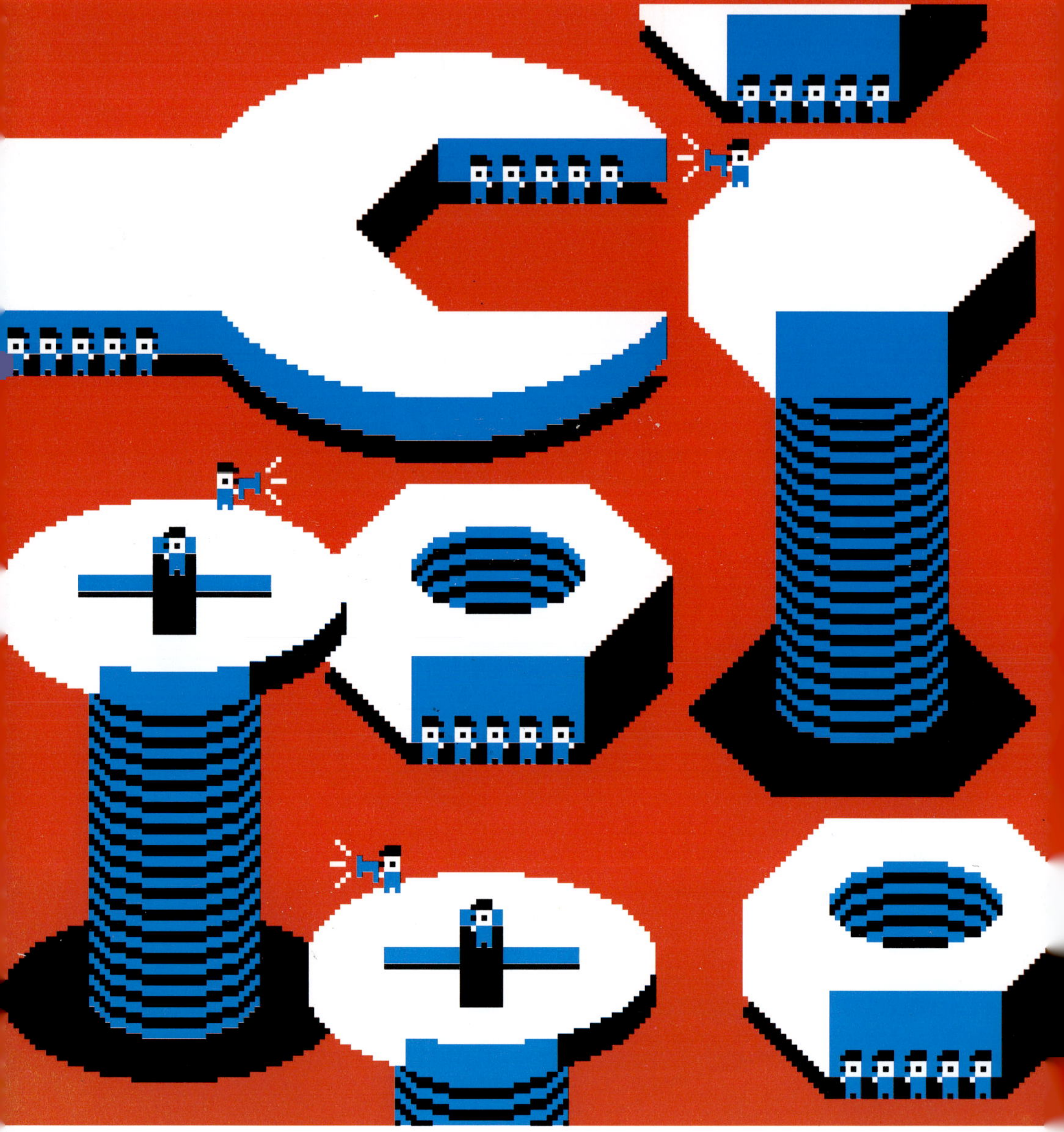

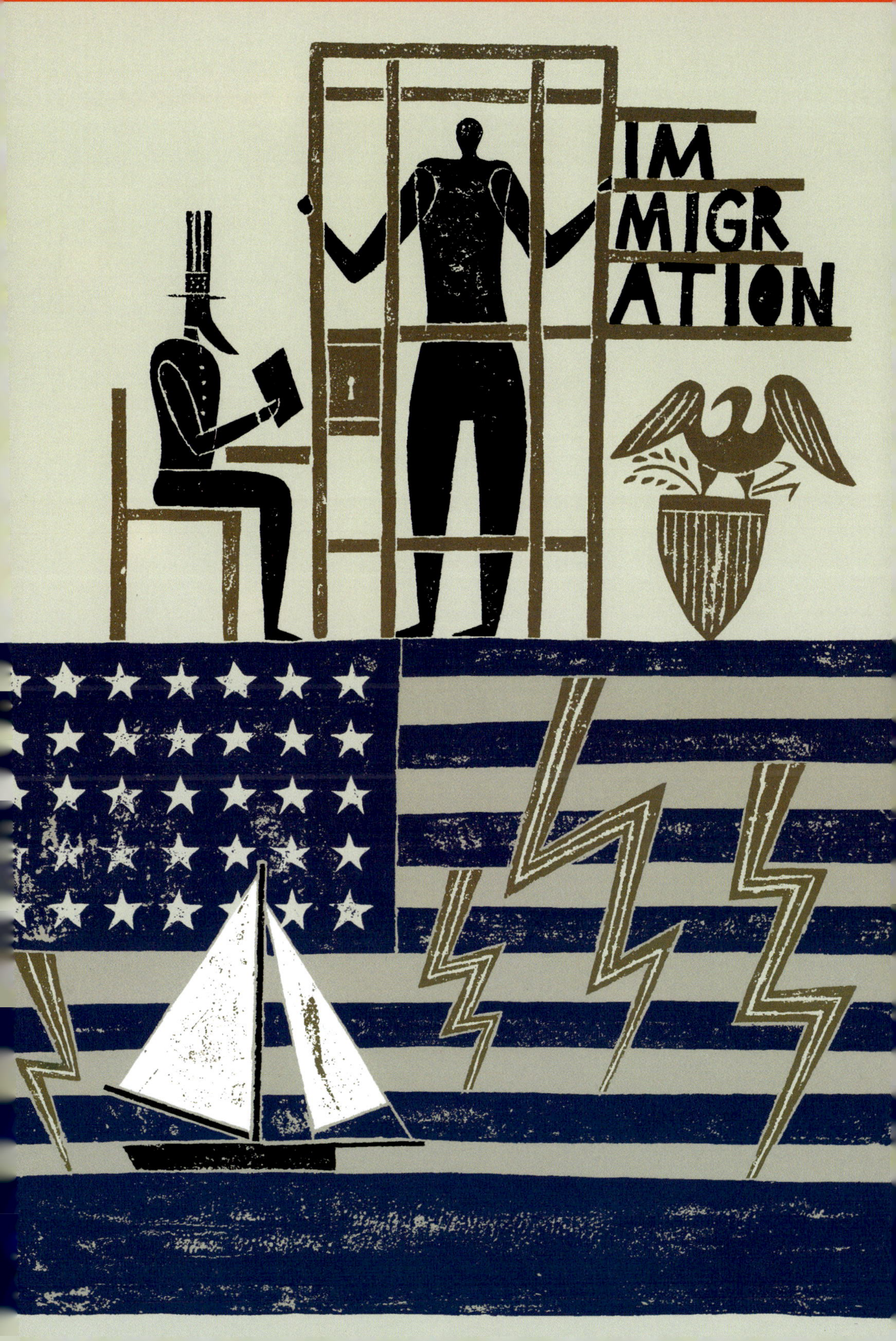

IM
MIGR
ATION

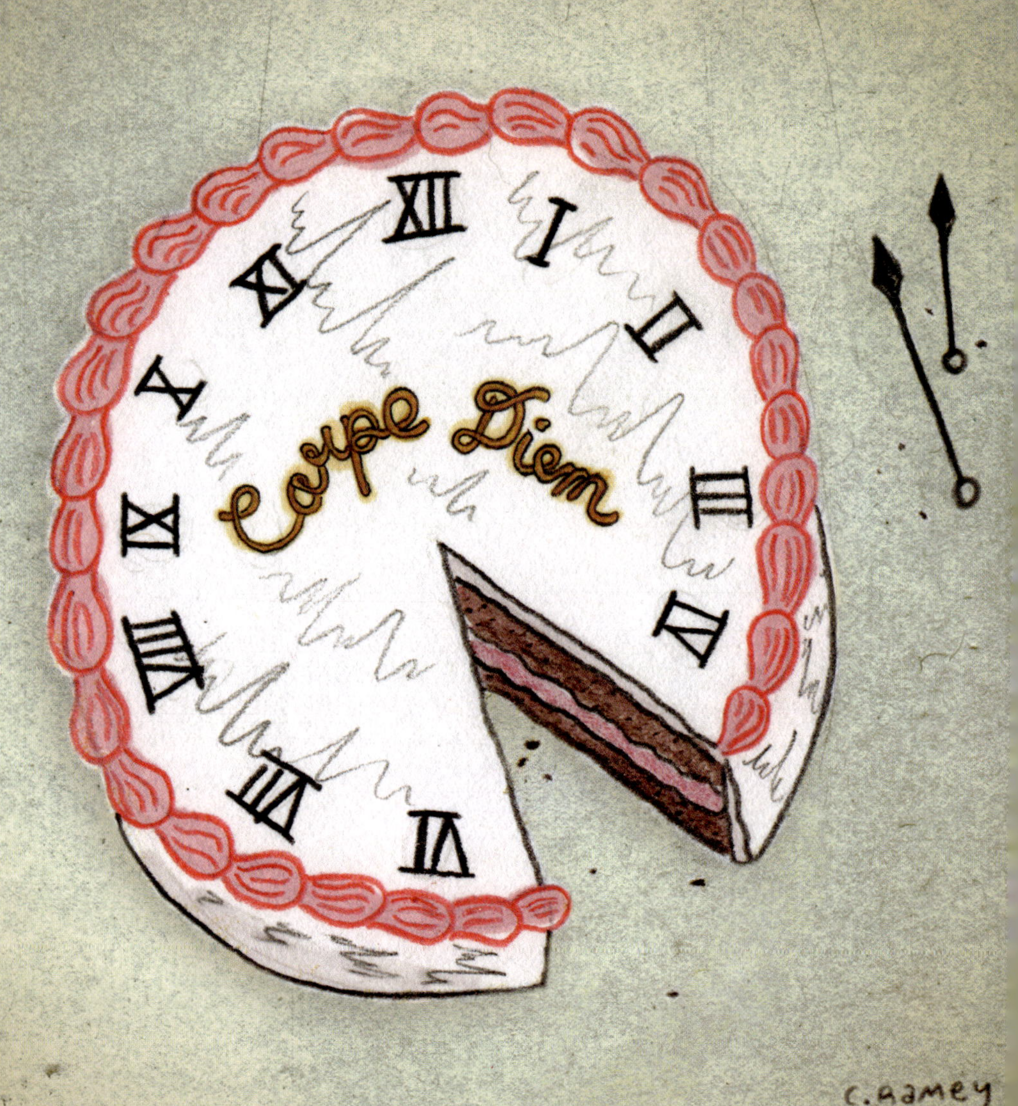
Carpe Diem

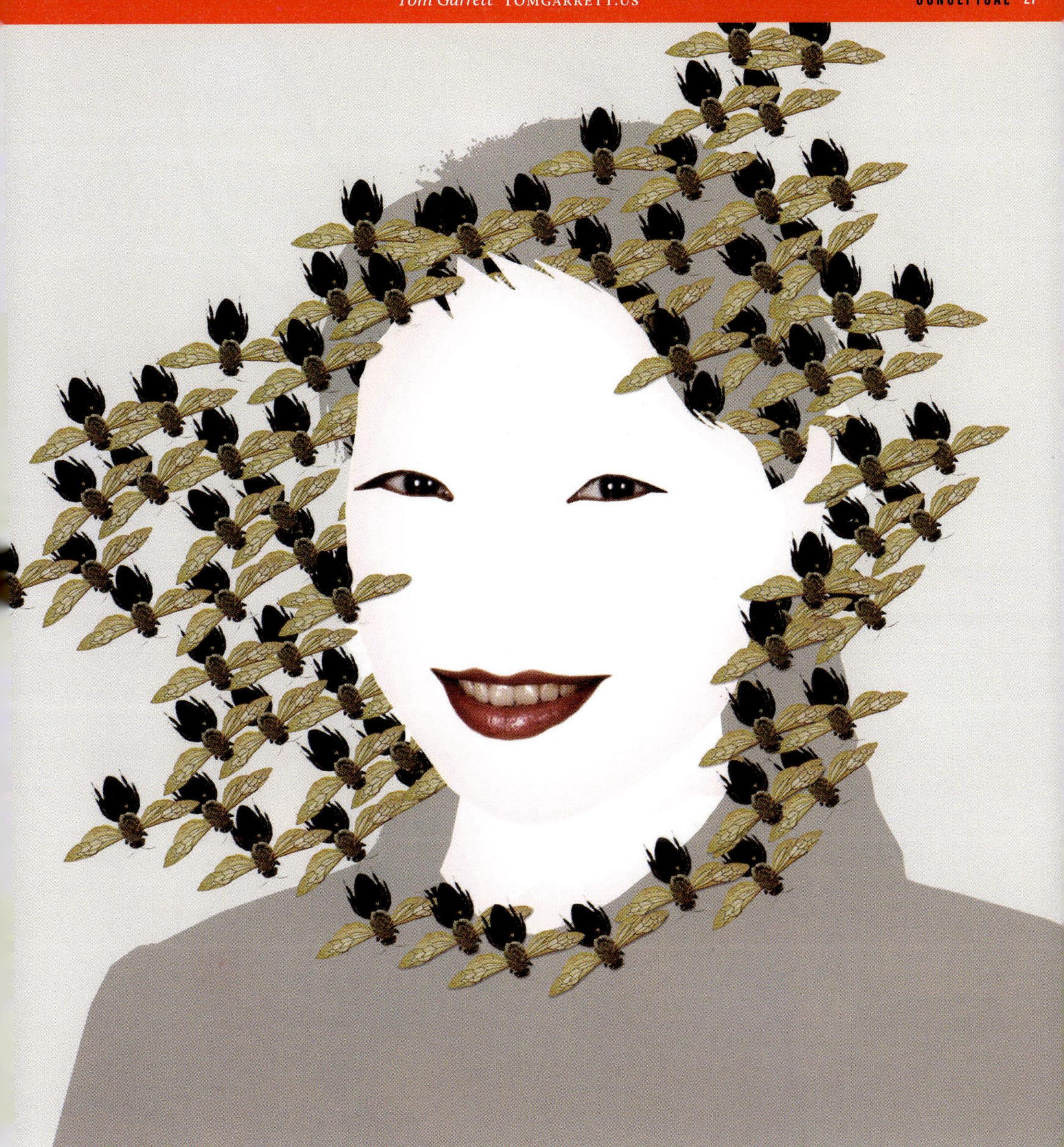

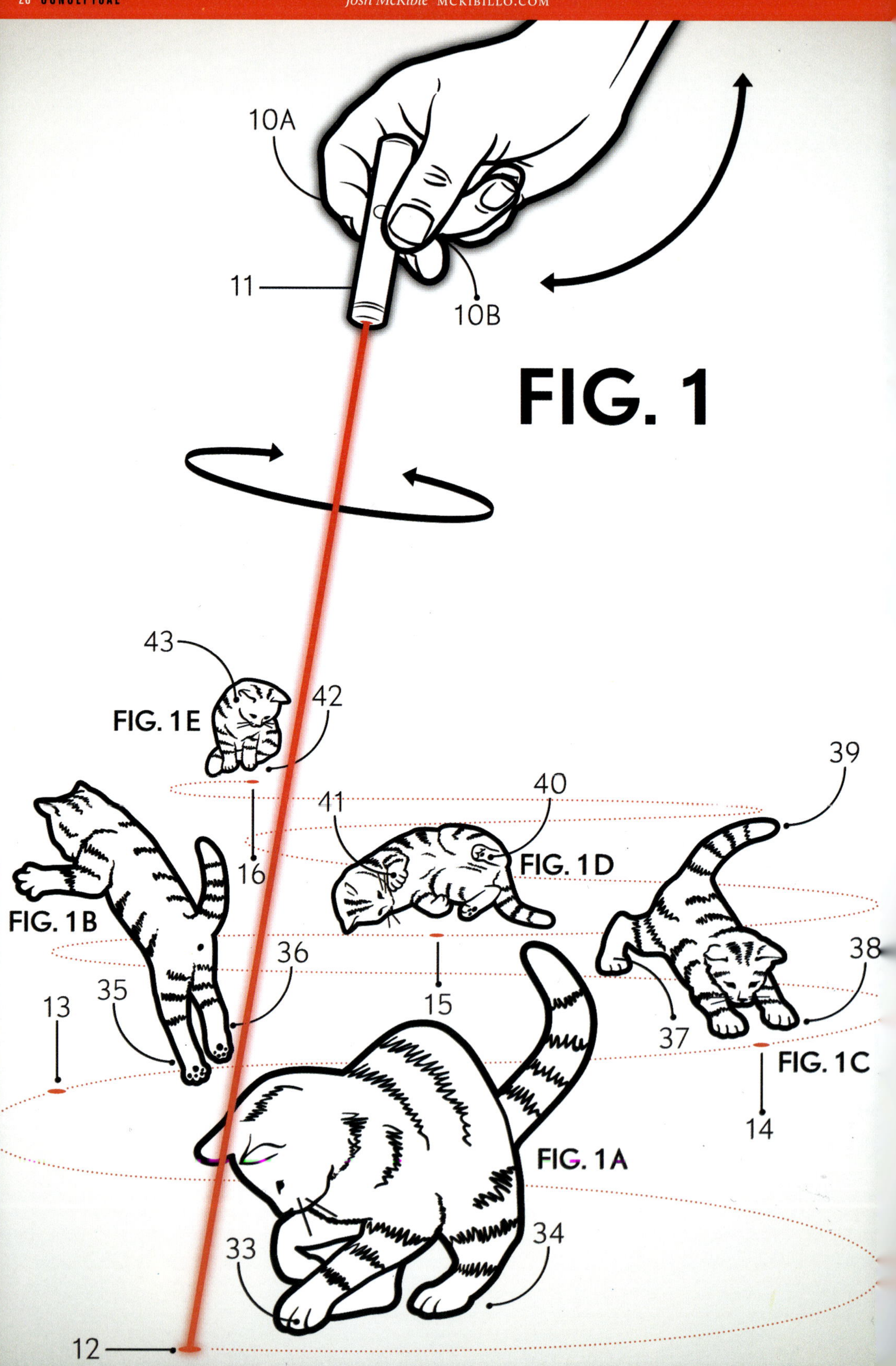
10A
11
10B
FIG. 1
43
FIG. 1E
42
41
40
FIG. 1D
39
16
FIG. 1B
36
35
38
13
15
37
FIG. 1C
14
FIG. 1A
33
34
12

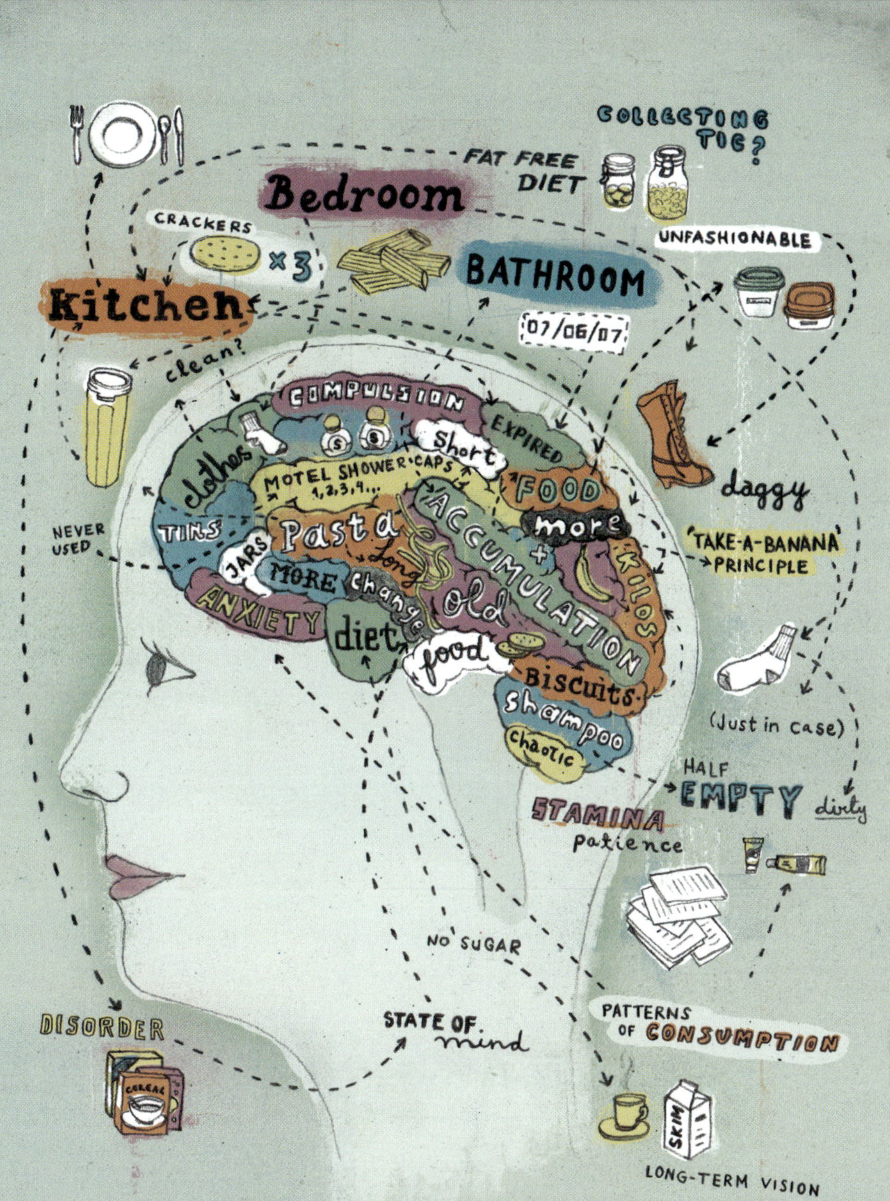
COLLECTING TIC?
FAT FREE DIET
Bedroom
CRACKERS
x3
UNFASHIONABLE
Kitchen
BATHROOM
07/06/07
clean?
COMPULSION
EXPIRED
Short
clothes
MOTEL SHOWER CAPS
1,2,3,4...
FOOD
daggy
NEVER USED
TINS
Pasta
ACCUMULATION
more
+
KILOS
TAKE-A-BANANA
PRINCIPLE
JARS
long
MORE
change
Old
ANXIETY
diet
food
Biscuits.
(Just in case)
shampoo
chaotic
HALF
EMPTY
dirty
STAMINA
patience
NO SUGAR
DISORDER
STATE OF.
mind
PATTERNS
OF CONSUMPTION
CEREAL
SKIM
LONG-TERM VISION

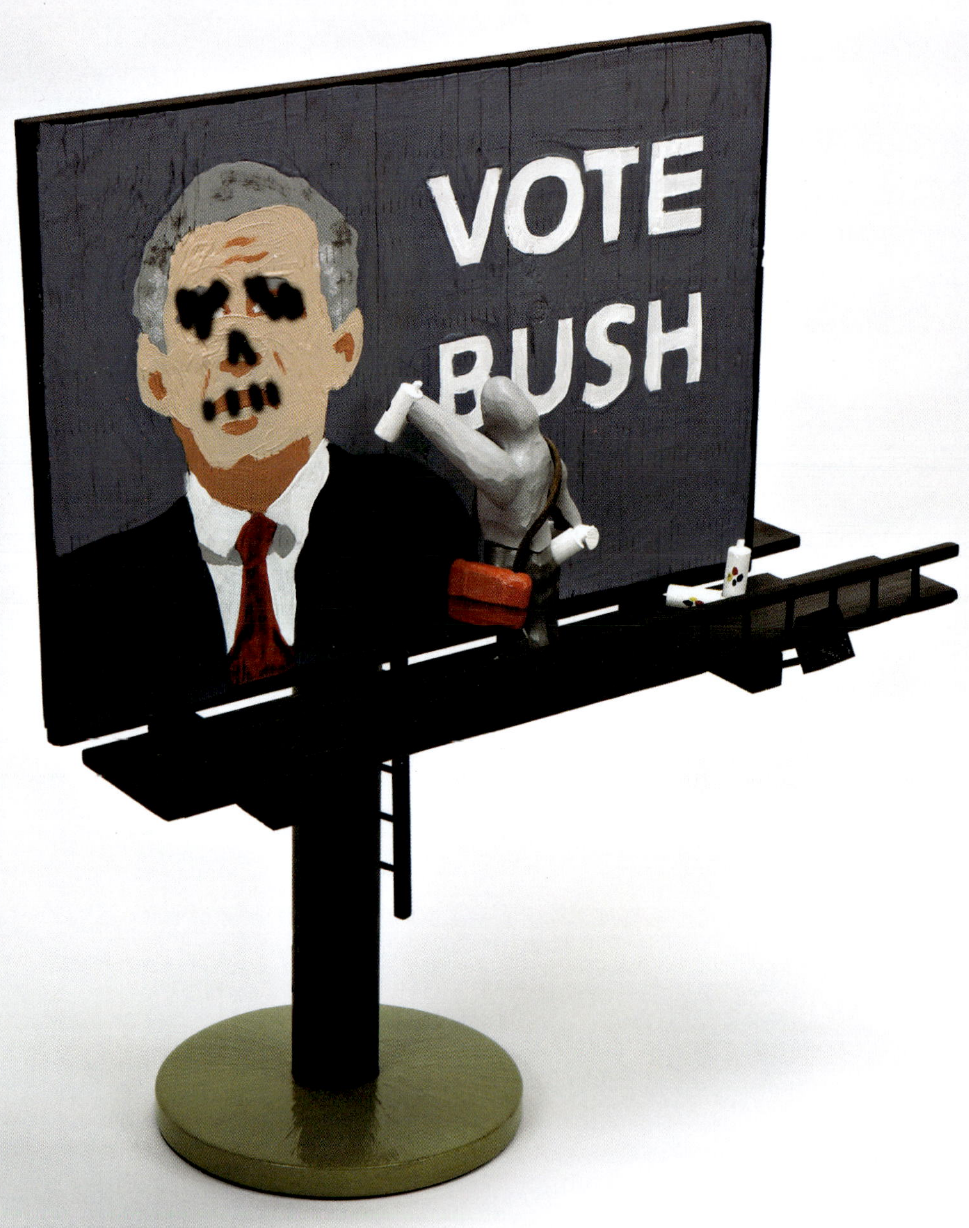
VOTE
BUSH

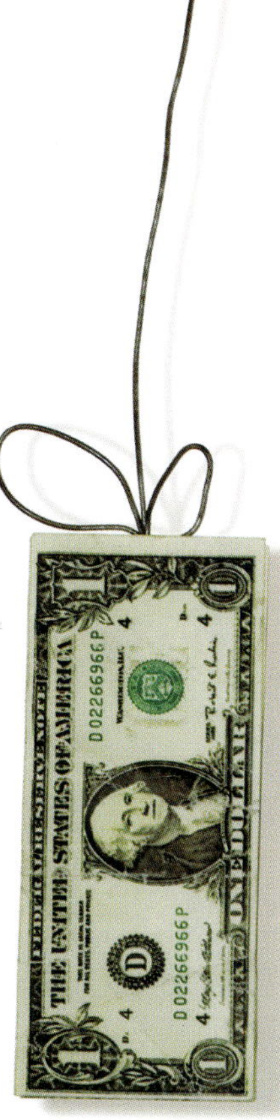

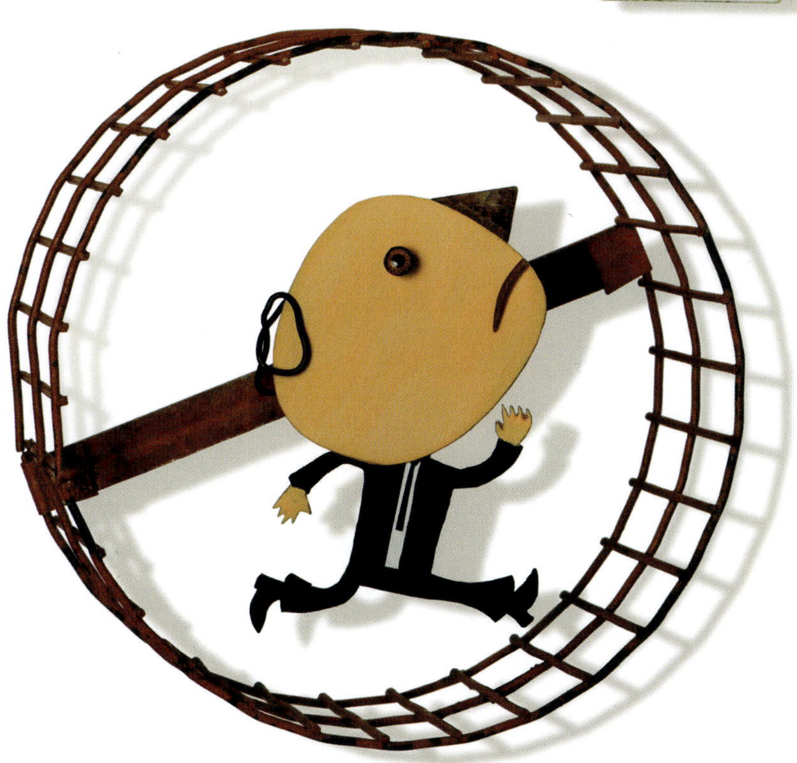

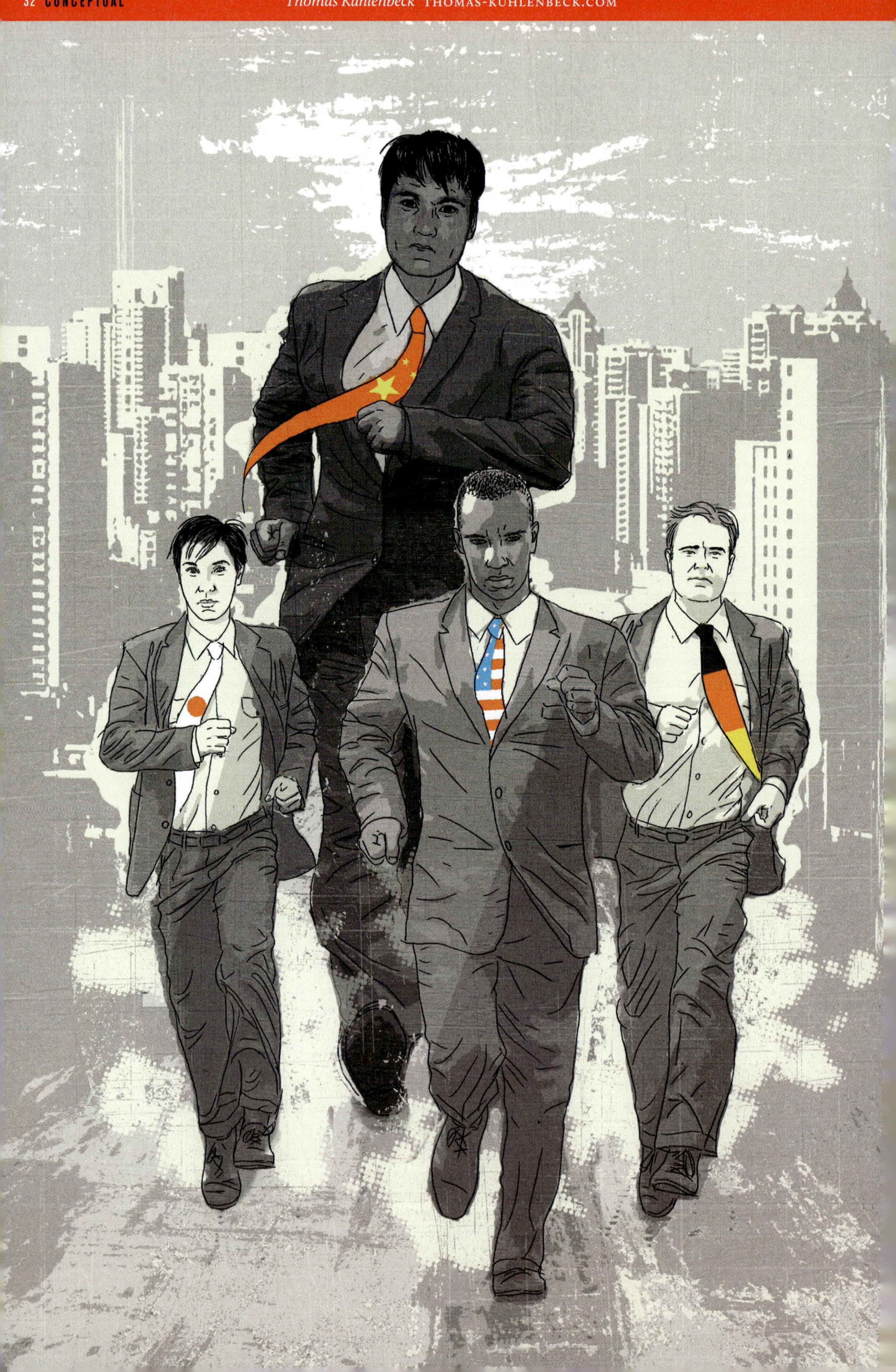

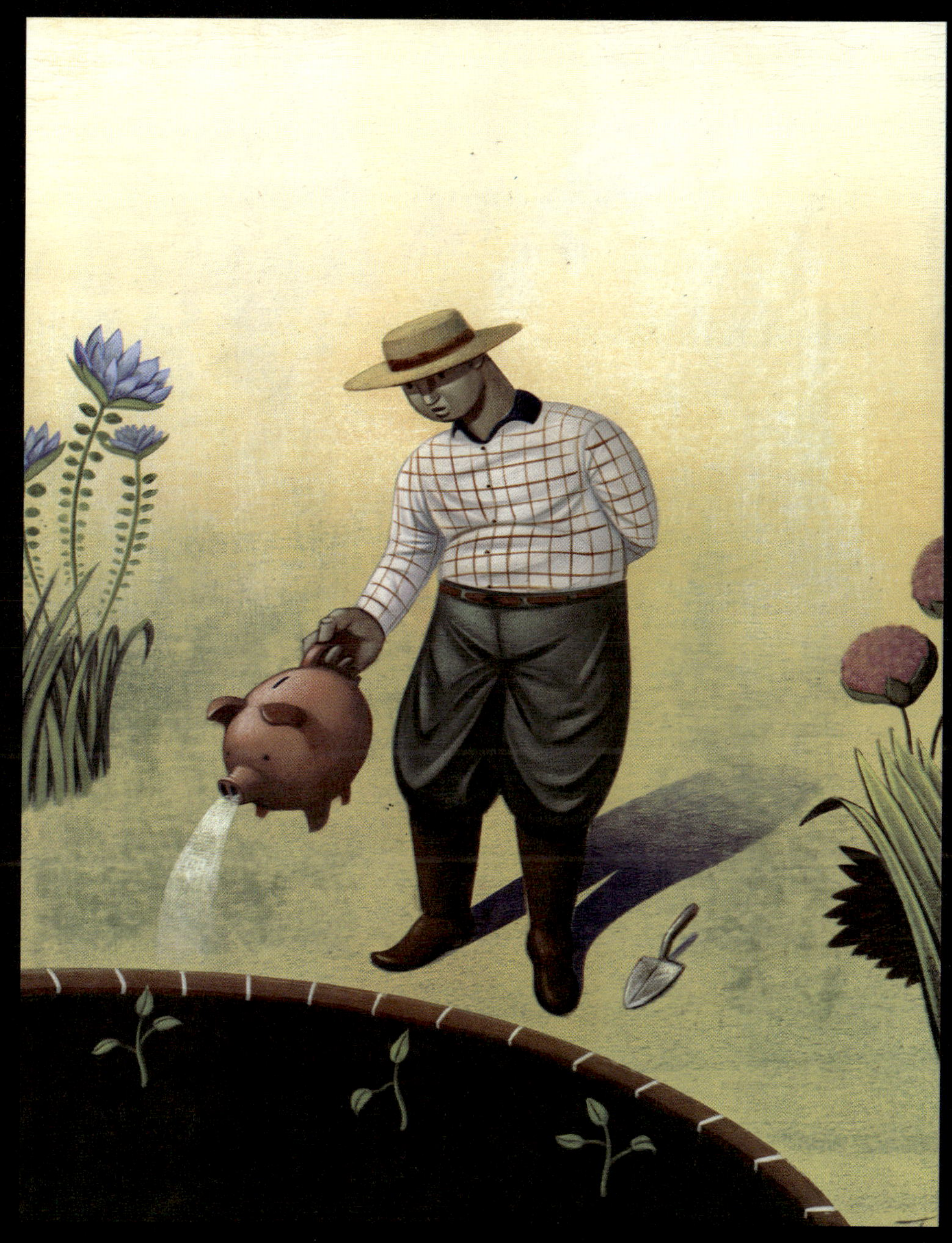

   Richard Borge RICHARDBORGE.COM

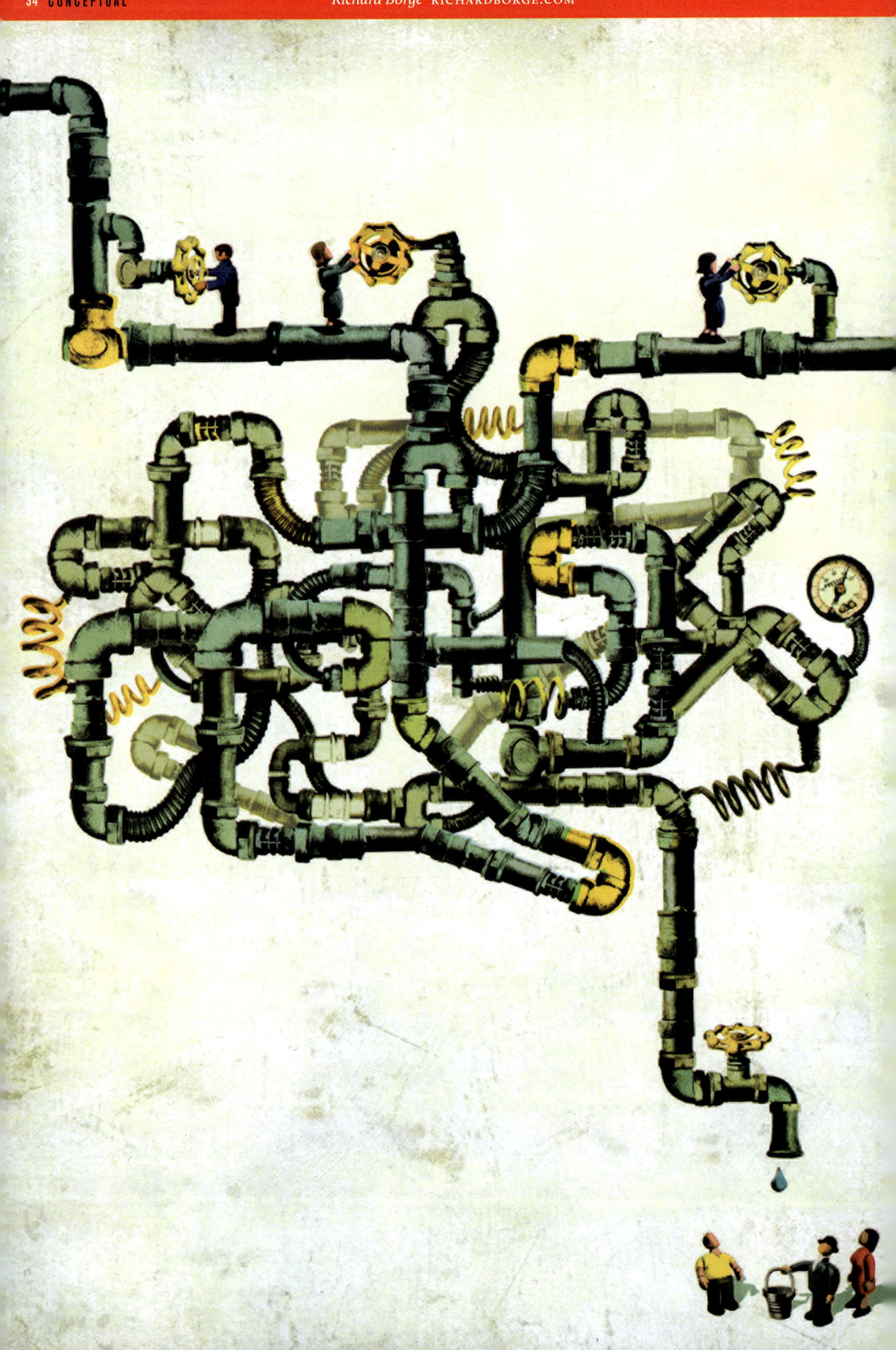

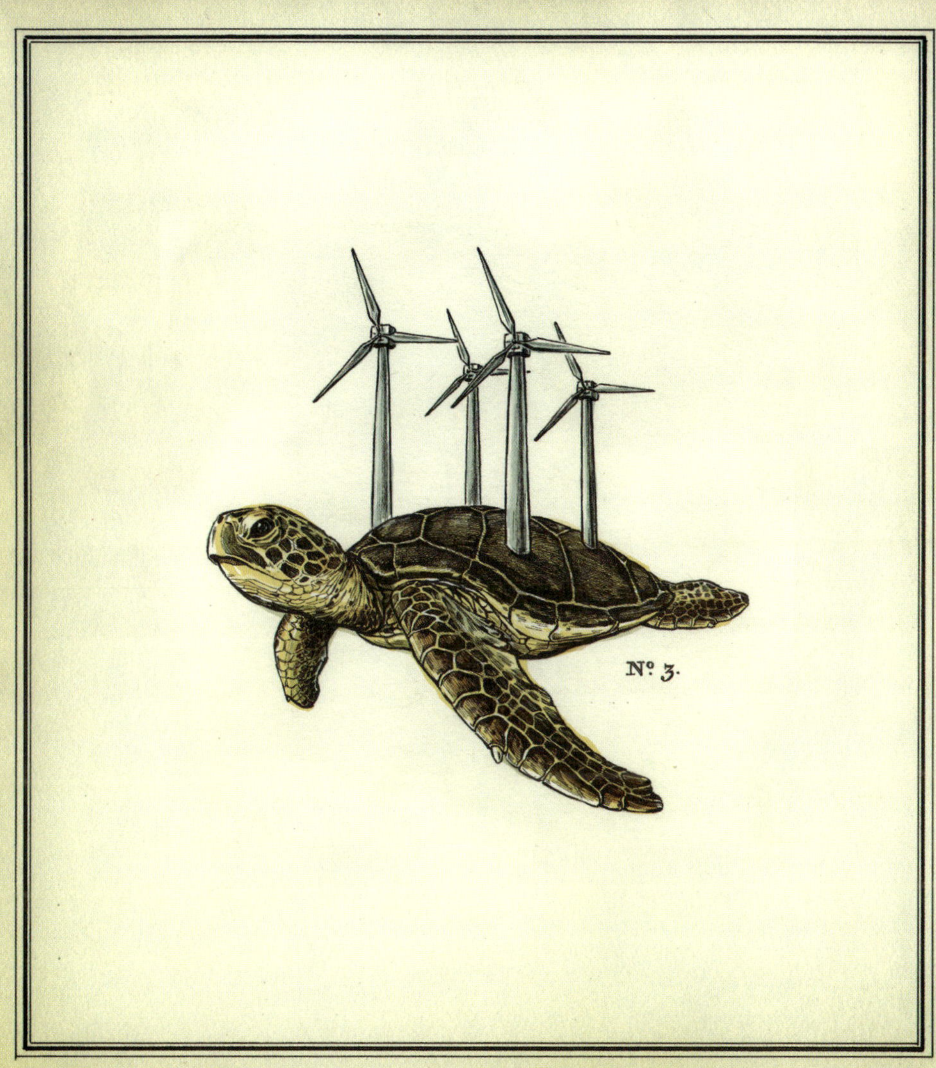
Nº 3.

Beppe Giacobbe BEPPEGIACOBBE.COM

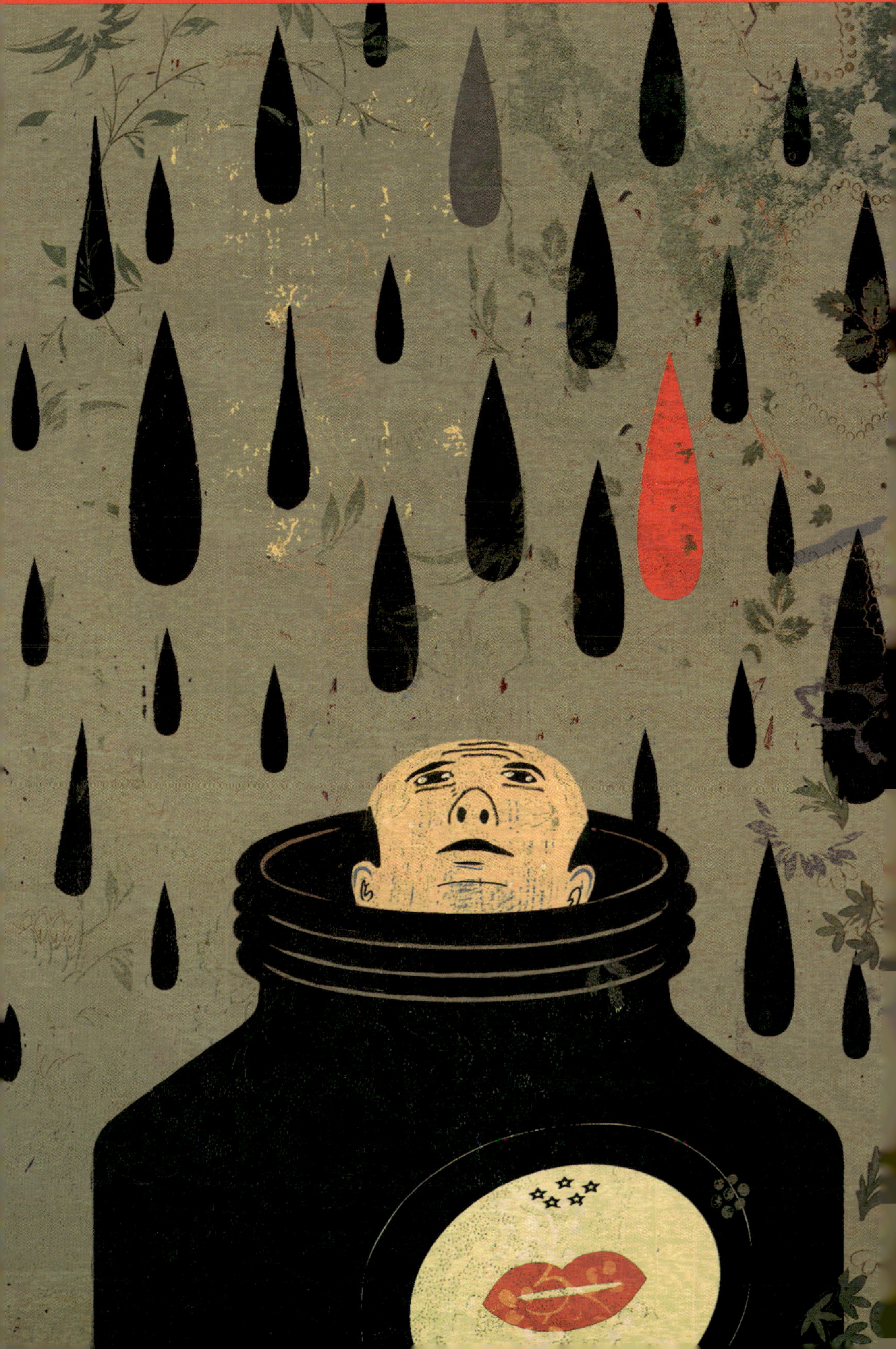

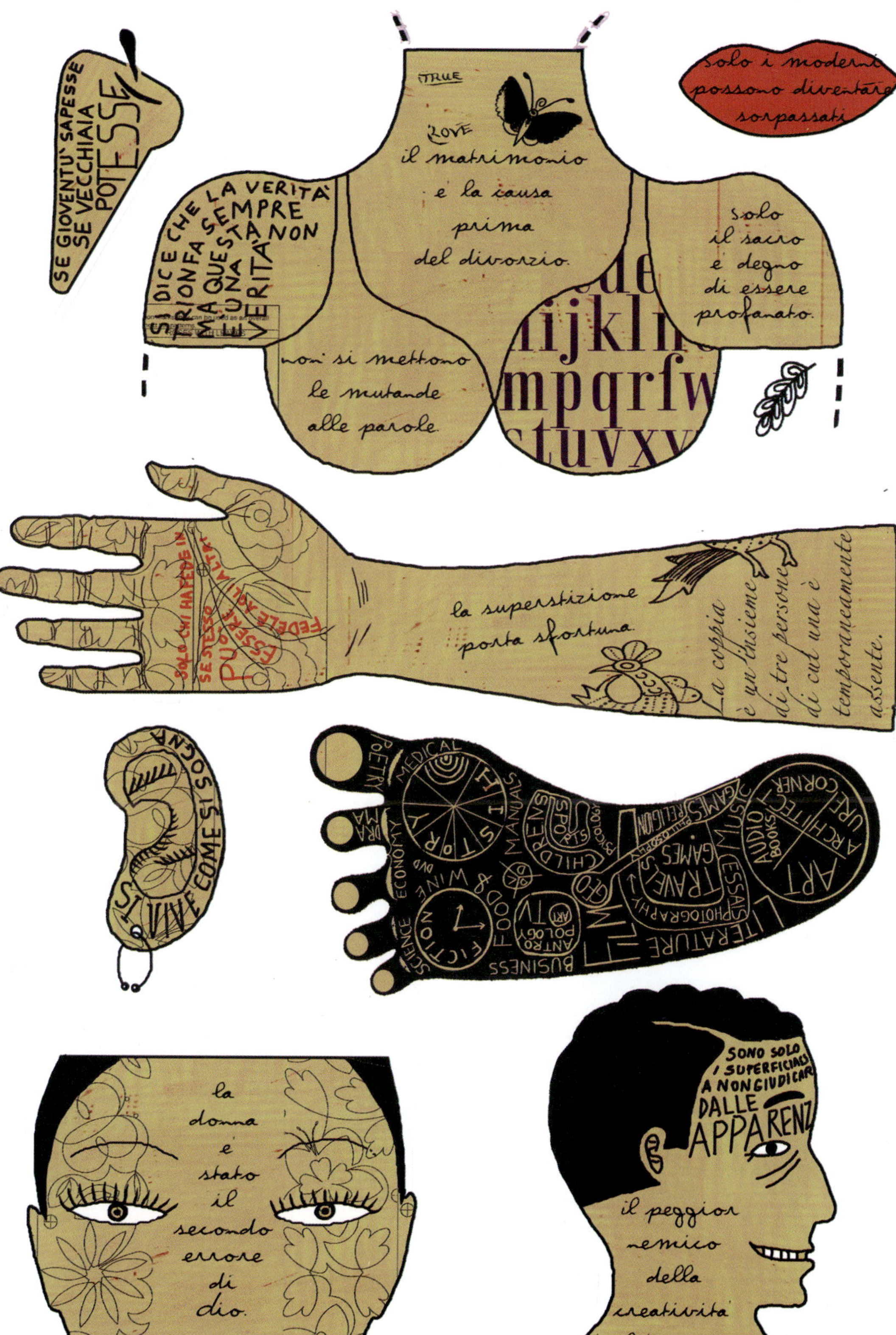
SE GIOVENTU' SAPESSE SE VECCHIAIA POTESSE
solo i moderni possono diventare sorpassati
SI DICE CHE LA VERITÀ TRIONFA SEMPRE MA QUESTA NON È UNA VERITÀ
TRUE
LOVE
il matrimonio è la causa prima del divorzio.
solo il sacro è degno di essere profanato.
non si mettono le mutande alle parole.
la superstizione porta sfortuna.
SOLO CHI HA FEDE IN SE STESSO PUÒ ESSERE FEDELE AGLI ALTRI
La coppia è un'insieme di tre persone di cui una è temporaneamente assente.
SI VIVE COME SI SOGNA
POETRY
MEDICAL
HISTORY
MANUALS
CHILDRENS
SPORTS
GAMES
RELIGION
PHILOSOPHY
PSYCHOLOGY
TRAVEL
MUSIC
ESSAIS
PHOTOGRAPHY
LITERATURE
FILM
ART
AUDIO BOOKS
ARCHITECT
URE CORNER
BUSINESS
ANTROPOLOGY
FICTION
SCIENCE
ECONOMY
FOOD & WINE
DVD
DRAMA
TV
ART
la donna e stato il secondo errore di dio.
SONO SOLO I SUPERFICIALI A NON GIUDICARE DALLE APPARENZE
il peggior nemico della creativita e il buon gusto

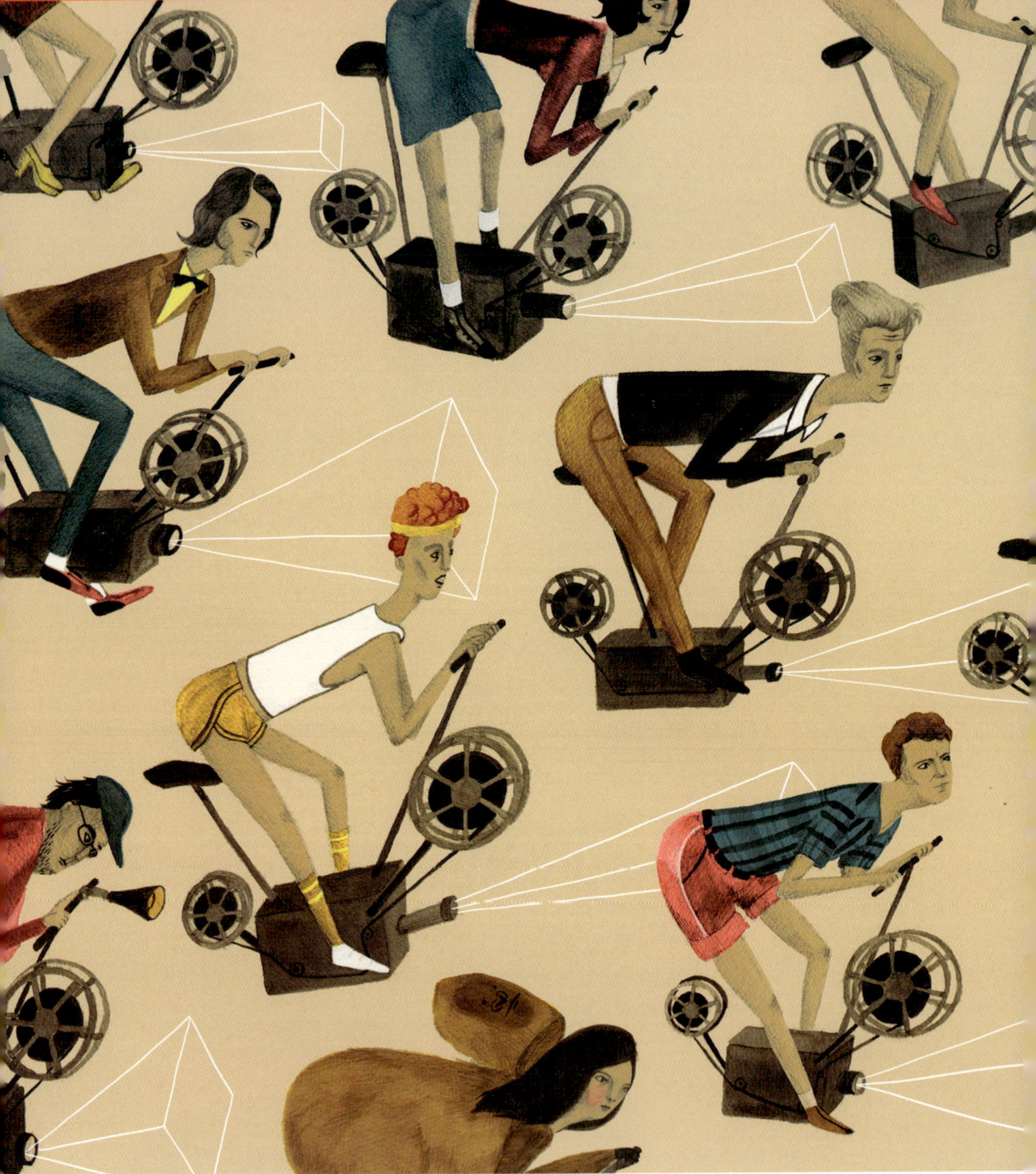

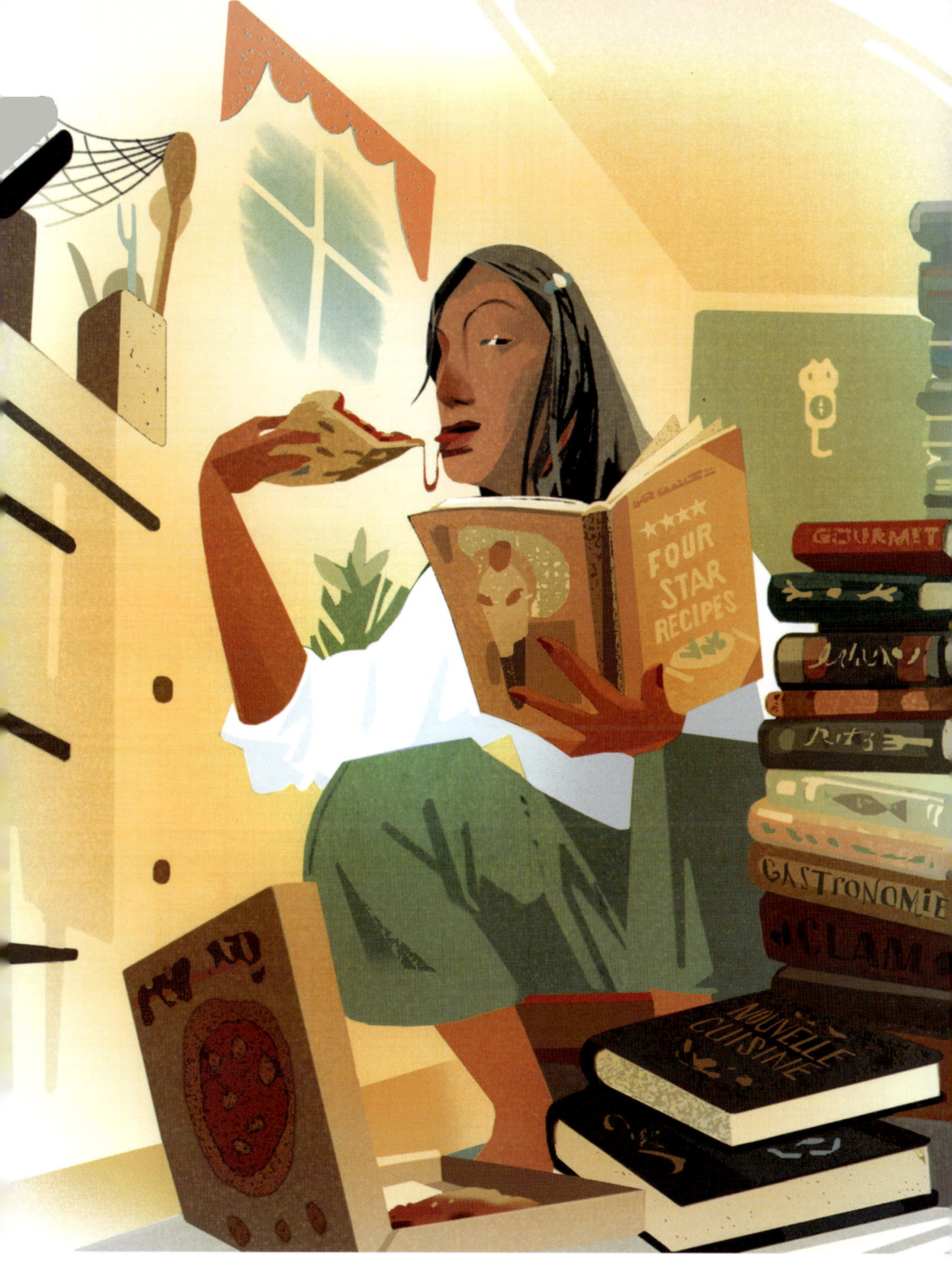
FOUR
STAR
RECIPES
GOURMET
GASTRONOMIE
CLAM
NOUVELLE
CUISINE

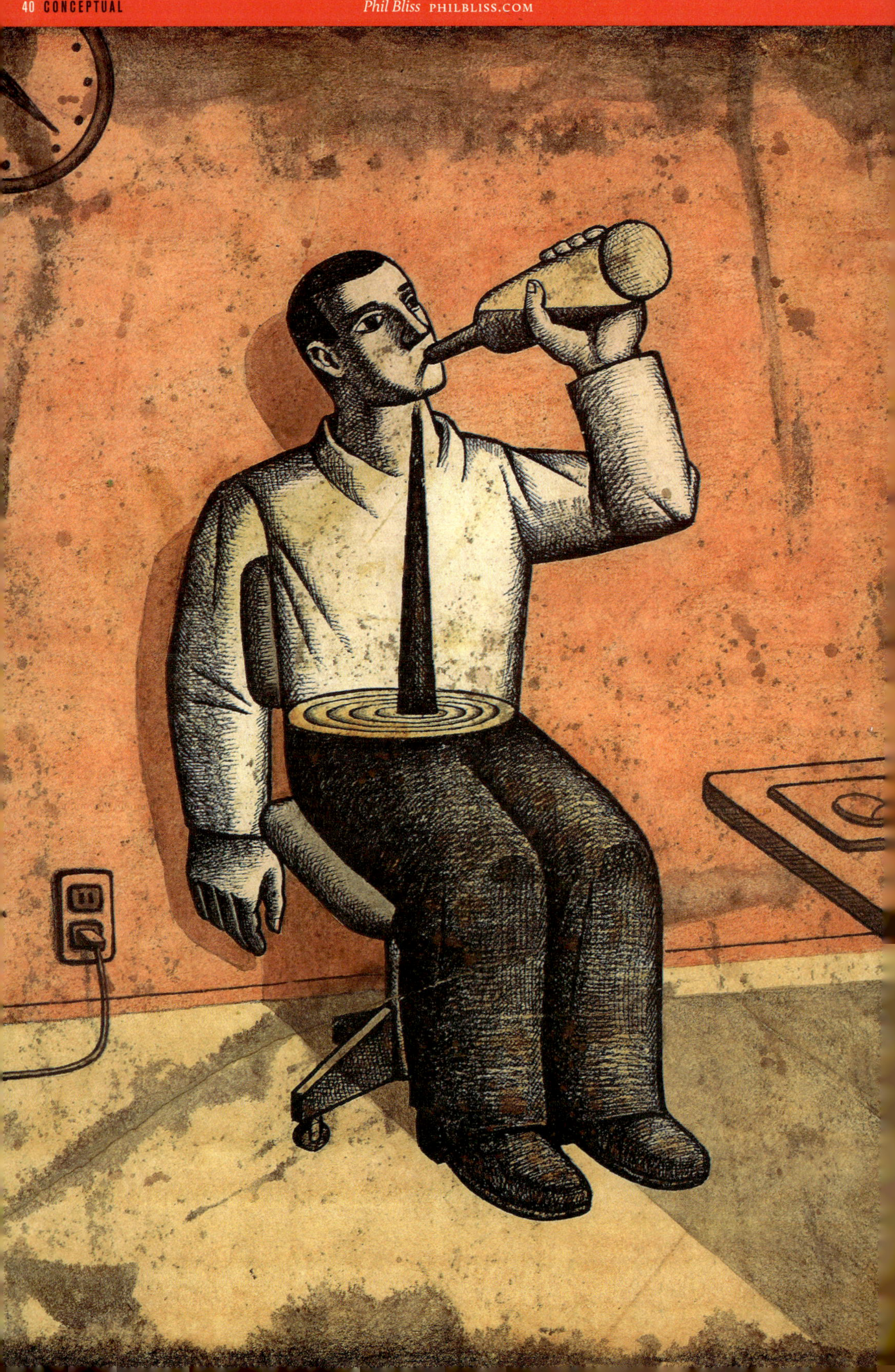

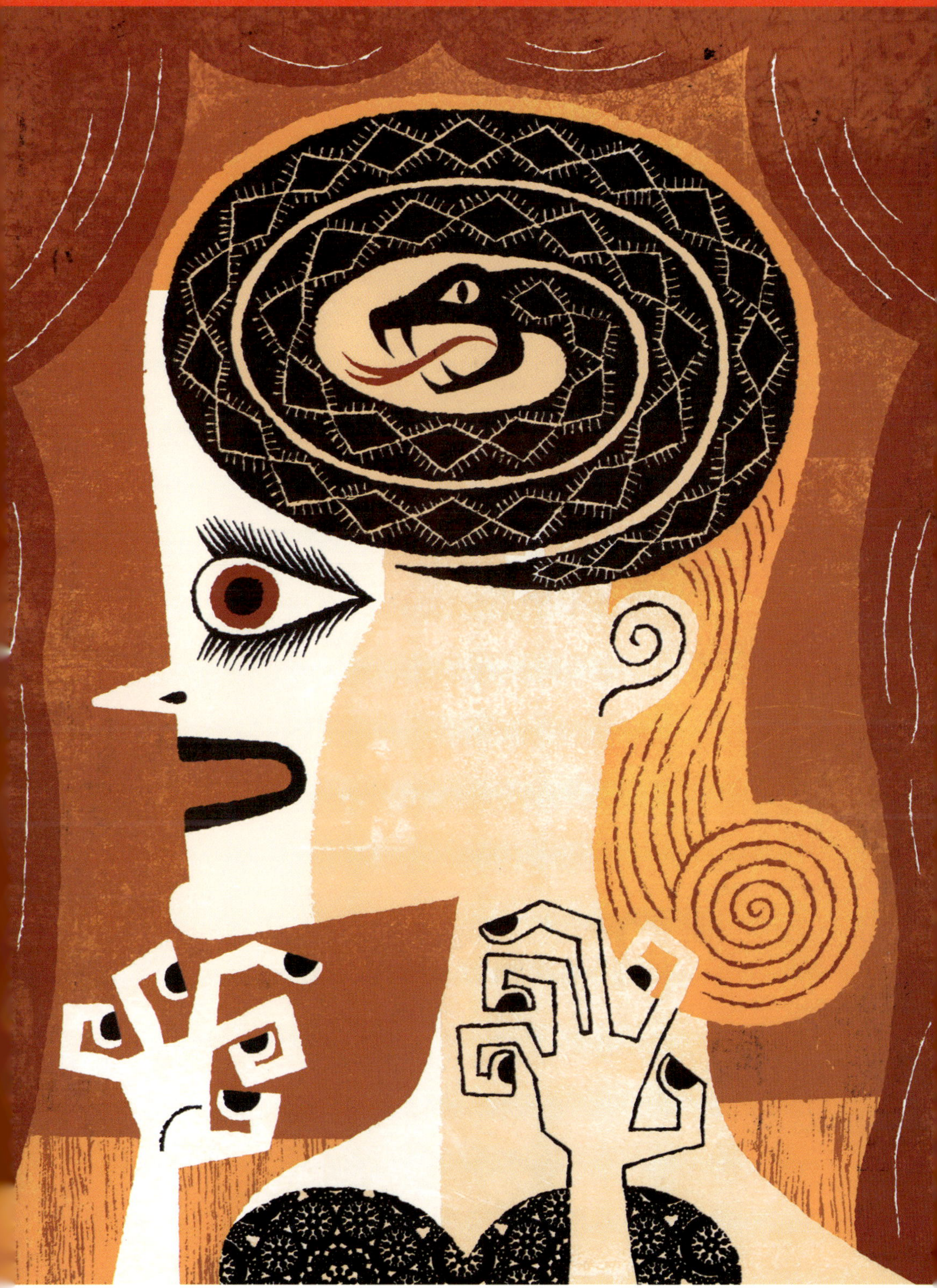

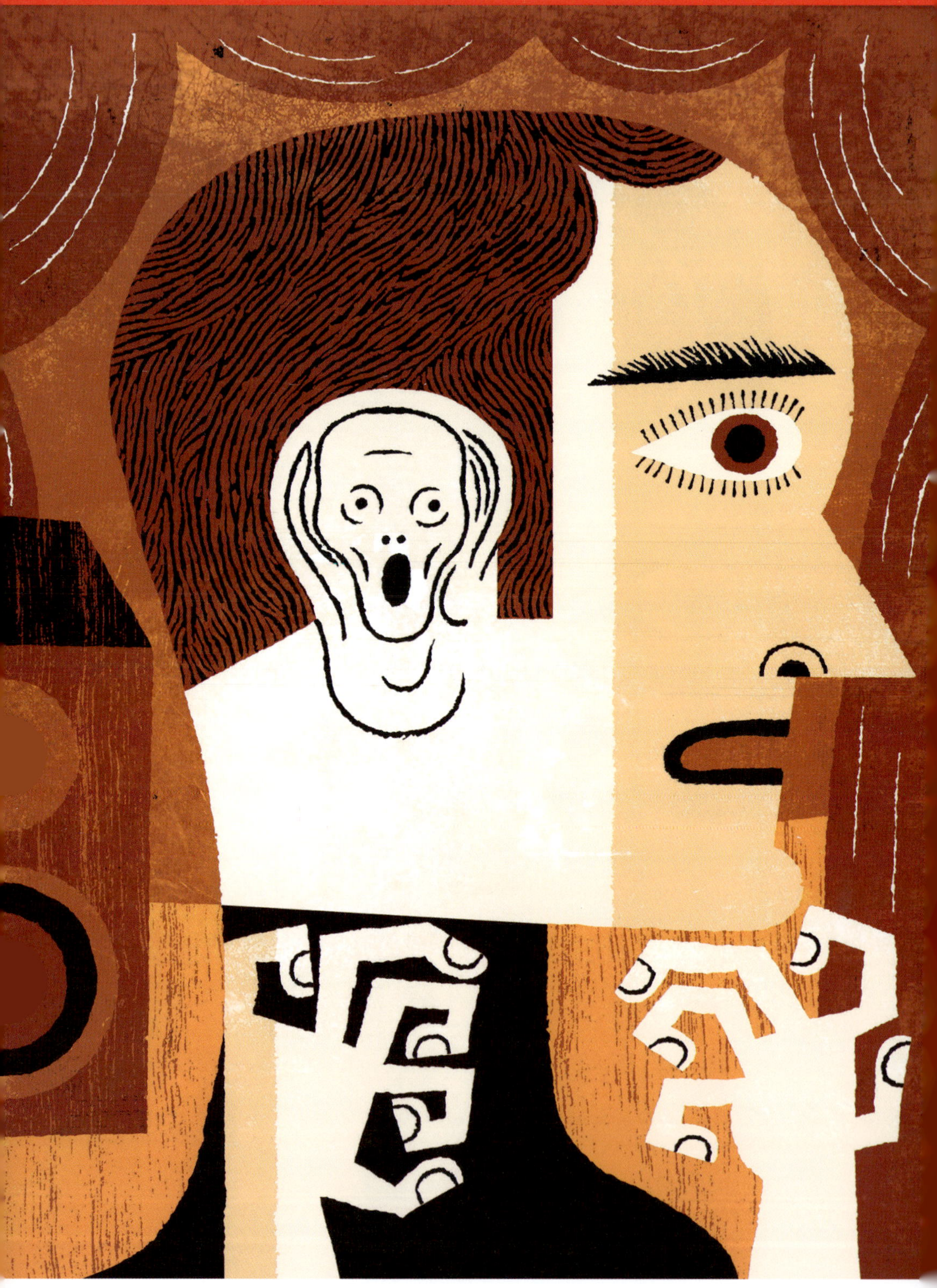

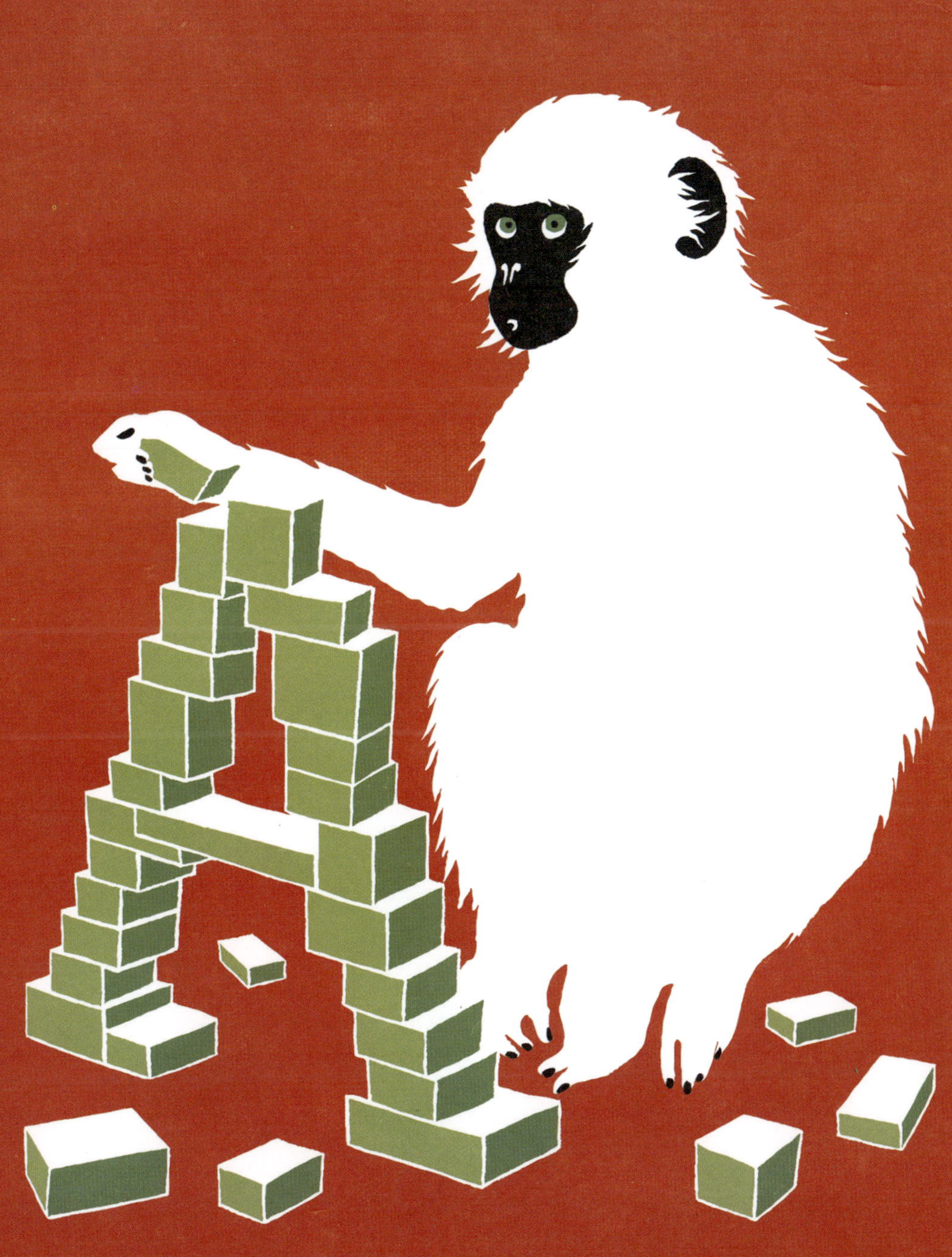

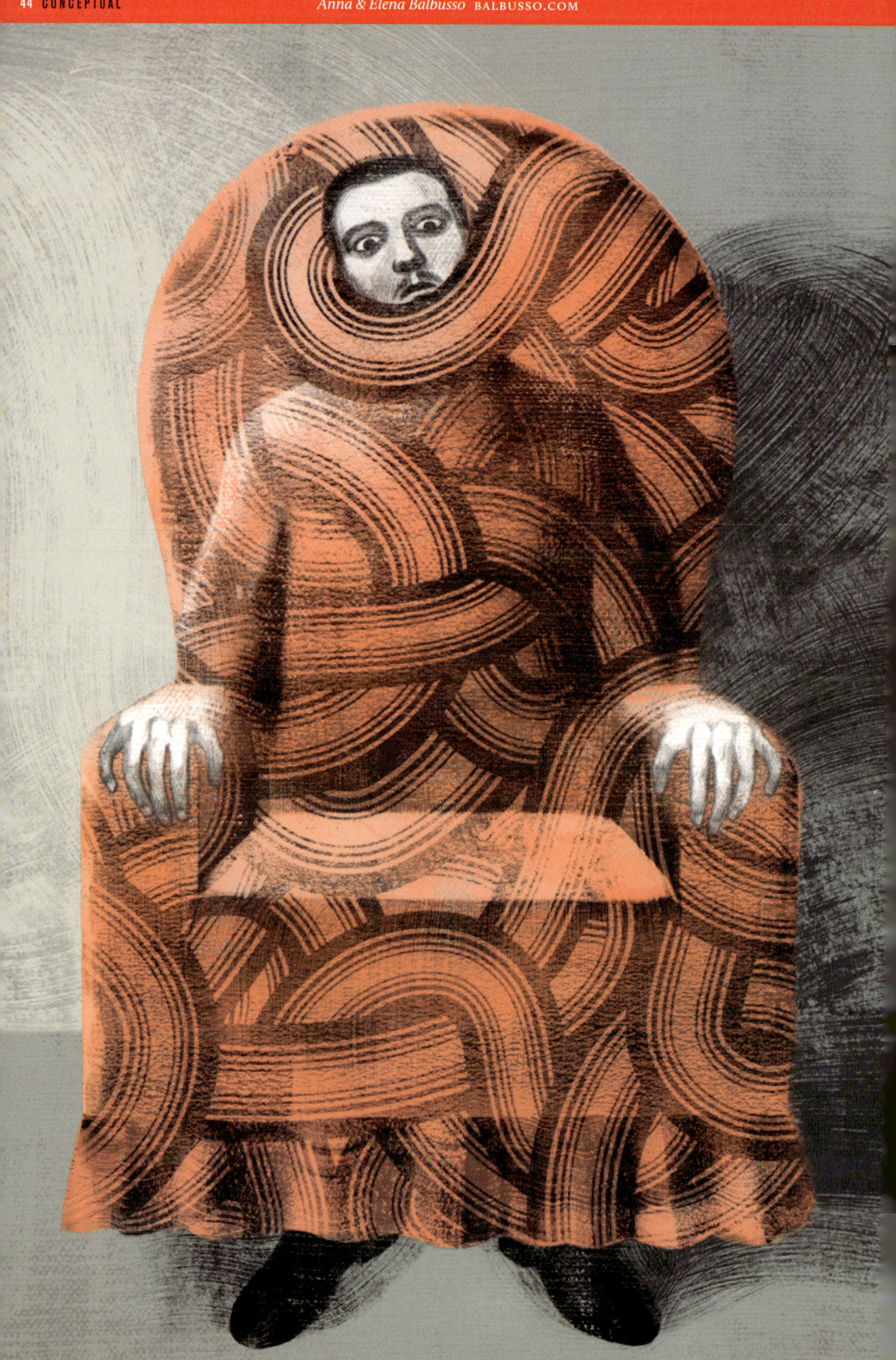

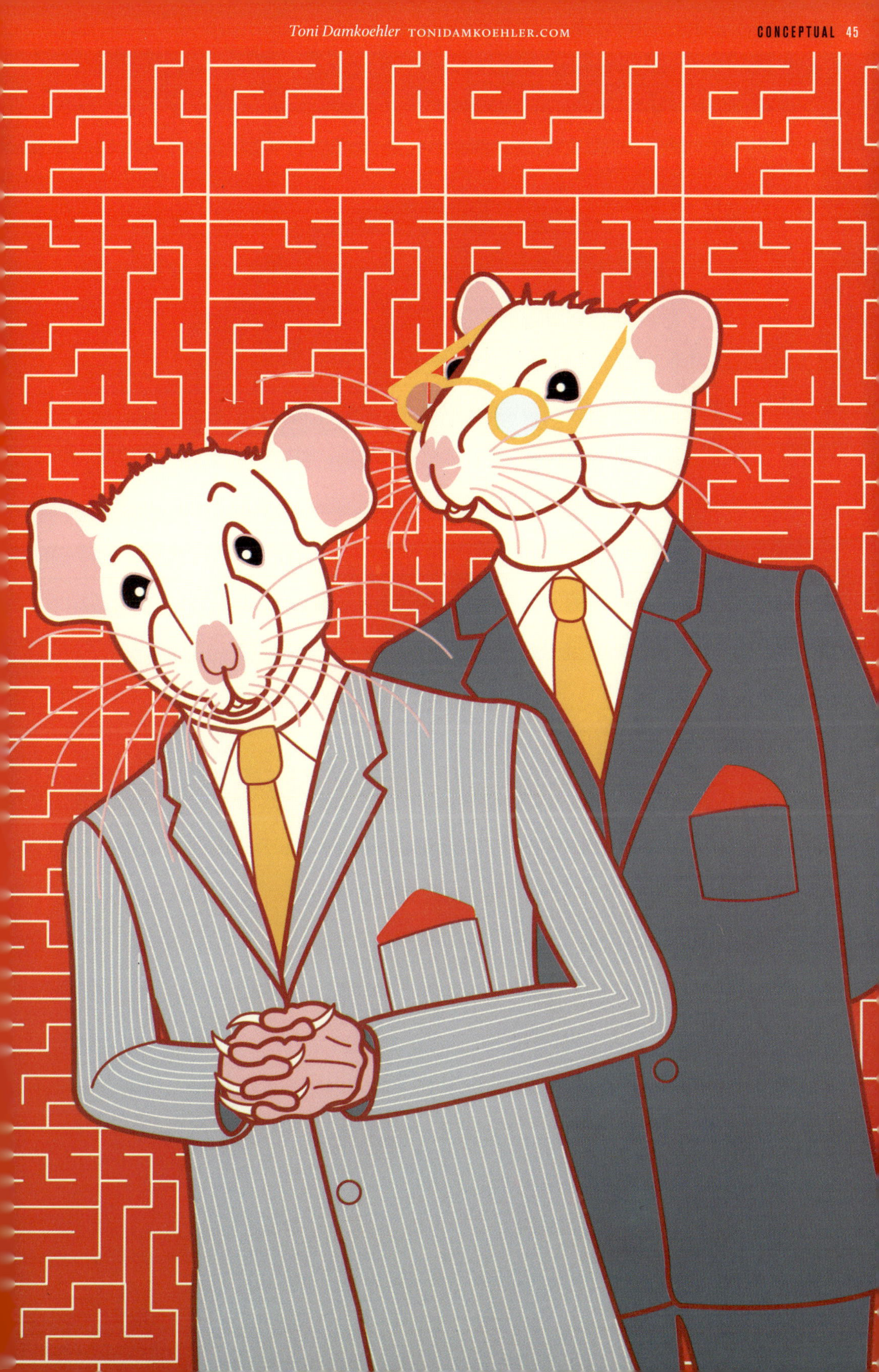

Scott Bakal SCOTTBAKAL.COM

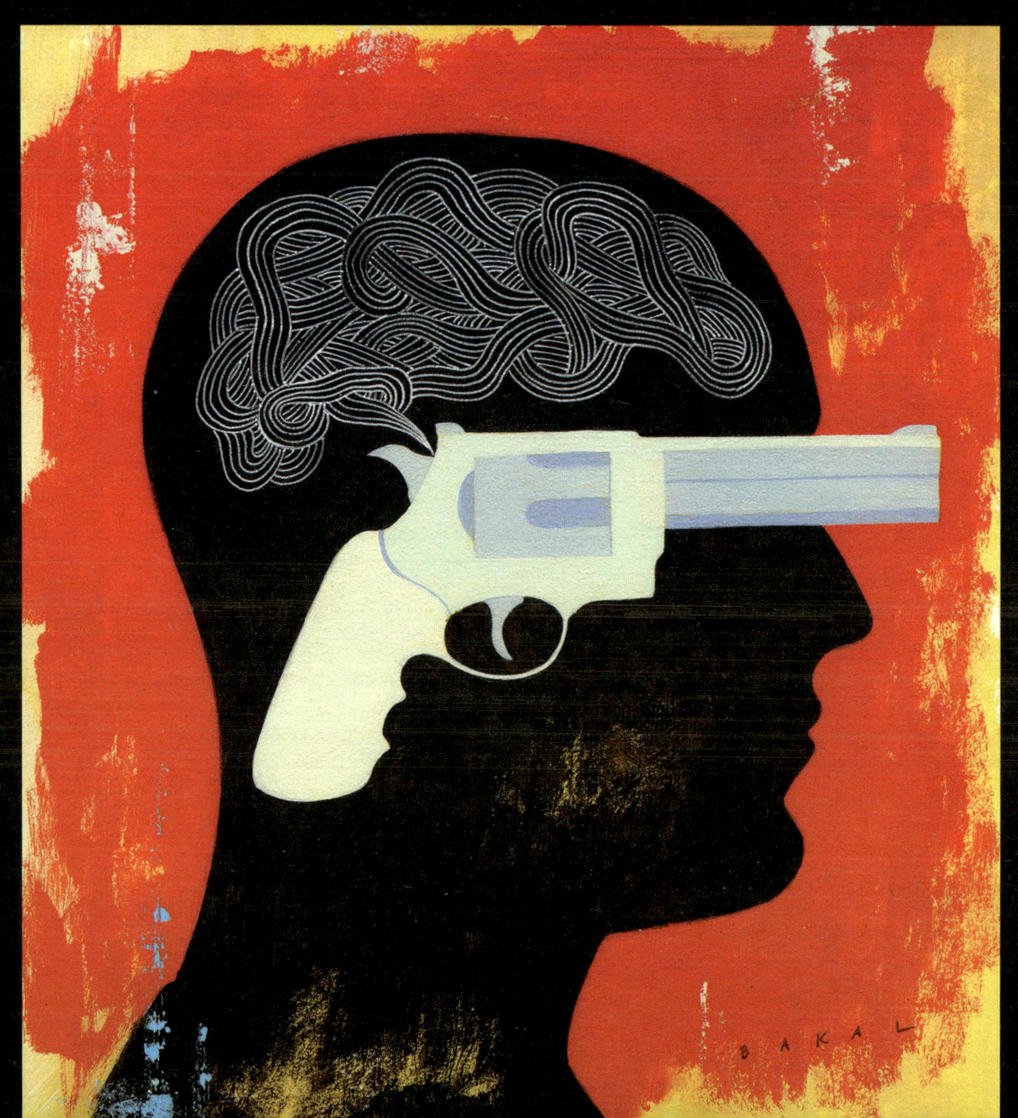

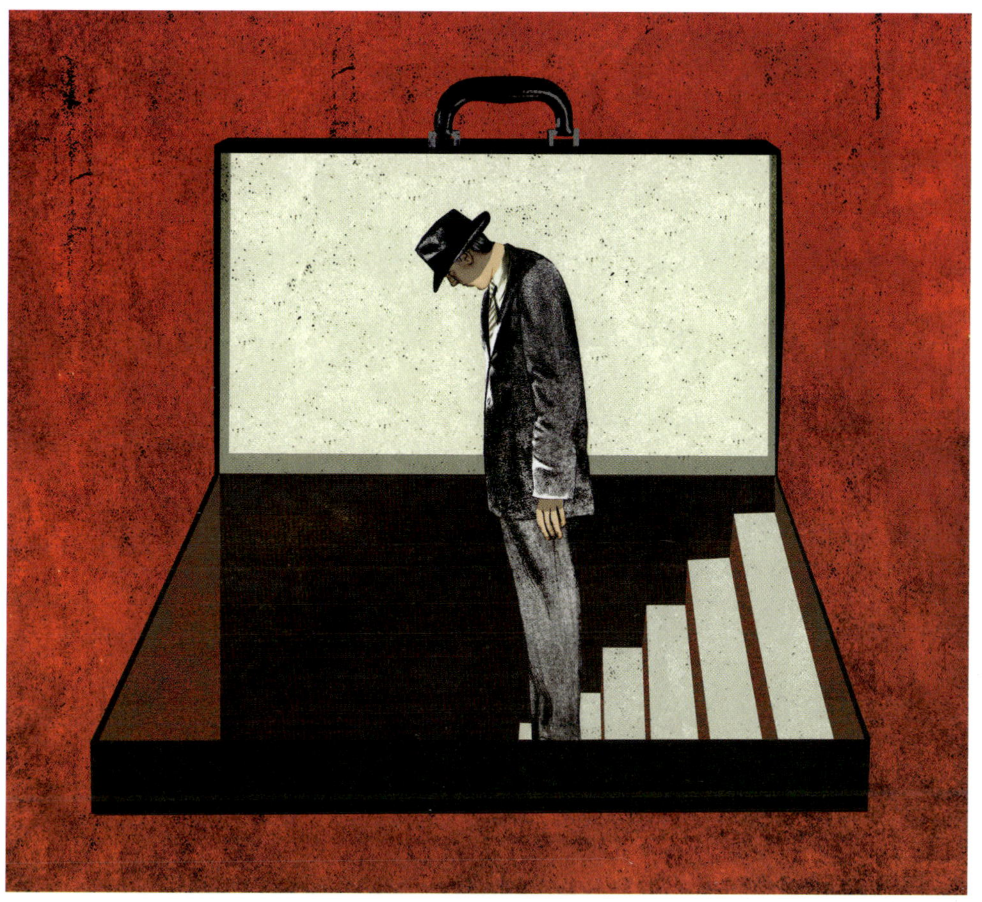

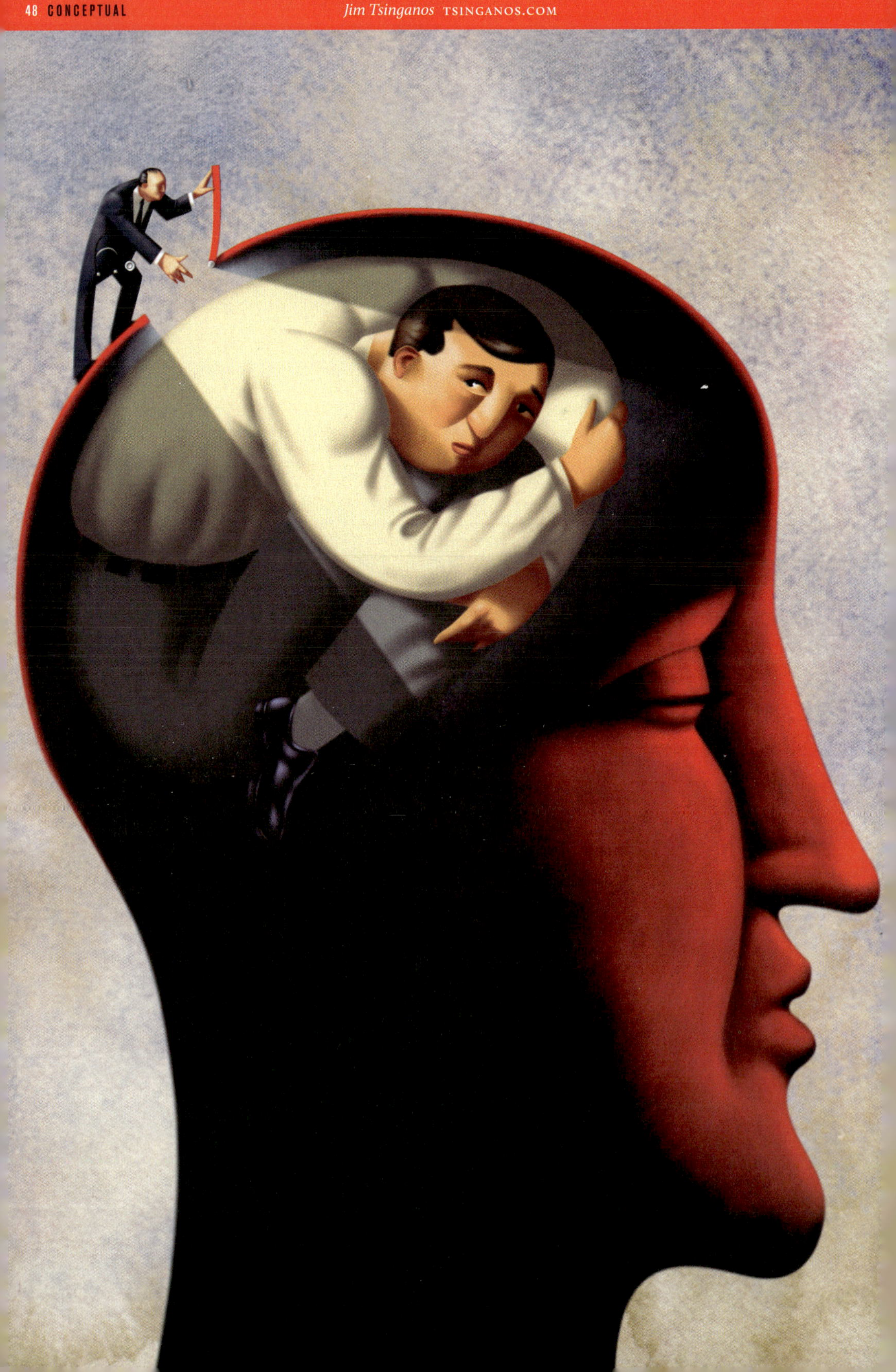

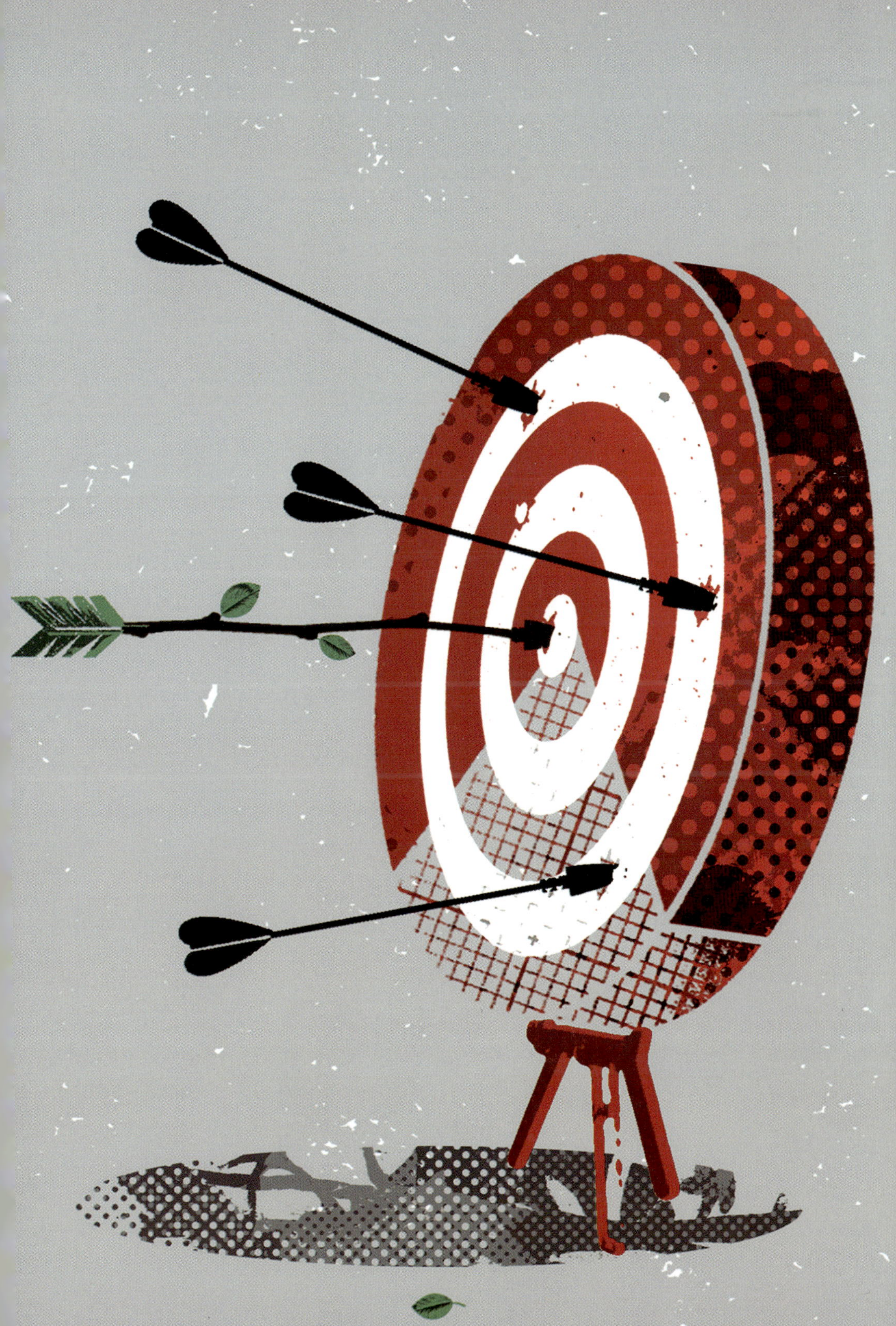

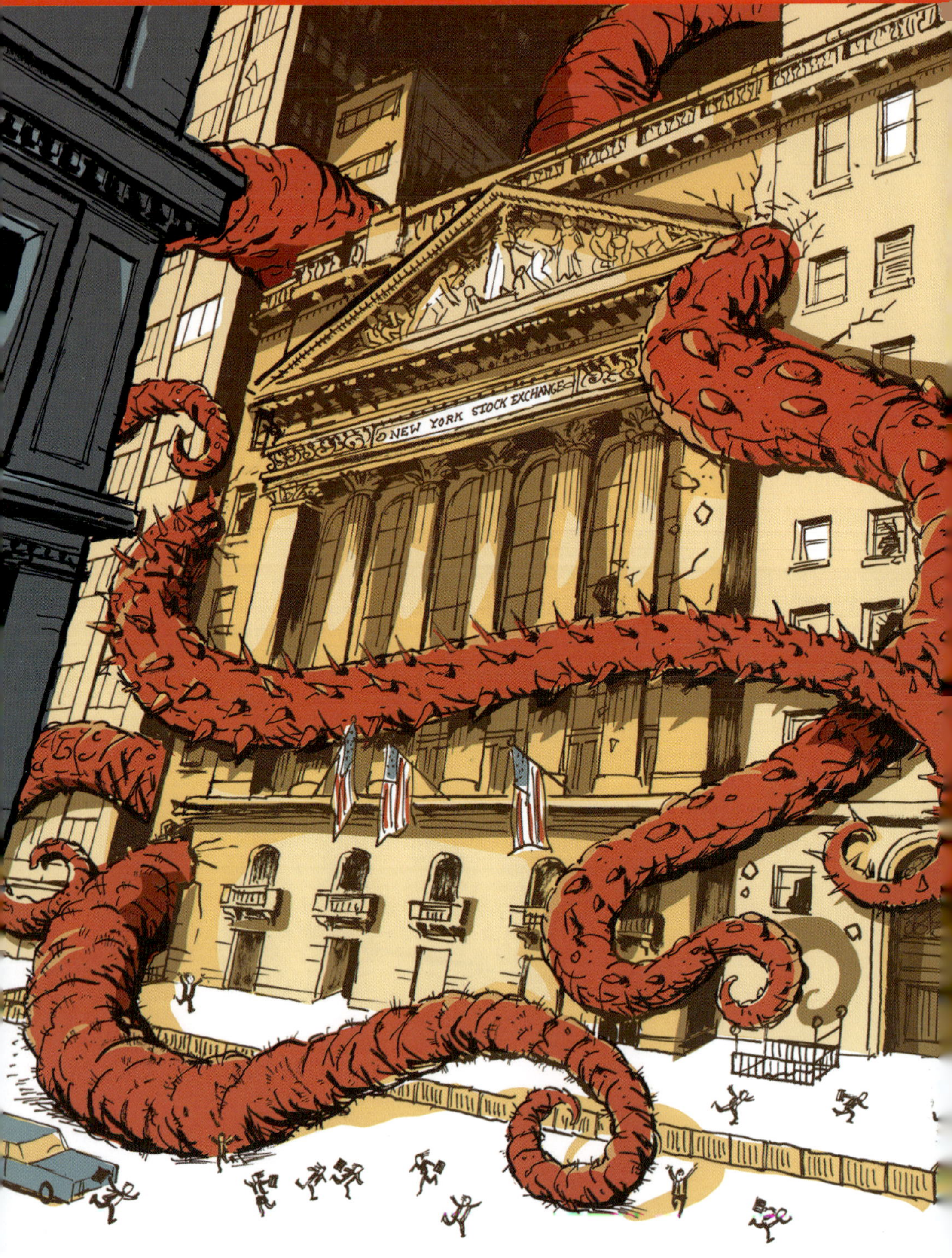
NEW YORK STOCK EXCHANGE

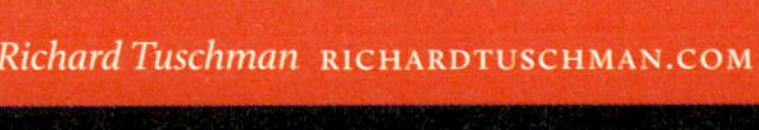

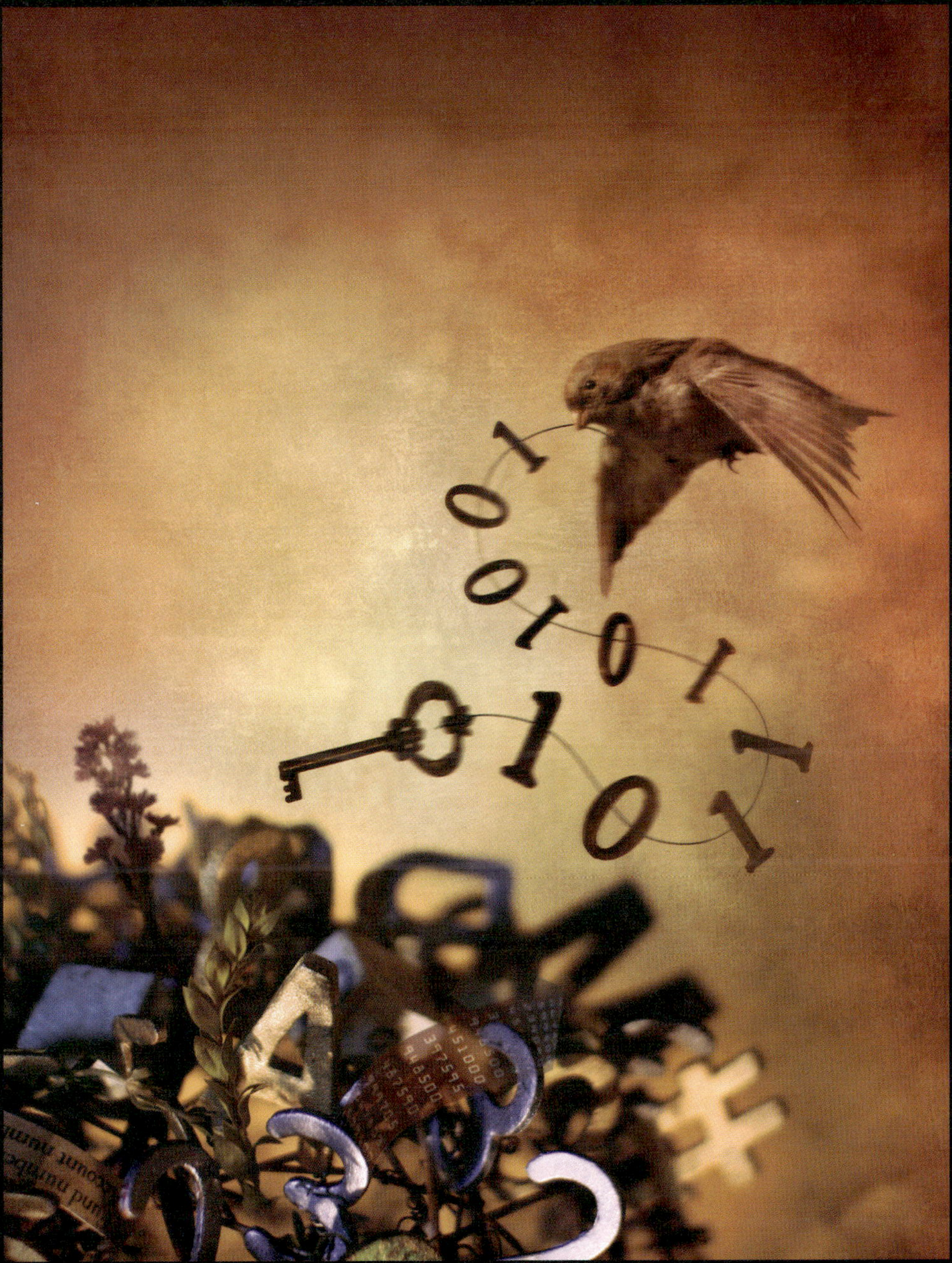

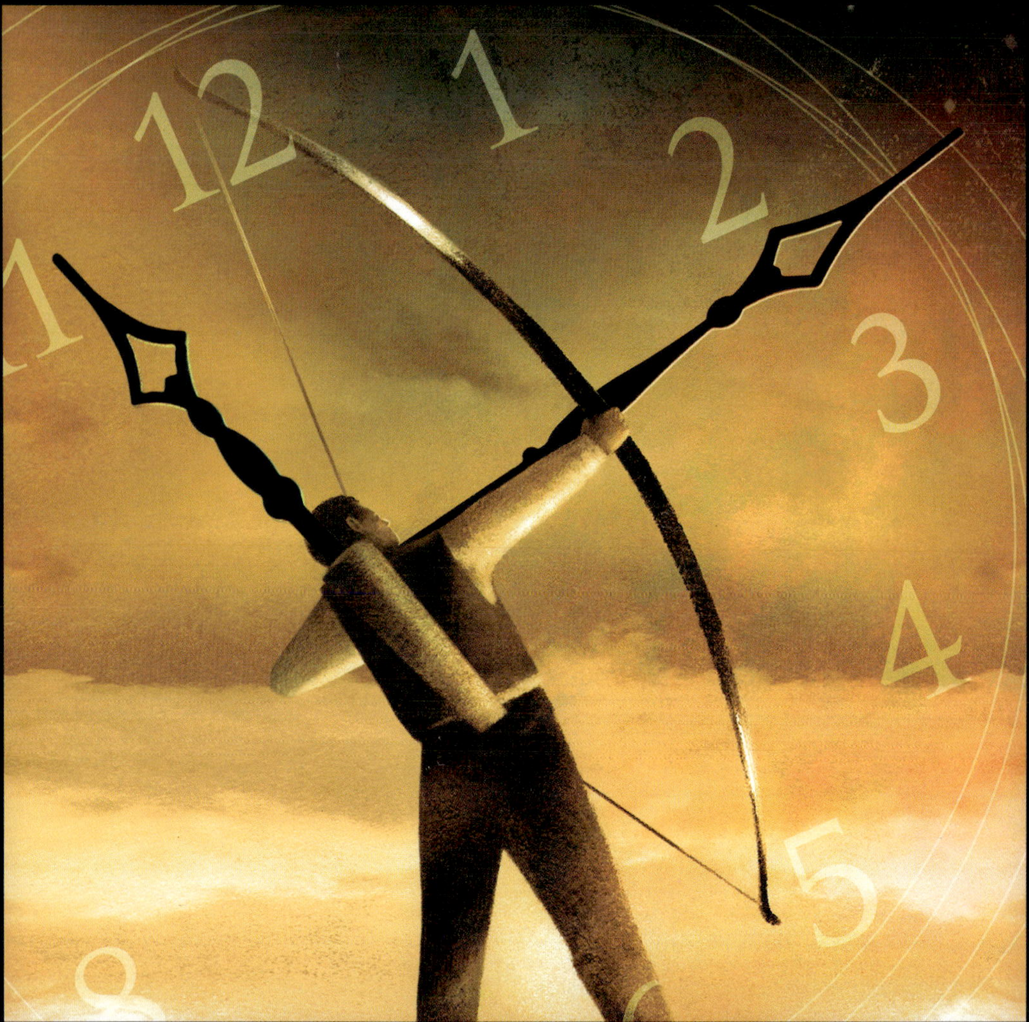

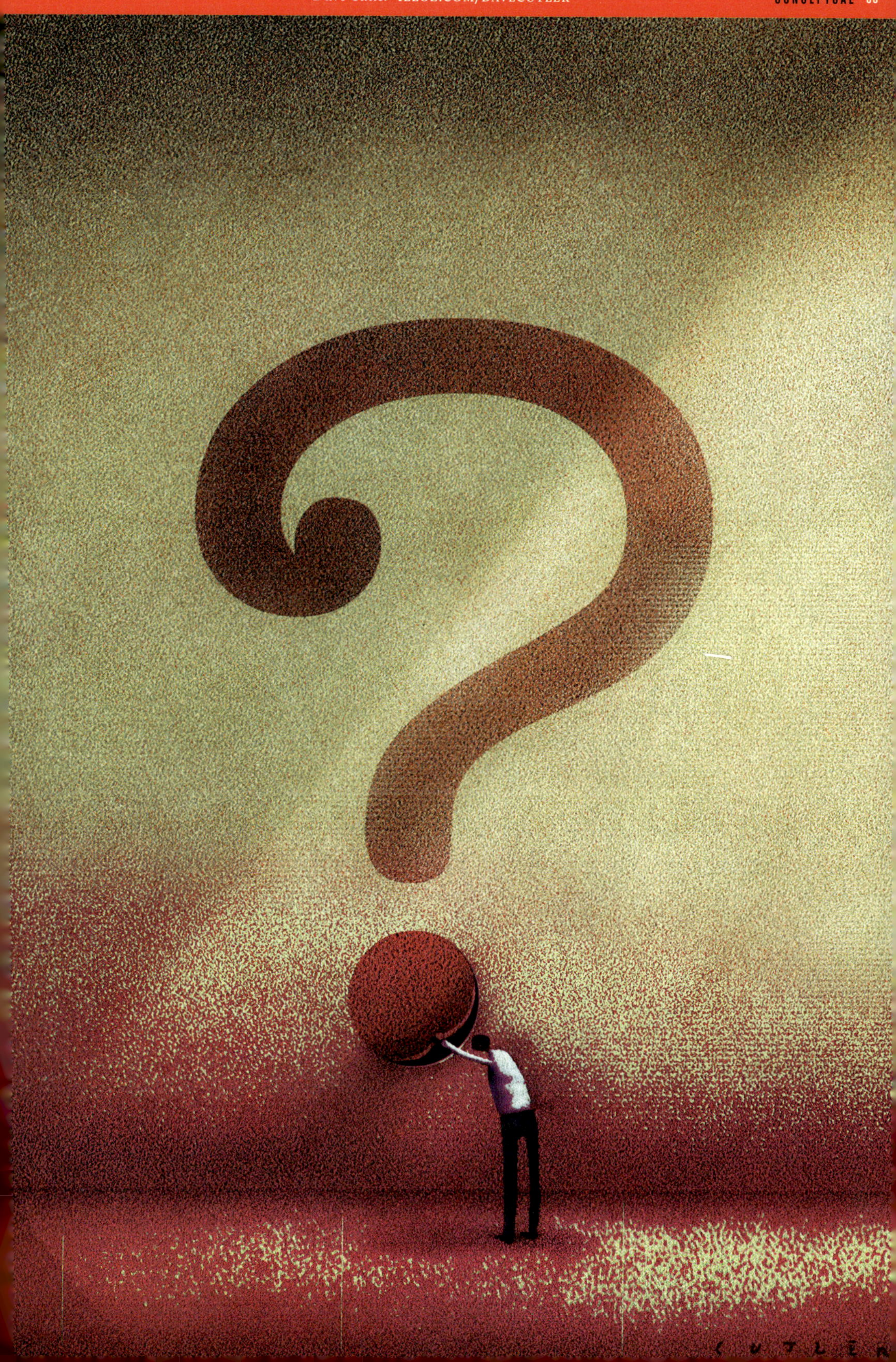

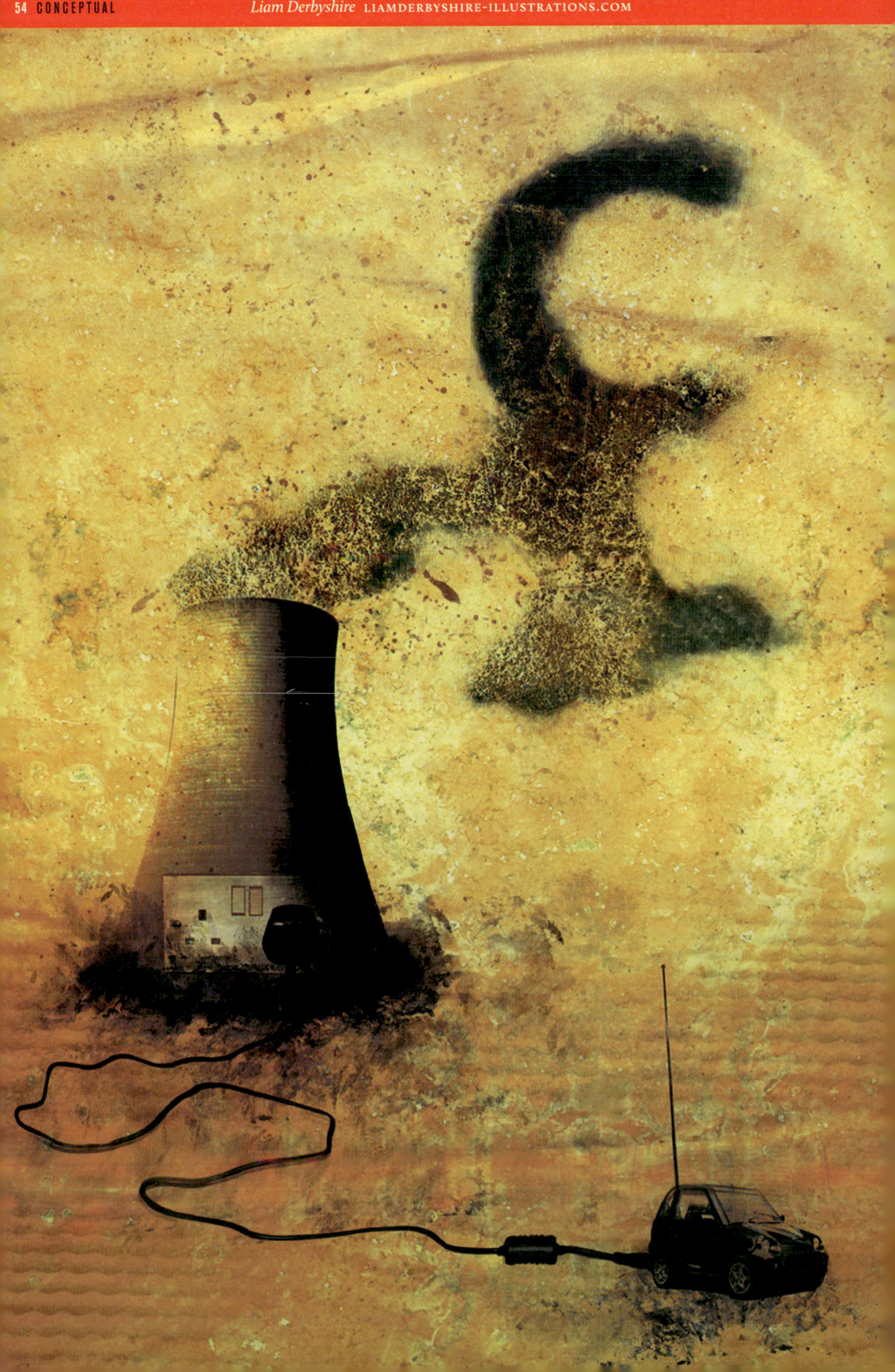

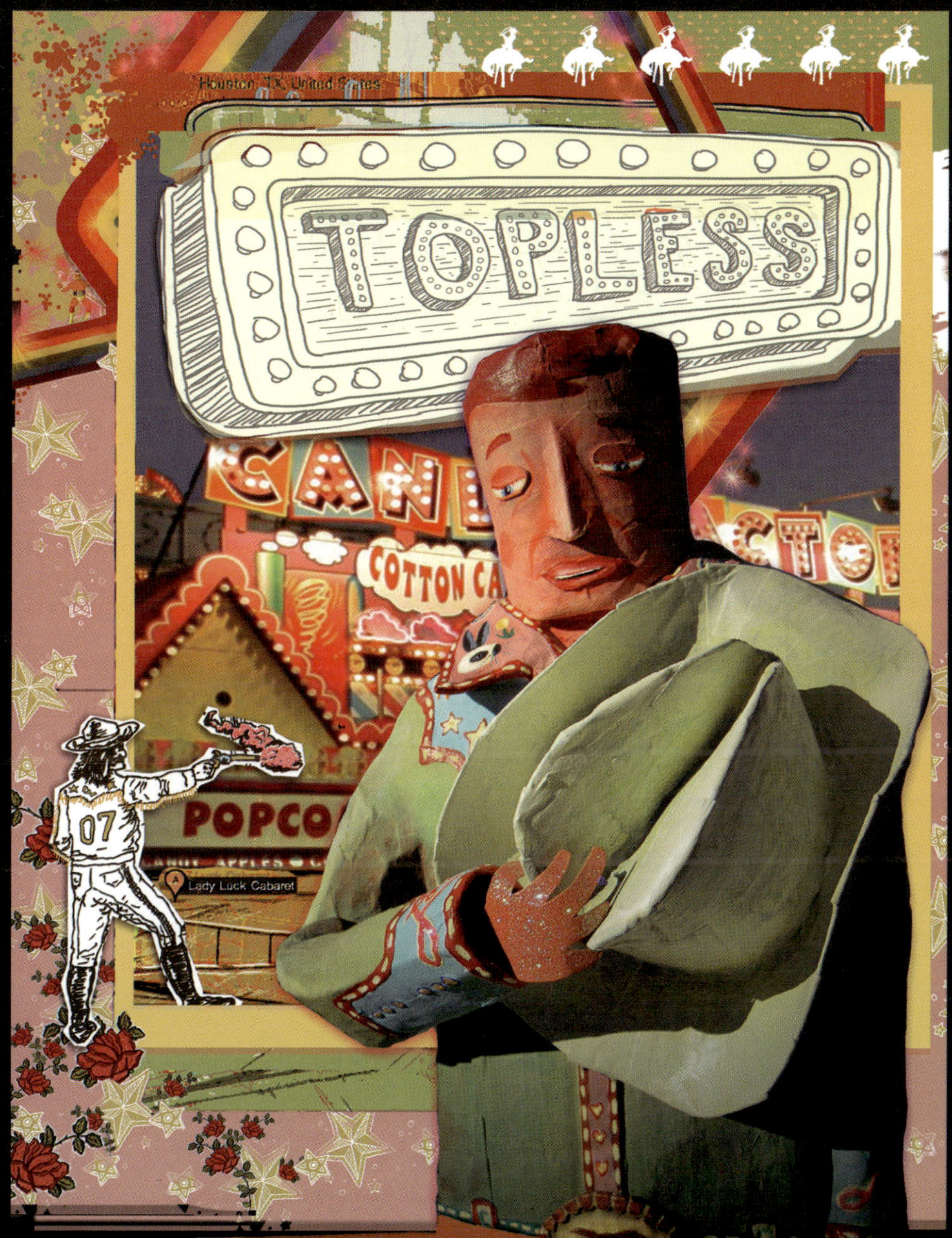
Houston, TX, United States
TOPLESS
CANDY
COTTON CA
CTO
POPCO
CANDY APPLES
Lady Luck Cabaret
07

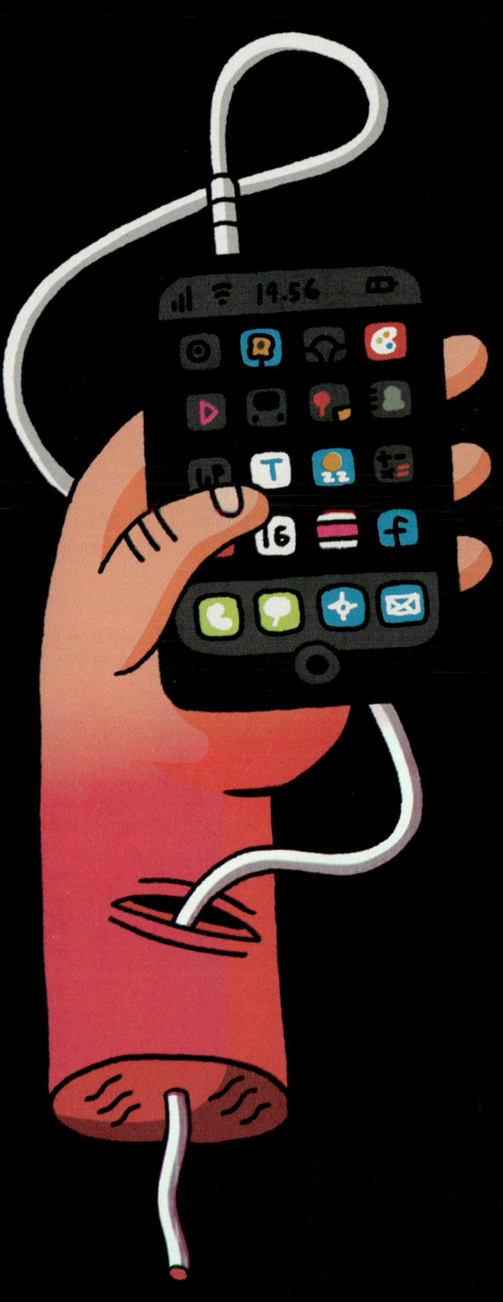

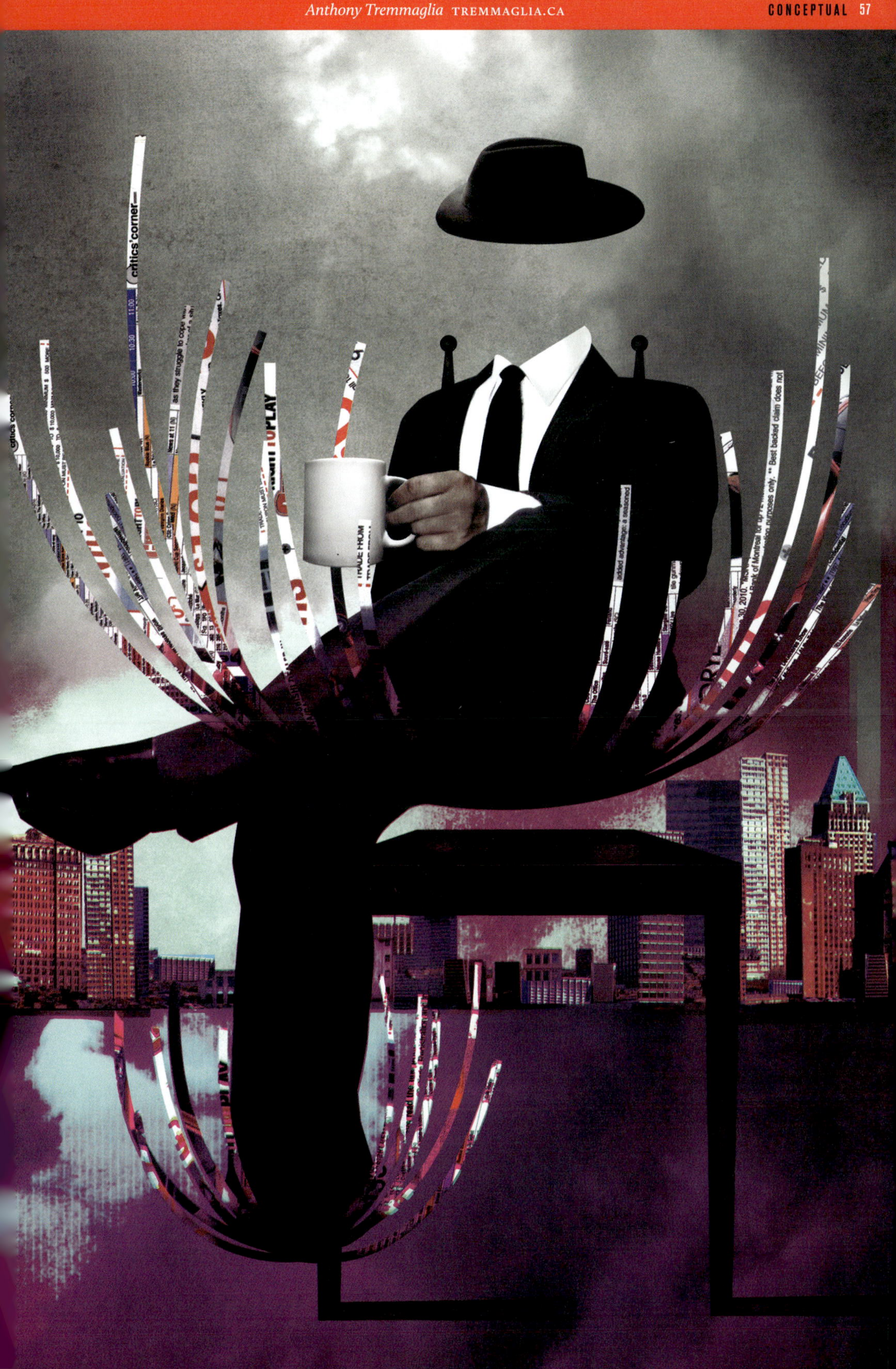

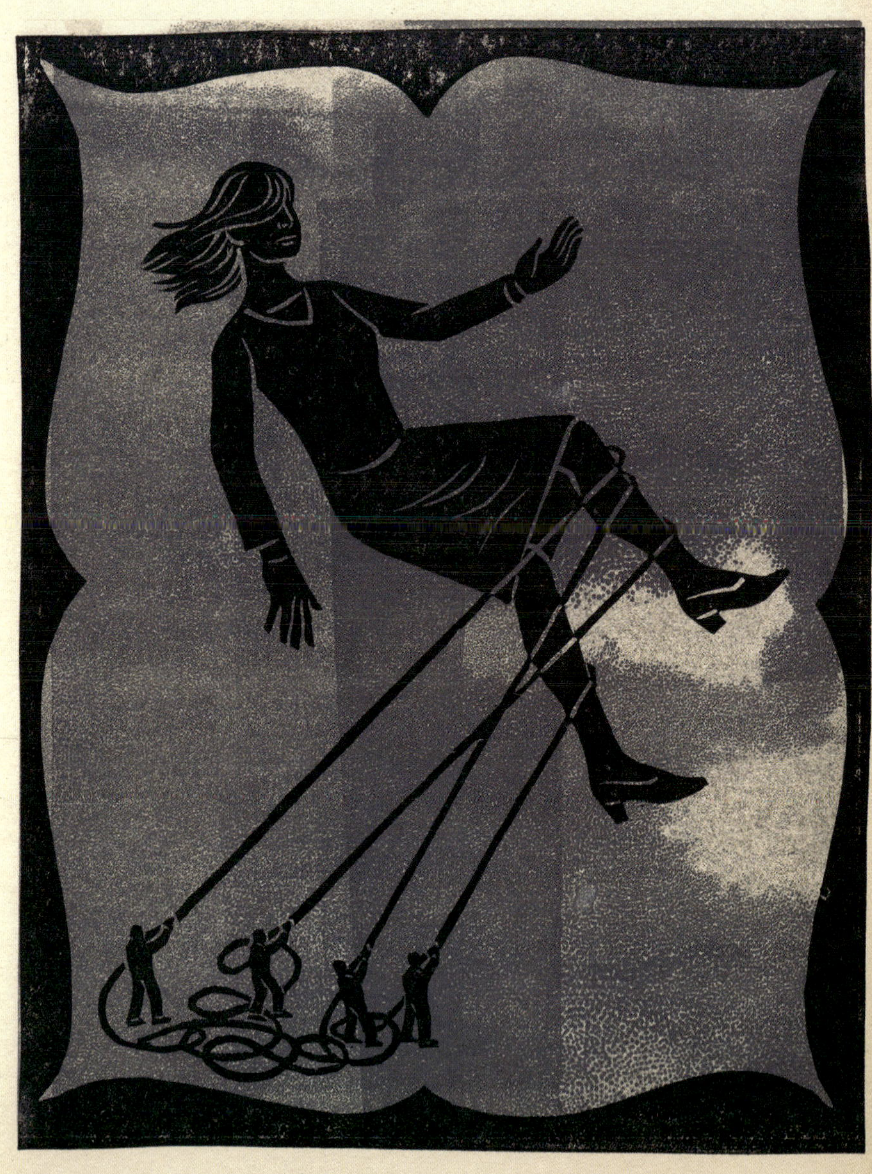

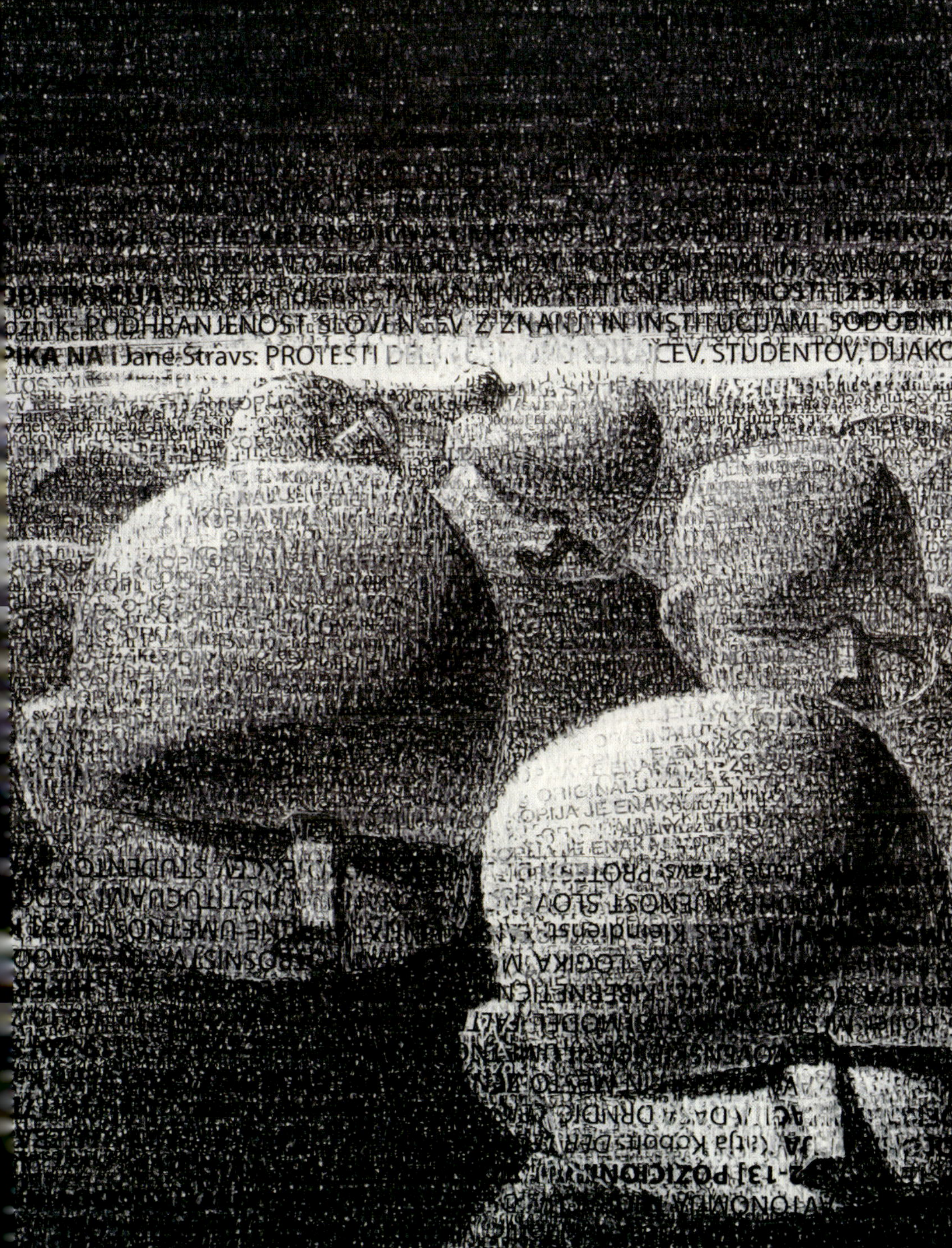

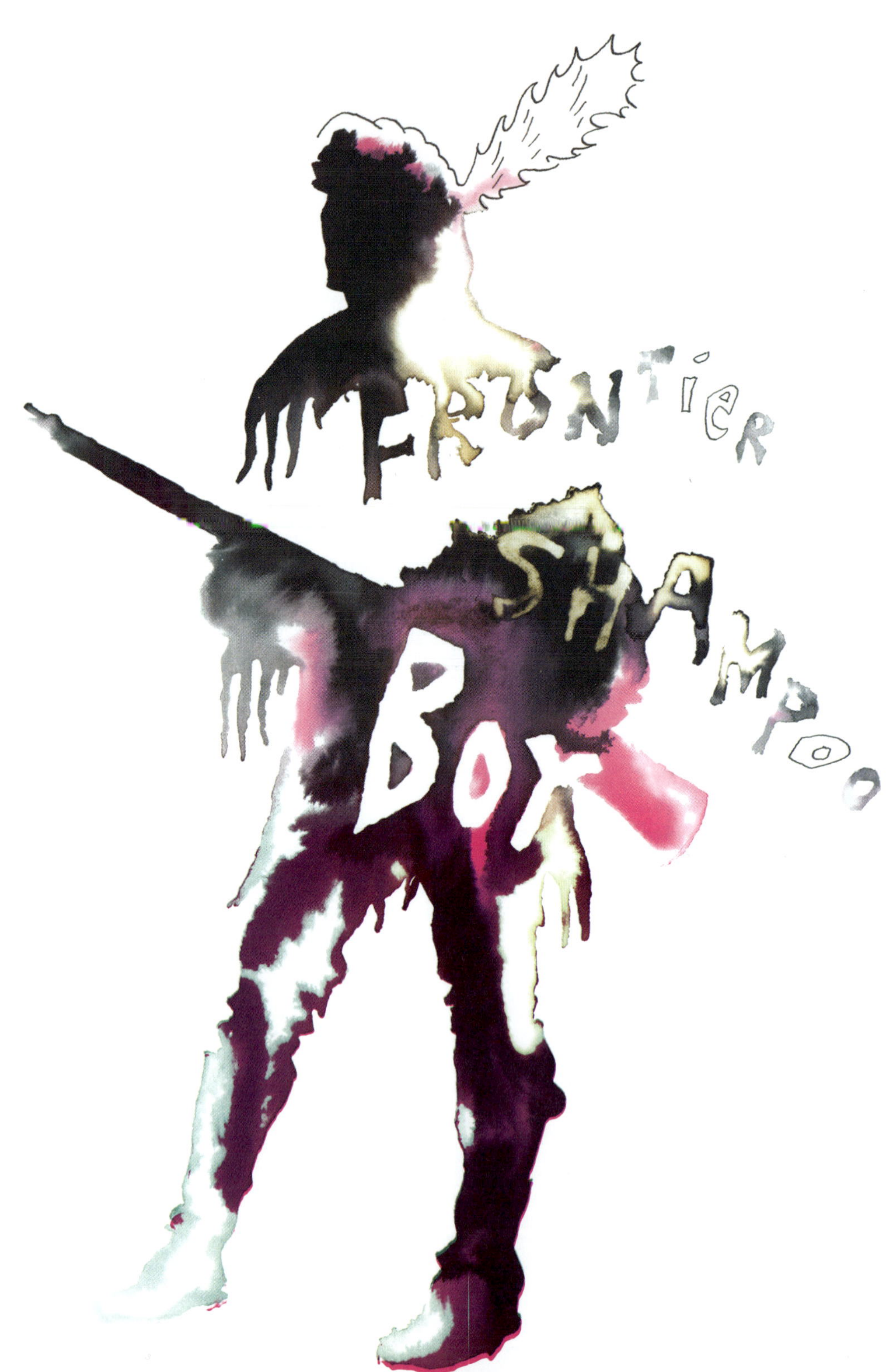

FRONTIER
SHAMPOO
BOX

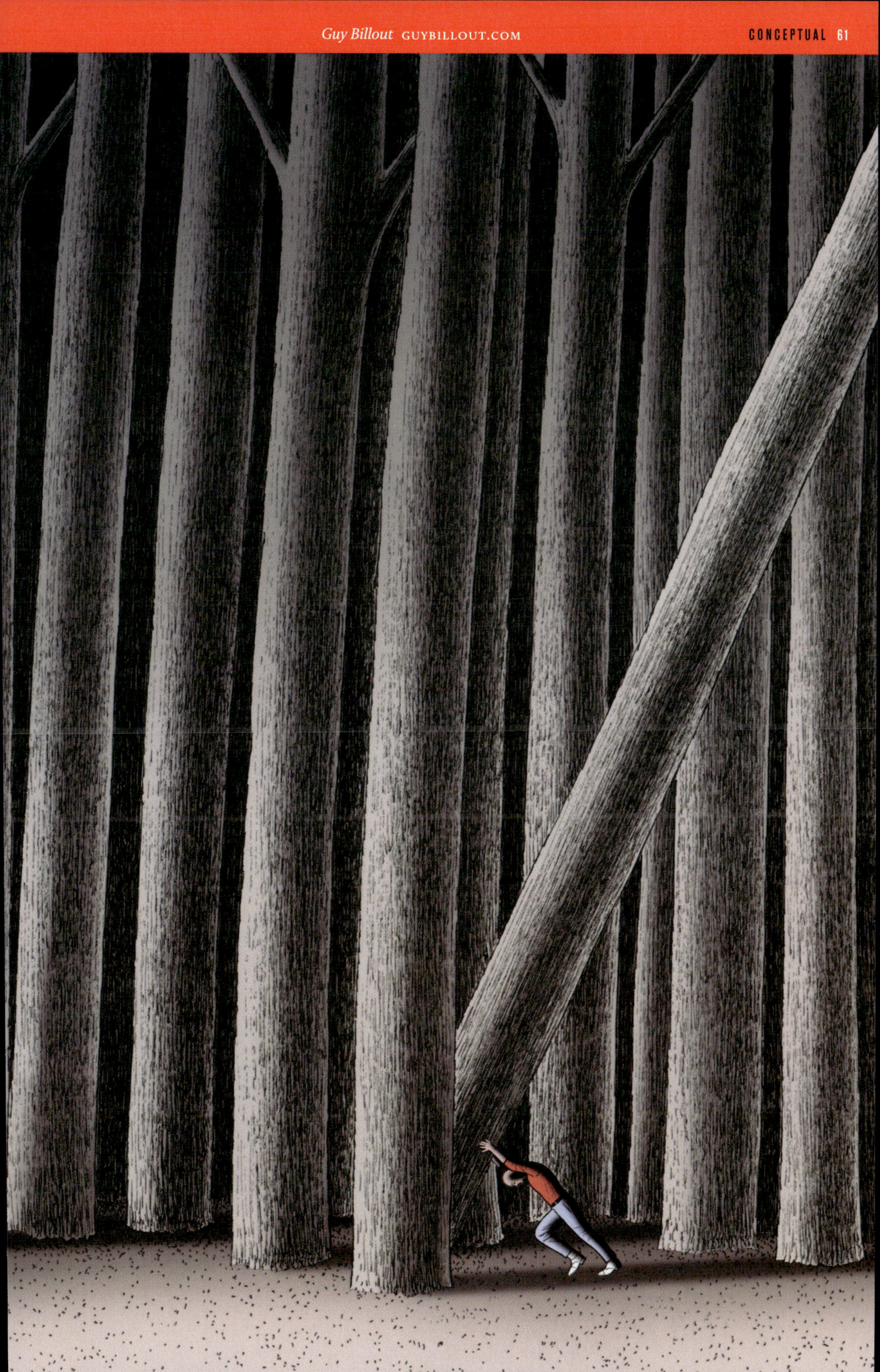

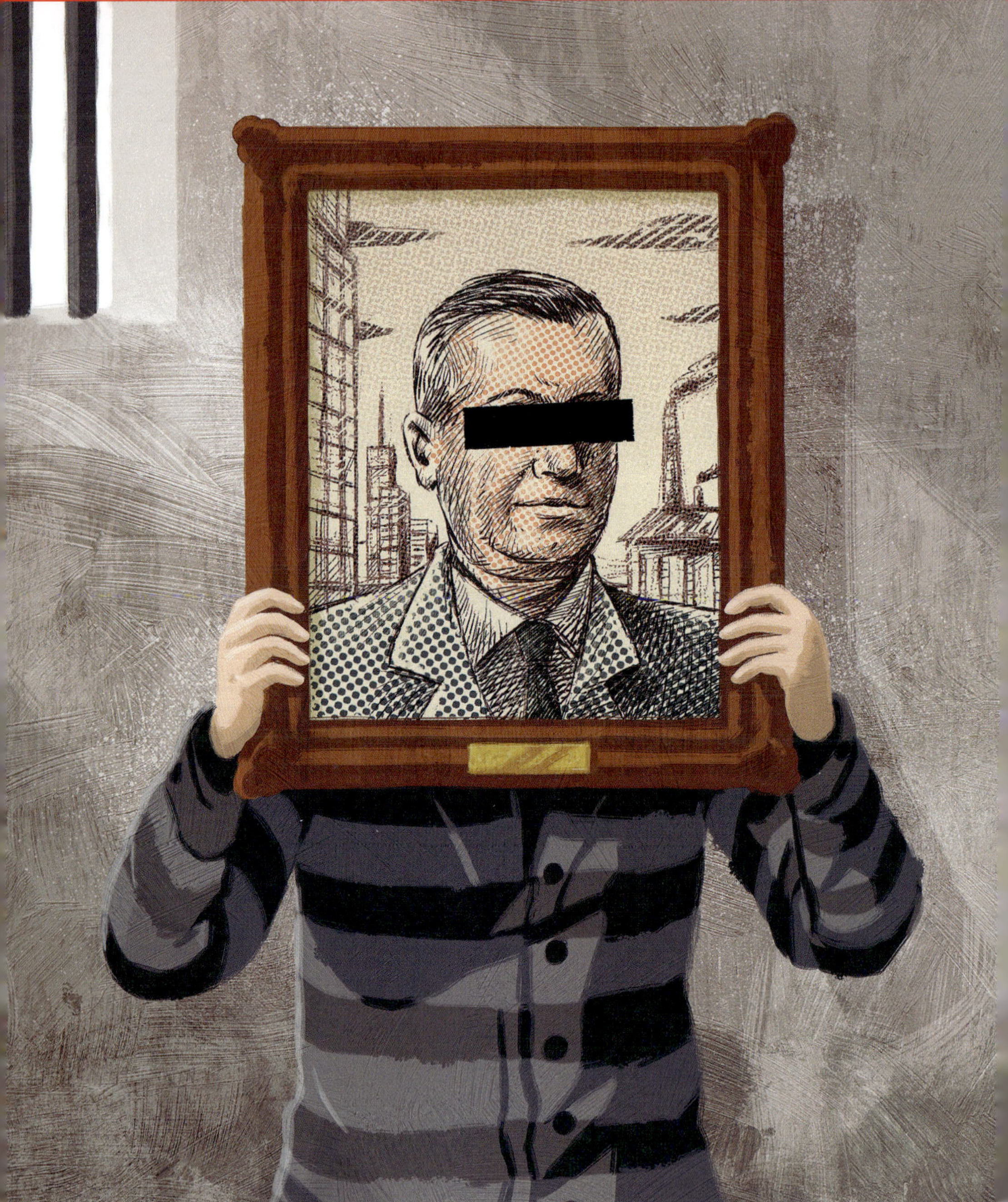

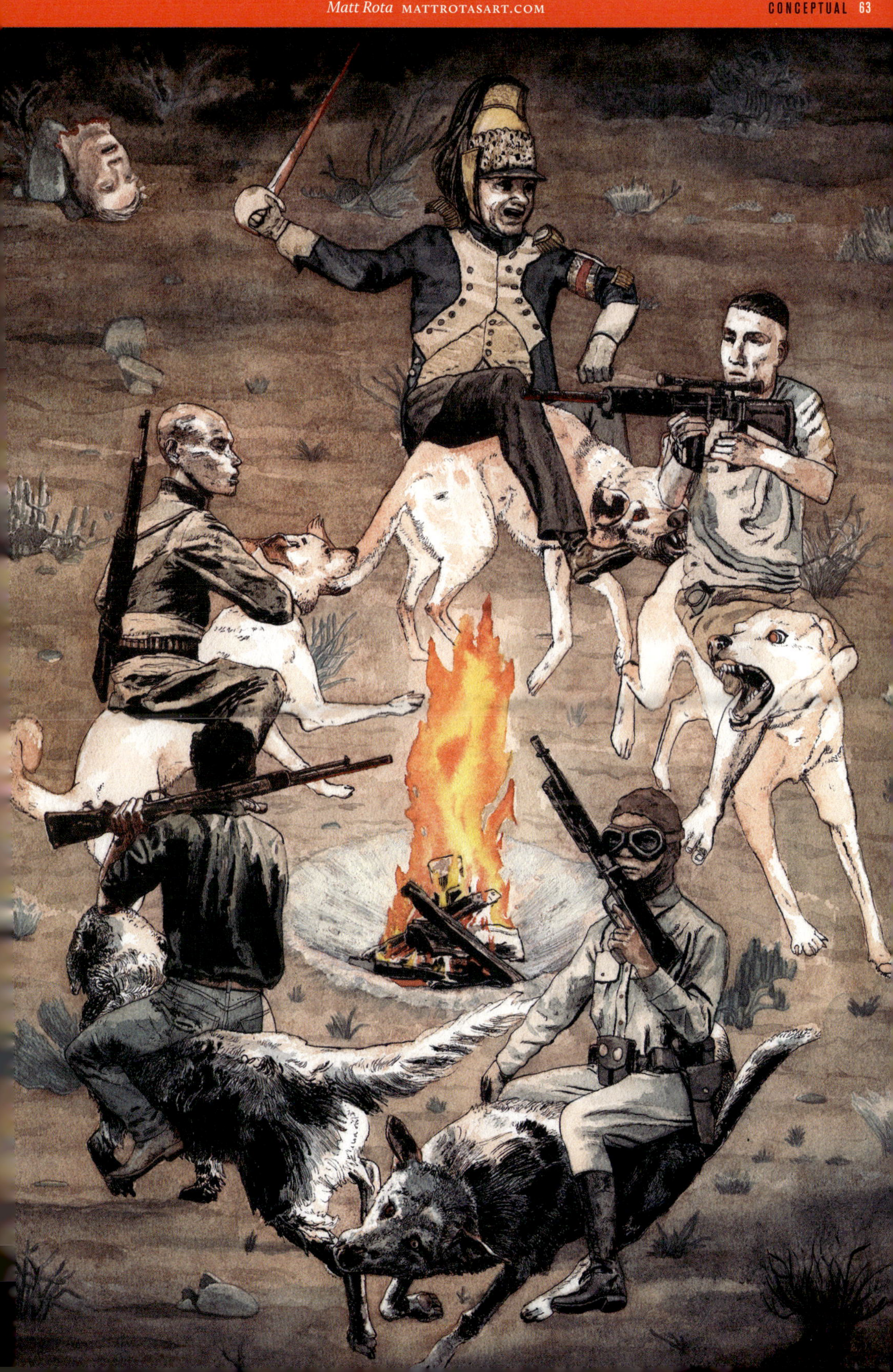

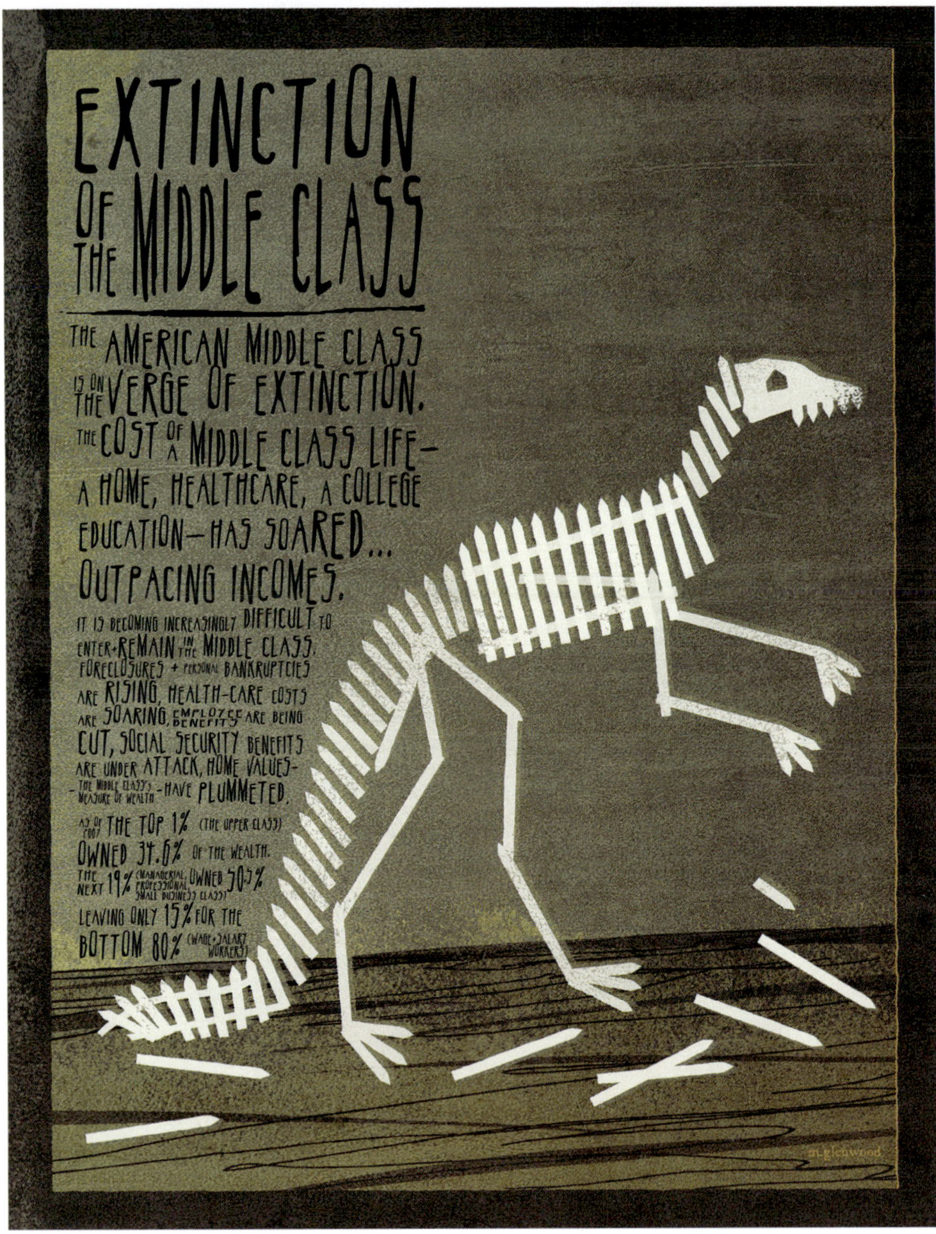
EXTINCTION OF THE MIDDLE CLASS
THE AMERICAN MIDDLE CLASS IS ON THE VERGE OF EXTINCTION. THE COST OF A MIDDLE CLASS LIFE — A HOME, HEALTHCARE, A COLLEGE EDUCATION — HAS SOARED... OUTPACING INCOMES.
IT IS BECOMING INCREASINGLY DIFFICULT TO ENTER + REMAIN IN THE MIDDLE CLASS. FORECLOSURES + PERSONAL BANKRUPTCIES ARE RISING, HEALTH-CARE COSTS ARE SOARING, EMPLOYEE BENEFITS ARE BEING CUT, SOCIAL SECURITY BENEFITS ARE UNDER ATTACK, HOME VALUES — THE MIDDLE CLASS'S MEASURE OF WEALTH — HAVE PLUMMETED.
AS OF 2007 THE TOP 1% (THE UPPER CLASS) OWNED 34.6% OF THE WEALTH. THE NEXT 19% (MANAGERIAL, PROFESSIONAL, SMALL BUSINESS CLASS) OWNED 50.5% LEAVING ONLY 15% FOR THE BOTTOM 80% (WAGE + SALARY WORKERS)
m.glenwood

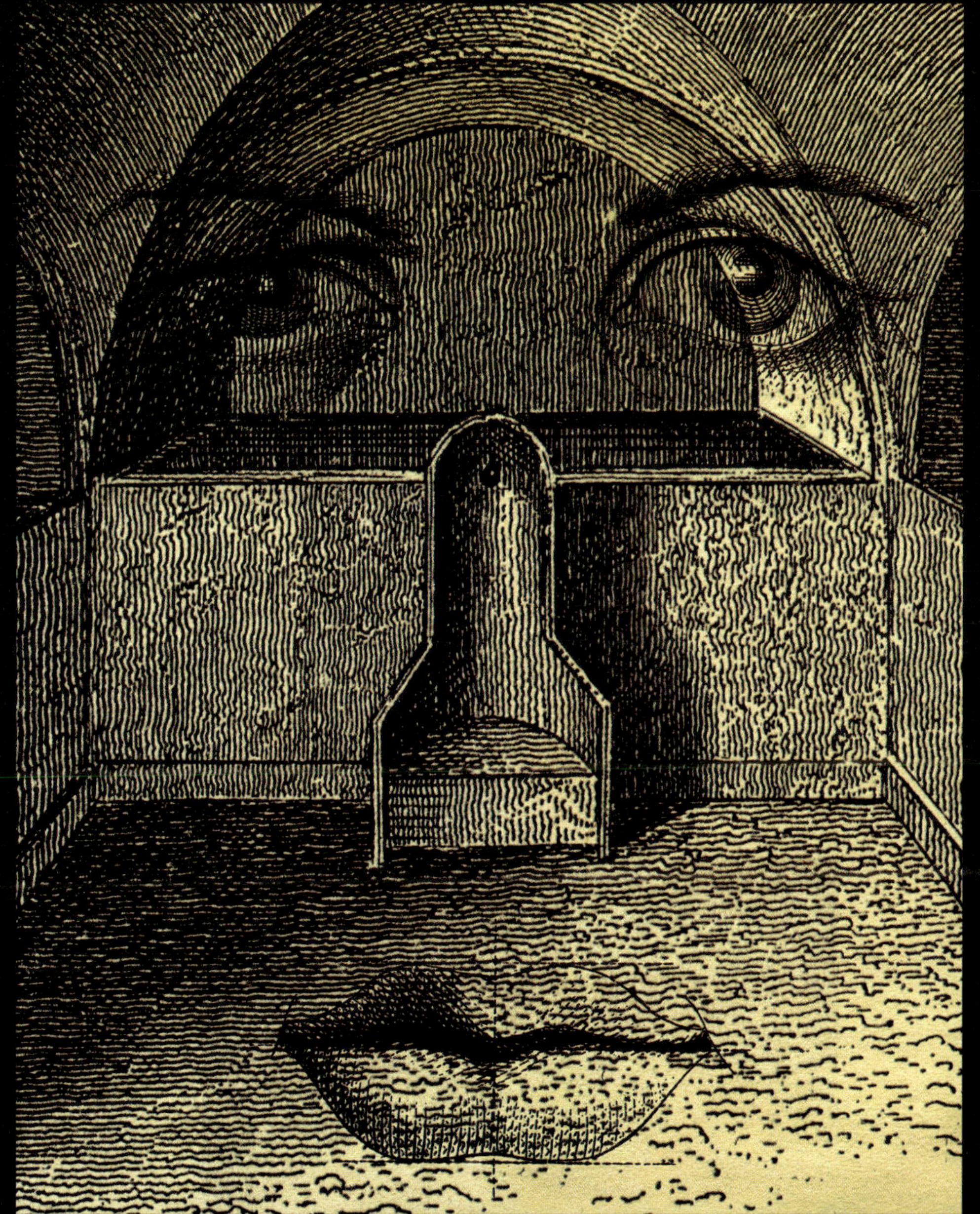

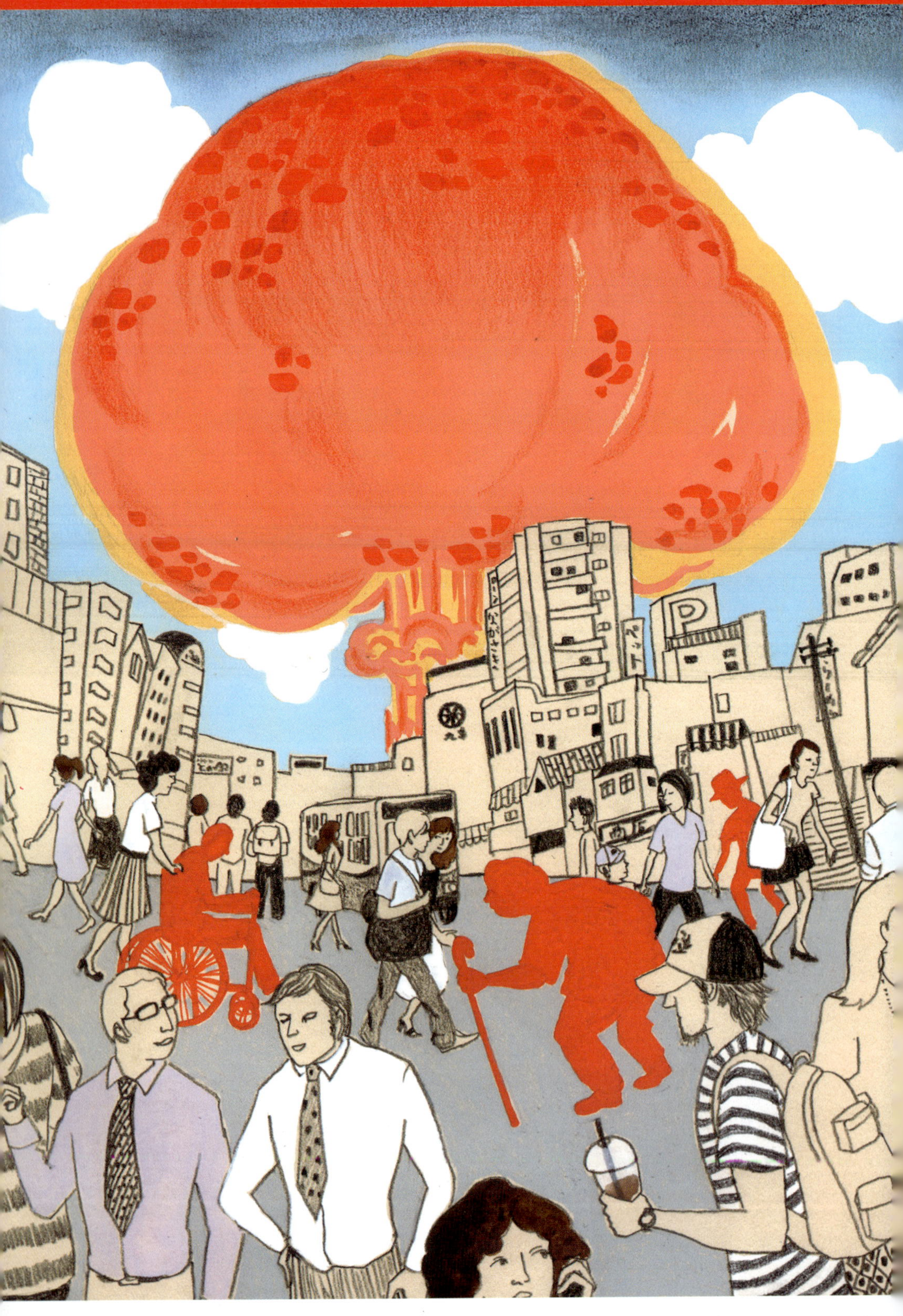

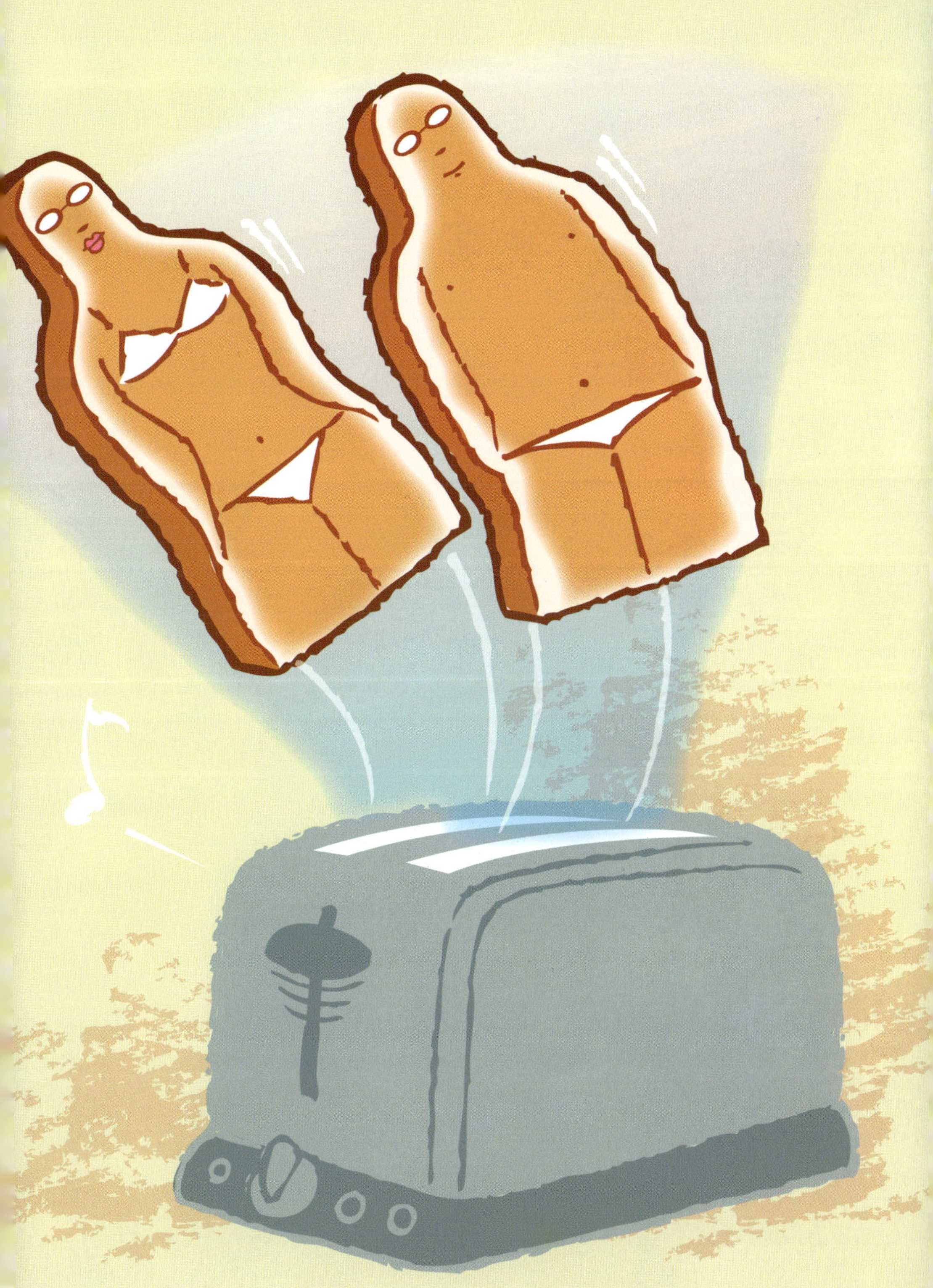

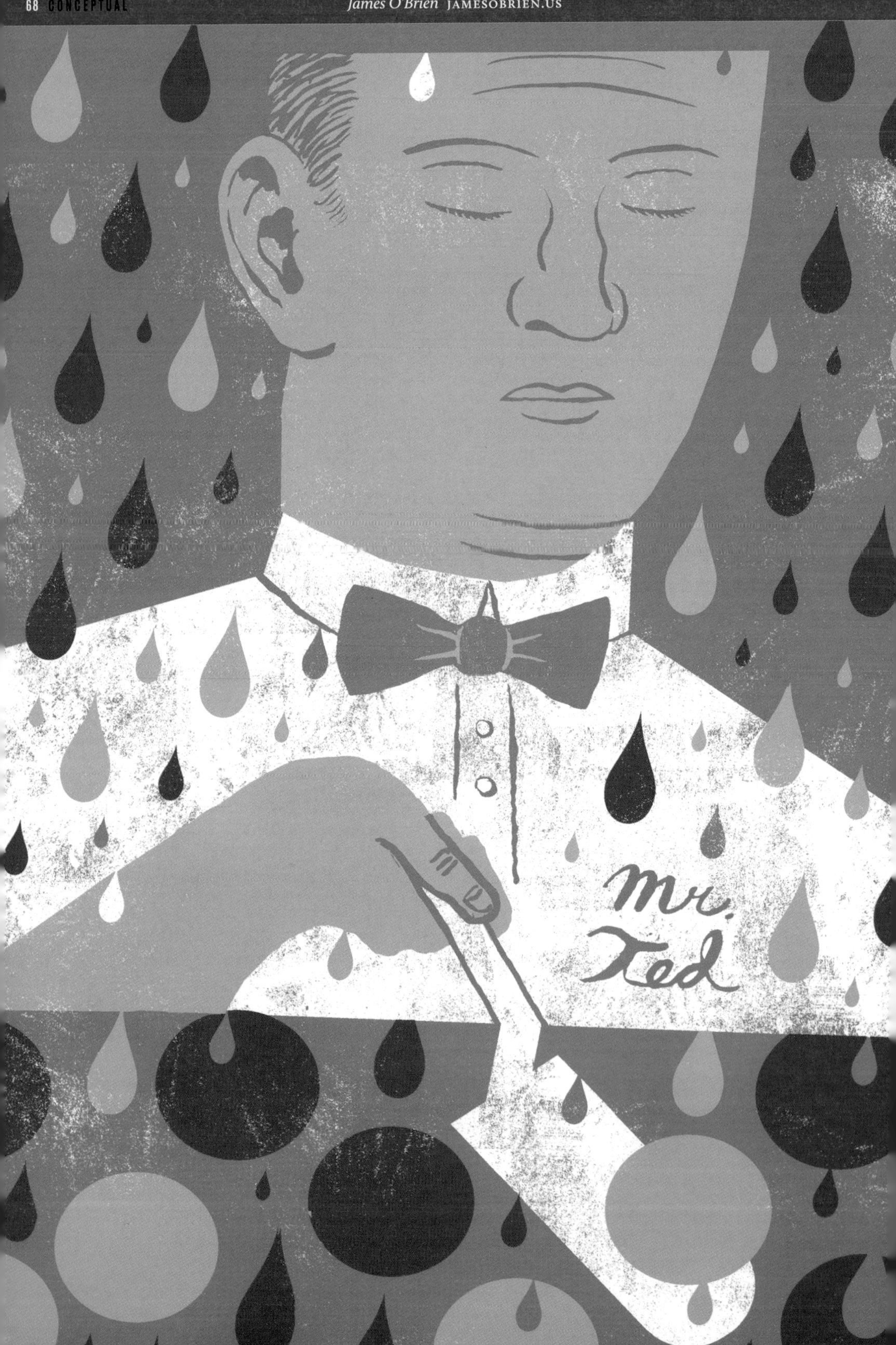
Mr.
Ted

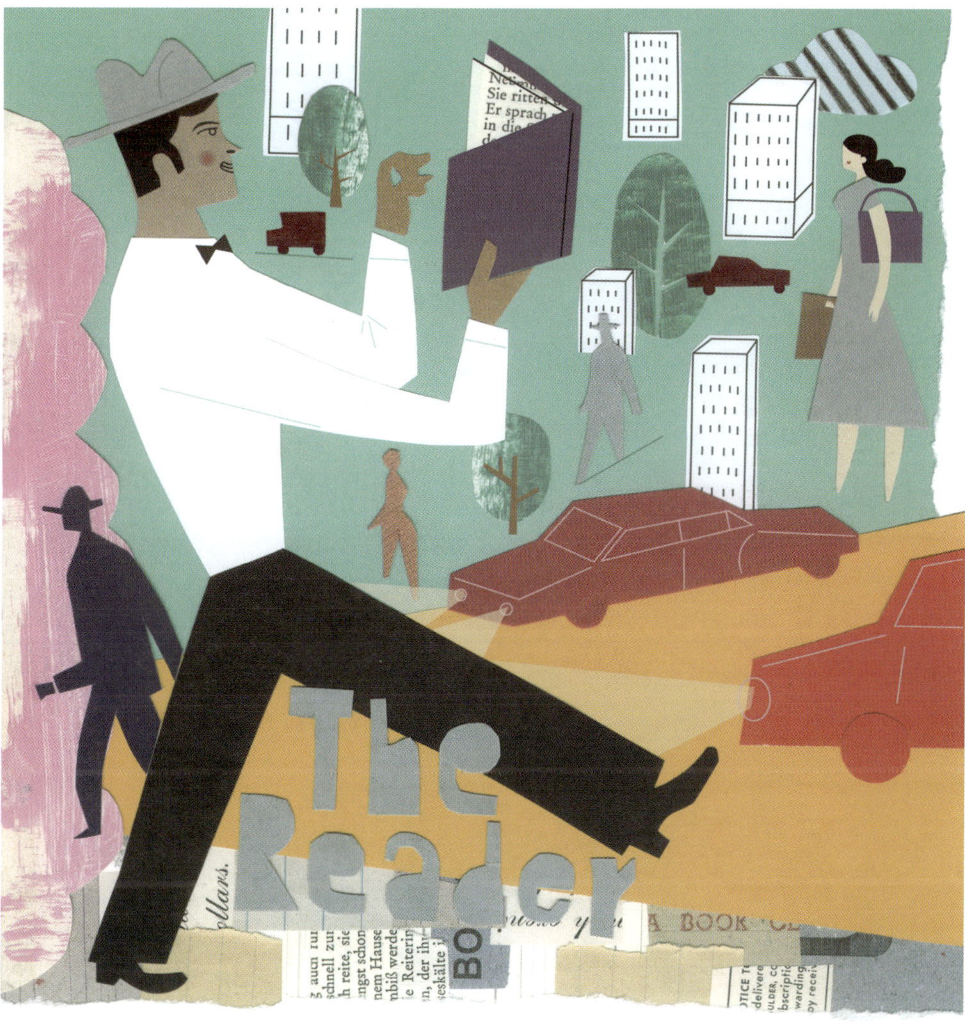
The Reader

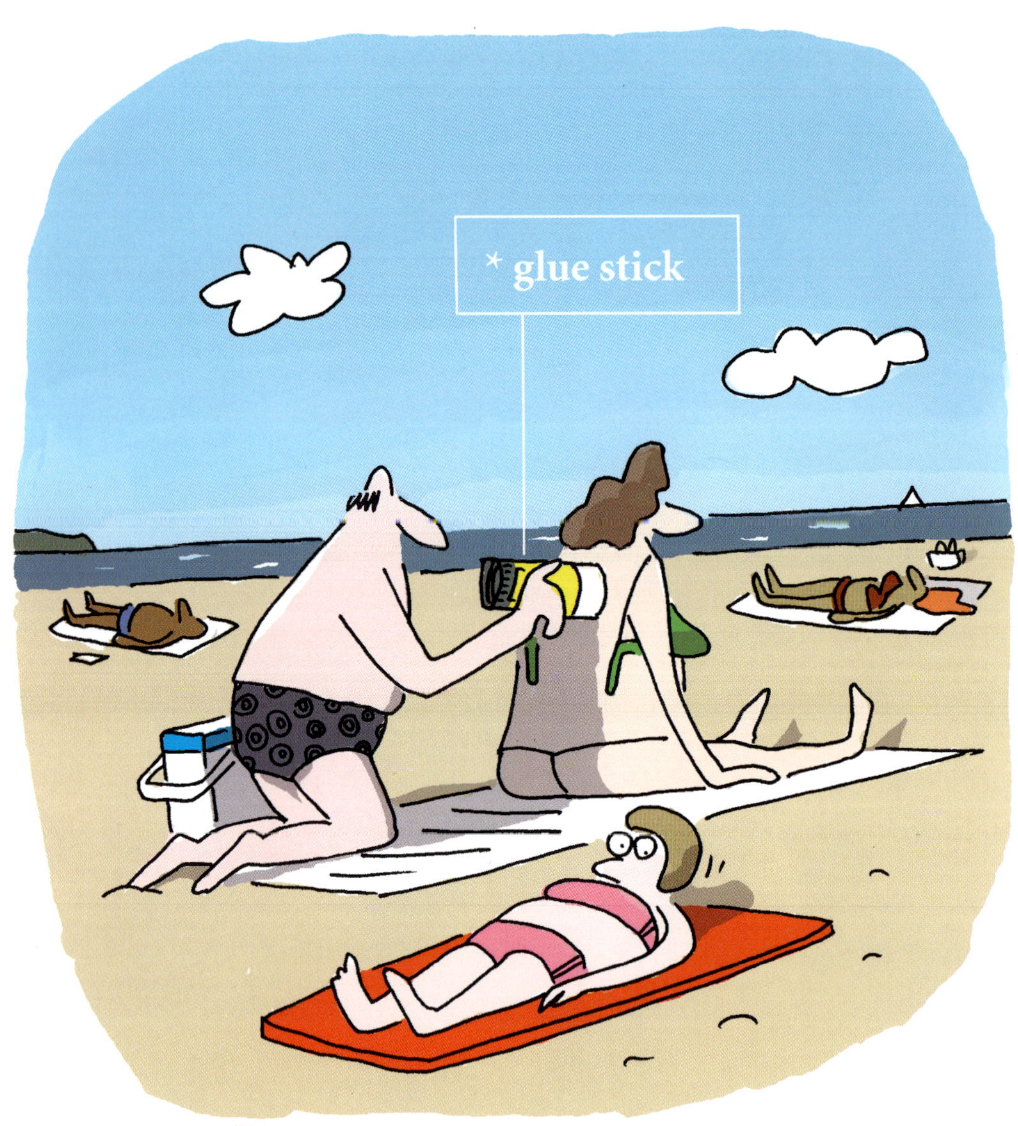
* glue stick

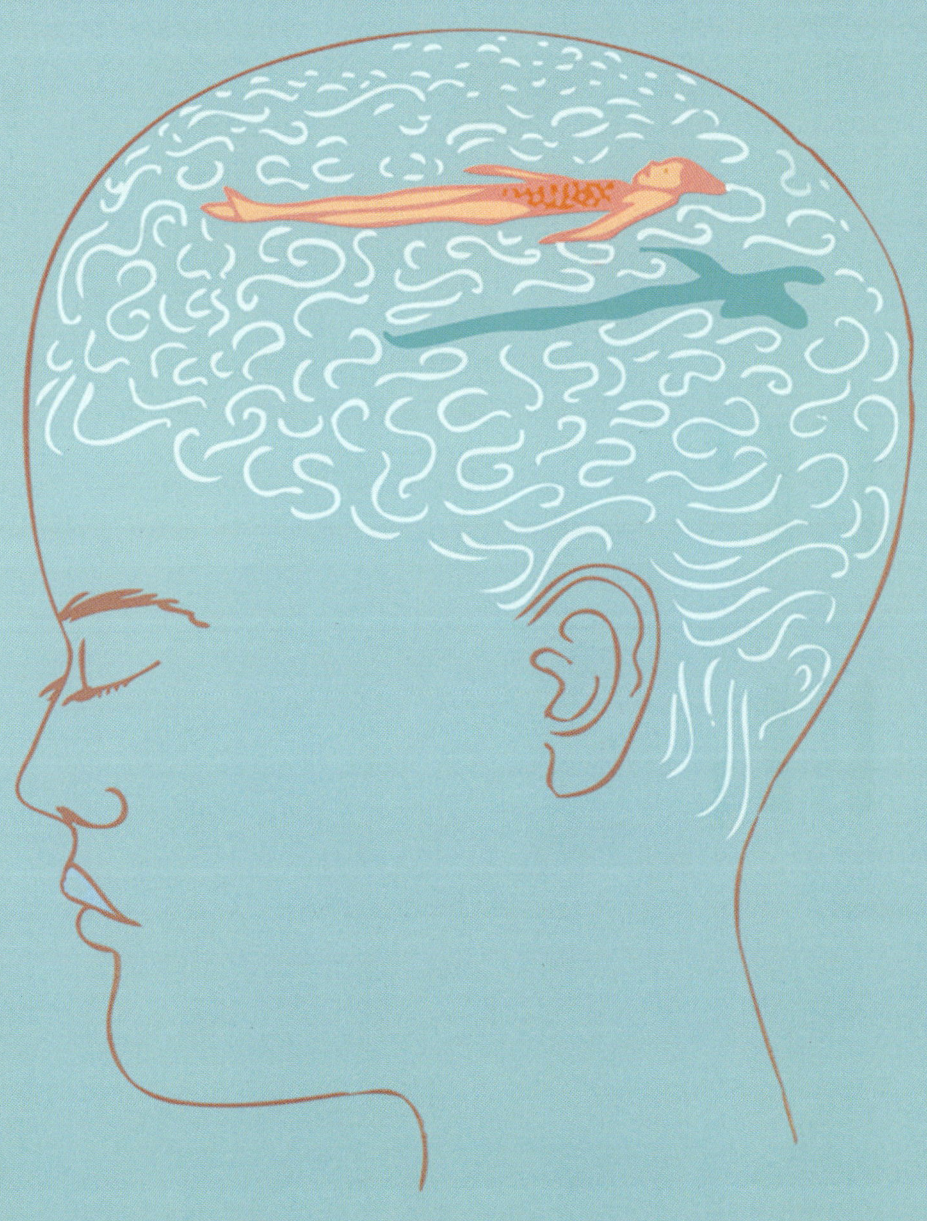

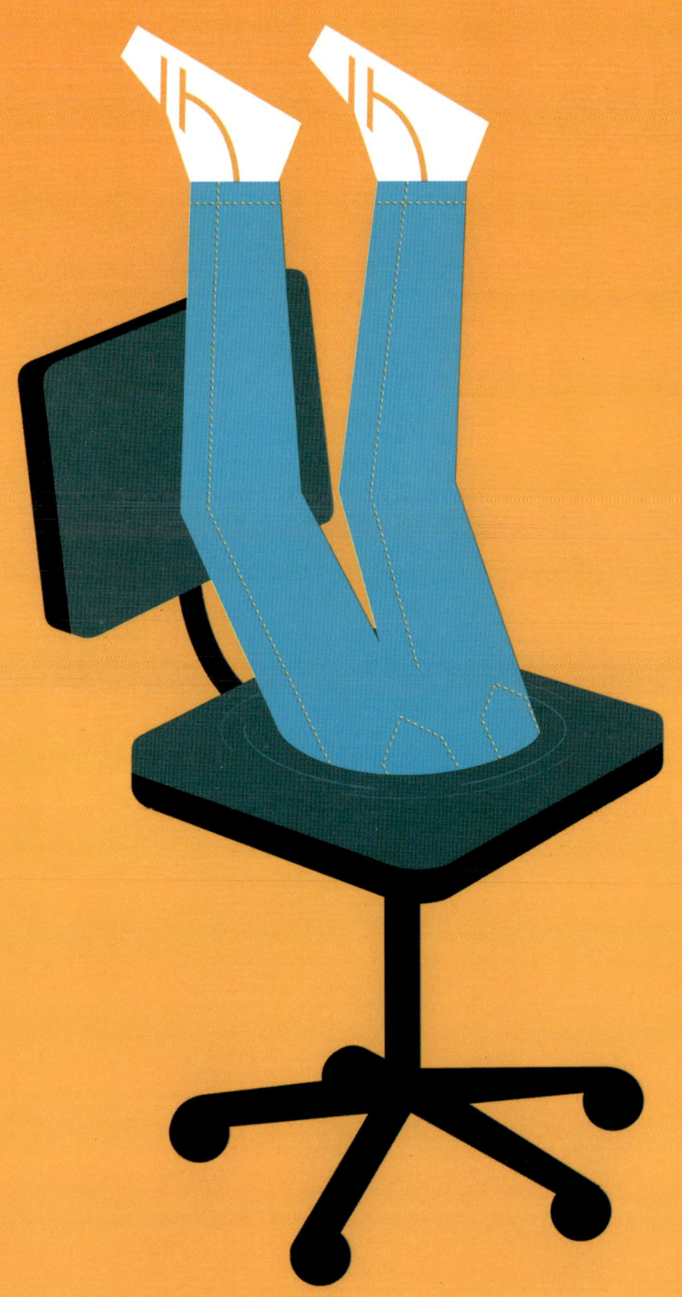

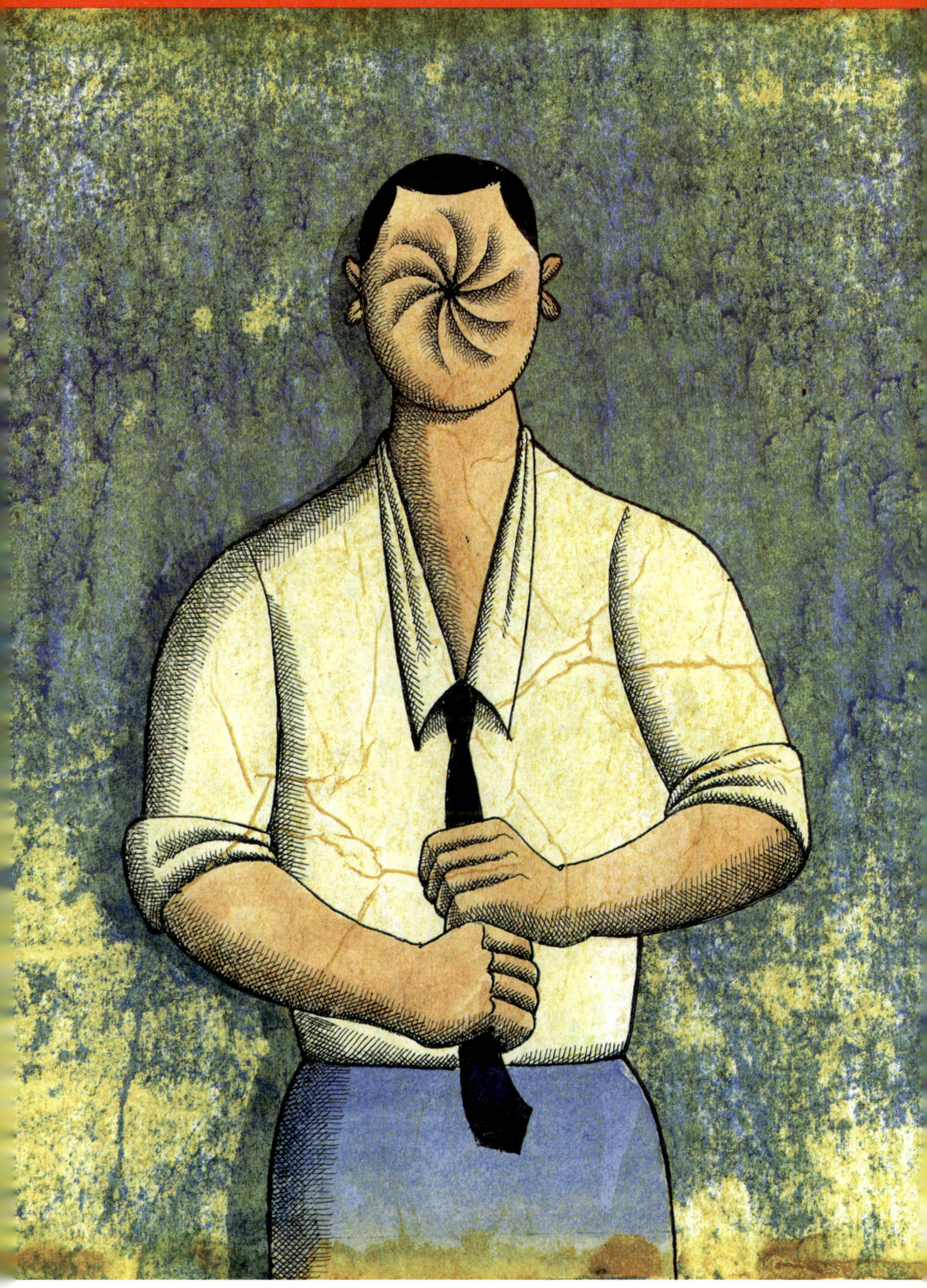

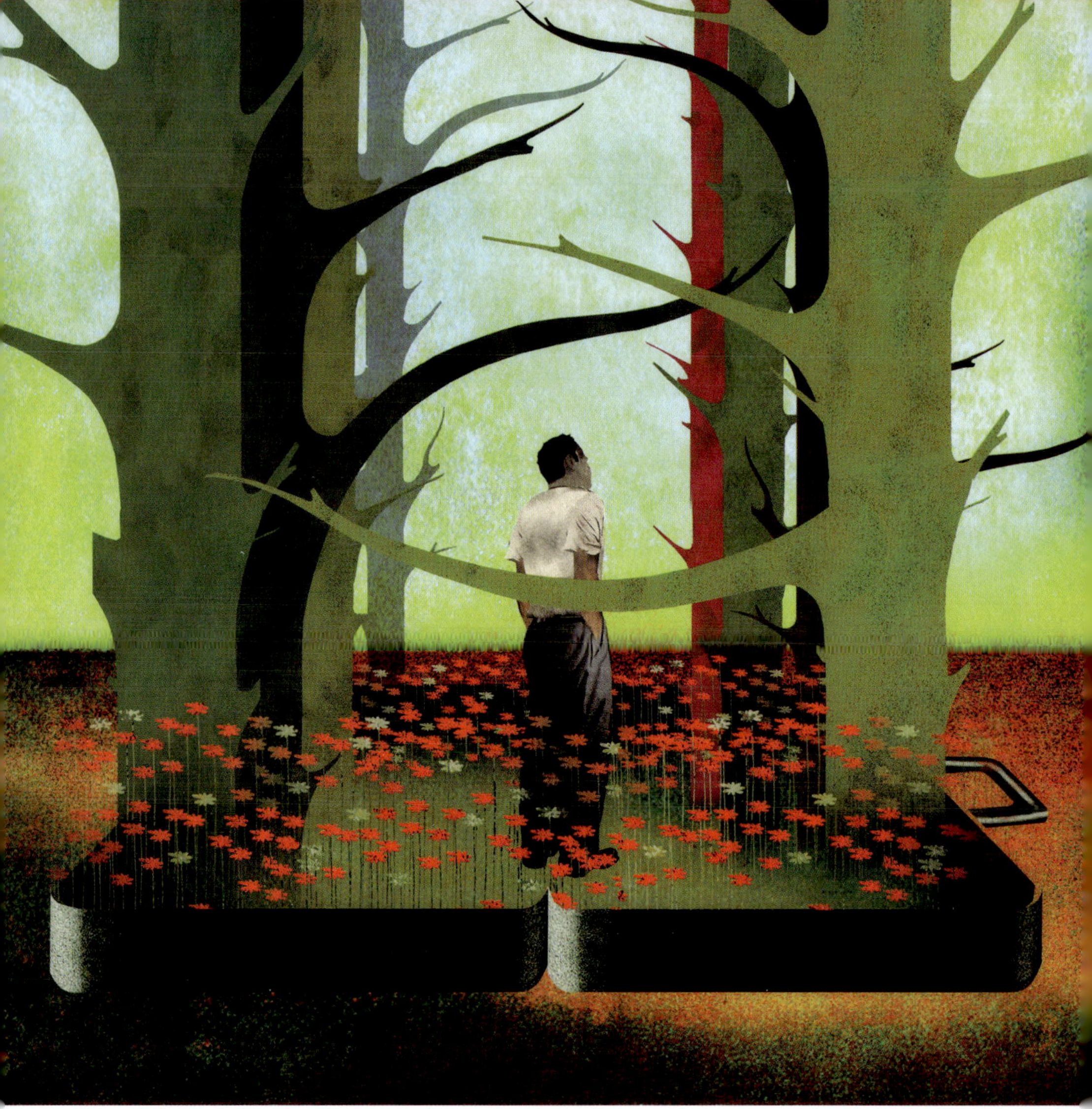

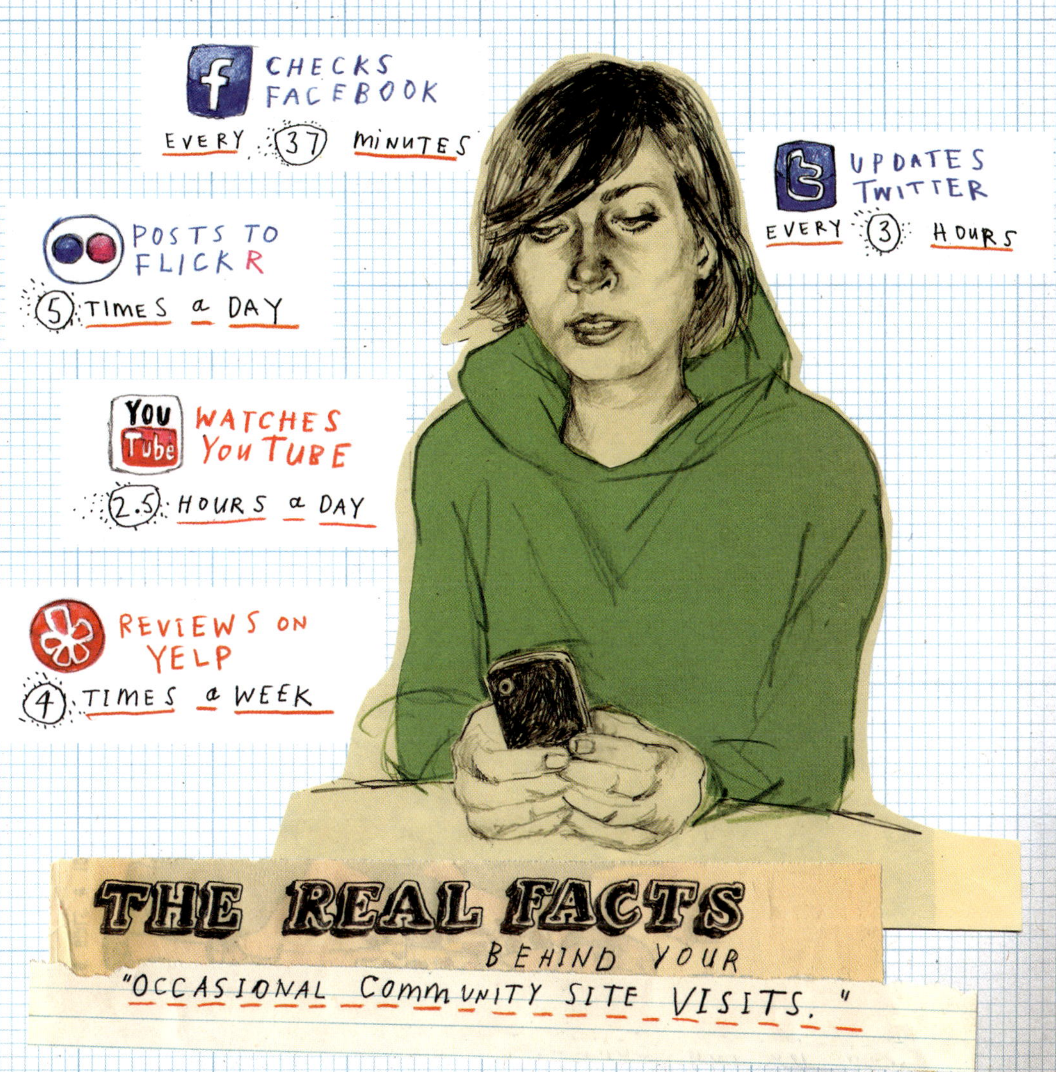
CHECKS FACEBOOK
EVERY 37 MINUTES
POSTS TO FLICKR
5 TIMES a DAY
WATCHES YouTUBE
2.5 HOURS a DAY
REVIEWS ON YELP
4 TIMES a WEEK
UPDATES TWITTER
EVERY 3 HOURS
THE REAL FACTS
BEHIND YOUR
"OCCASIONAL COMMUNITY SITE VISITS."

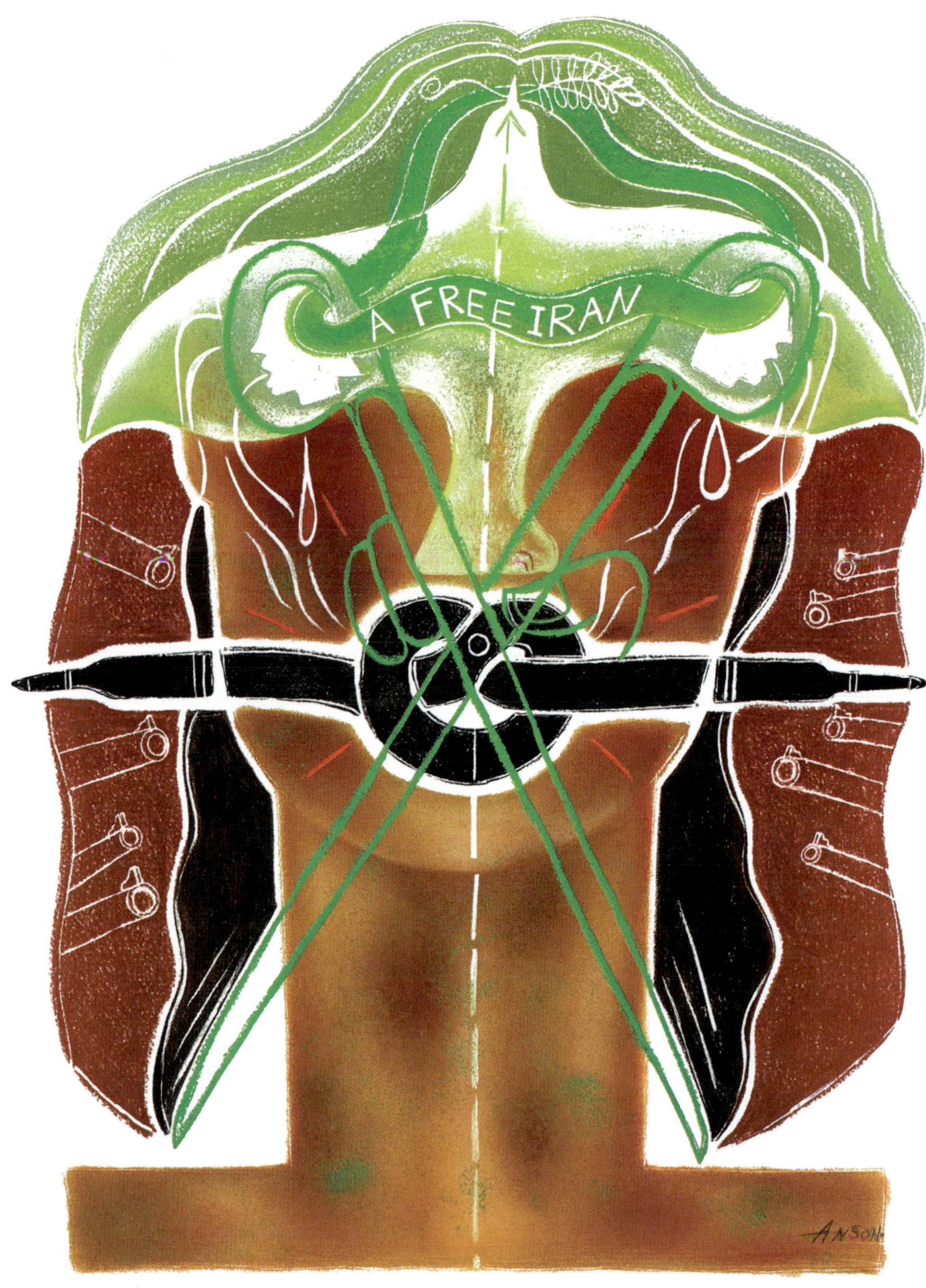
A FREE IRAN
ANSON

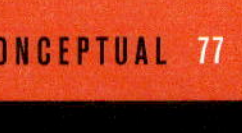

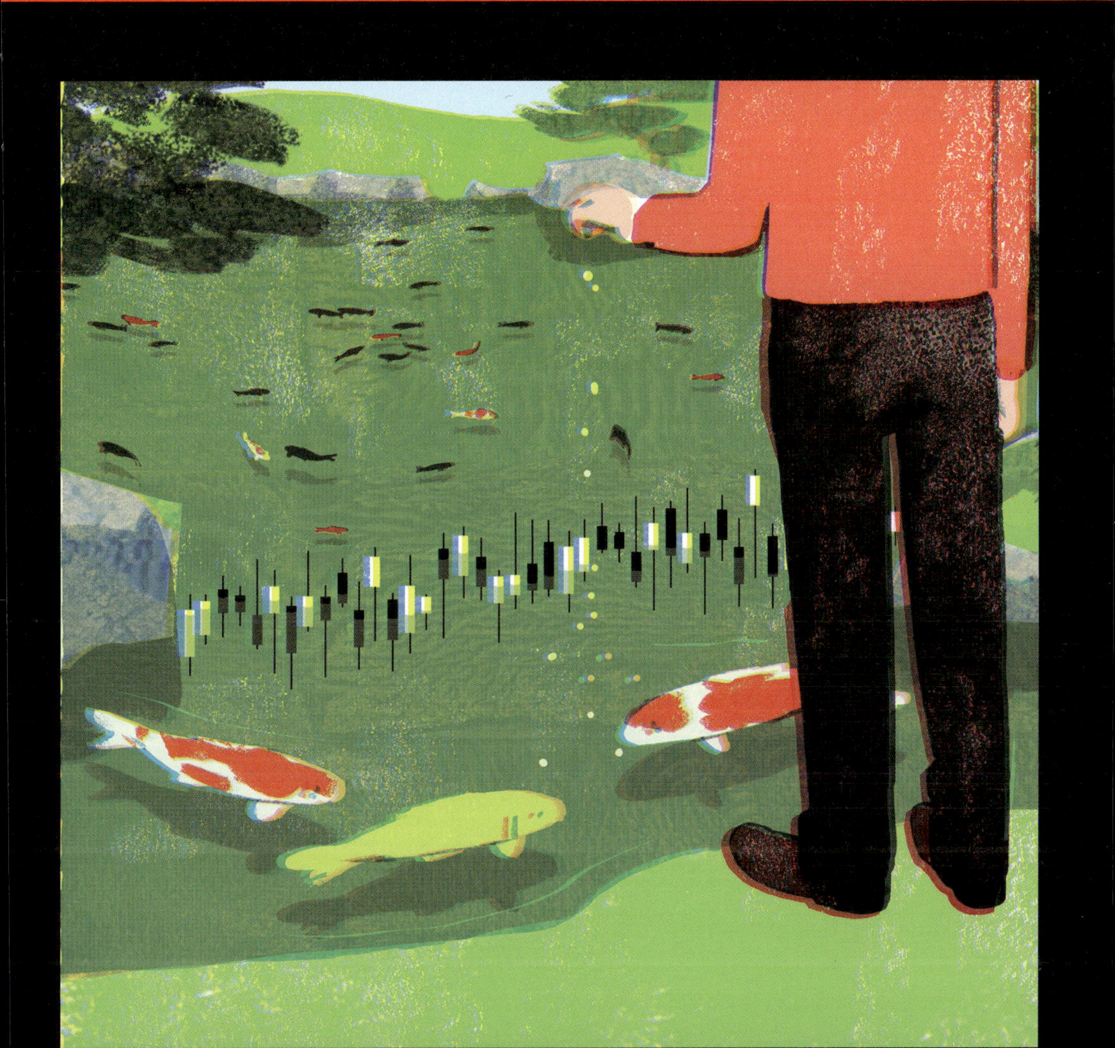

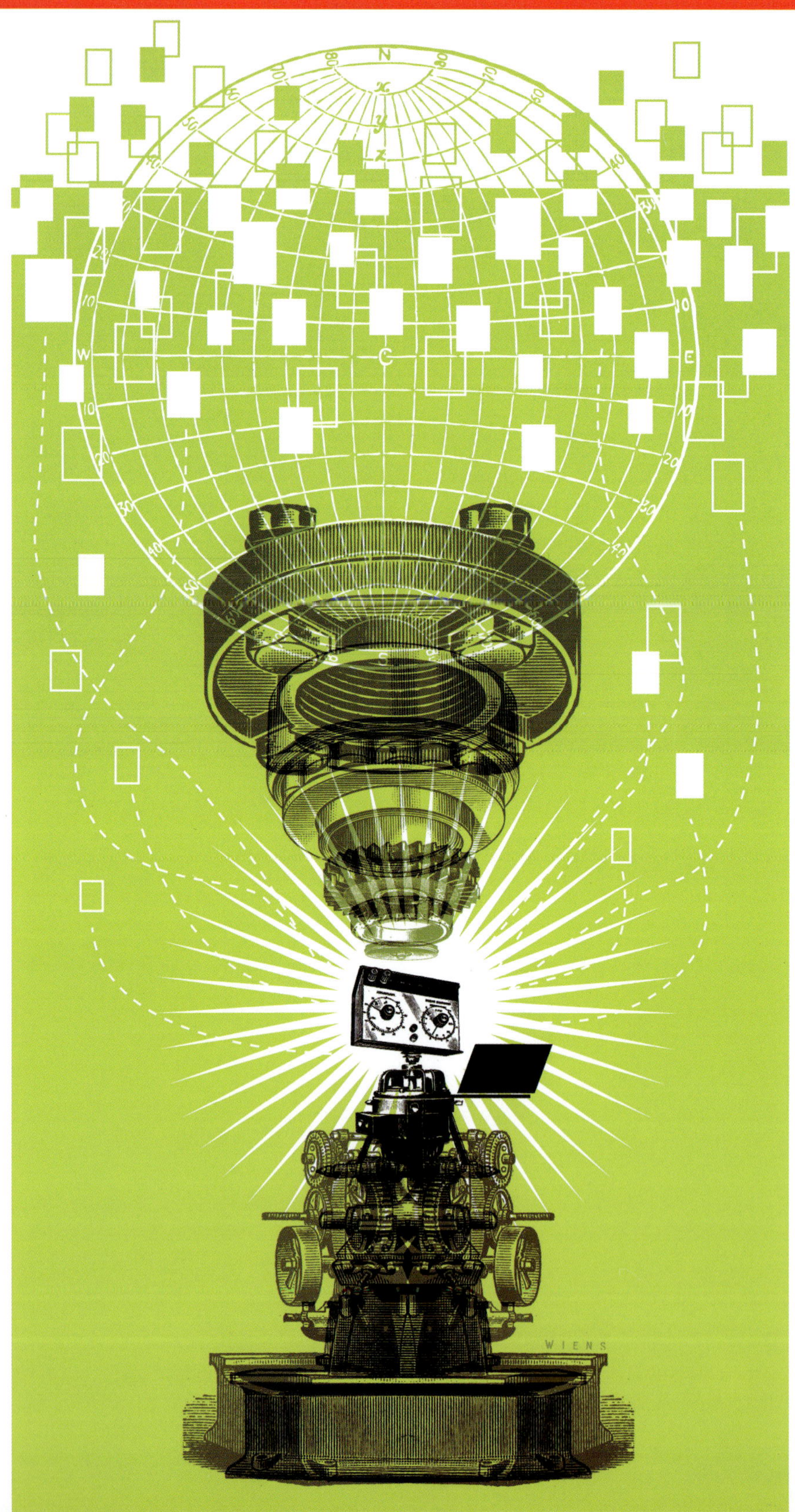

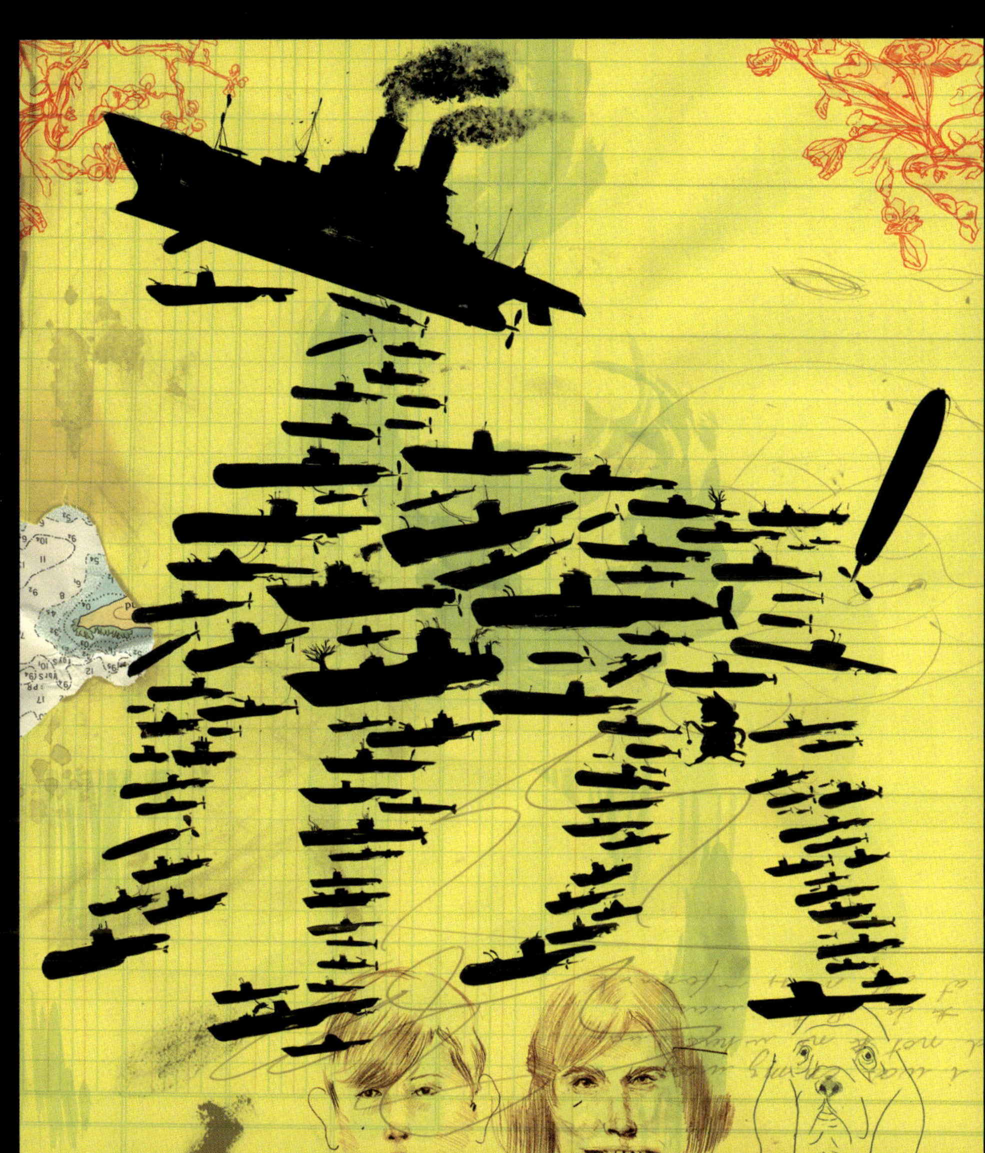

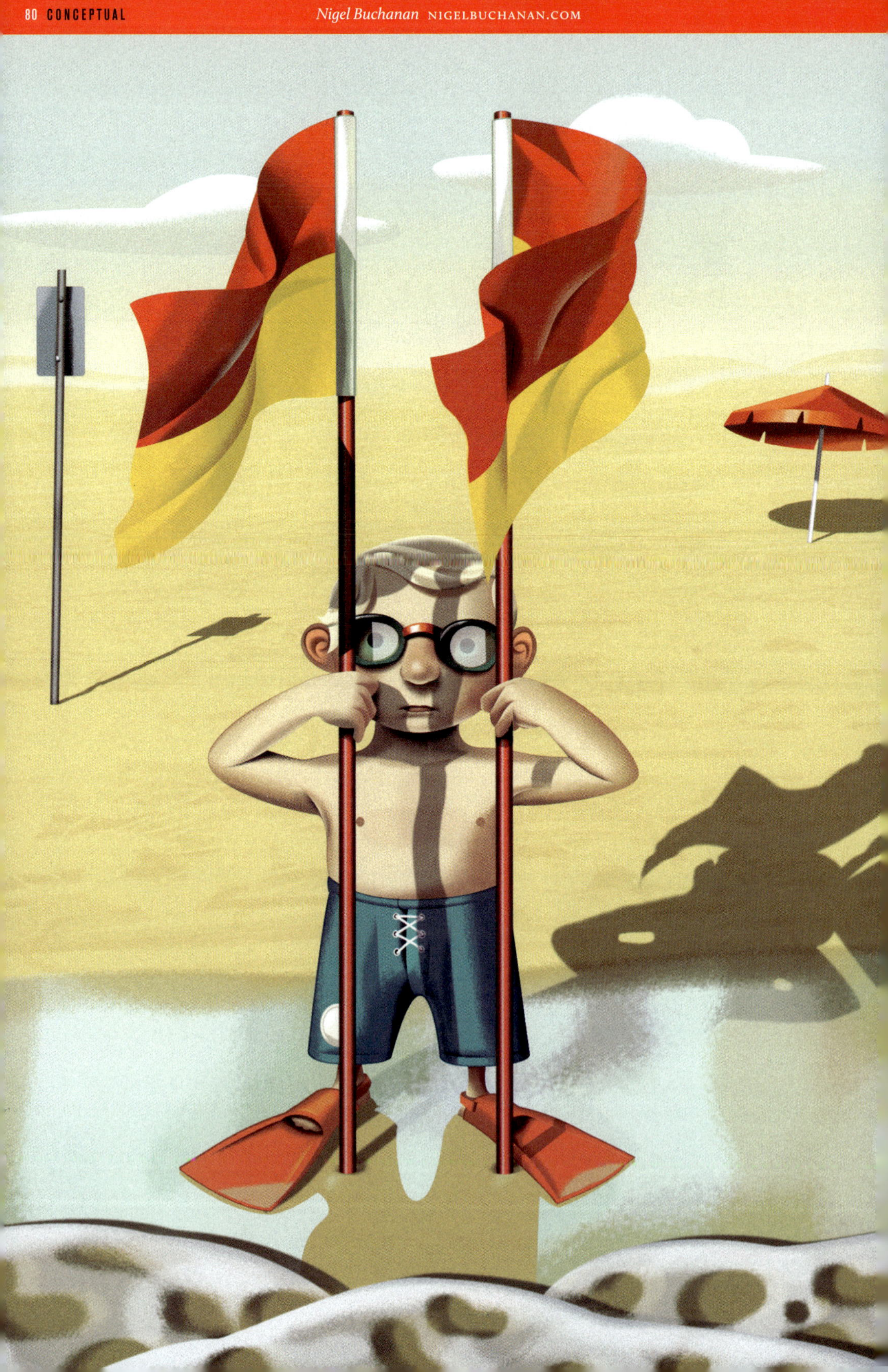

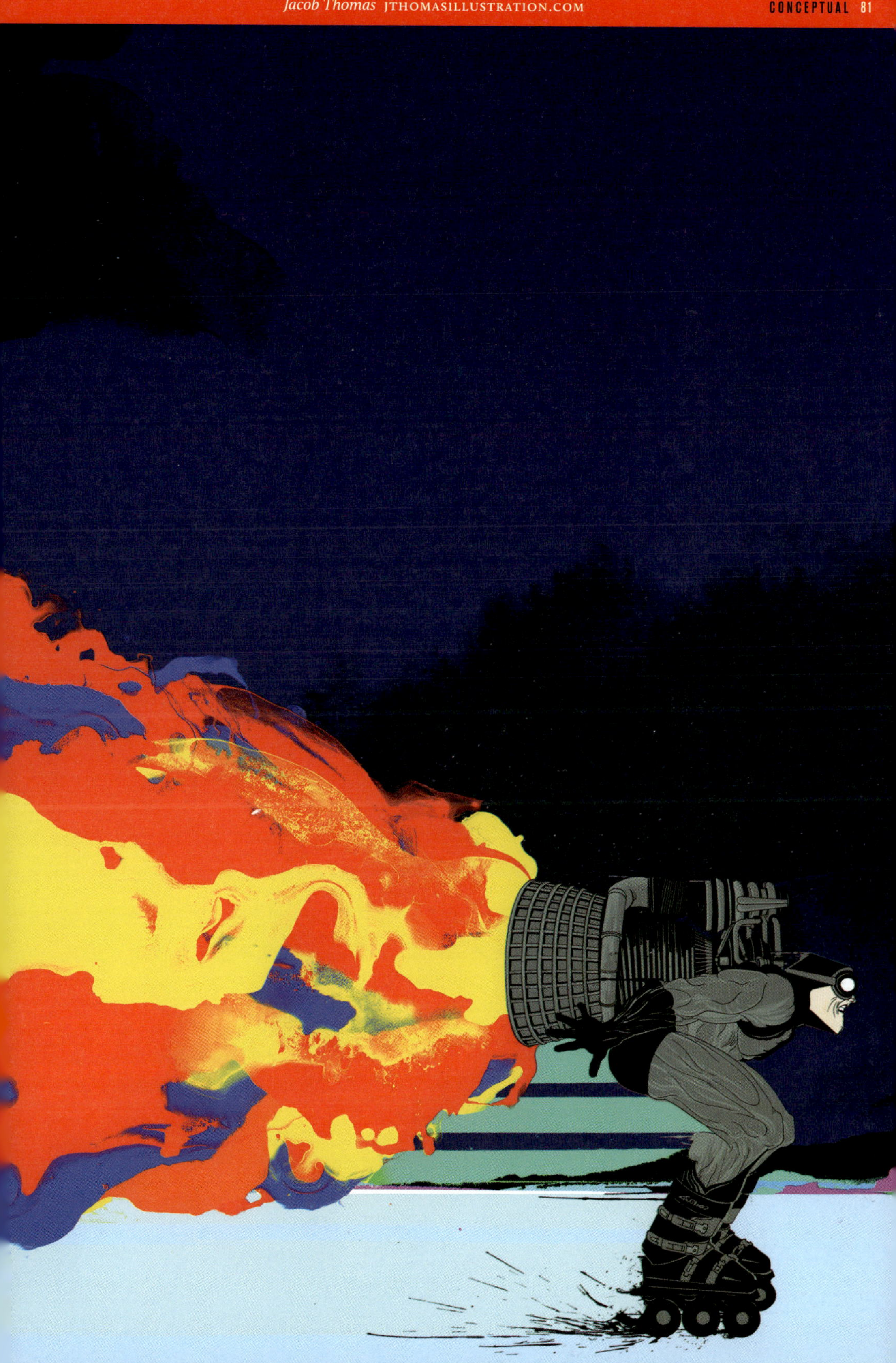

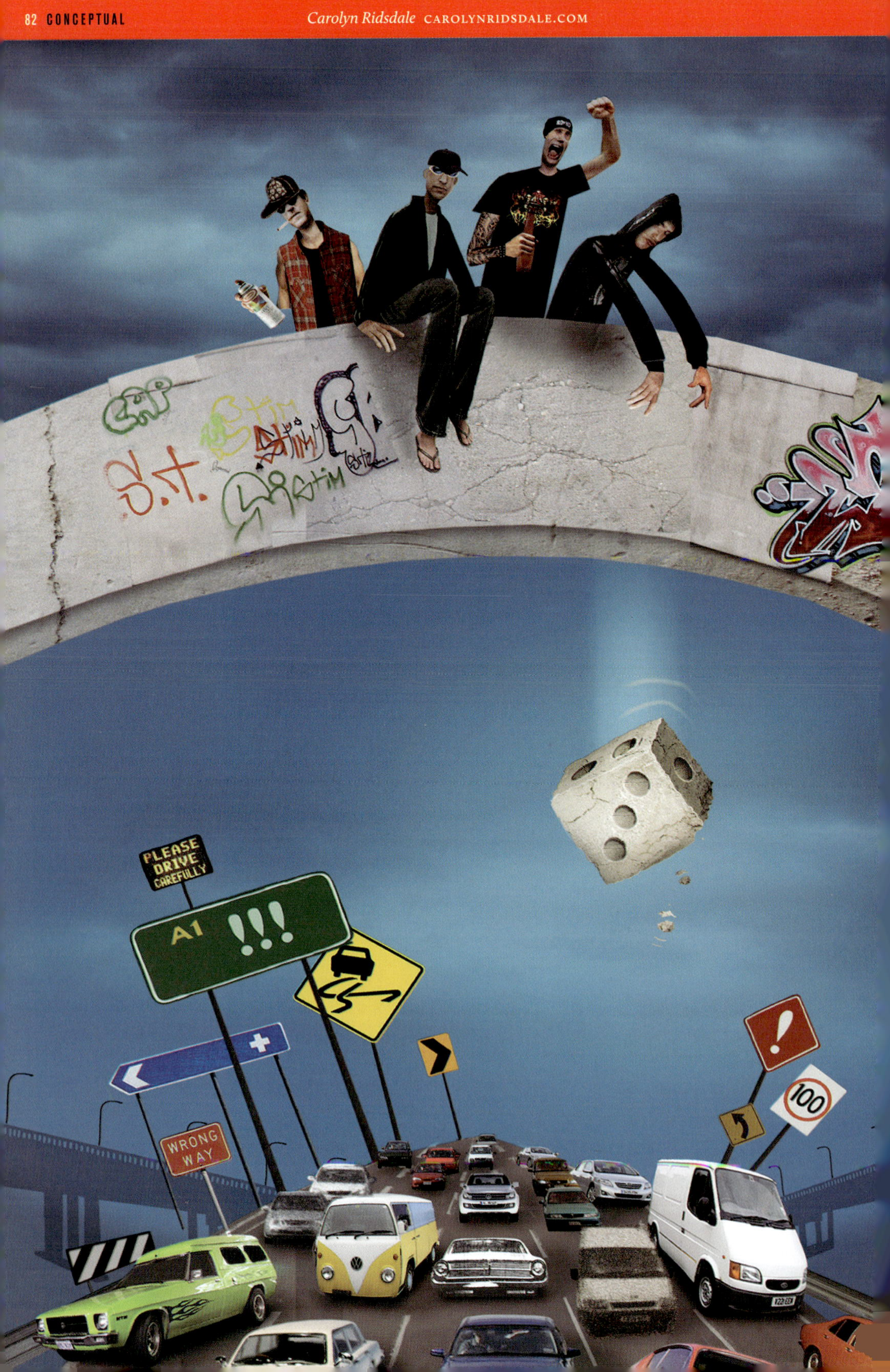
PLEASE DRIVE CAREFULLY
A1 !!!
WRONG WAY
100

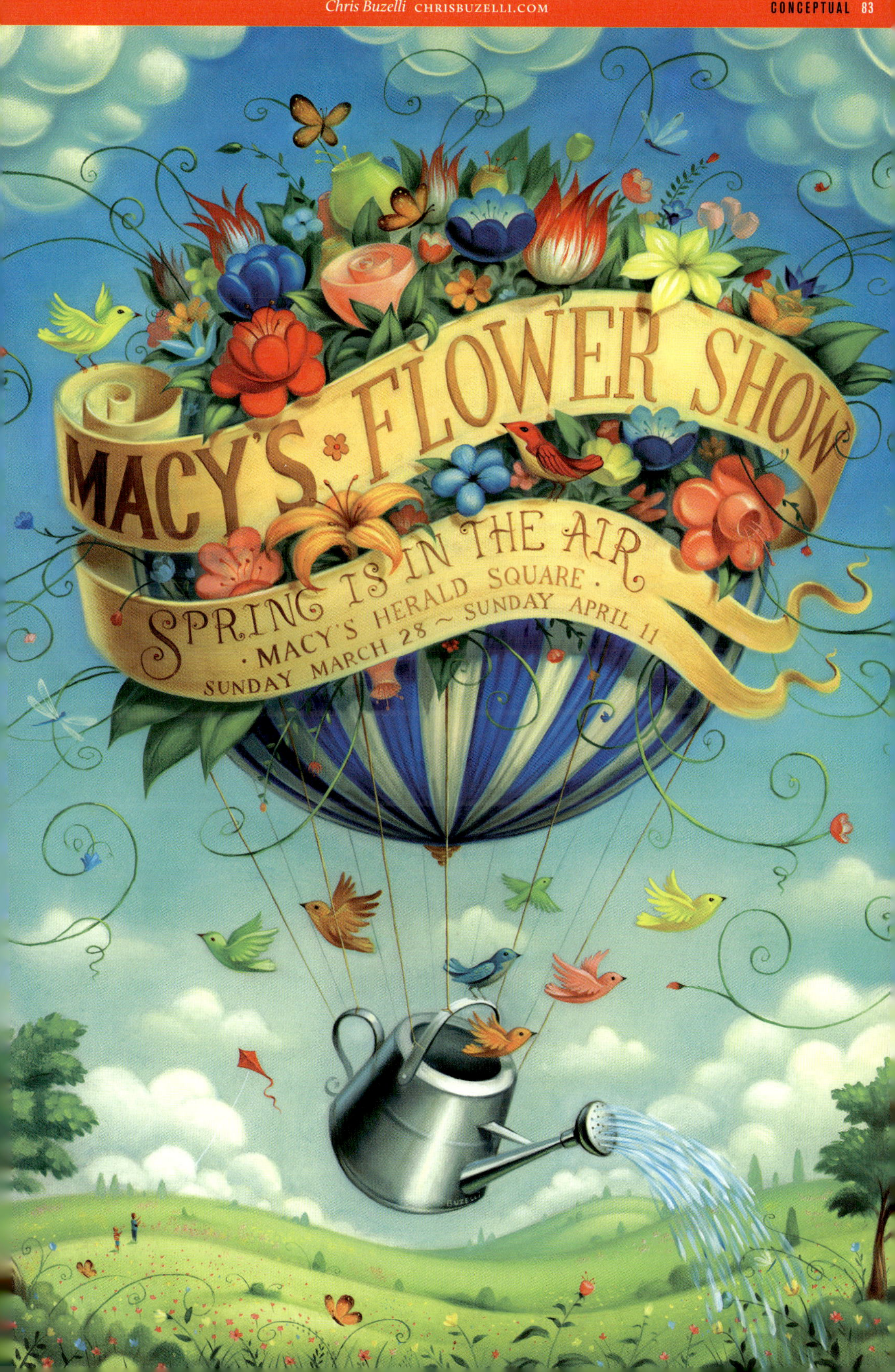
MACY'S · FLOWER SHOW
SPRING IS IN THE AIR
· MACY'S HERALD SQUARE ·
SUNDAY MARCH 28 ~ SUNDAY APRIL 11

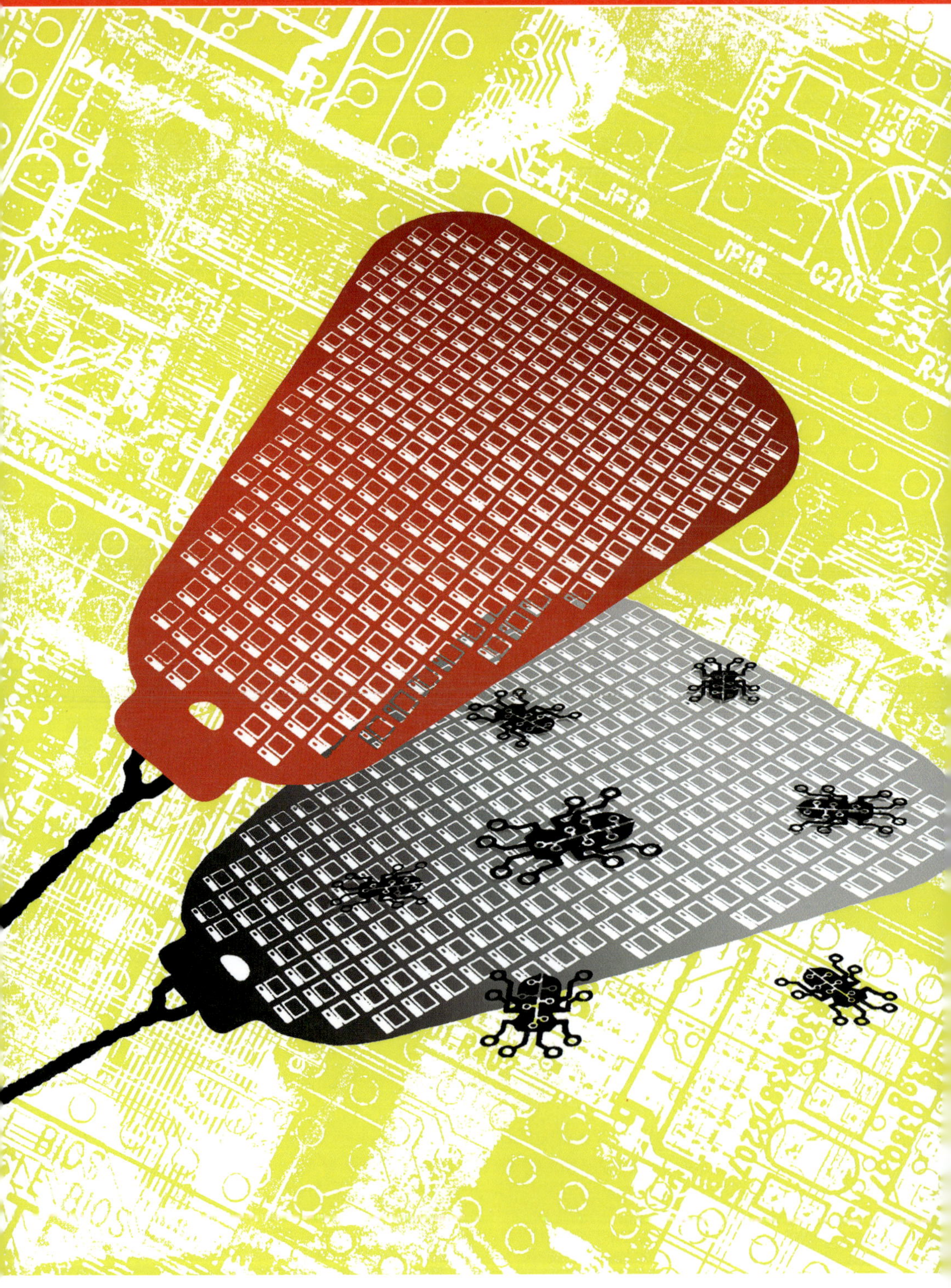

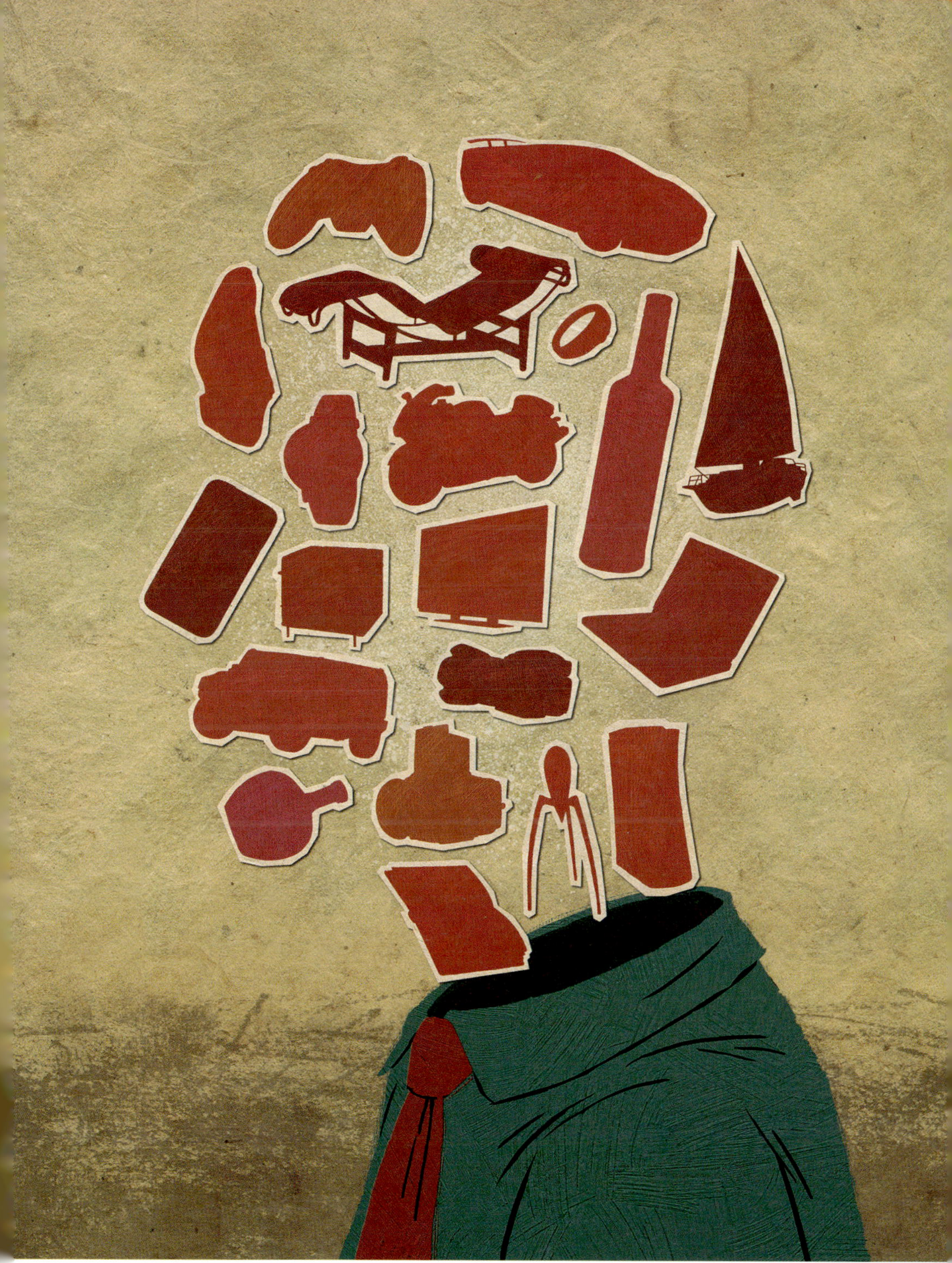

 Jonathan McHugh BEEPENCIL.COM

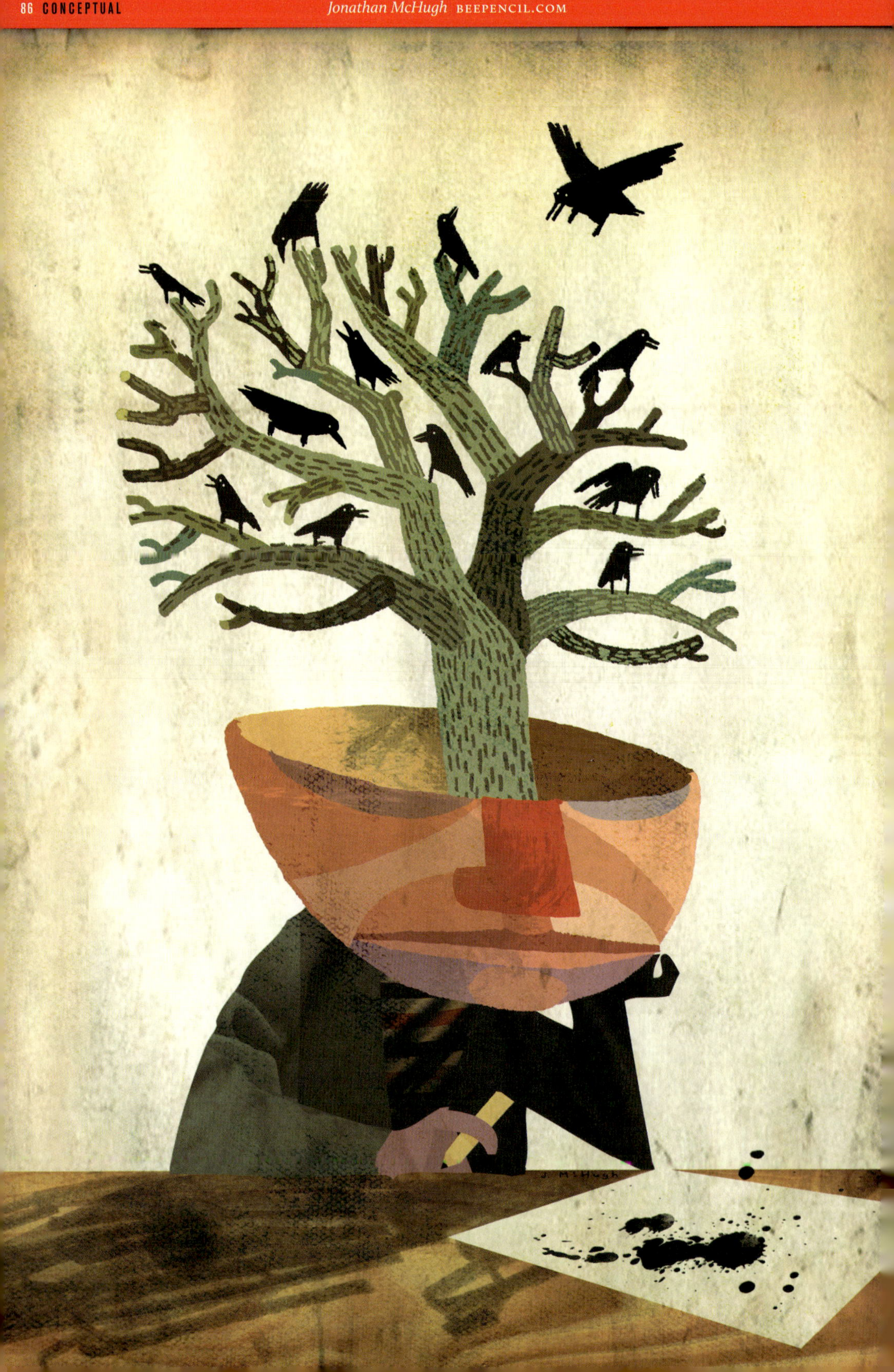

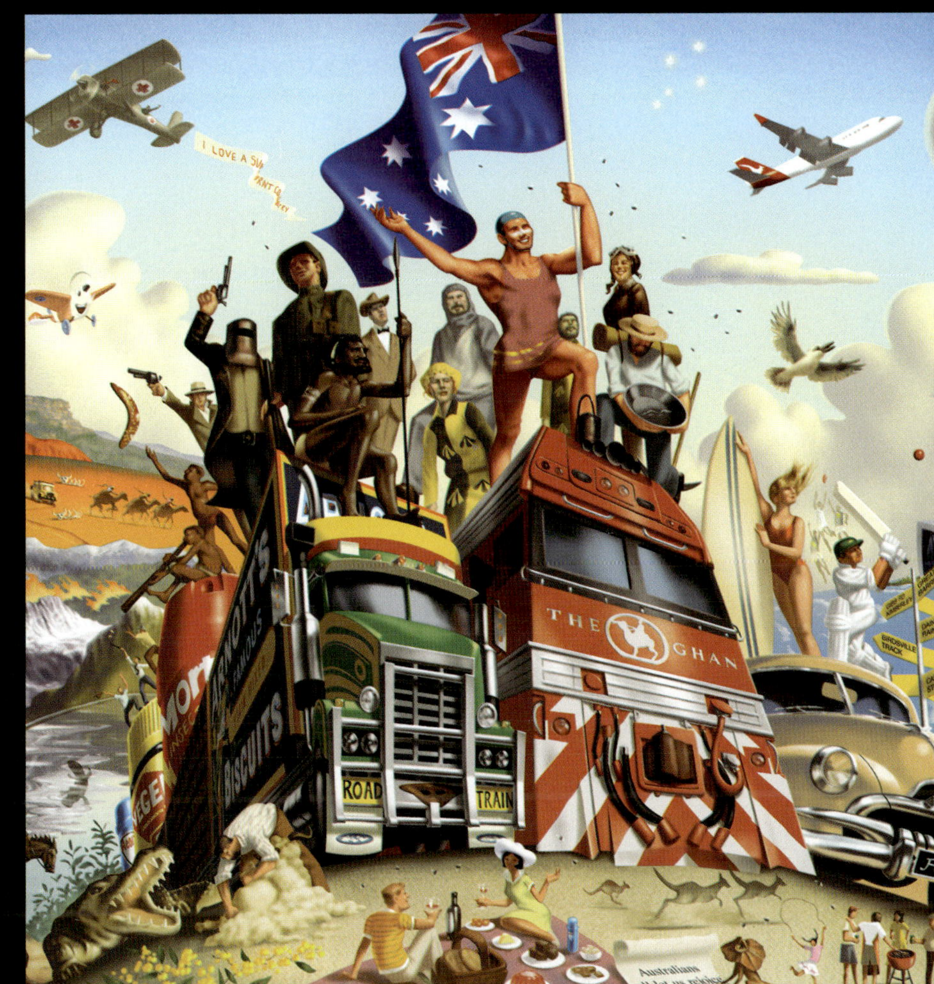
I LOVE A SU...
...RNT C... ...RFY
ARNOTT'S
BISCUITS
Mon...
...GE...
ROAD TRAIN
THE GHAN
GREAT BARRIER REEF
DAINTREE RAINFOREST
BIRDSVILLE TRACK
CANNING STOCK ROUTE
FJ
Australians
all let us rejoice
for we are young
and free

Tibor Kárpáti TIBORKARPATI.COM

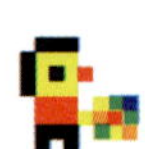

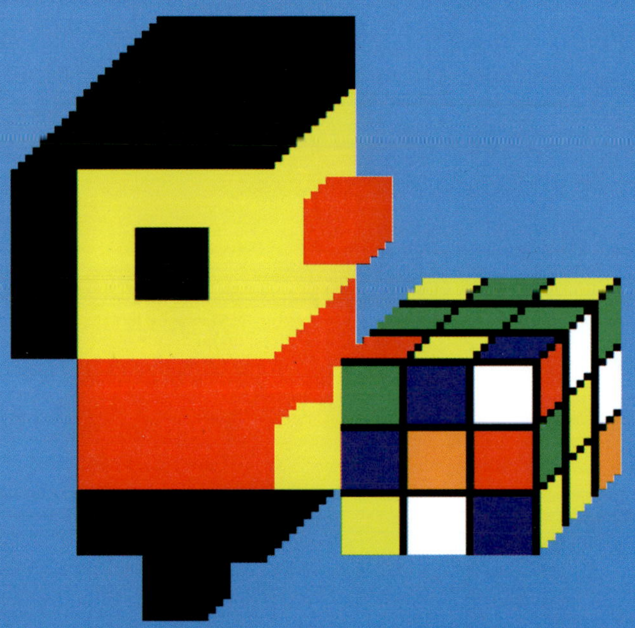

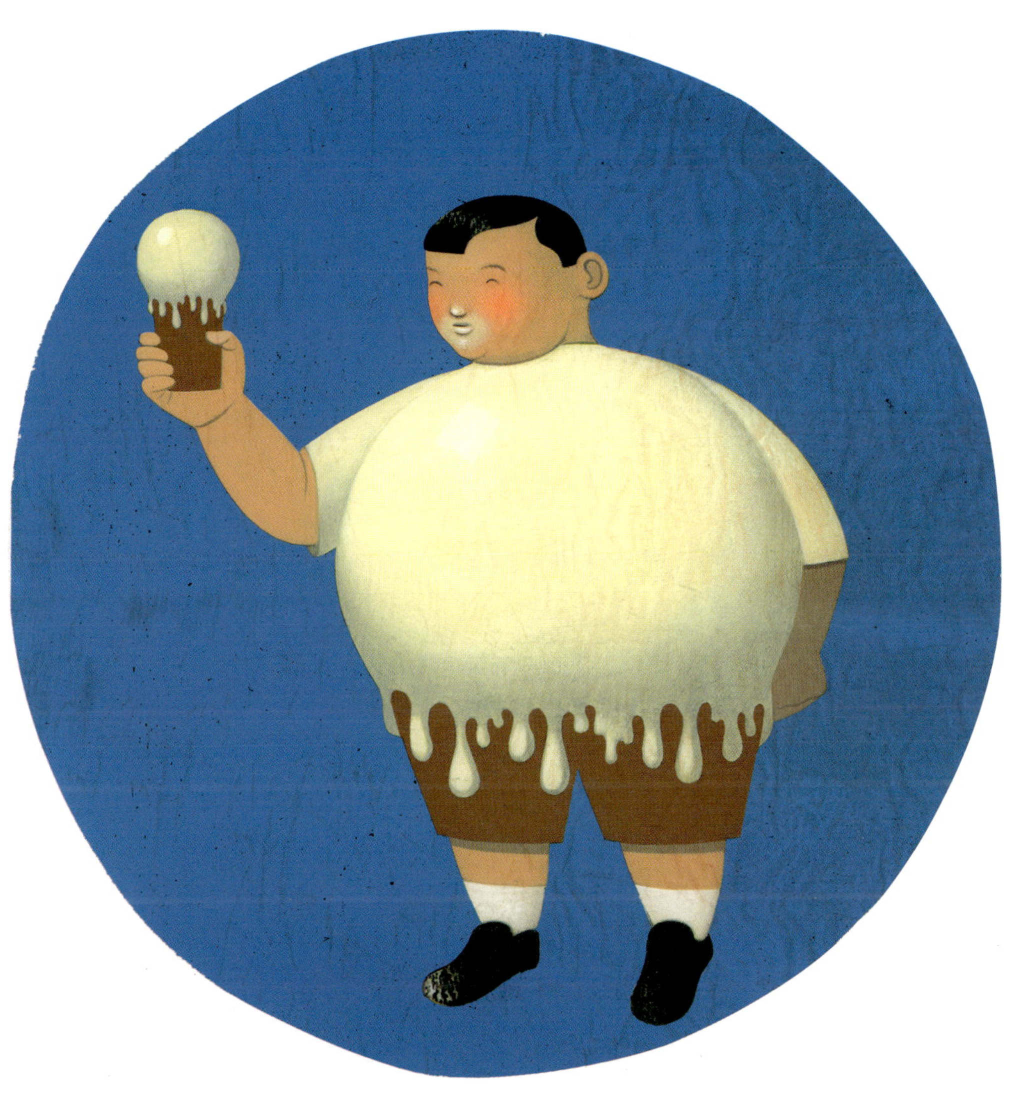

 Beck NEWTOONSONTHEBLOG.INFO

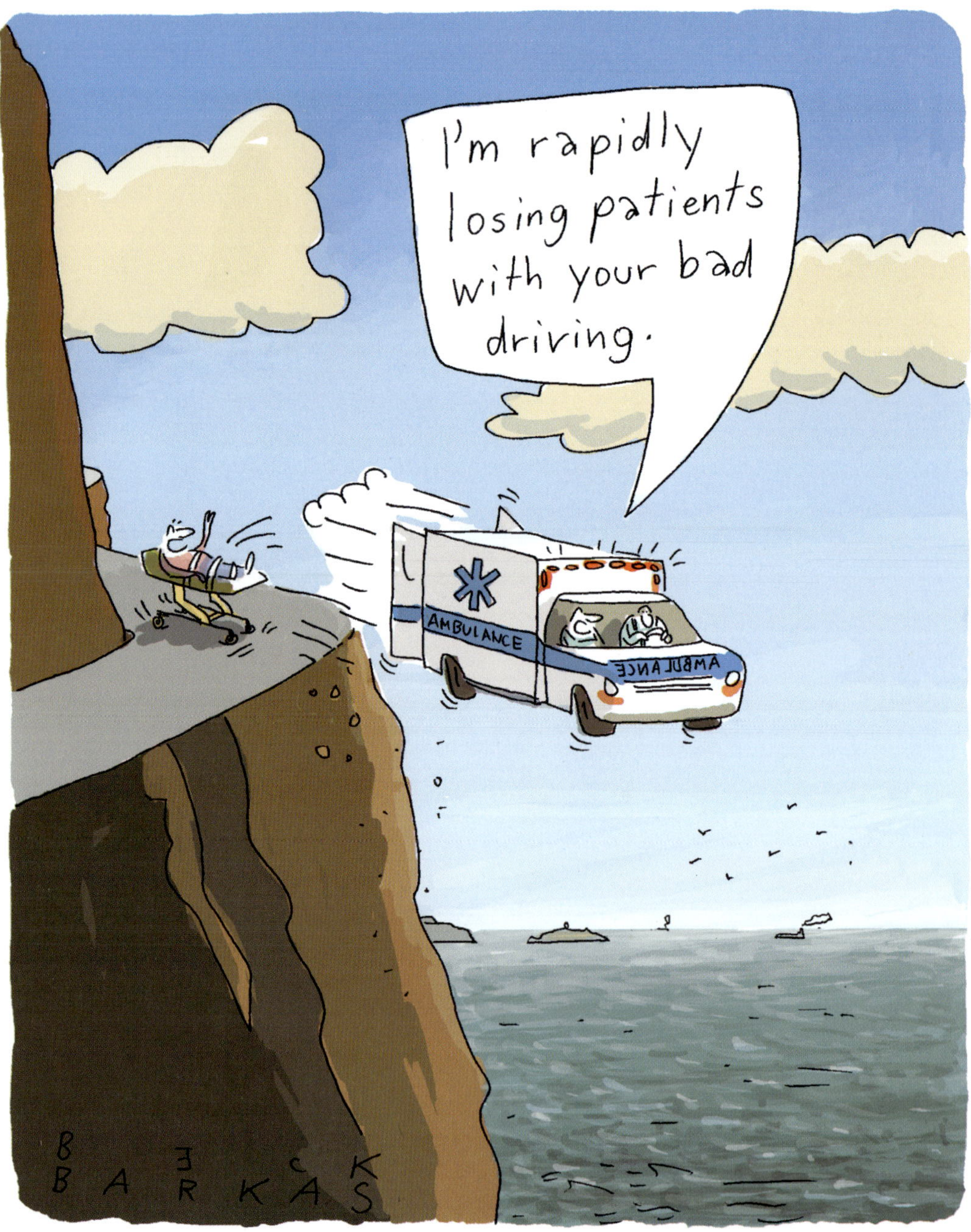

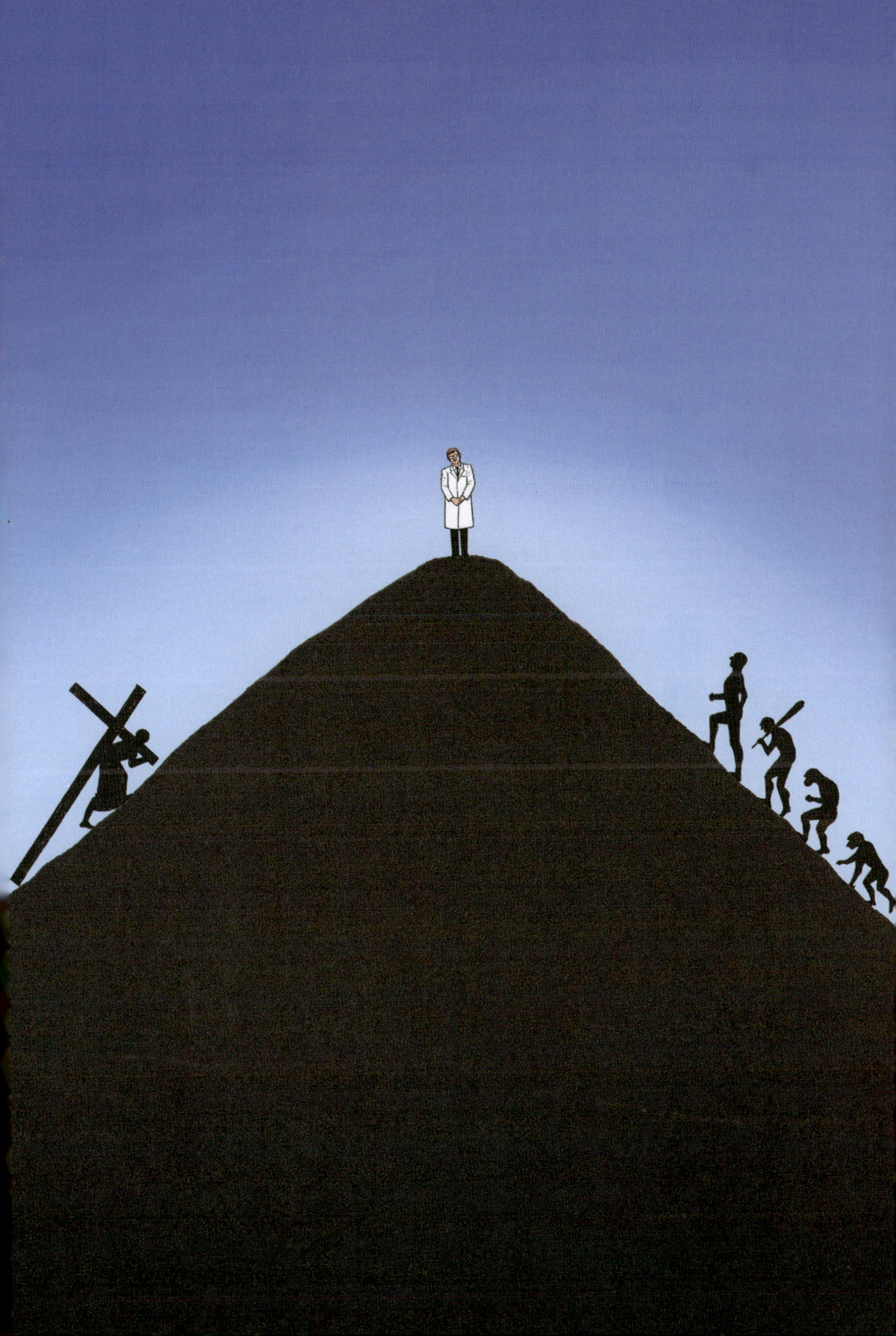

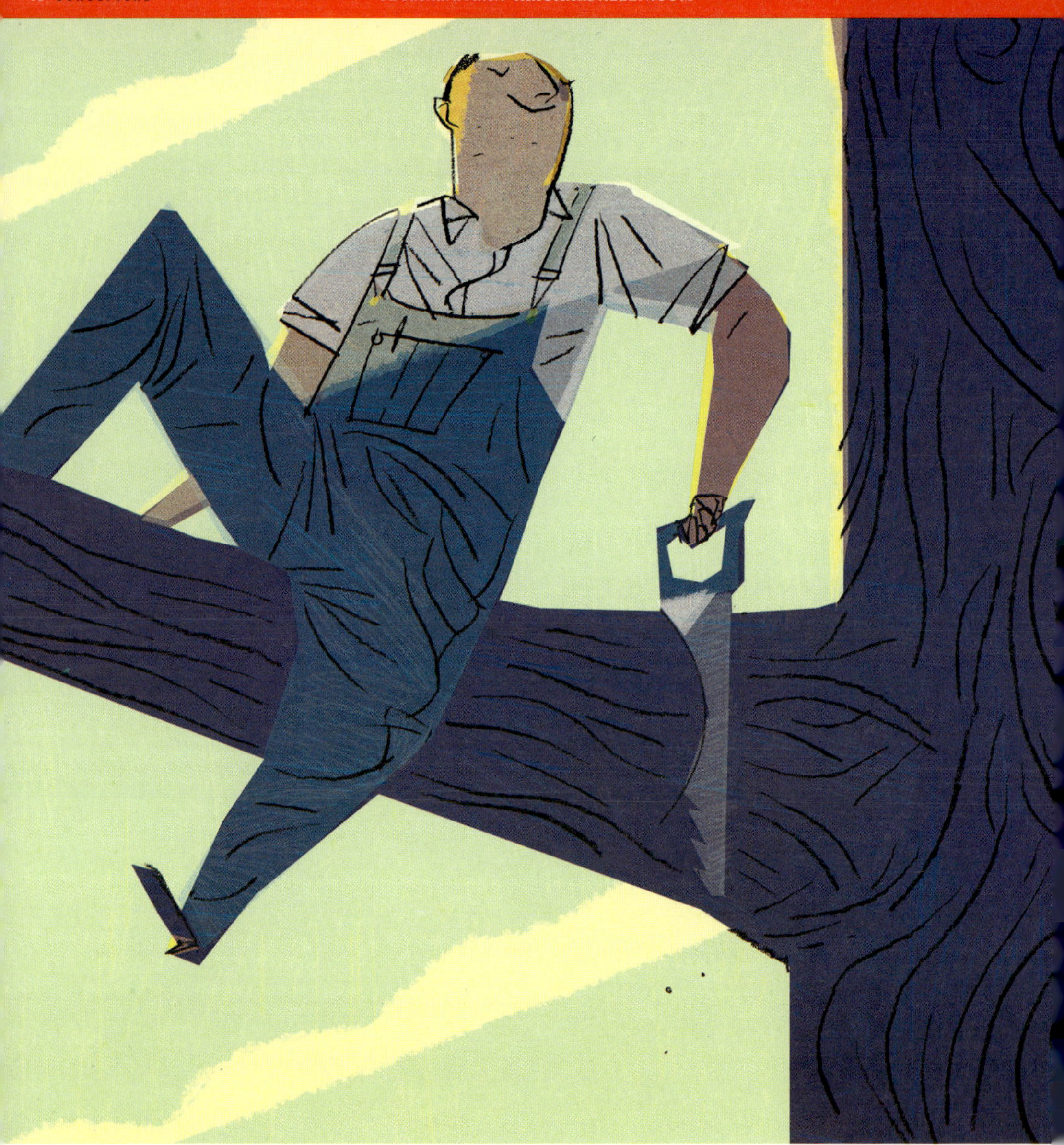

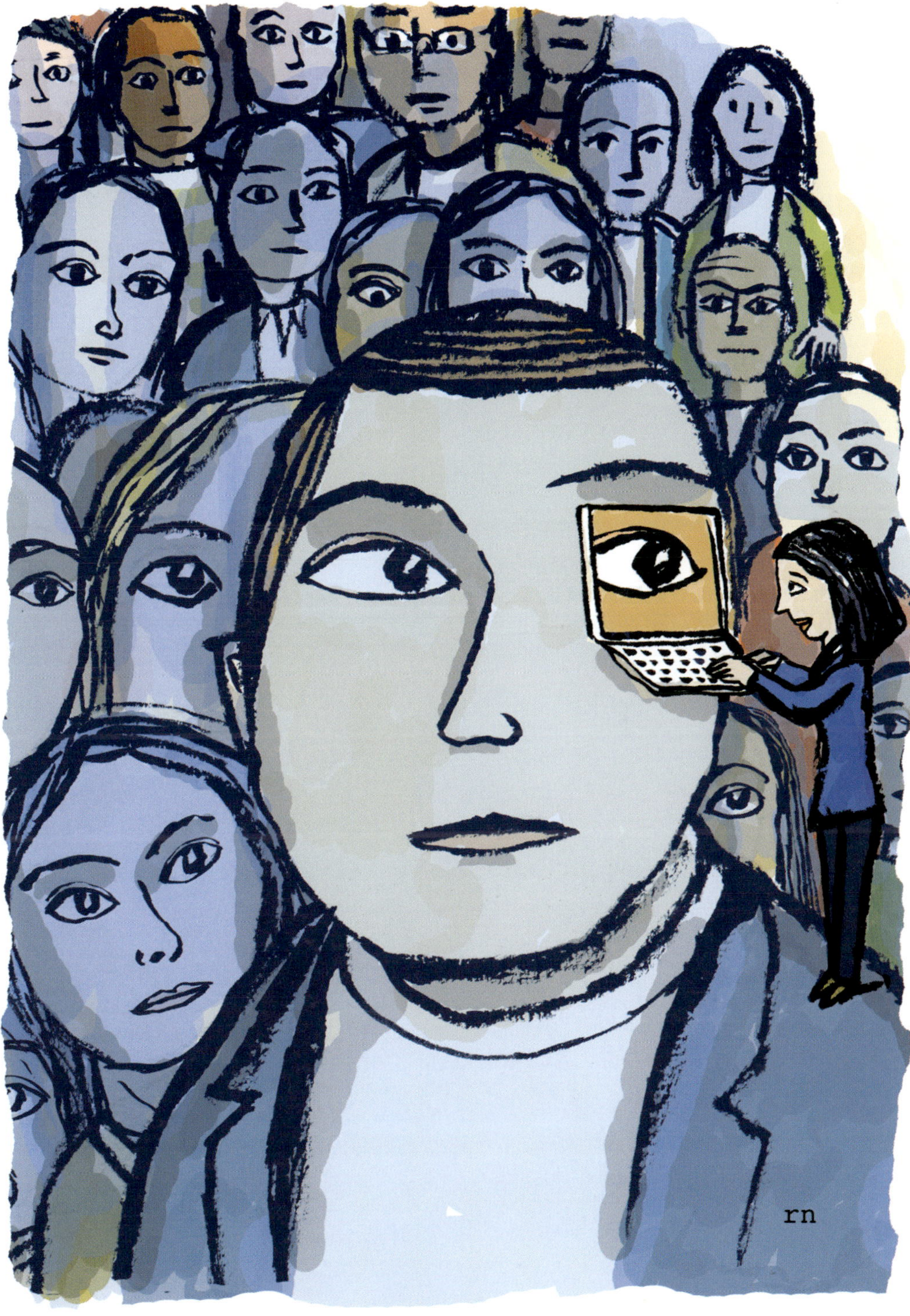

   Robin Hursthouse ROBINHURSTHOUSE.CO.UK

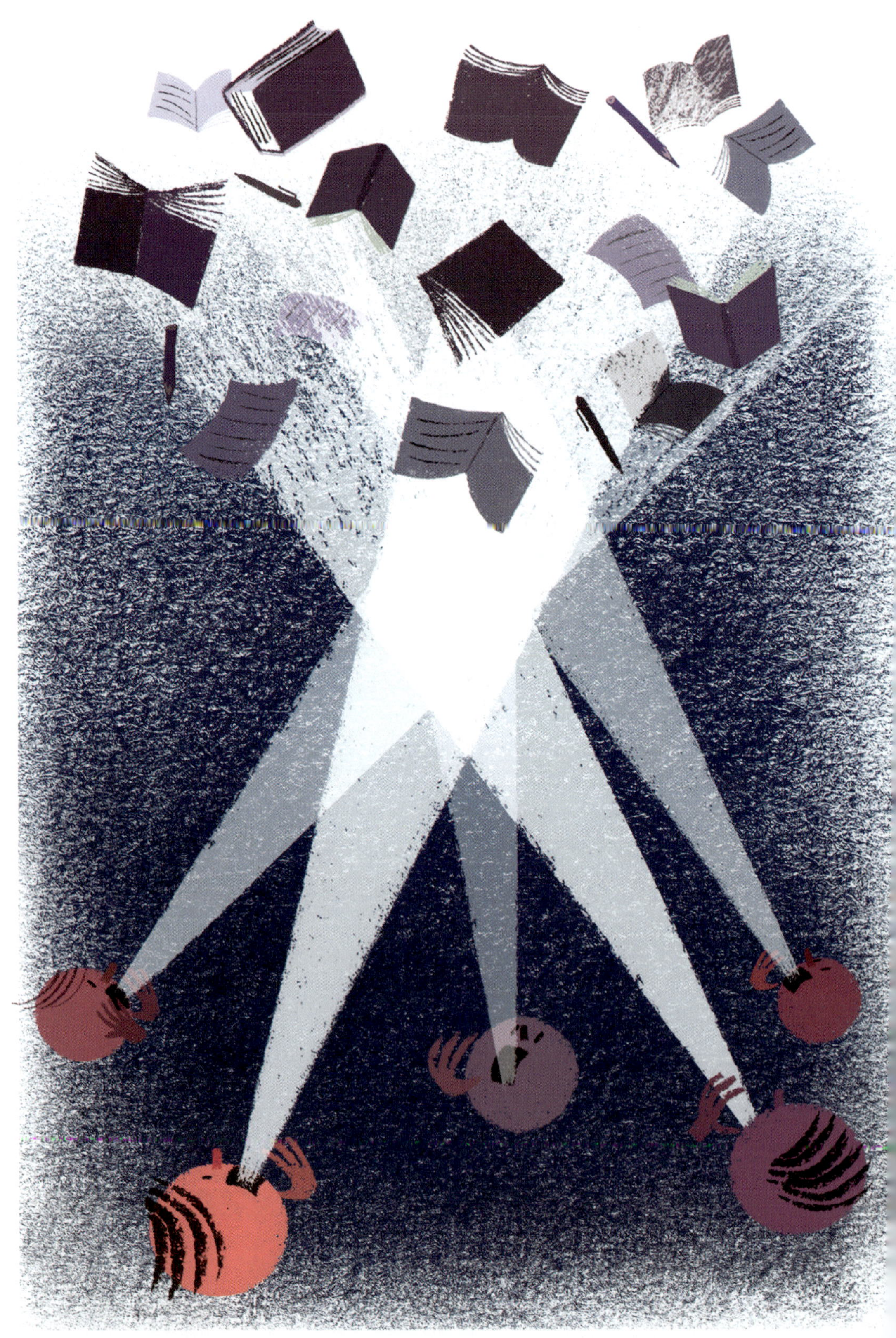

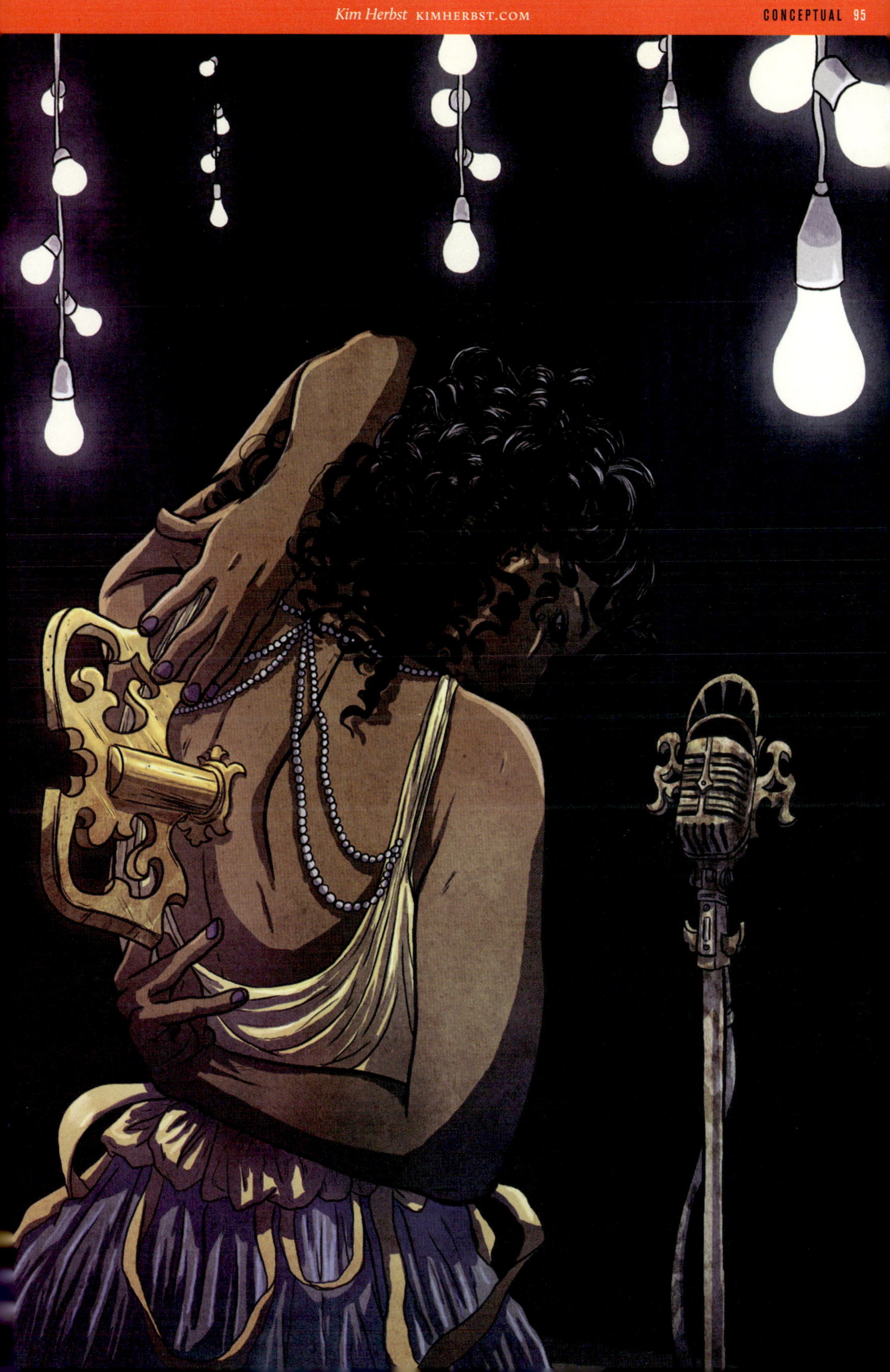

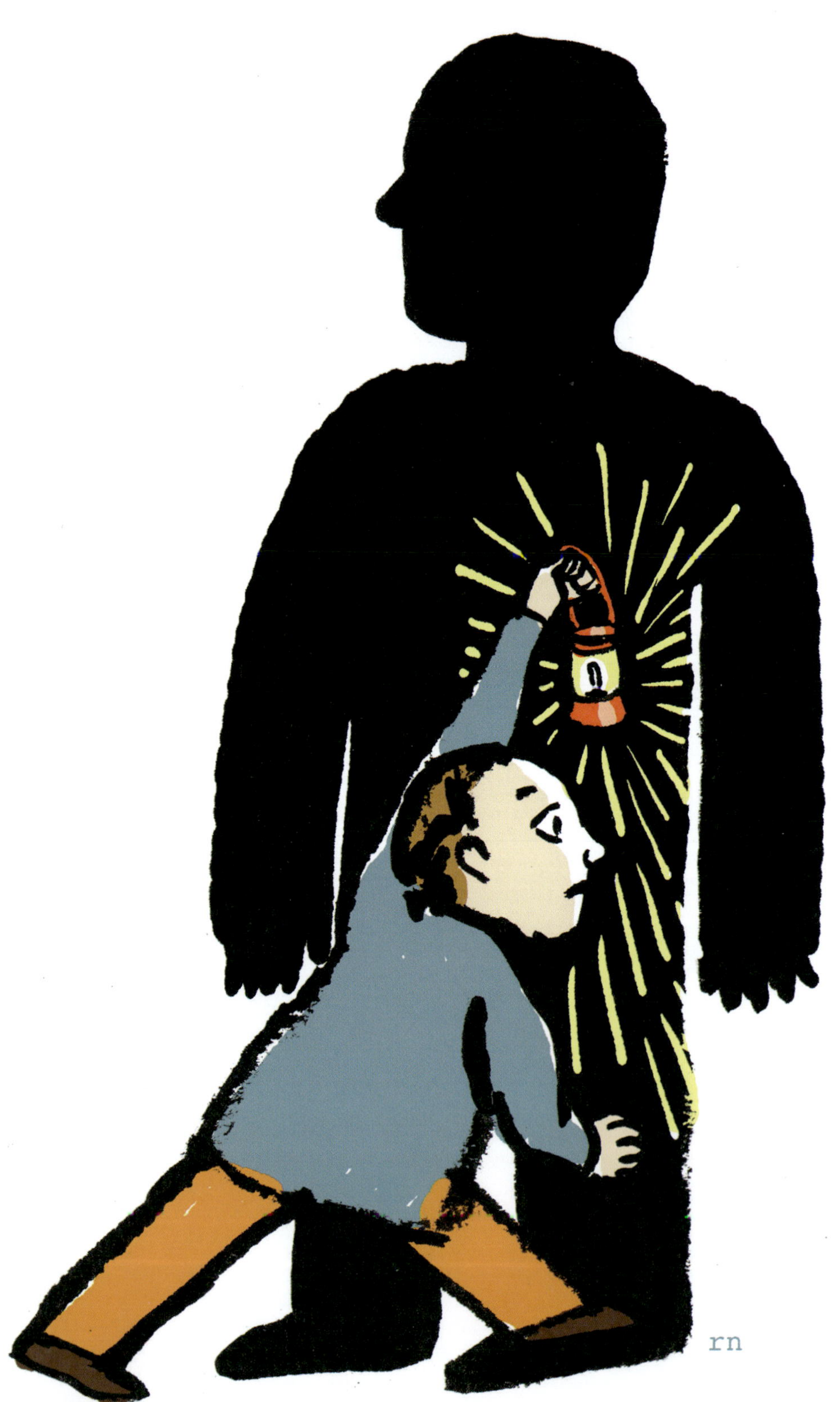

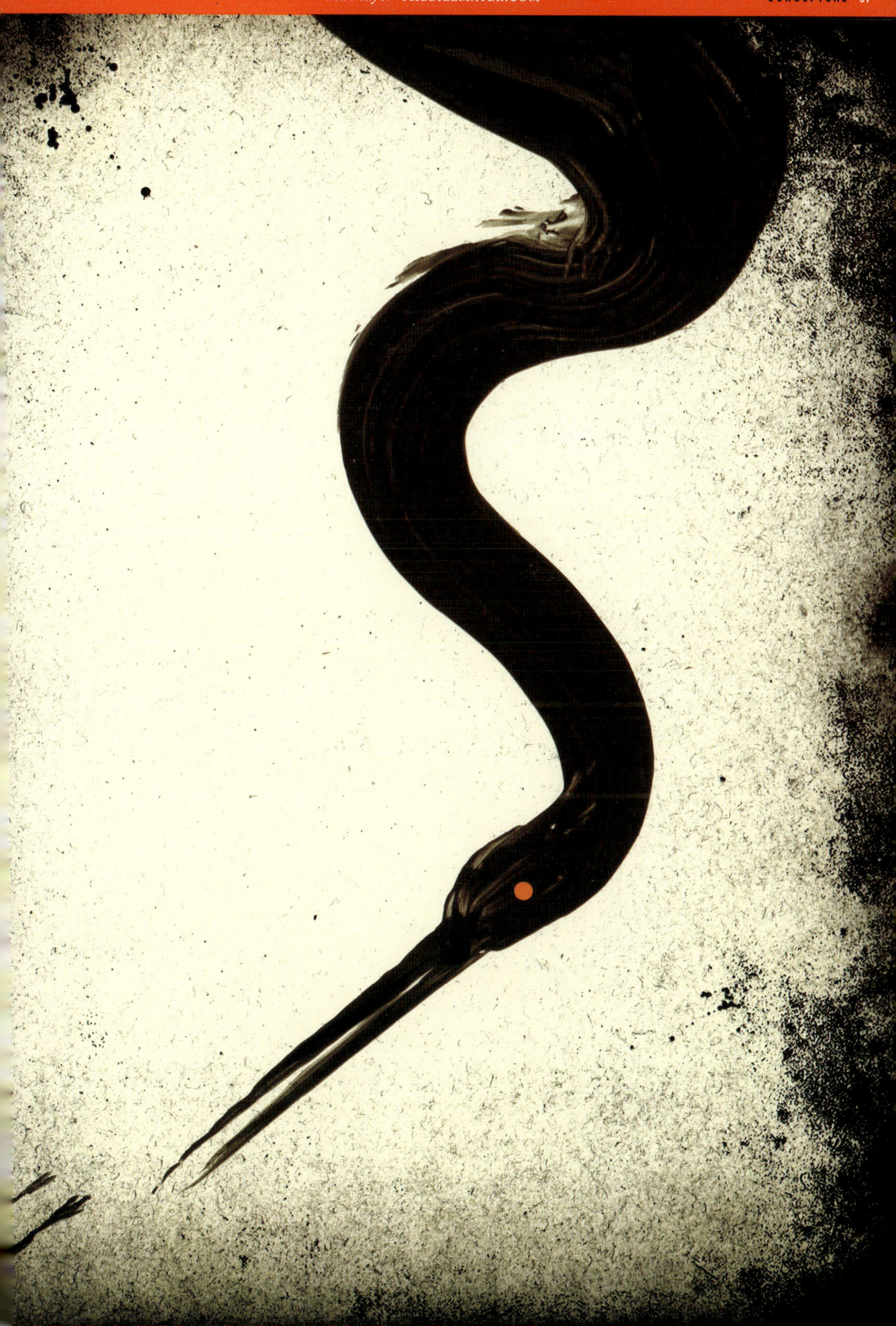

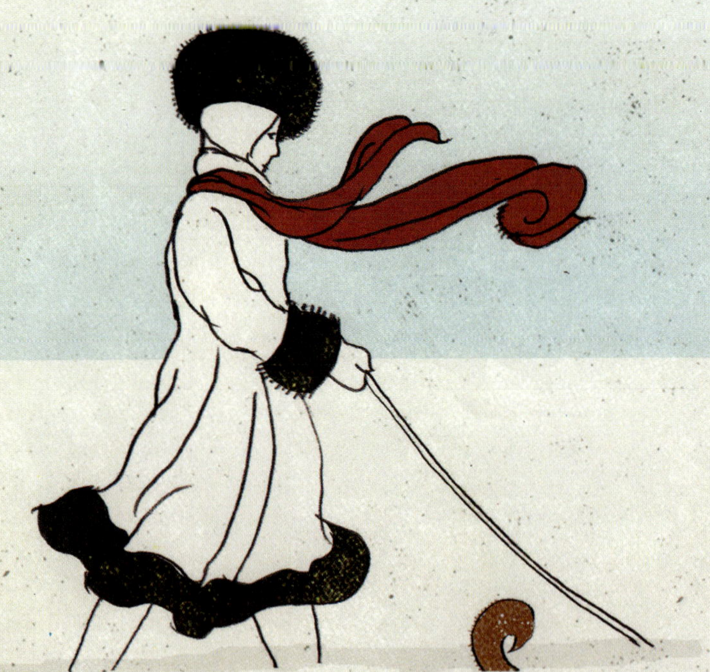
PRICE $5.99
MAR. 1, 2010
THE NEW YORKER
Stauffe

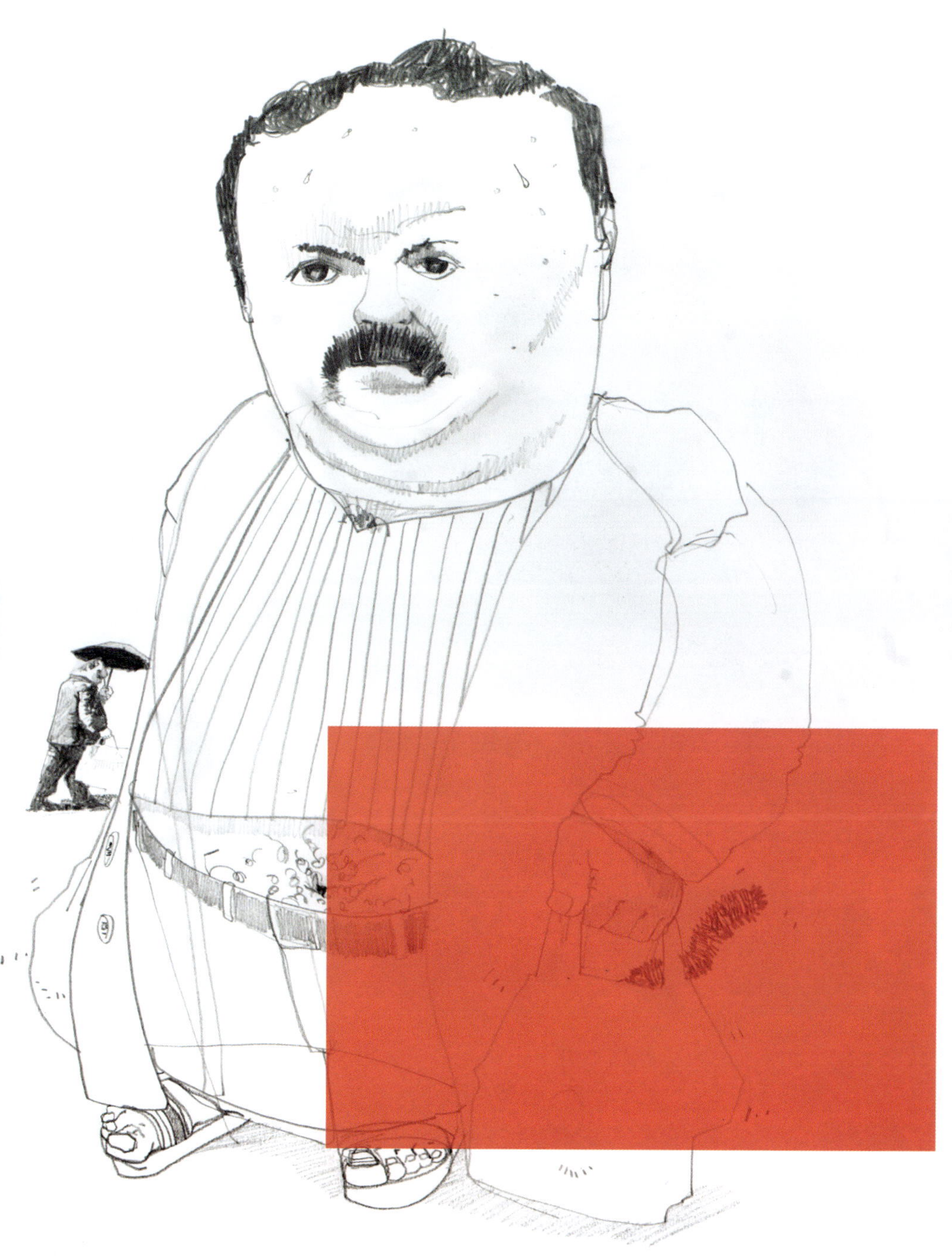

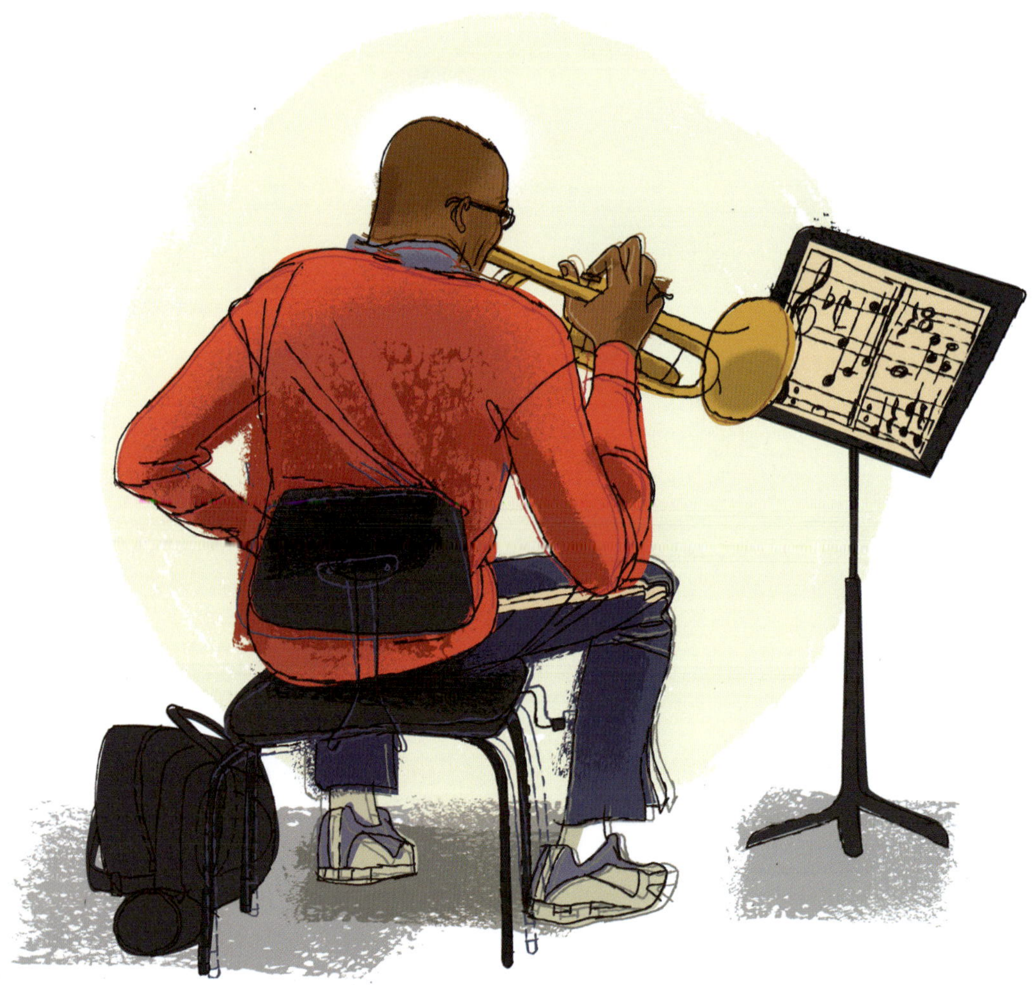

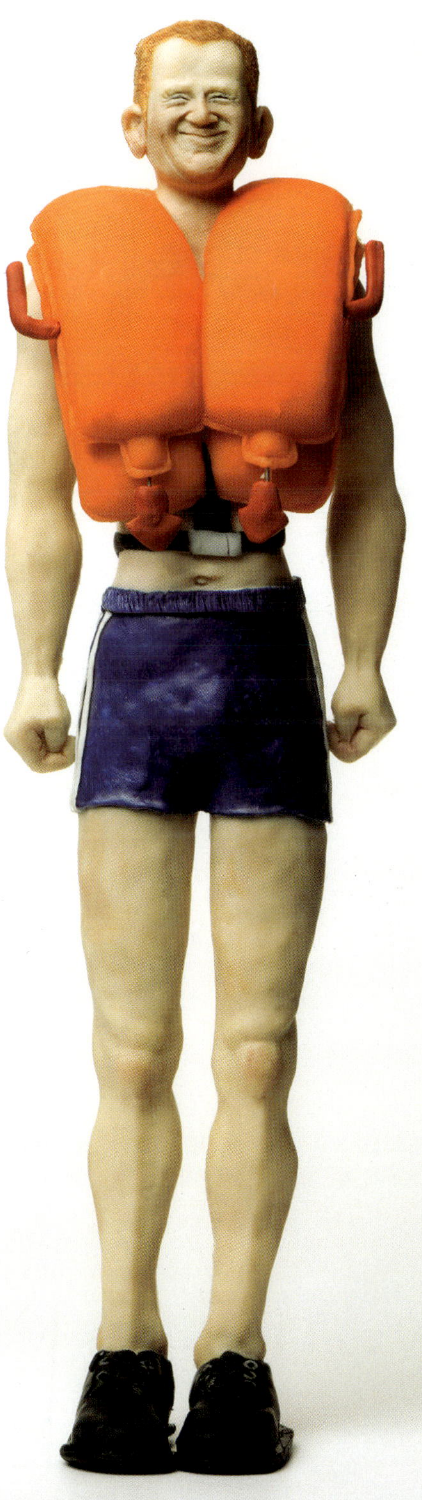

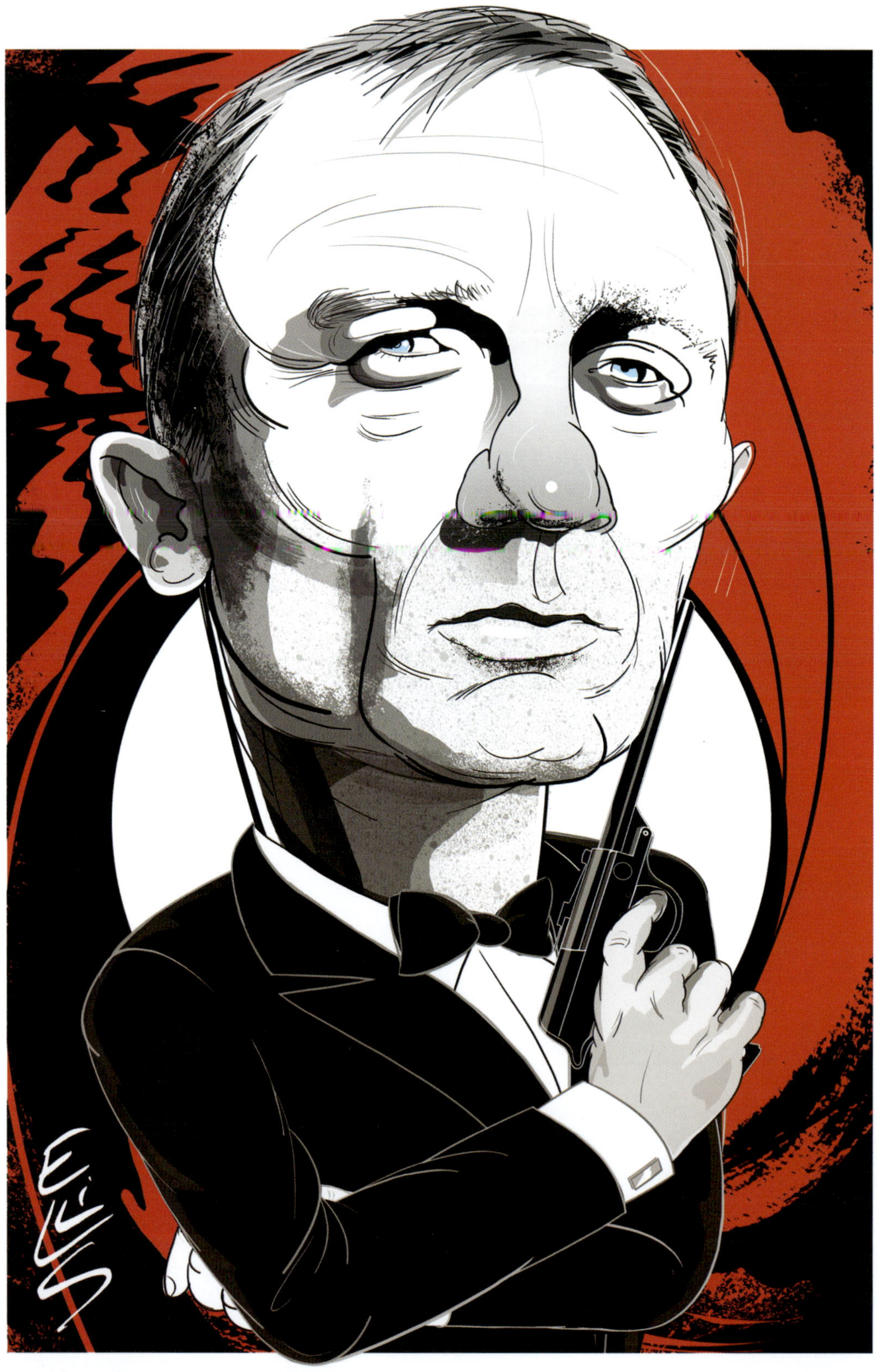

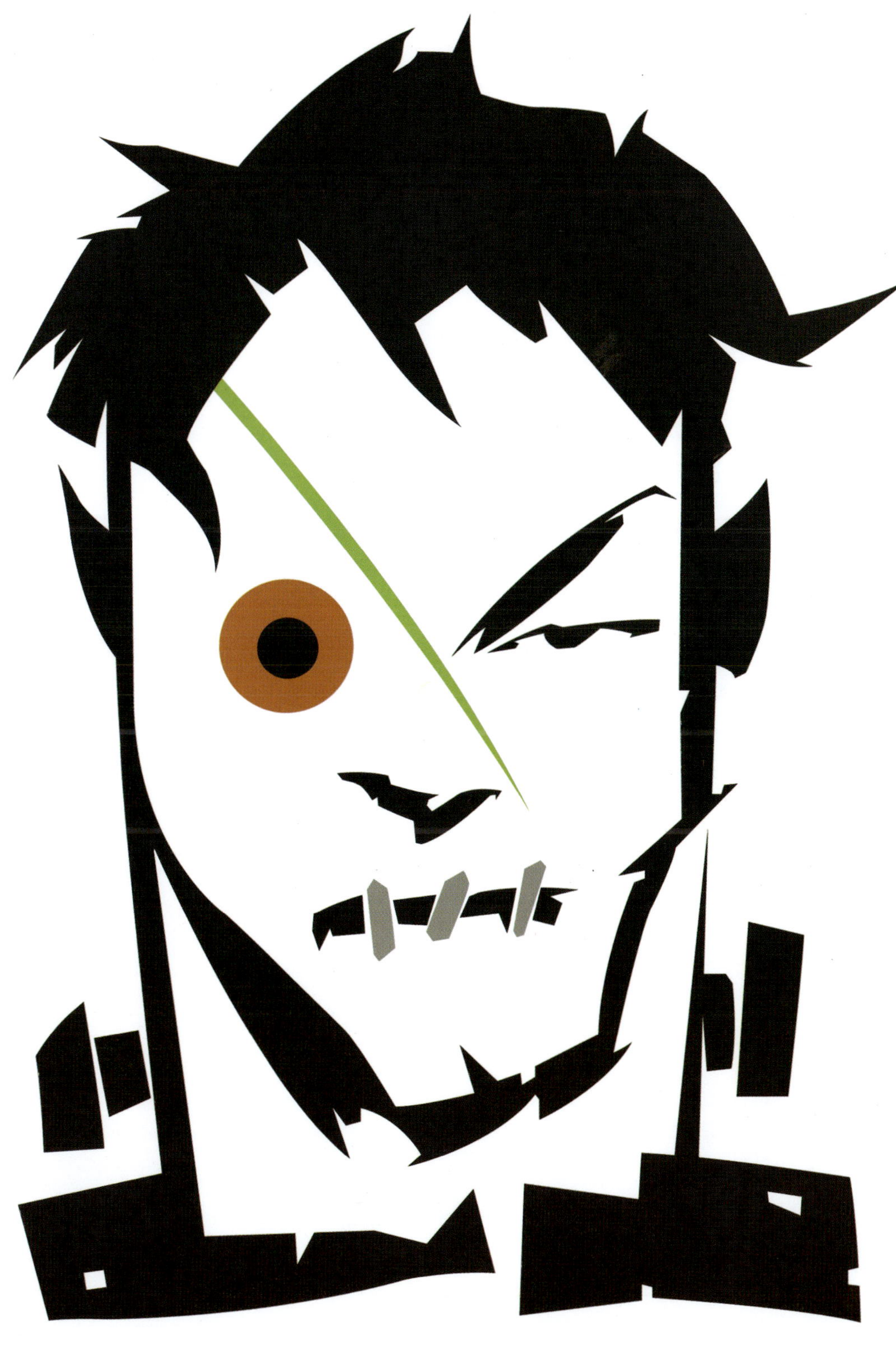

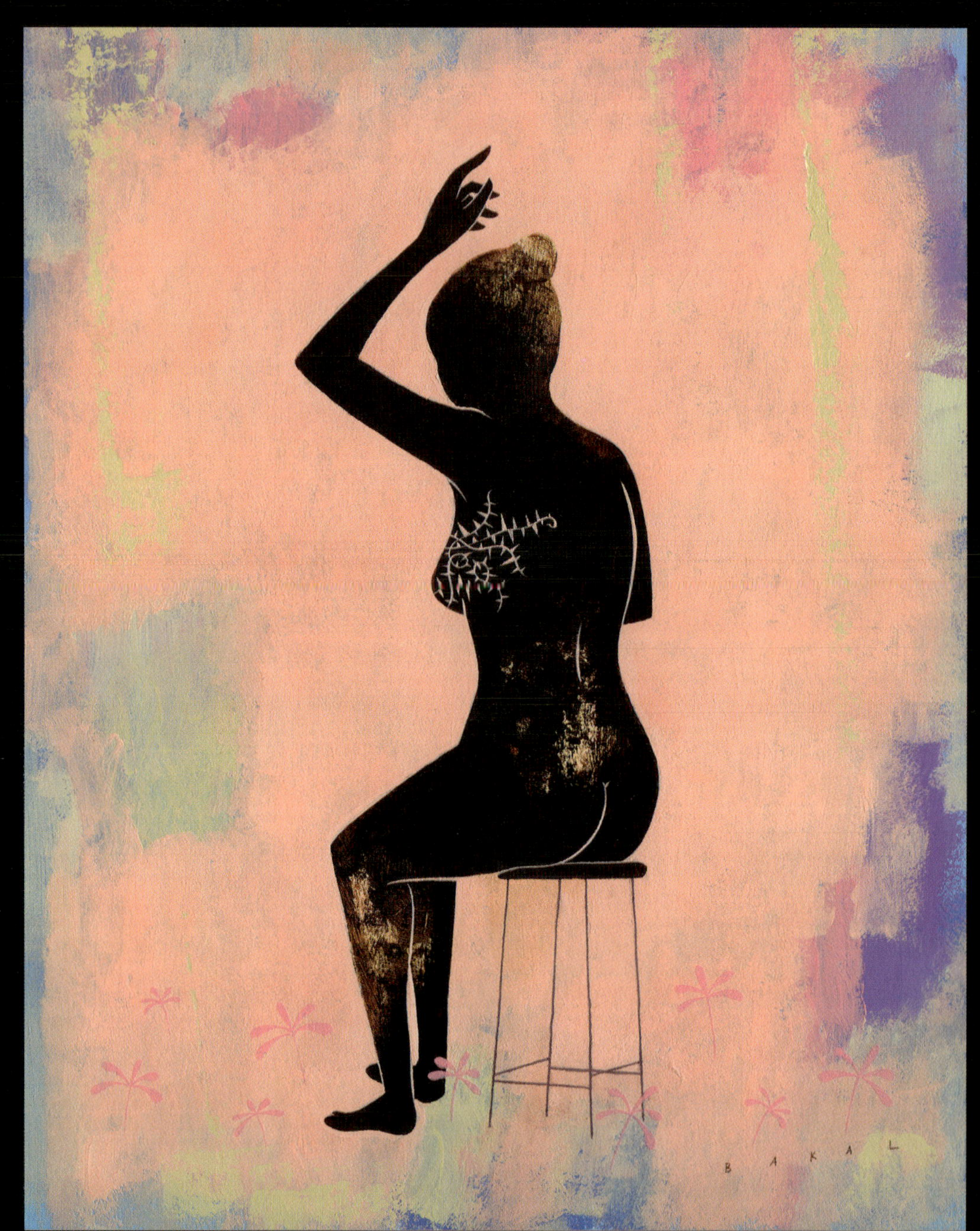
BAKAL

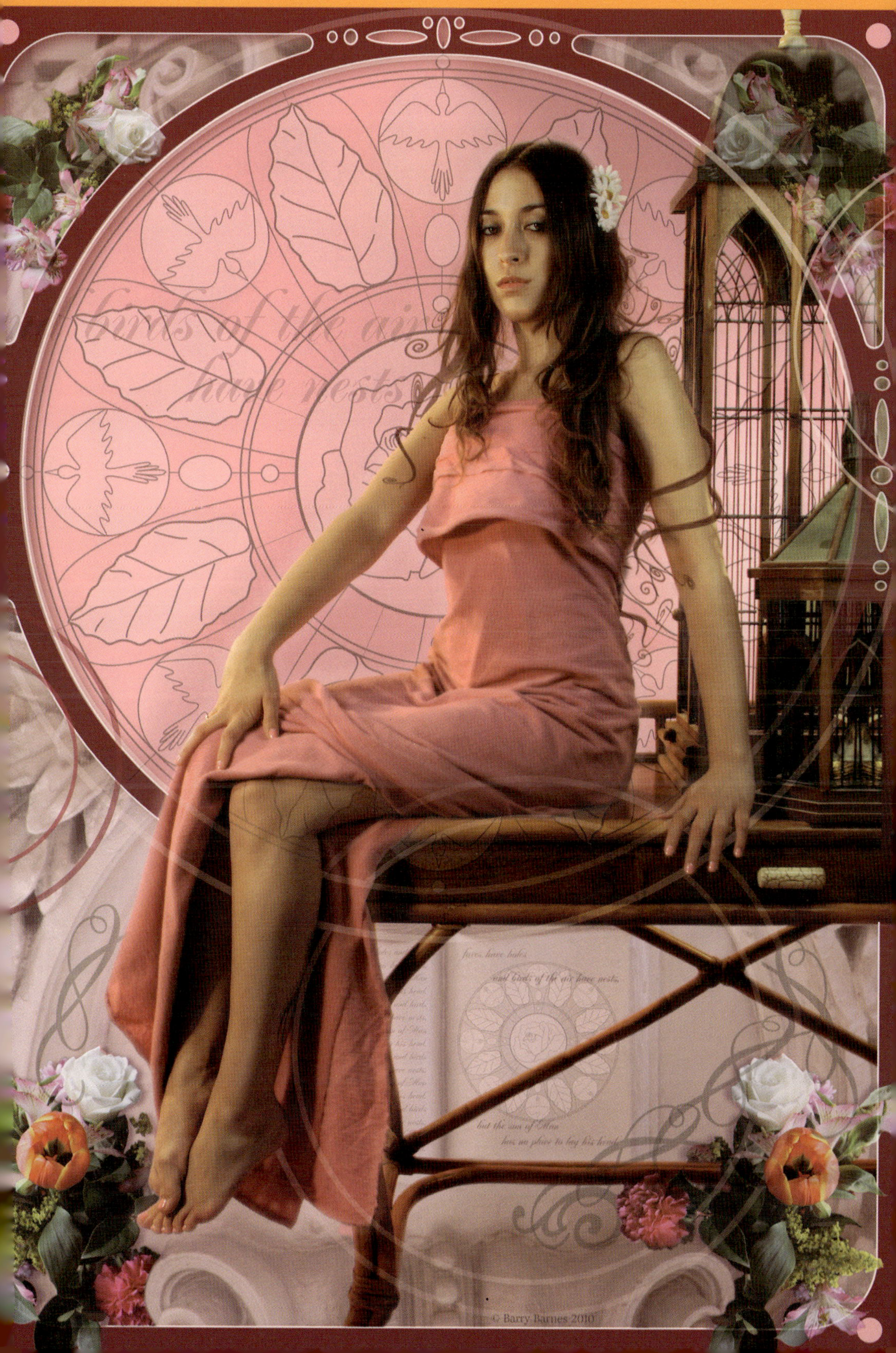

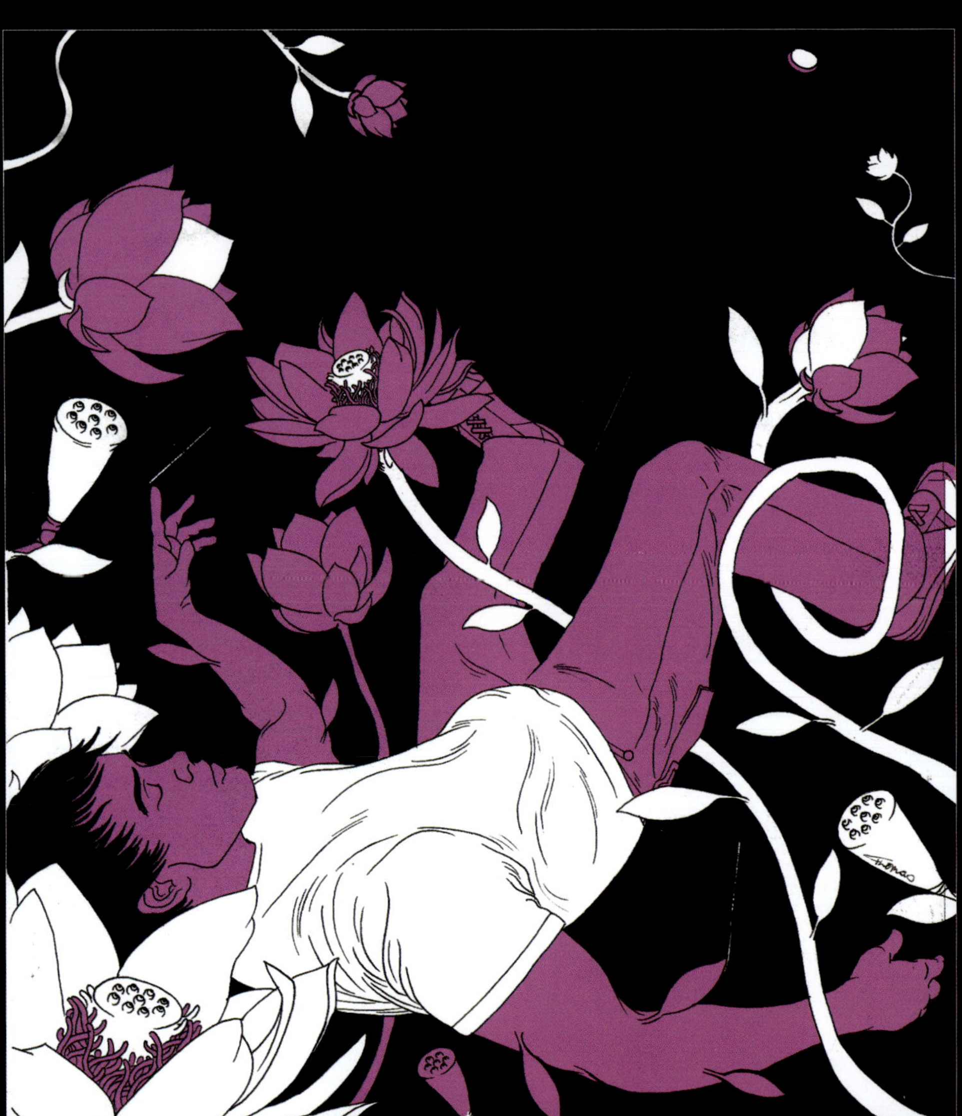

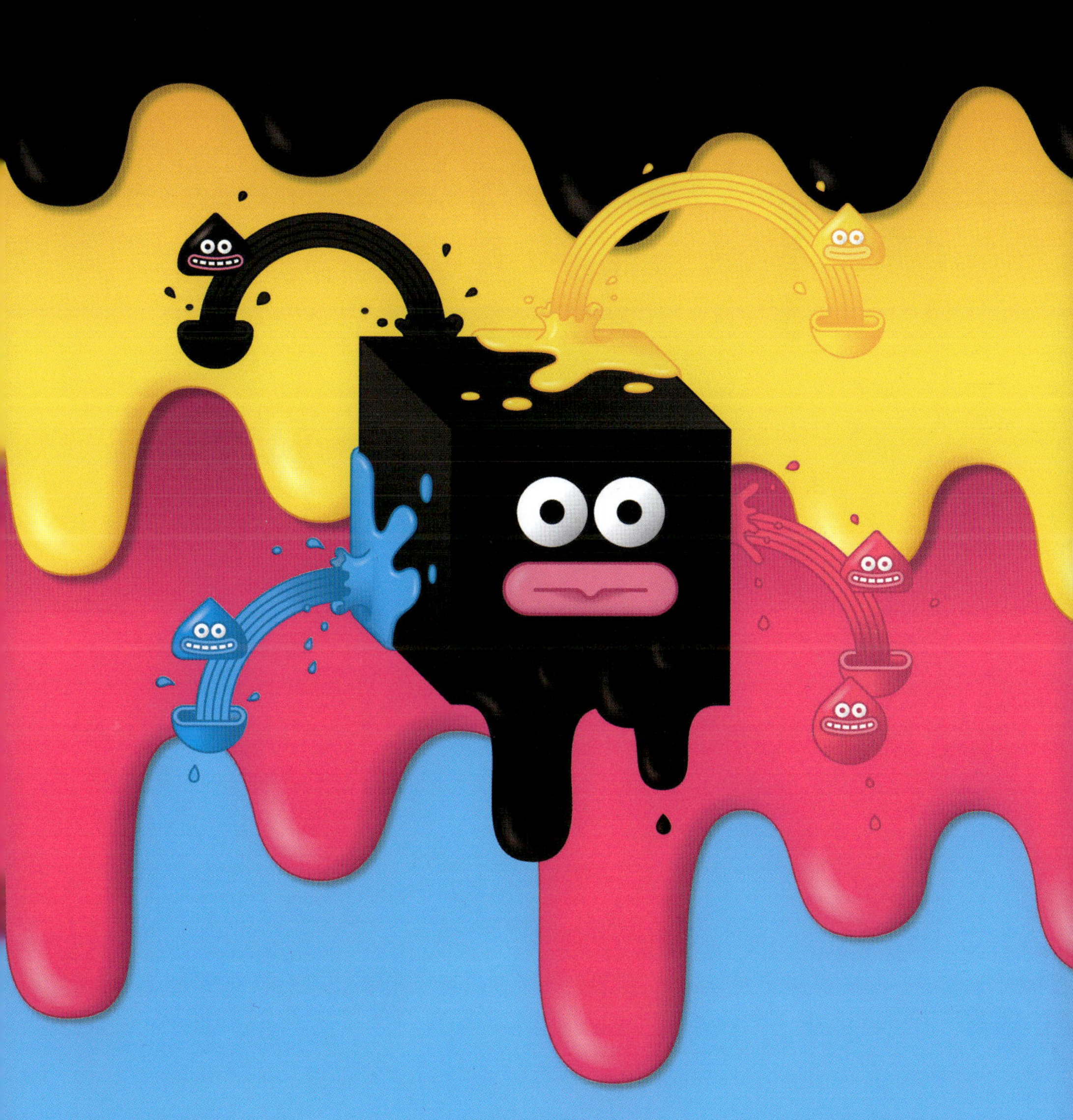

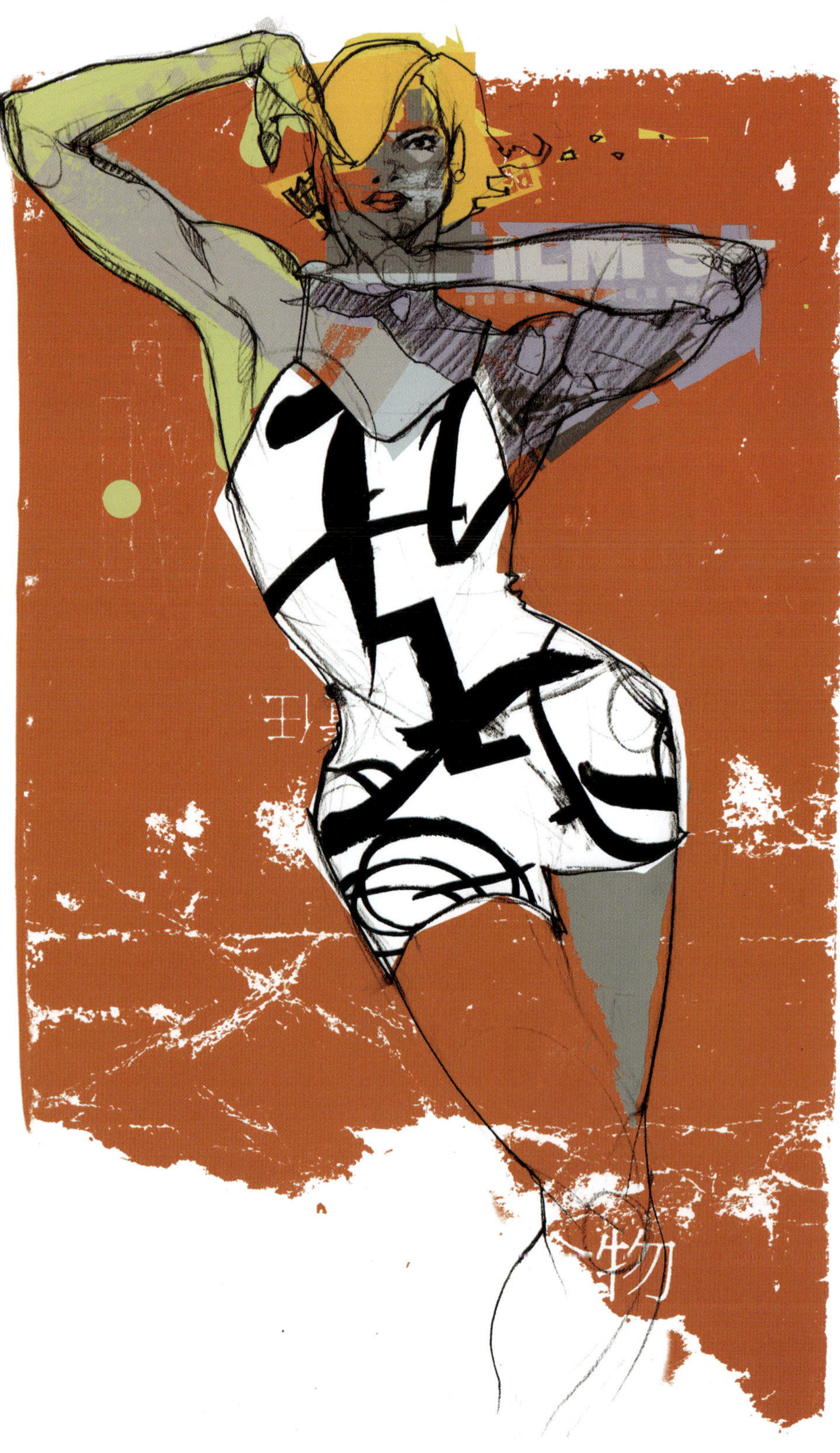

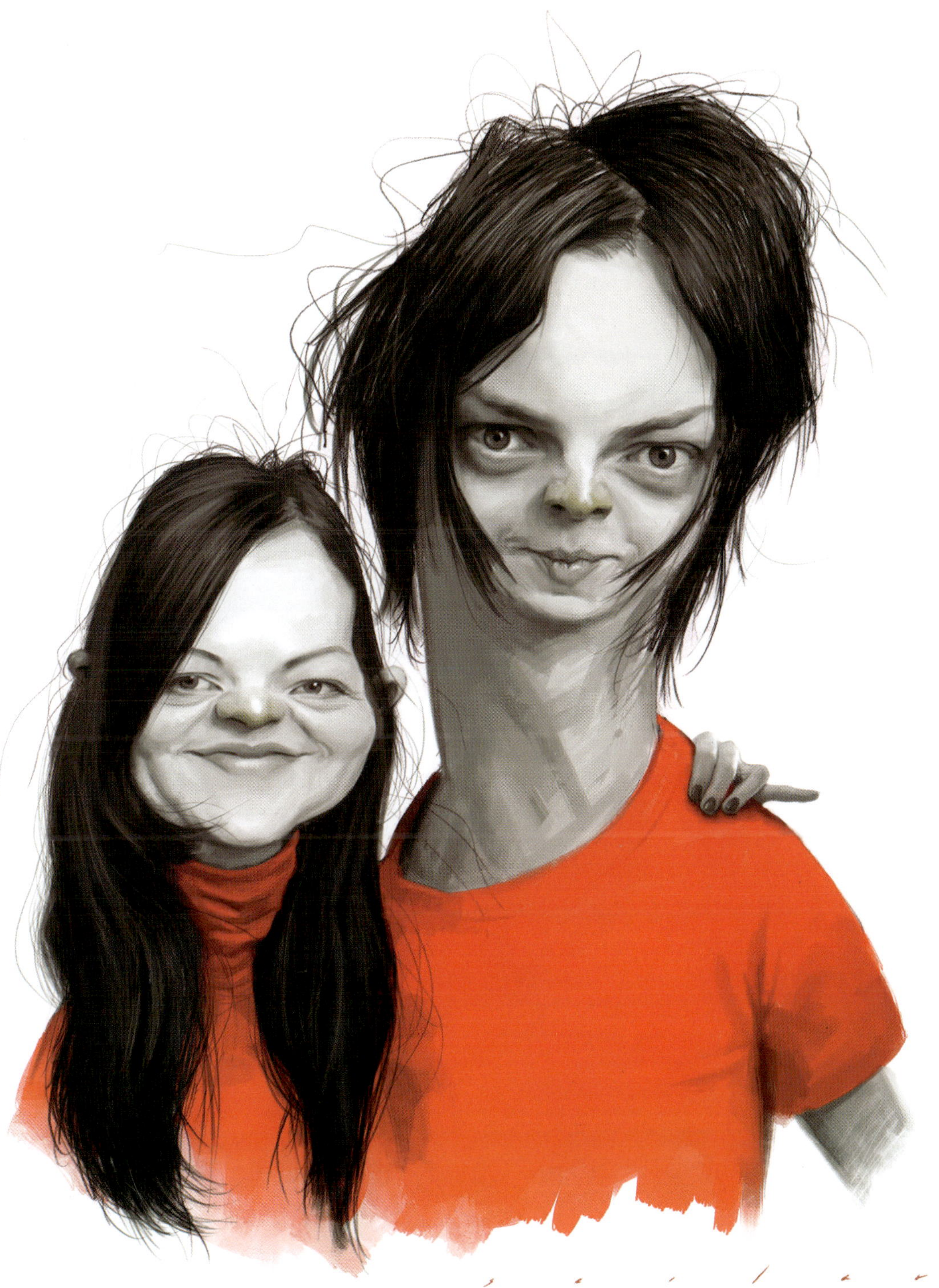

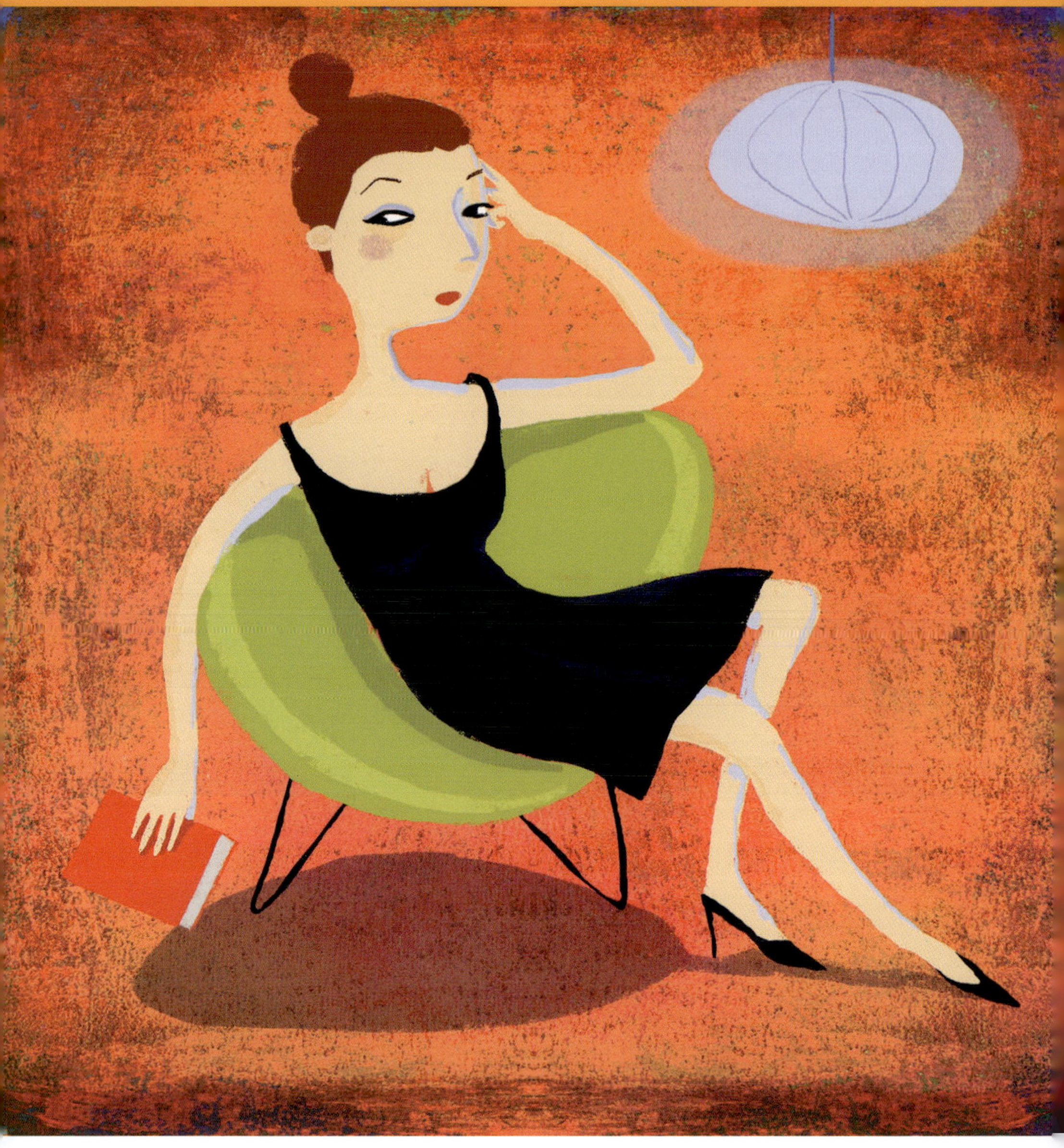

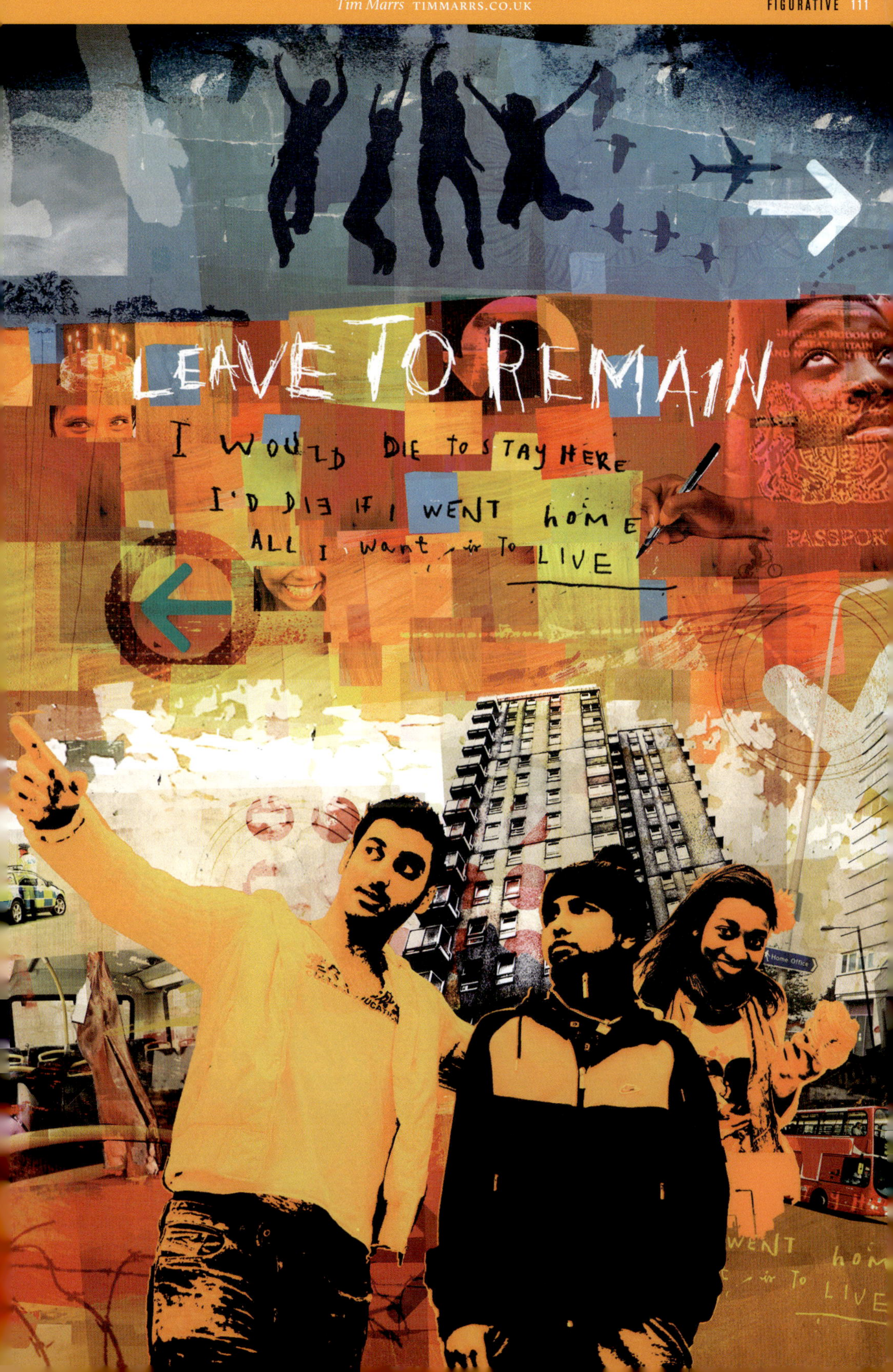
LEAVE TO REMAIN
I WOULD DIE TO STAY HERE
I'D DIE IF I WENT HOME
ALL I WANT IS TO LIVE
PASSPORT
Home Office
WENT
hom
r TO
LIVE

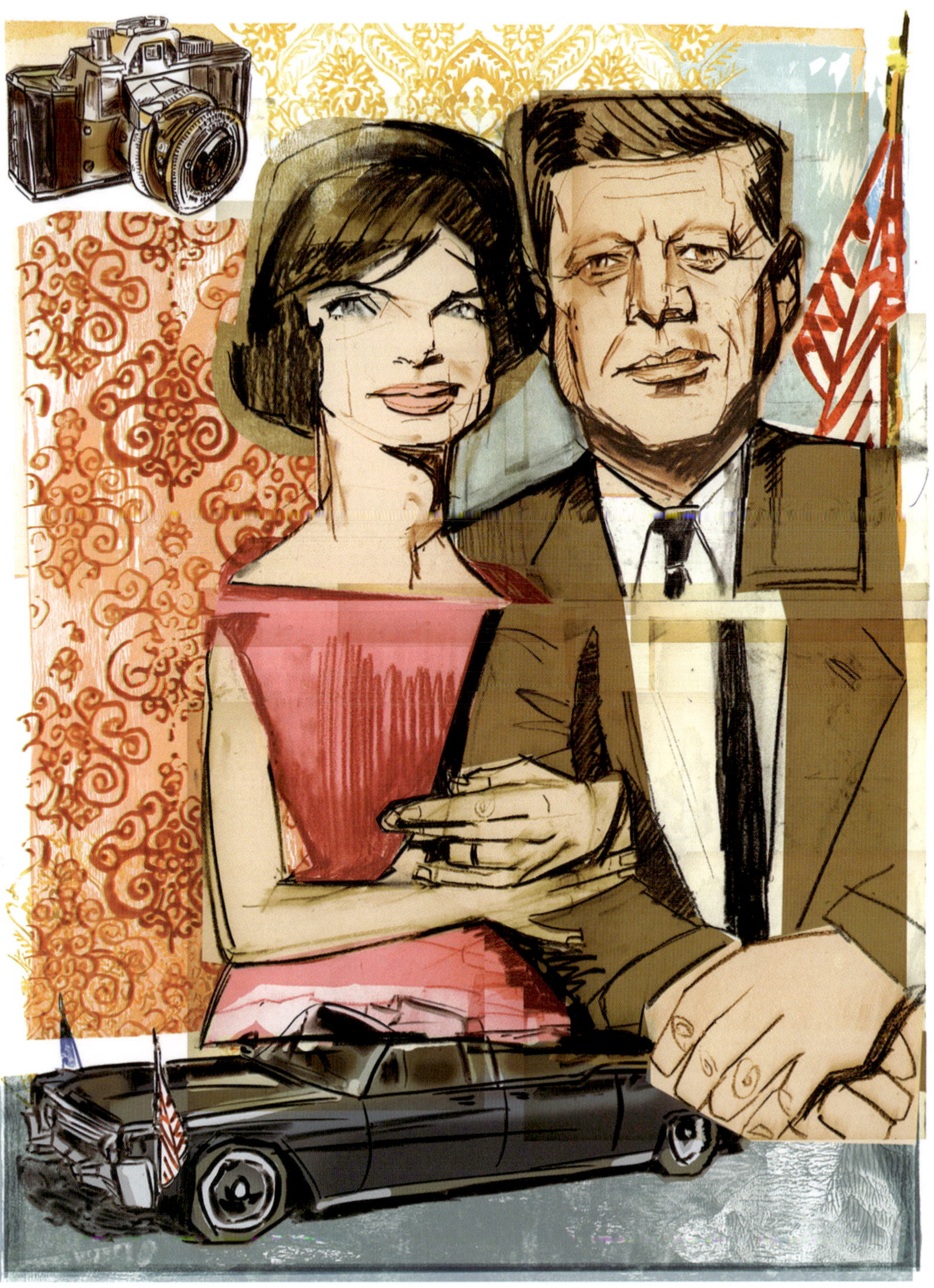

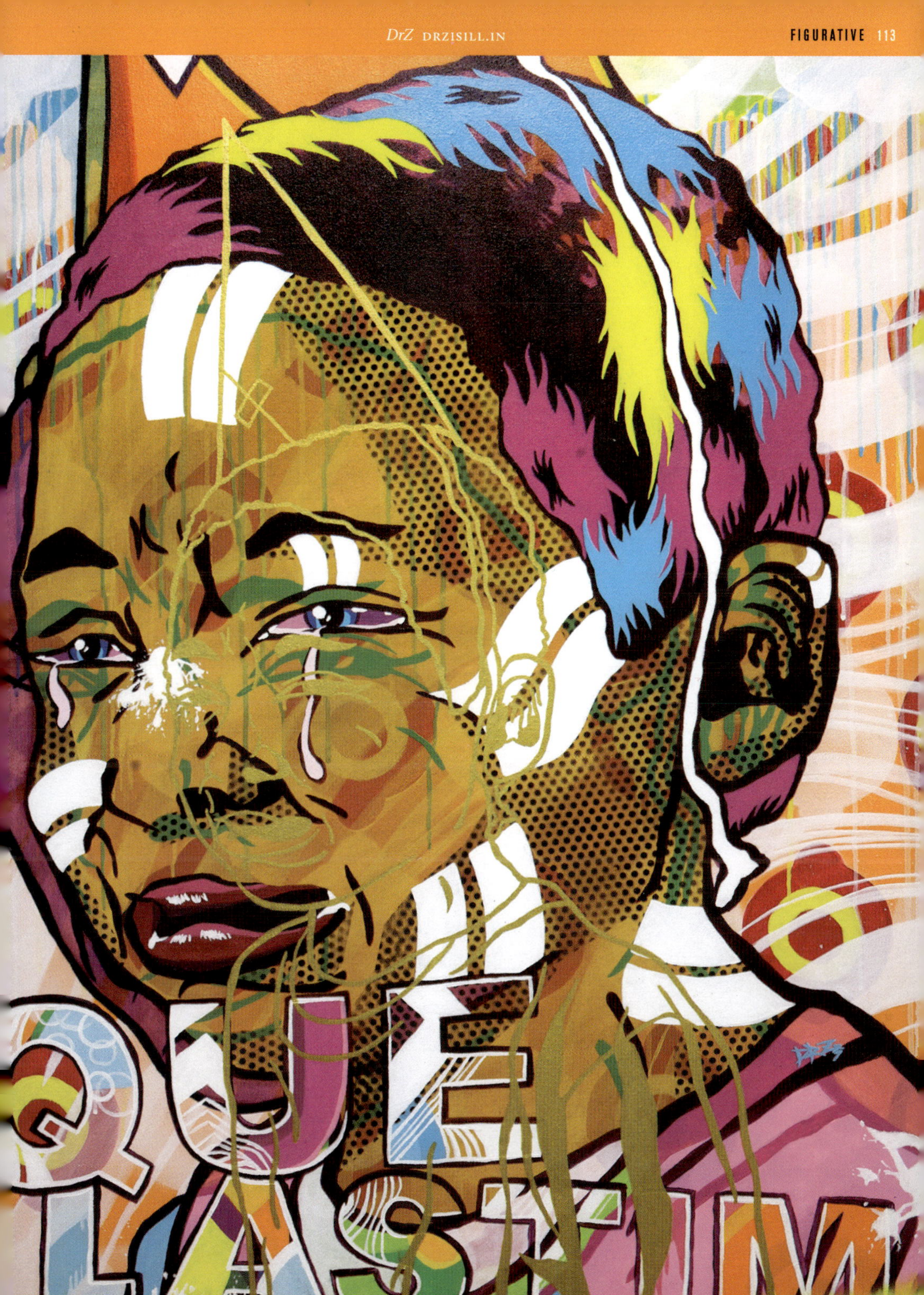
QUE
LASSIM

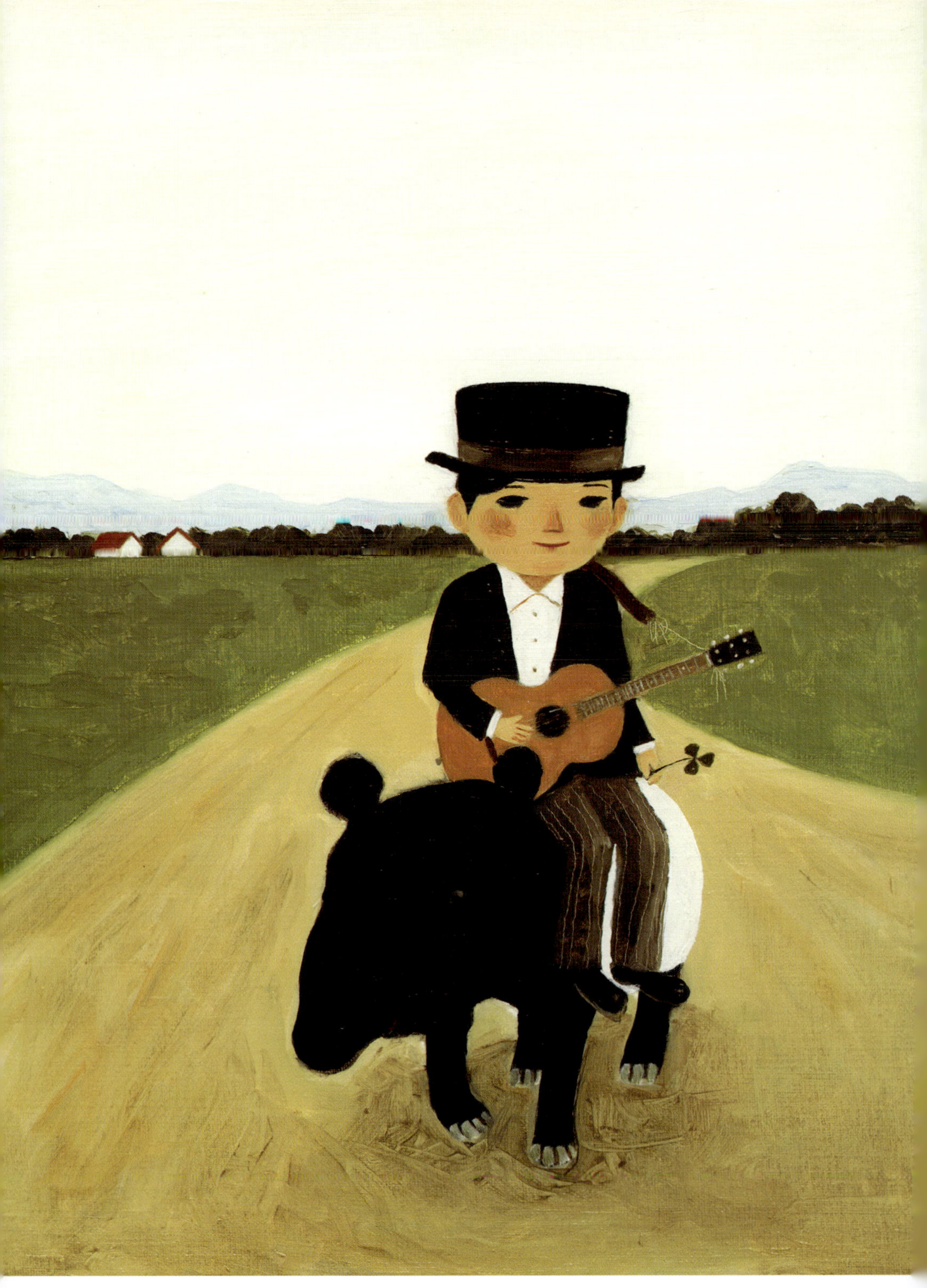

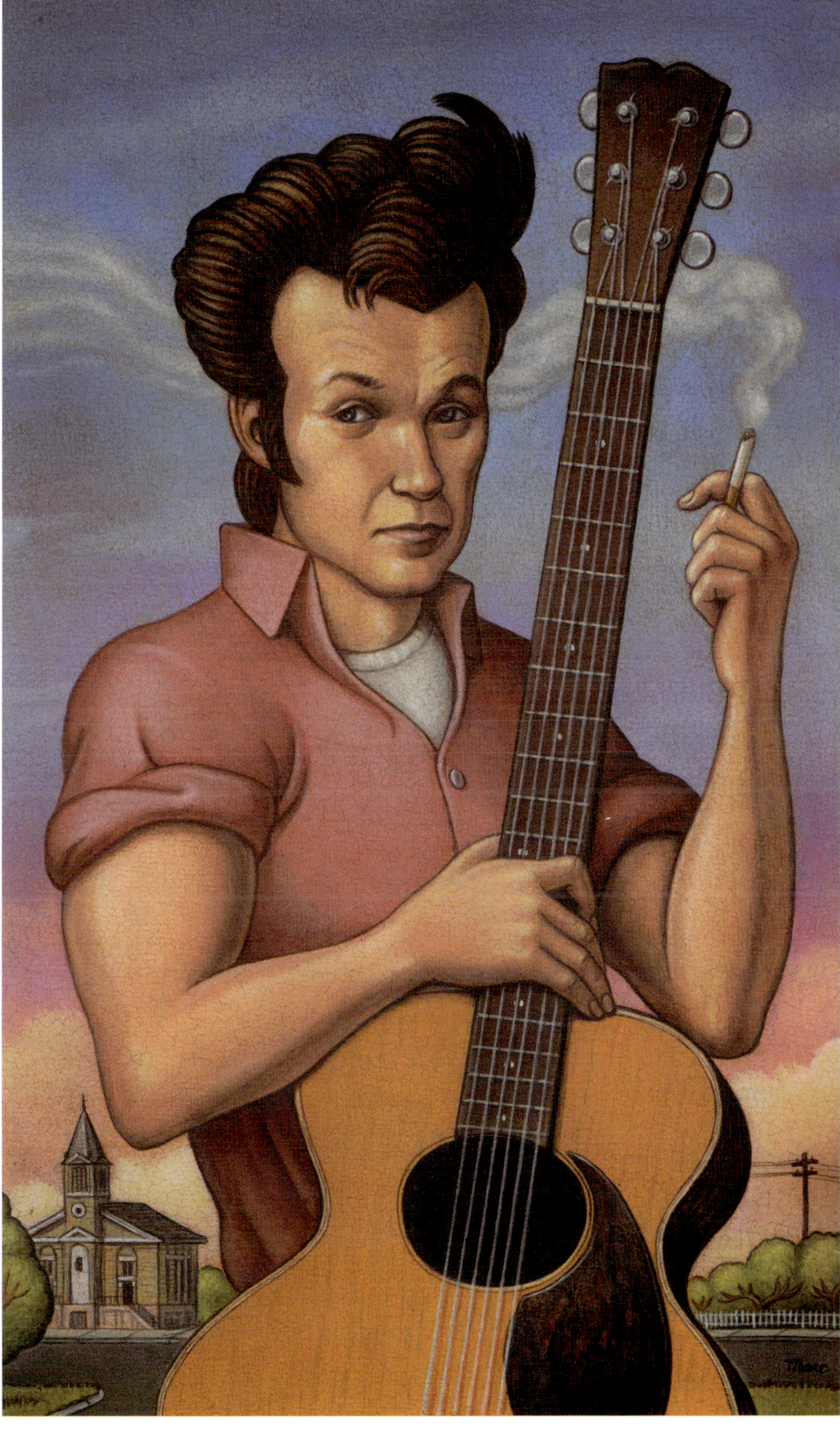

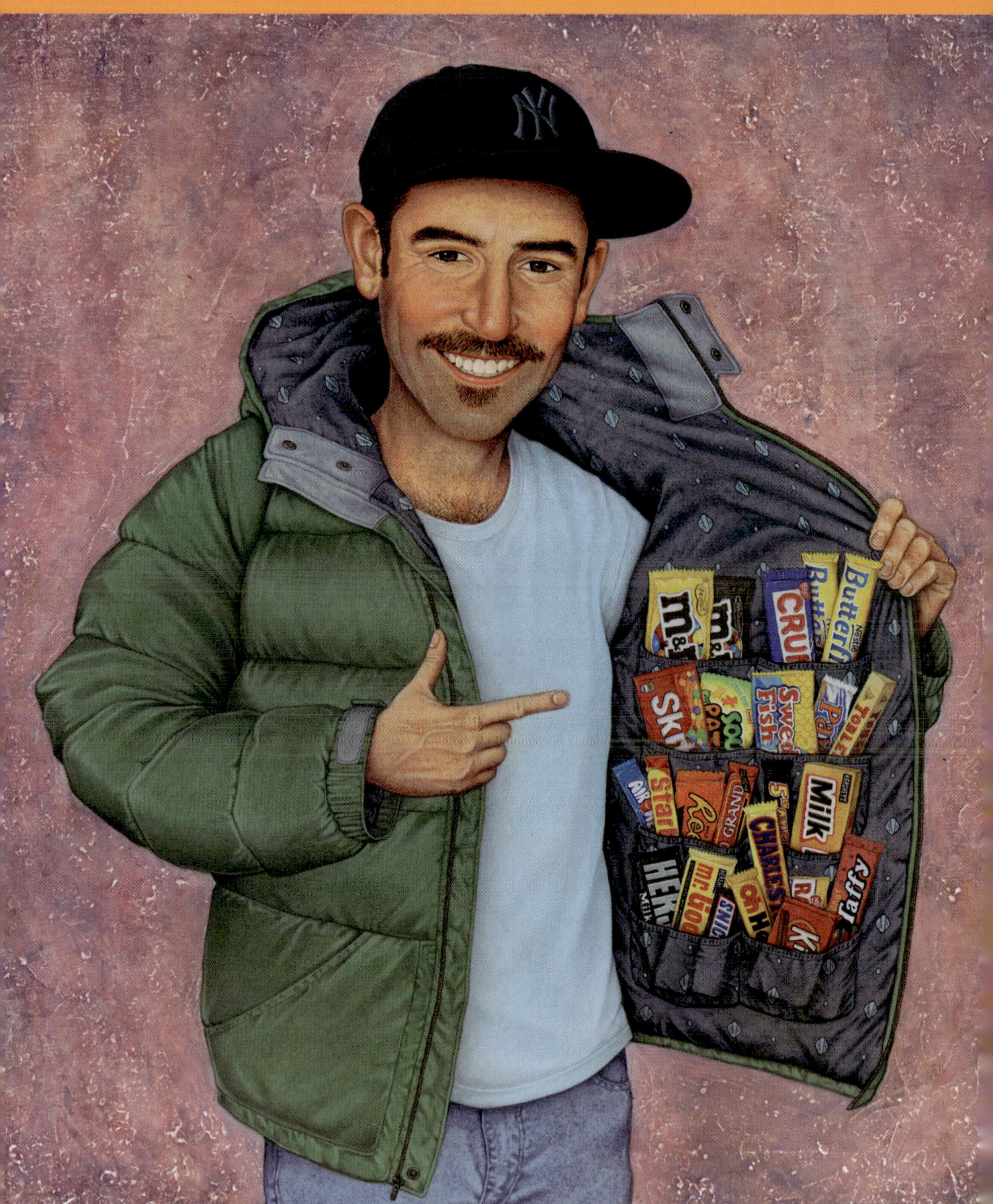

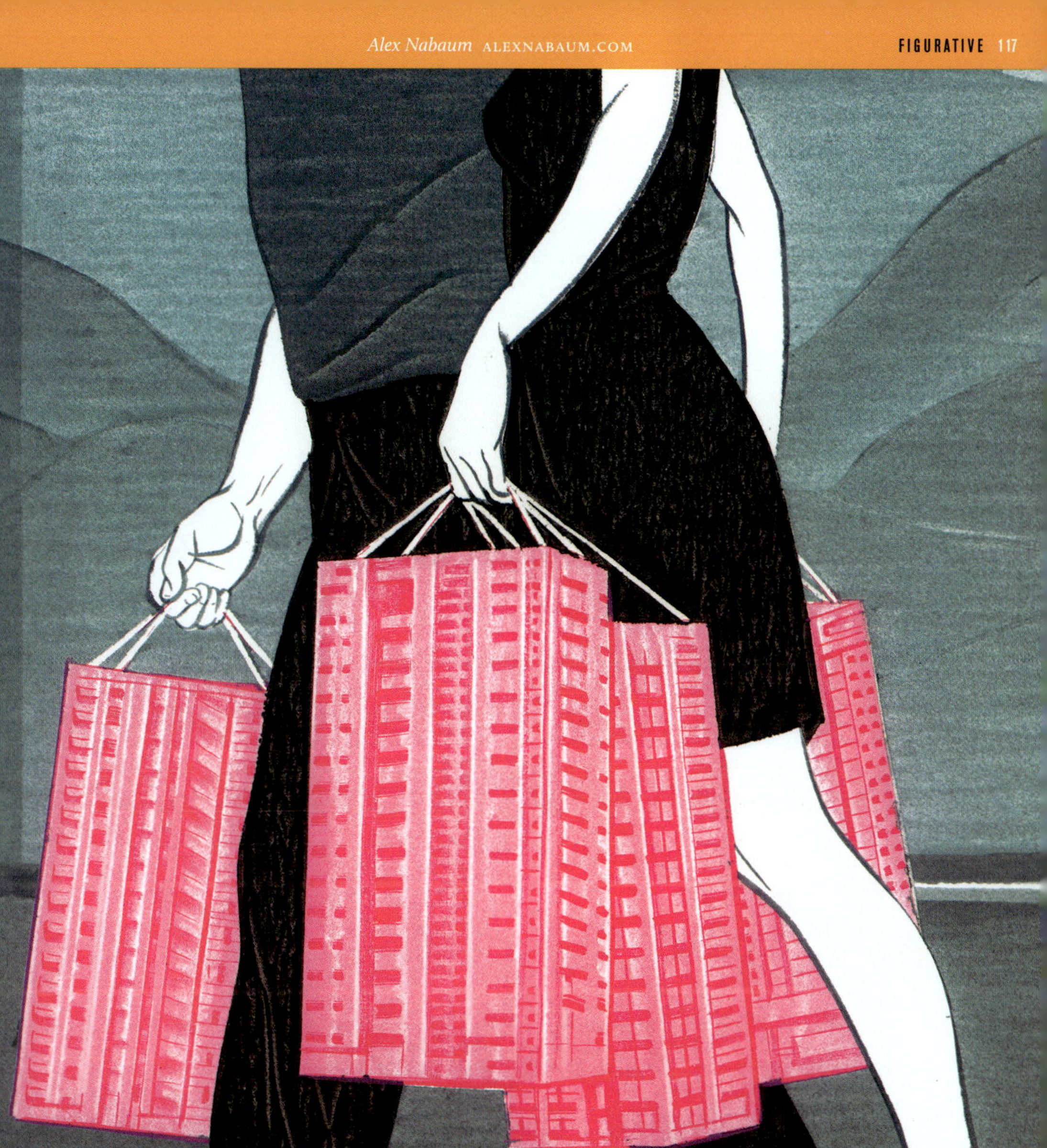

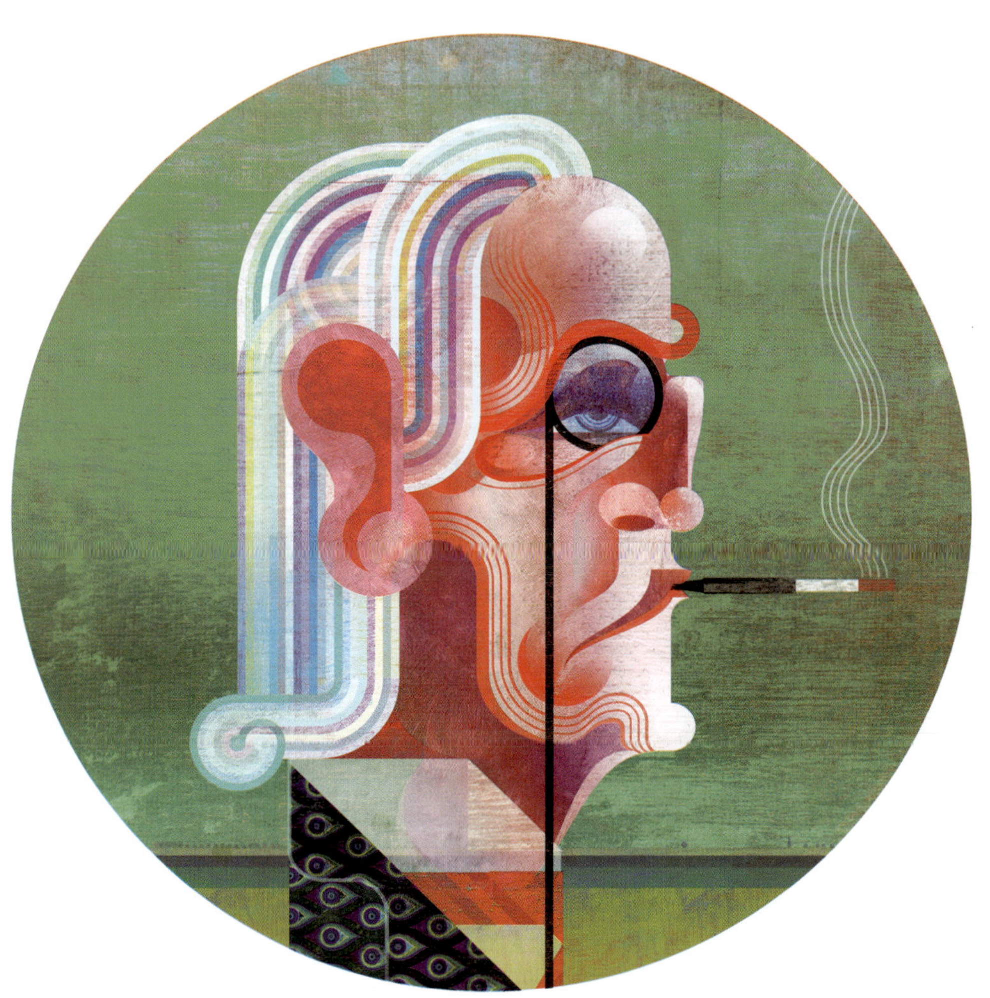

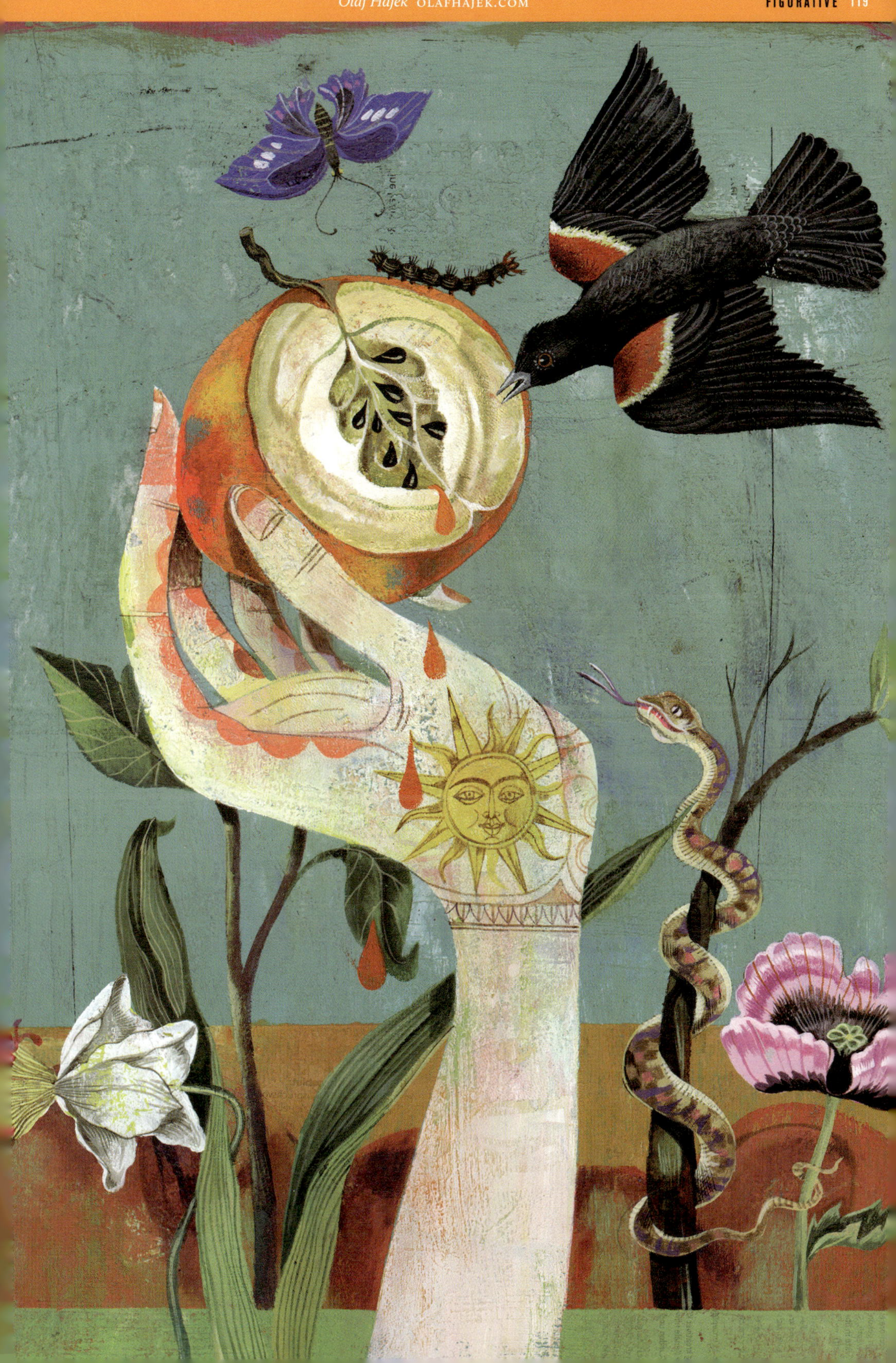

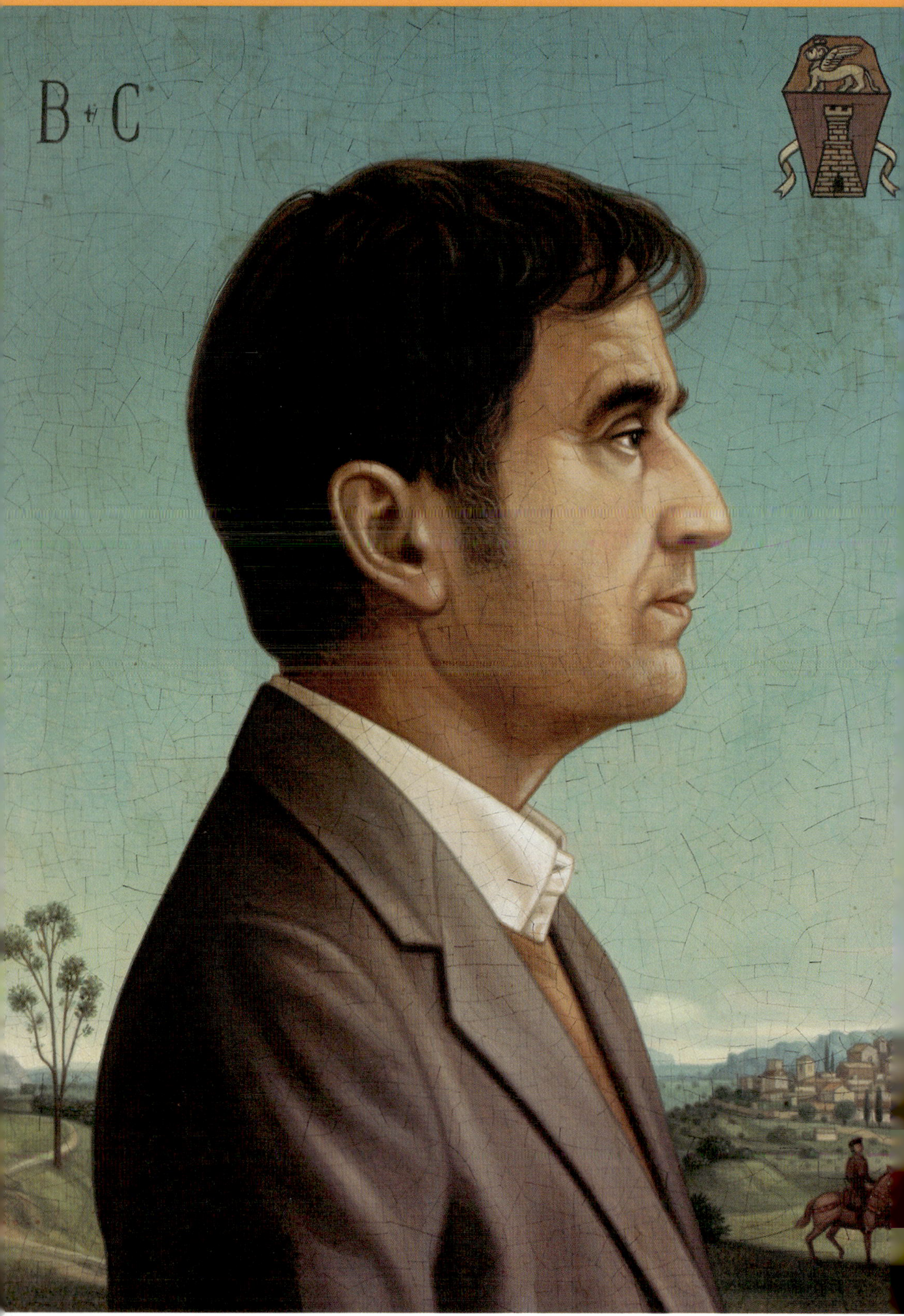

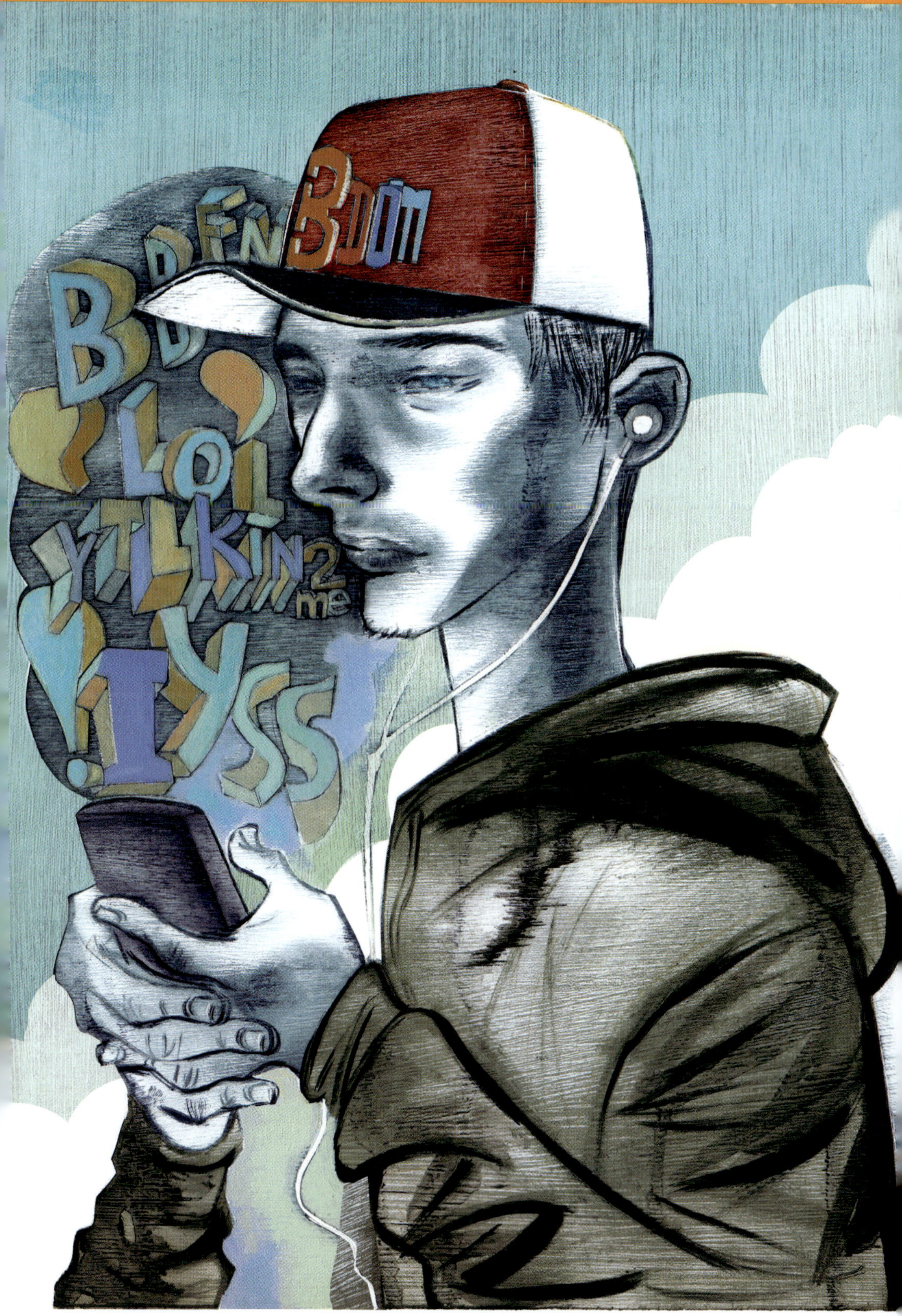
Boom
BDFN
B
LOL
YTLKin 2 me
TYSS

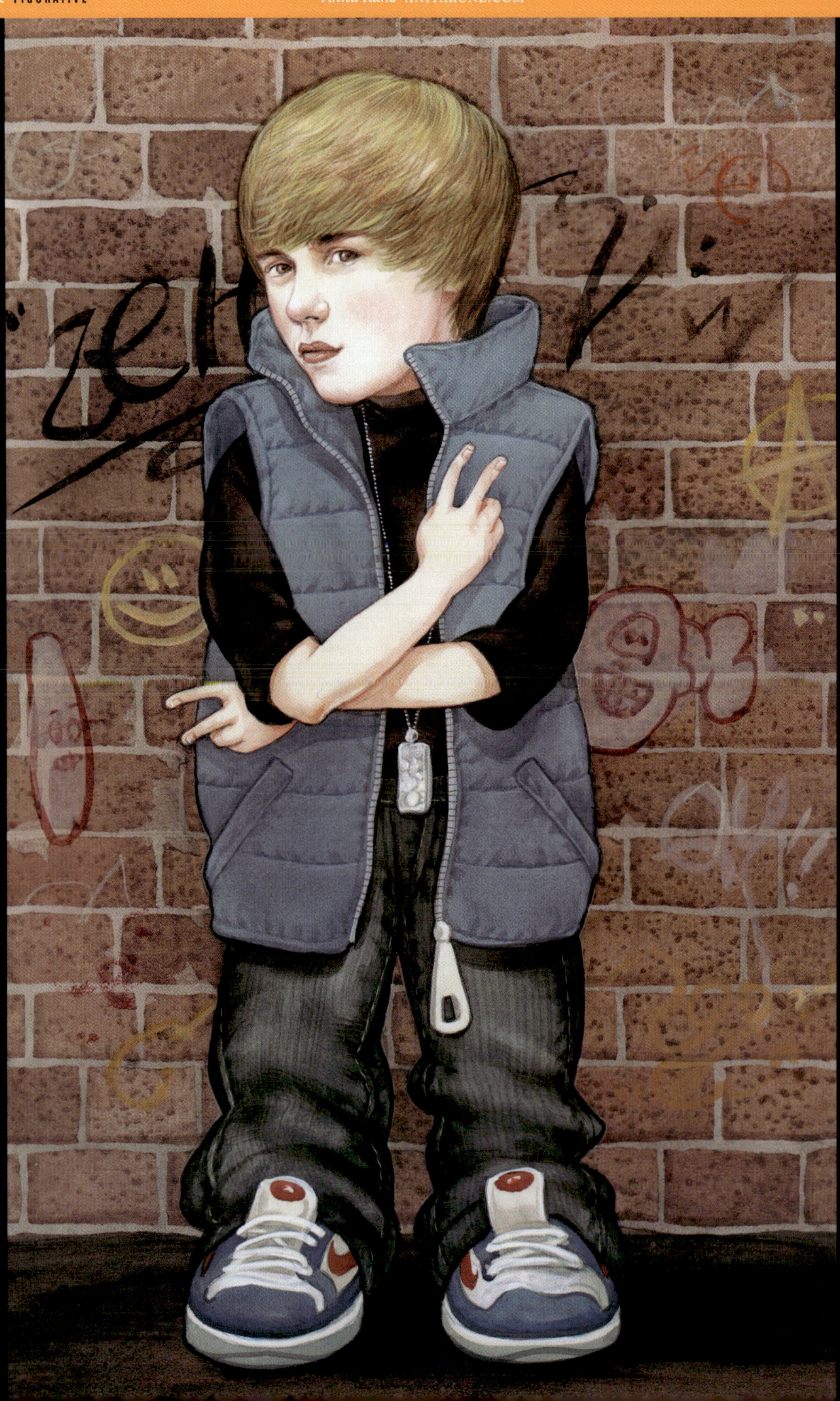

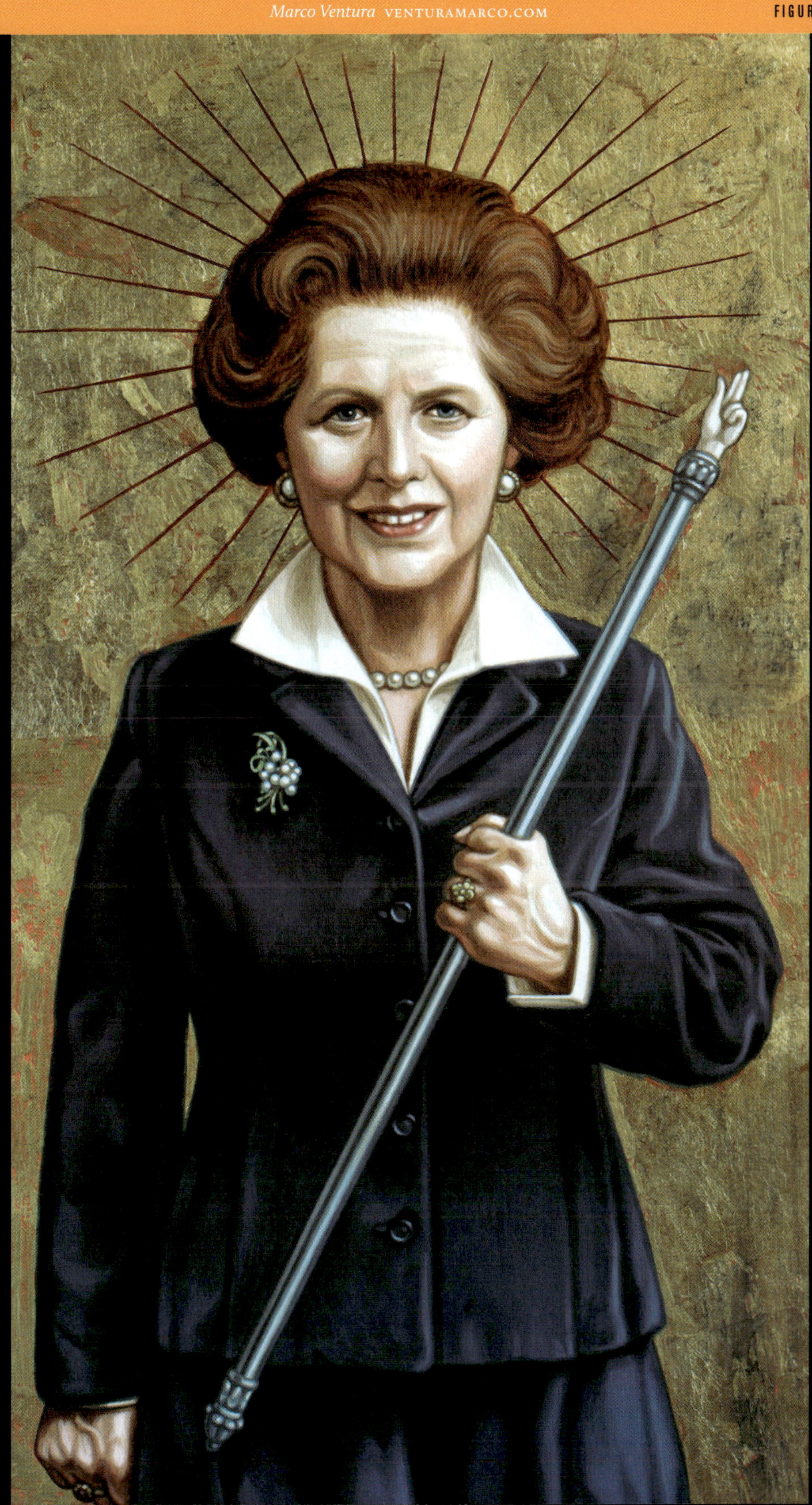

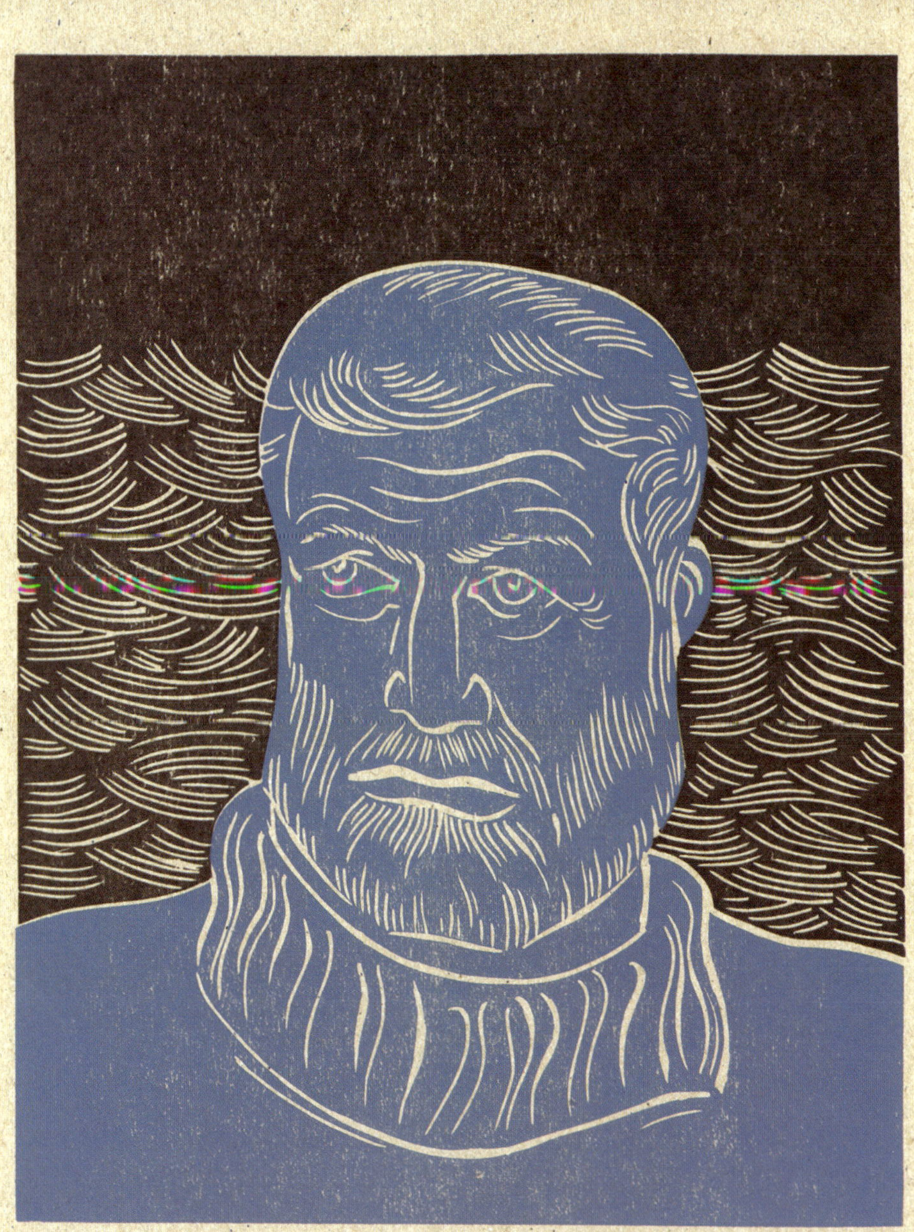

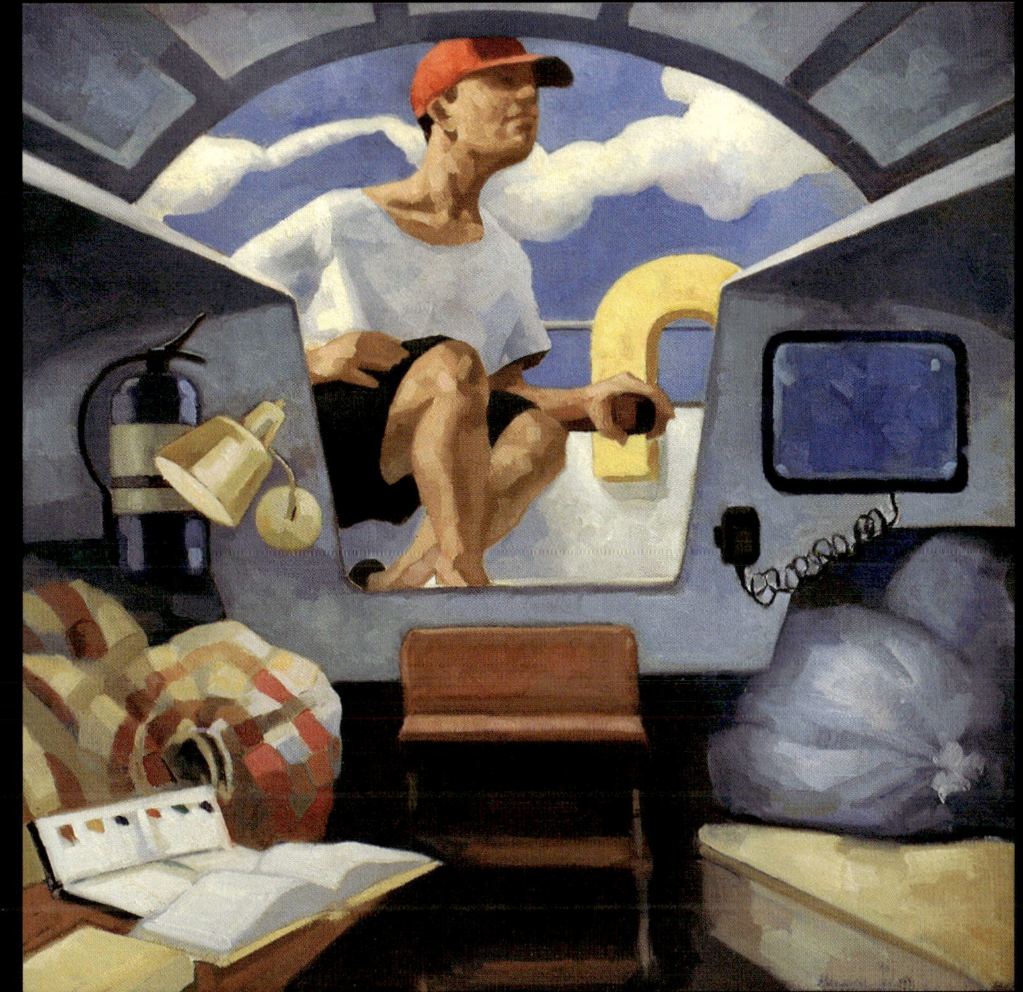

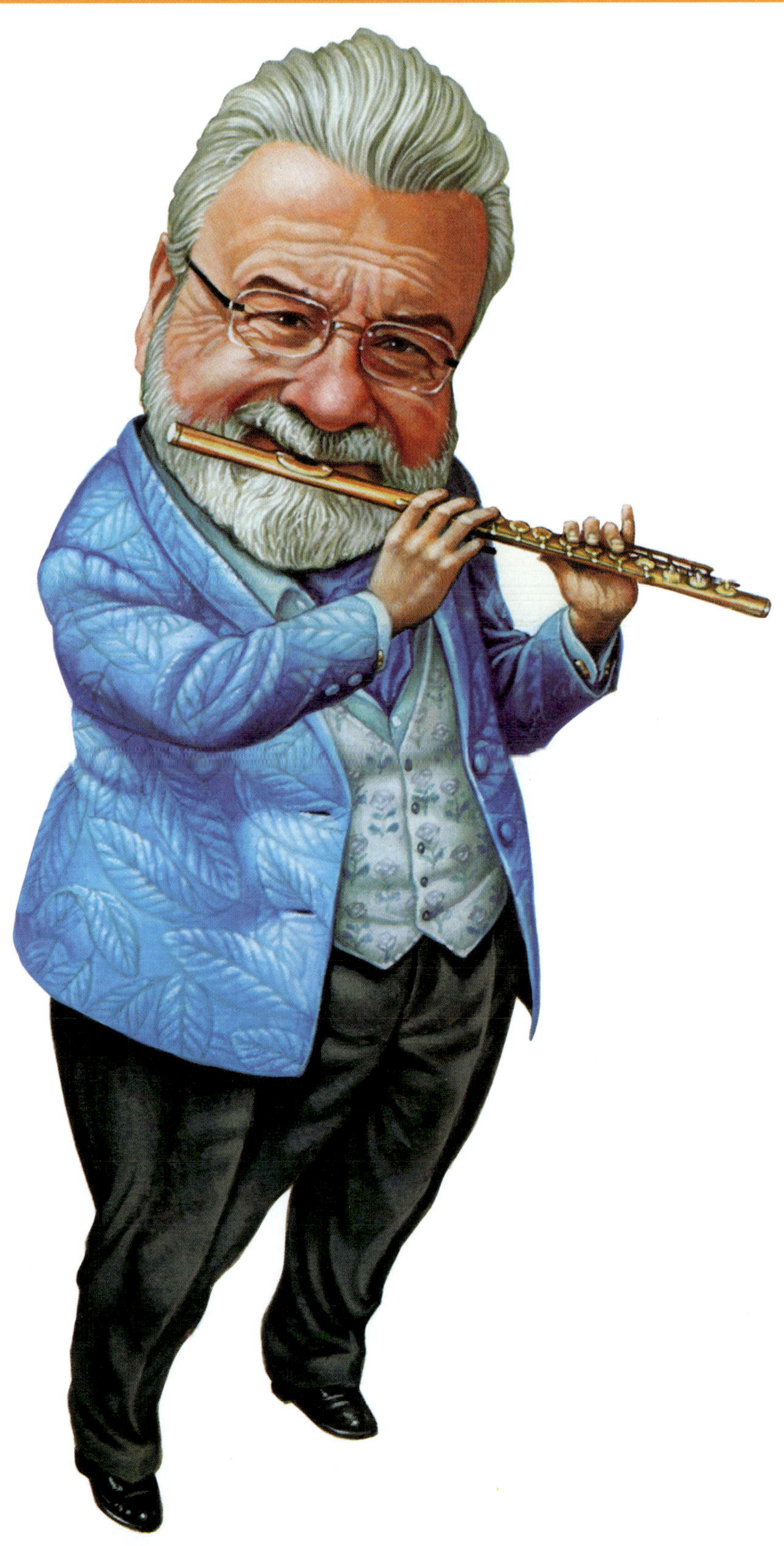

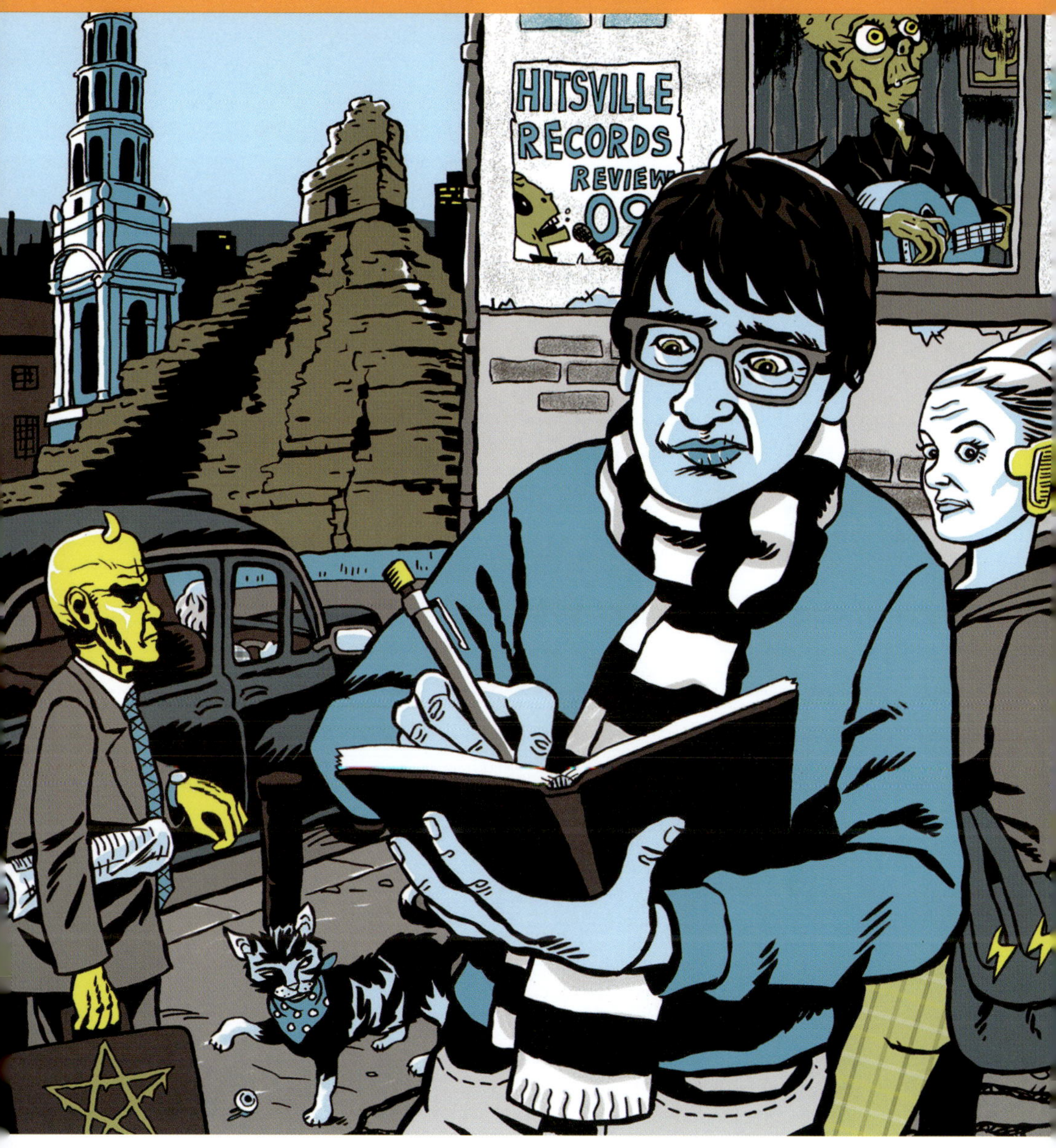

HITSVILLE
RECORDS
REVIEW
09

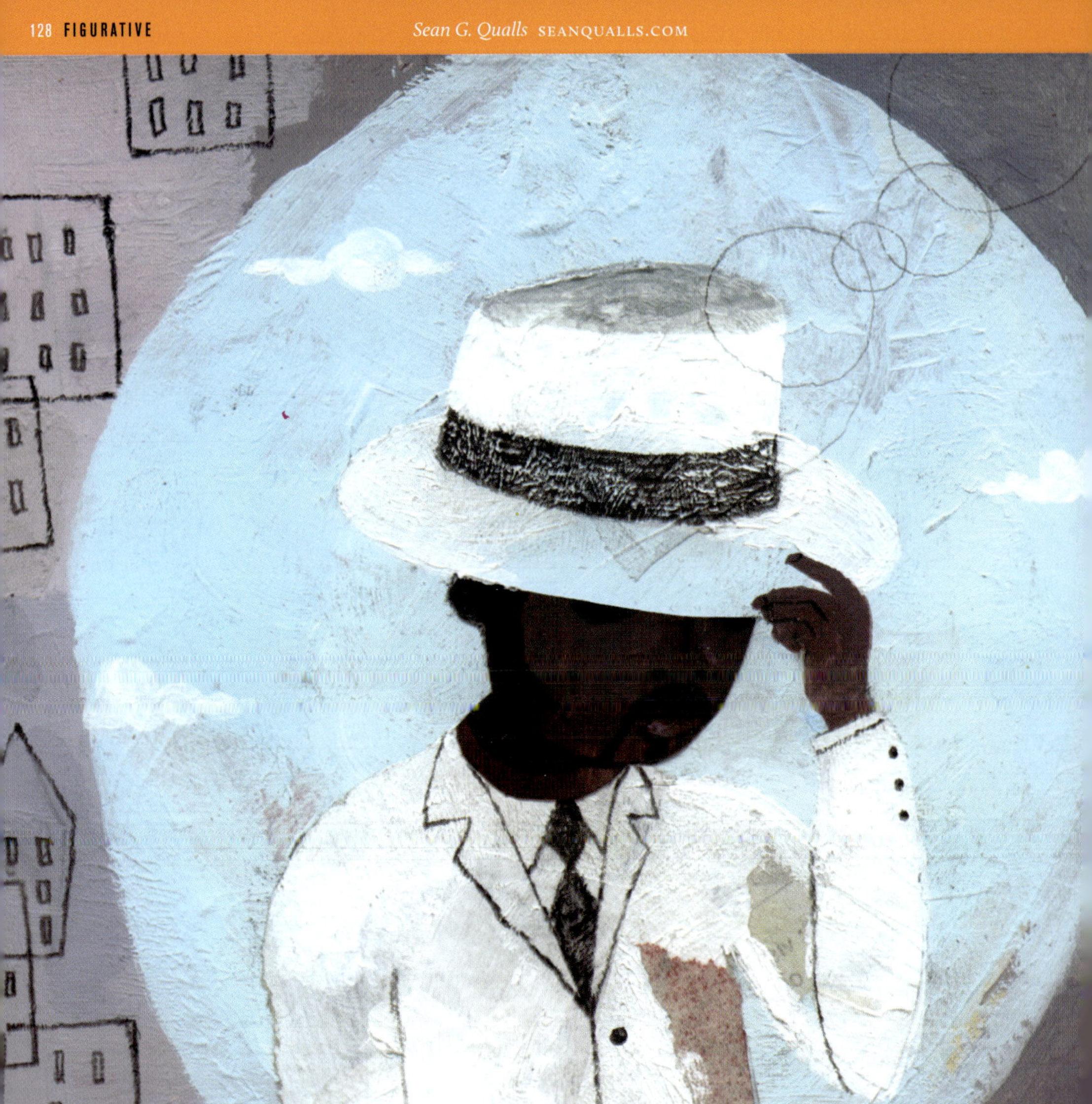
QUALLS

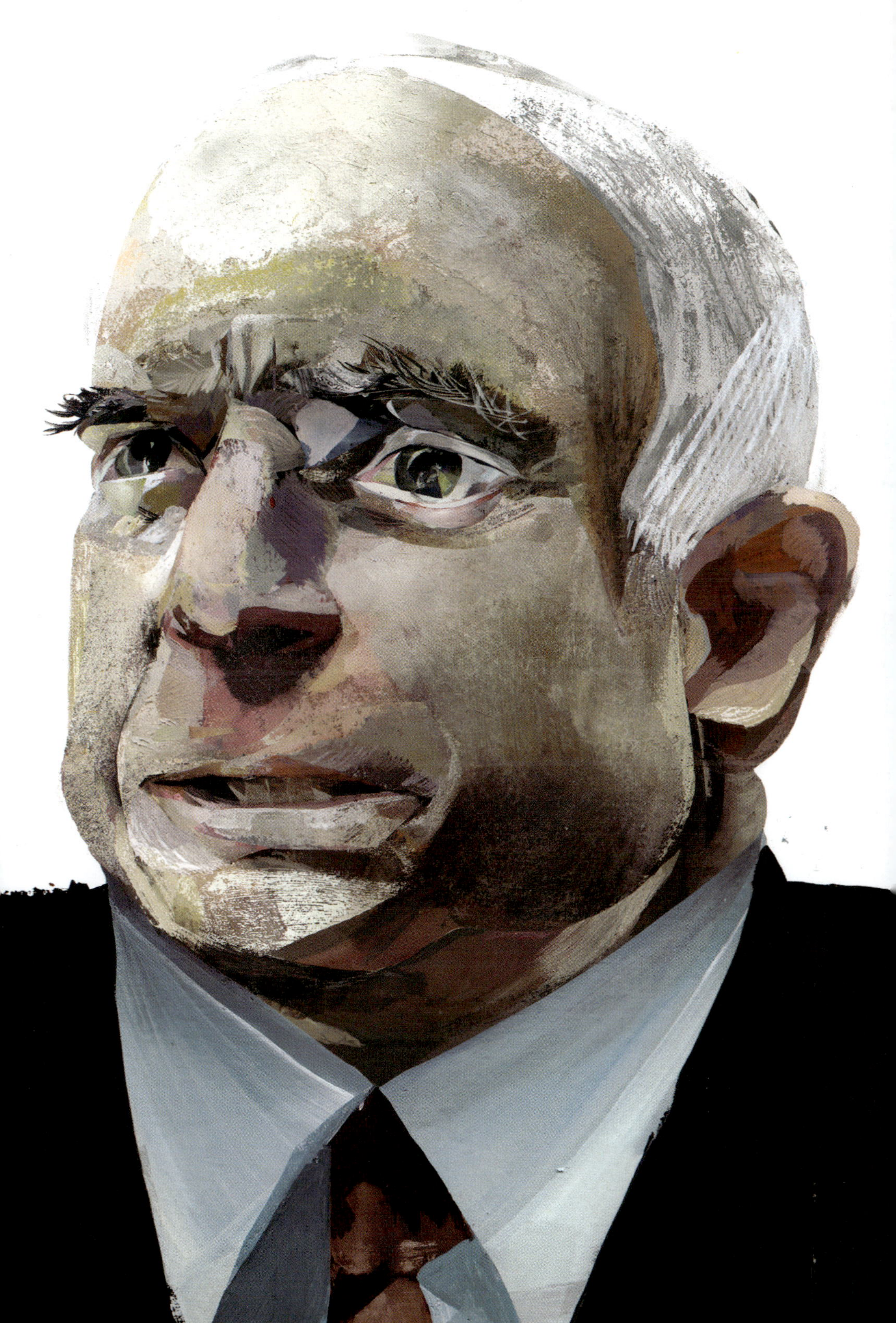

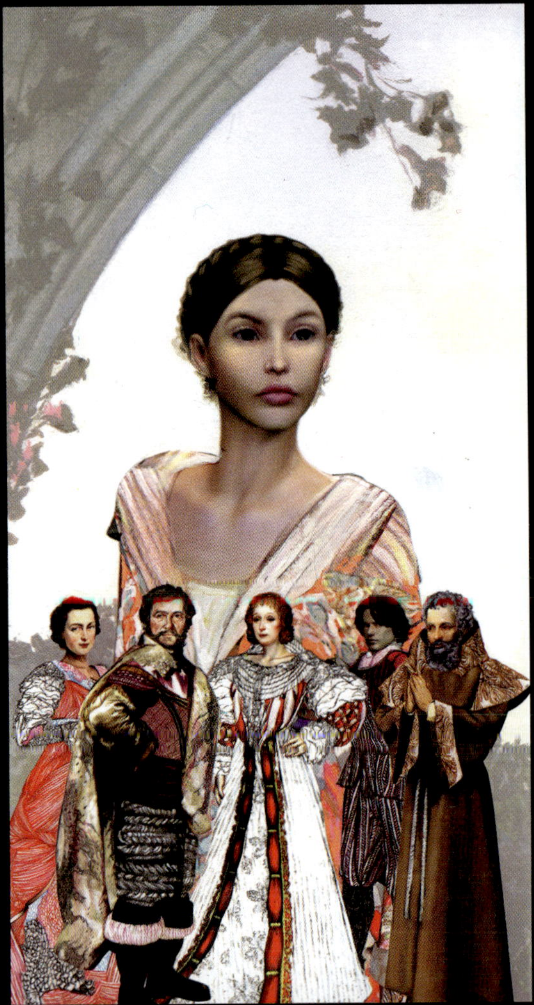

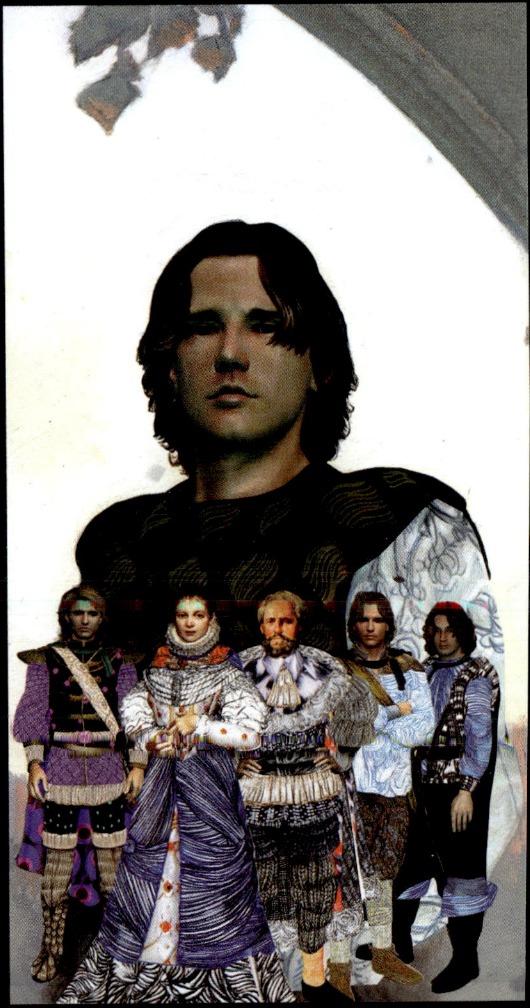

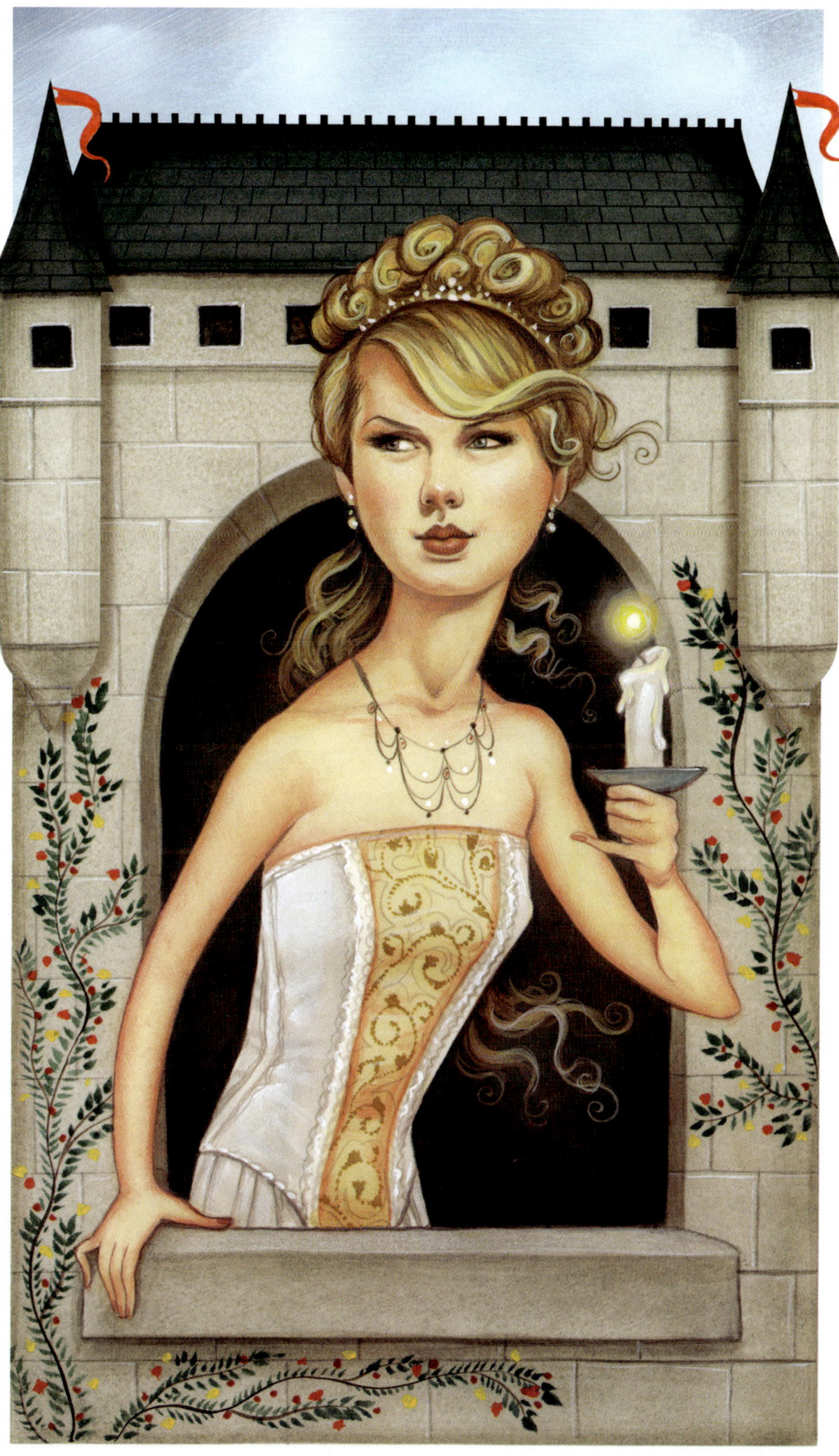

 Lance Jackson

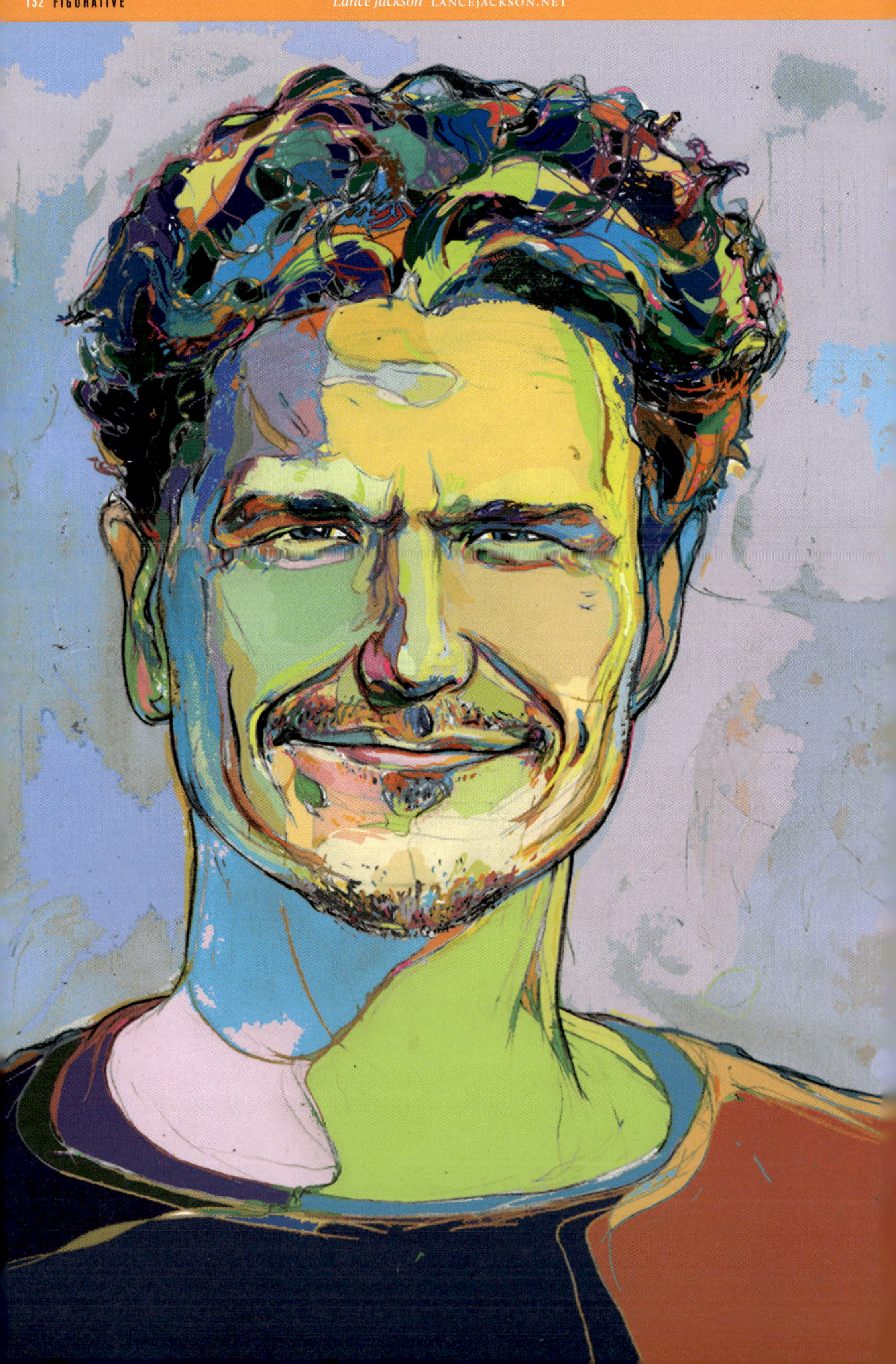

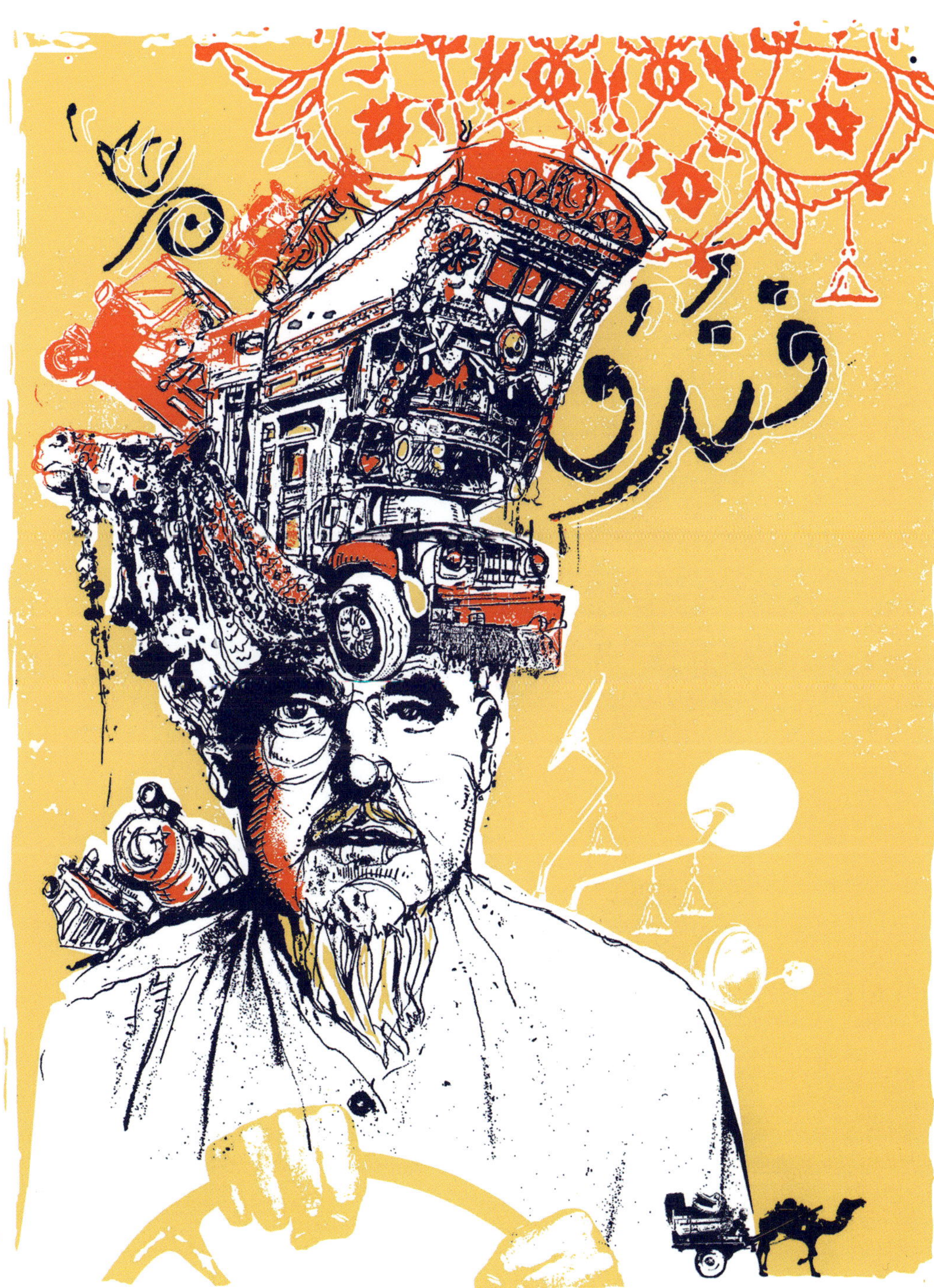

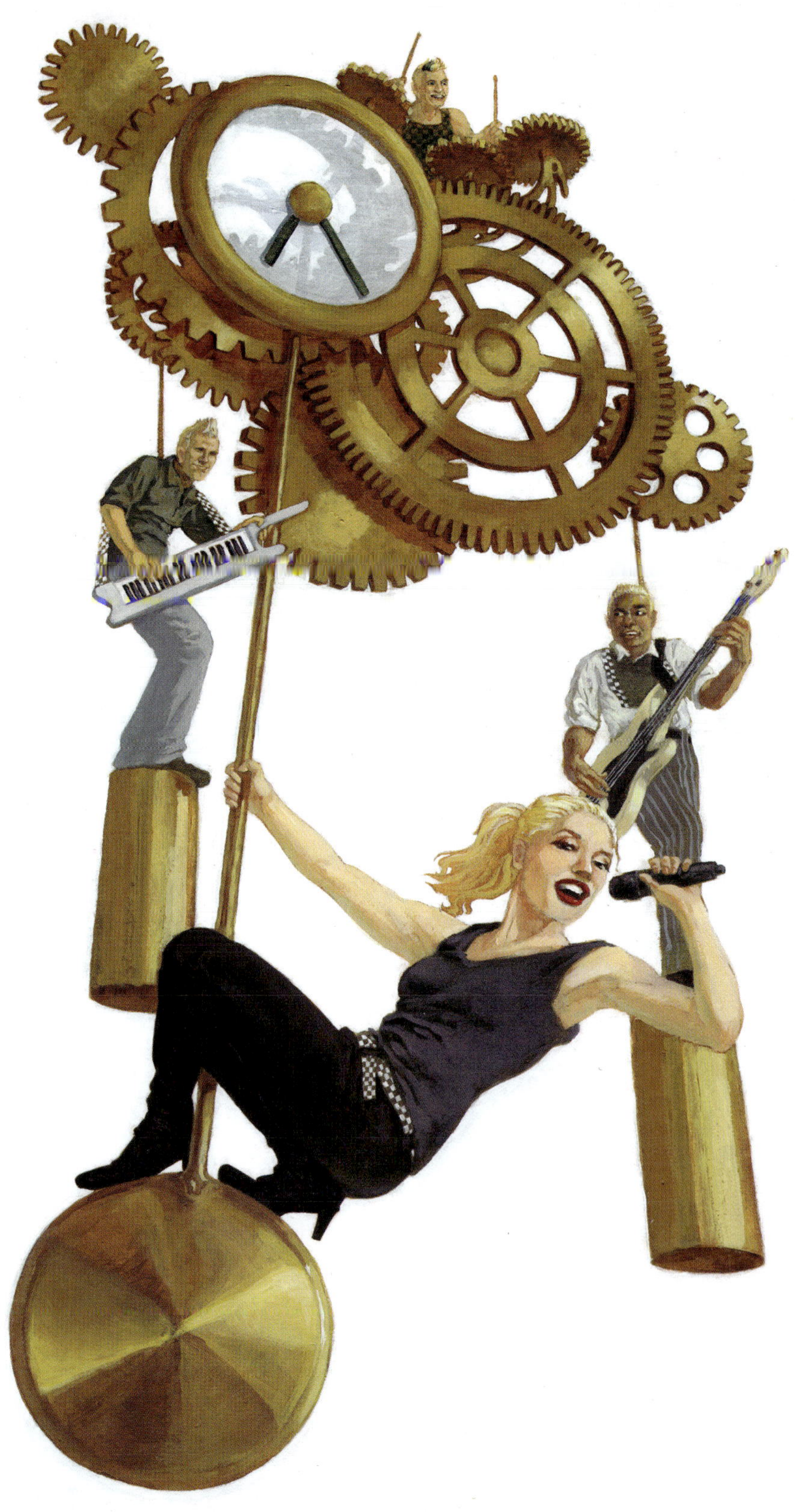

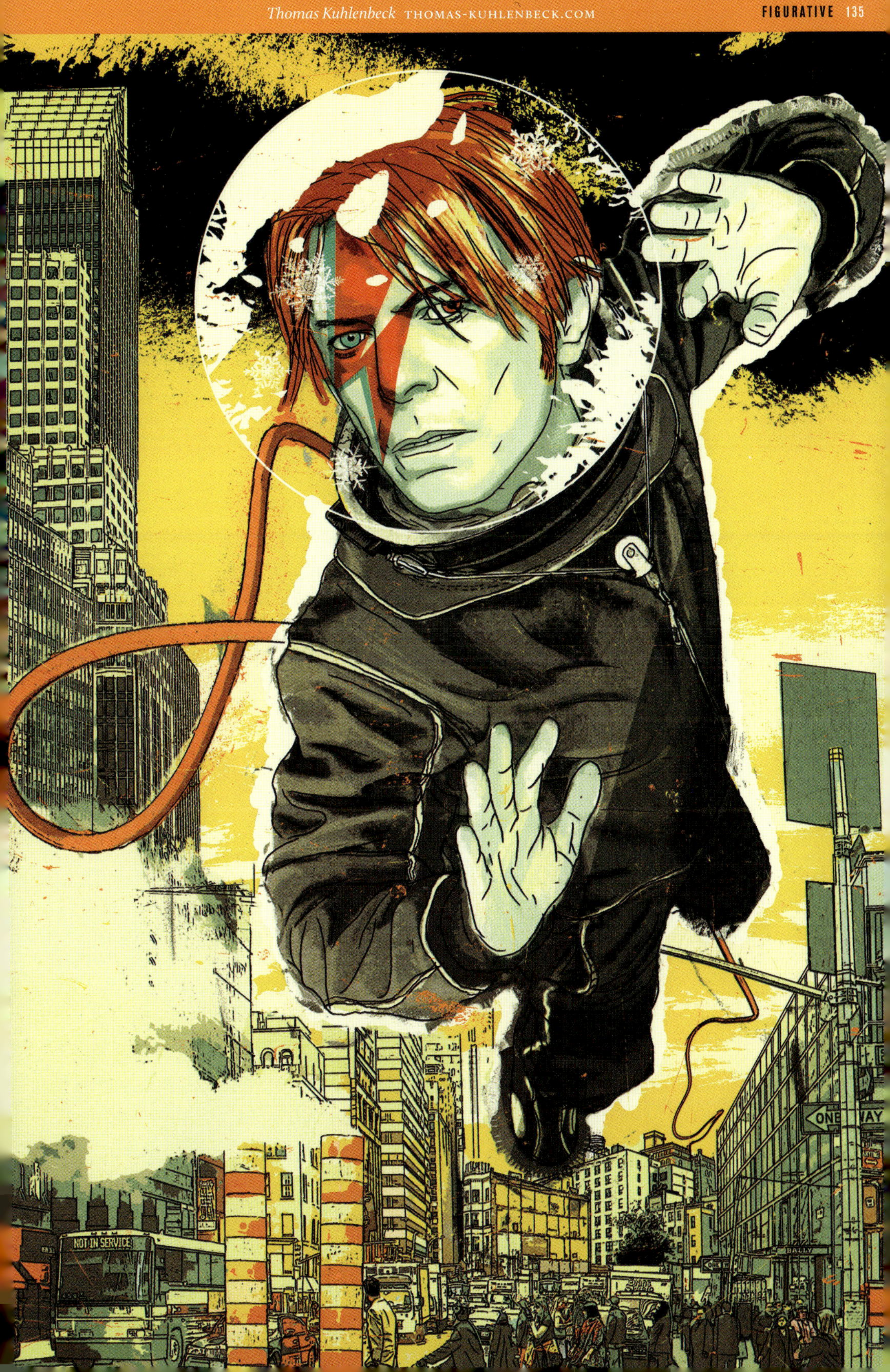

NOT IN SERVICE
ONE WAY
BALLY

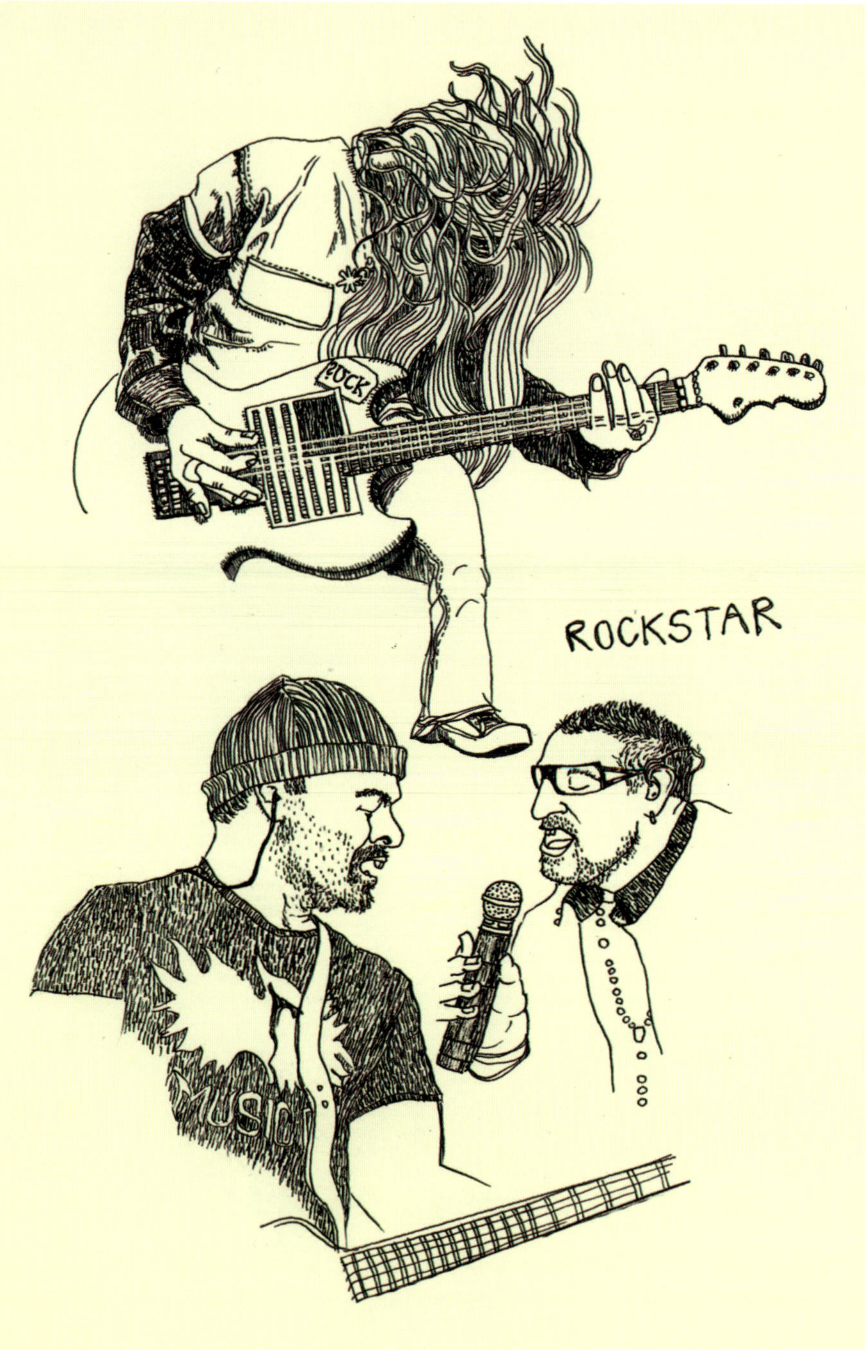
ROCKSTAR

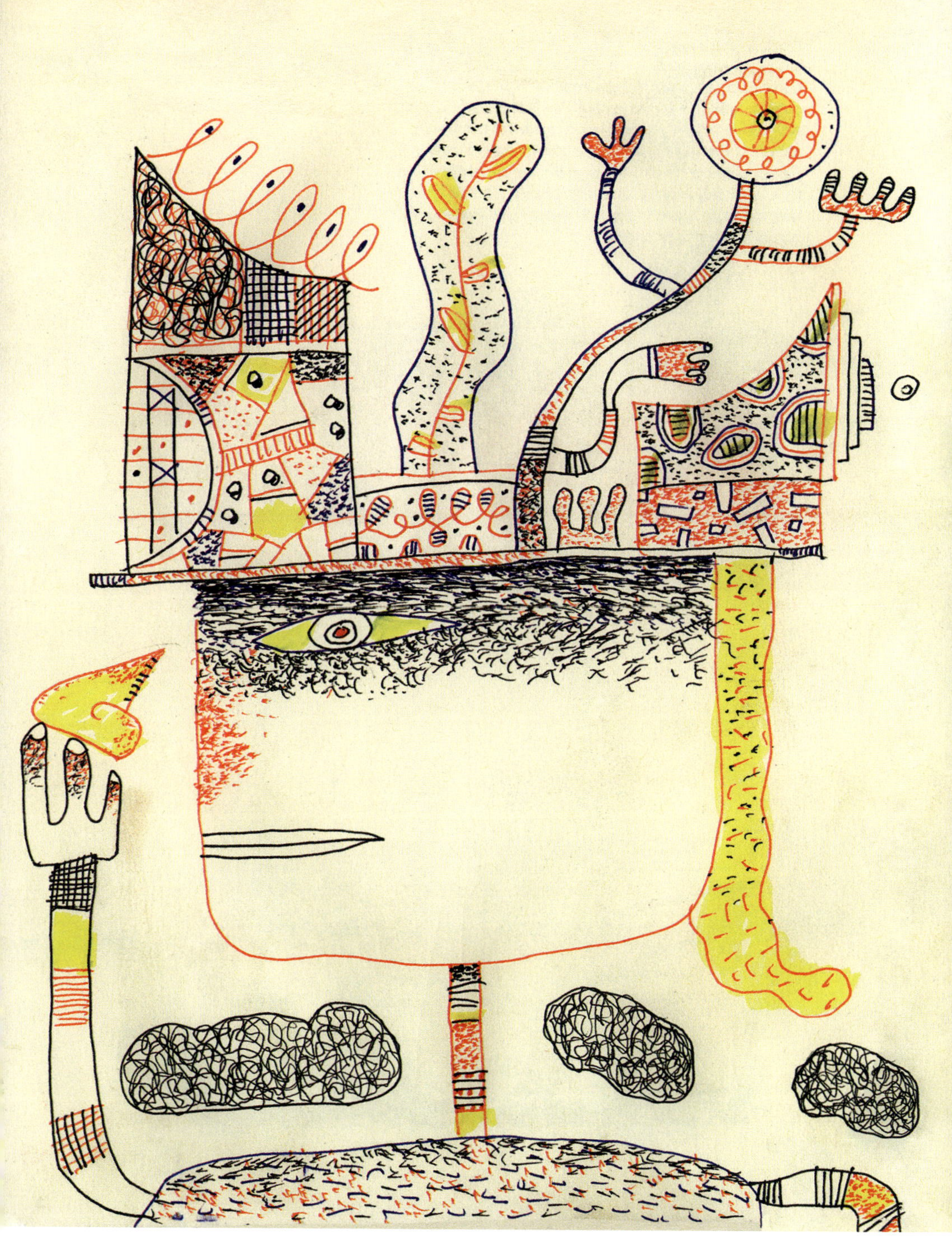

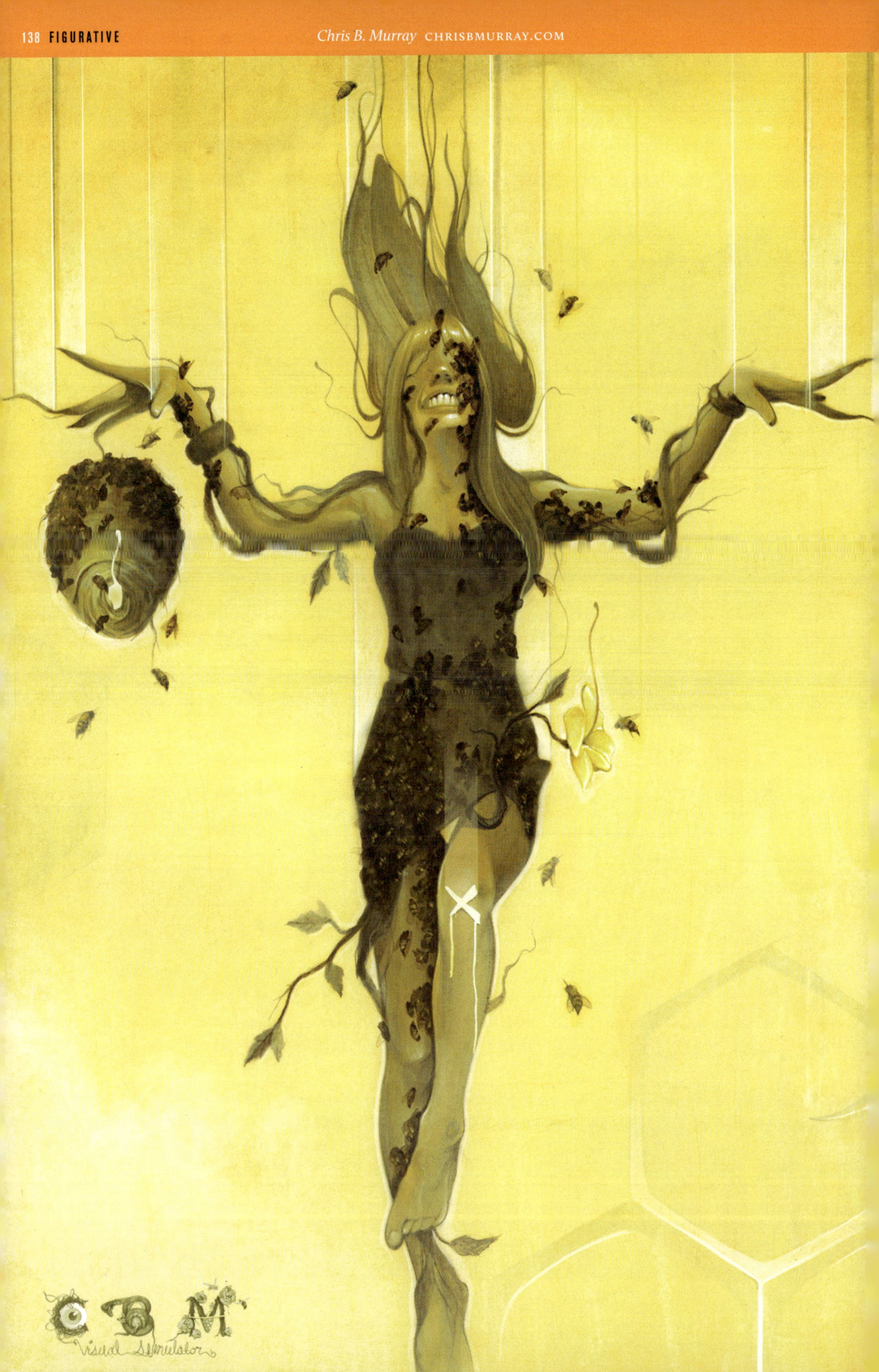
OBM
visual simulator

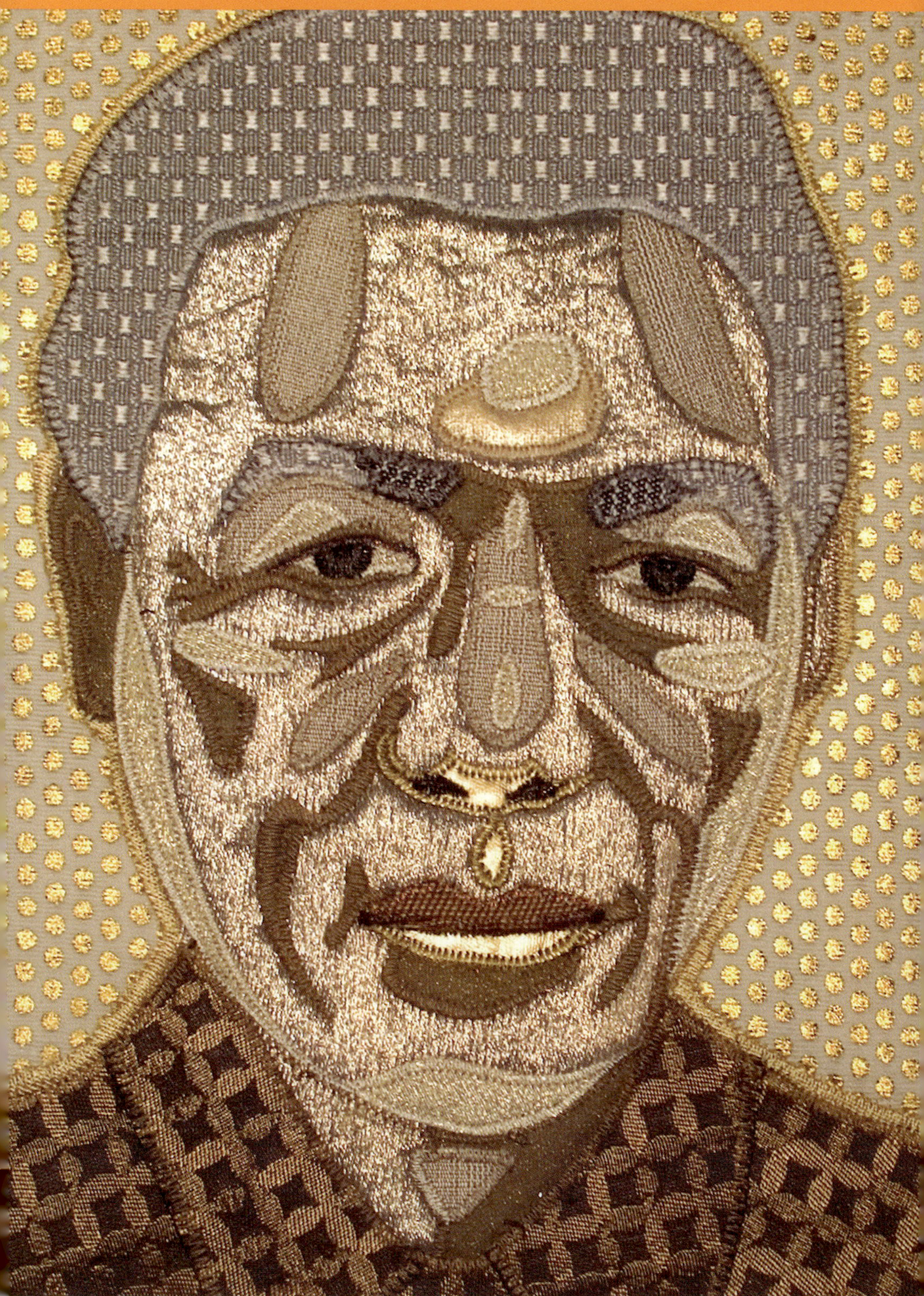

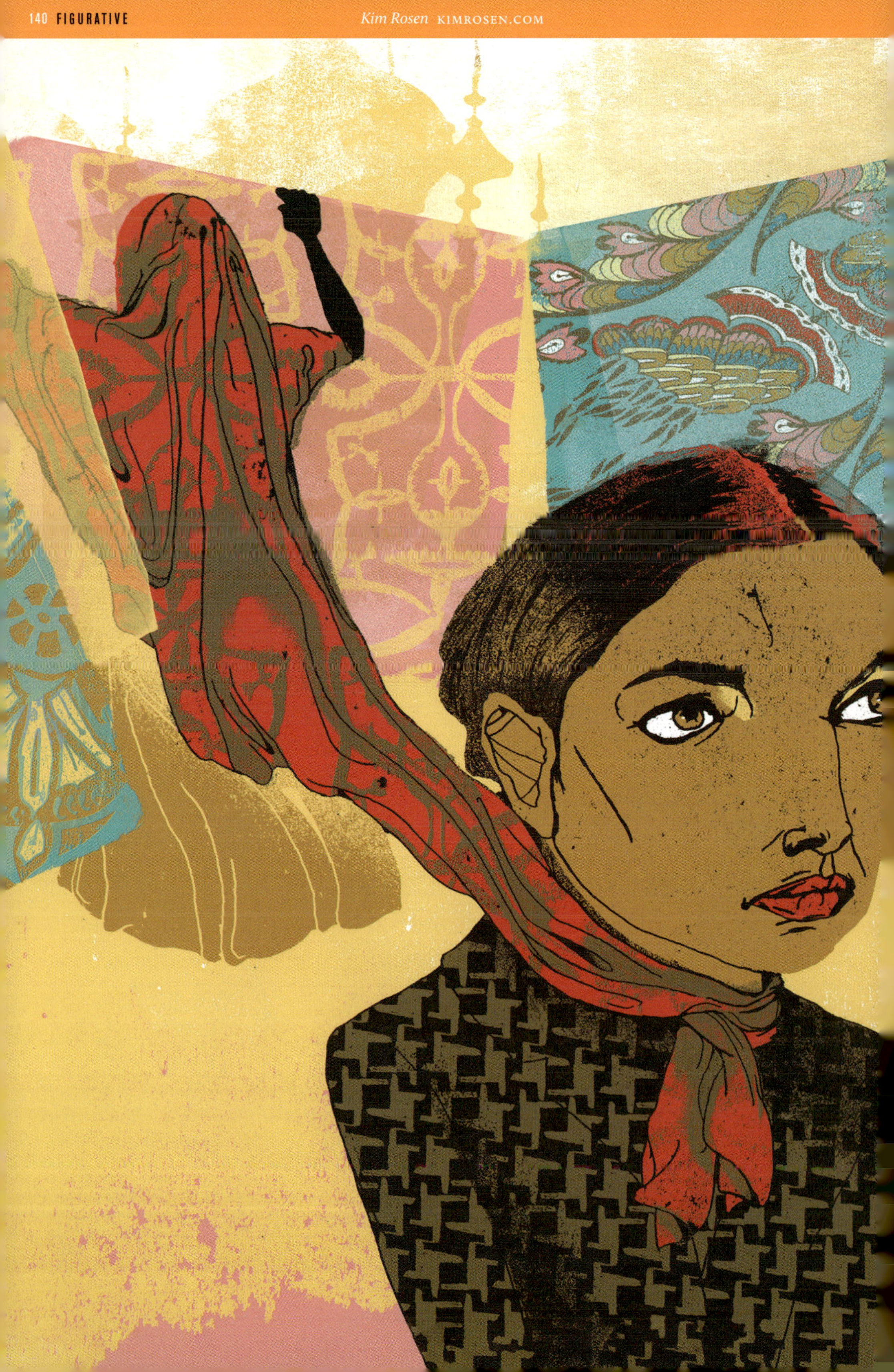

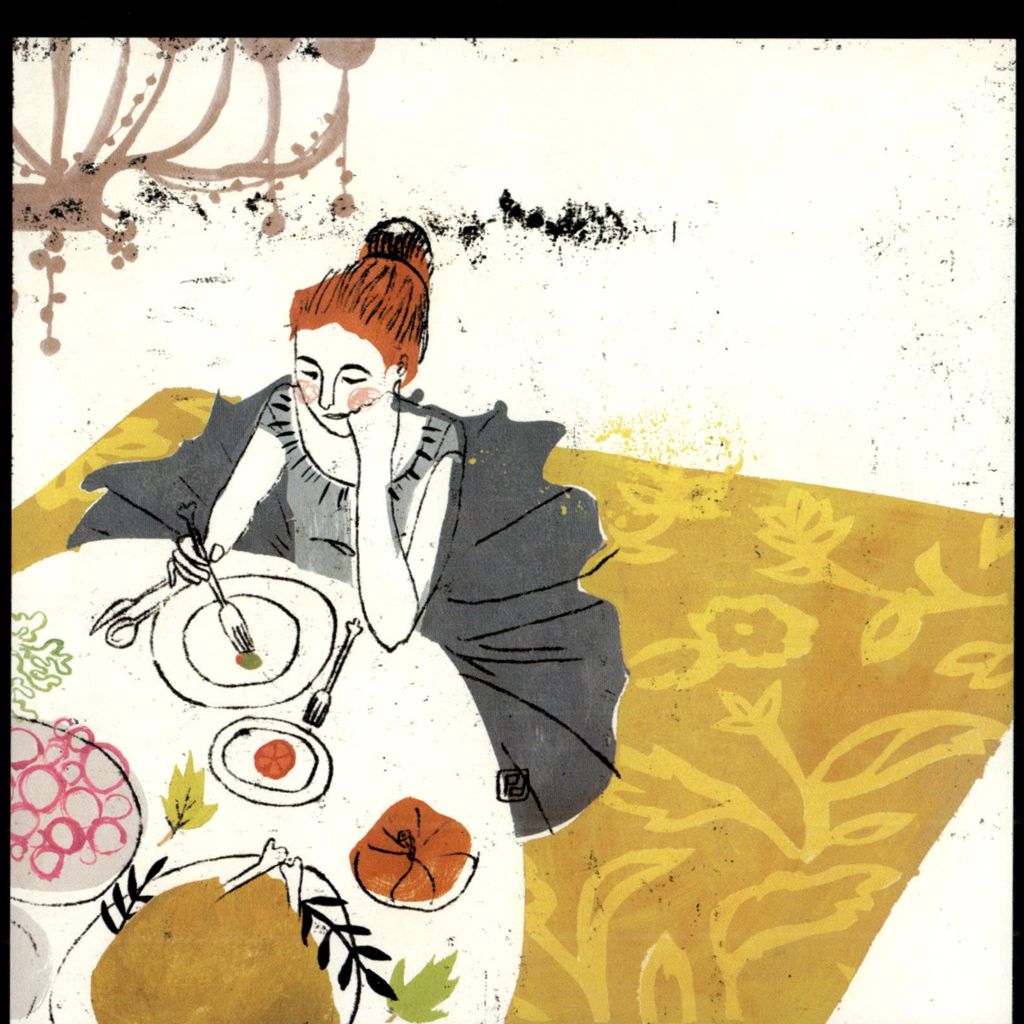

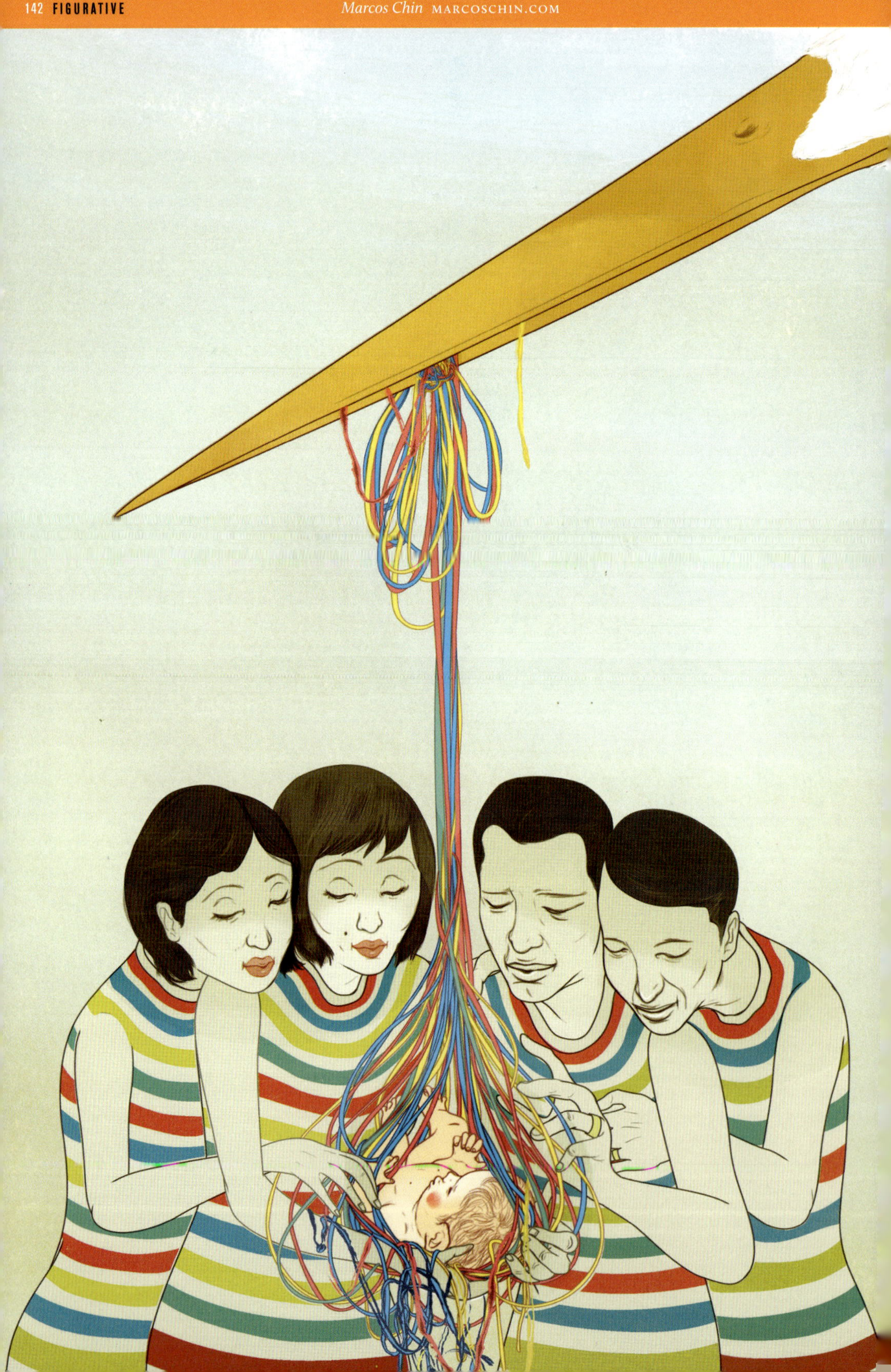

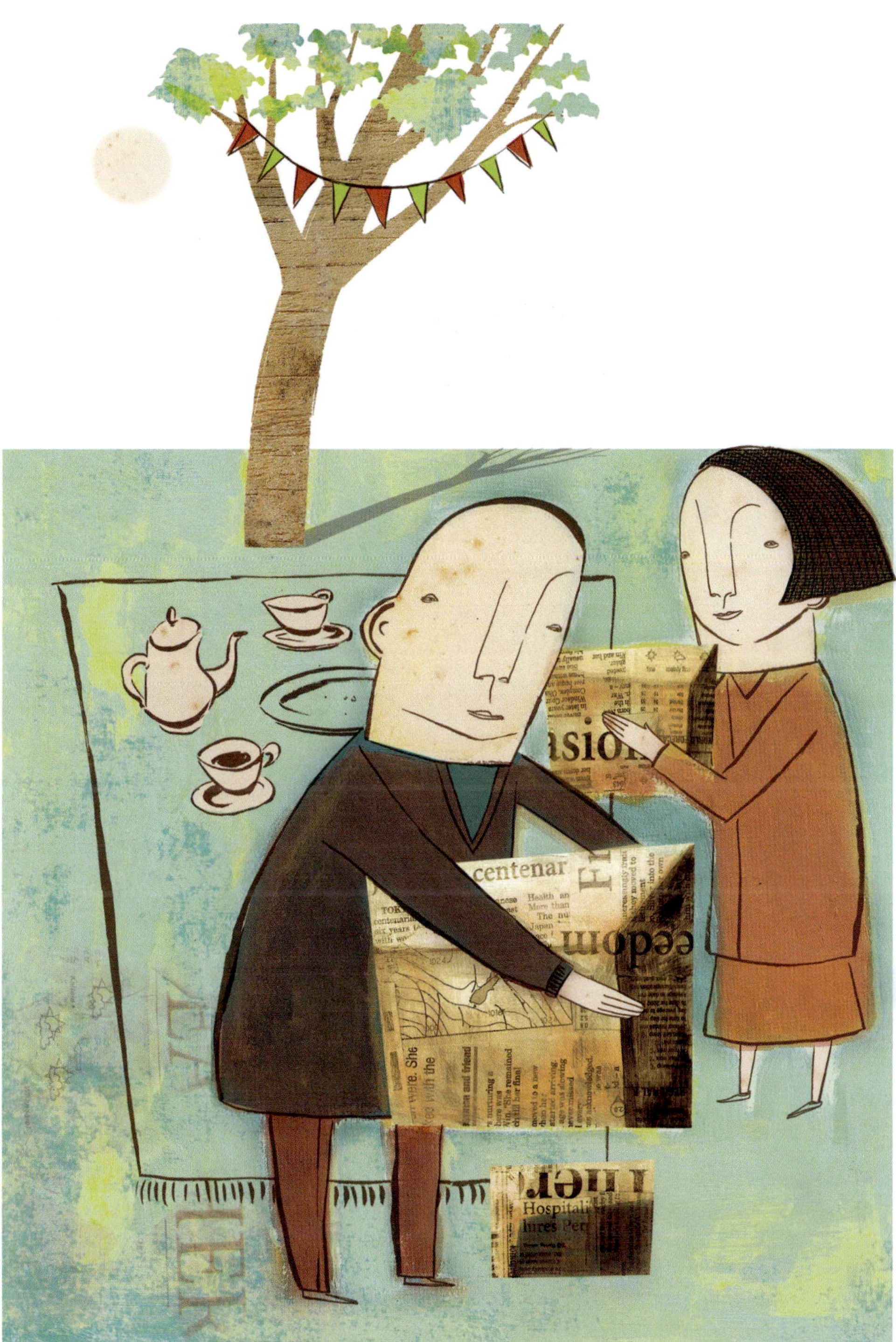

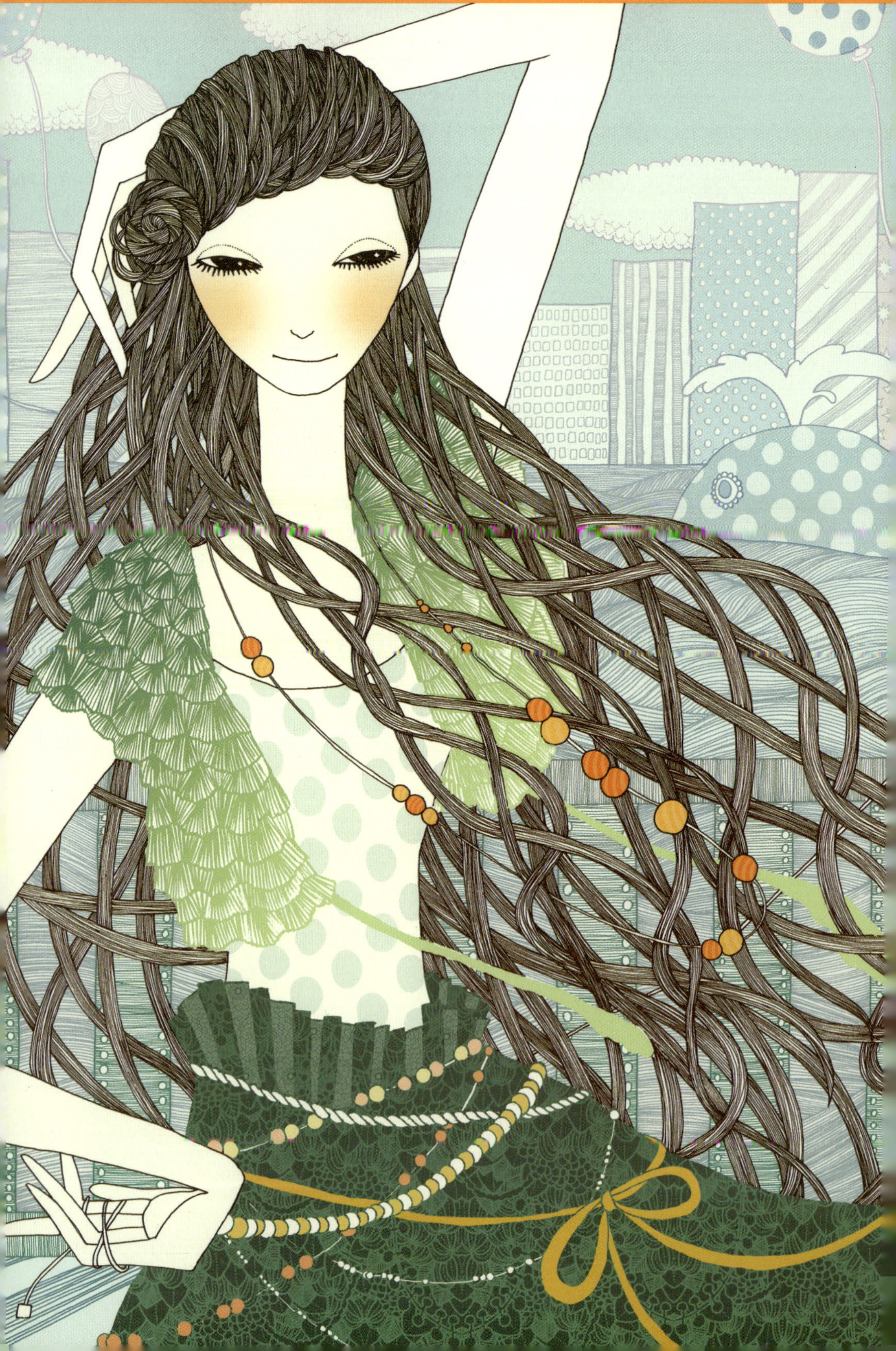

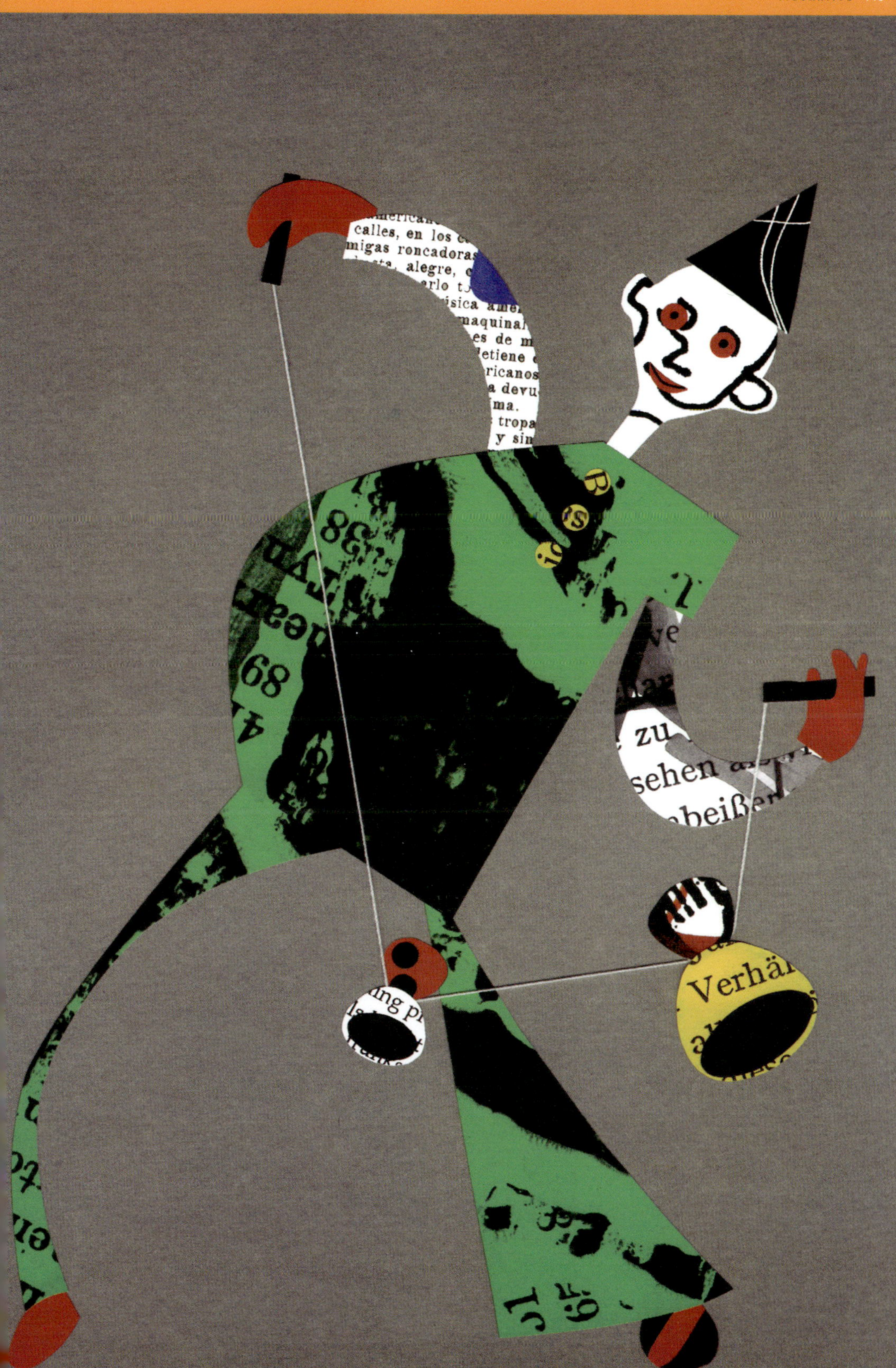
calles, en los c
migas roncadoras
ta, alegre,
erlo t
ísica ame
maquinal
es de m
etiene
ricanos
a devu
ma.
tropa
y sin
zu
sehen a
beißen
Verhä

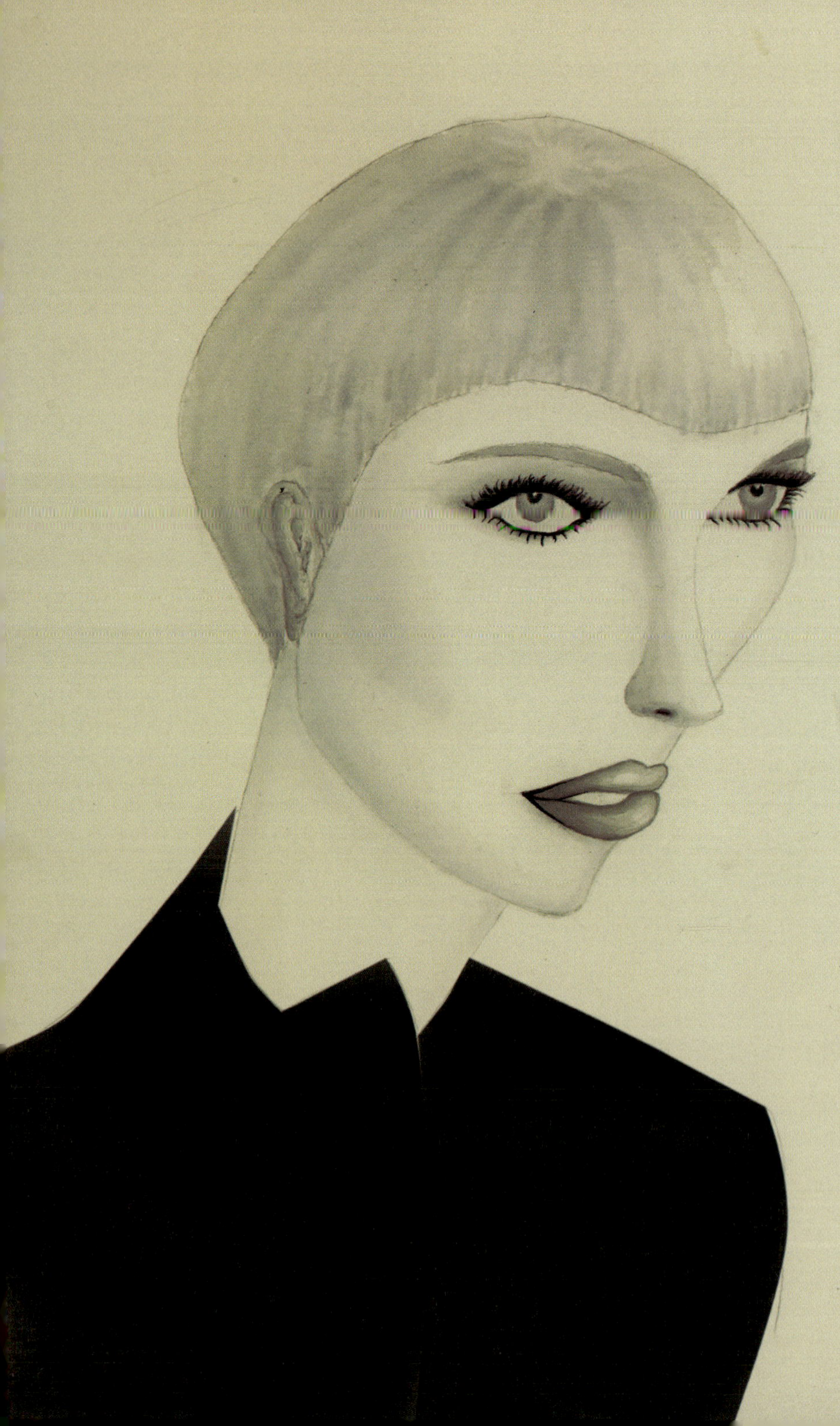

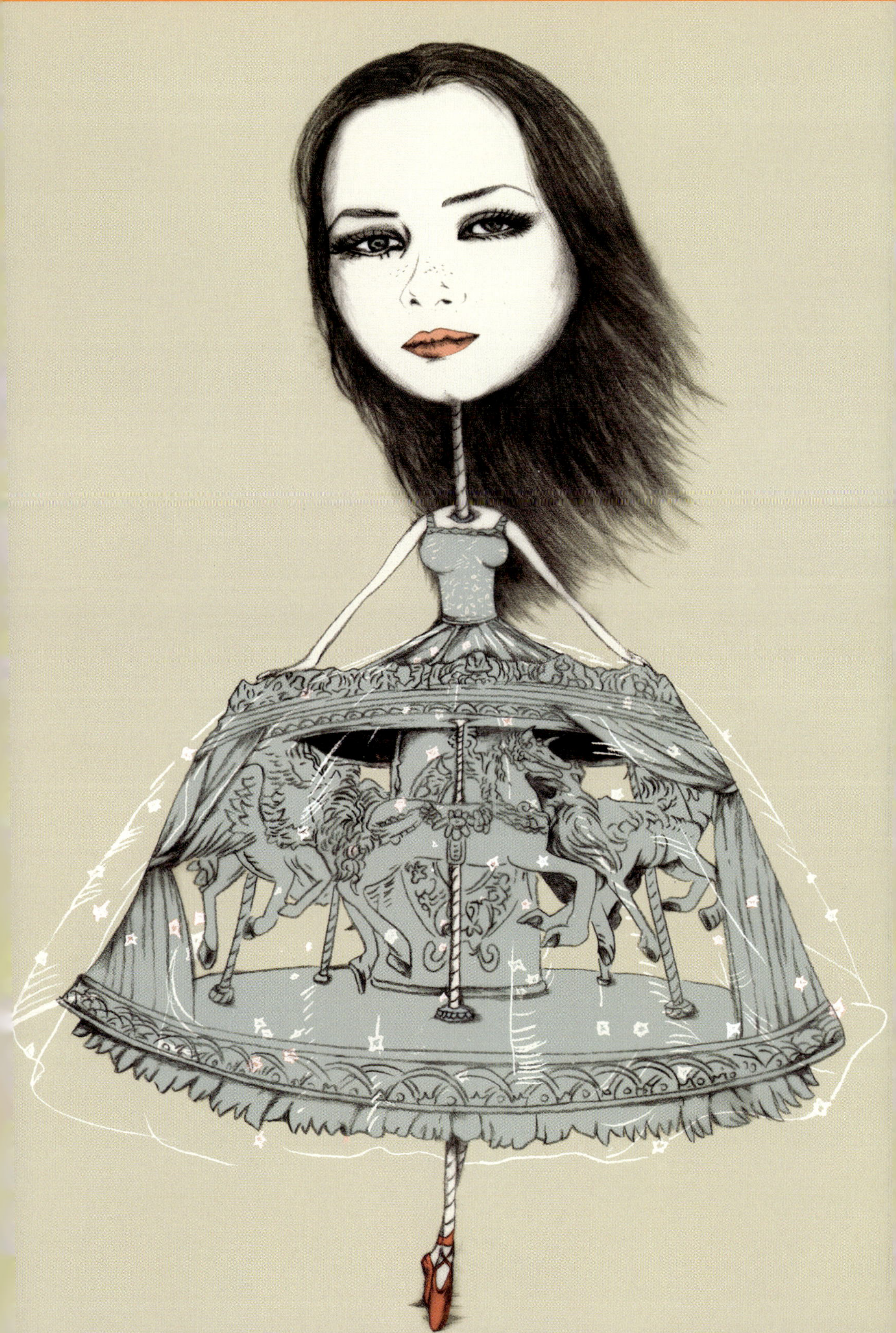

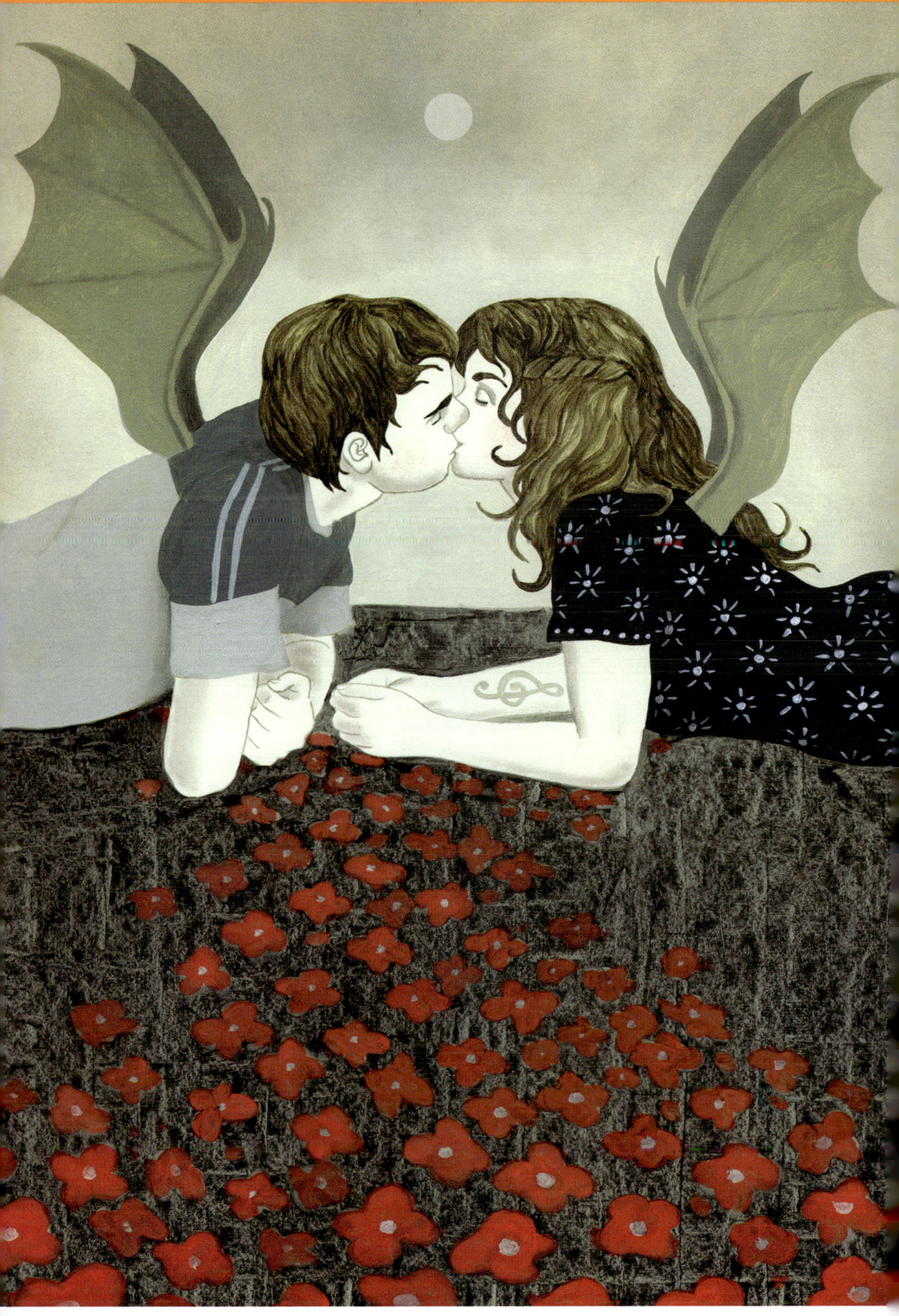

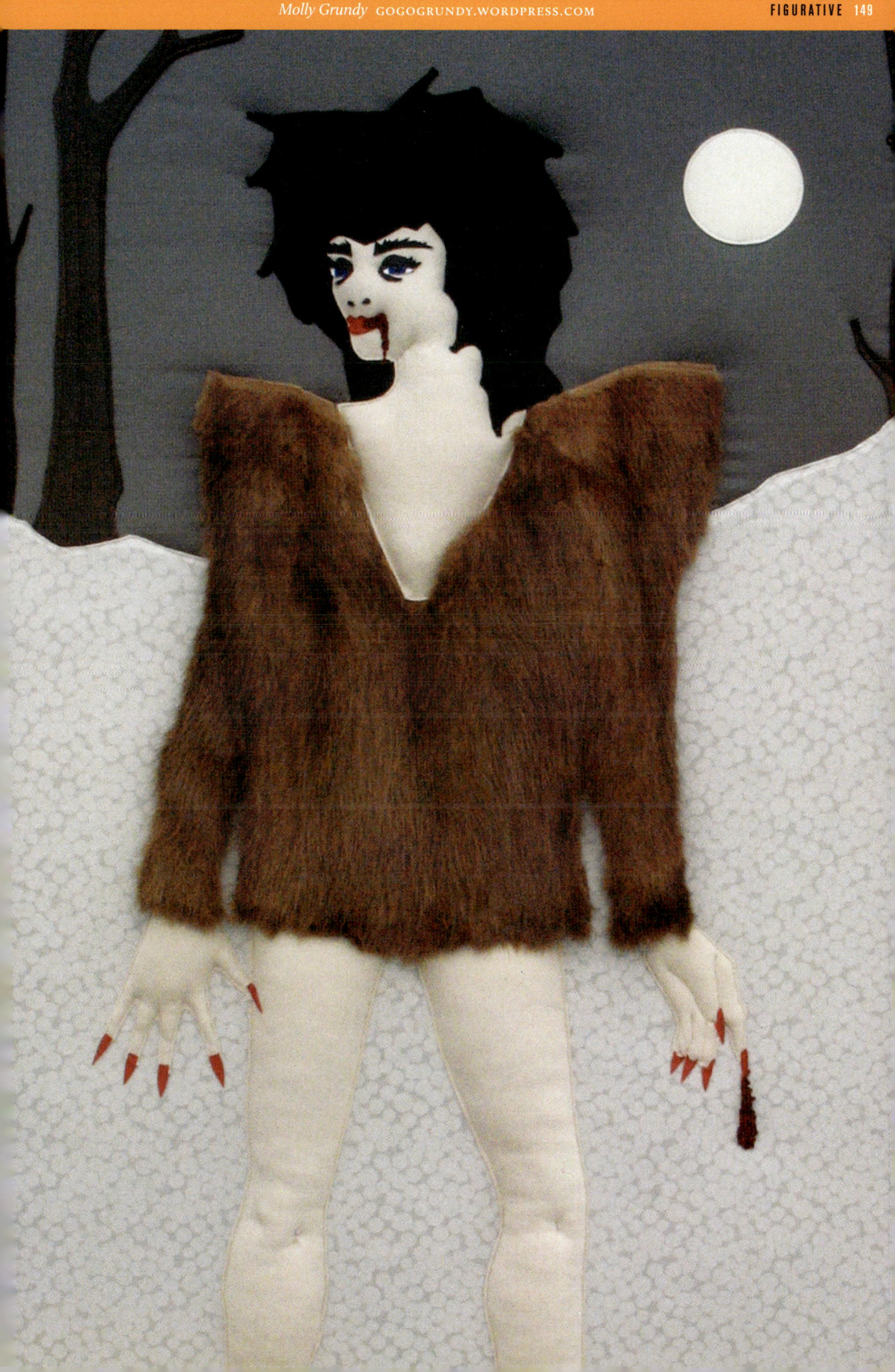

 Alenka Sottler SOTTLER.SI

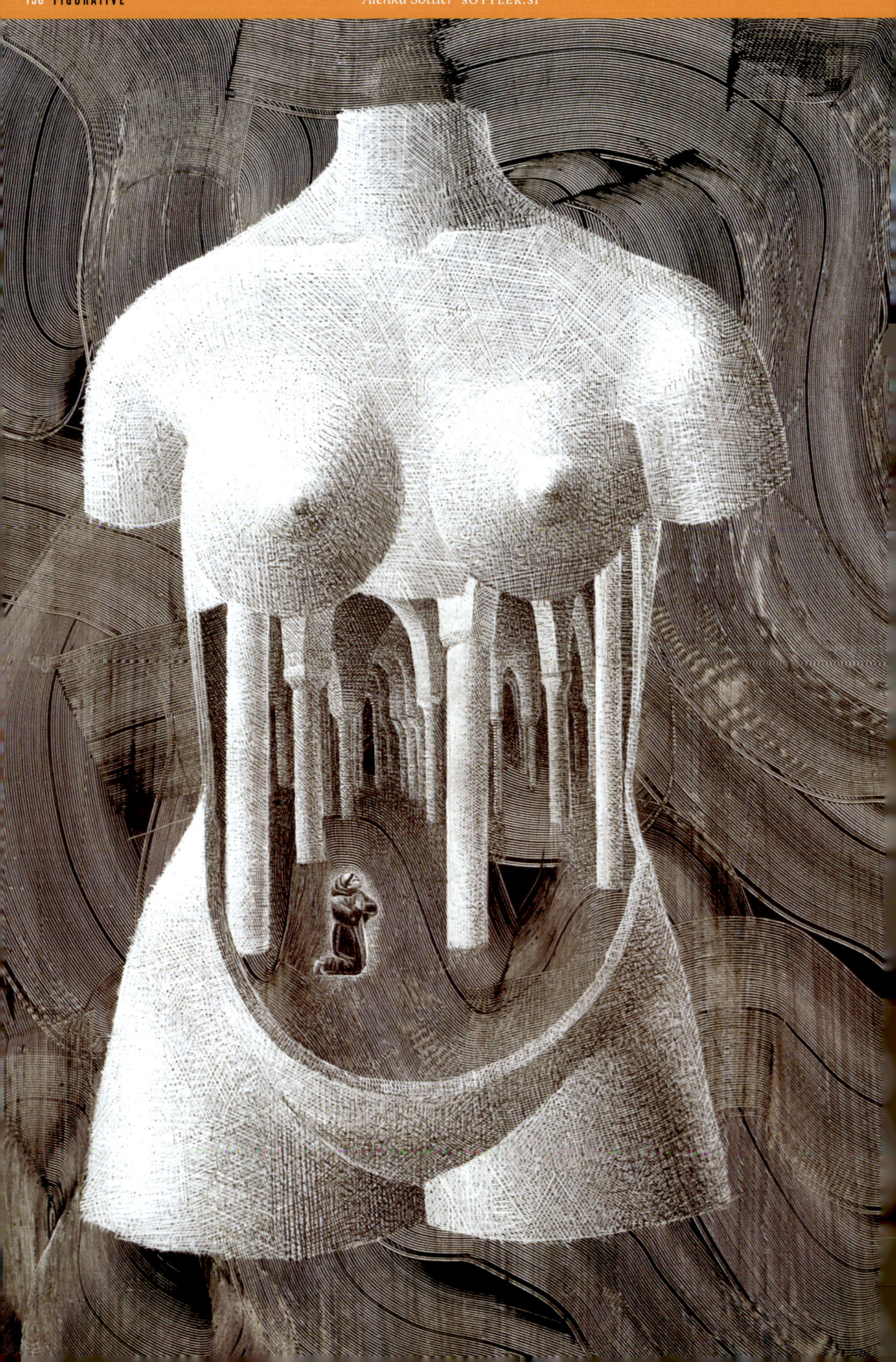

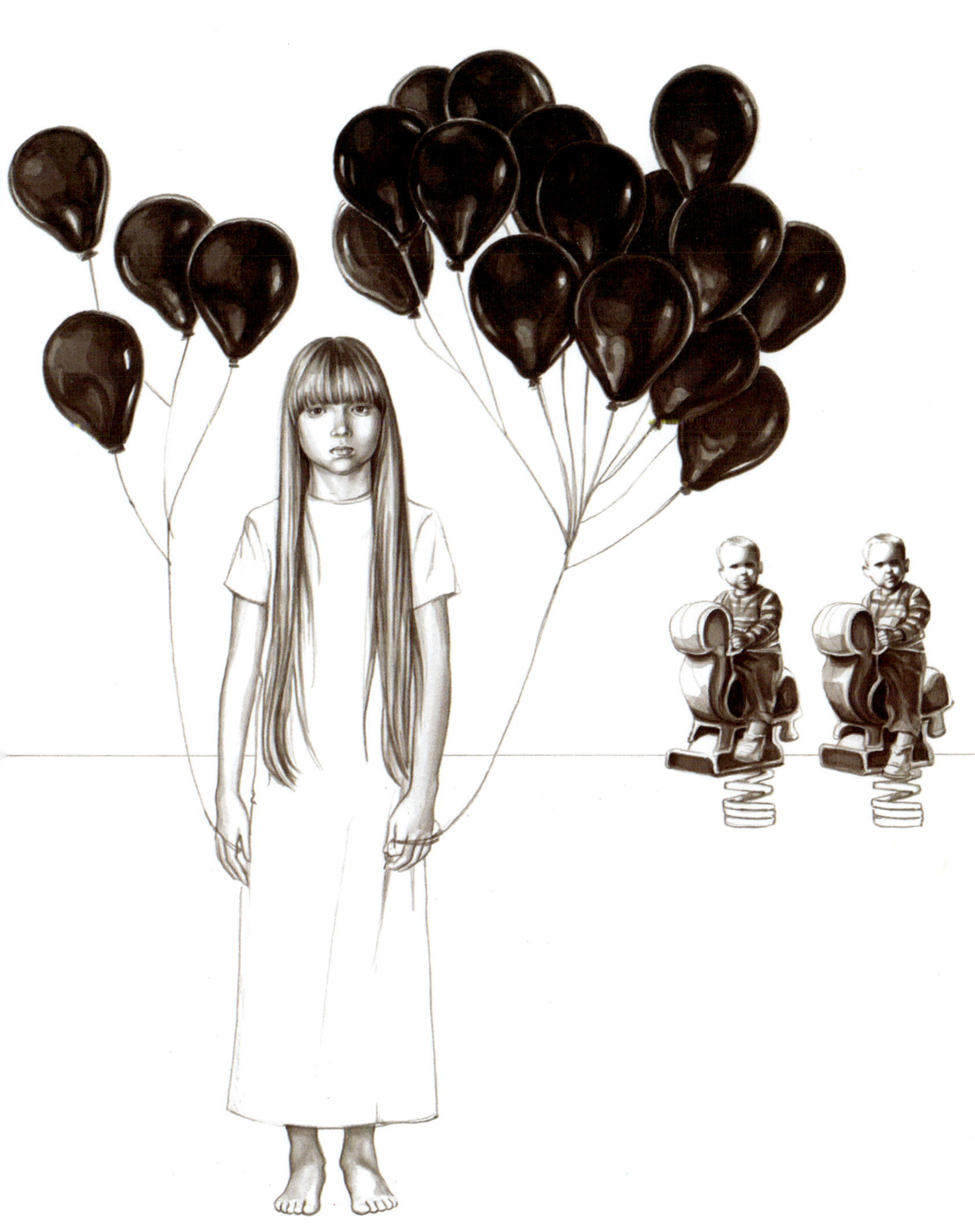

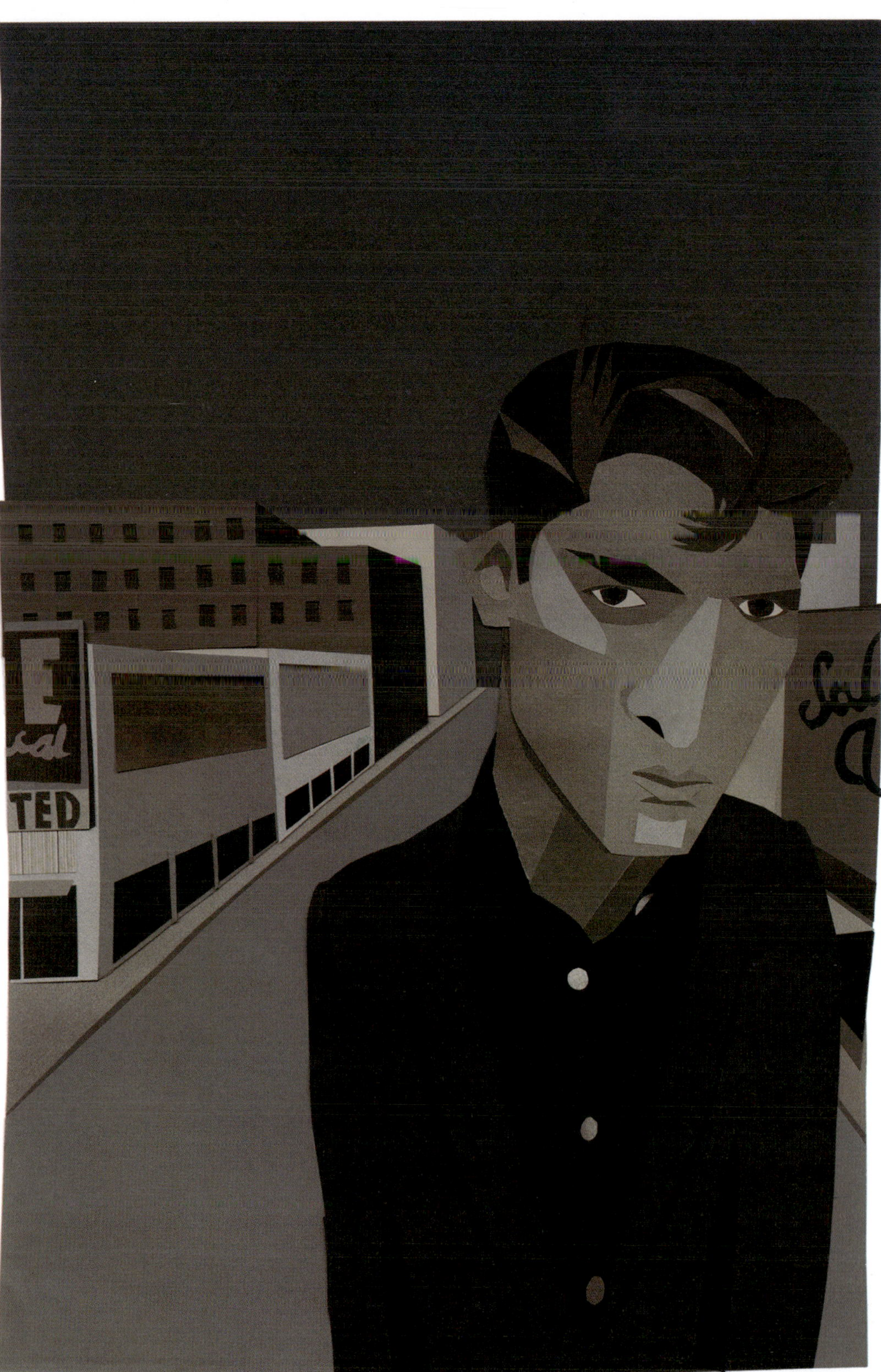
TED
SALE

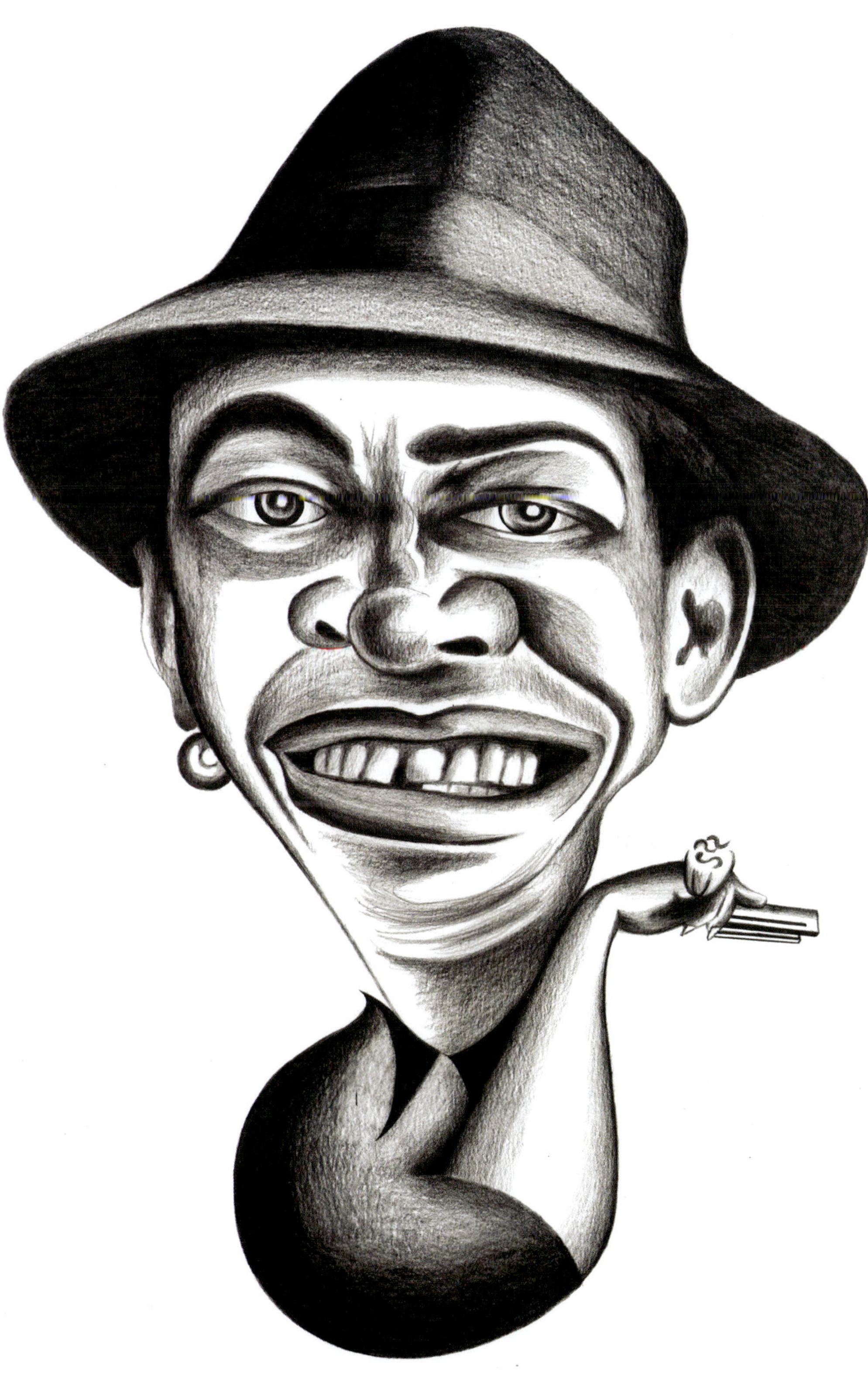

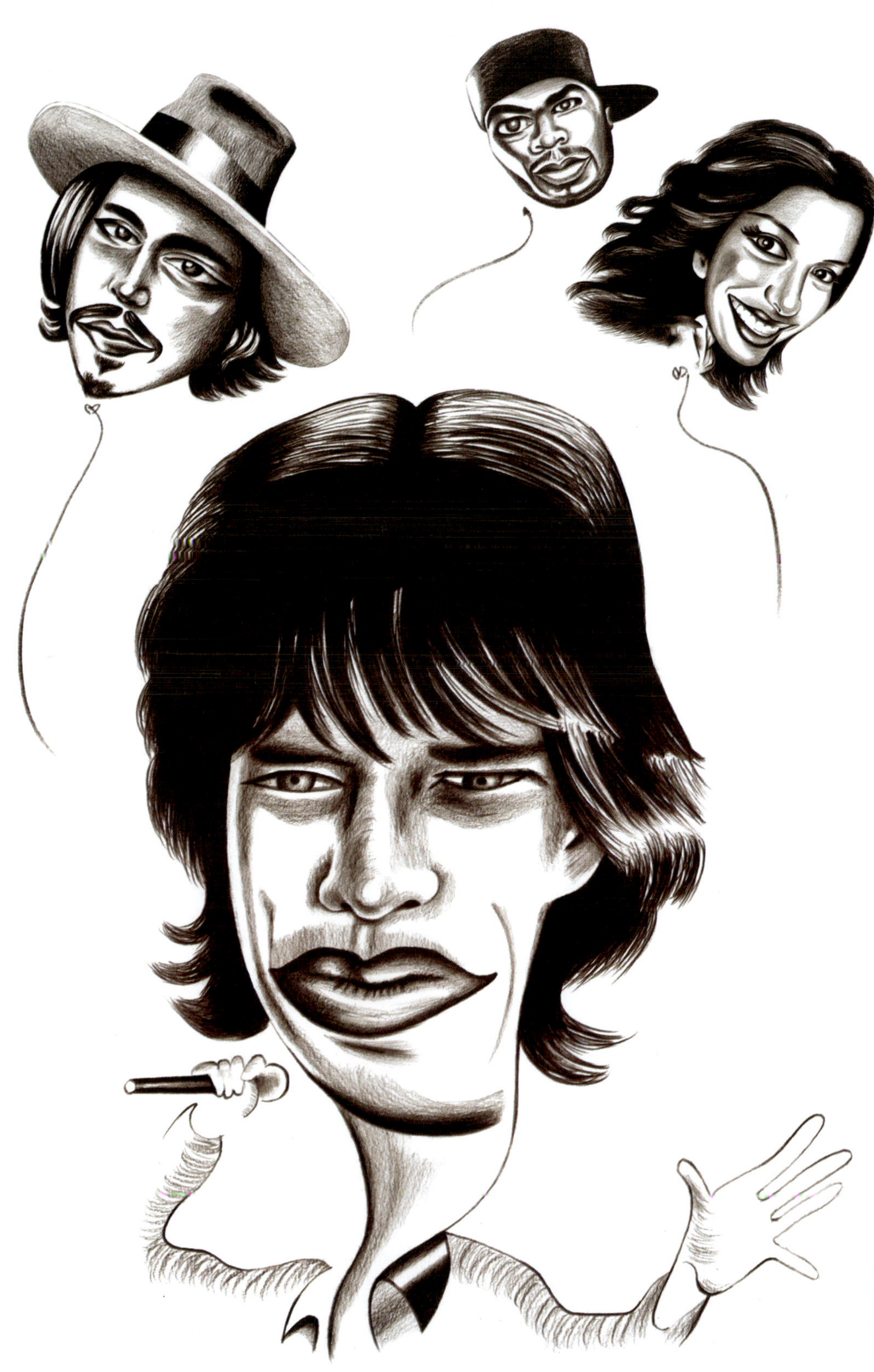

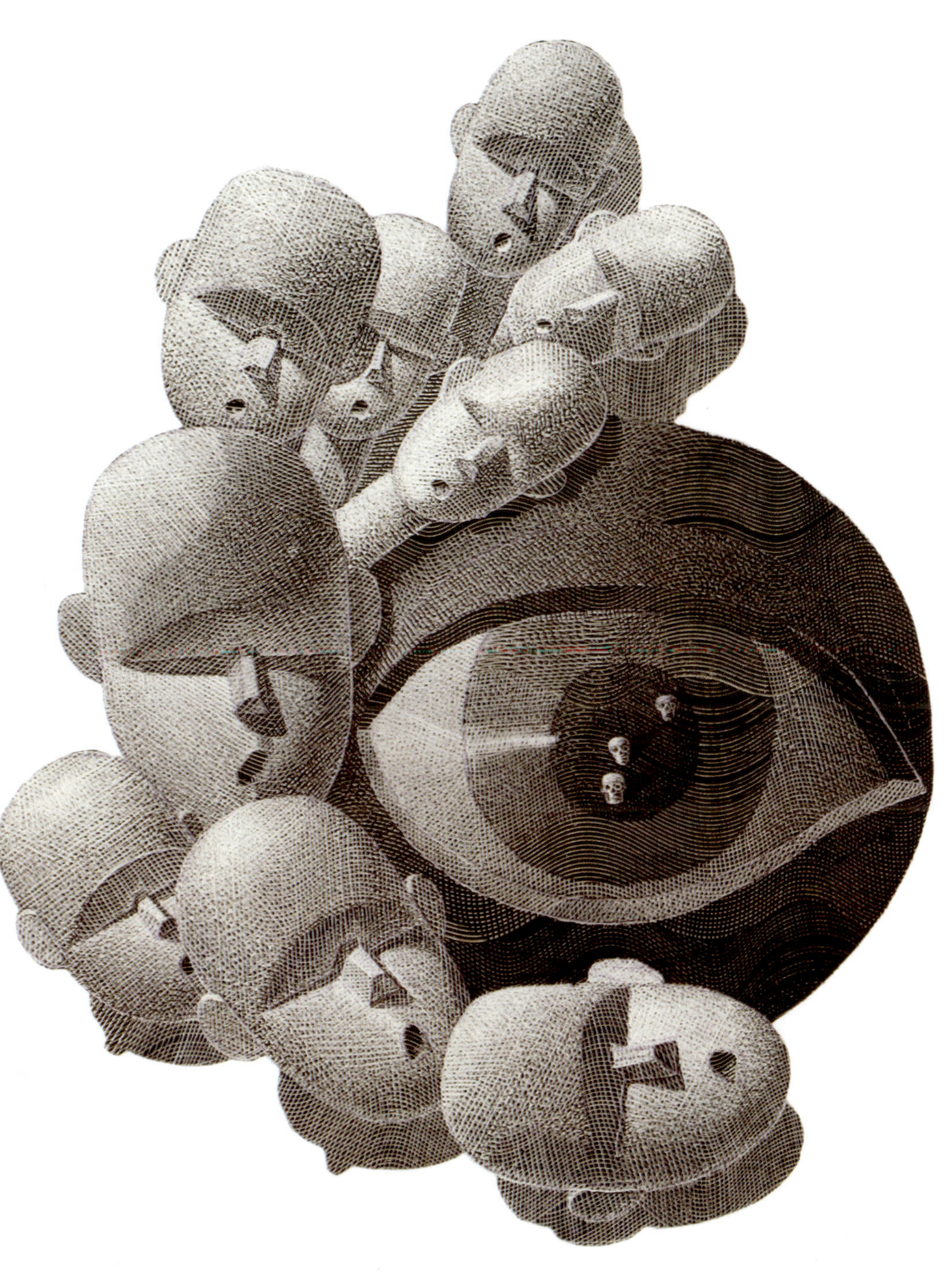

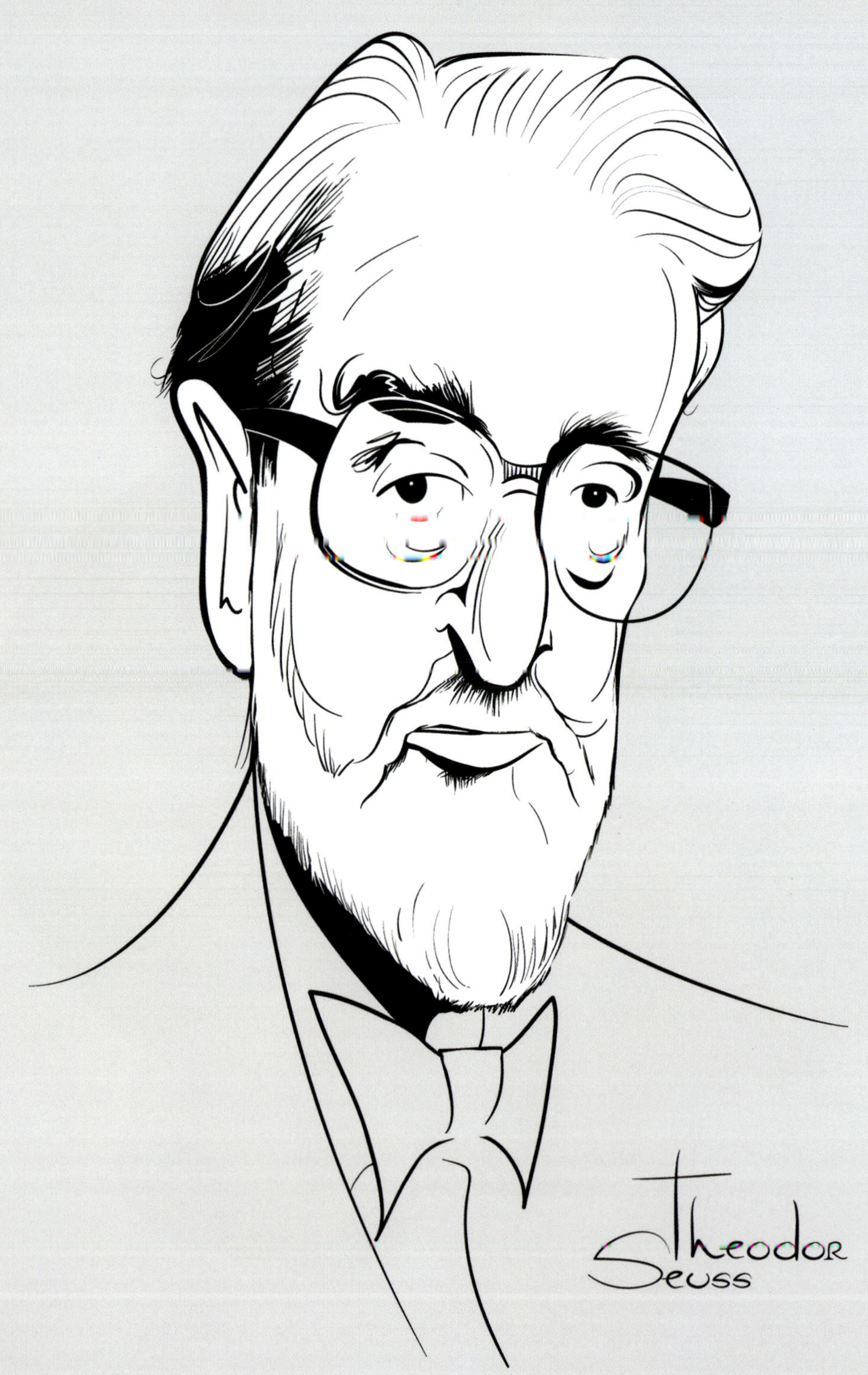
Theodor
Seuss

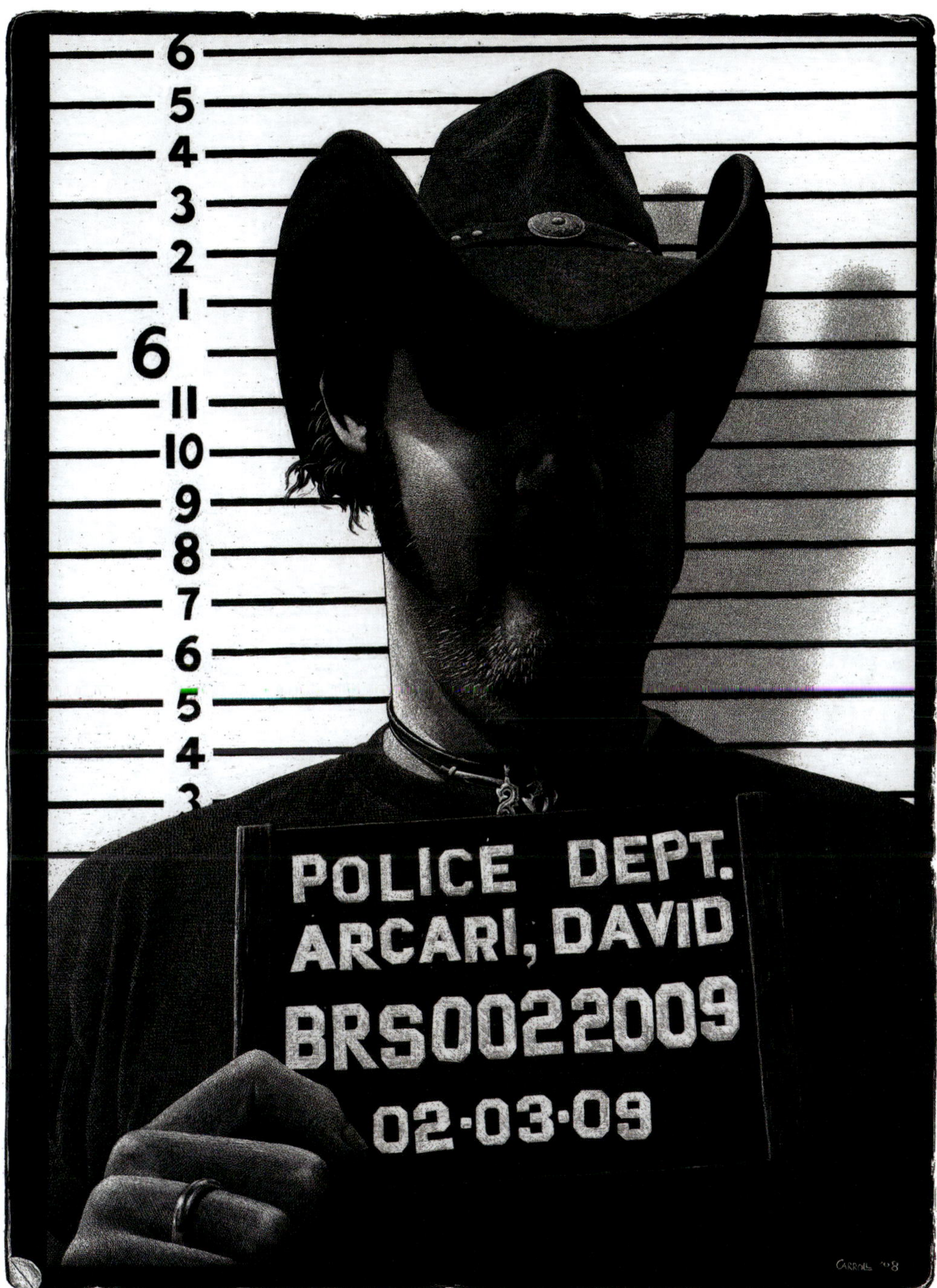
POLICE DEPT.
ARCARI, DAVID
BRS0022009
02-03-09
CARROLL '08

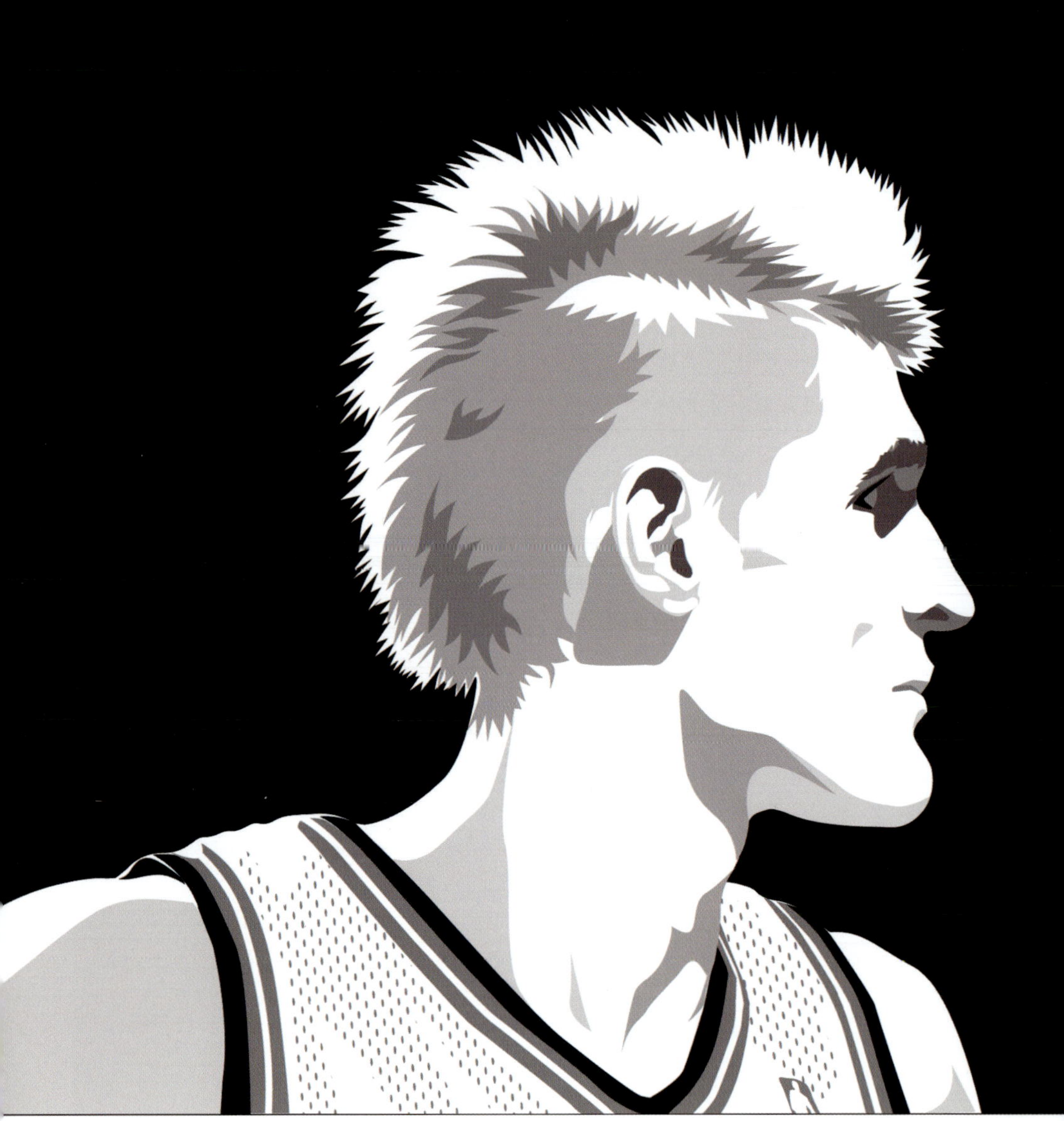

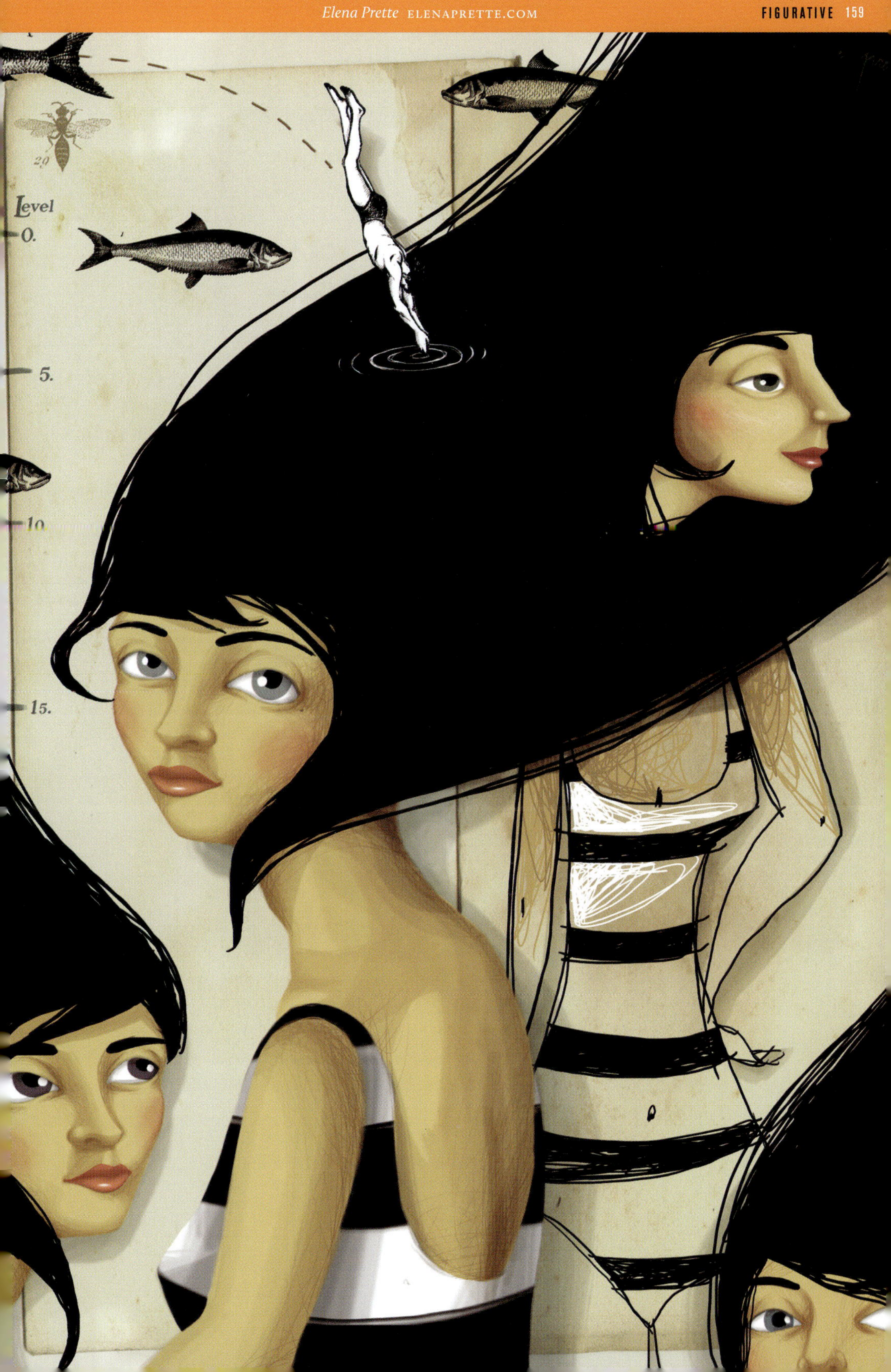

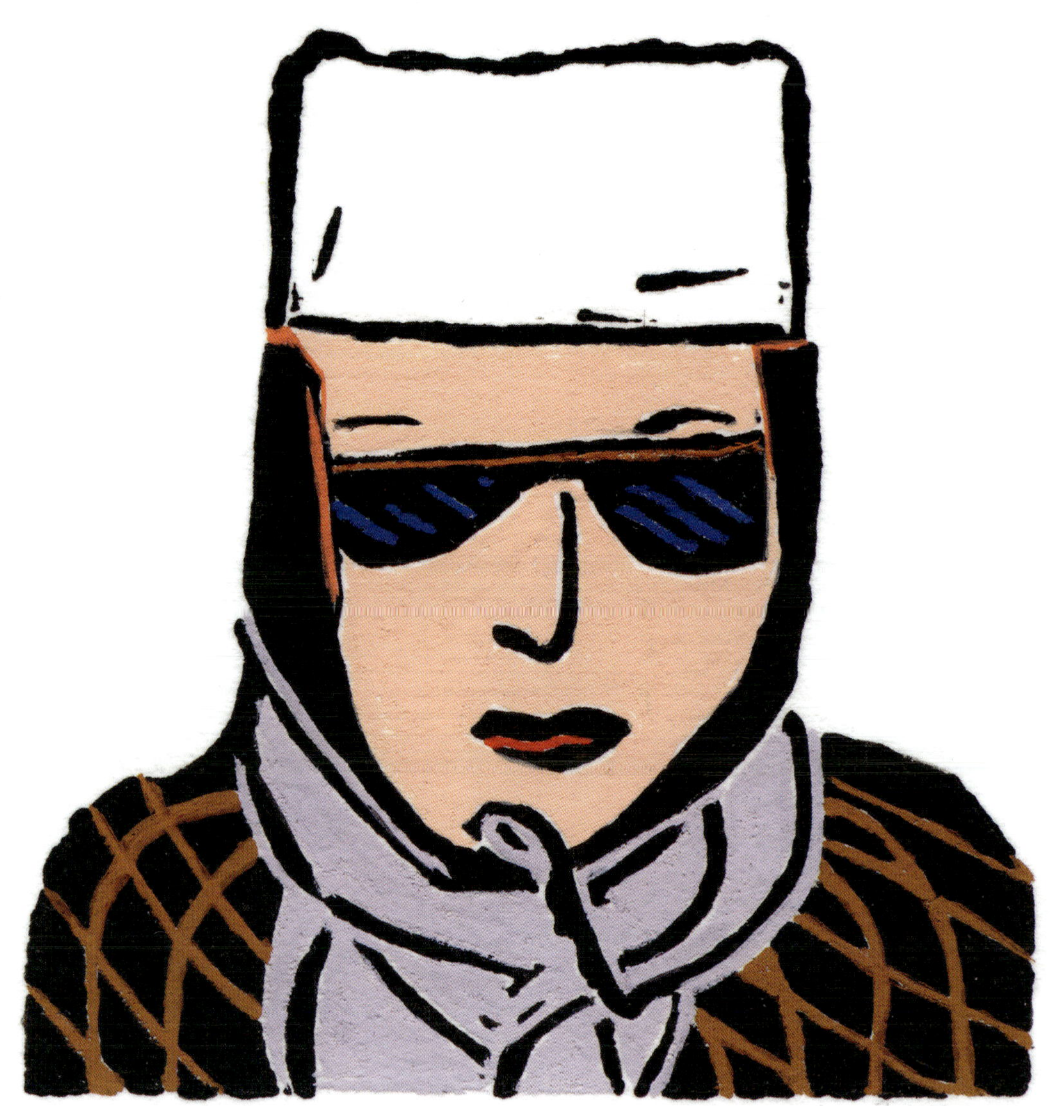

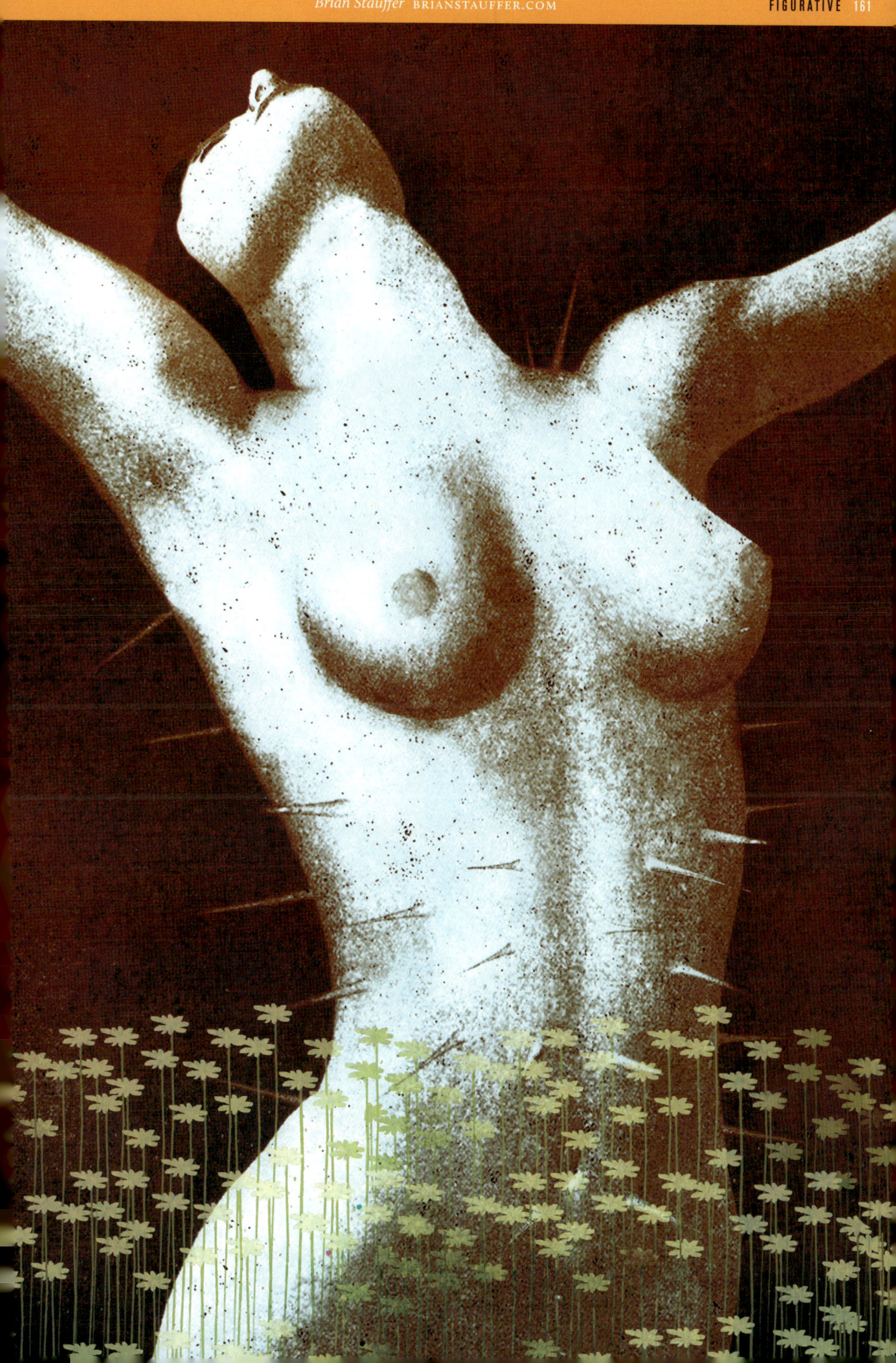

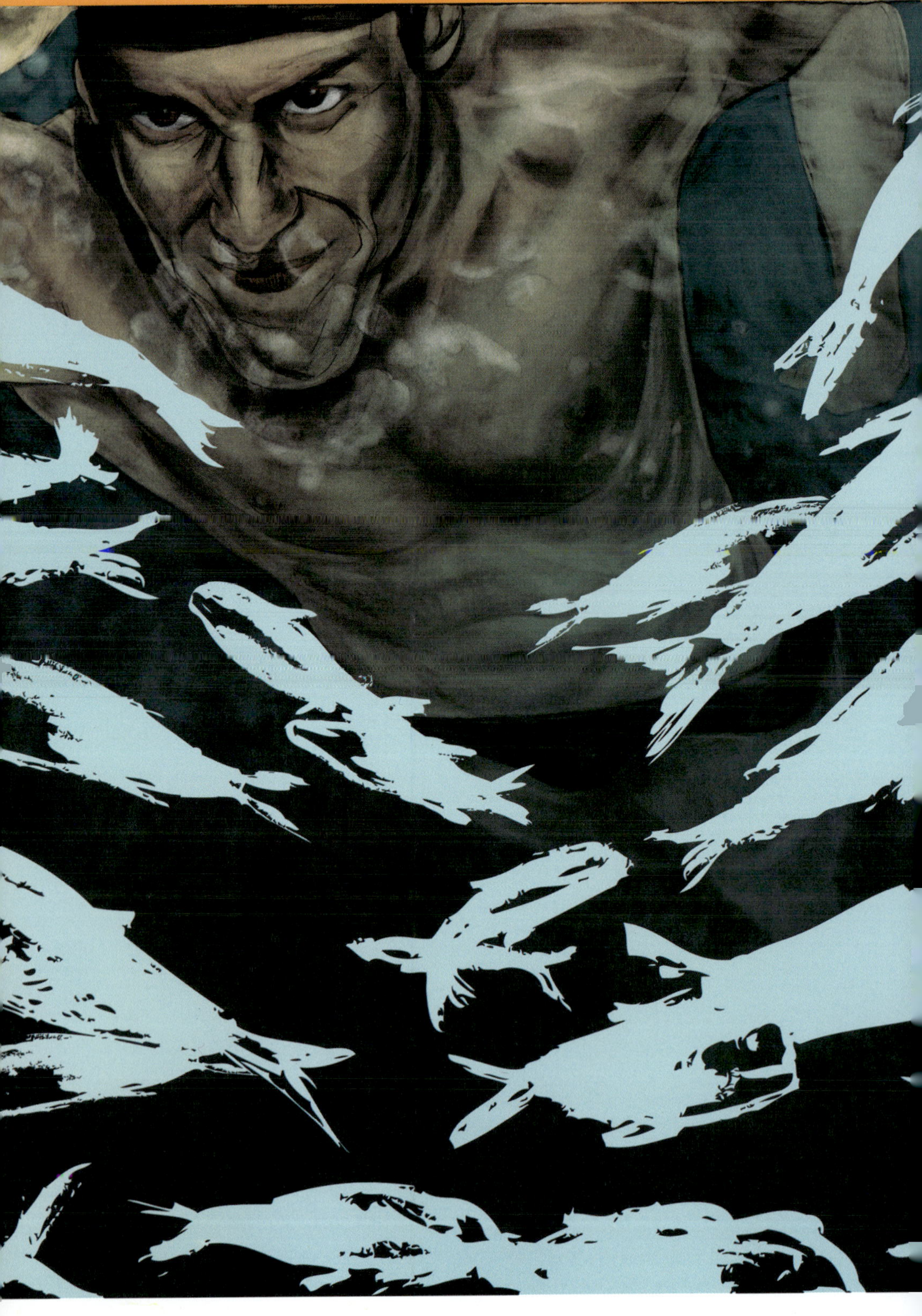

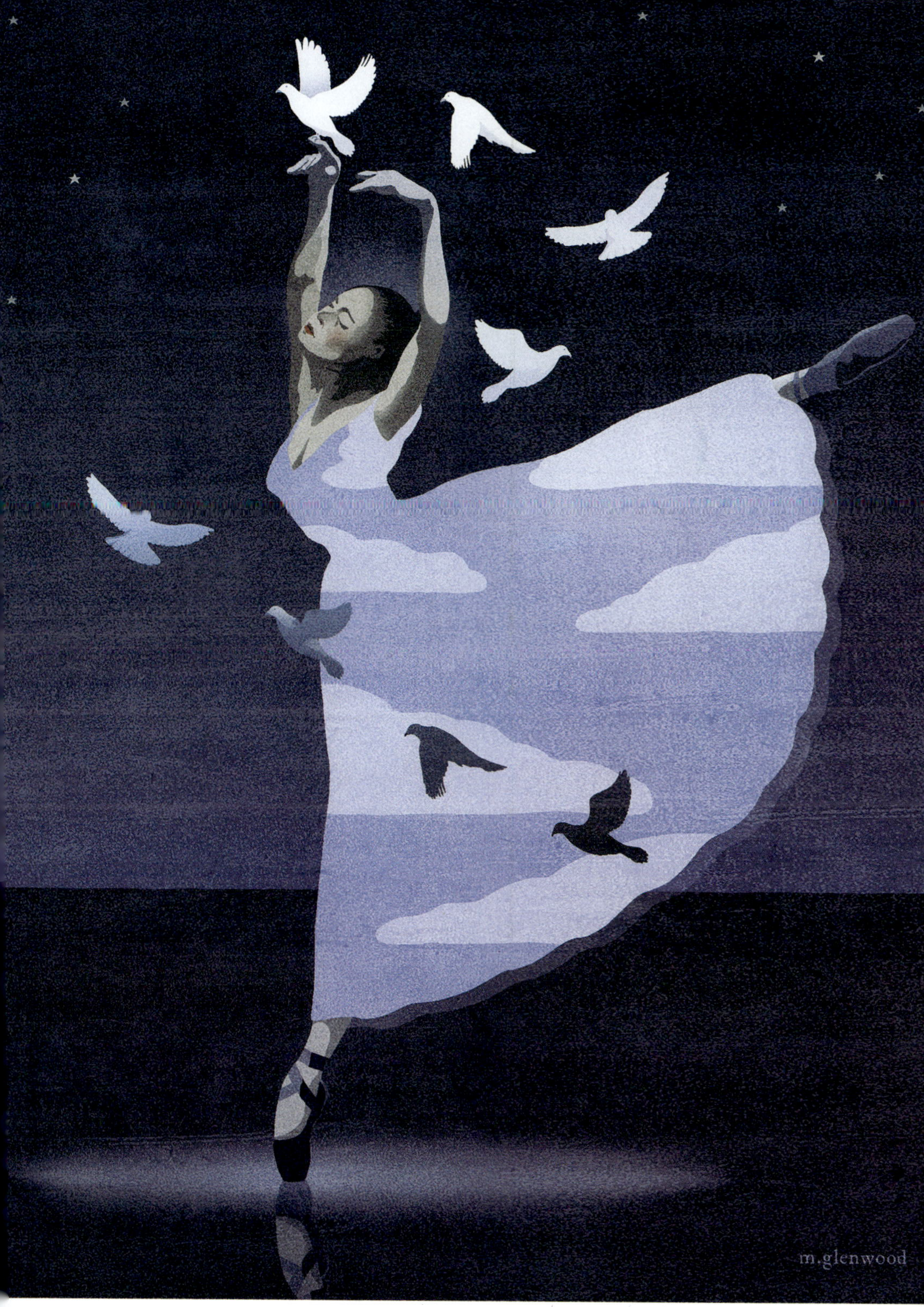
m.glenwood

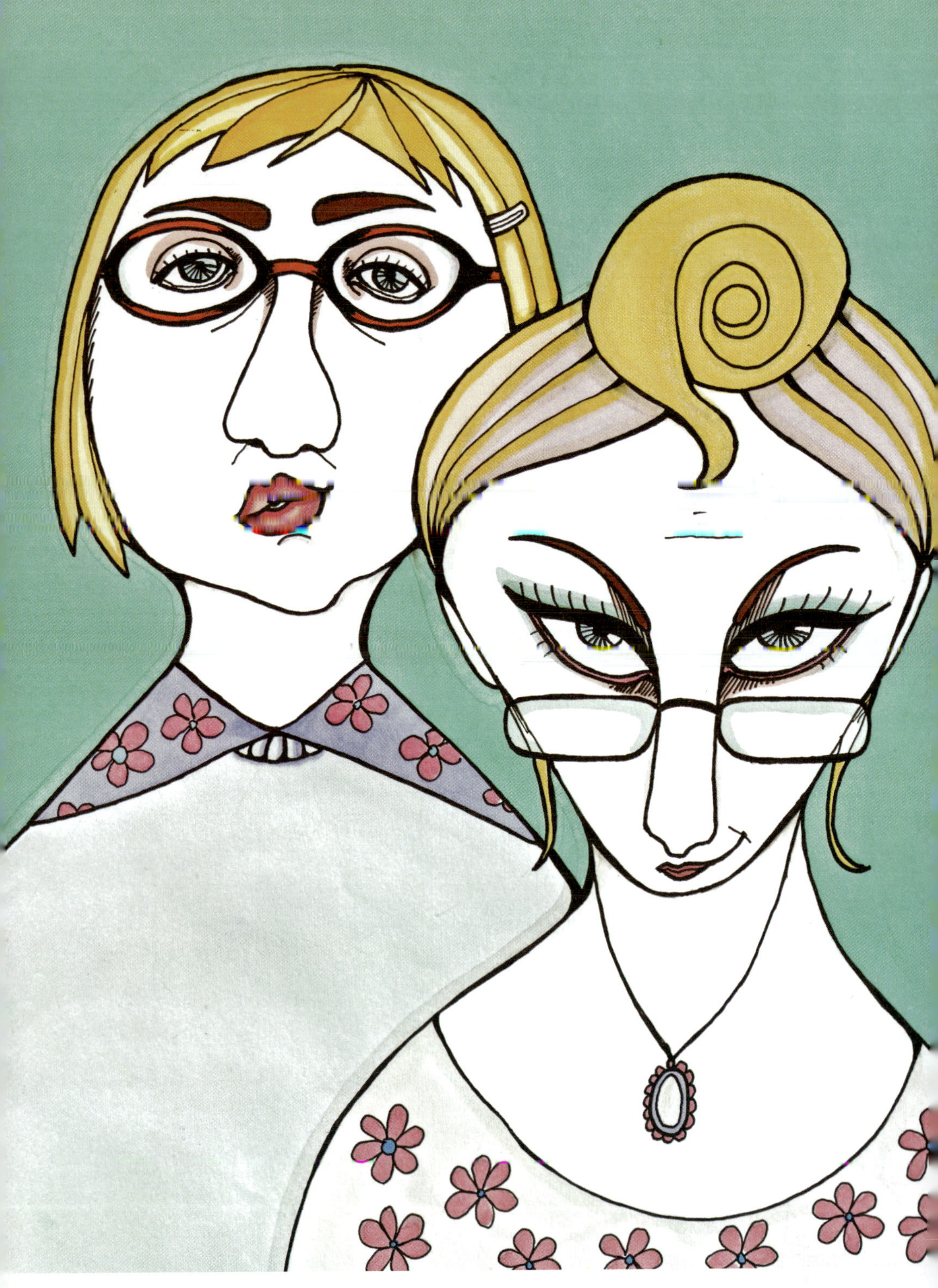

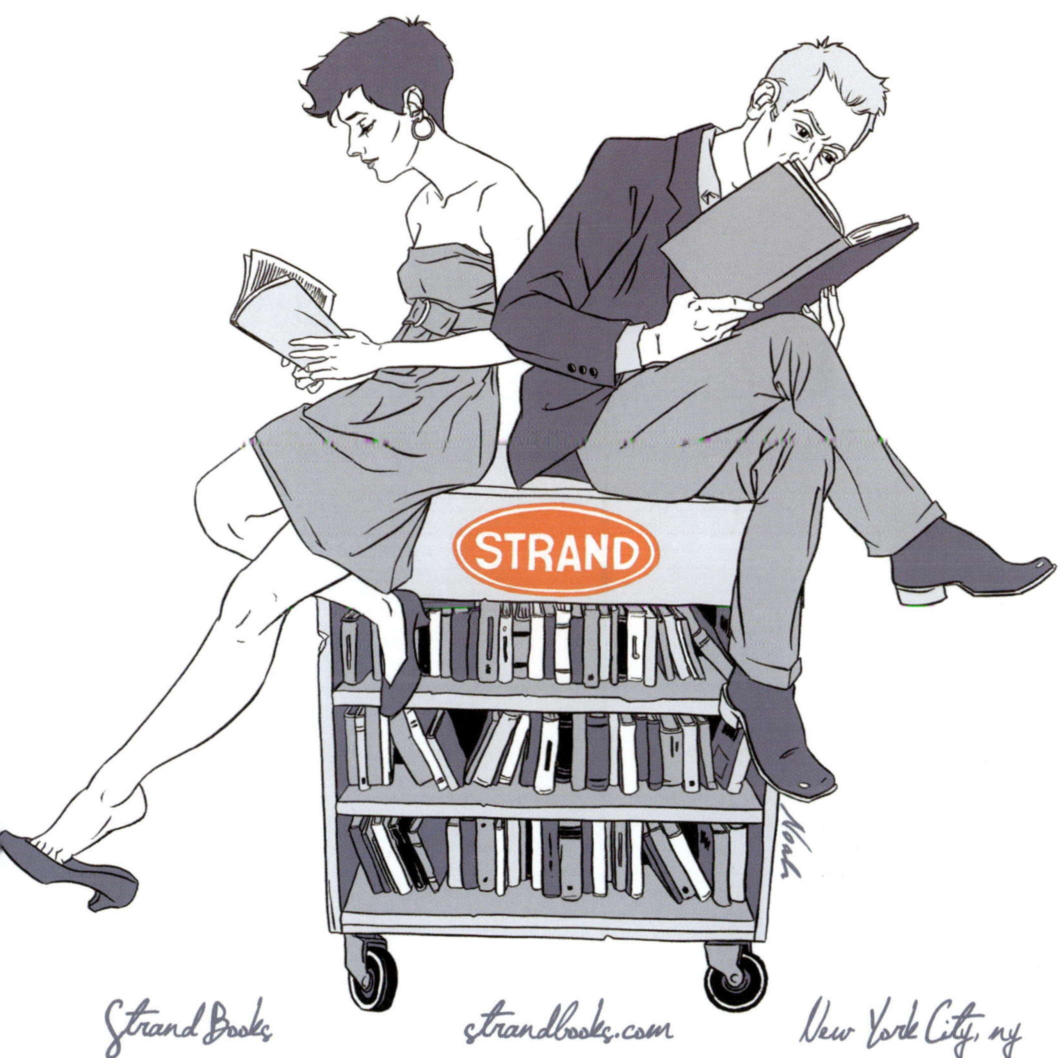

Strand Books   strandbooks.com   New York City, NY

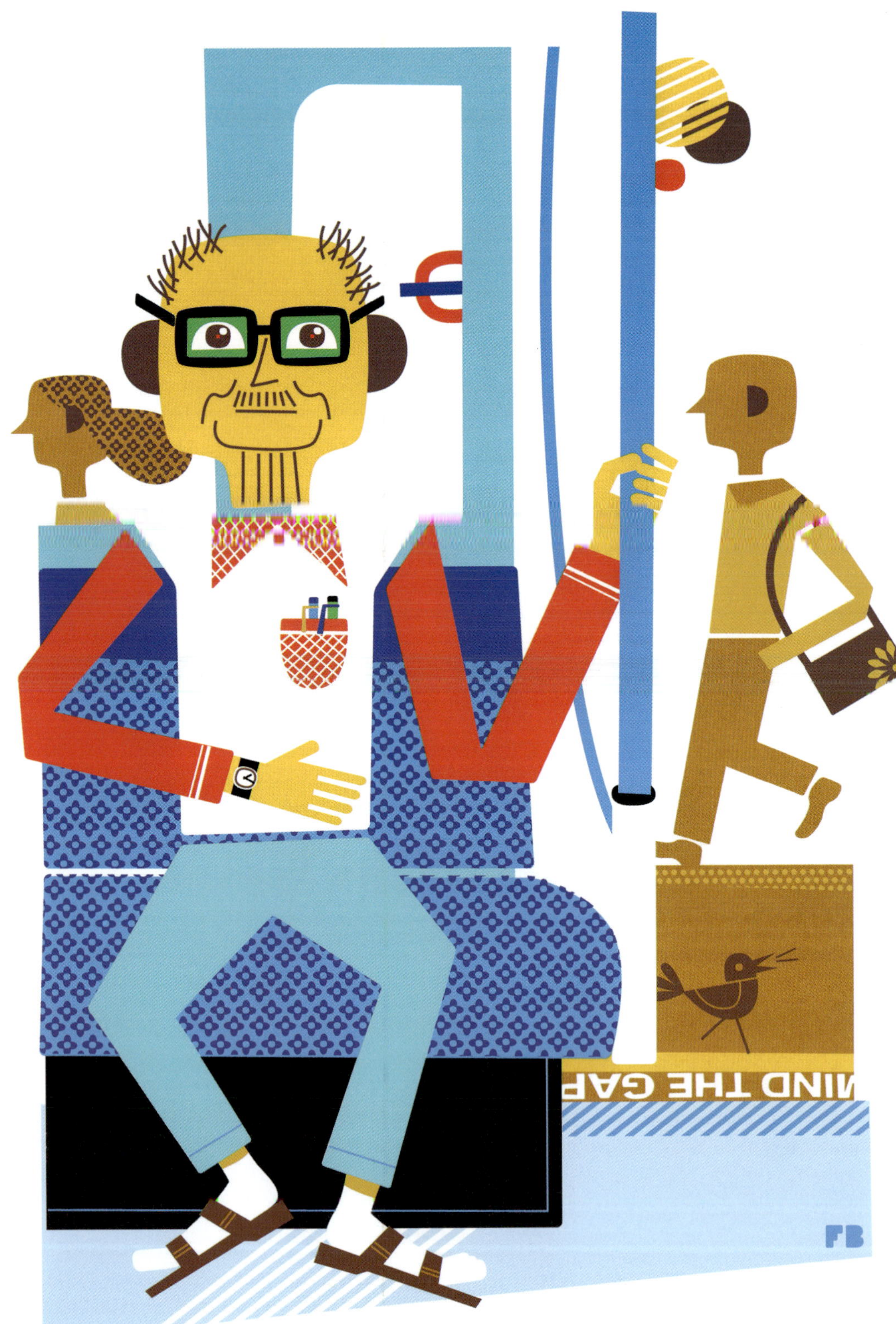
MIND THE GAP

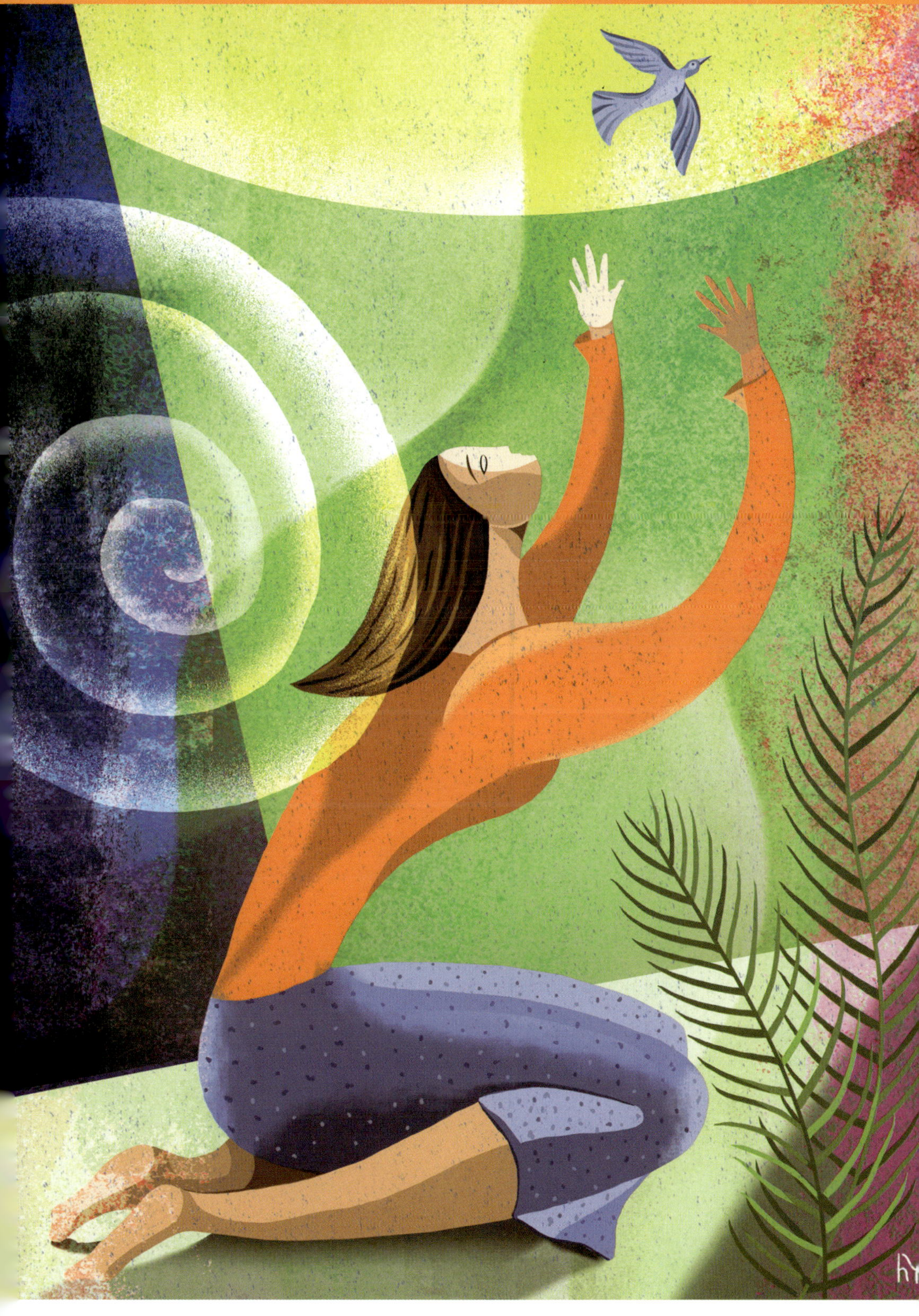

 Marian Heibel Richardson MARIANRICHARDSON.COM

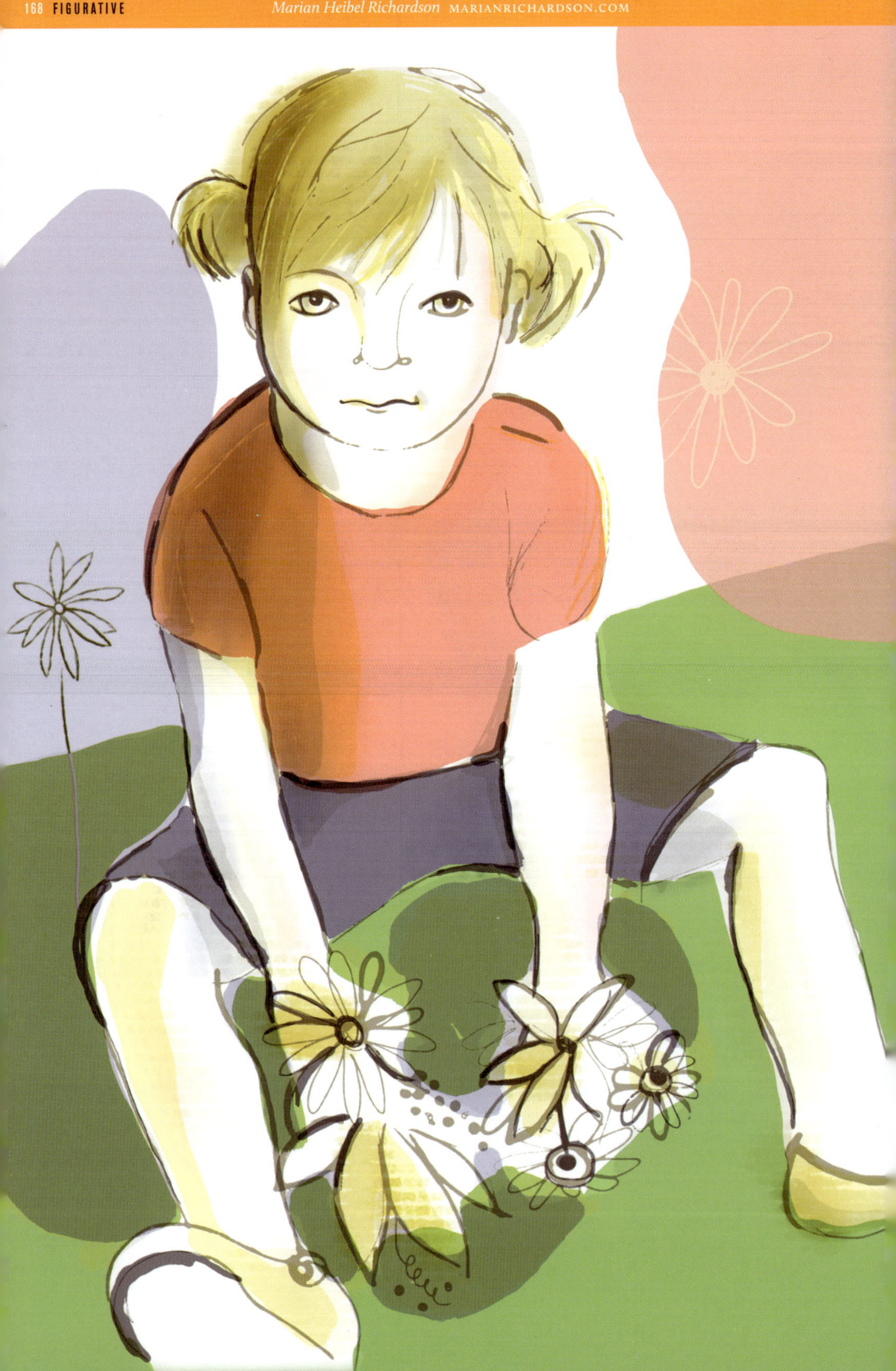

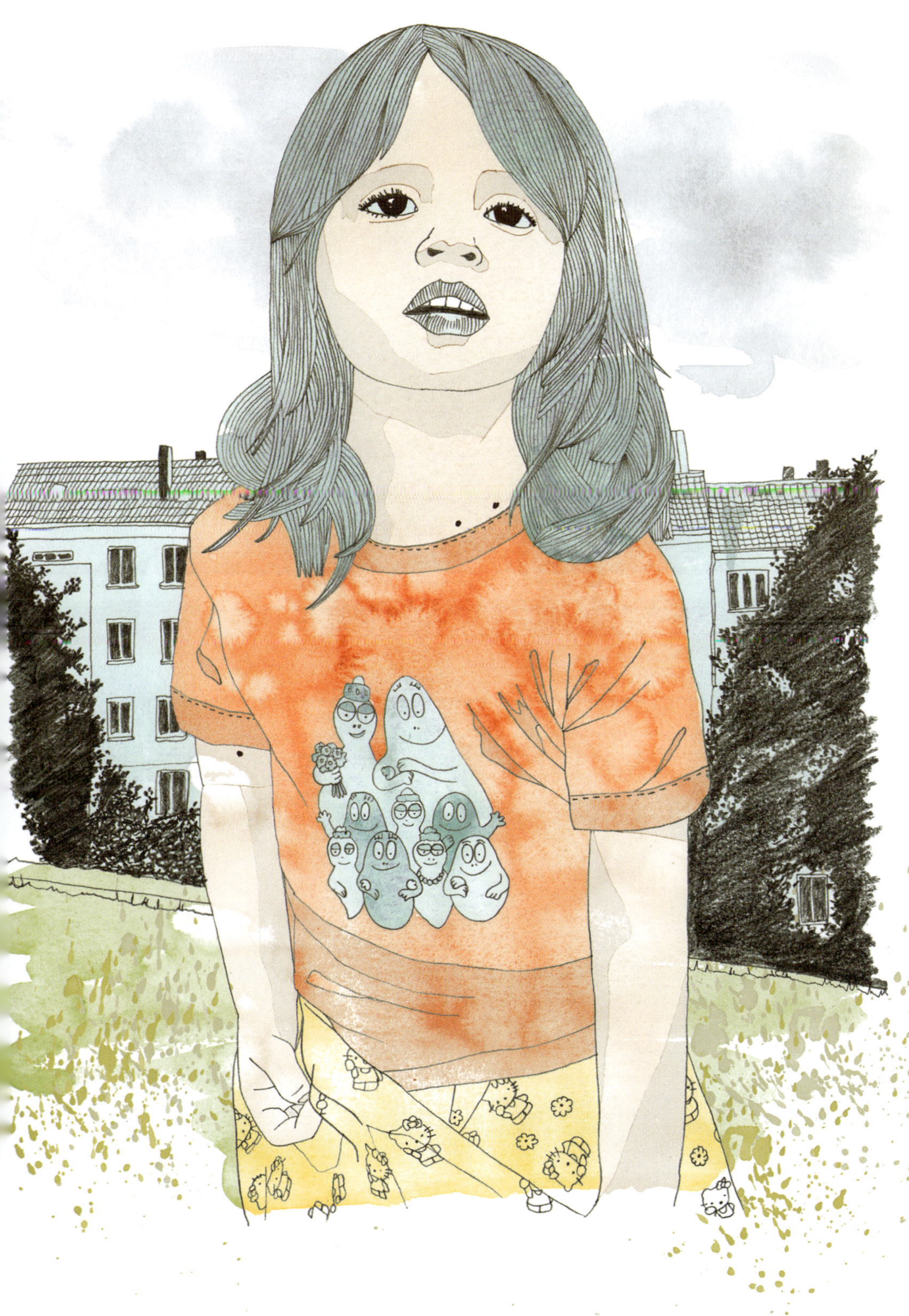

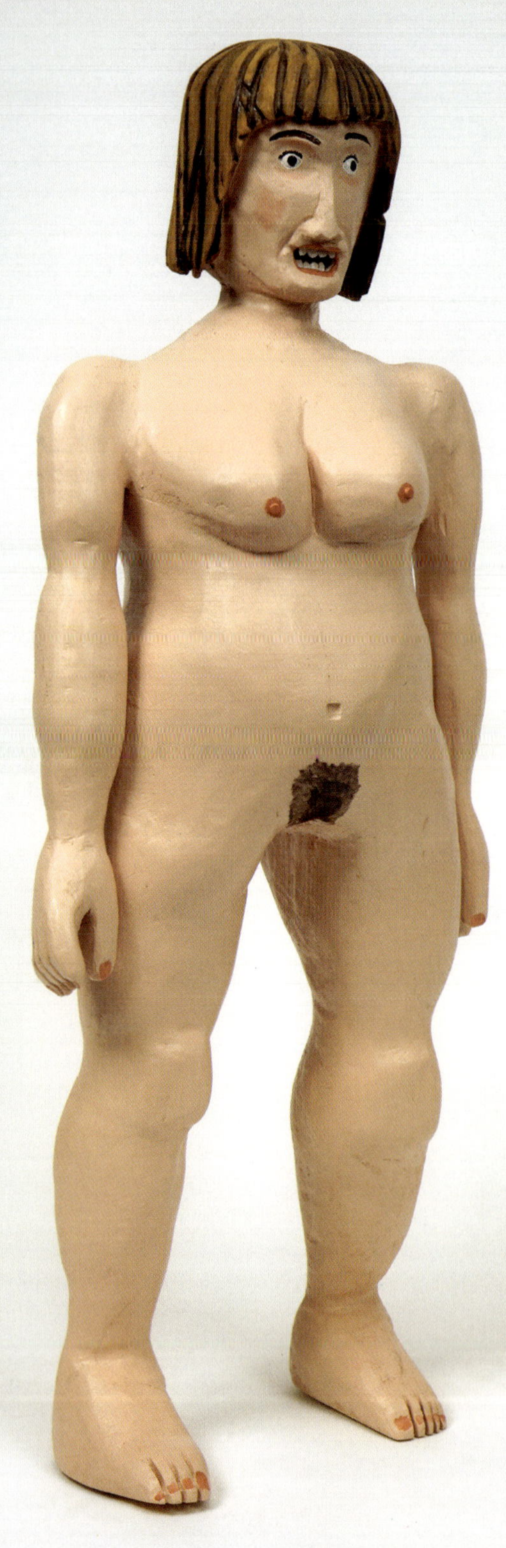

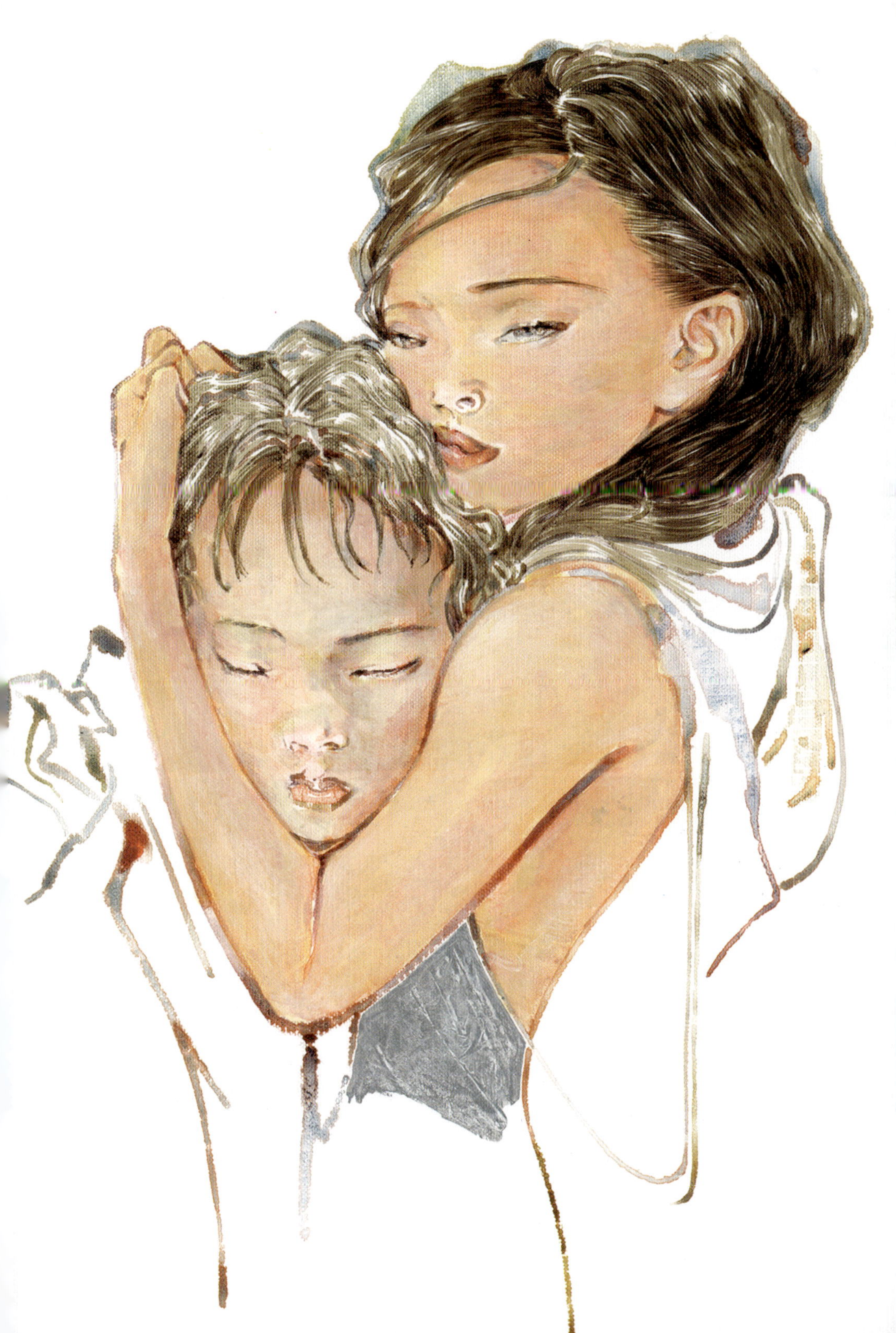

 Lina Chen

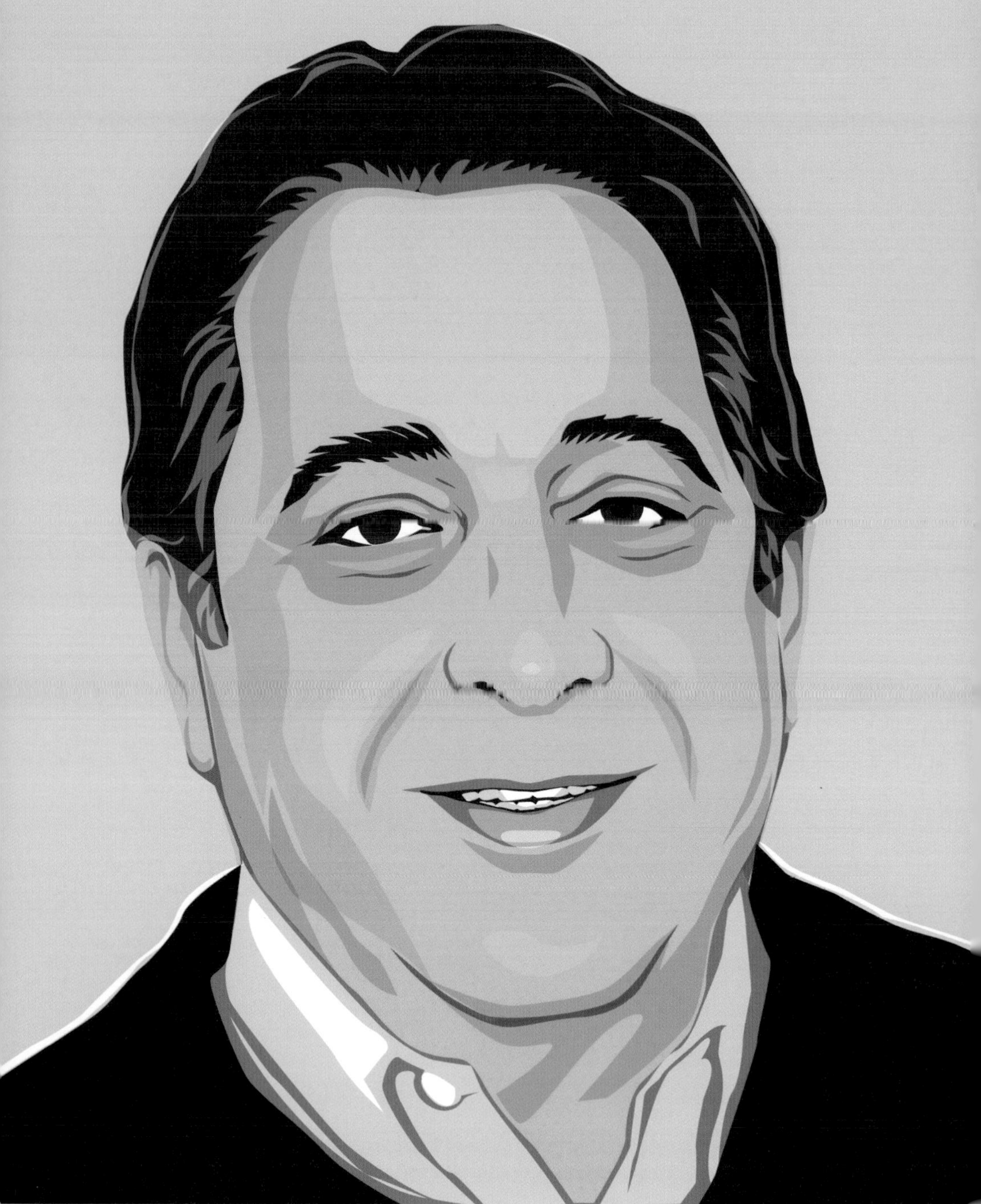

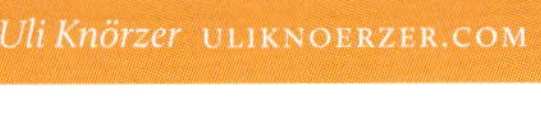

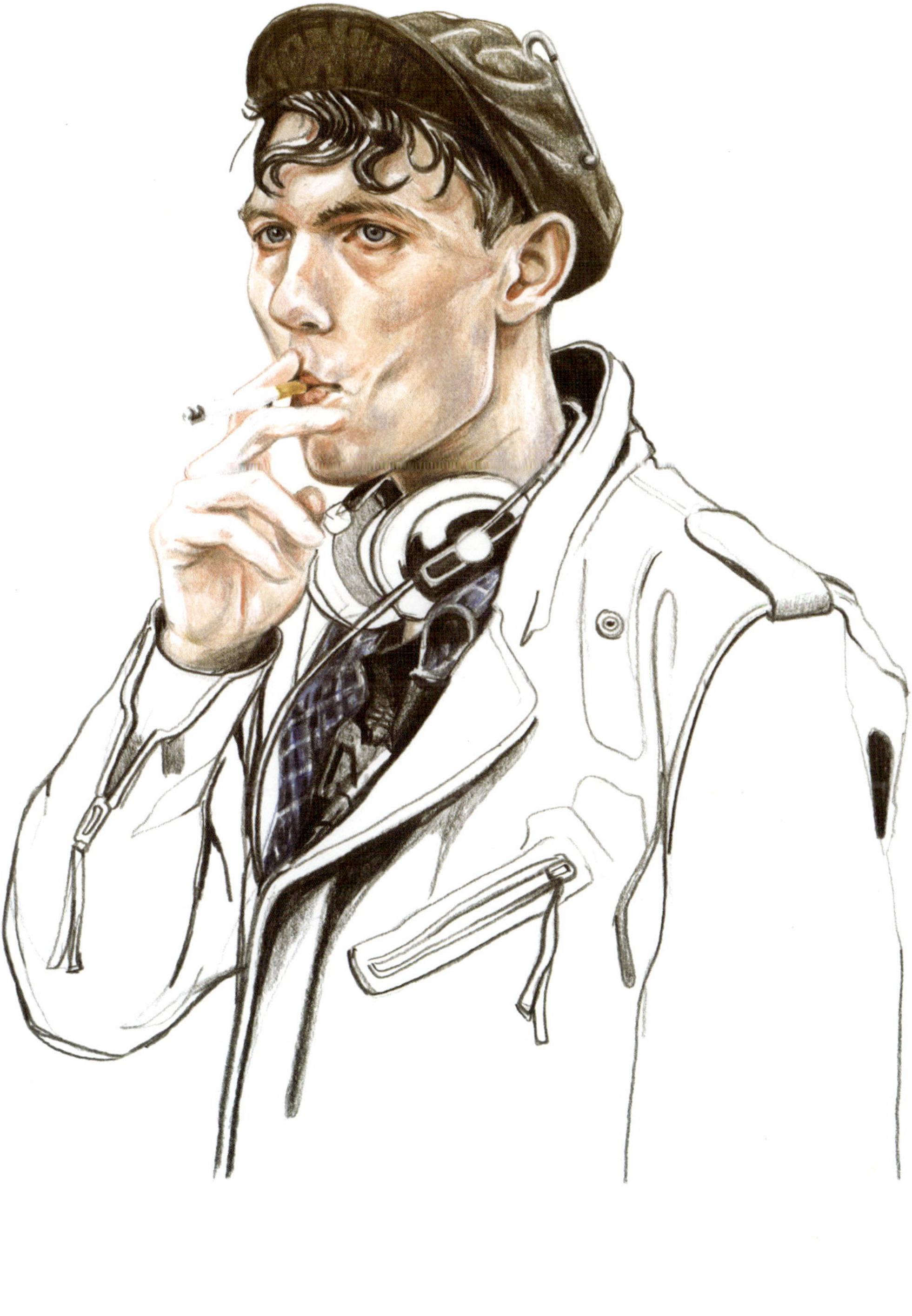

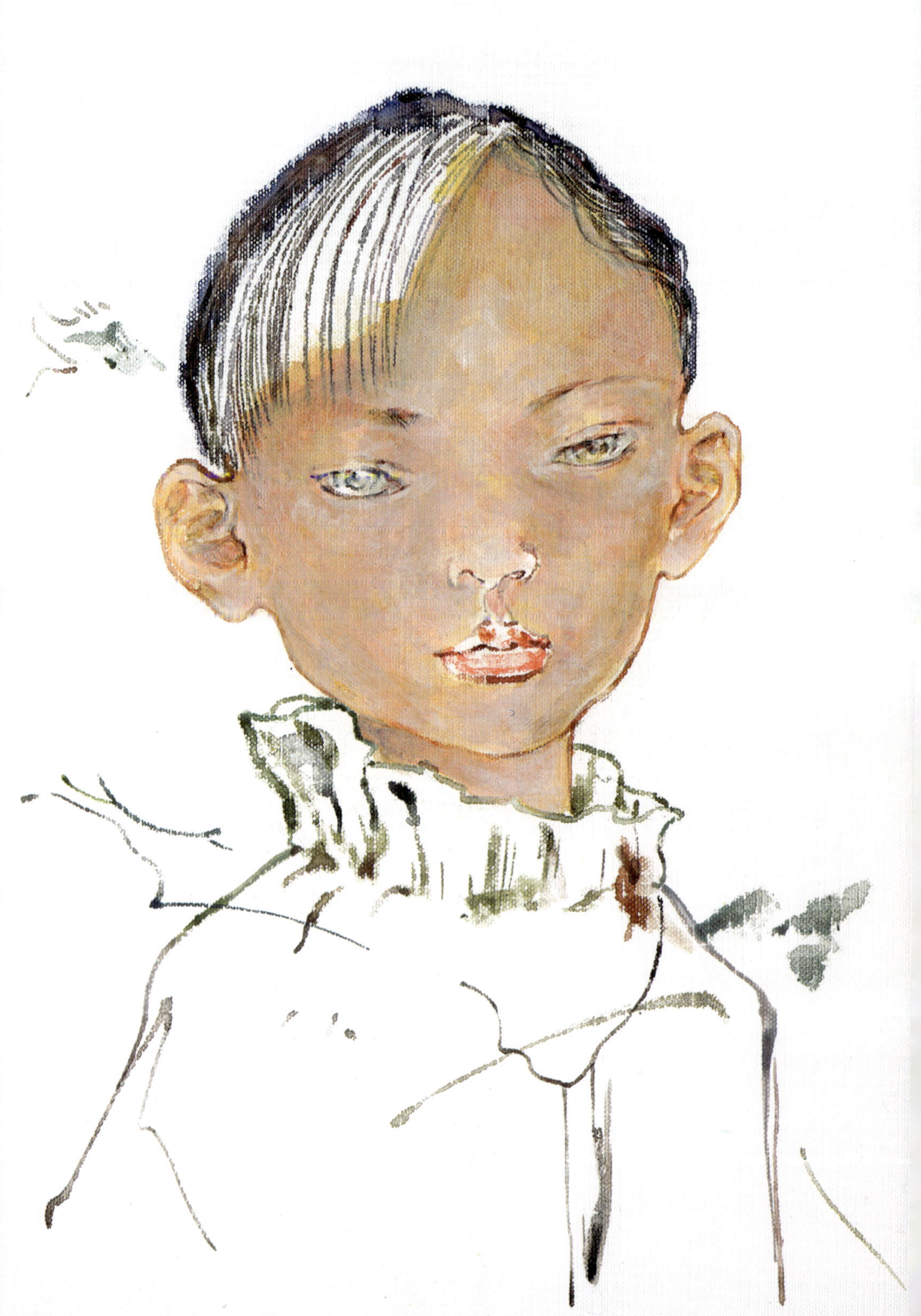

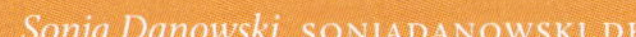
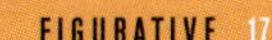

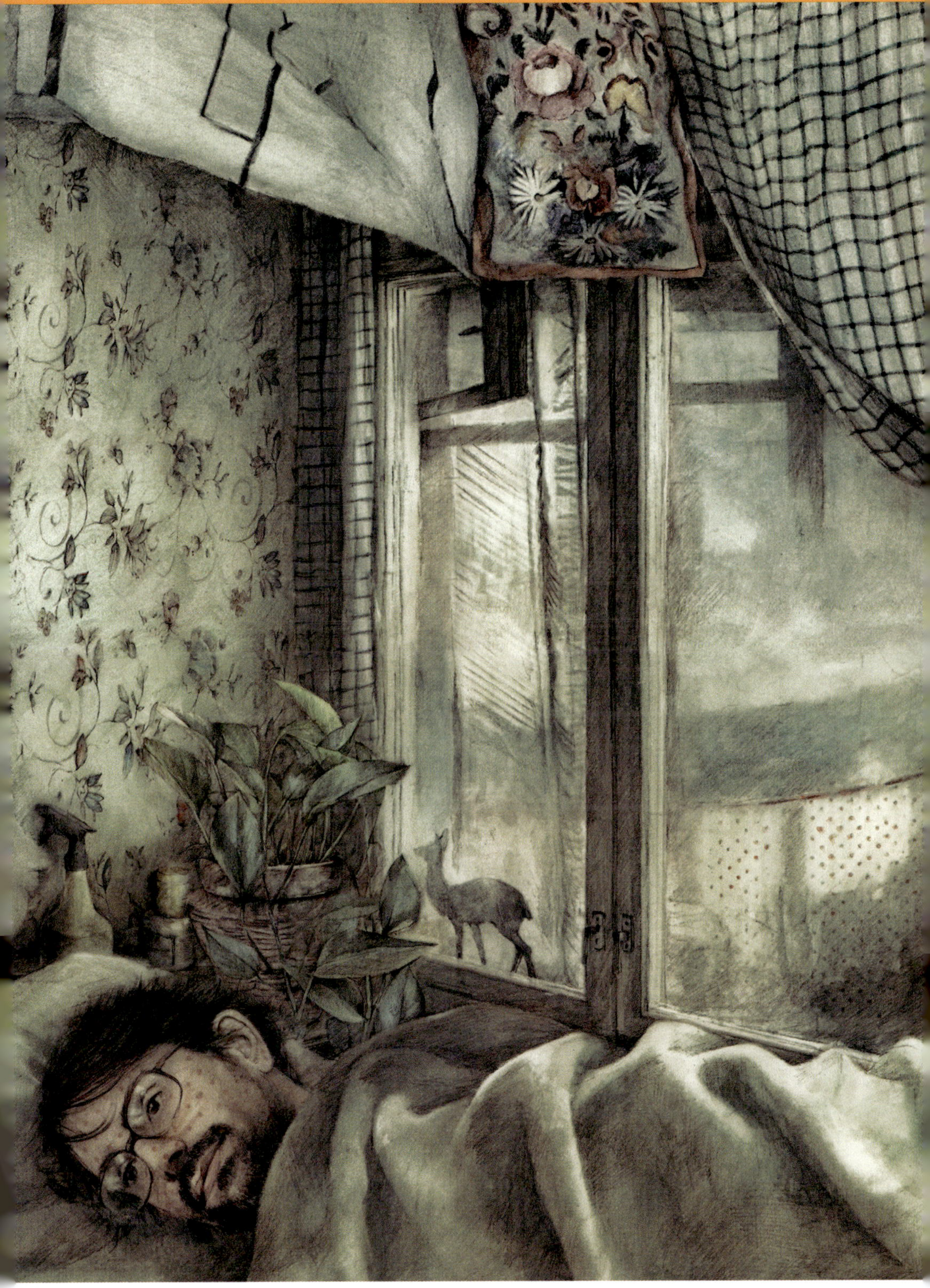

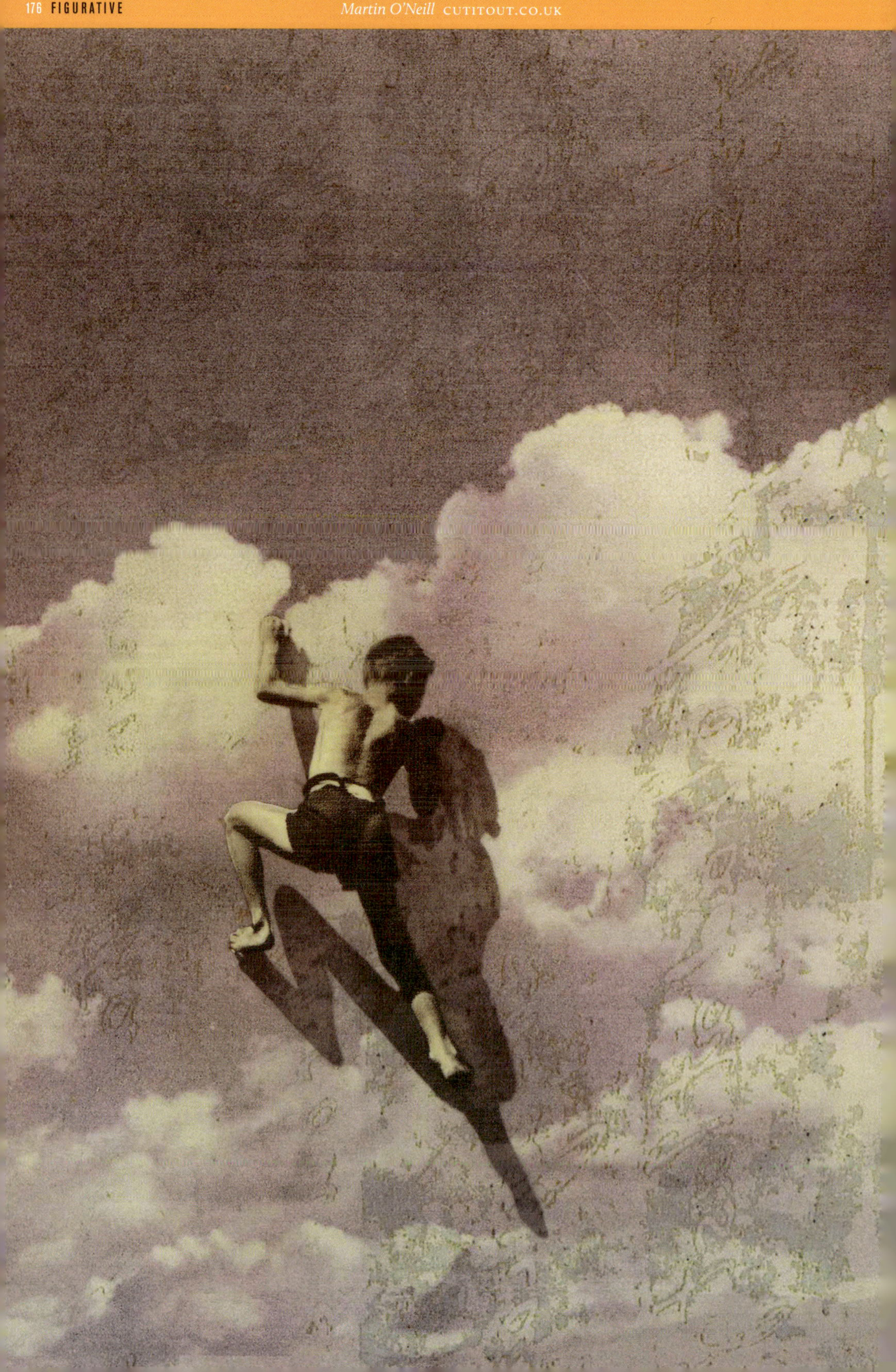

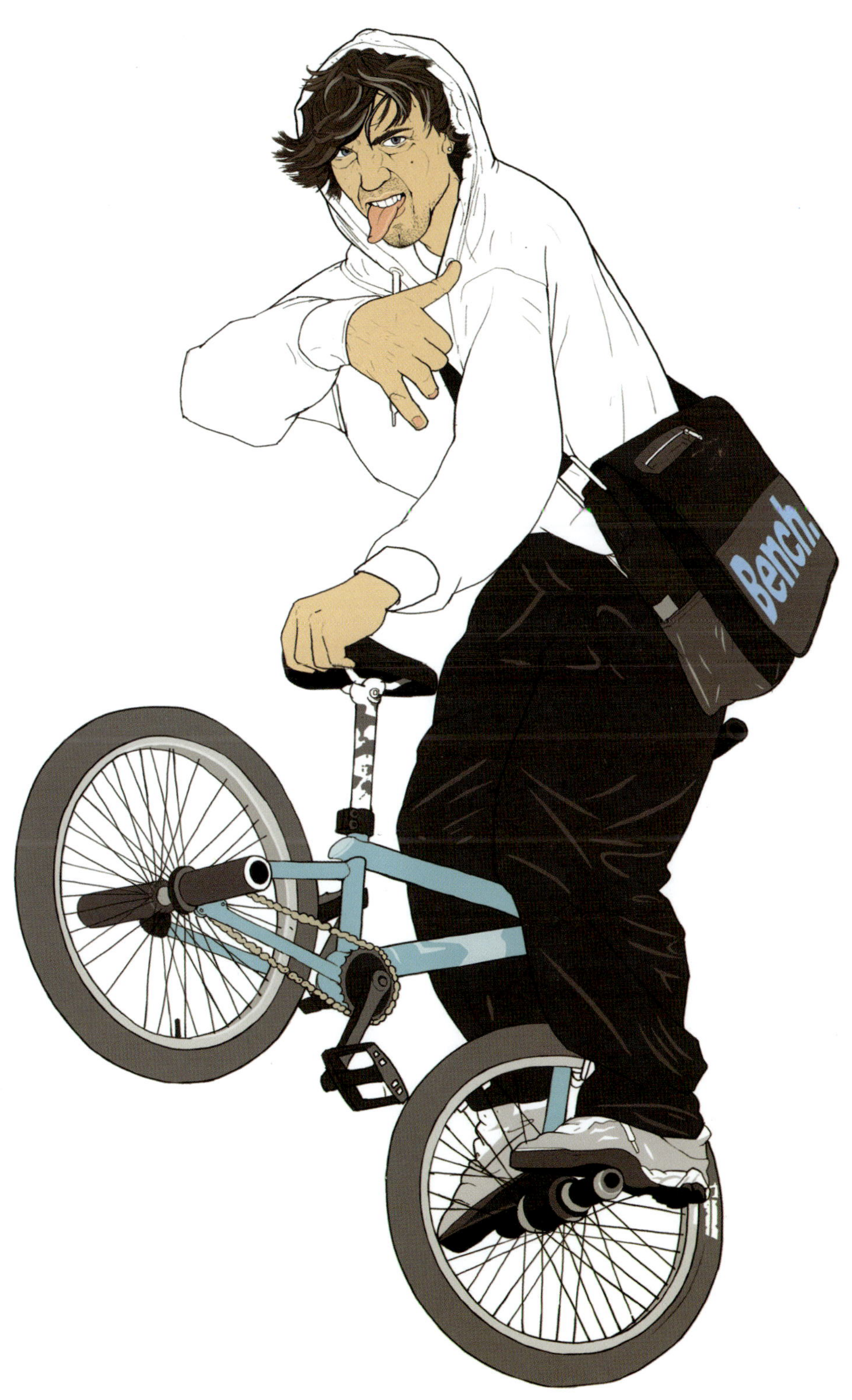
Bench.

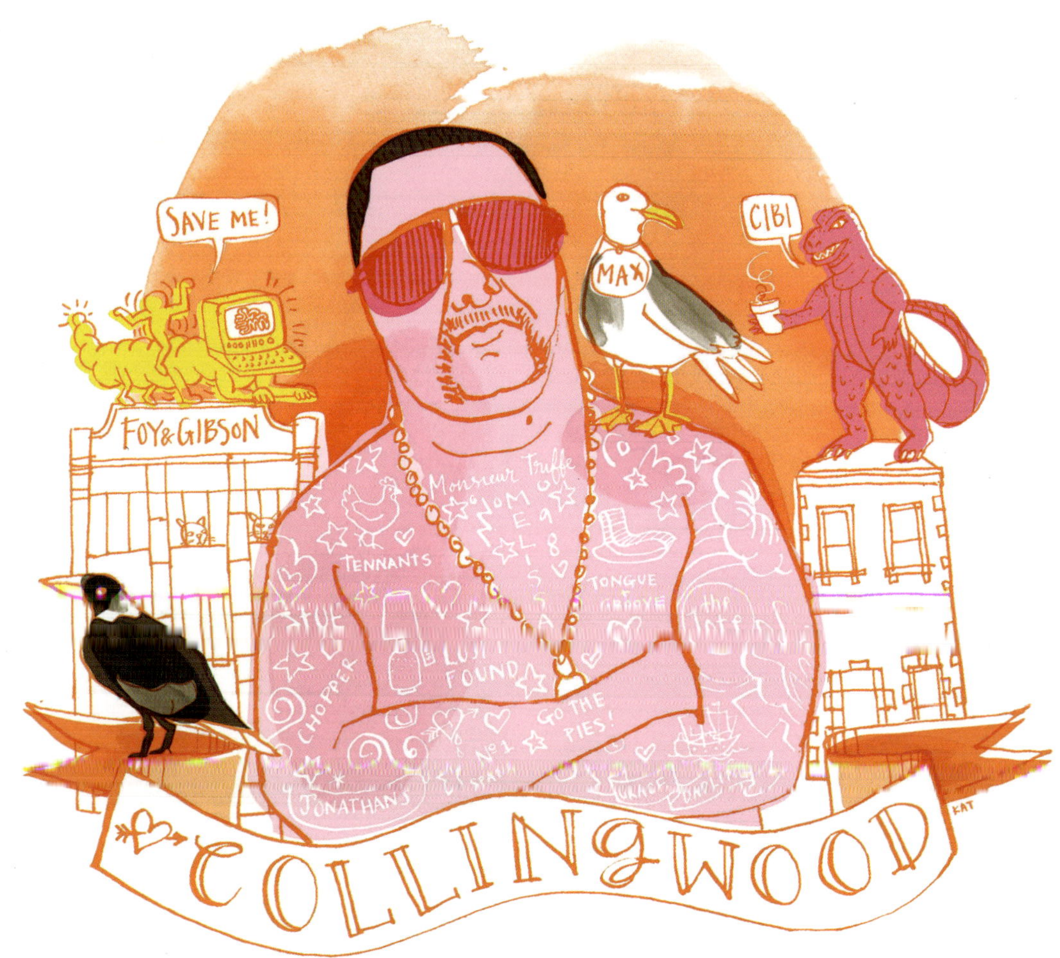
SAVE ME!
FOY & GIBSON
MAX
CIBI
Monsieur Truffe
TENNANTS
CHOPPER
LOST FOUND
TONGUE
No 1
GO THE PIES!
JONATHAN'S
COLLINGWOOD
KAT

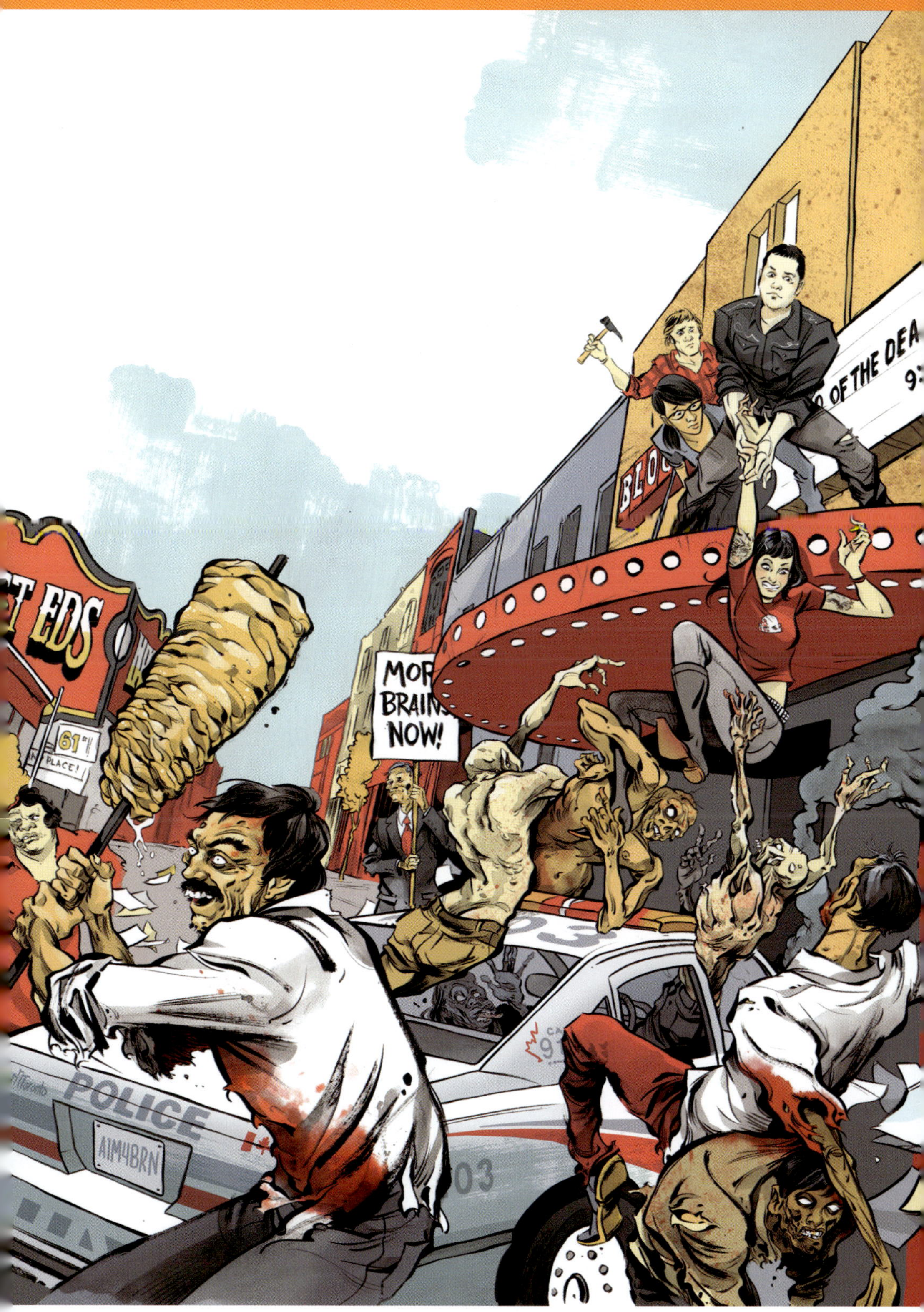
OF THE DEA
BLOO
MORE BRAINS NOW!
EDS
61¢ PLACE!
Toronto POLICE
A1M4BRN
03

  Richard Tuschman RICHARDTUSCHMAN.COM

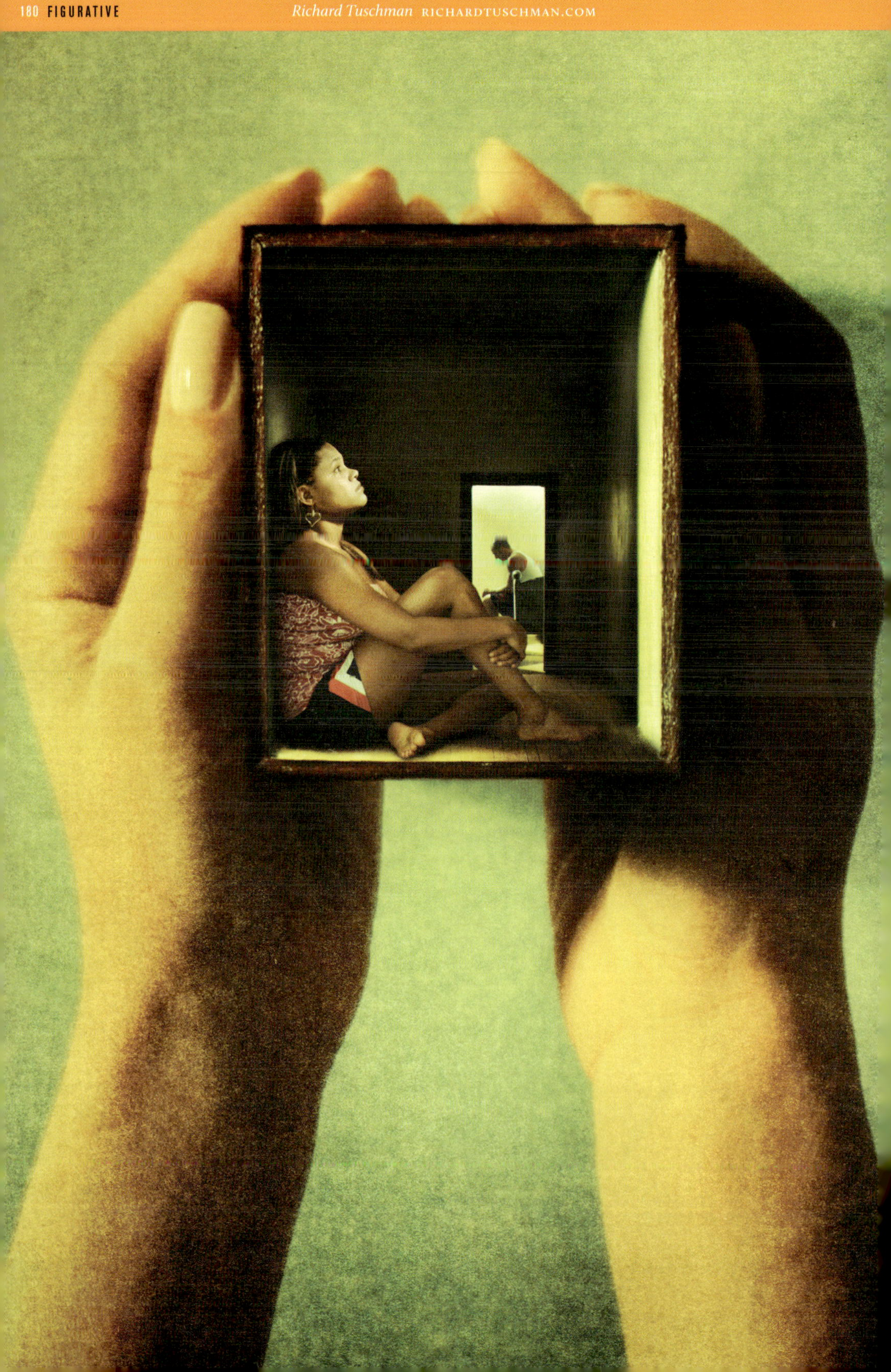

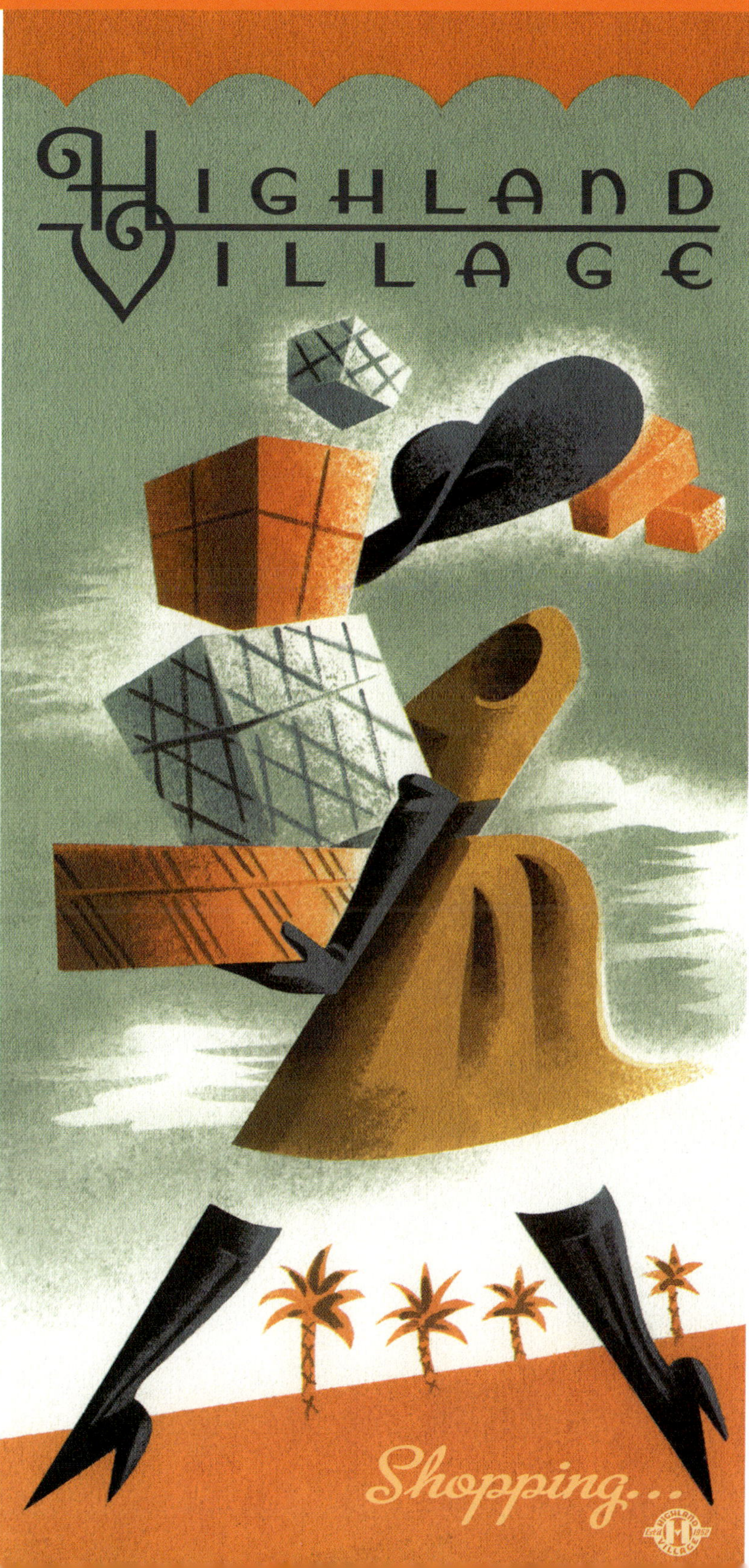
HIGHLAND VILLAGE
Shopping...

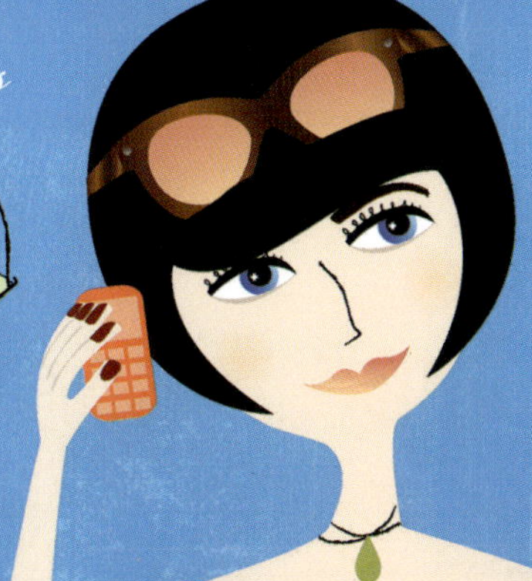

skirt! rules

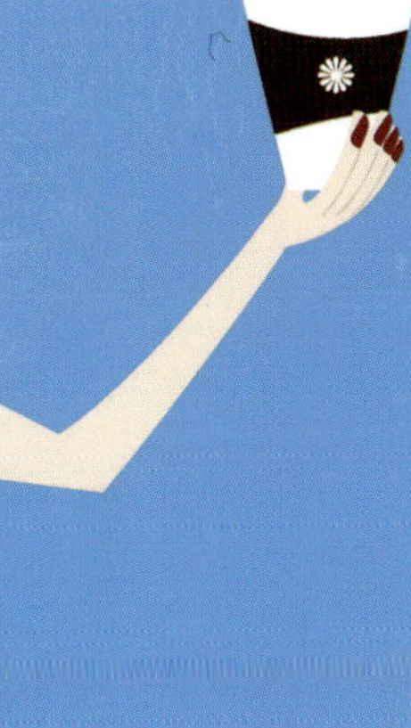

Thou shalt not talk on a *cell phone* while ordering a latte.

skirt! rules

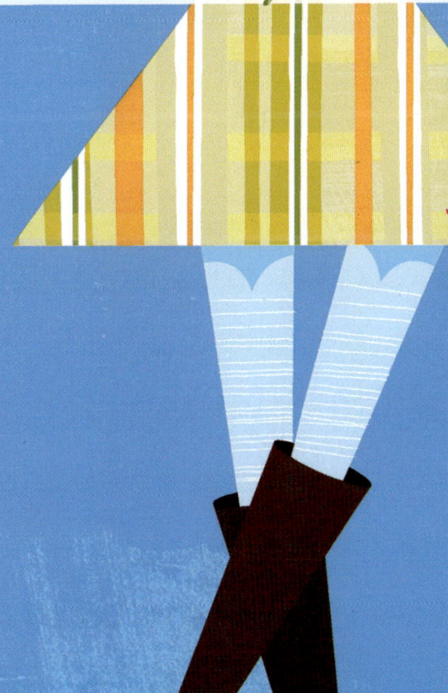

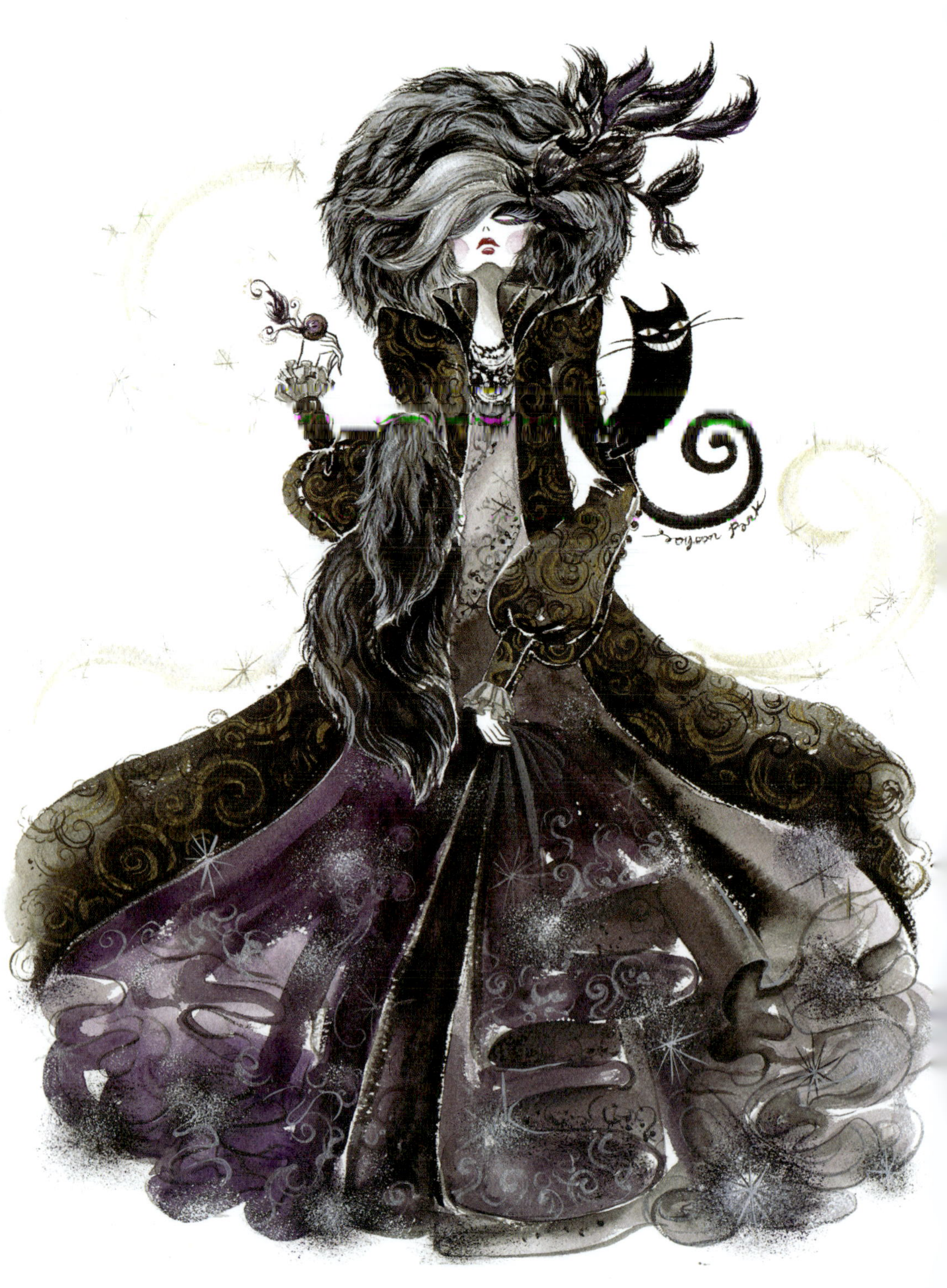

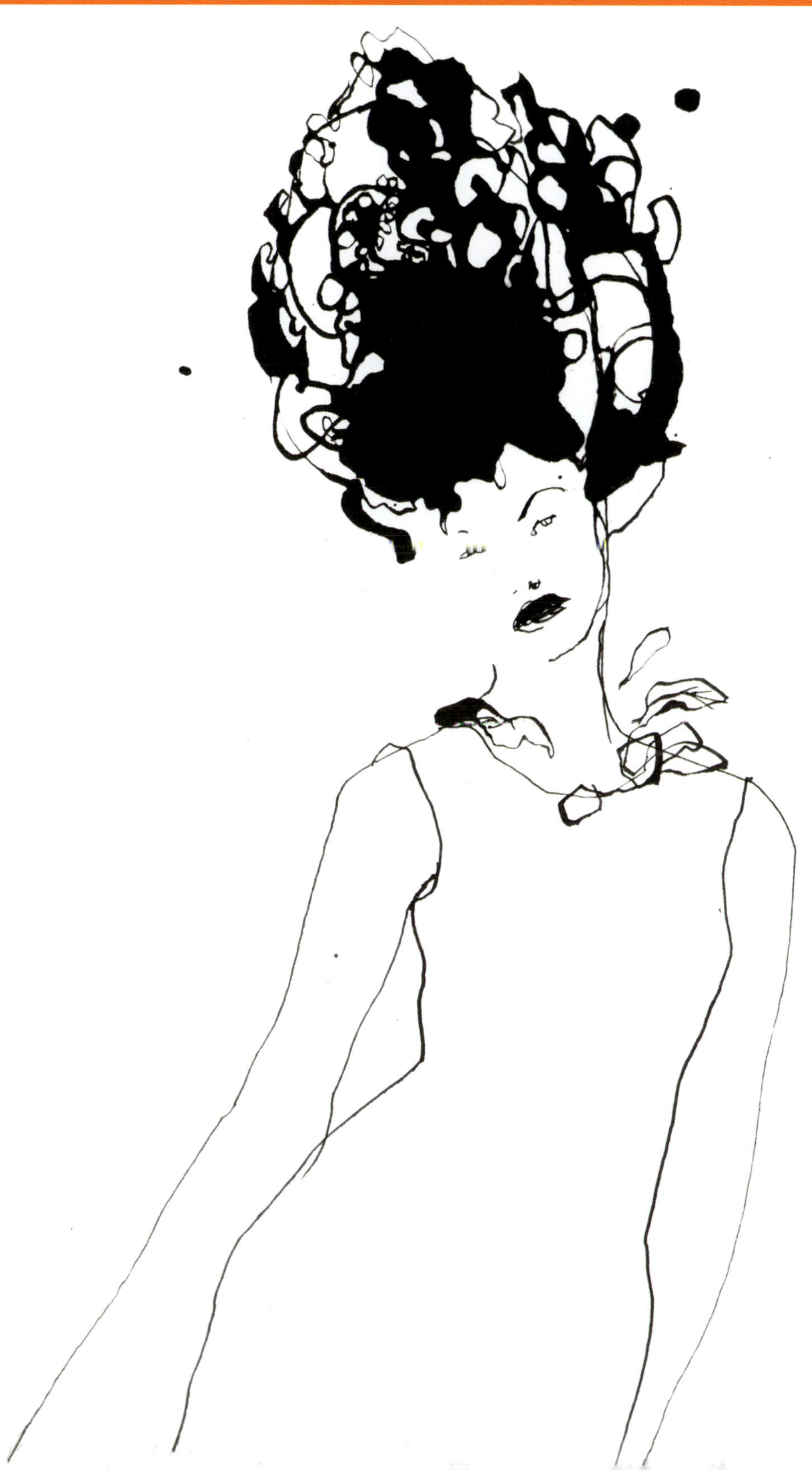

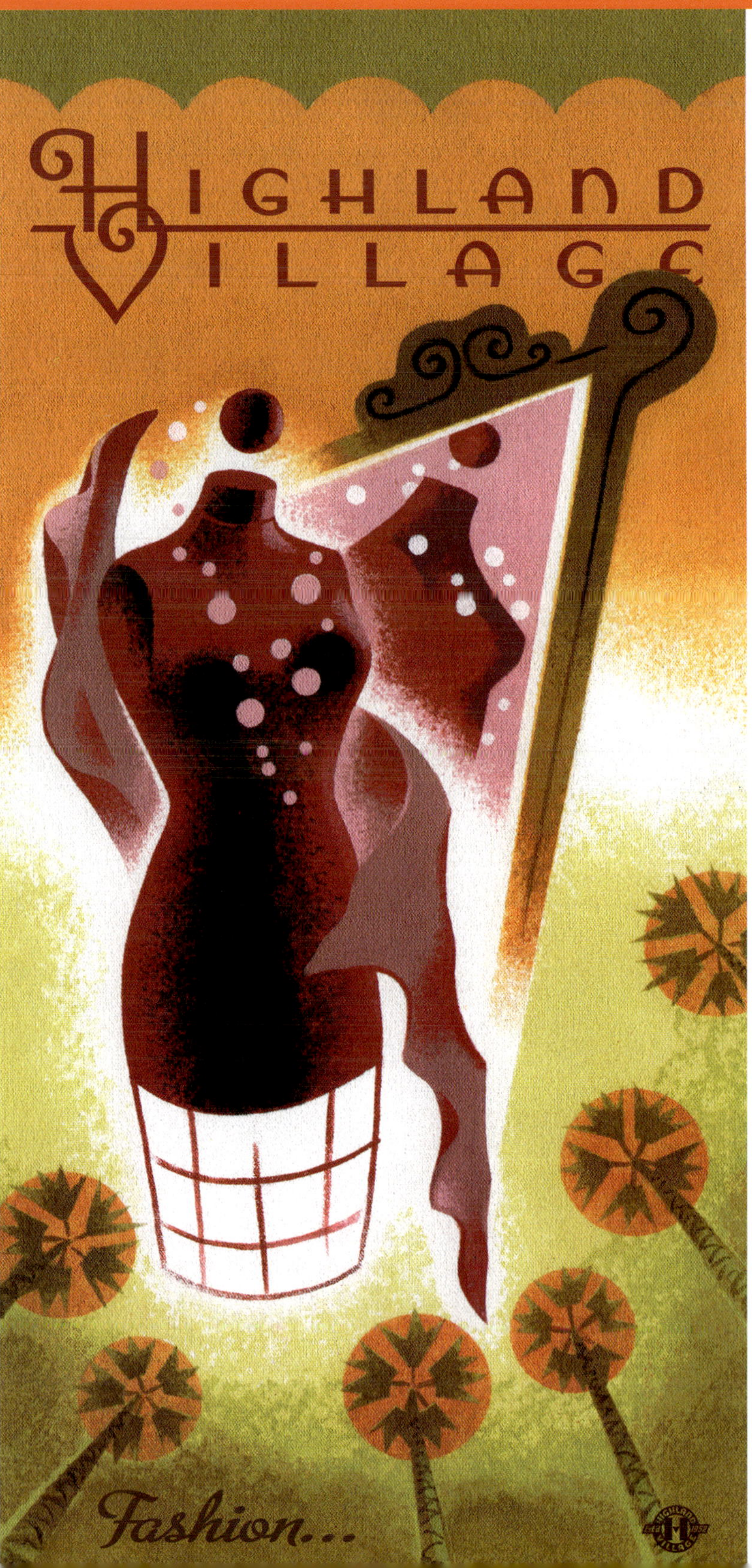

HIGHLAND VILLAGE
Fashion...

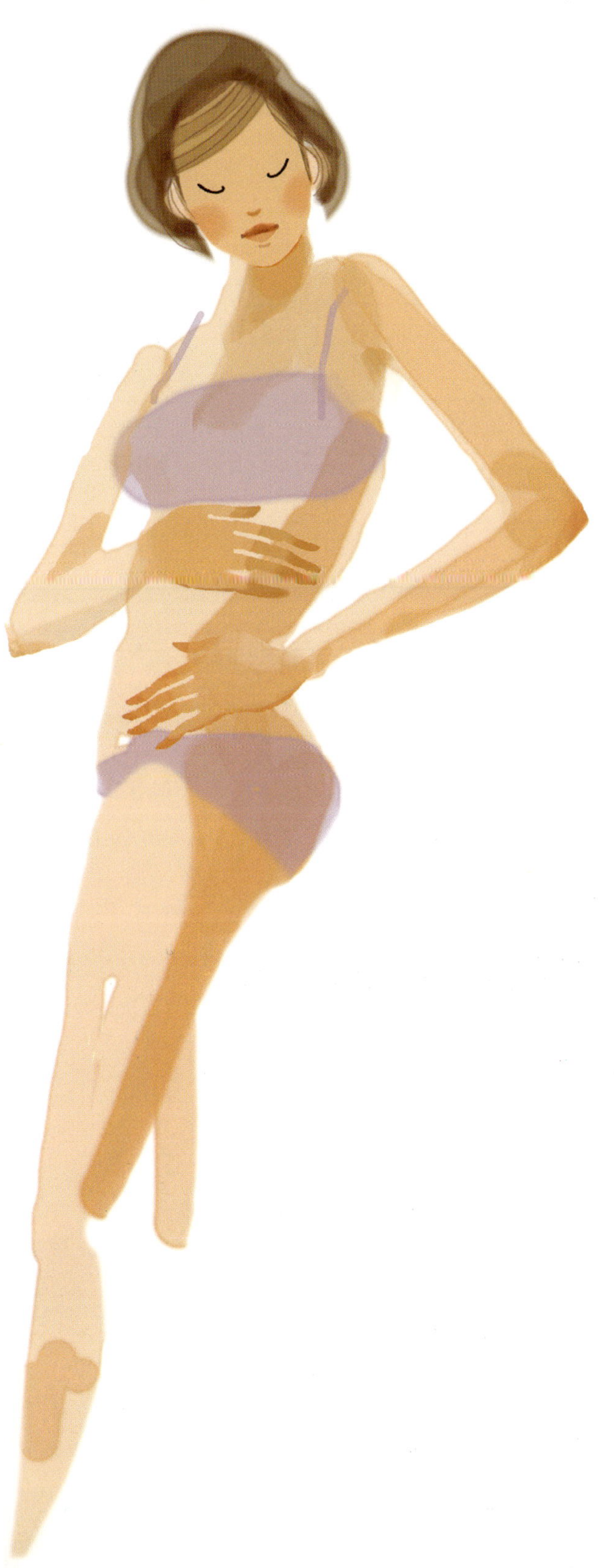

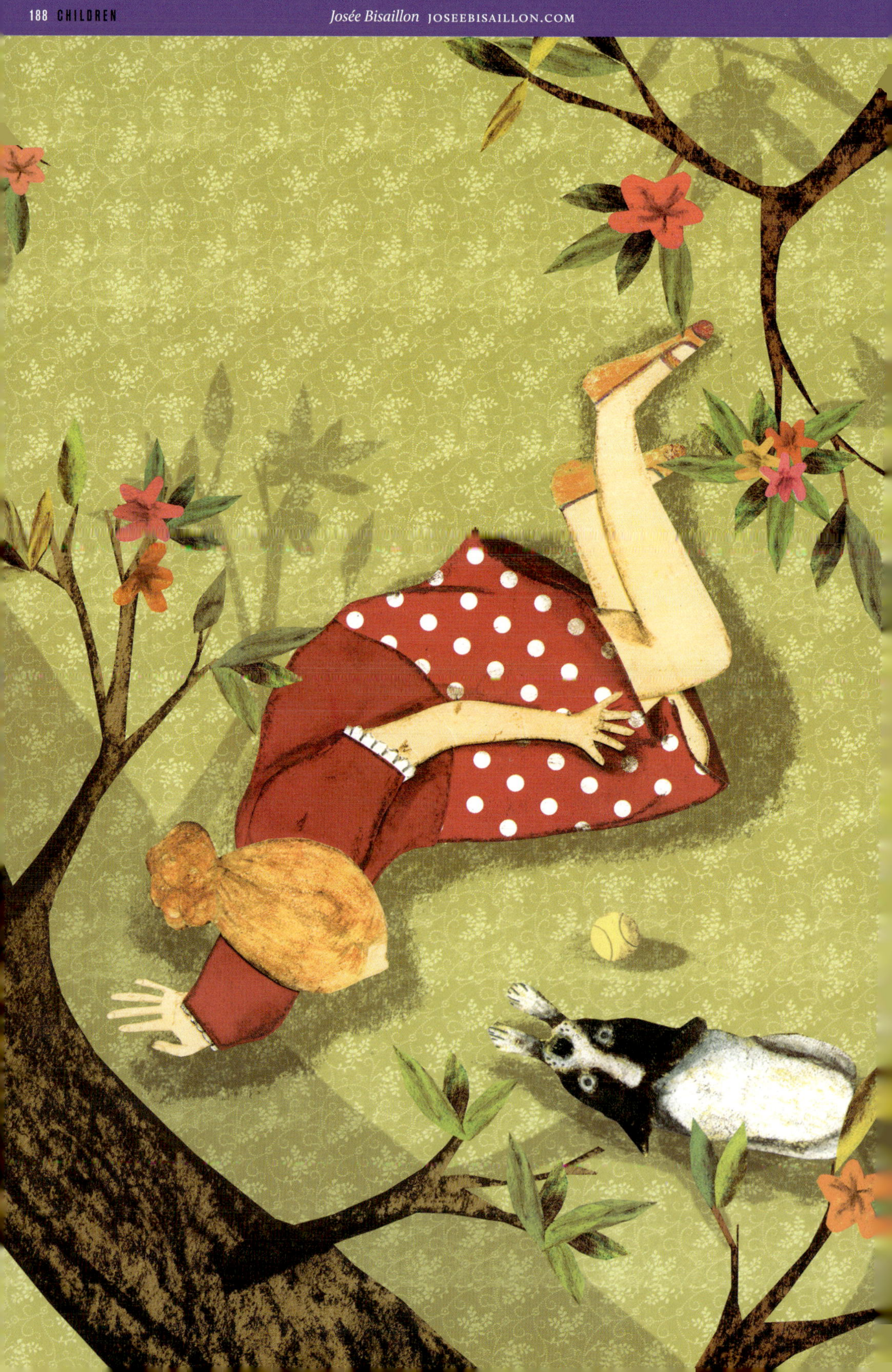

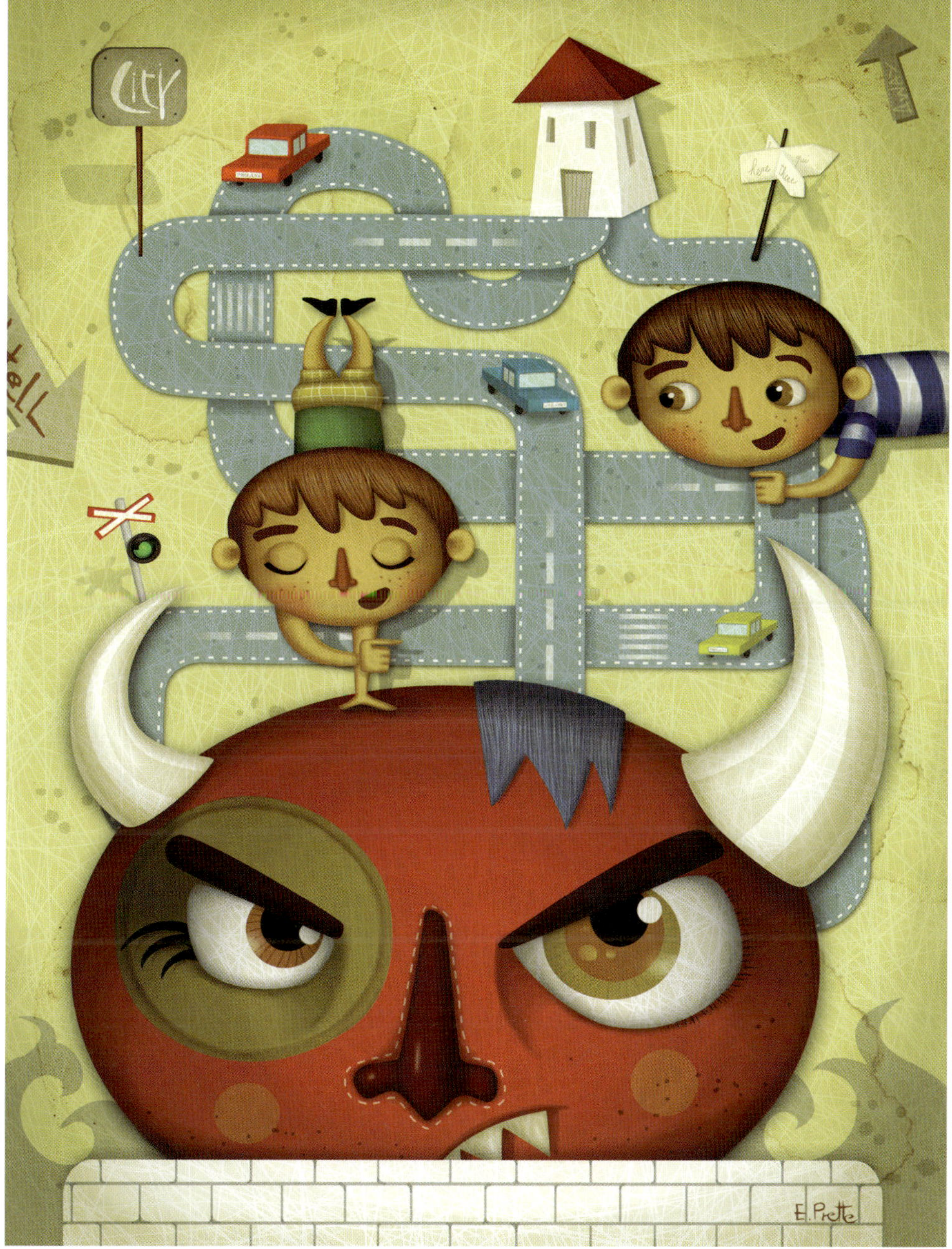
City
here there
E. Prette

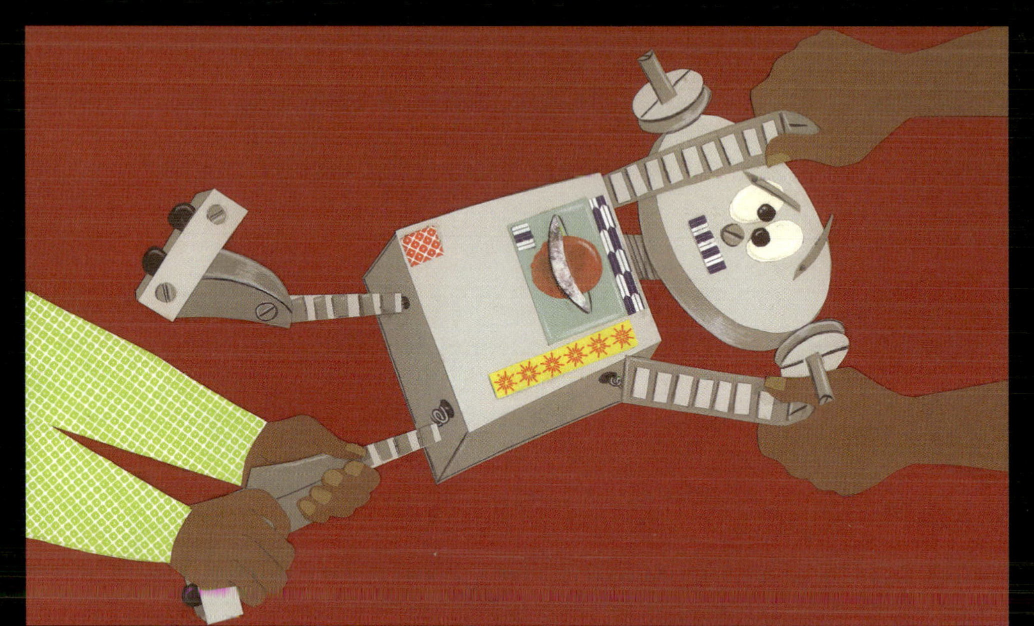

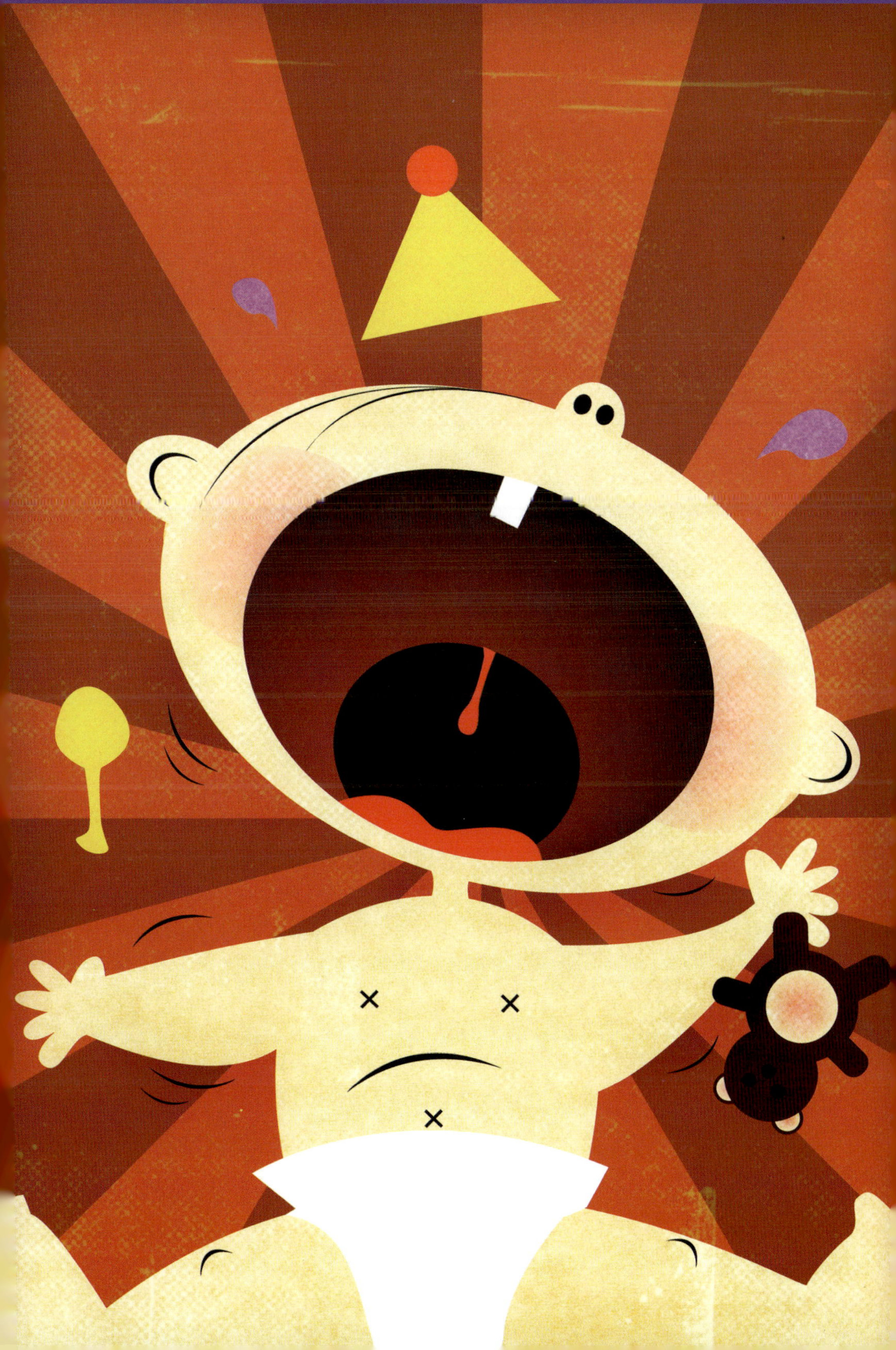

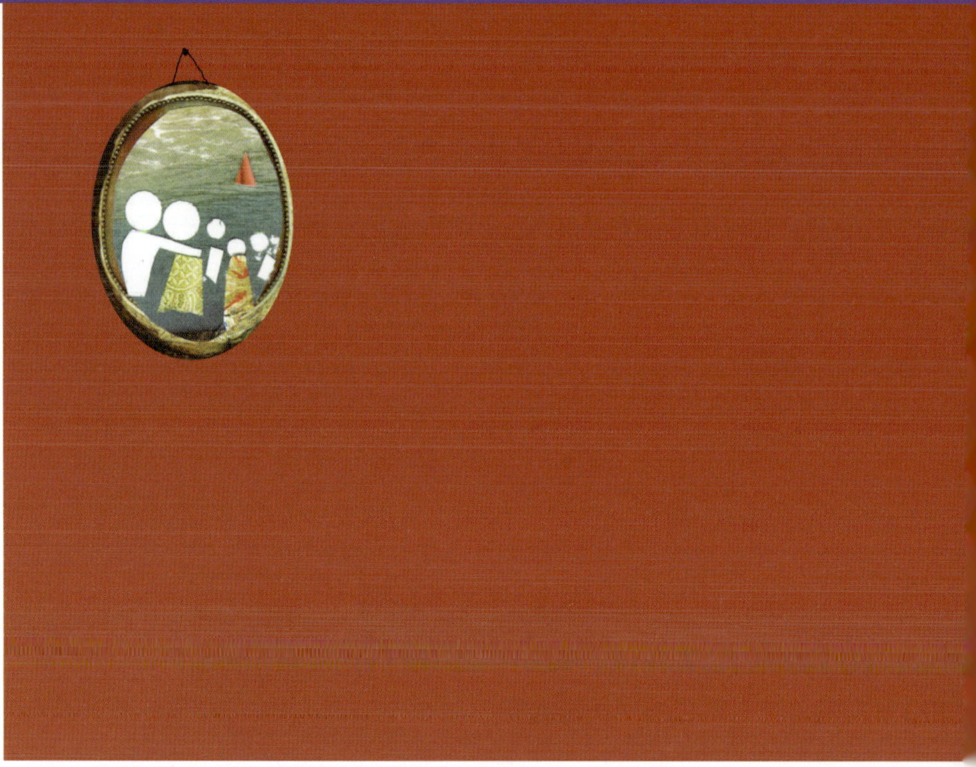

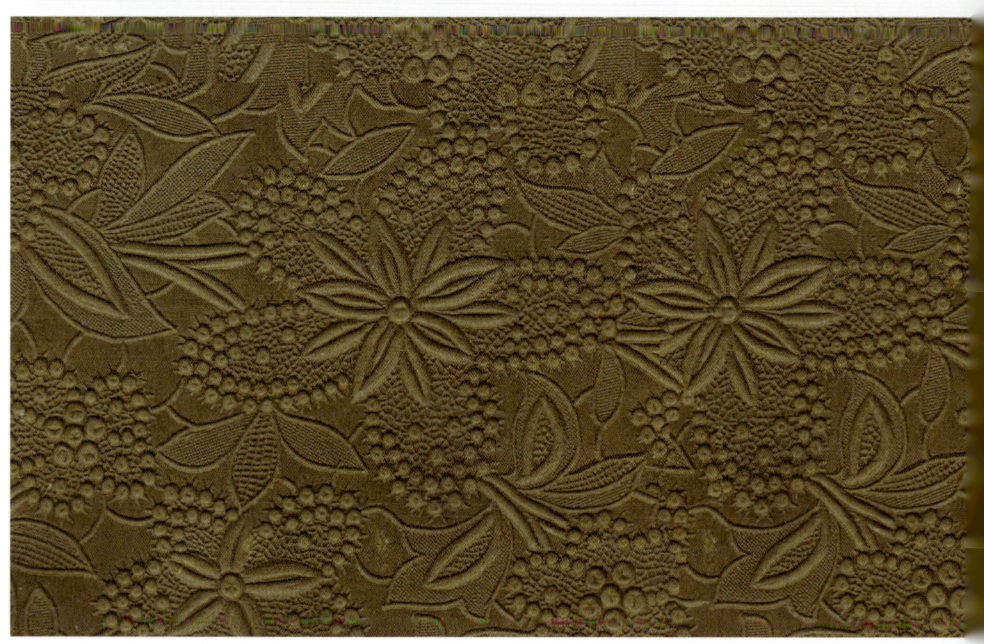

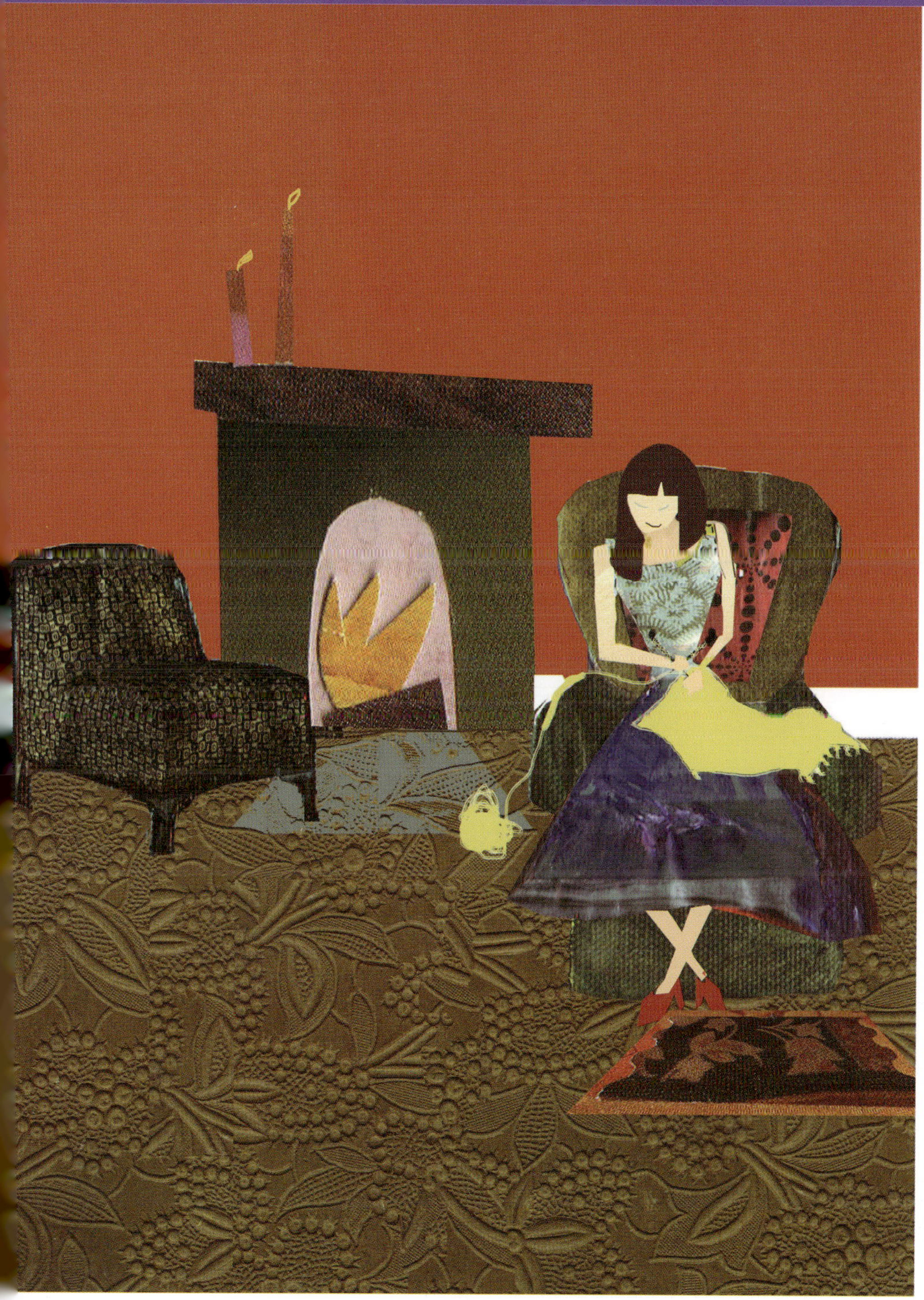

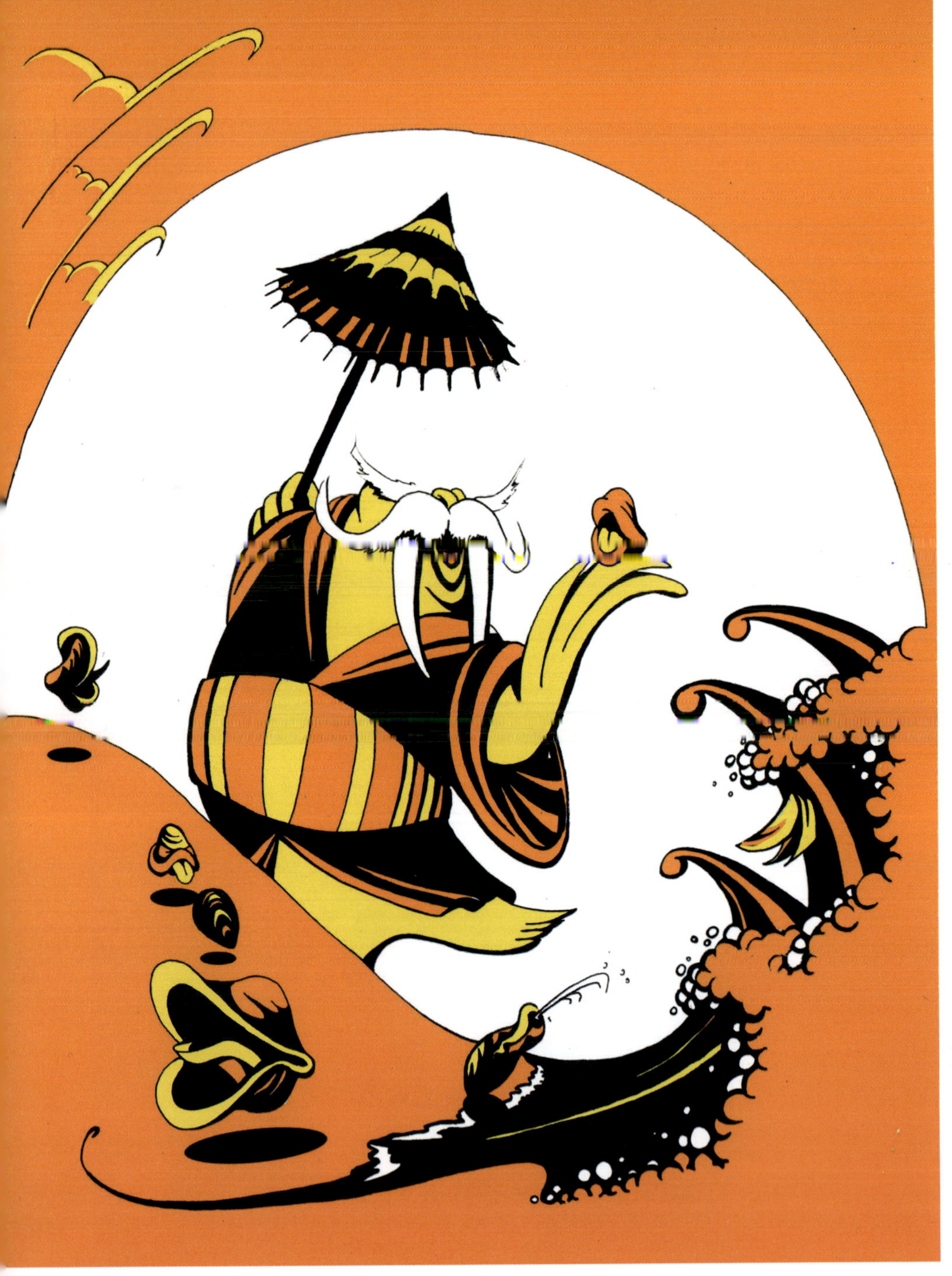

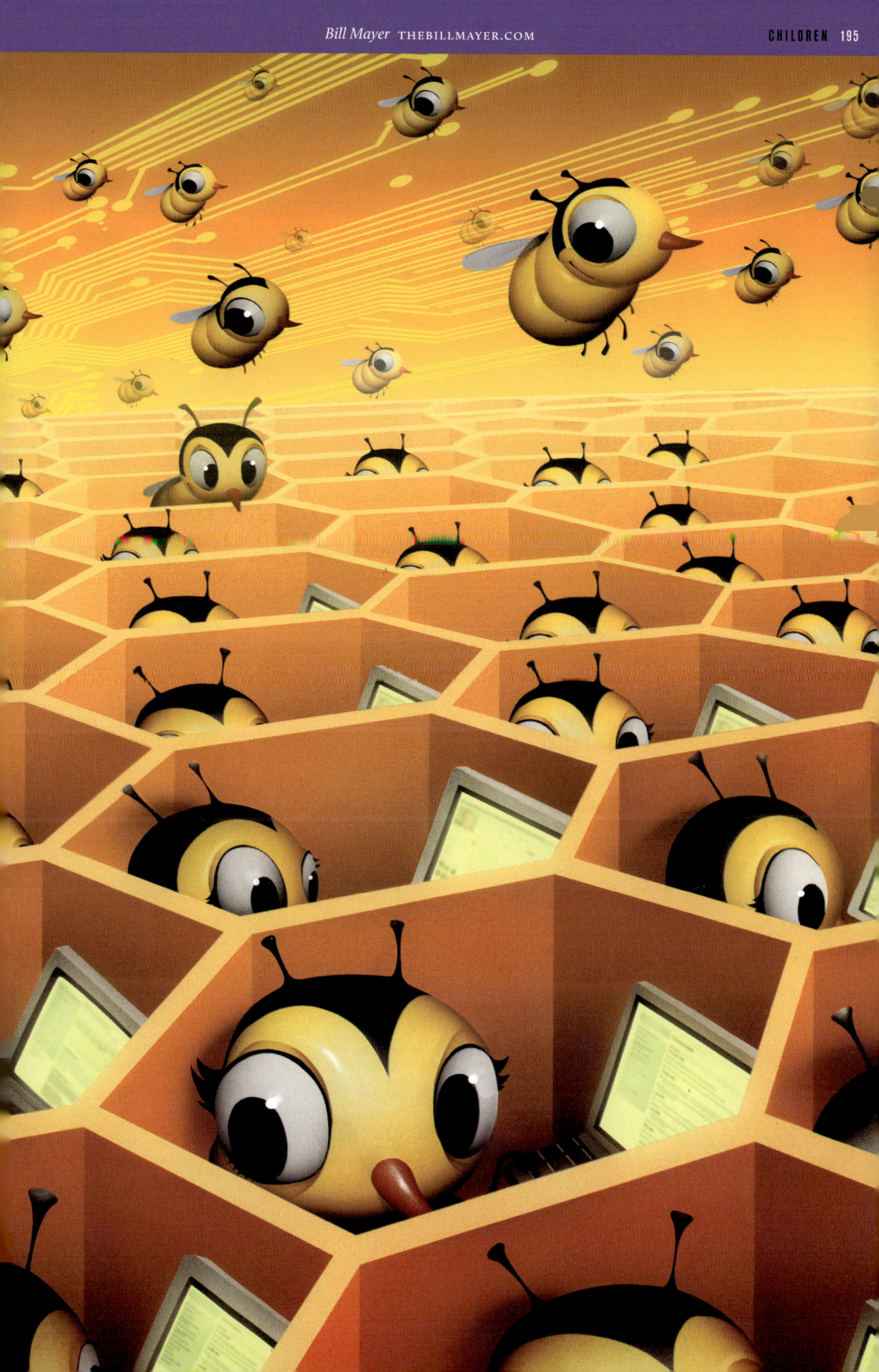

   Sarajo Frieden SARAJOFRIEDEN.COM

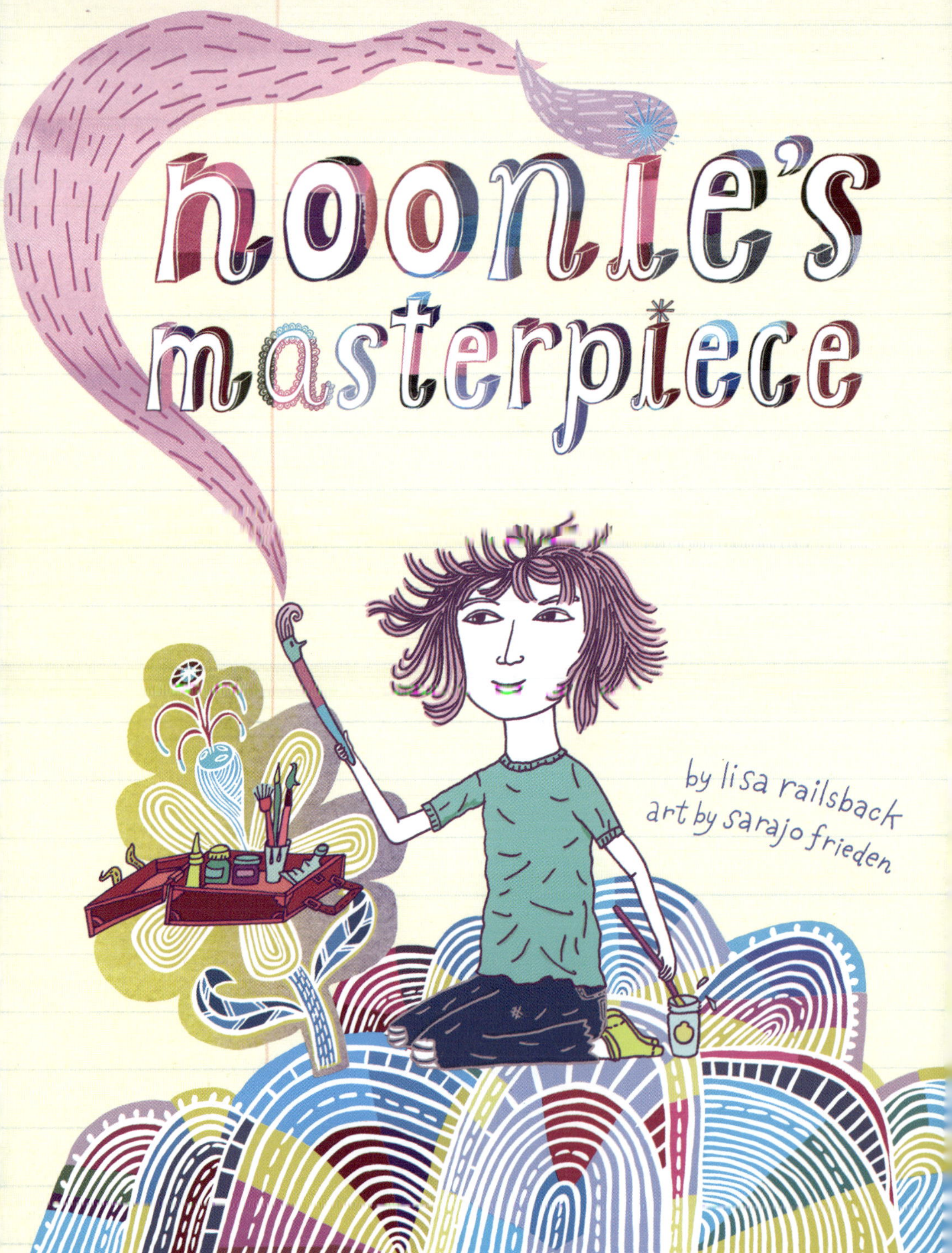

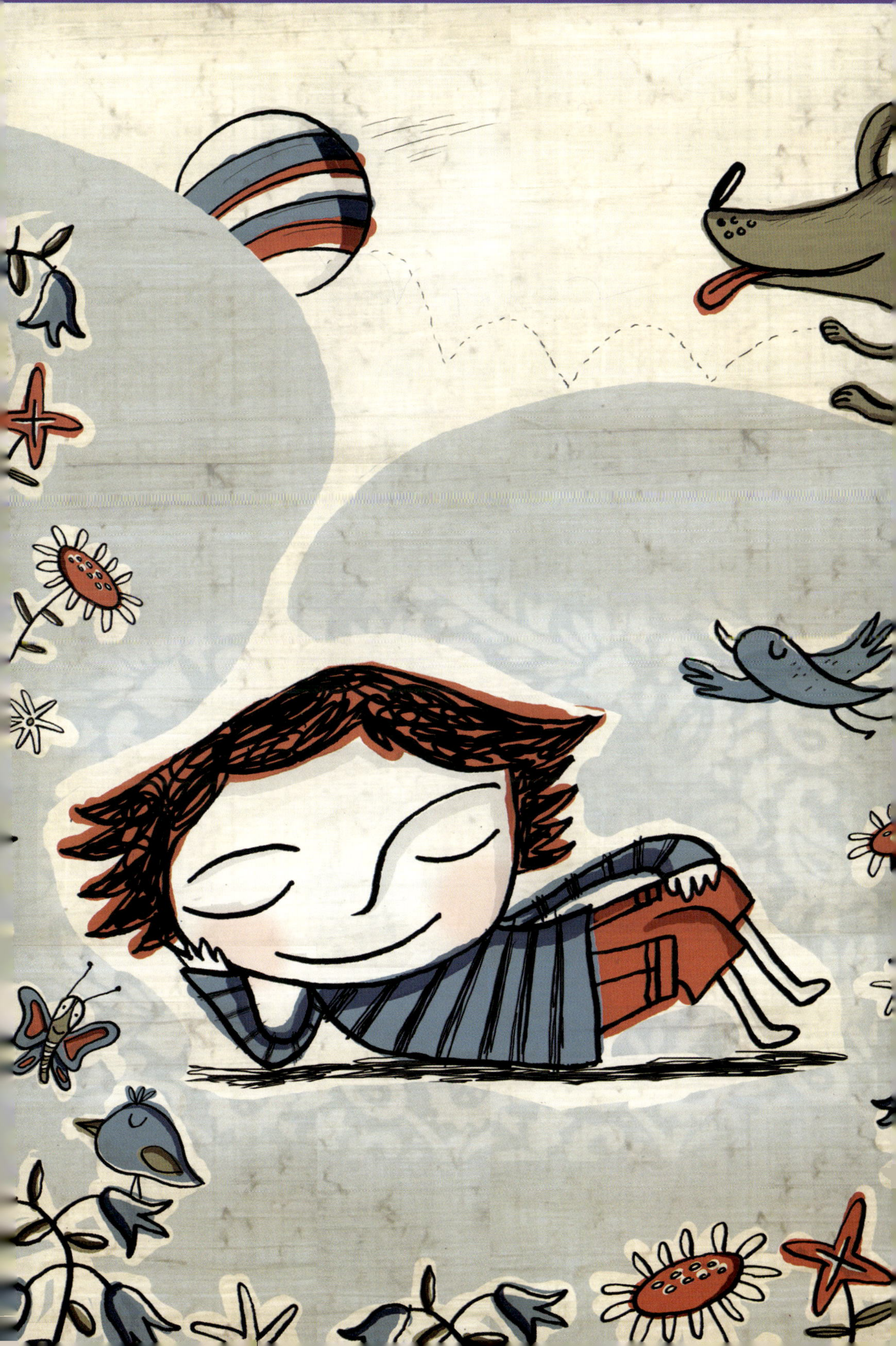

 Kat Chadwick KATCHADWICK.COM

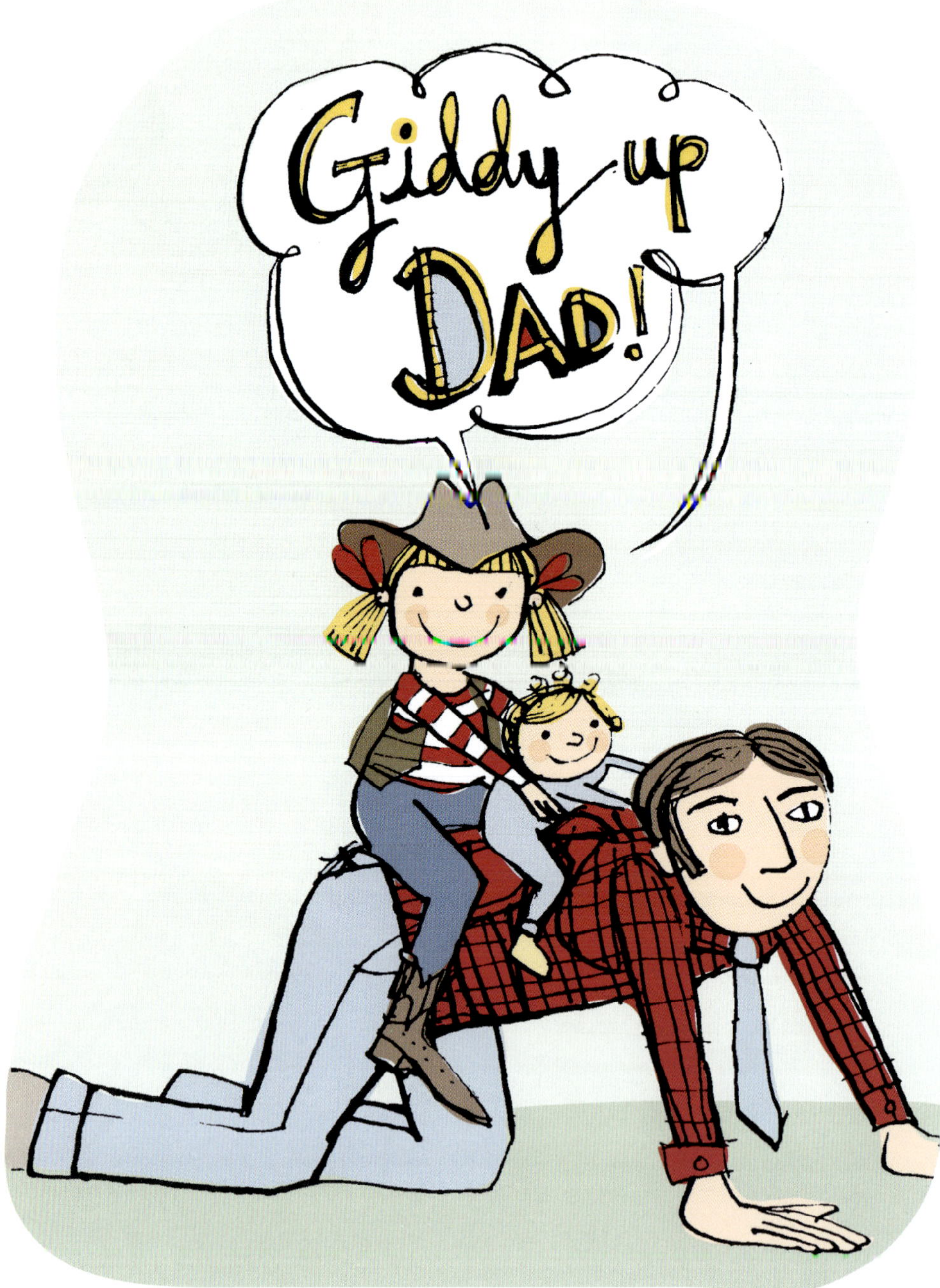

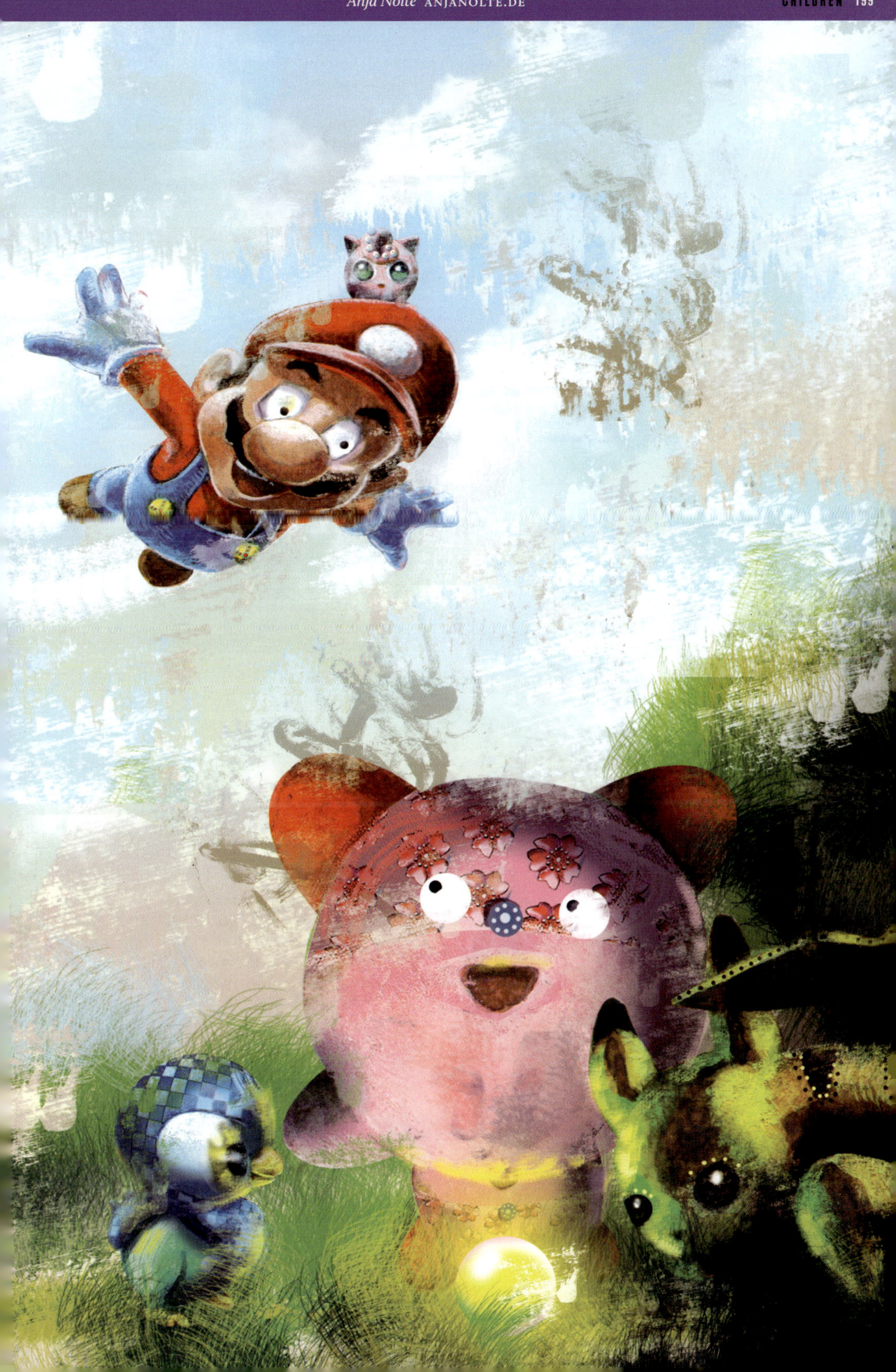

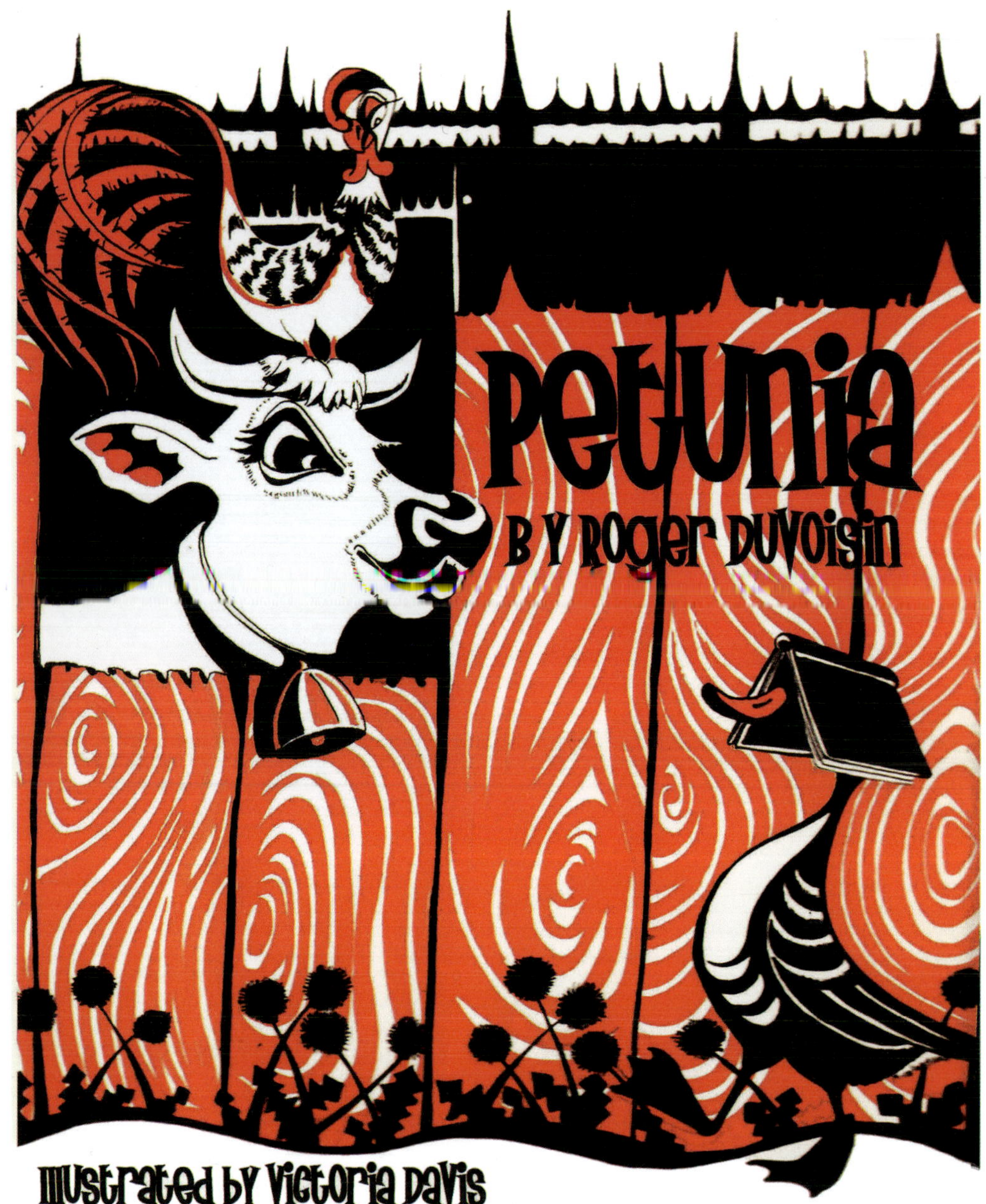
PETUNIA
BY ROGER DUVOISIN
ILLUSTRATED BY VICTORIA DAVIS

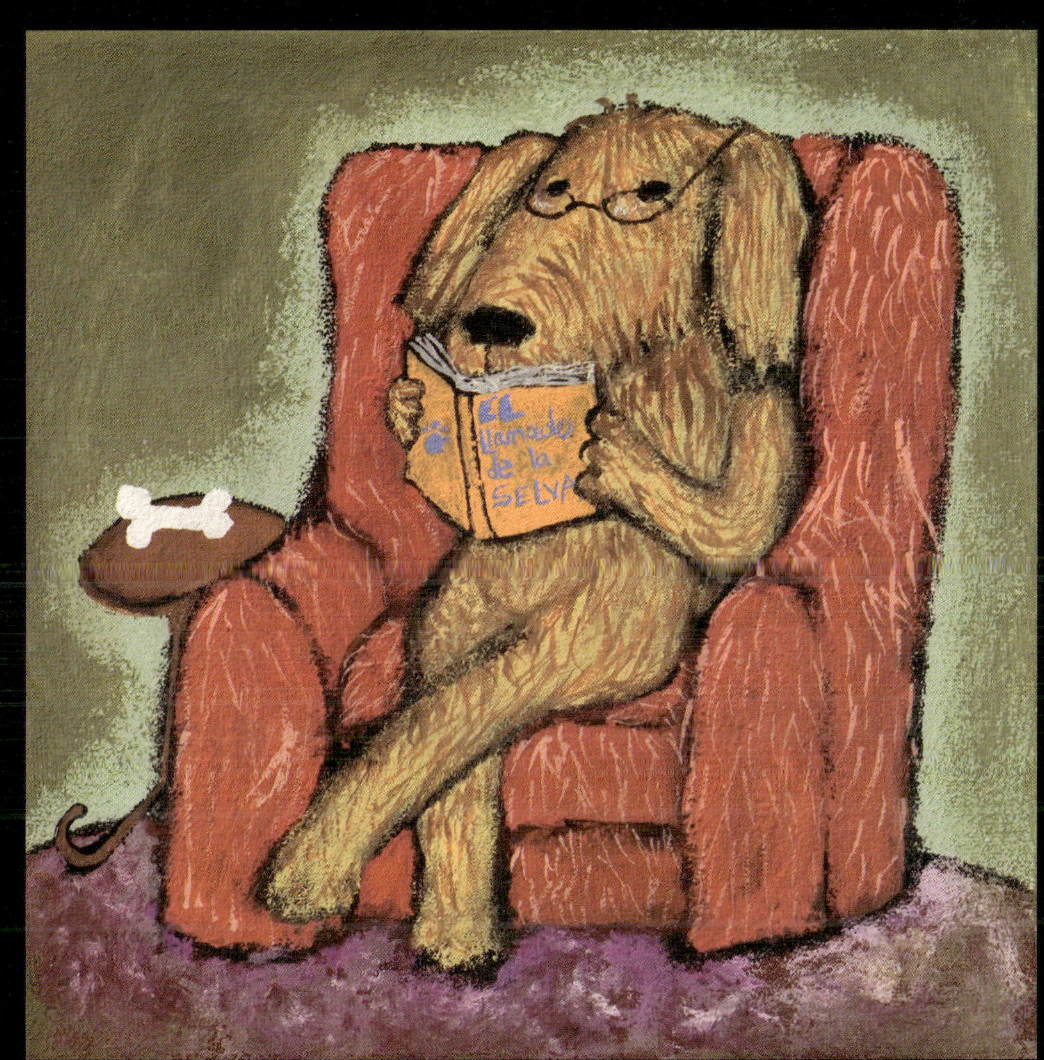
EL
llamado
de la
SELVA

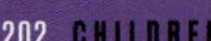

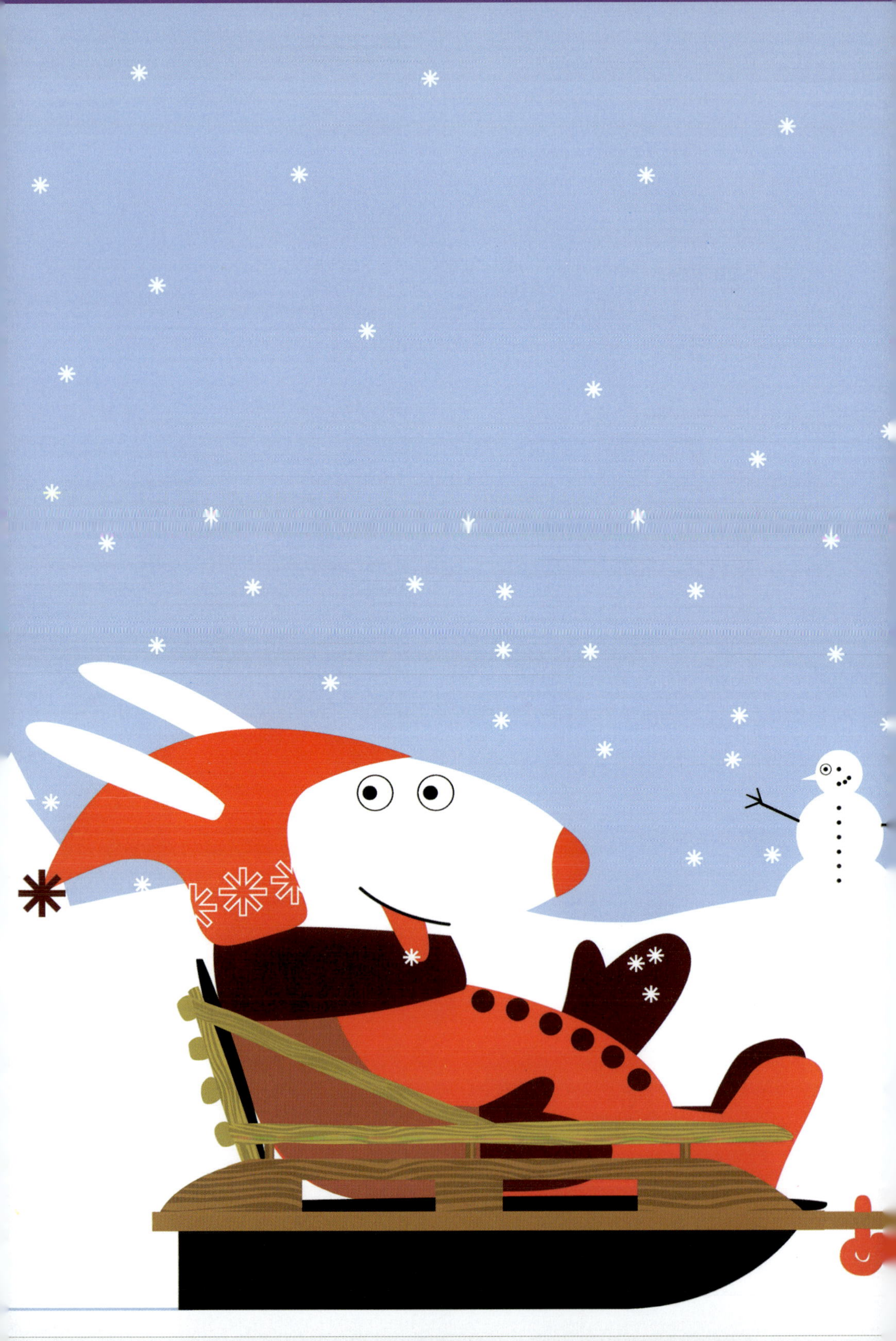

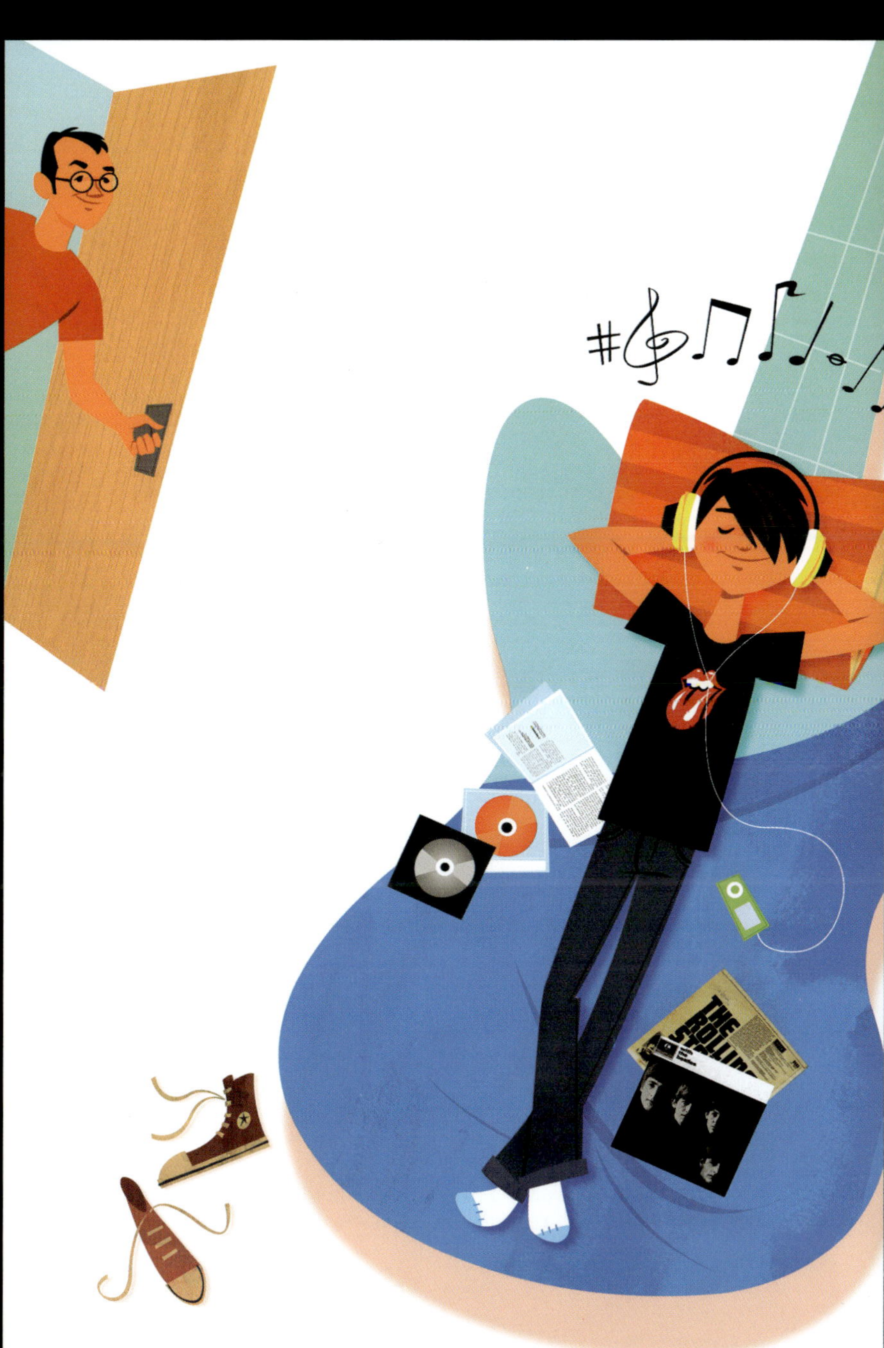

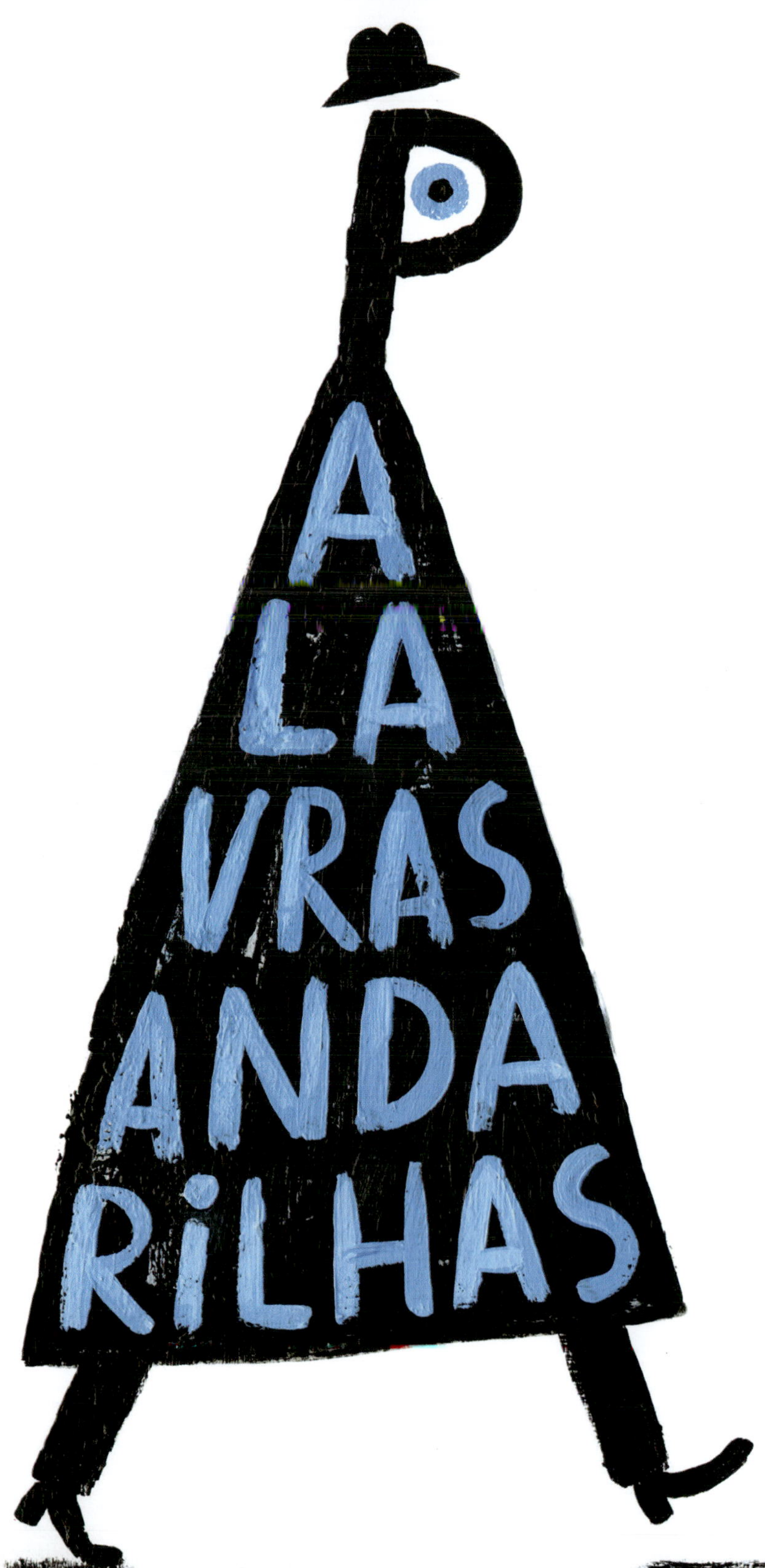
PALAVRAS ANDARILHAS

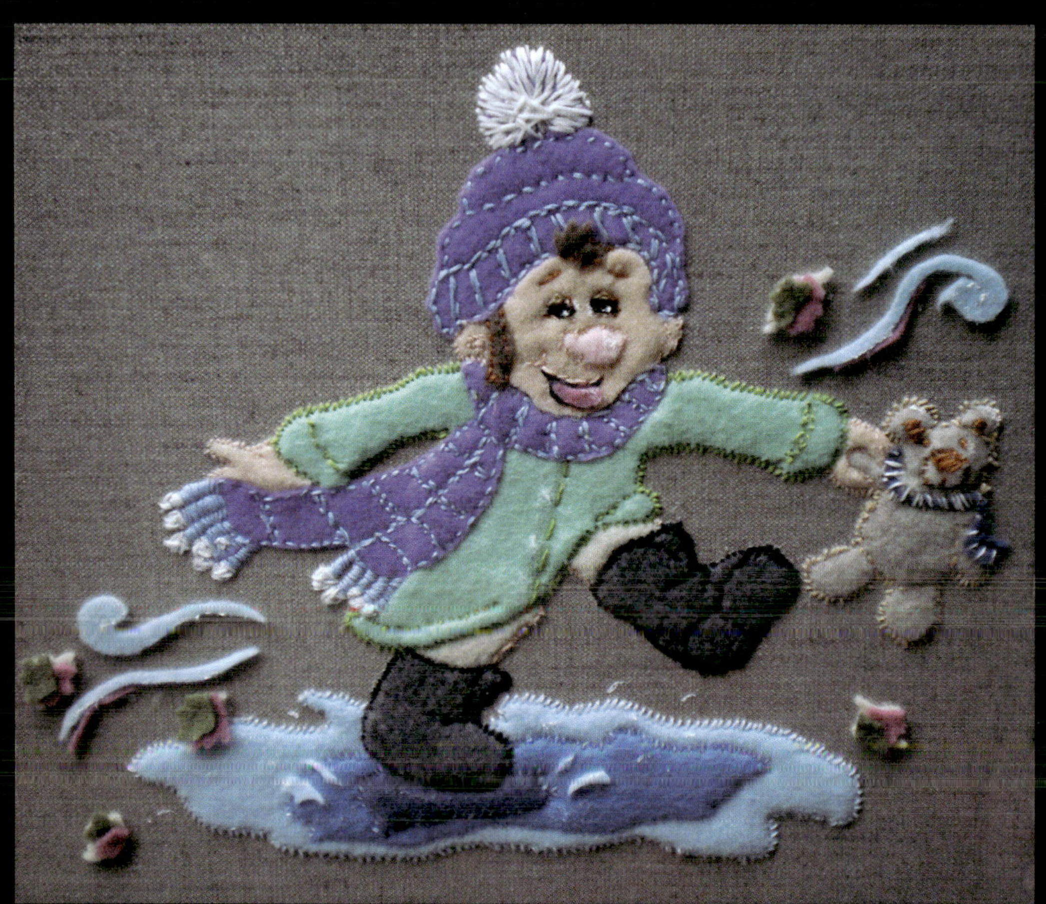

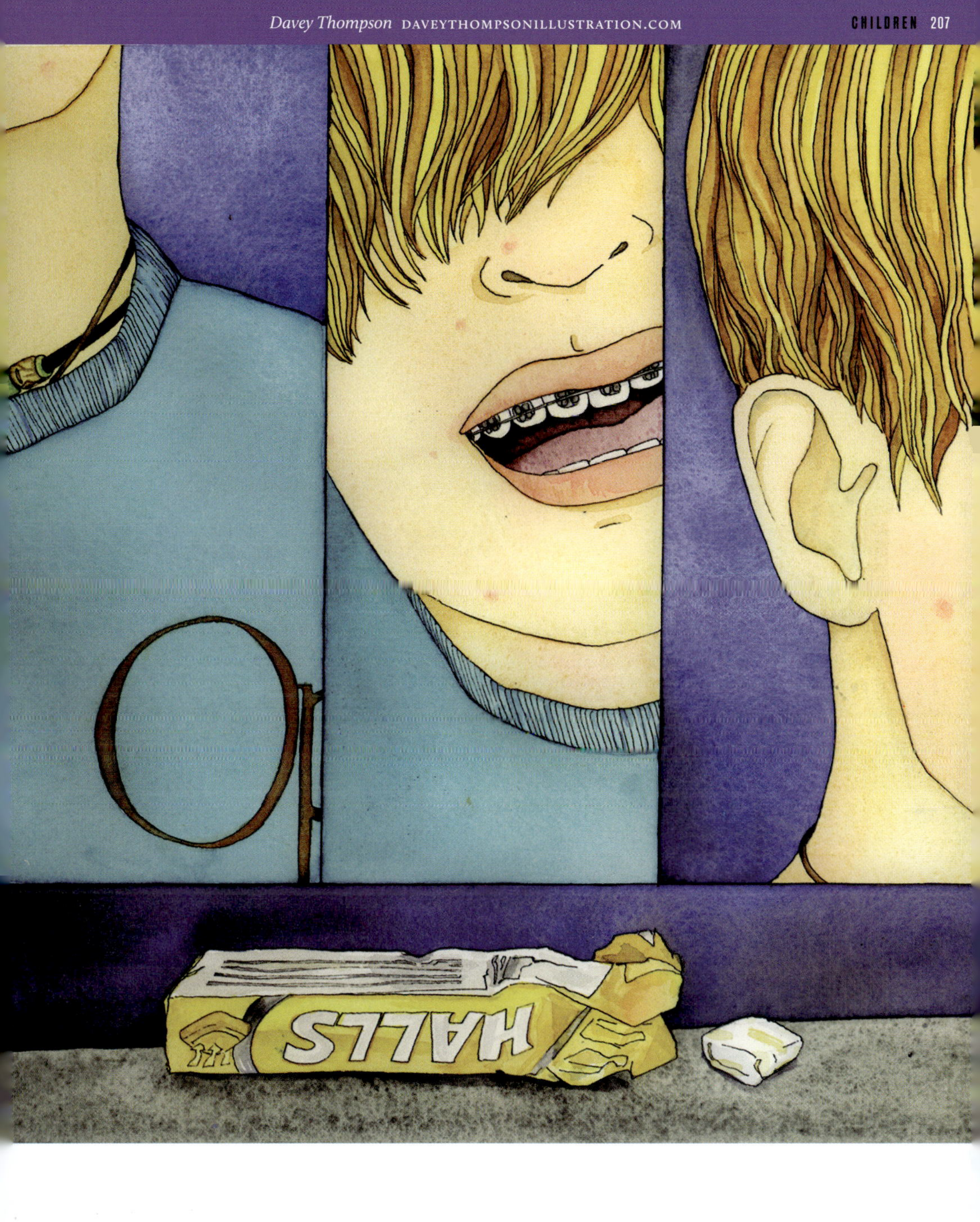
HALLS

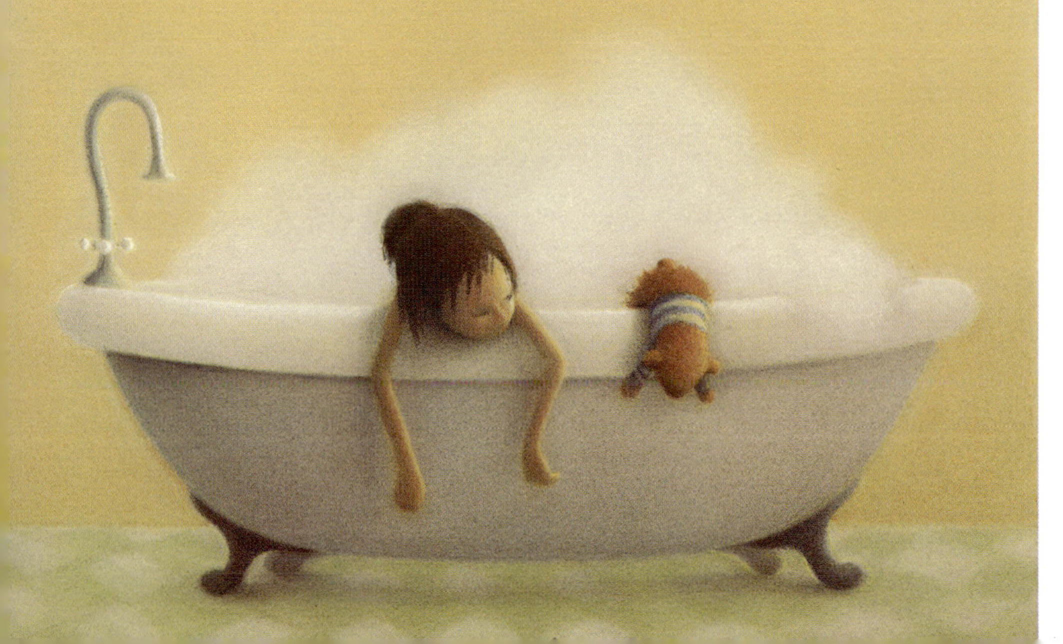

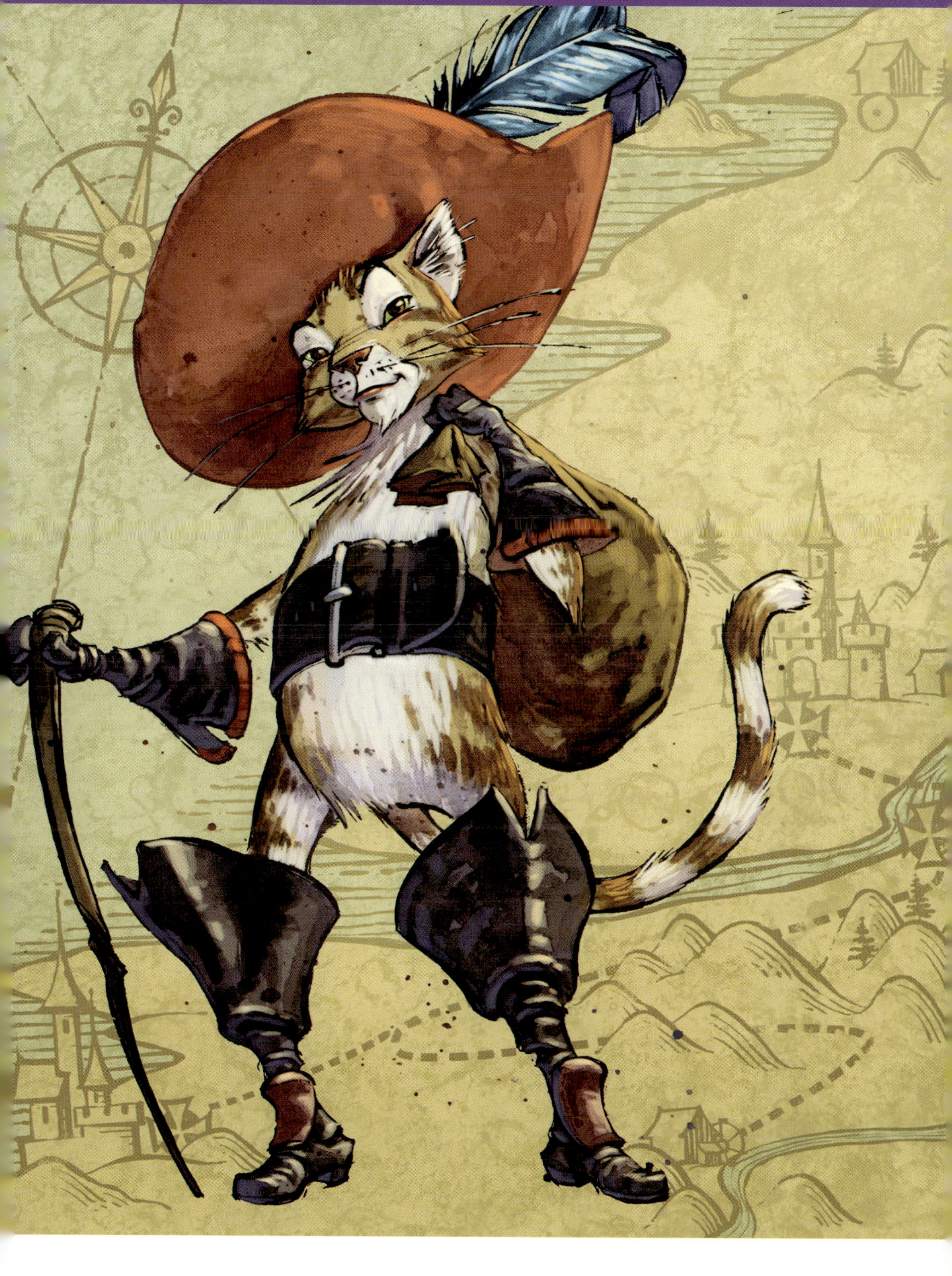

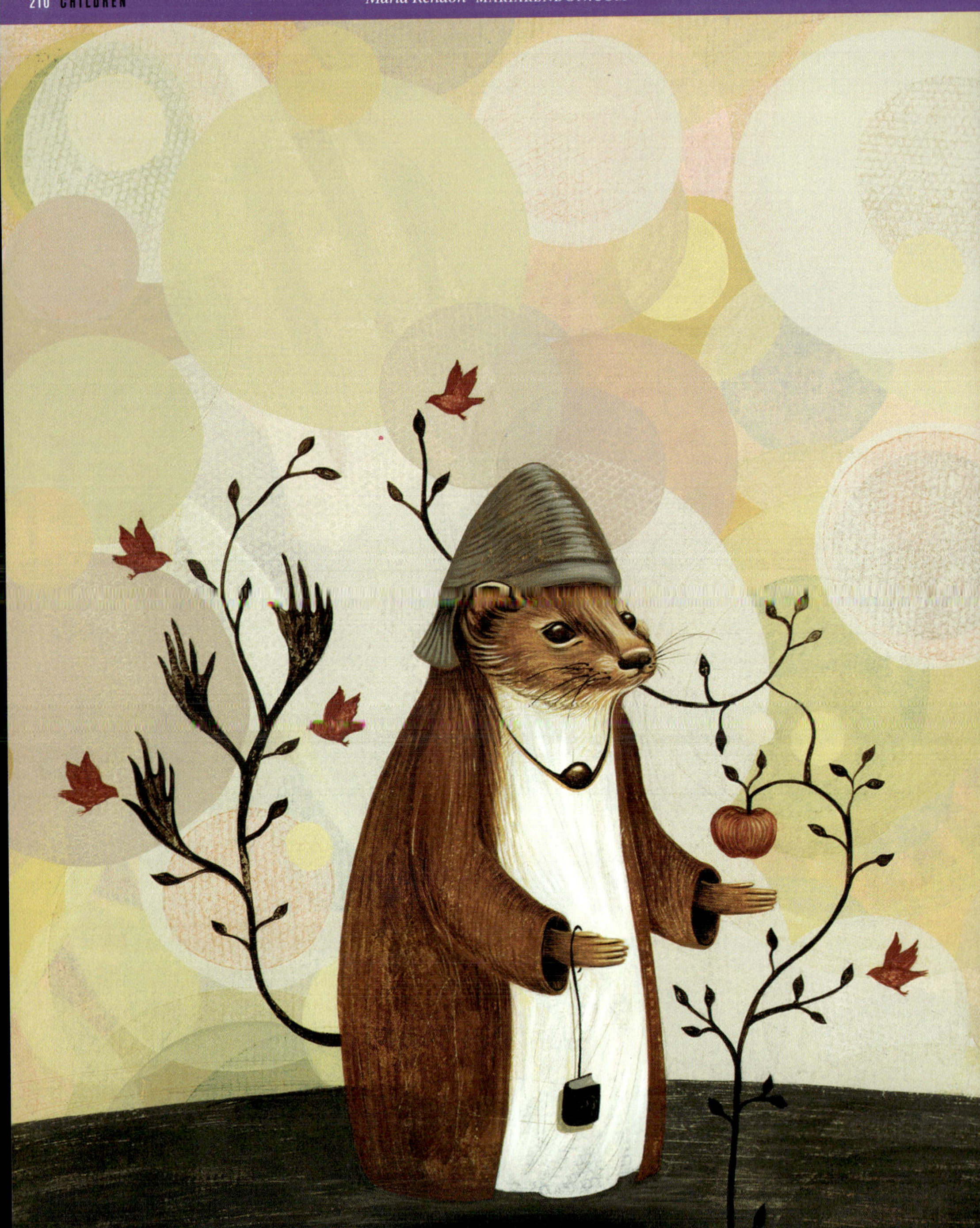

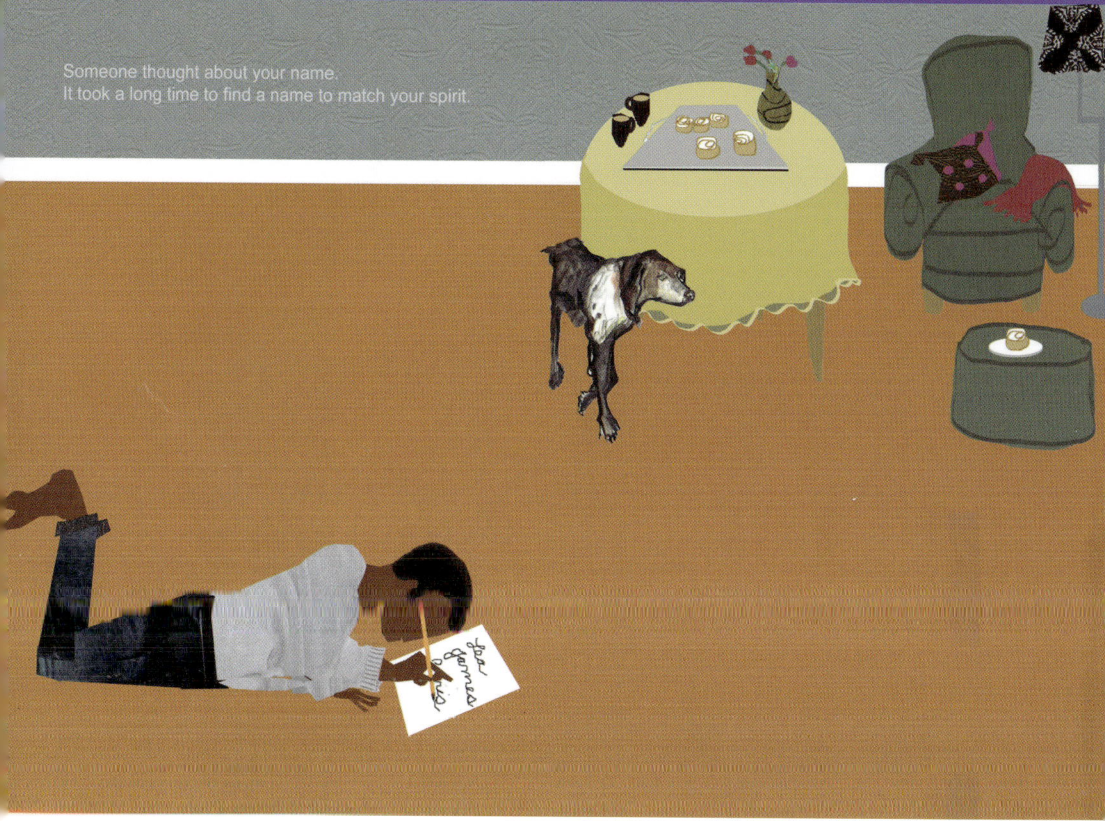
Someone thought about your name.
It took a long time to find a name to match your spirit.

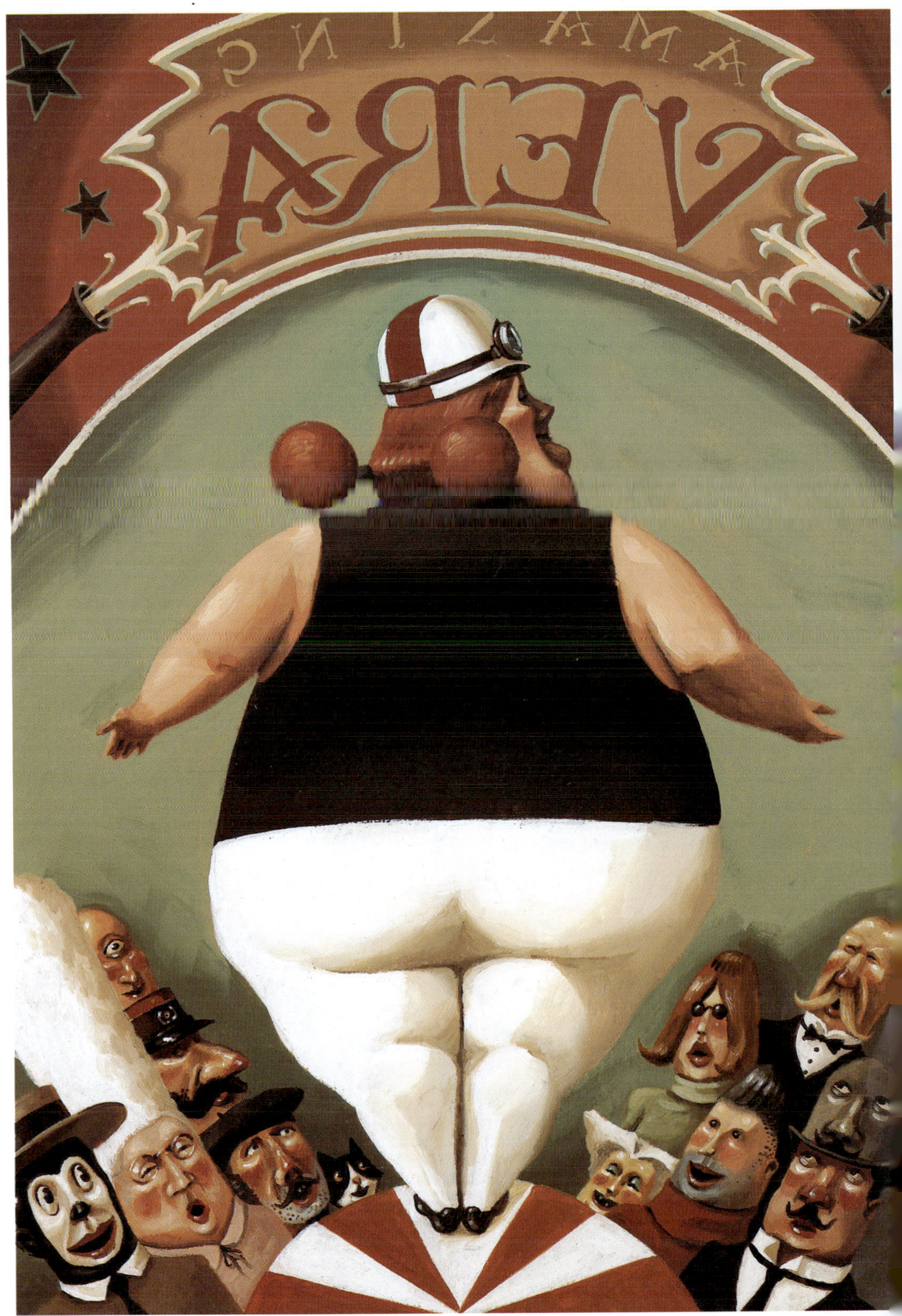

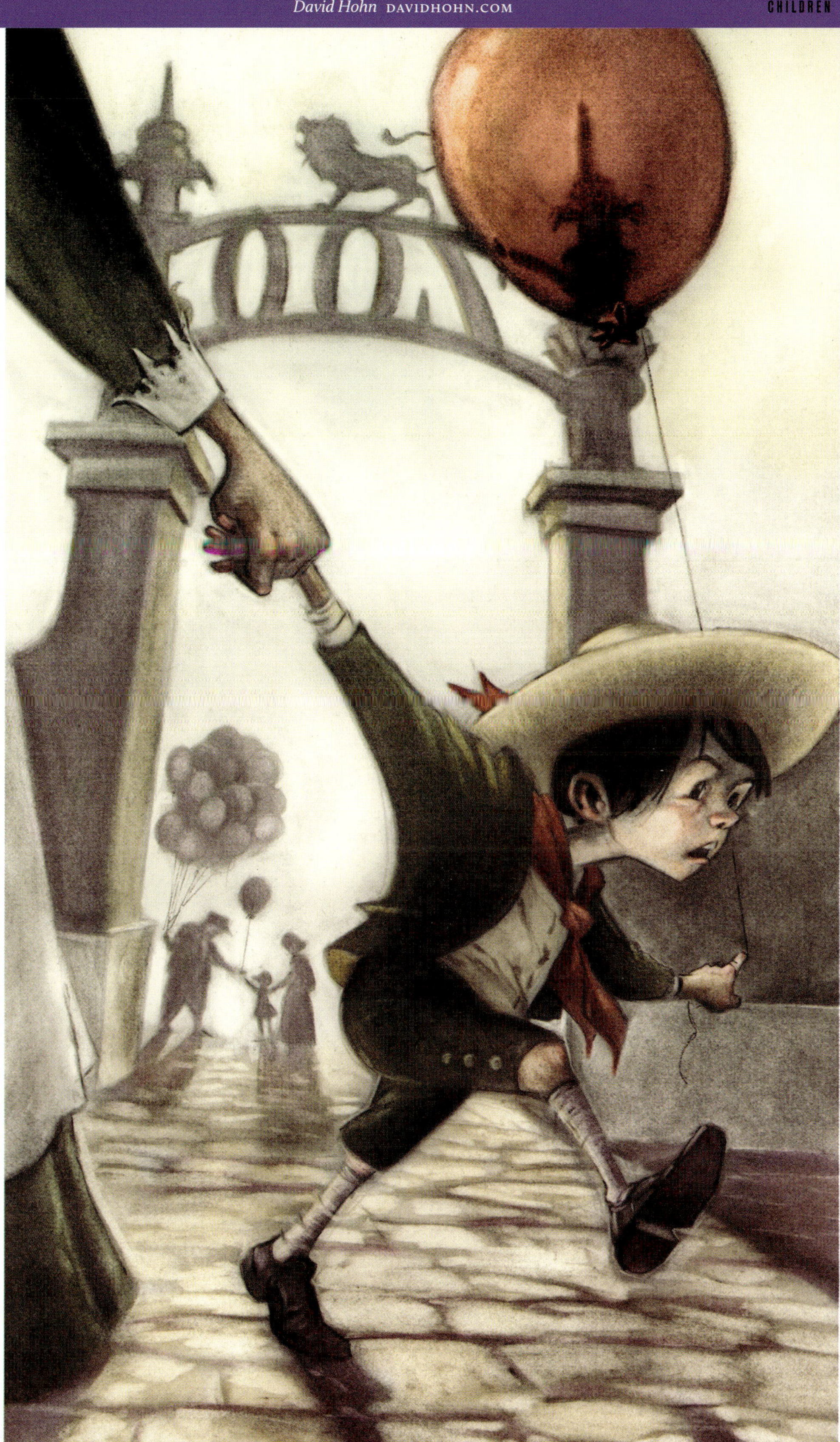

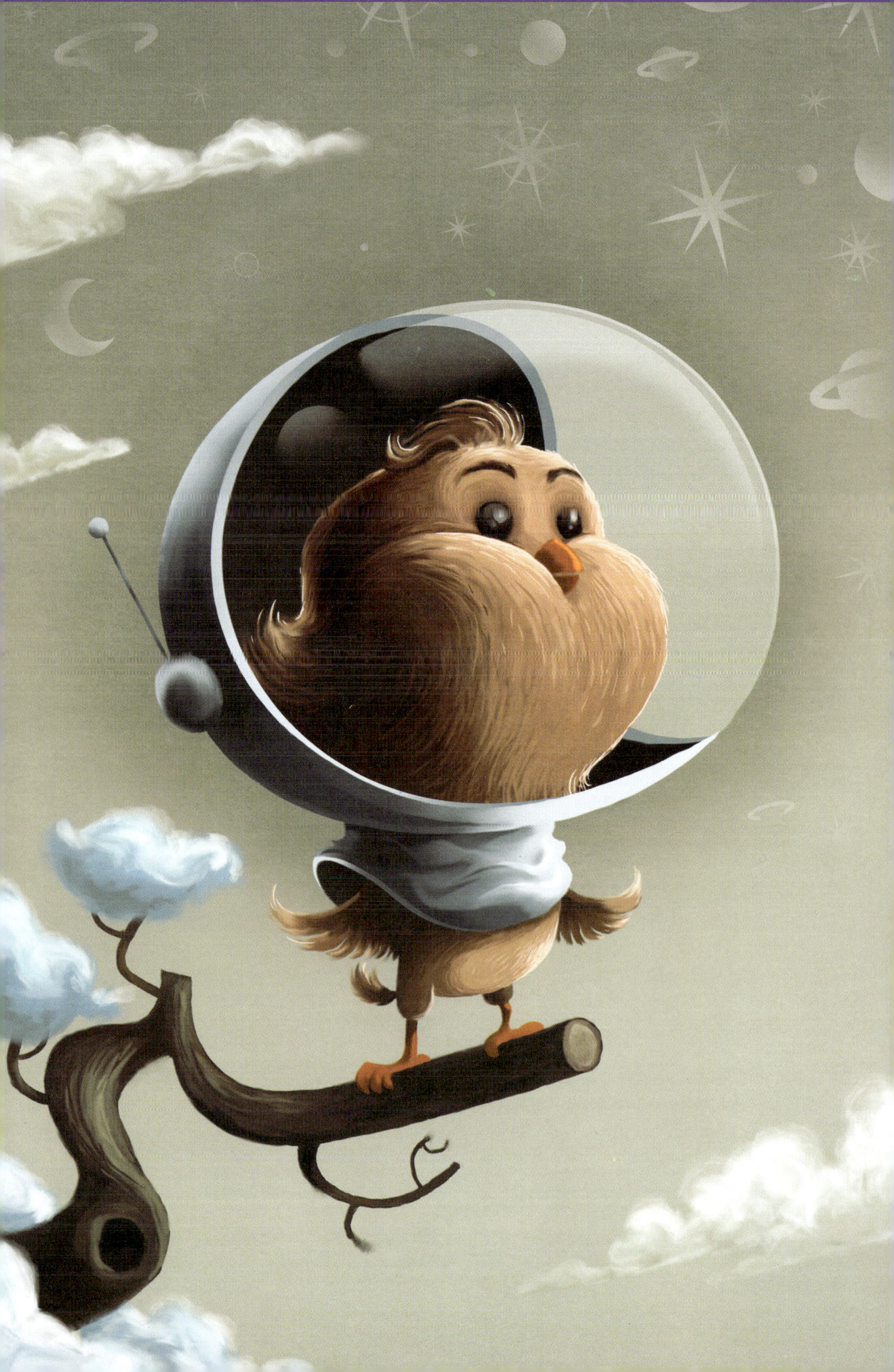

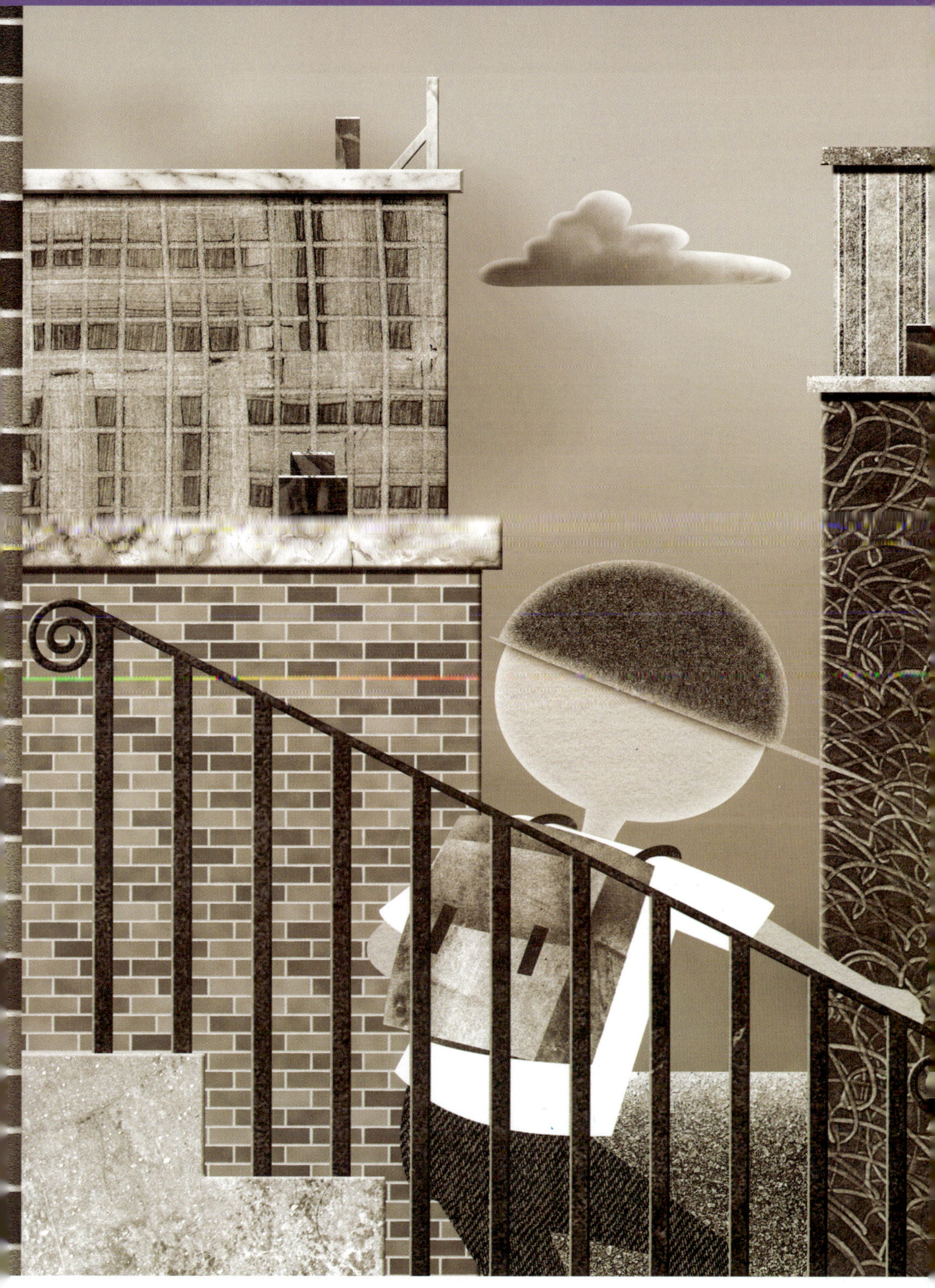

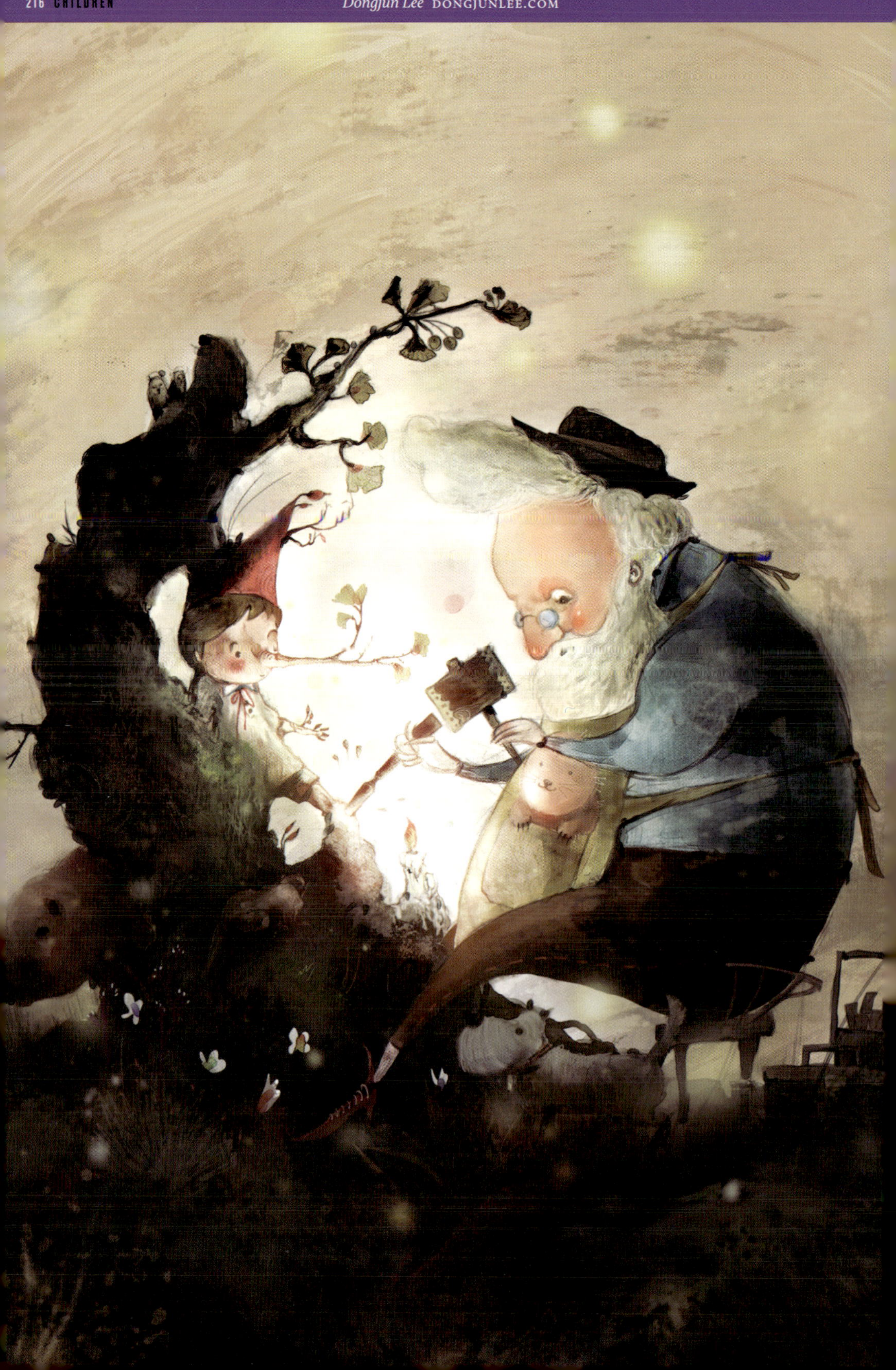

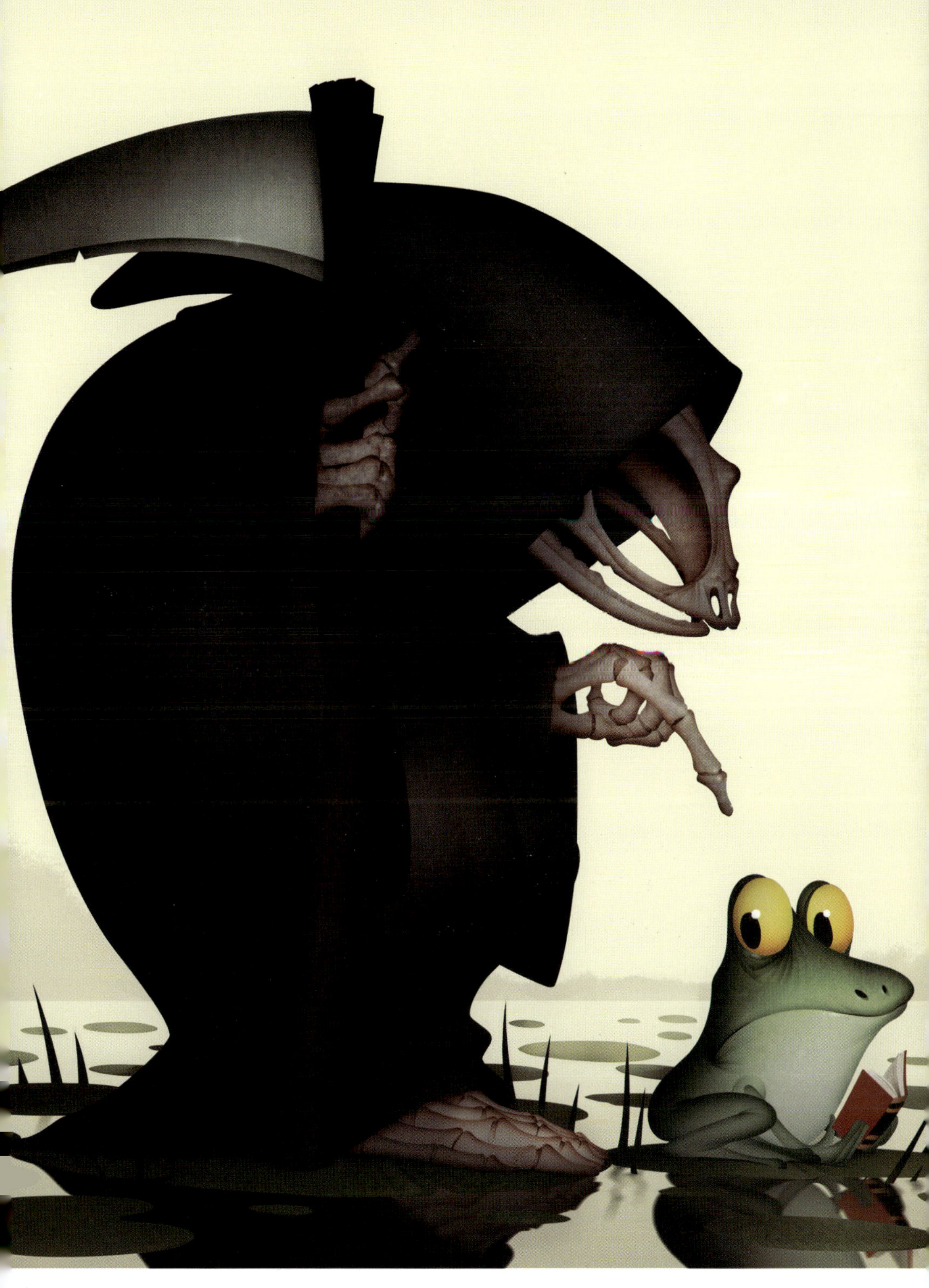

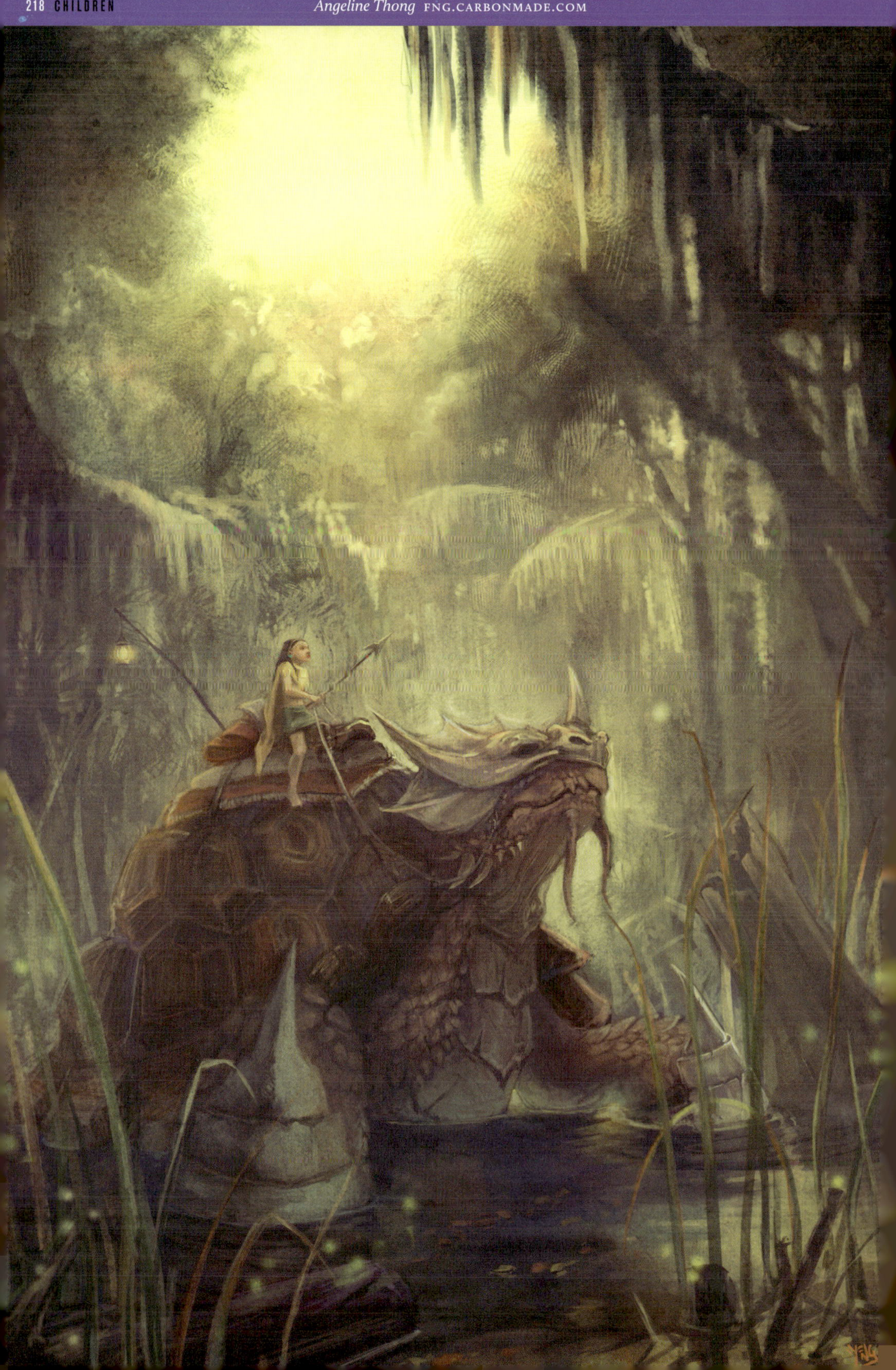

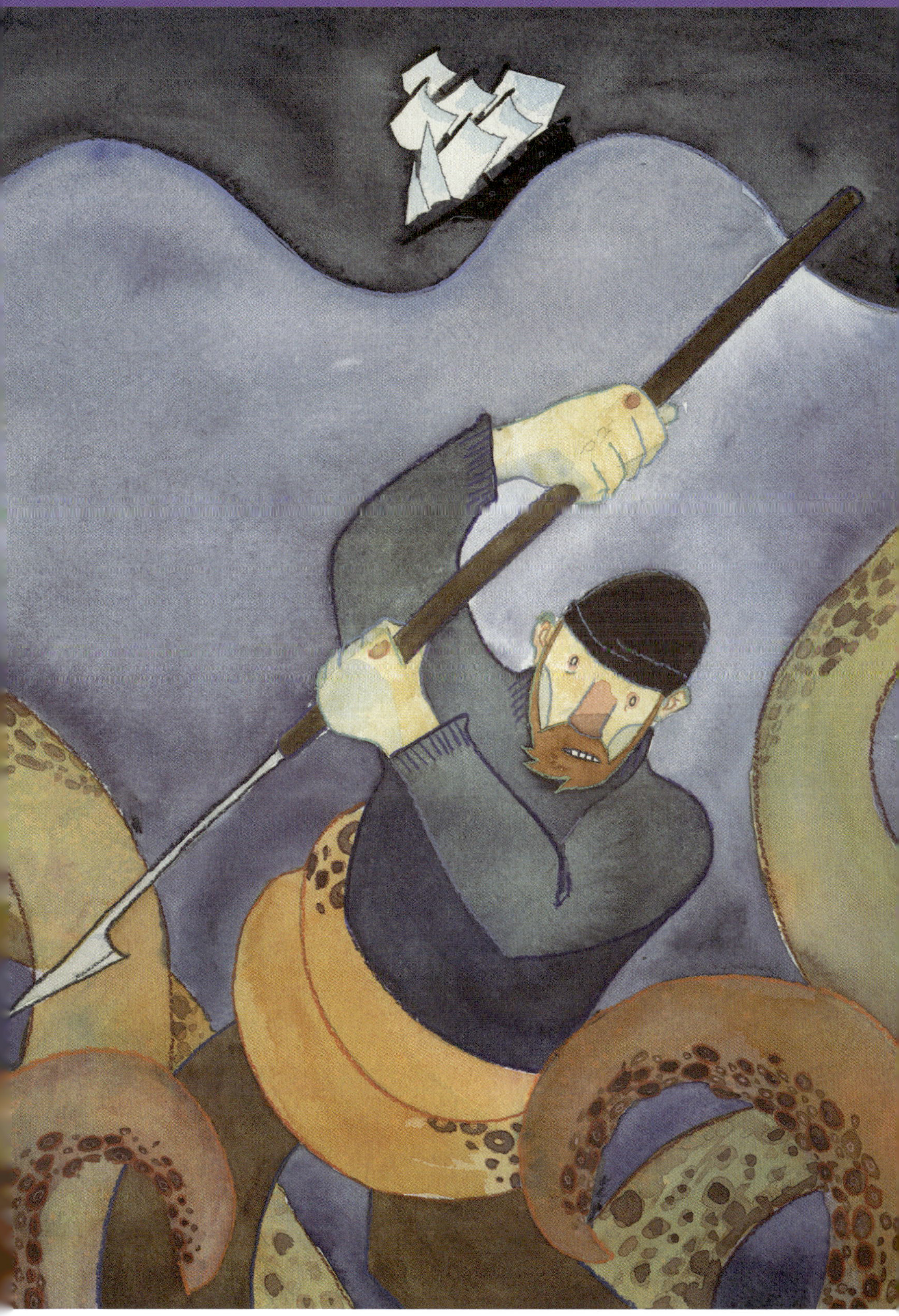

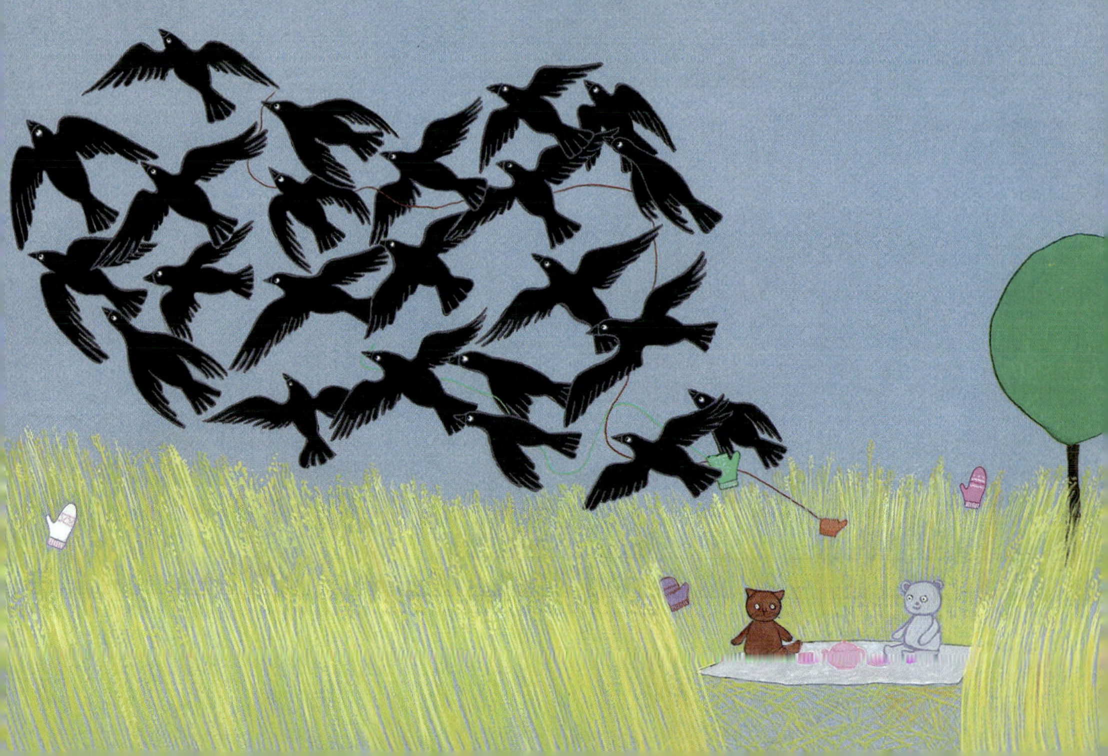

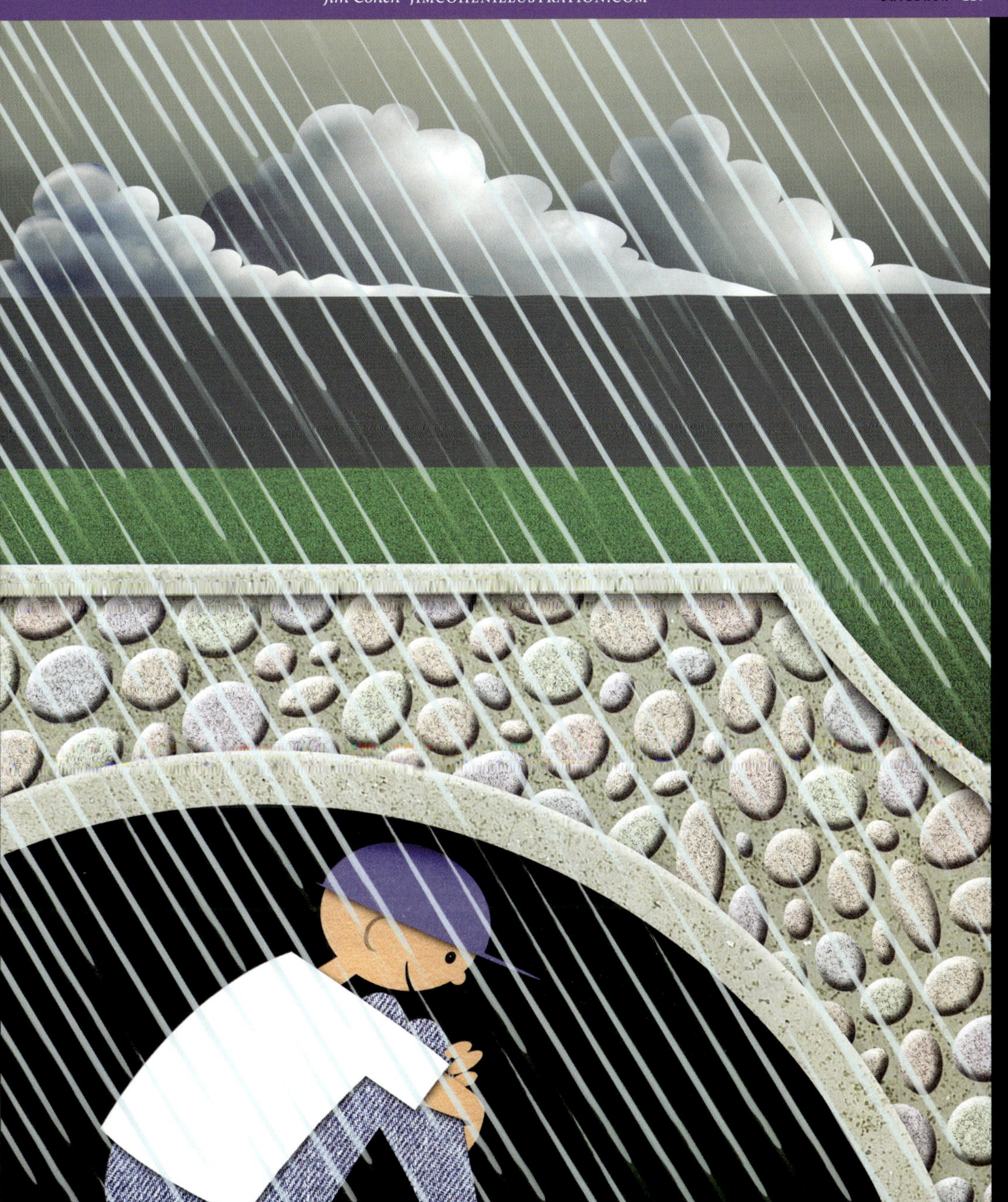

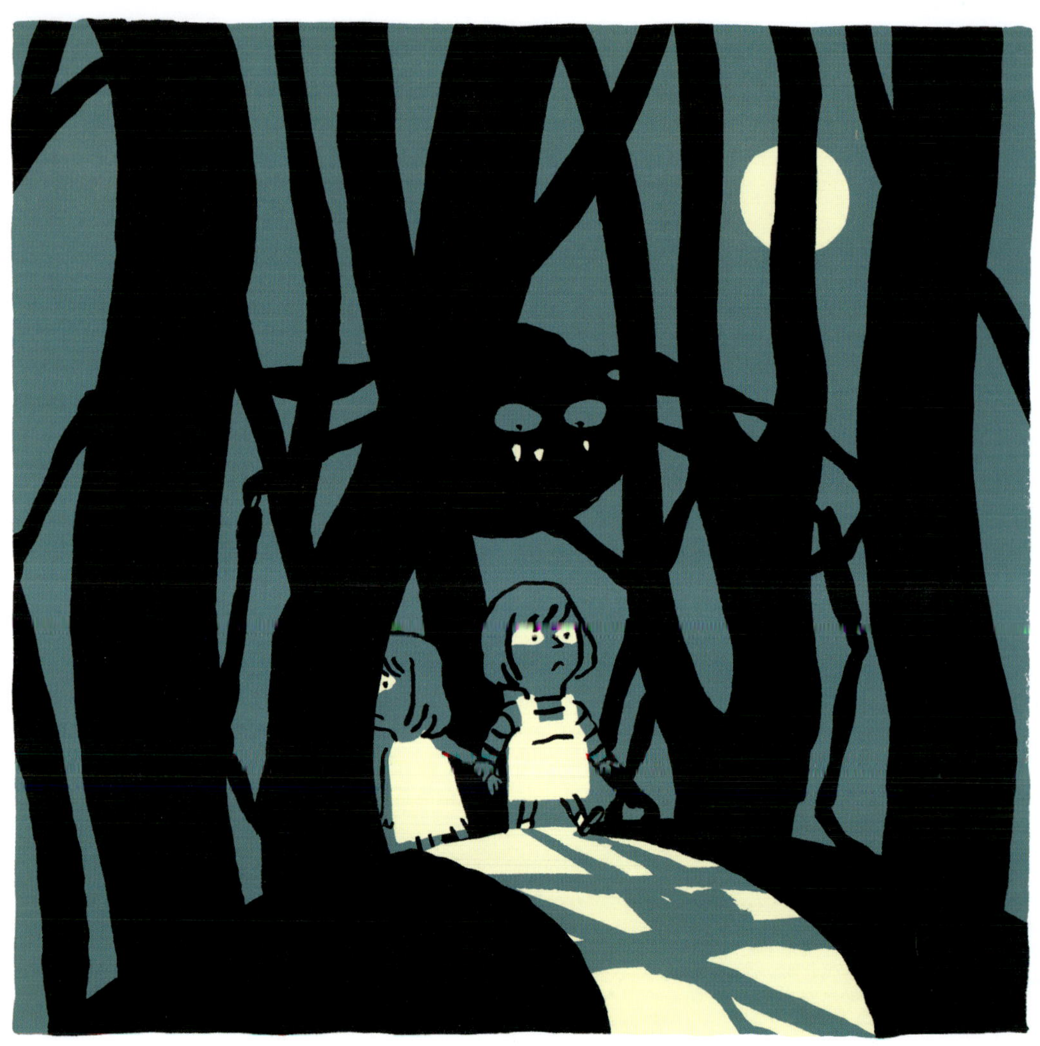

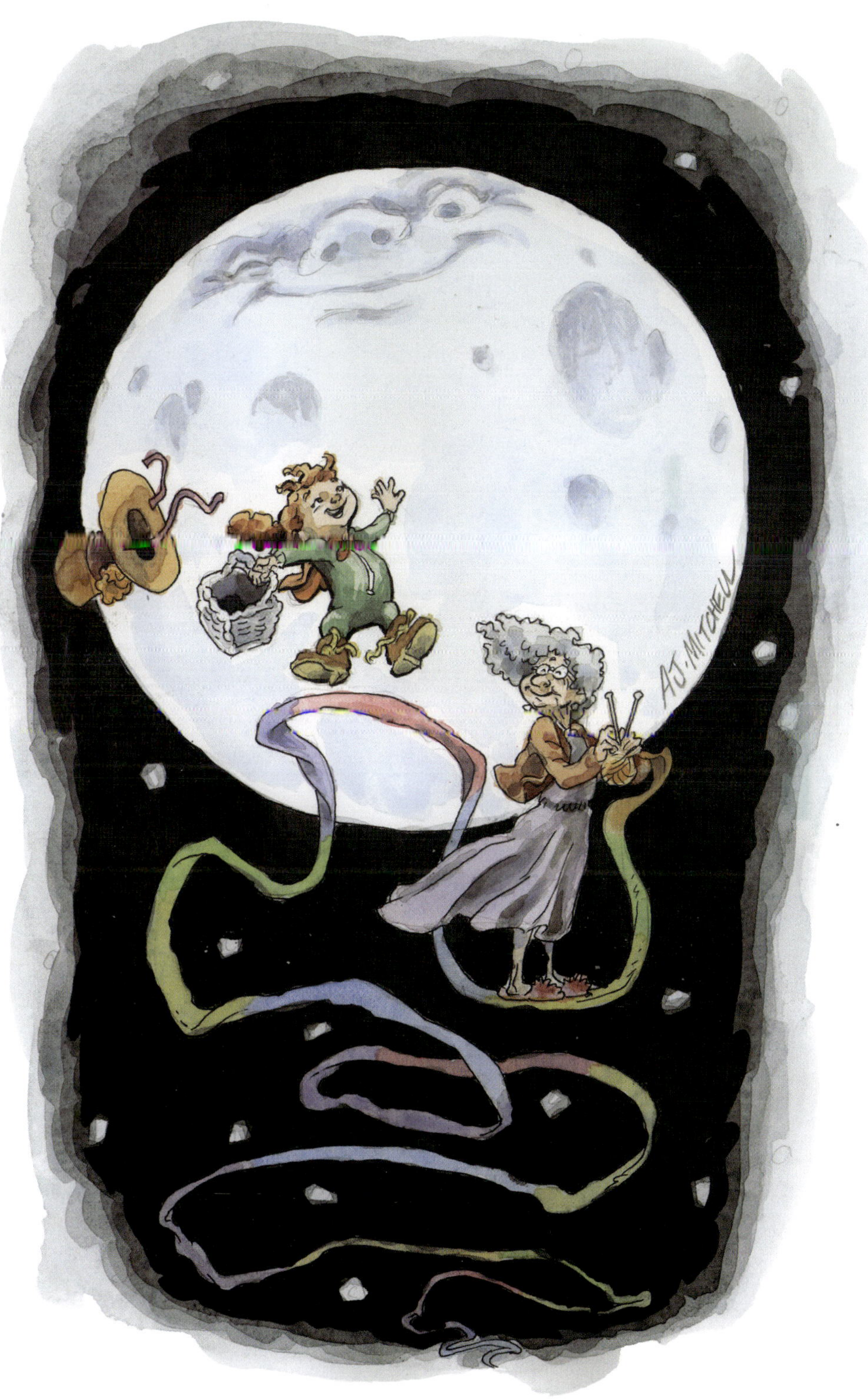

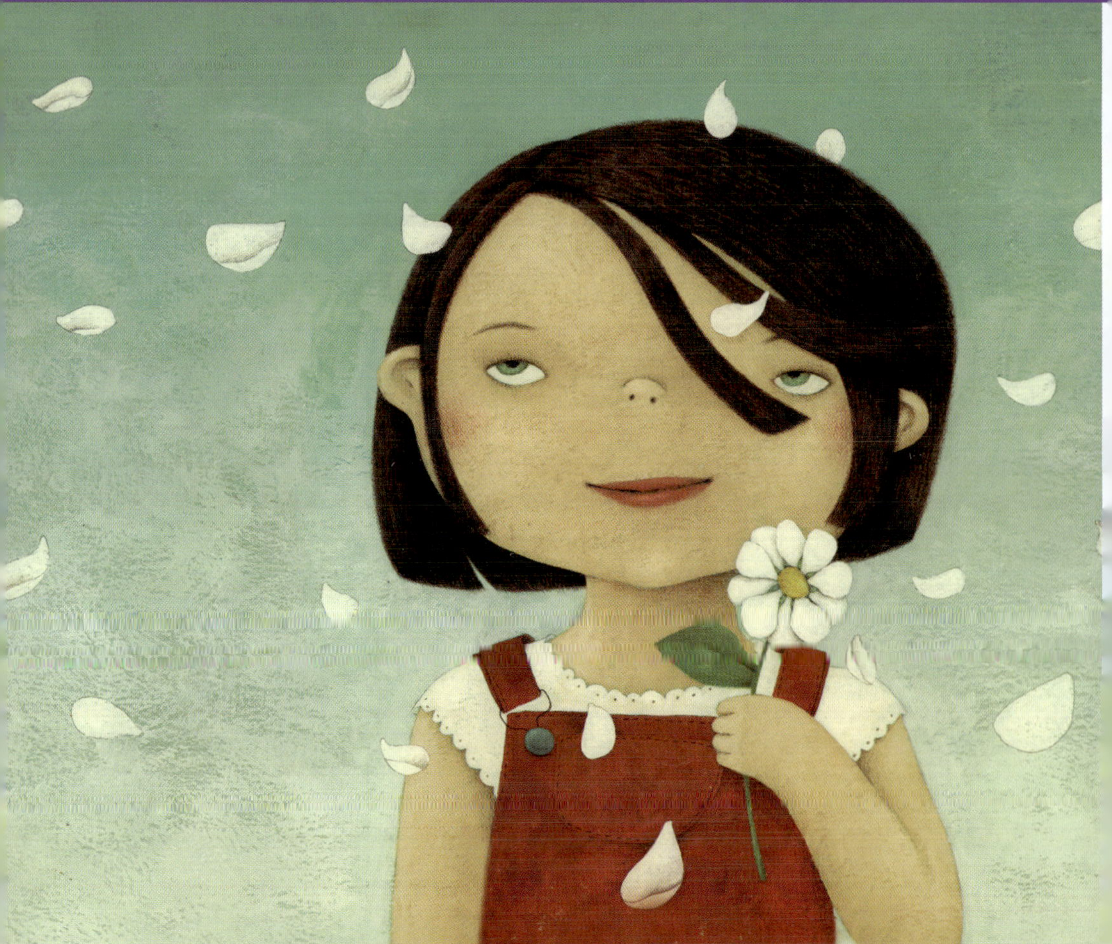

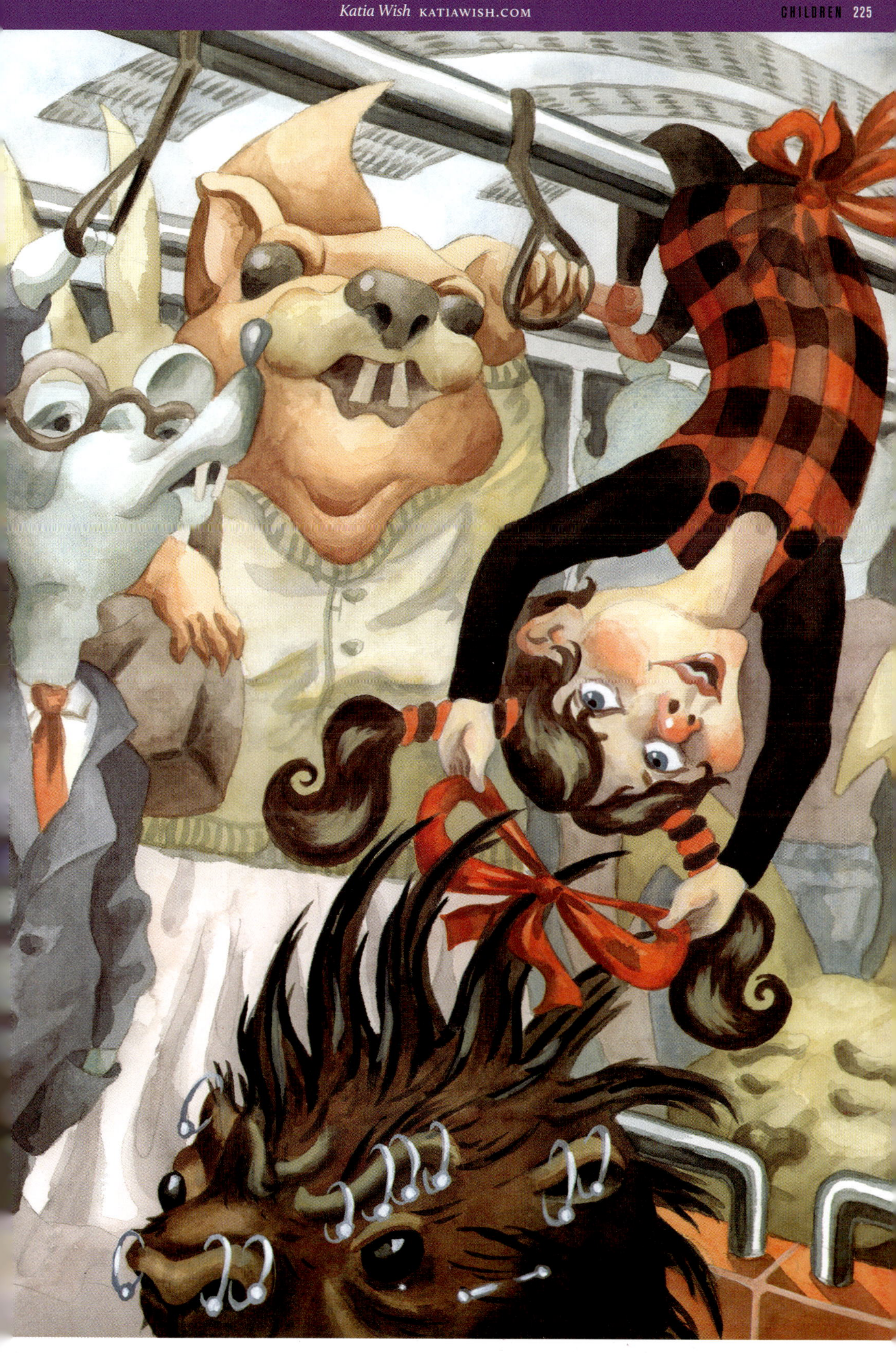

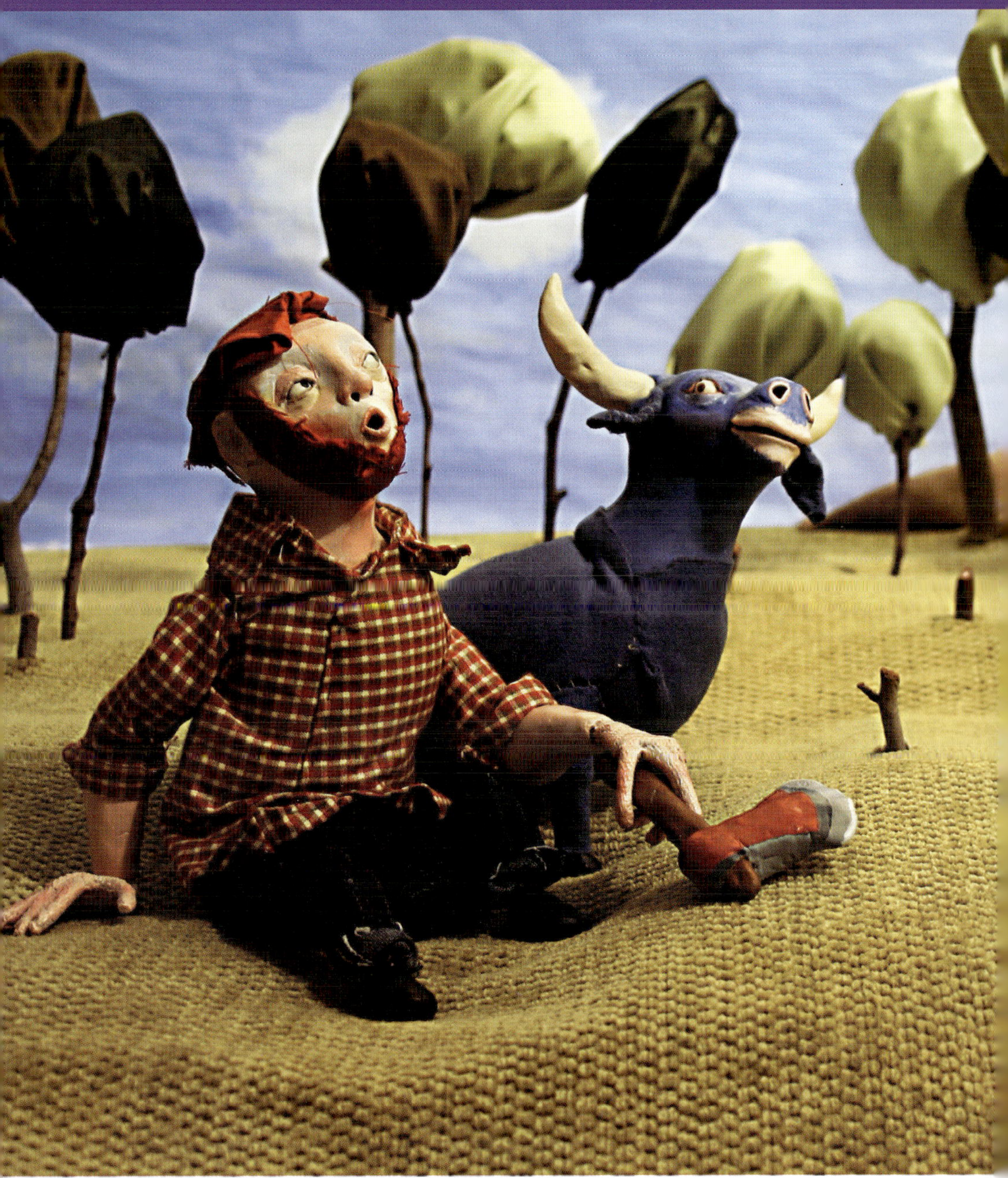

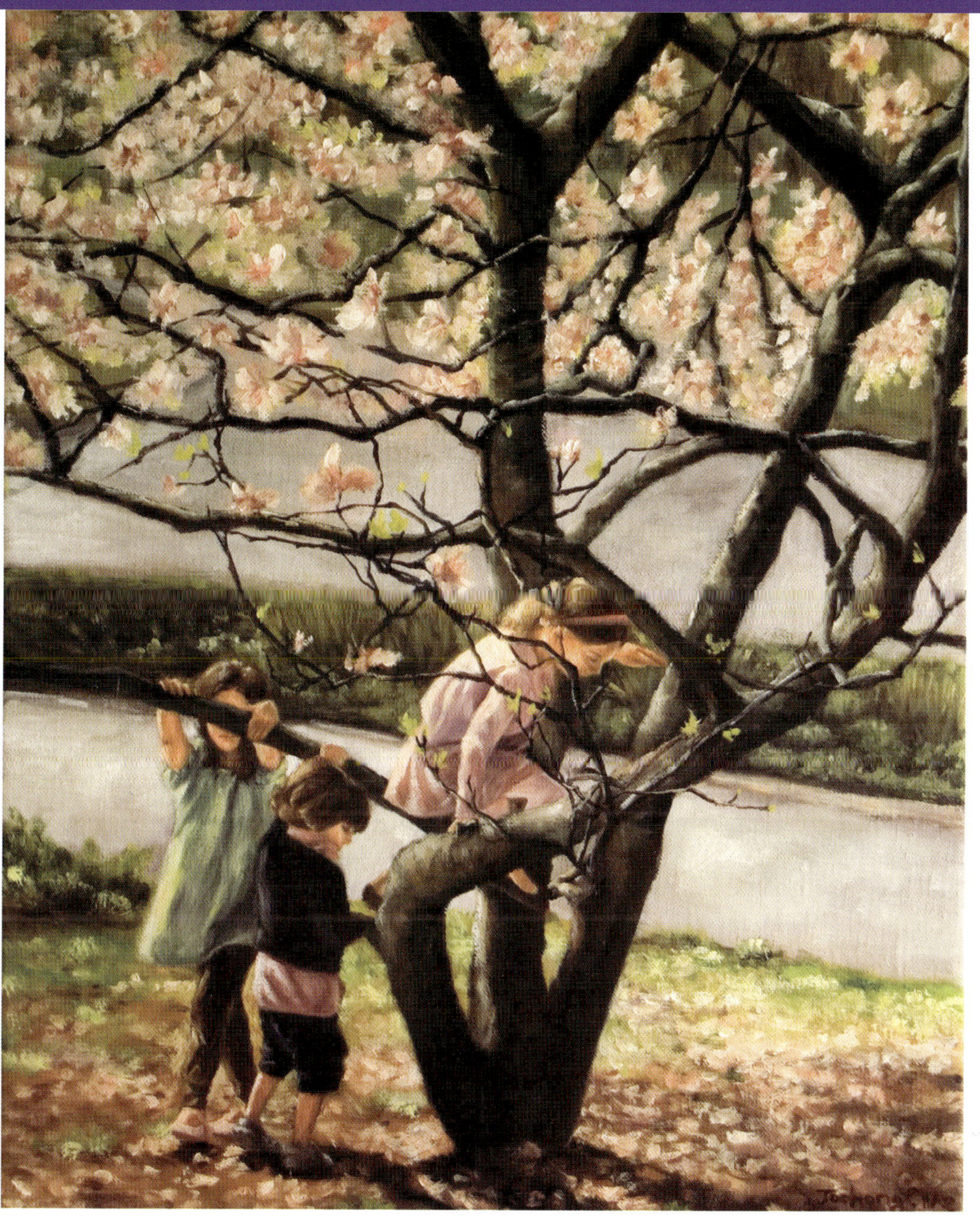

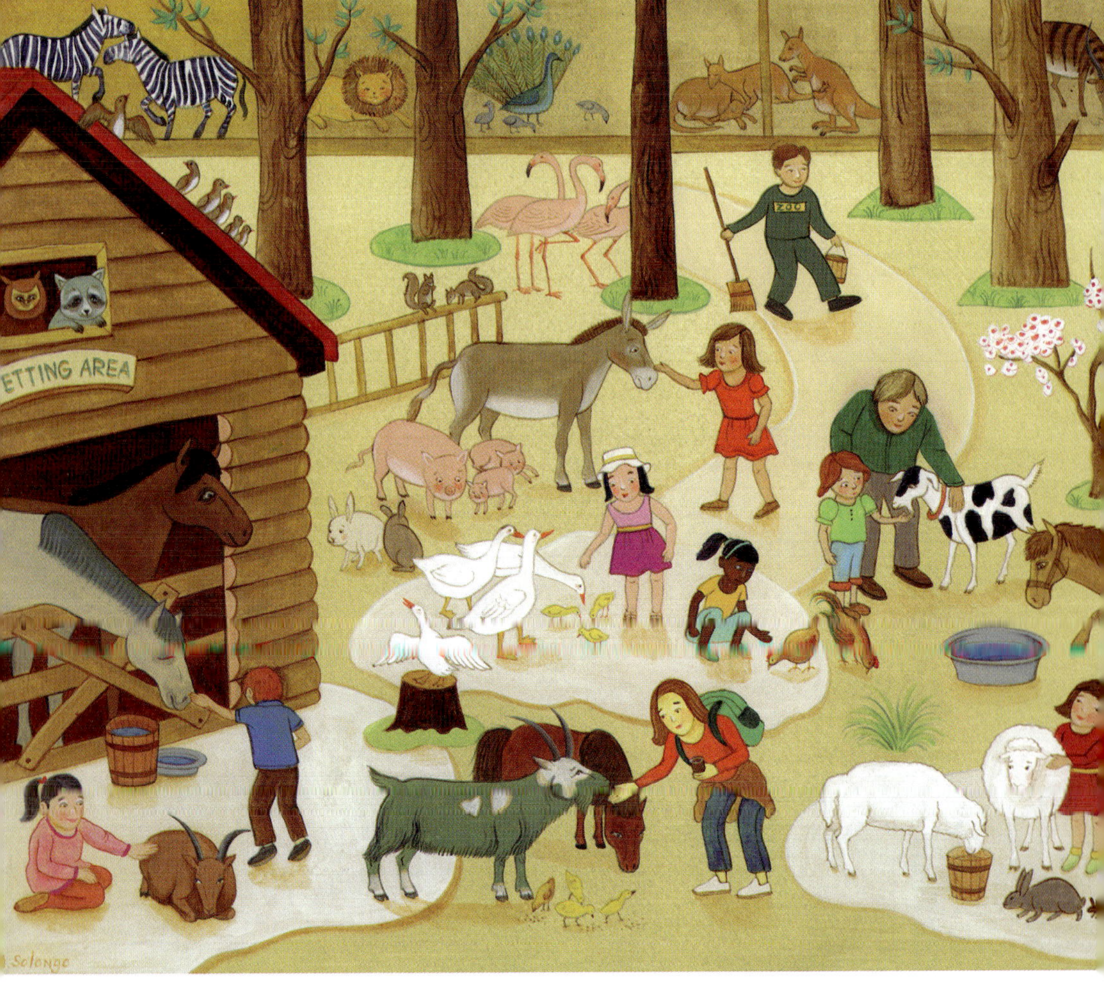
ETTING AREA
ZOO
Solongo

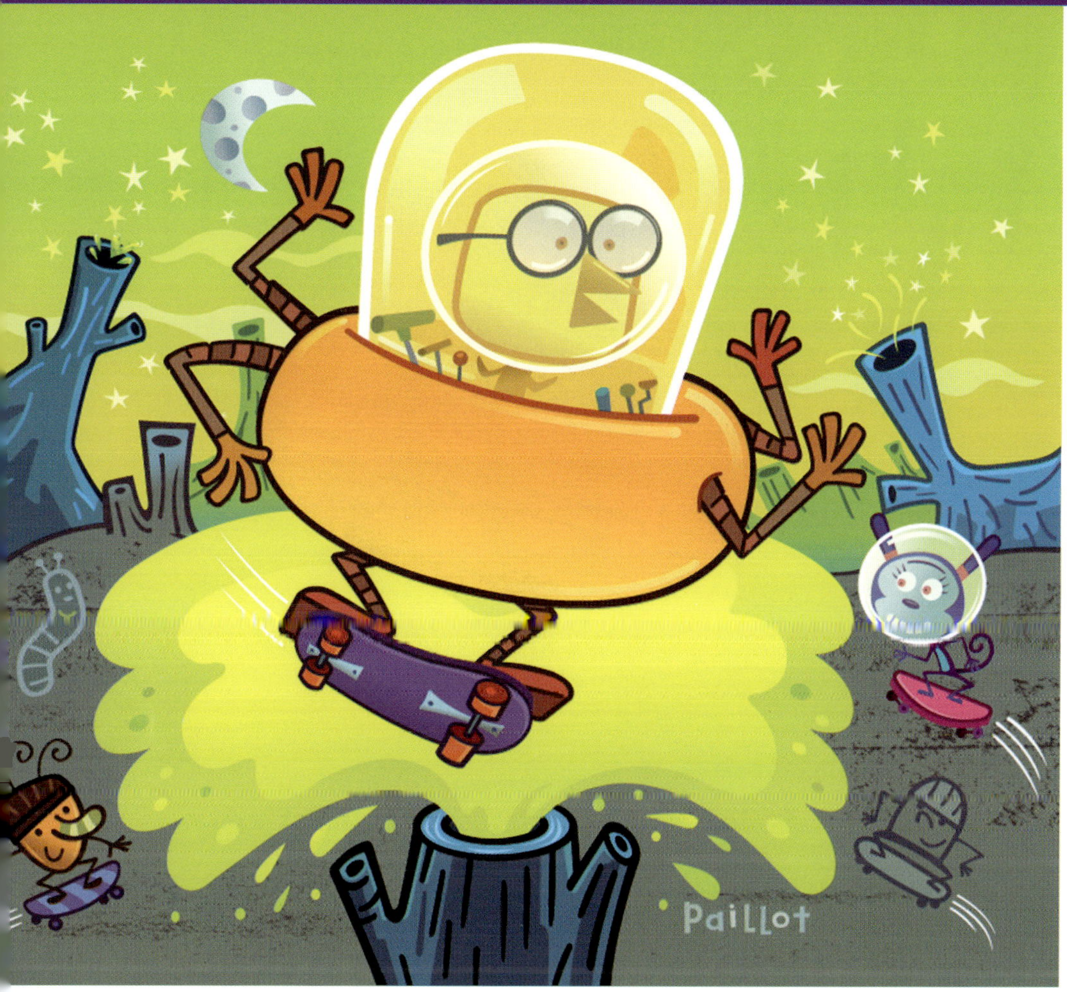
Paillot

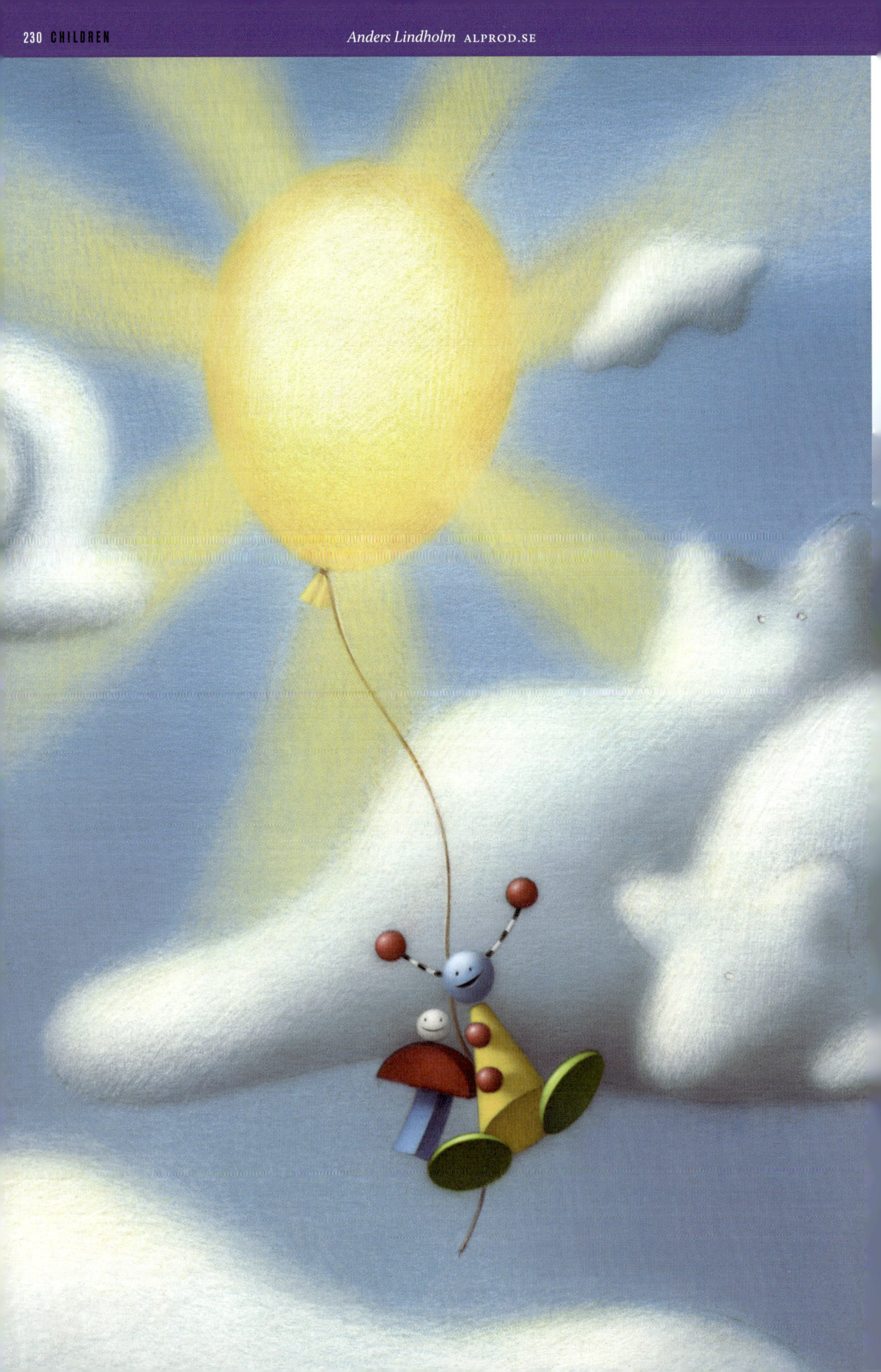

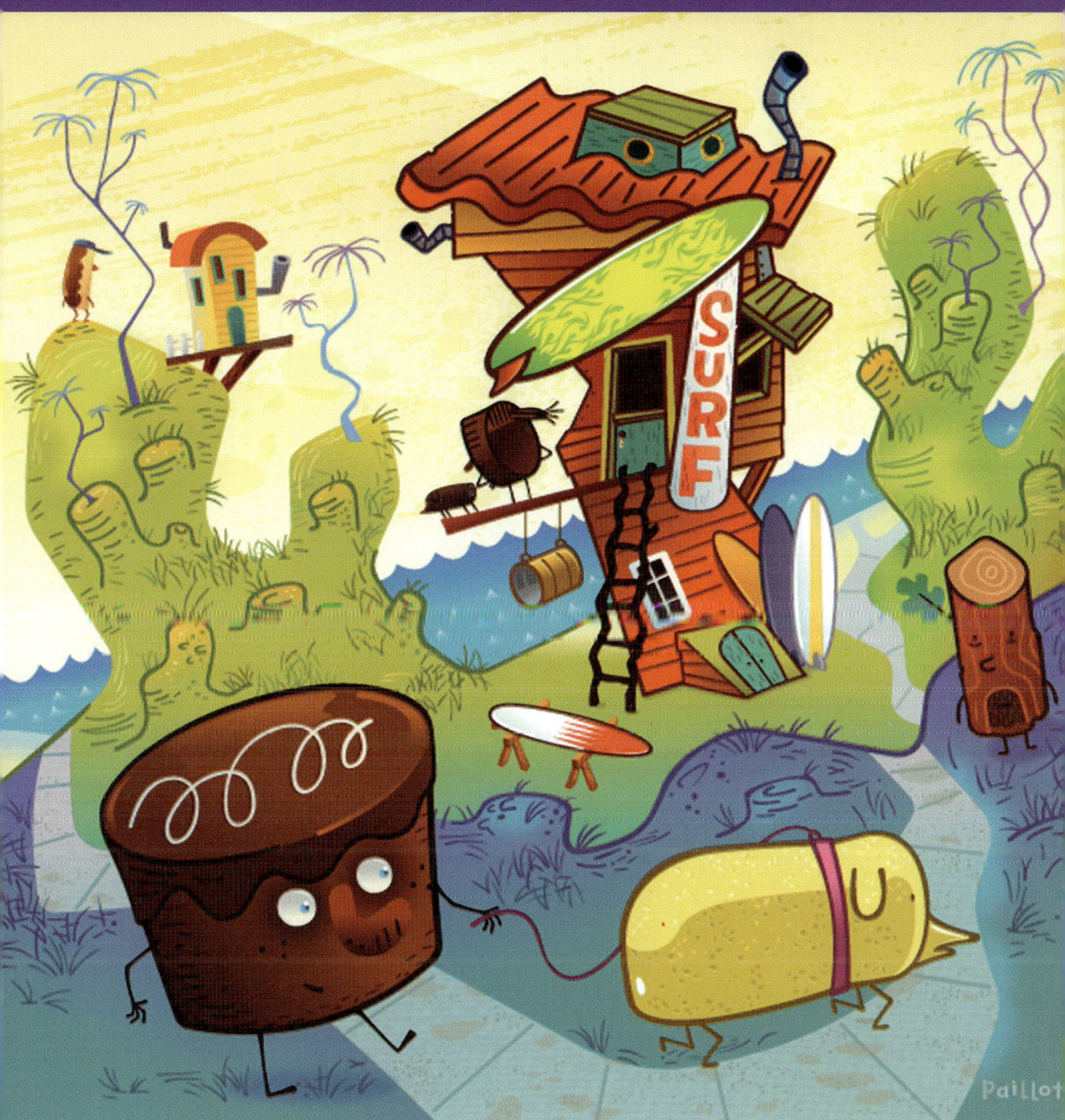
SURF

Andrew Mitchell AJMITCHELLART.COM

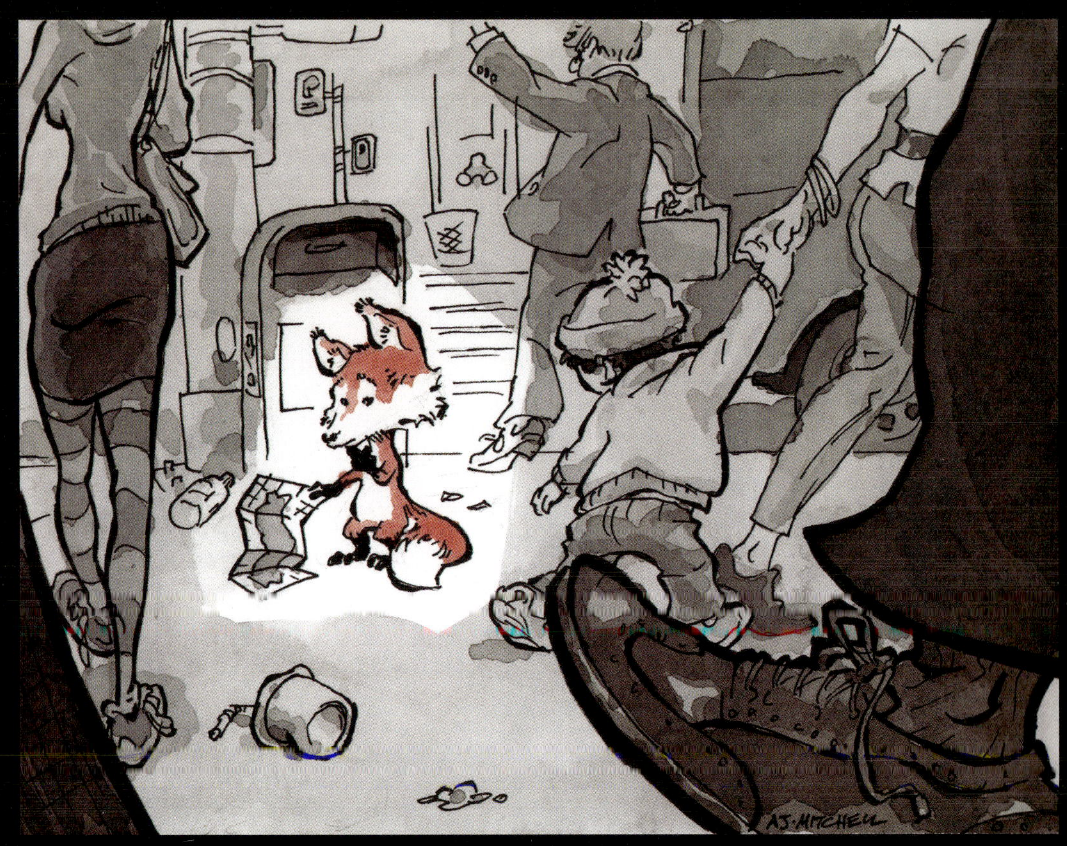

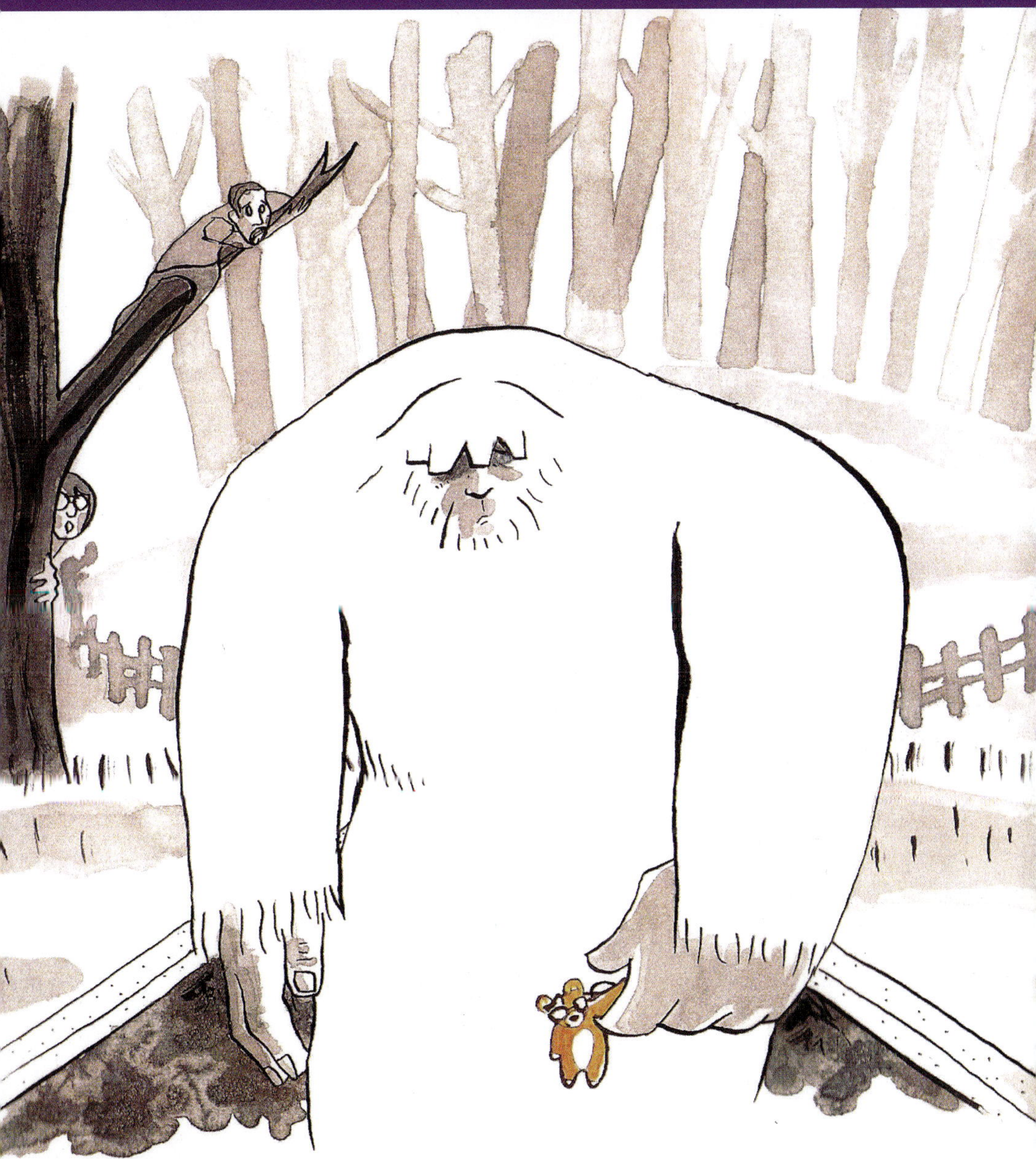

Chris French GRAFICPACIFIC.COM

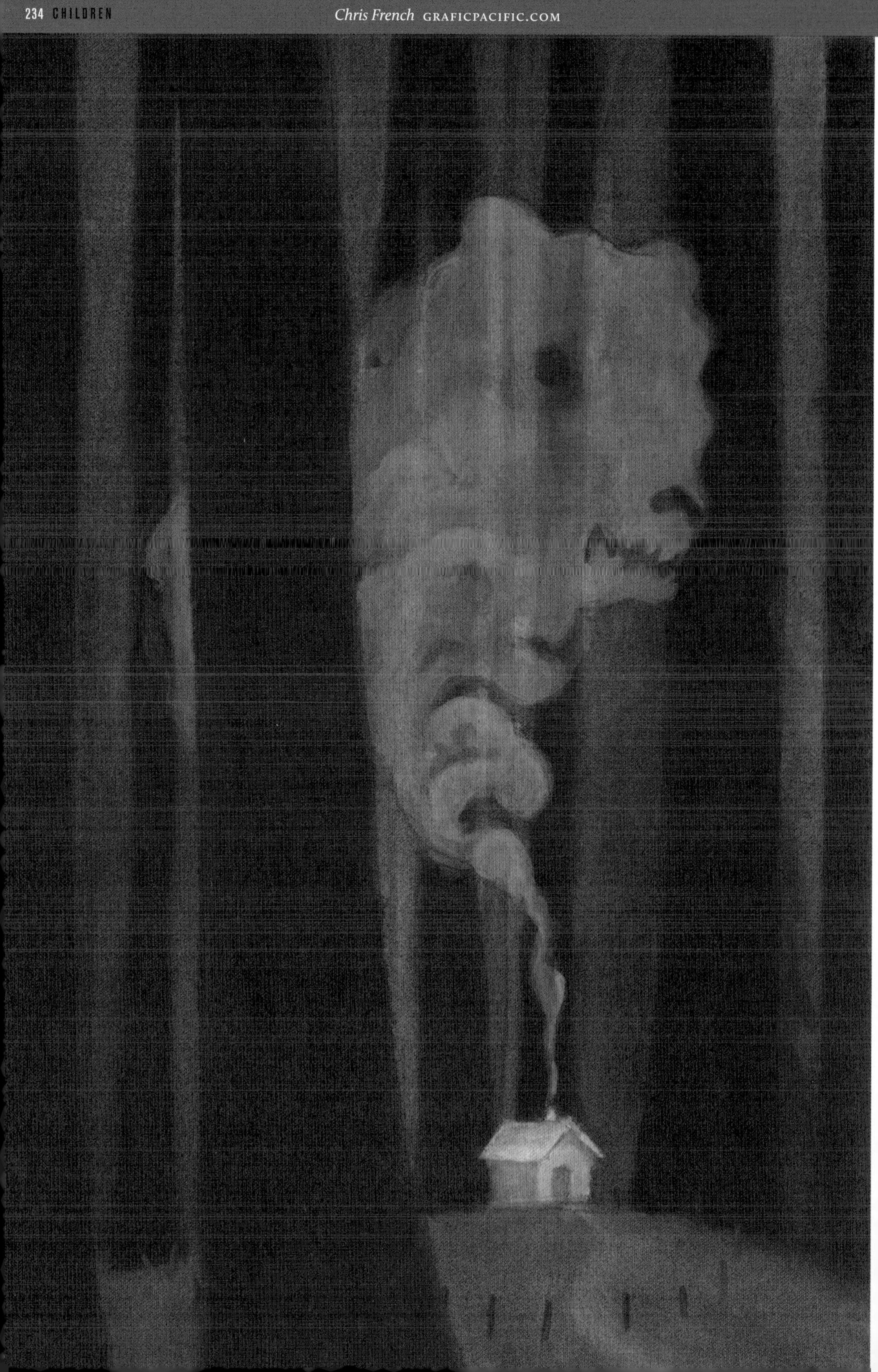

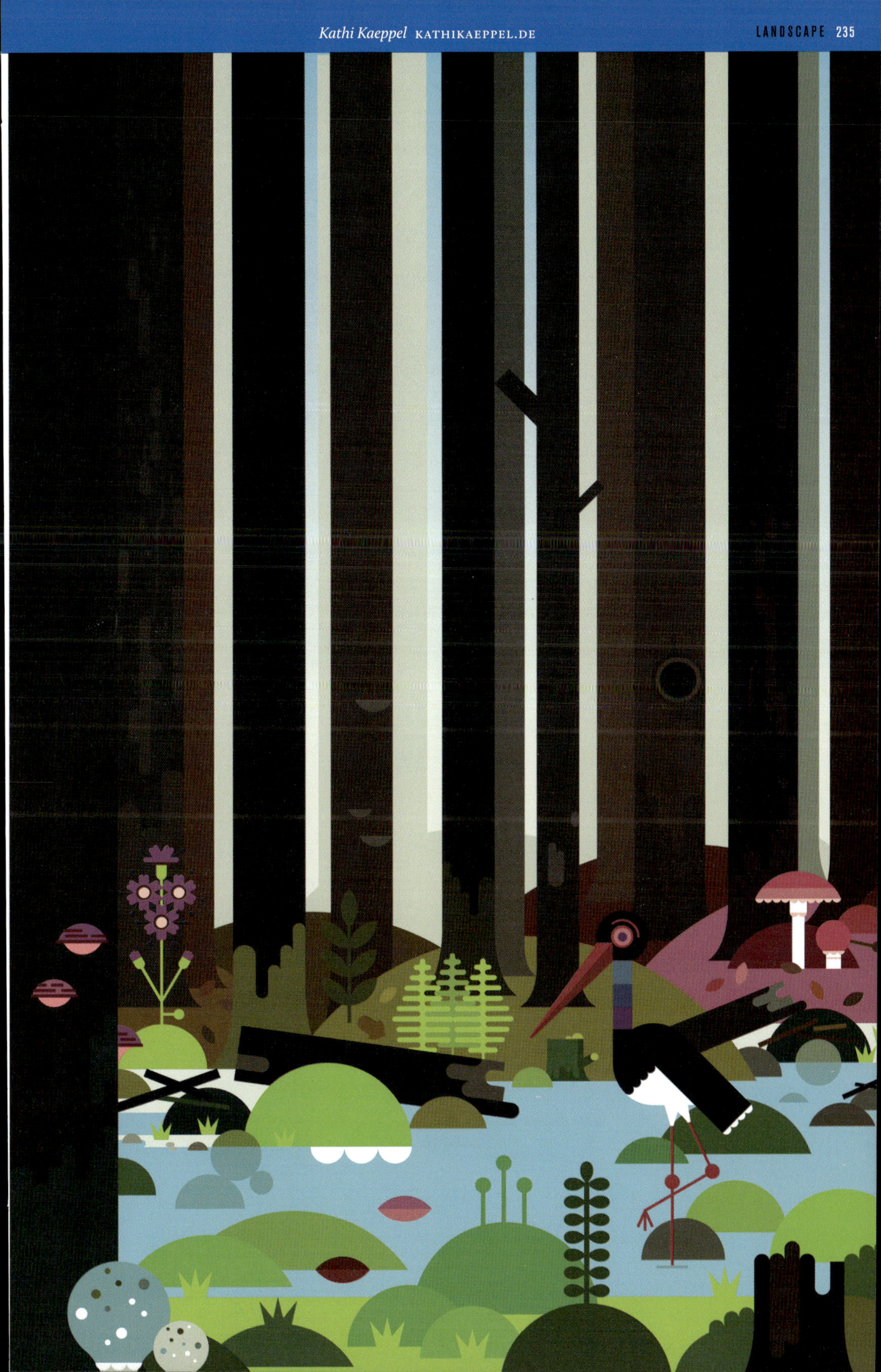

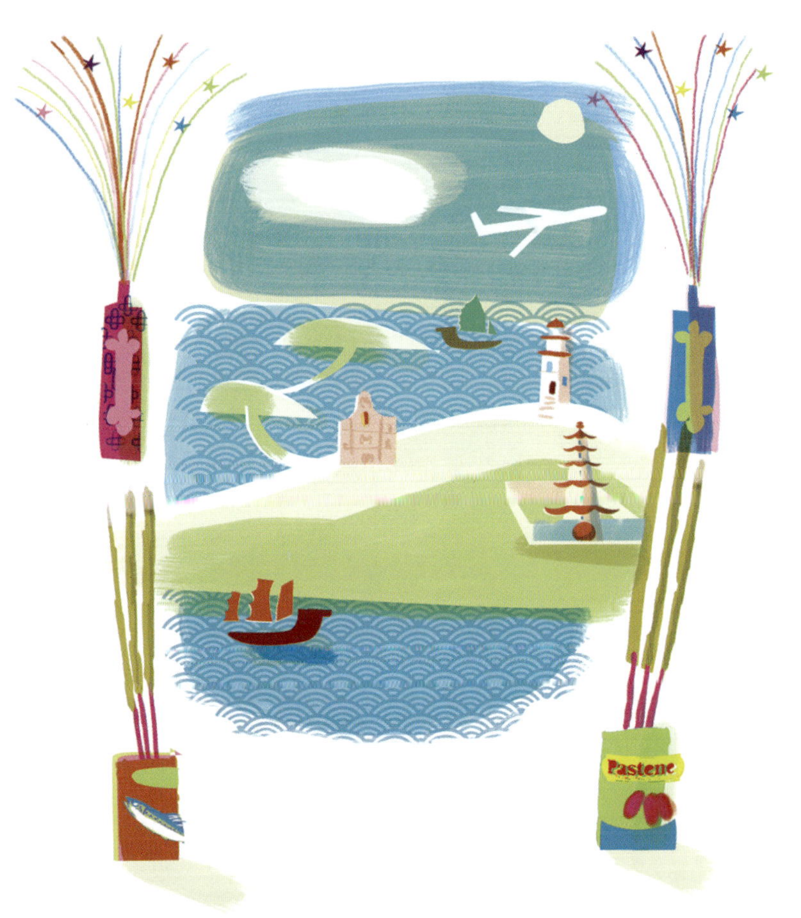

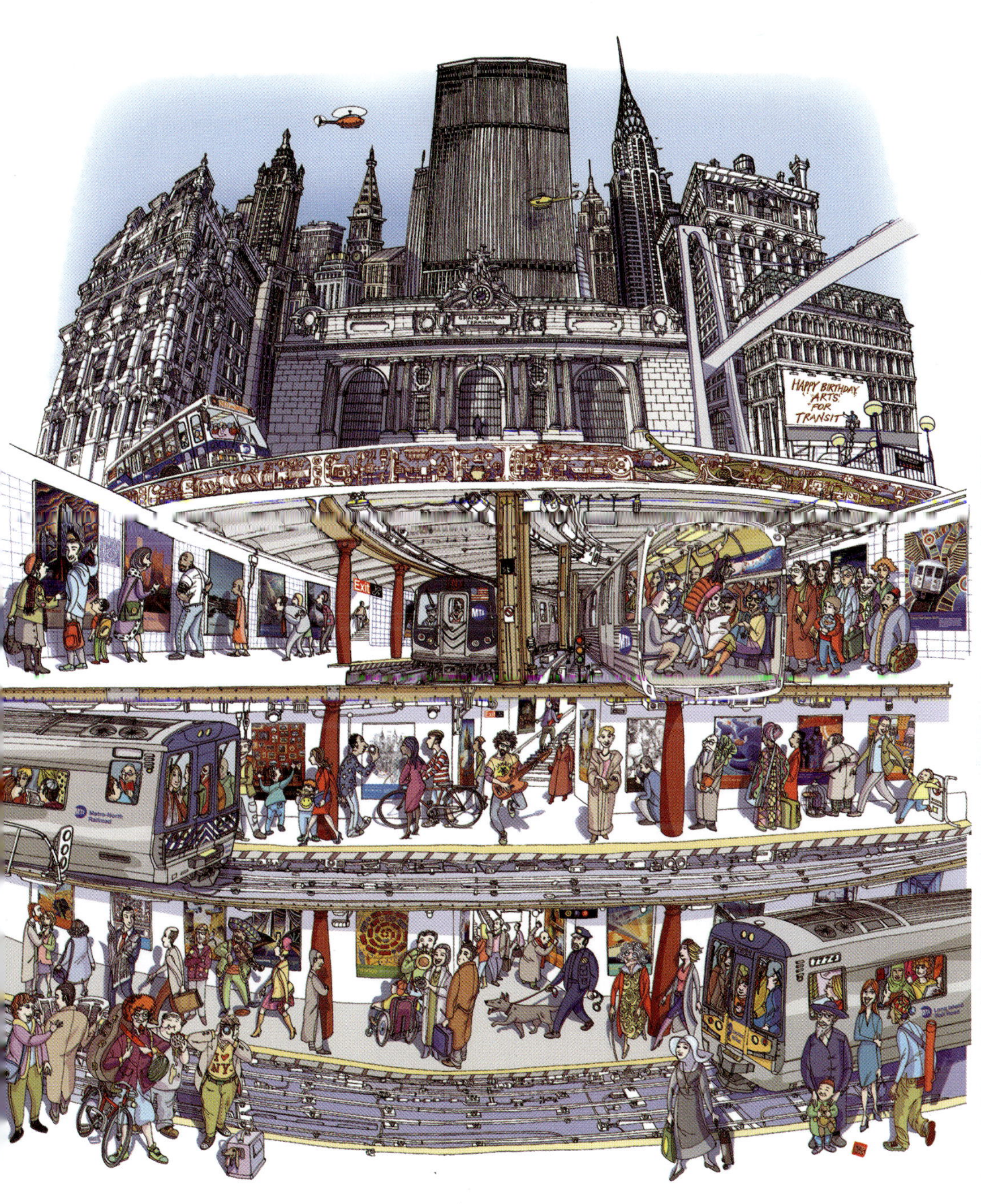
HAPPY BIRTHDAY
ARTS
FOR
TRANSIT
Exit
Metro-North
Railroad
MTA
I ♥ NY

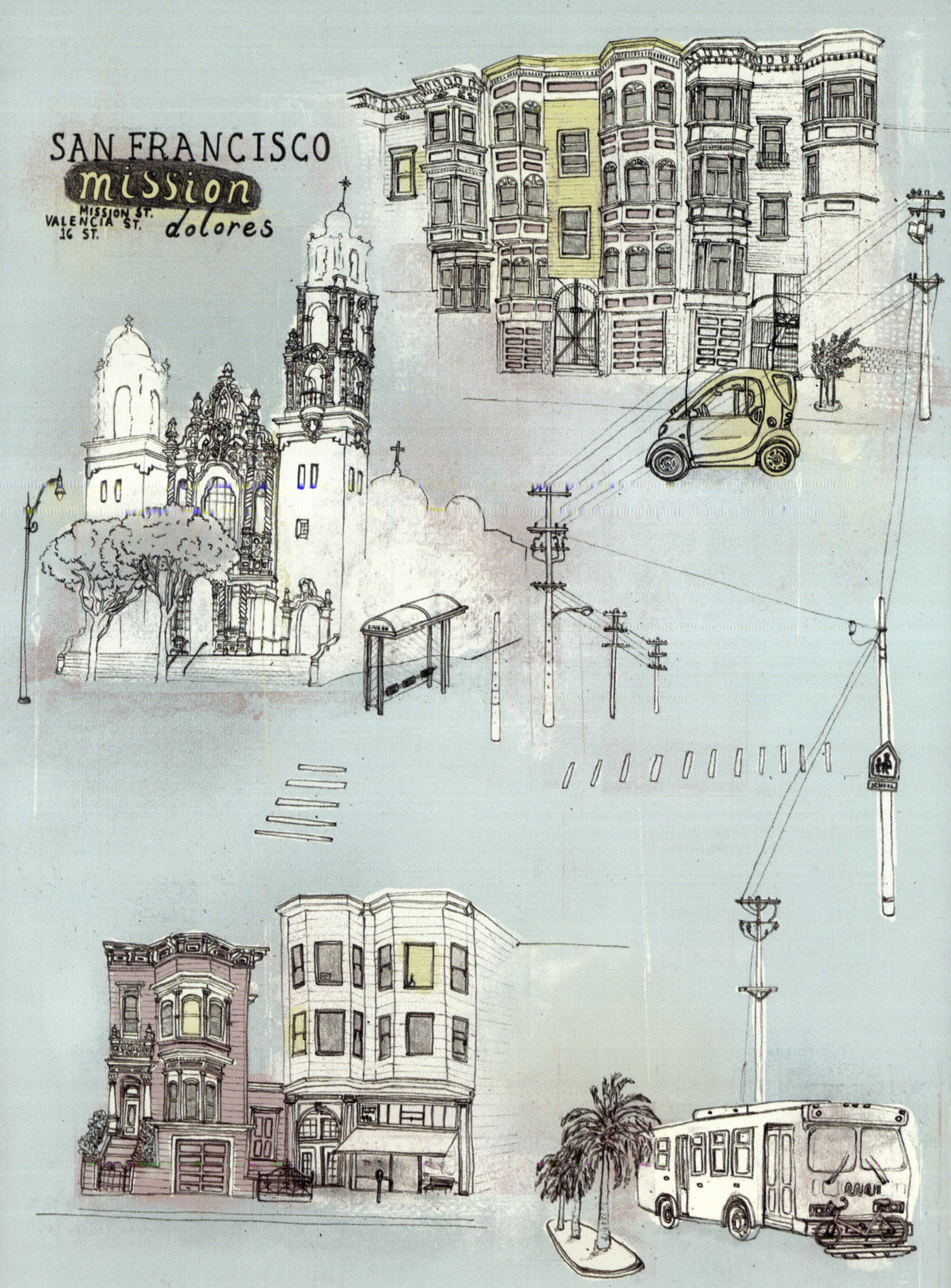
SAN FRANCISCO
mission
dolores
MISSION ST.
VALENCIA ST.
16 ST.

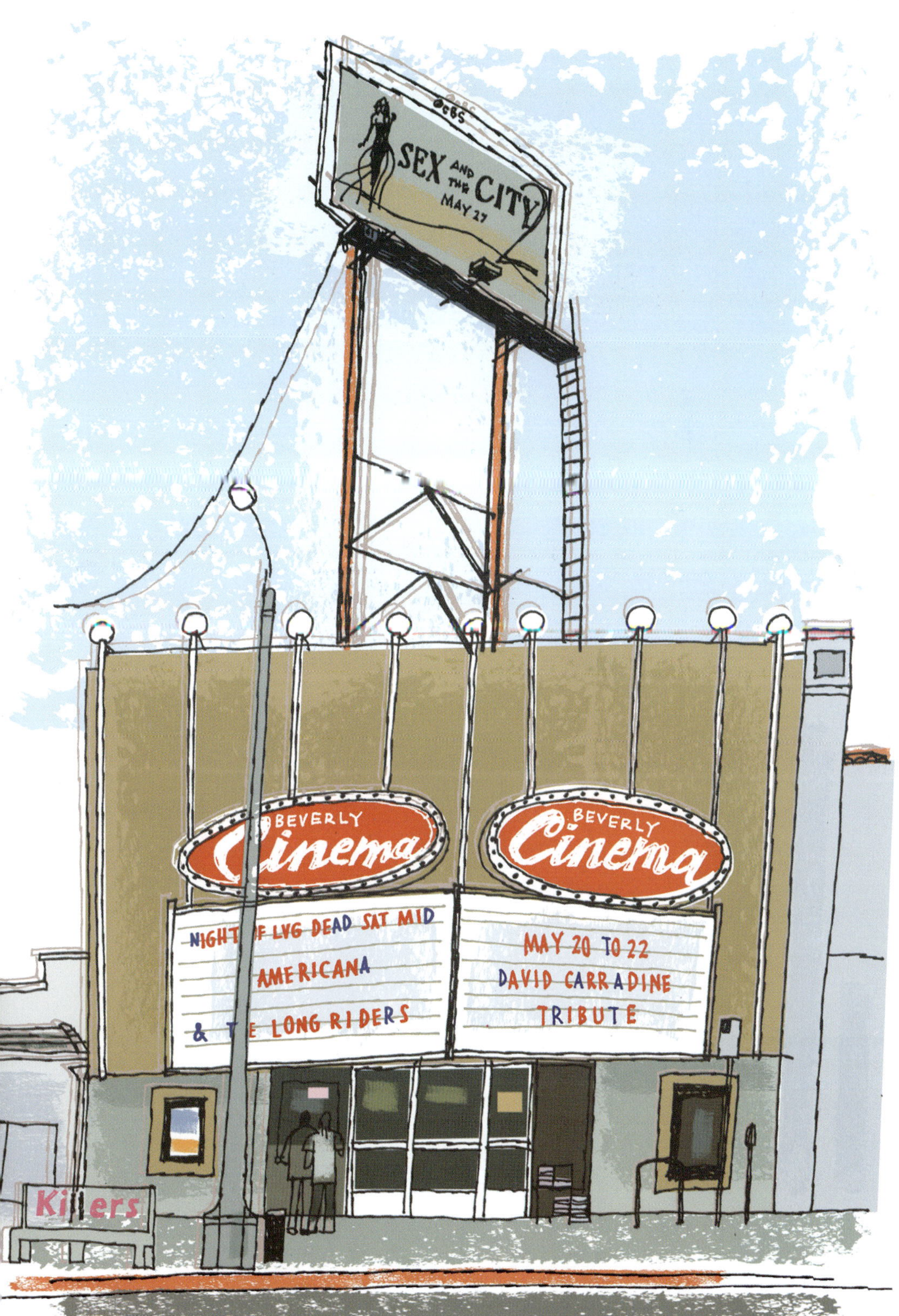
CBS
SEX AND THE CITY MAY 27
BEVERLY
Cinema
BEVERLY
Cinema
NIGHT OF LVG DEAD SAT MID
AMERICANA
& THE LONG RIDERS
MAY 20 TO 22
DAVID CARRADINE
TRIBUTE
Killers

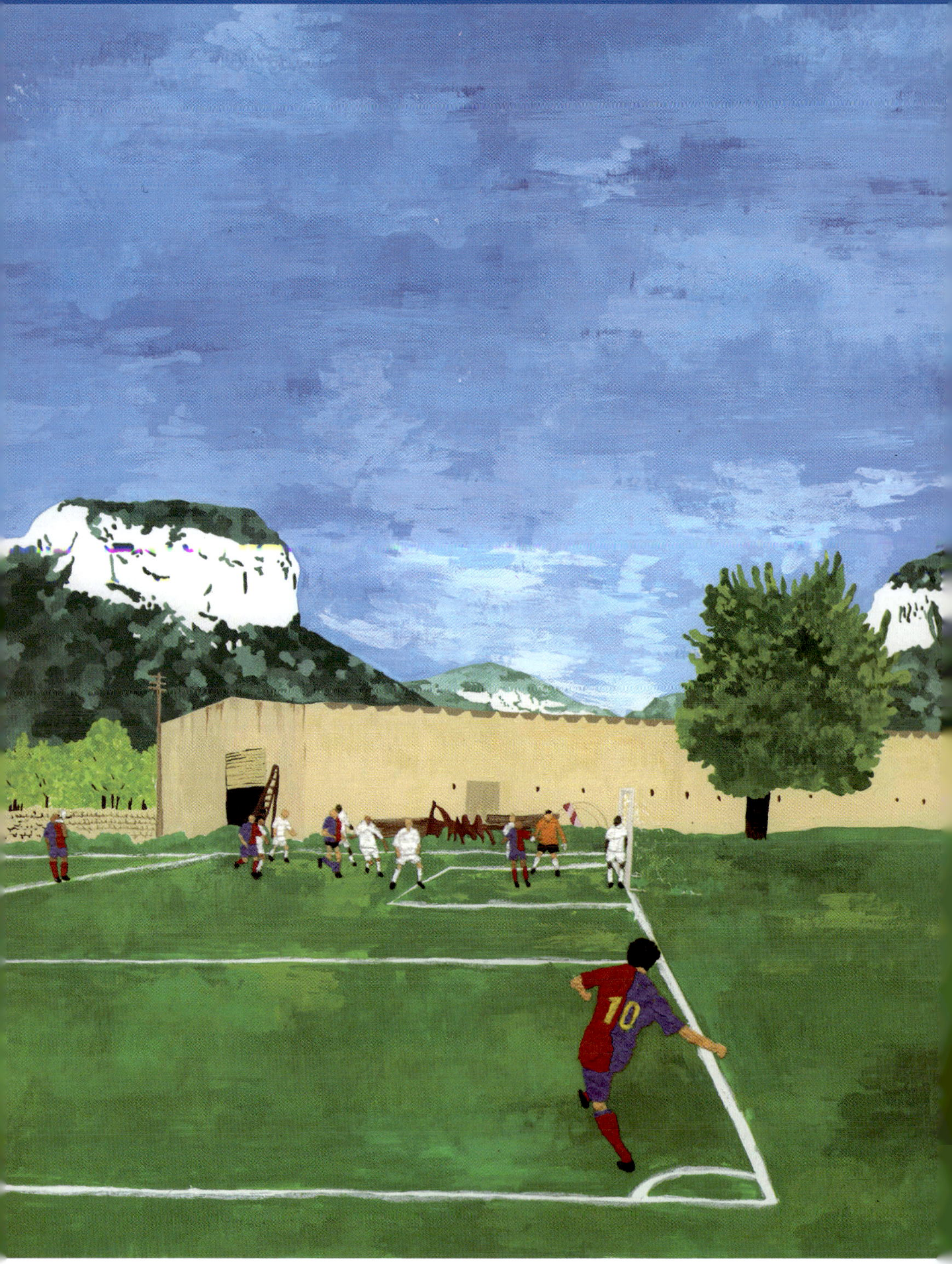

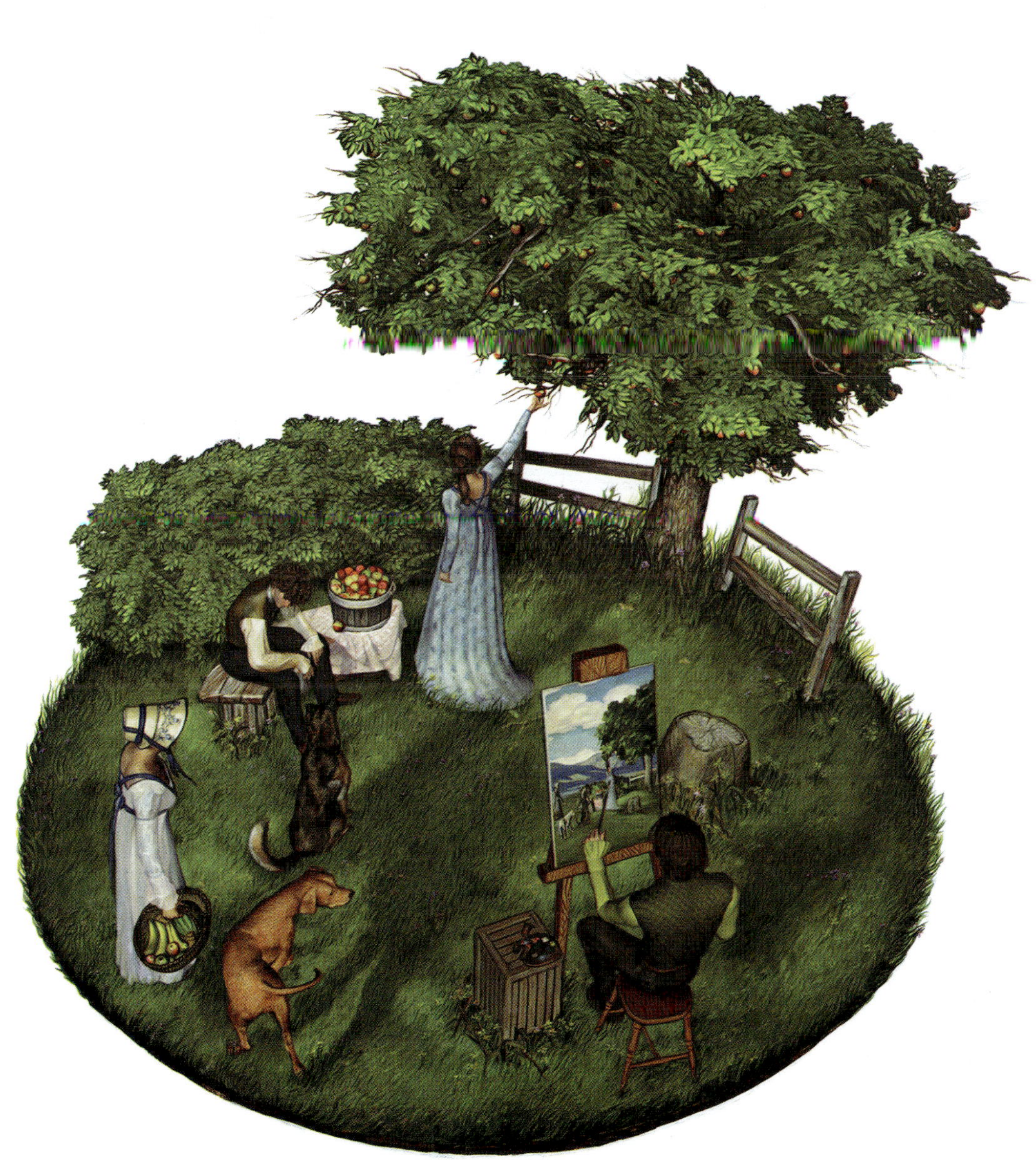

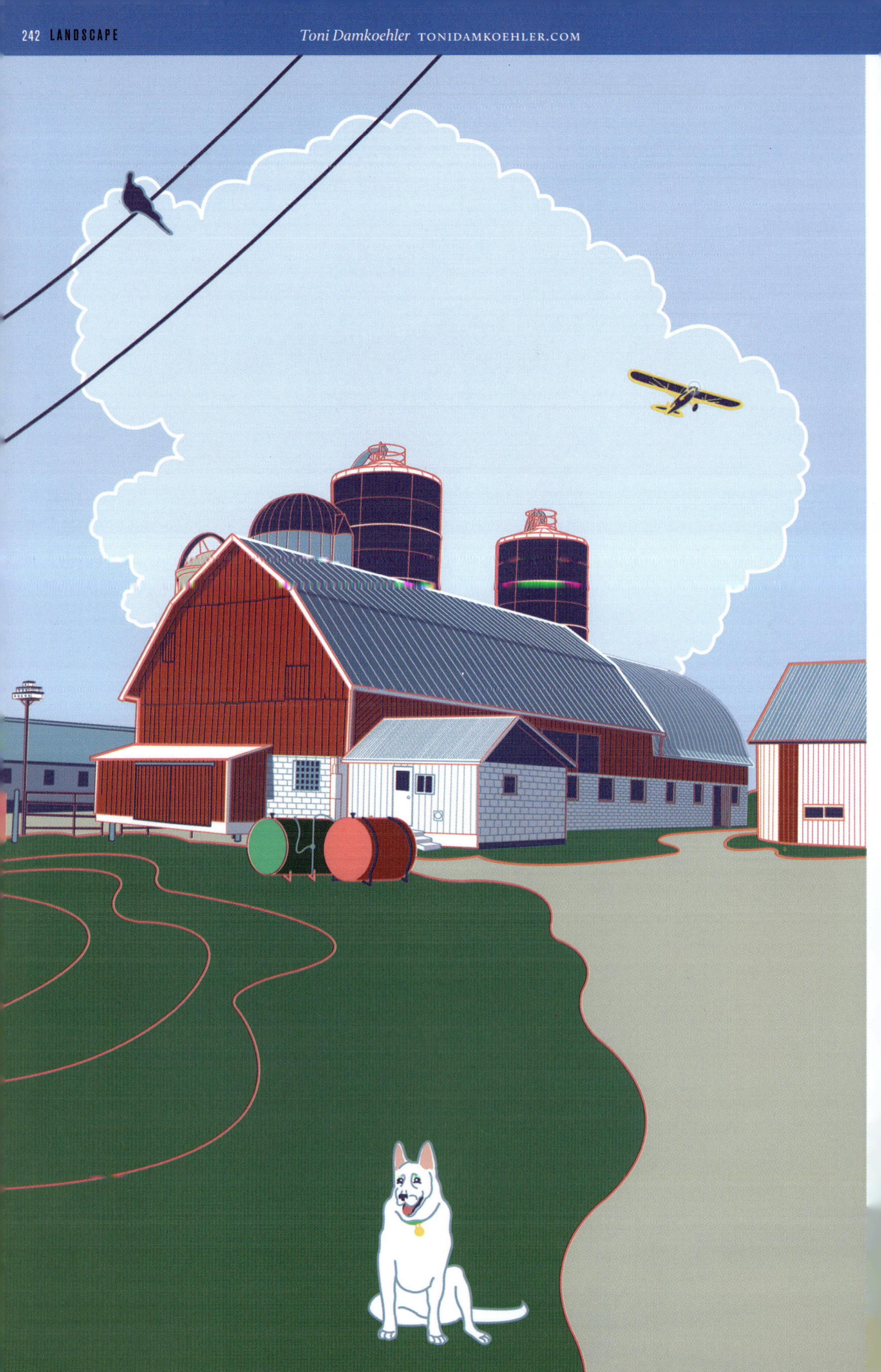

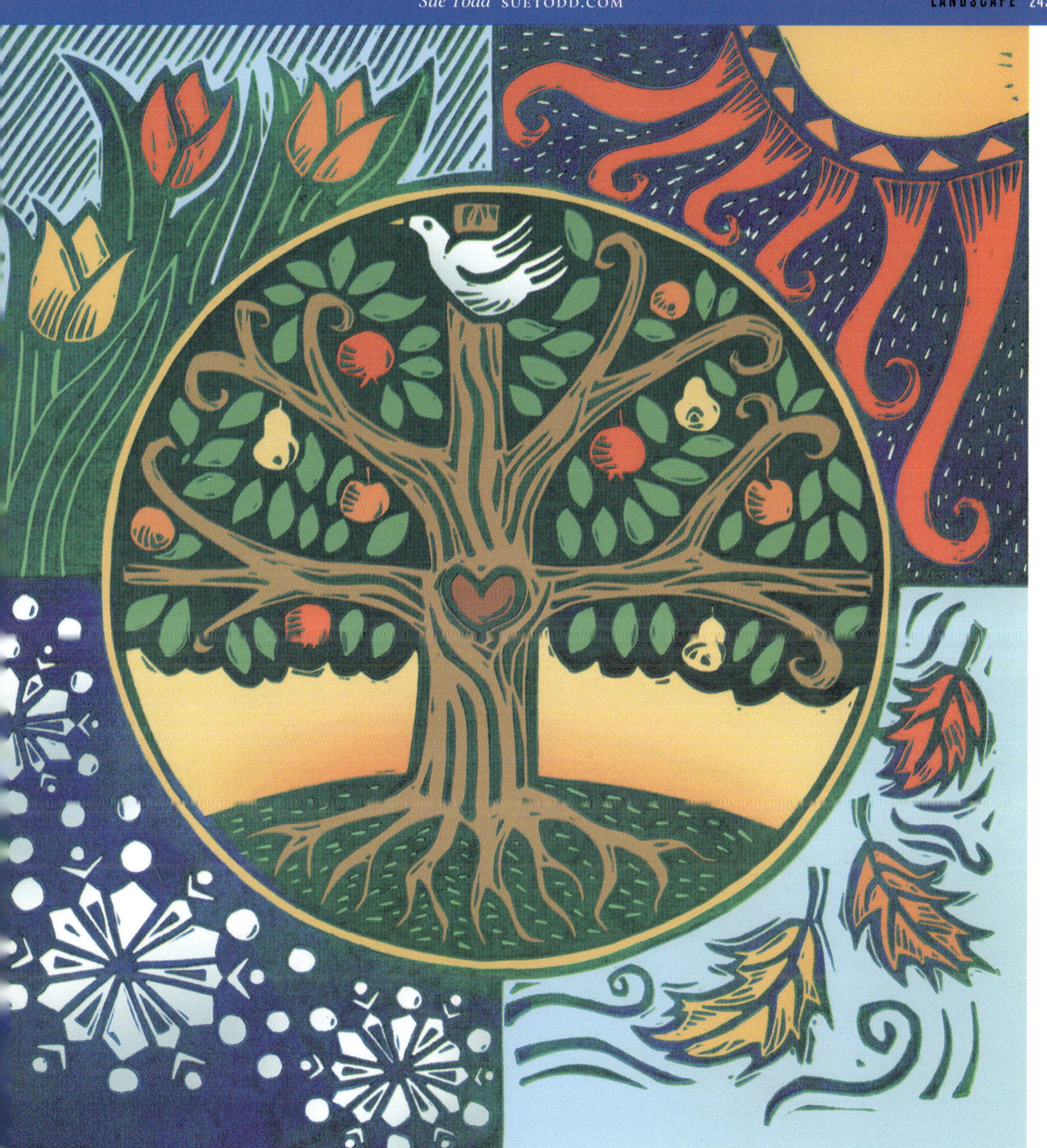

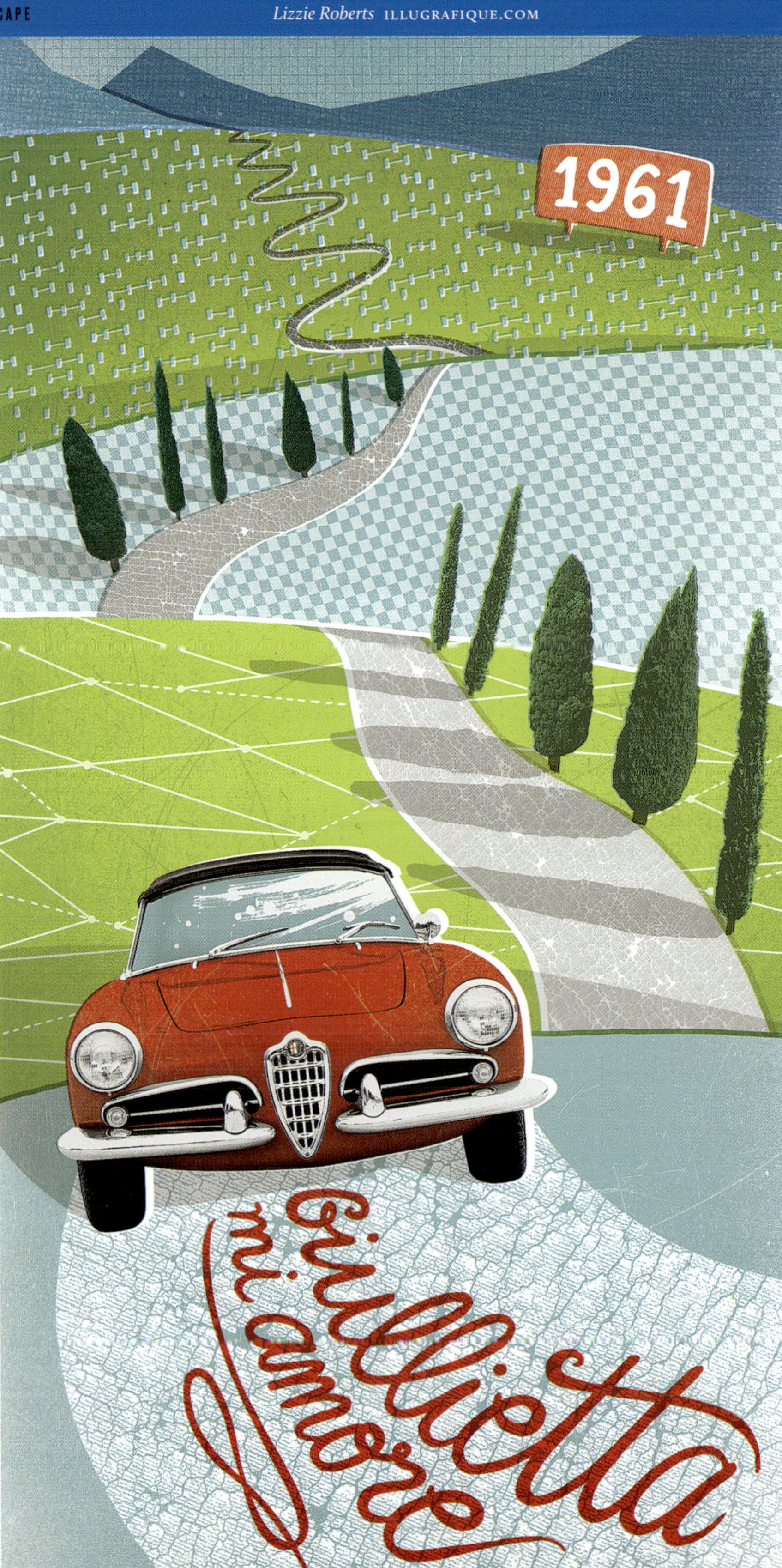
1961
Giulietta mi amore

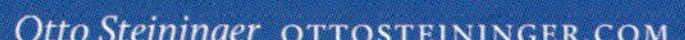
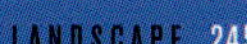

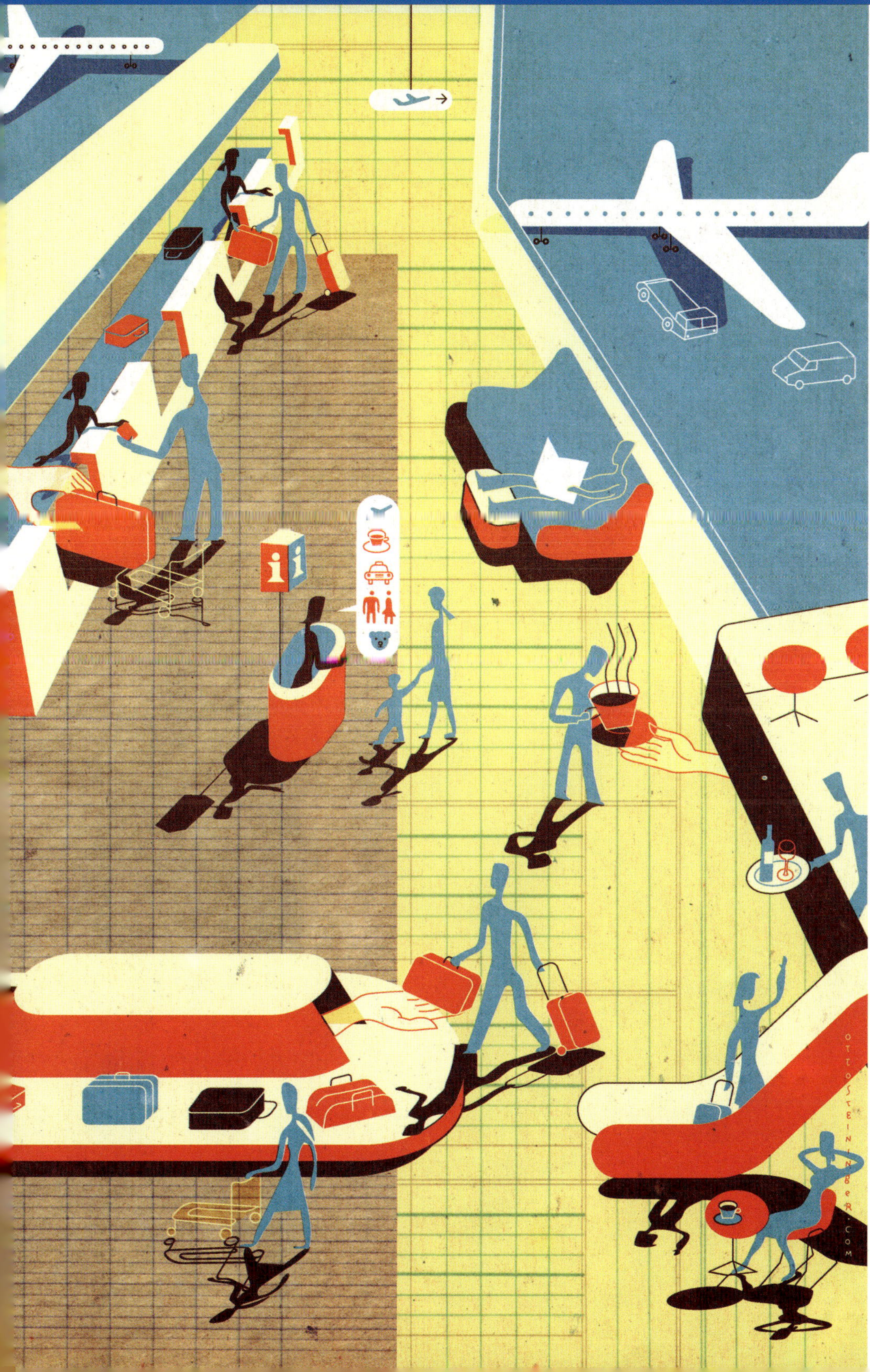

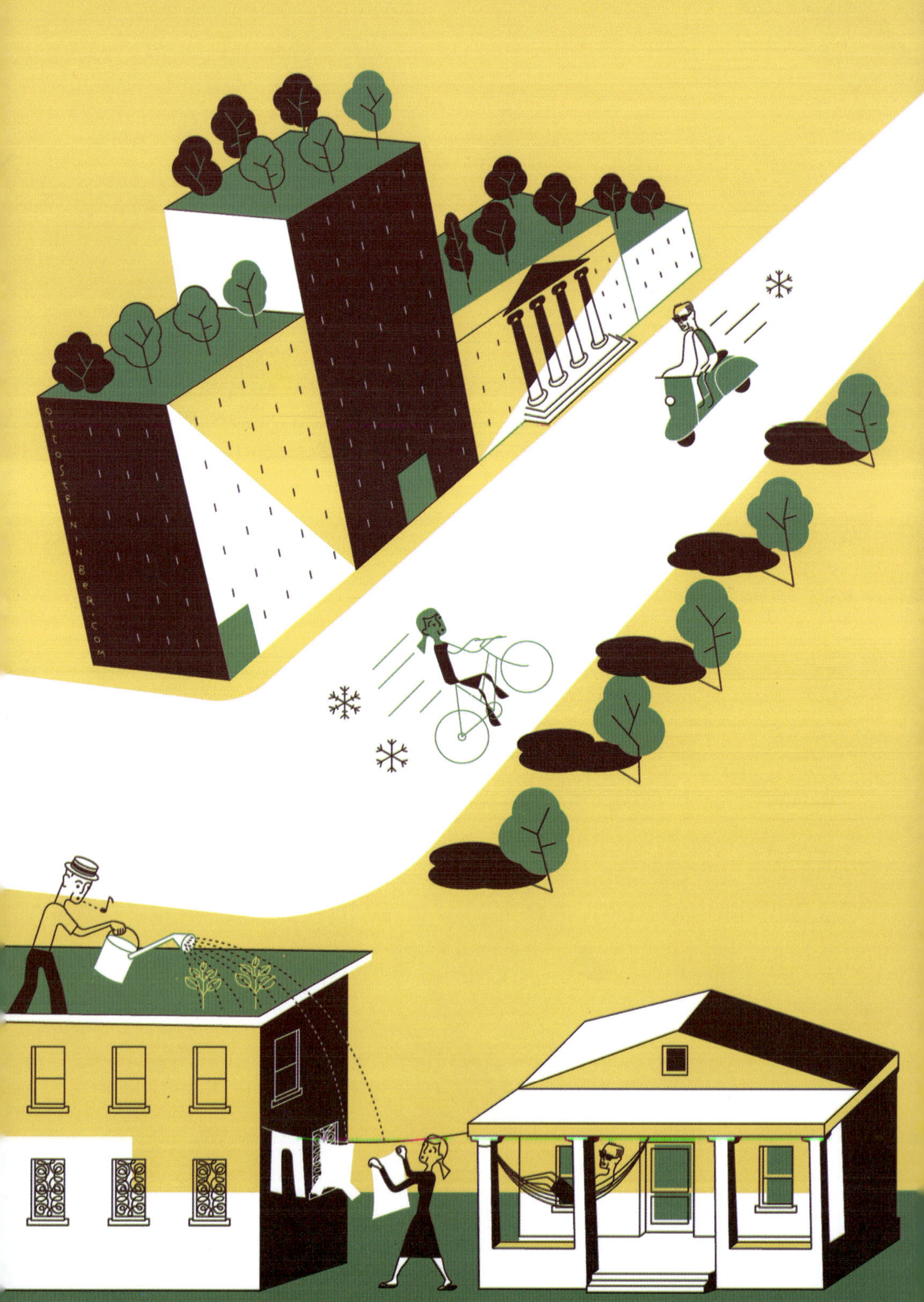
OTTOSTEININGER.COM

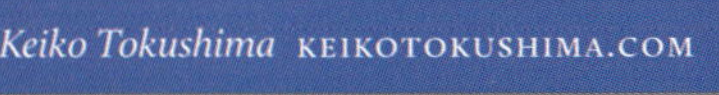

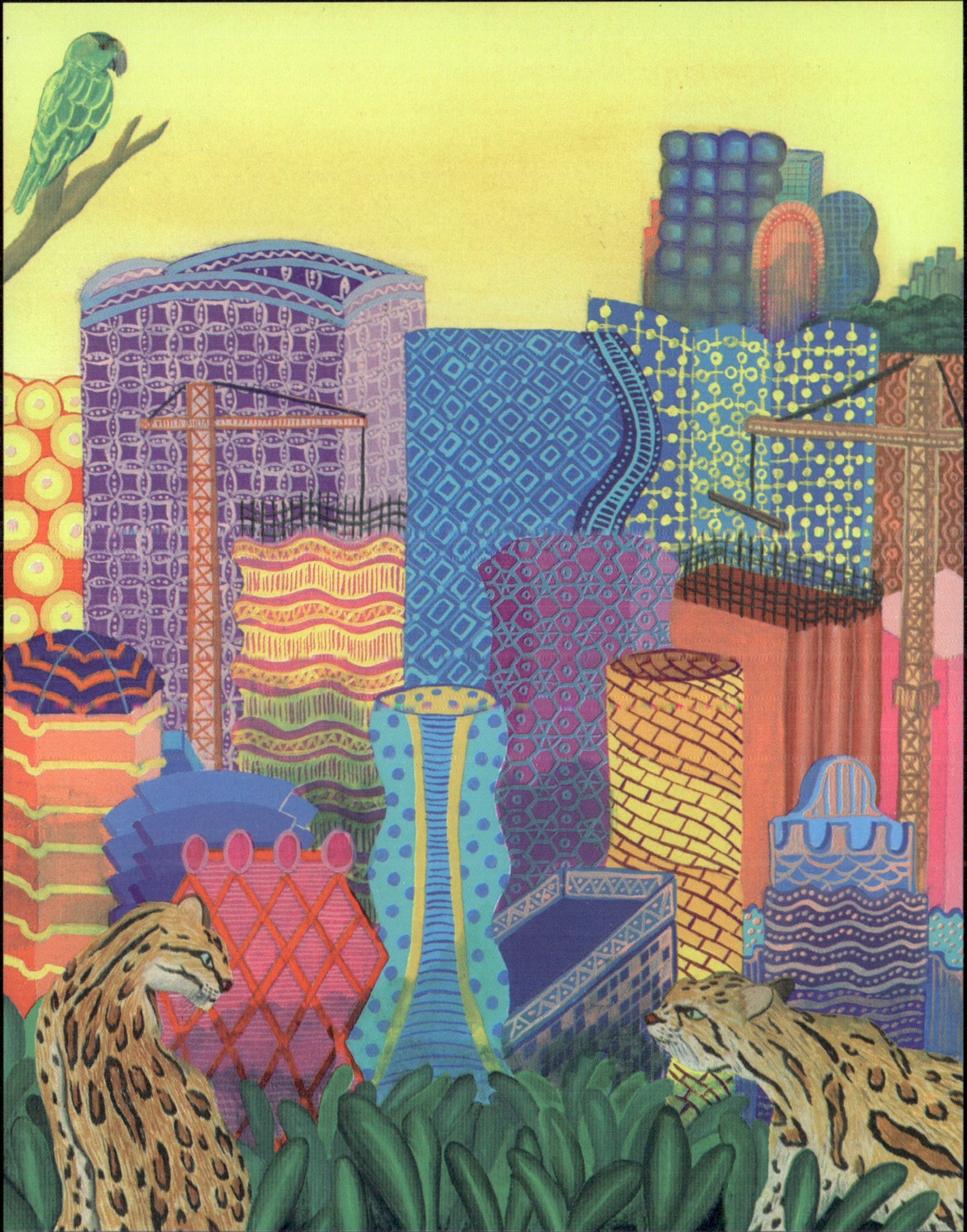

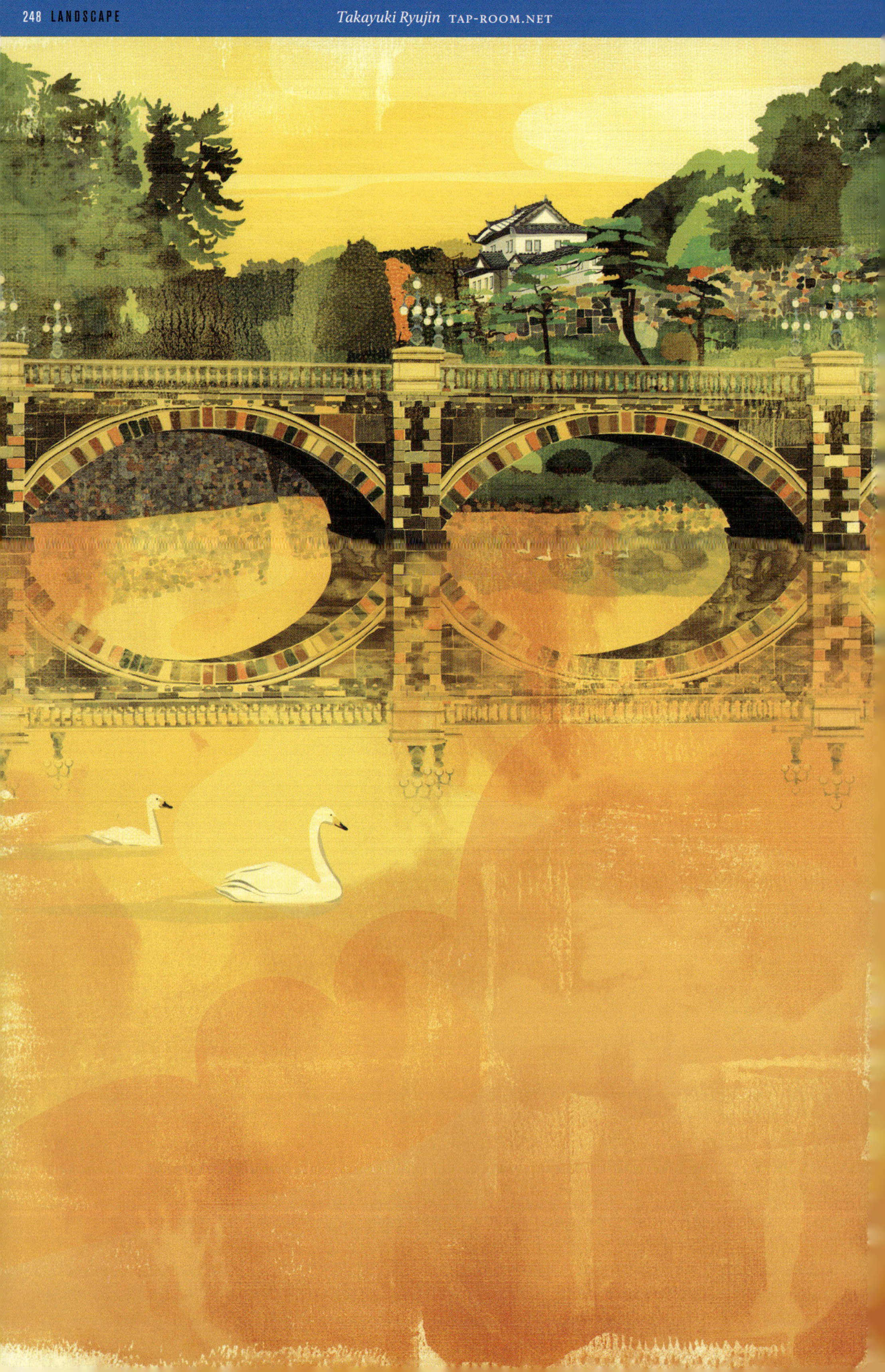

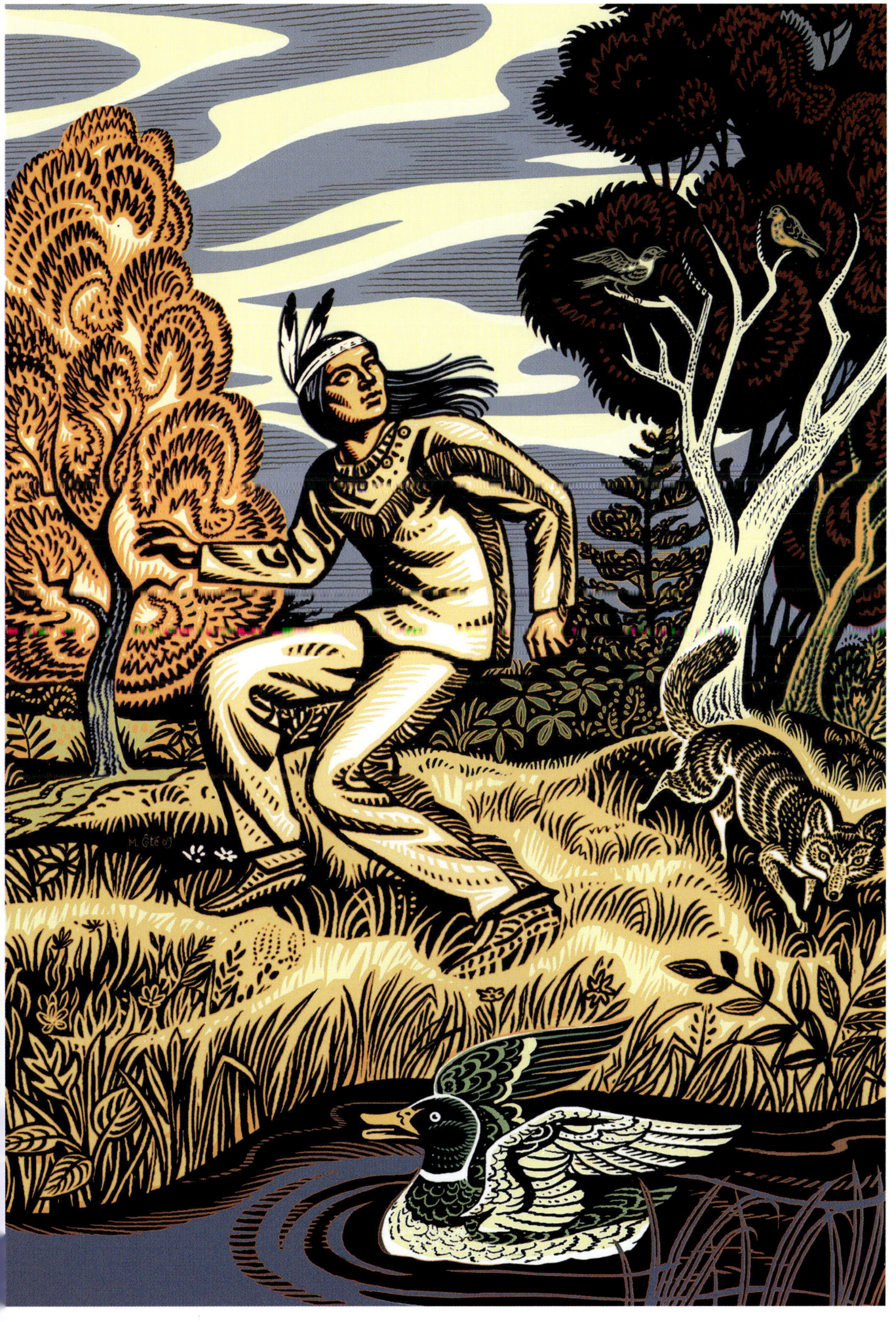

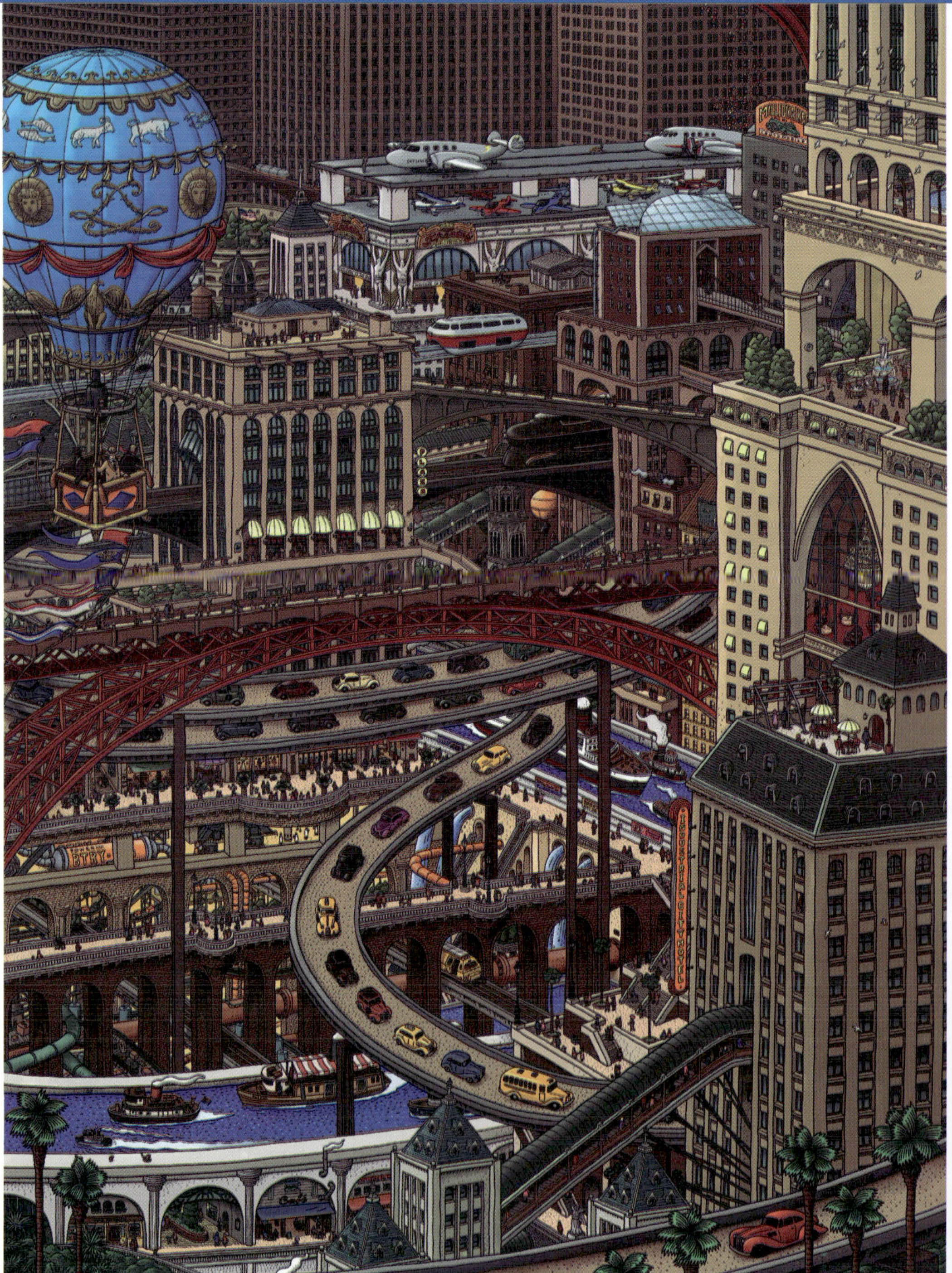

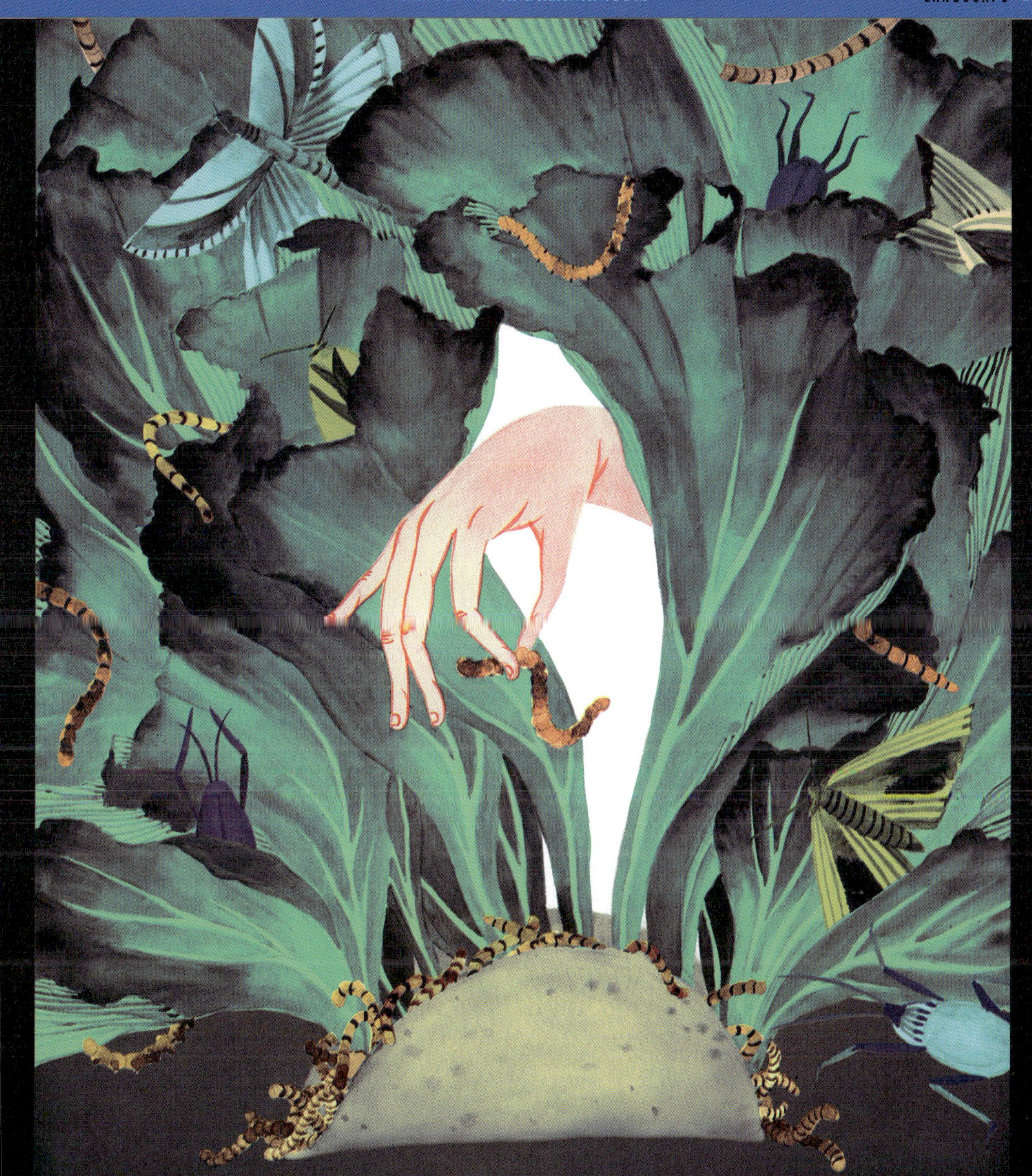

 Lars Henkel REFLEKTORIUM.DE

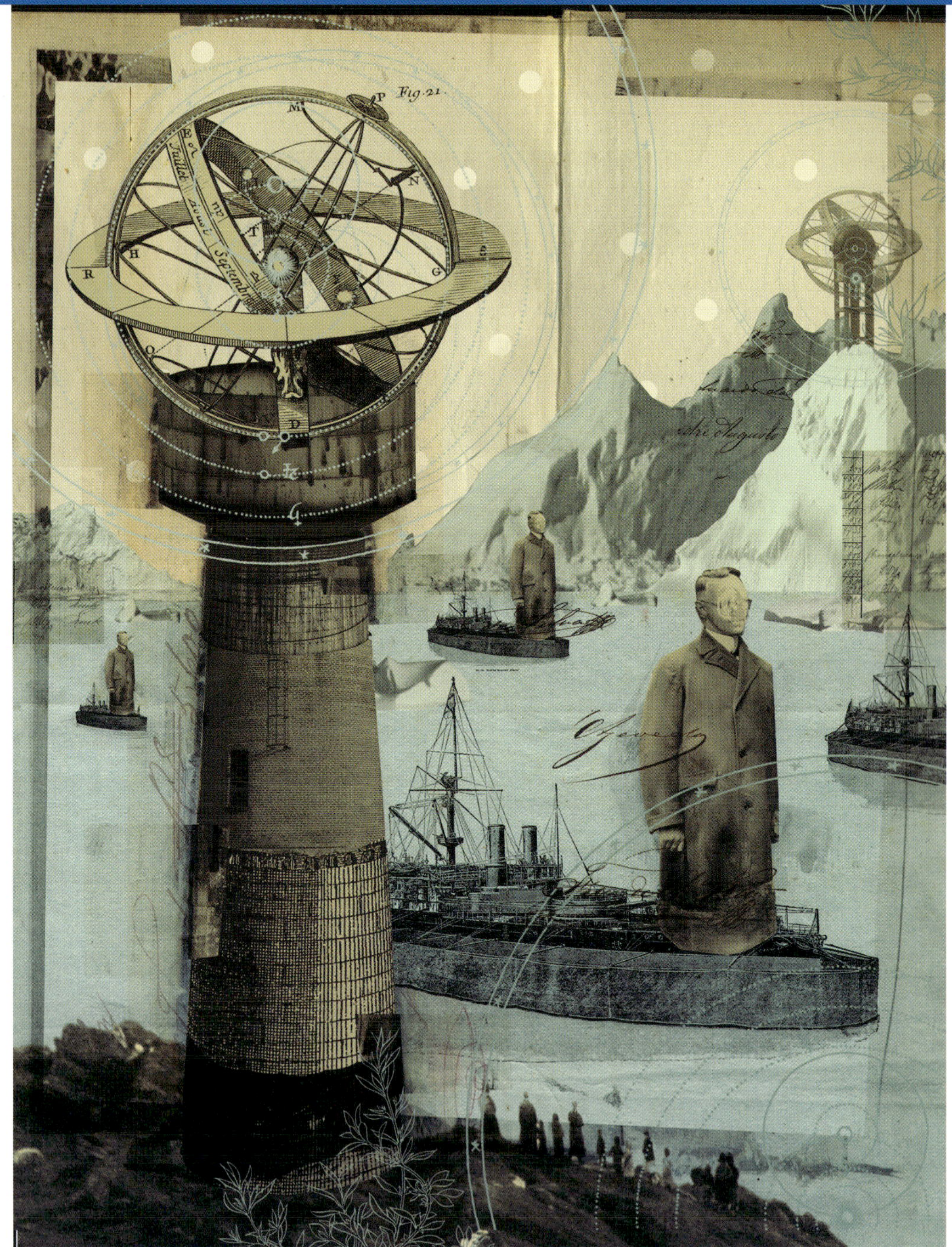

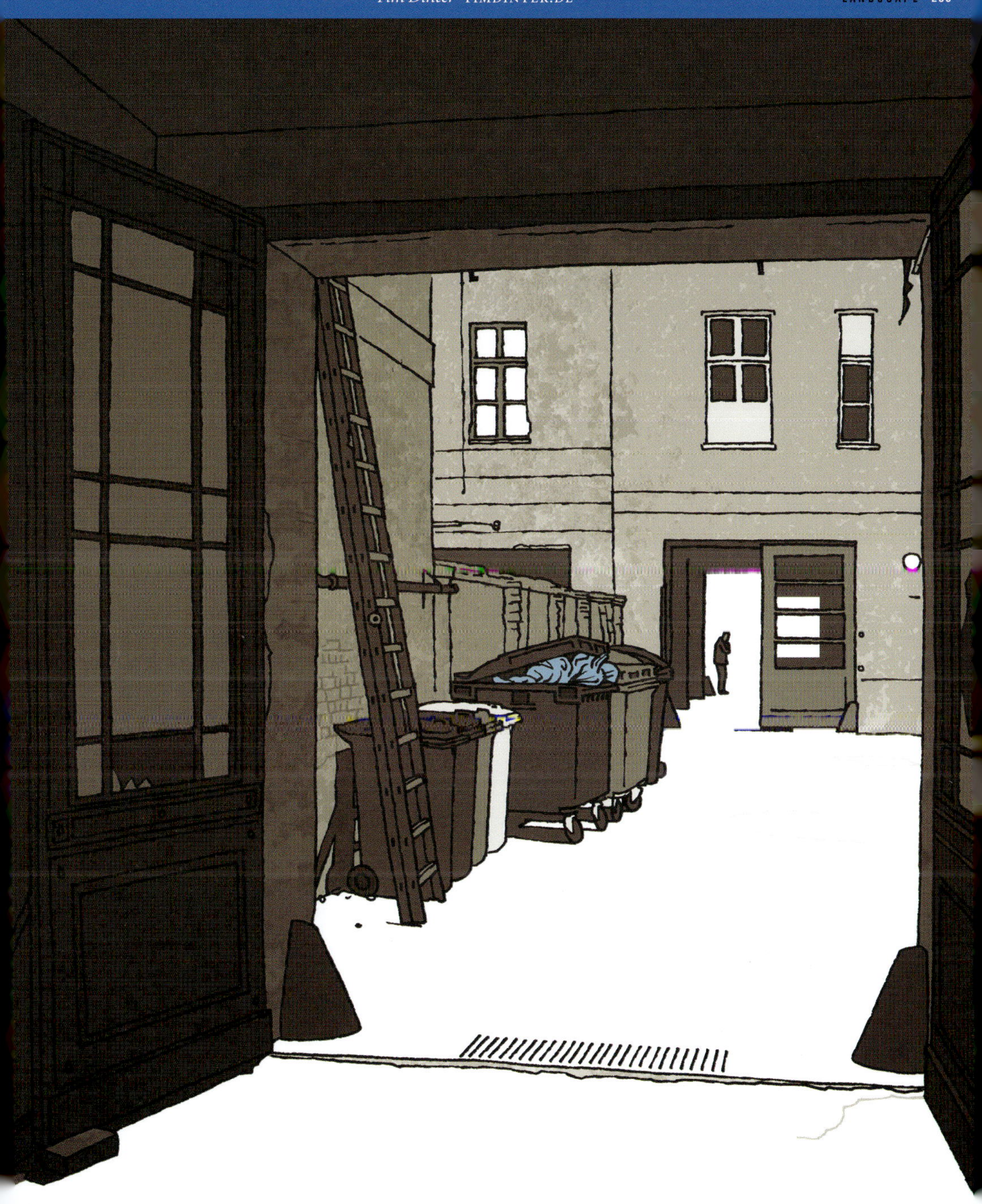

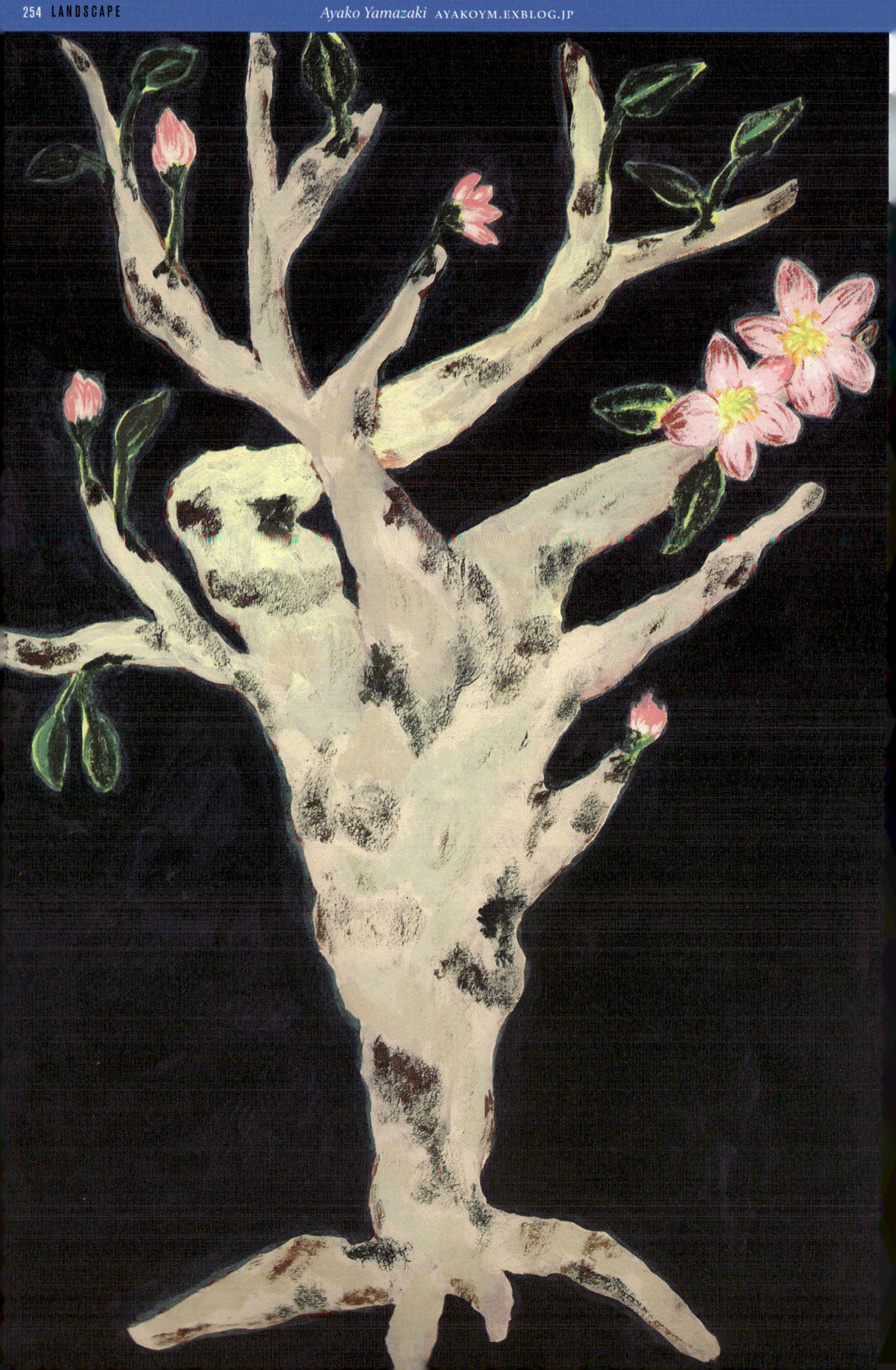

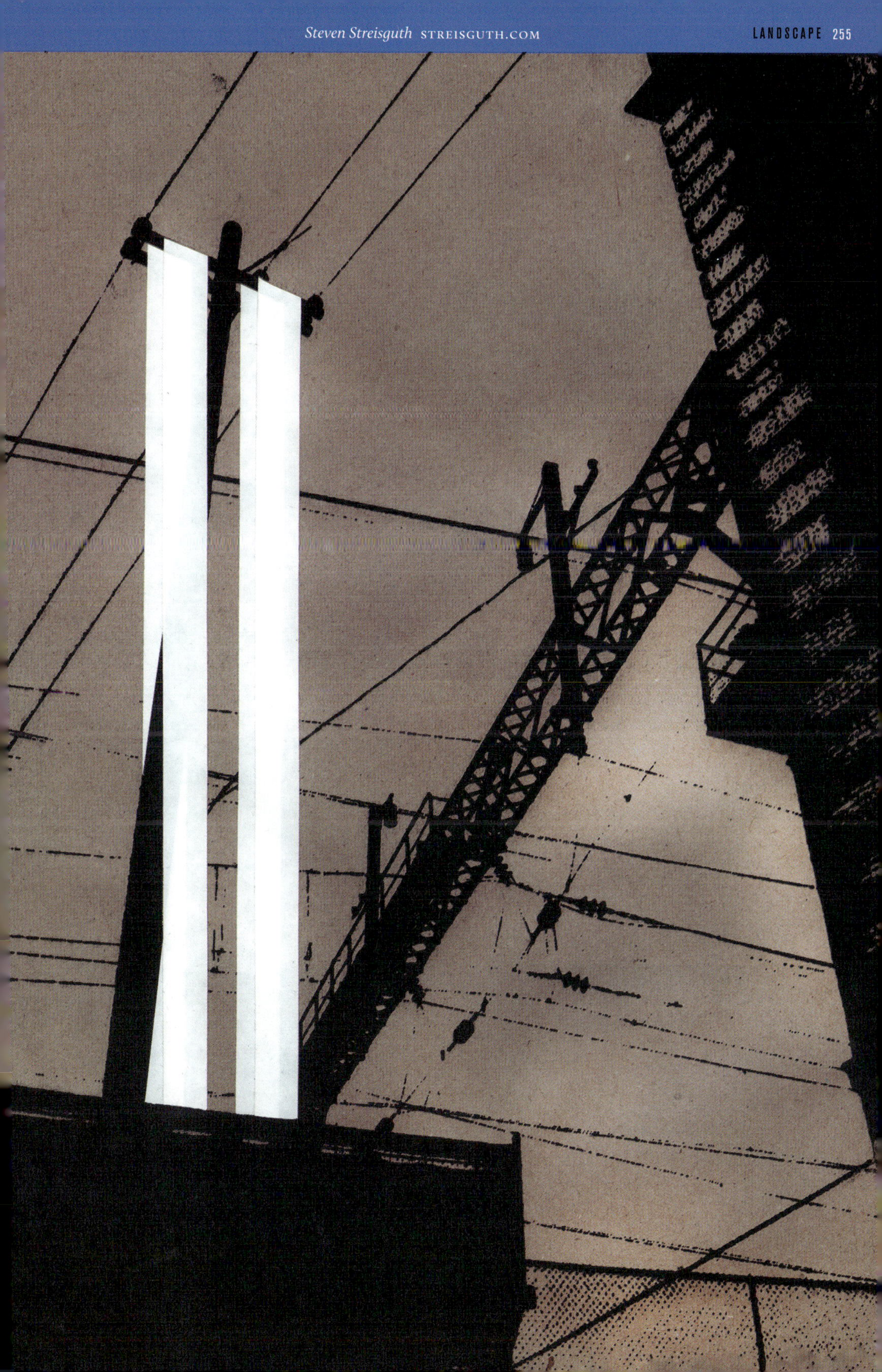

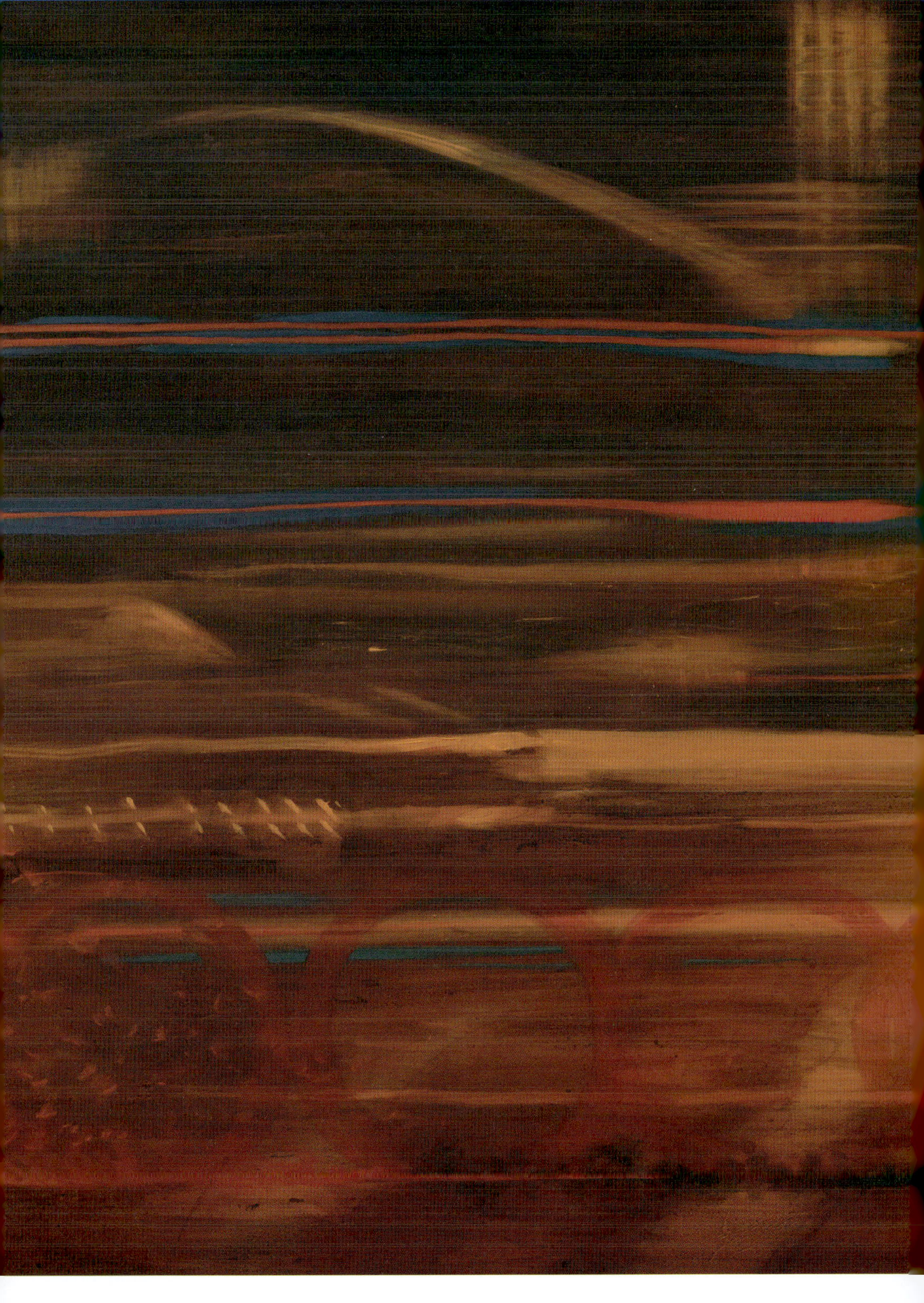

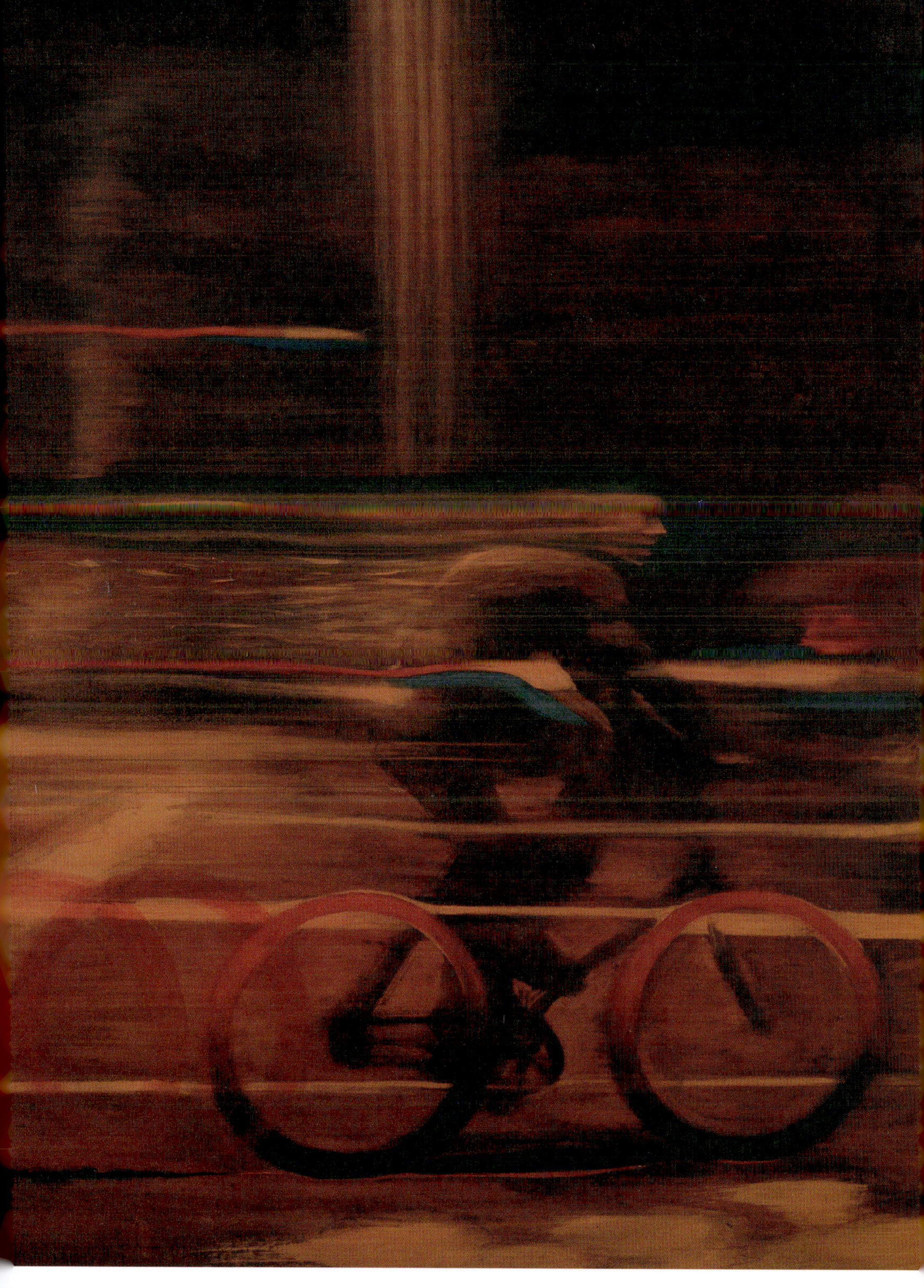

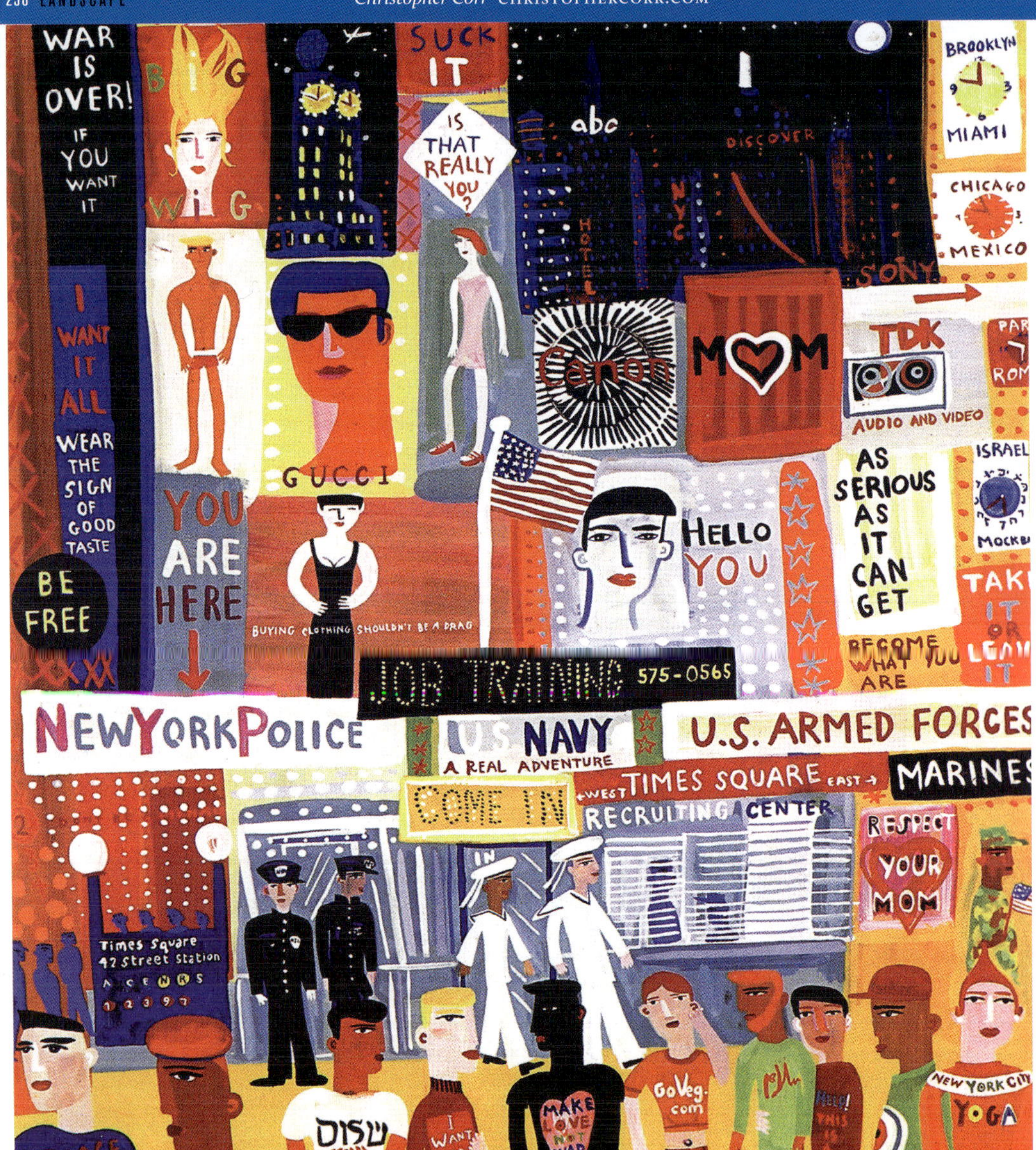
WAR IS OVER! IF YOU WANT IT
BIG WIG
I WANT IT ALL
WEAR THE SIGN OF GOOD TASTE
BE FREE
XXX
YOU ARE HERE
GUCCI
BUYING CLOTHING SHOULDN'T BE A DRAG
SUCK IT
IS THAT REALLY YOU?
abc
NYC
HOTEL
DISCOVER
Canon
M♥M
TDK
AUDIO AND VIDEO
SONY
BROOKLYN
MIAMI
CHICAGO
MEXICO
PAR ROM
ISRAEL
MOCKBA
HELLO YOU
AS SERIOUS AS IT CAN GET
BECOME WHAT YOU ARE
TAKE IT OR LEAVE IT
JOB TRAINING   575-0565
NewYorkPolice
U.S. NAVY
A REAL ADVENTURE
U.S. ARMED FORCES
COME IN
IN
WEST TIMES SQUARE EAST
RECRUITING CENTER
MARINES
RESPECT YOUR MOM
Times Square
42 Street Station
A C E N R S
1 2 3 9 7
שלום
I WANT TO BE HAPPY
MAKE LOVE NOT WAR
GoVeg.com
HELP! THIS IS
NEW YORK CITY YOGA
PEACE

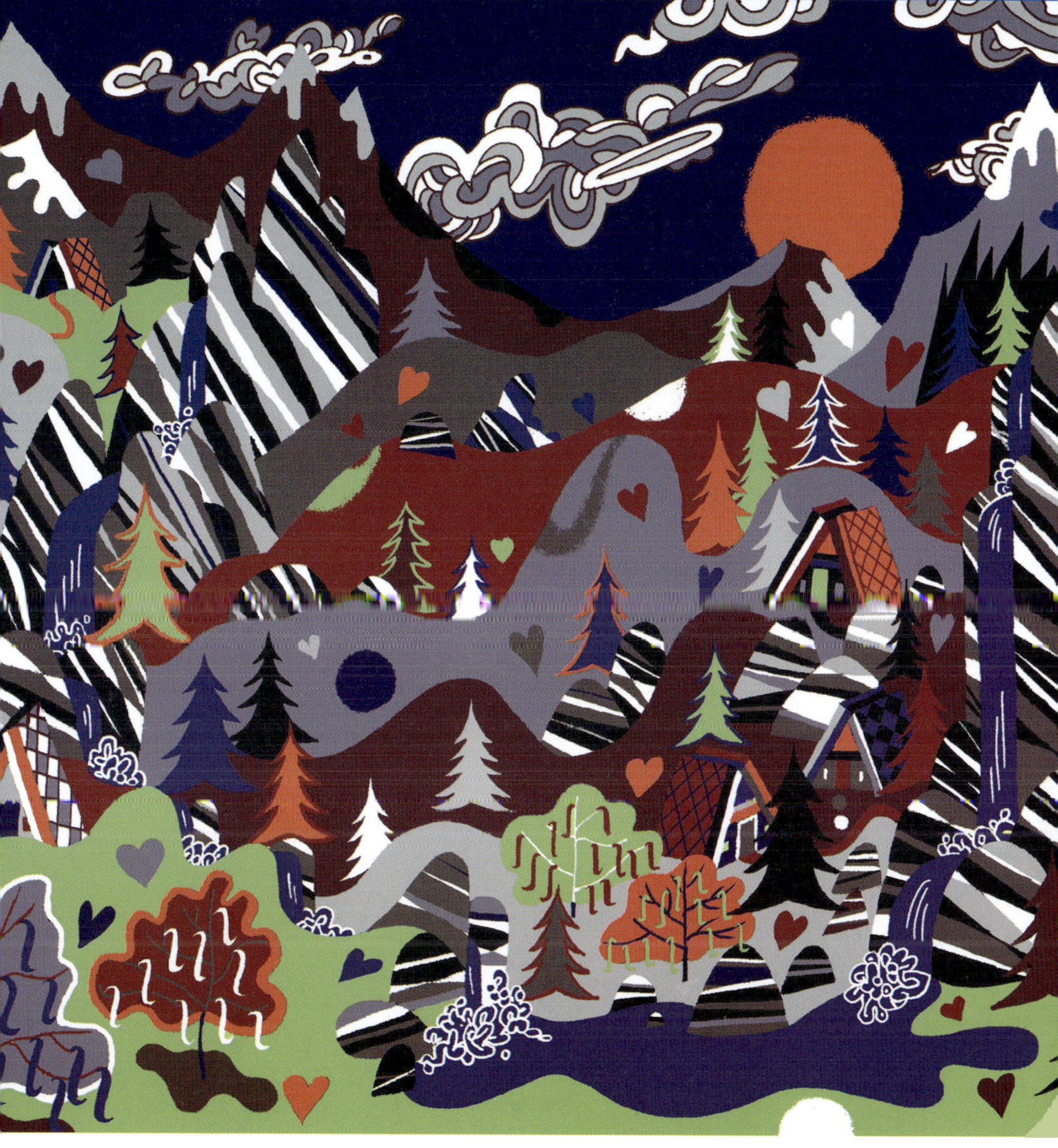

Kate Miller KATE-MILLER.COM

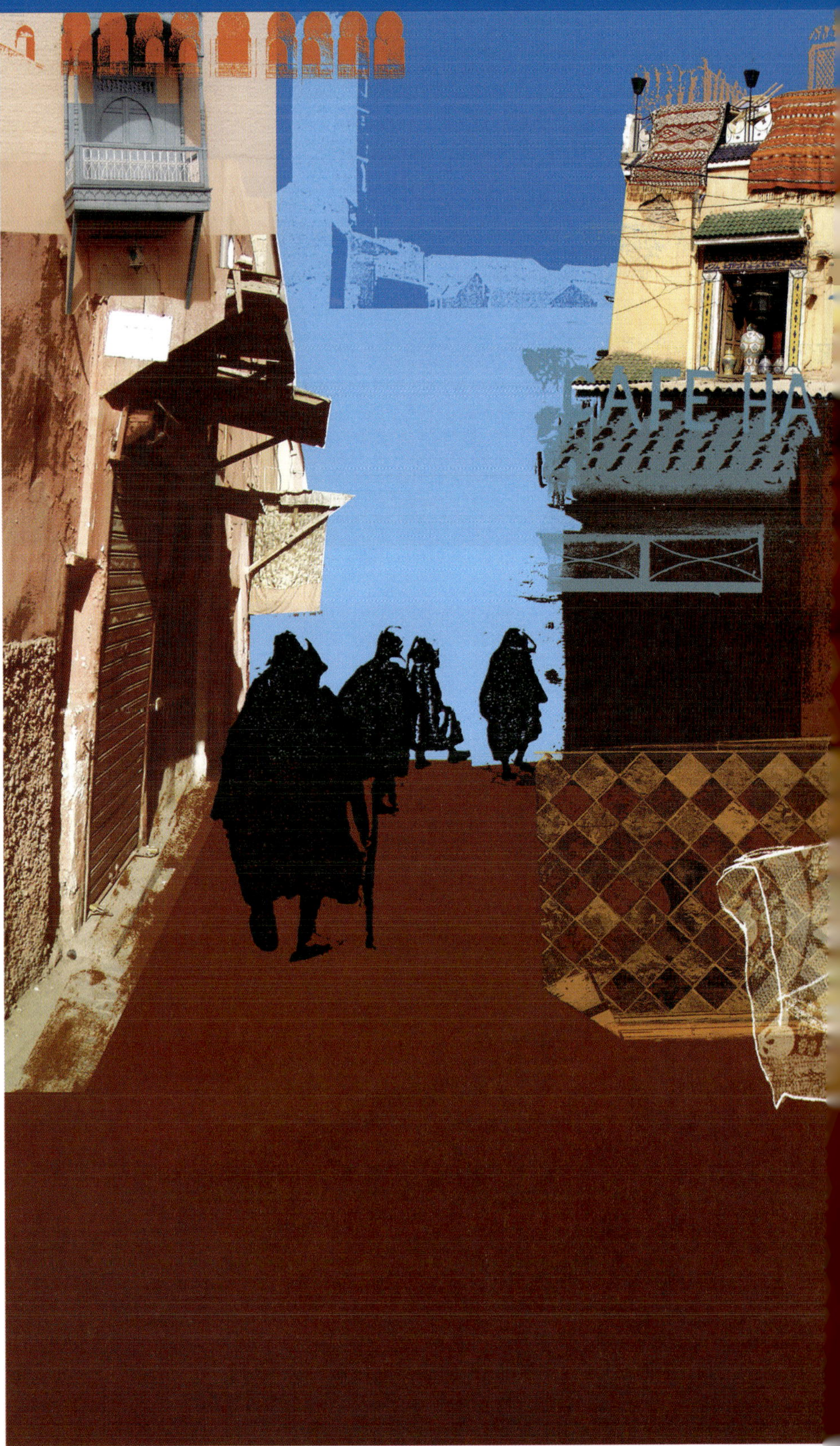

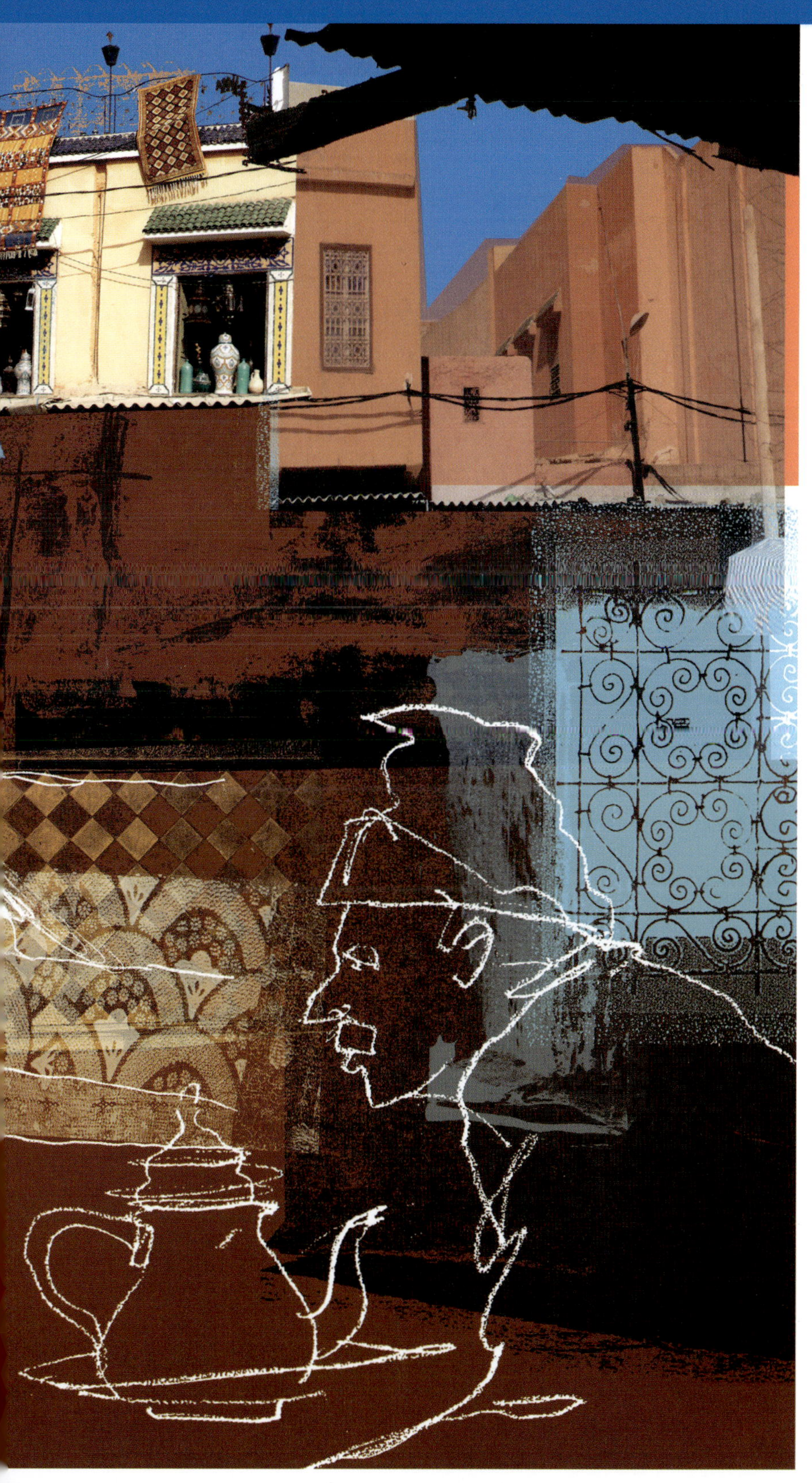

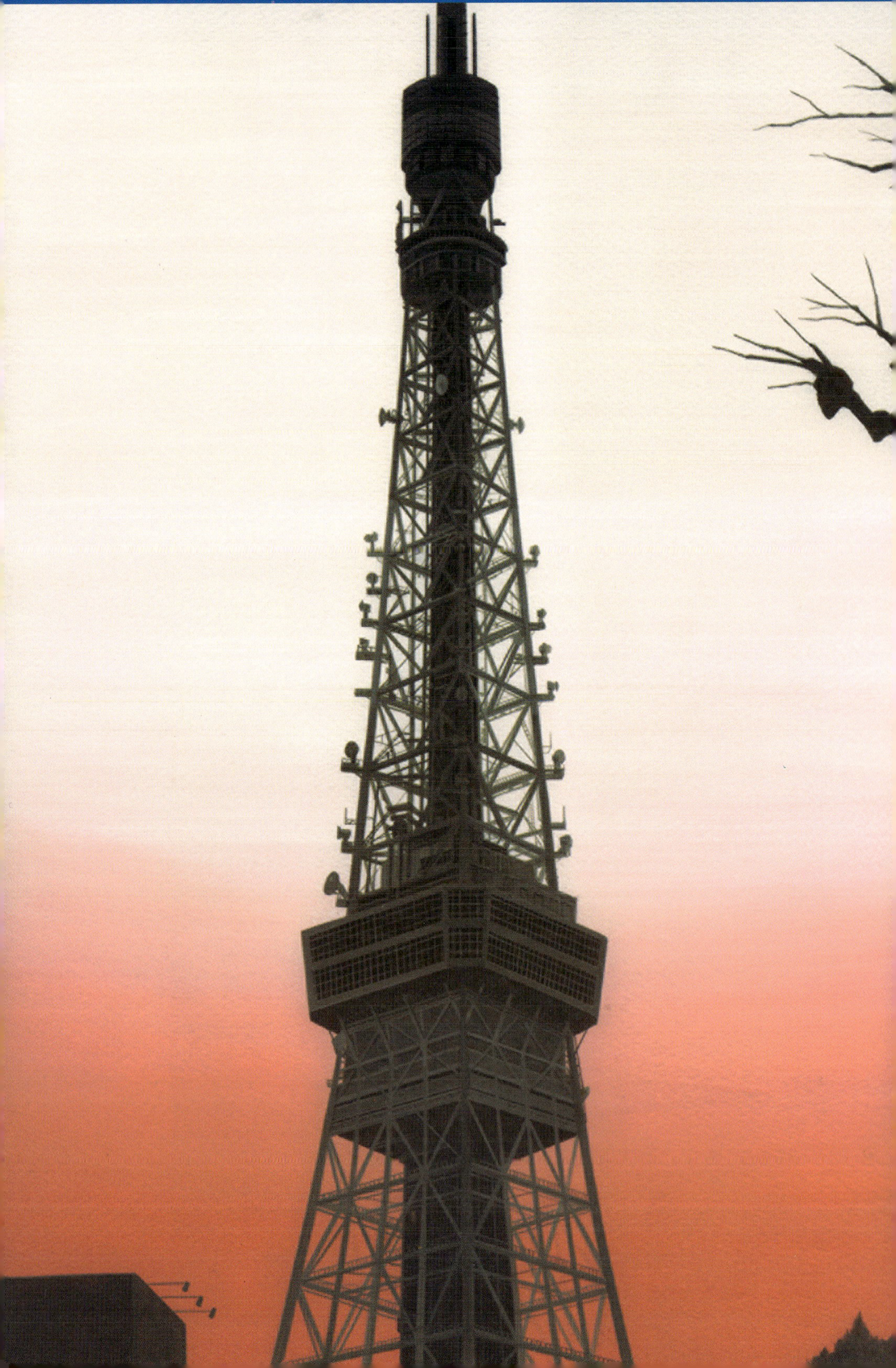

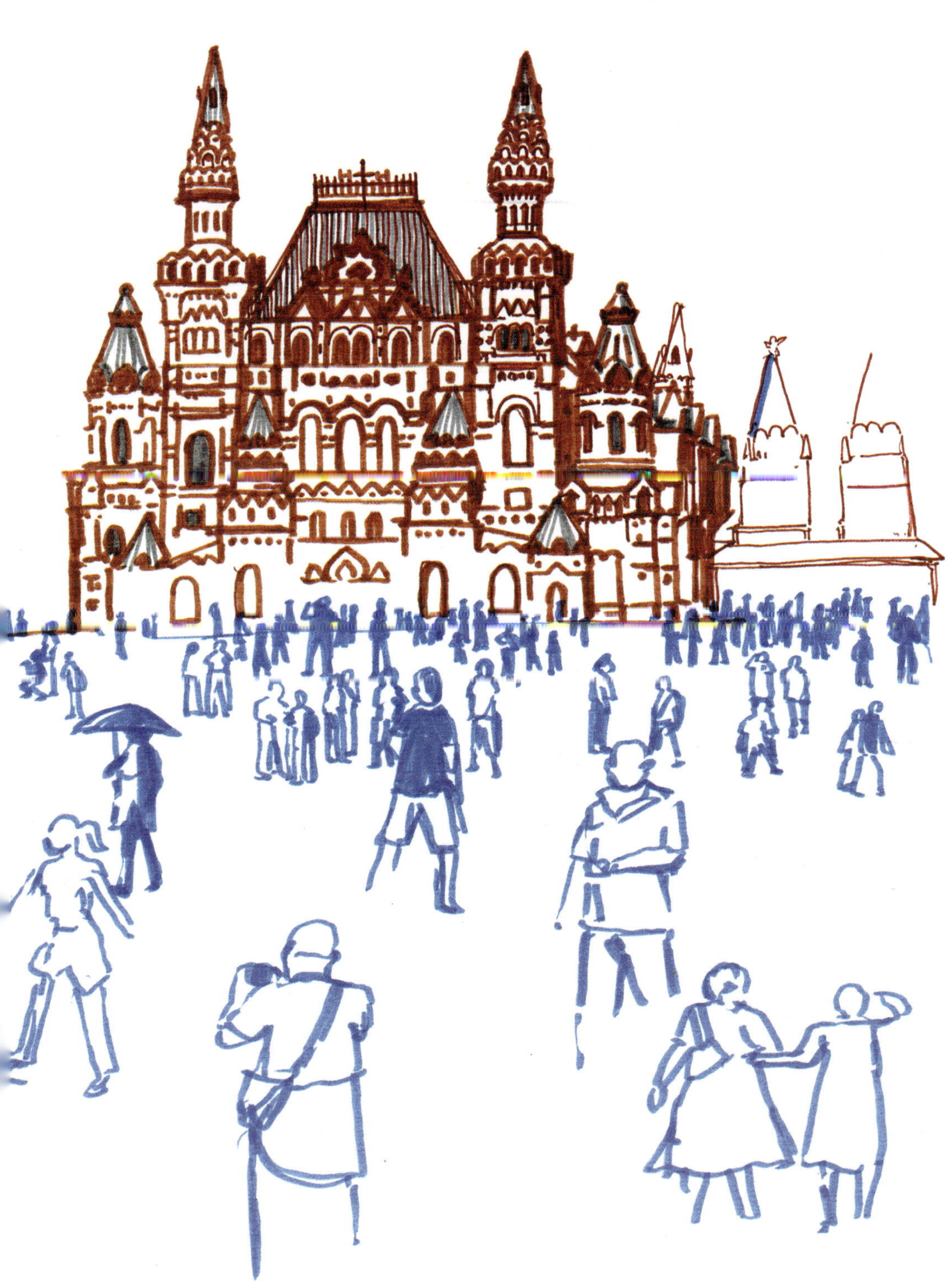

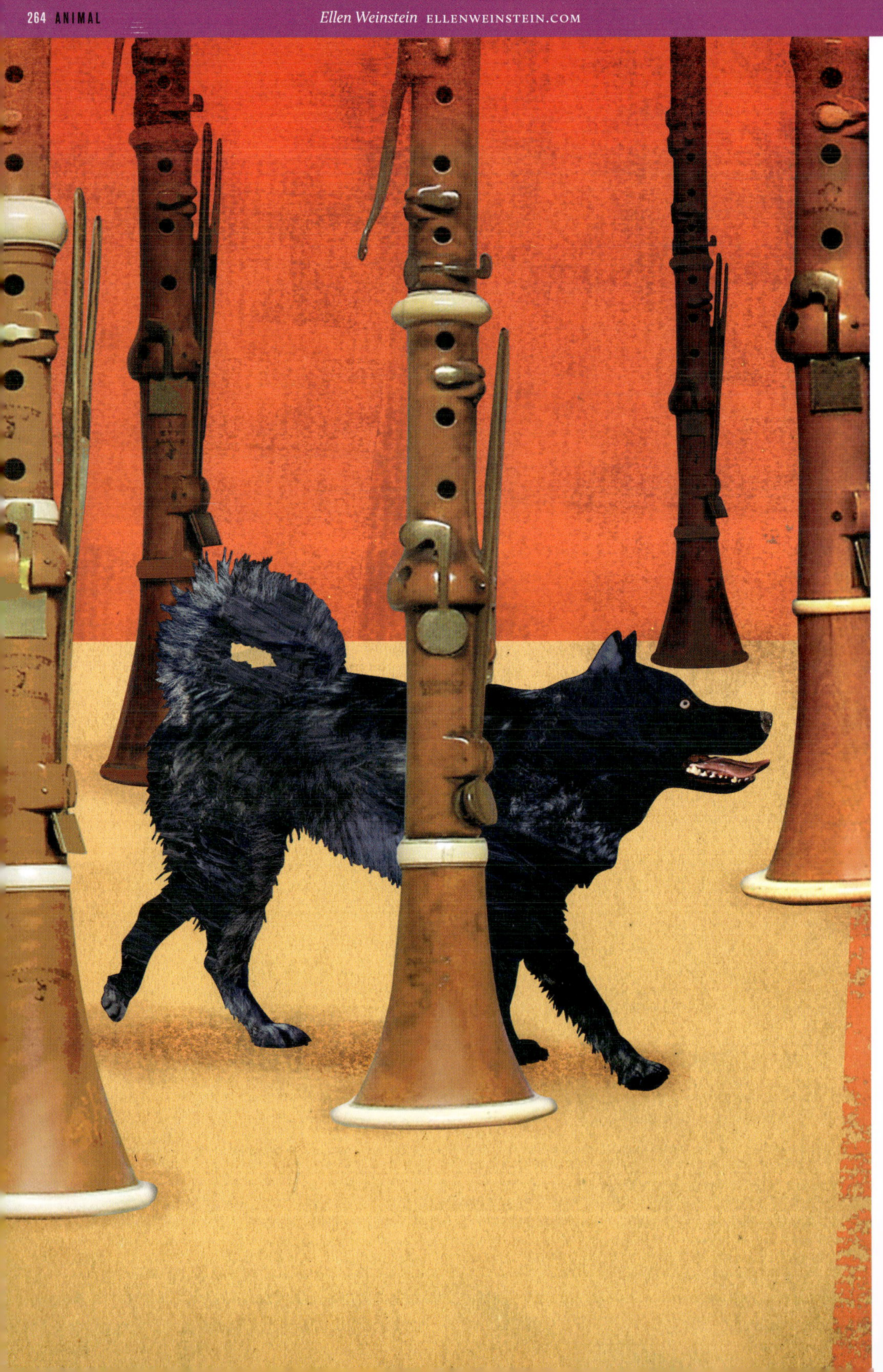

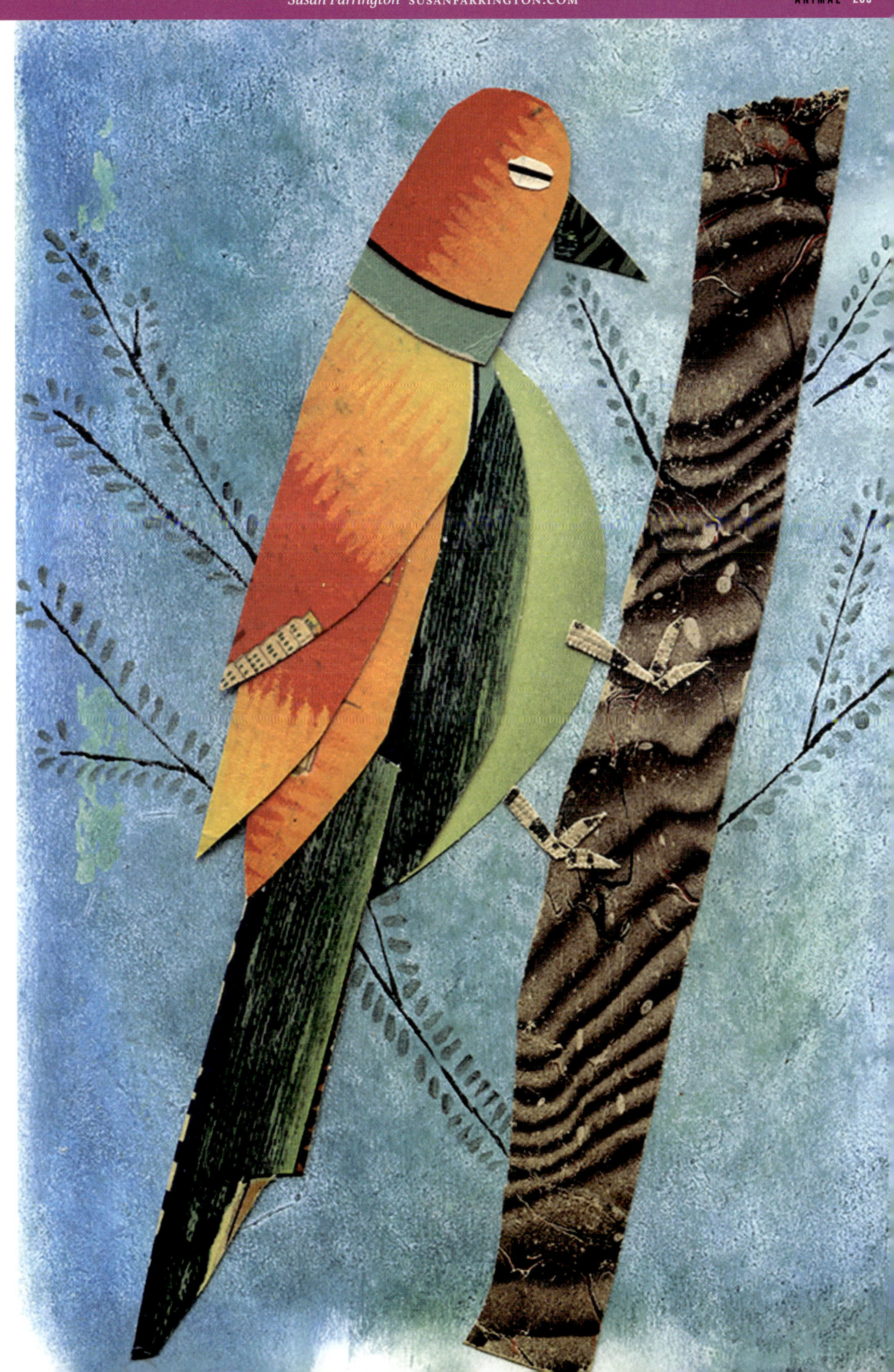

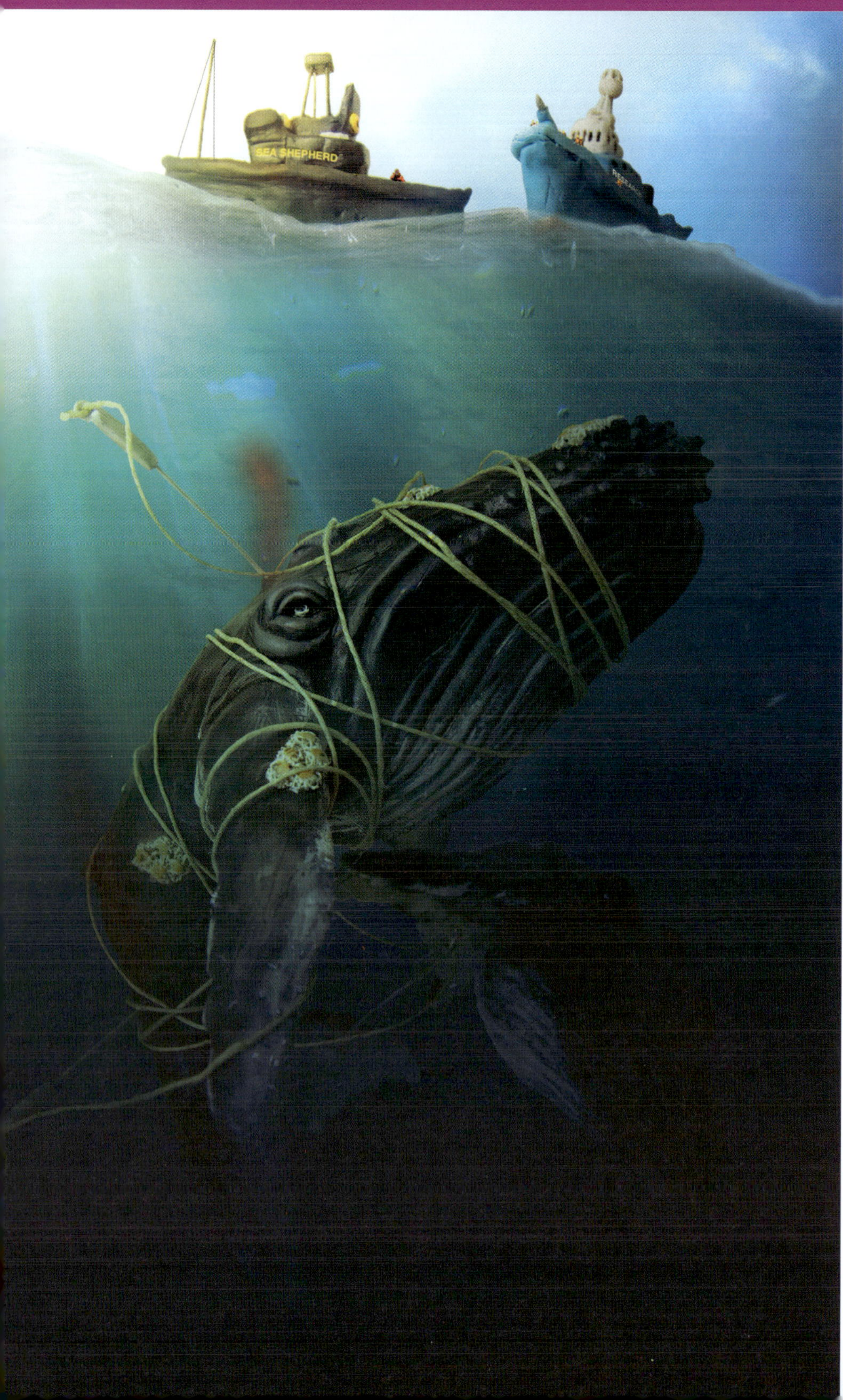
SEA SHEPHERD

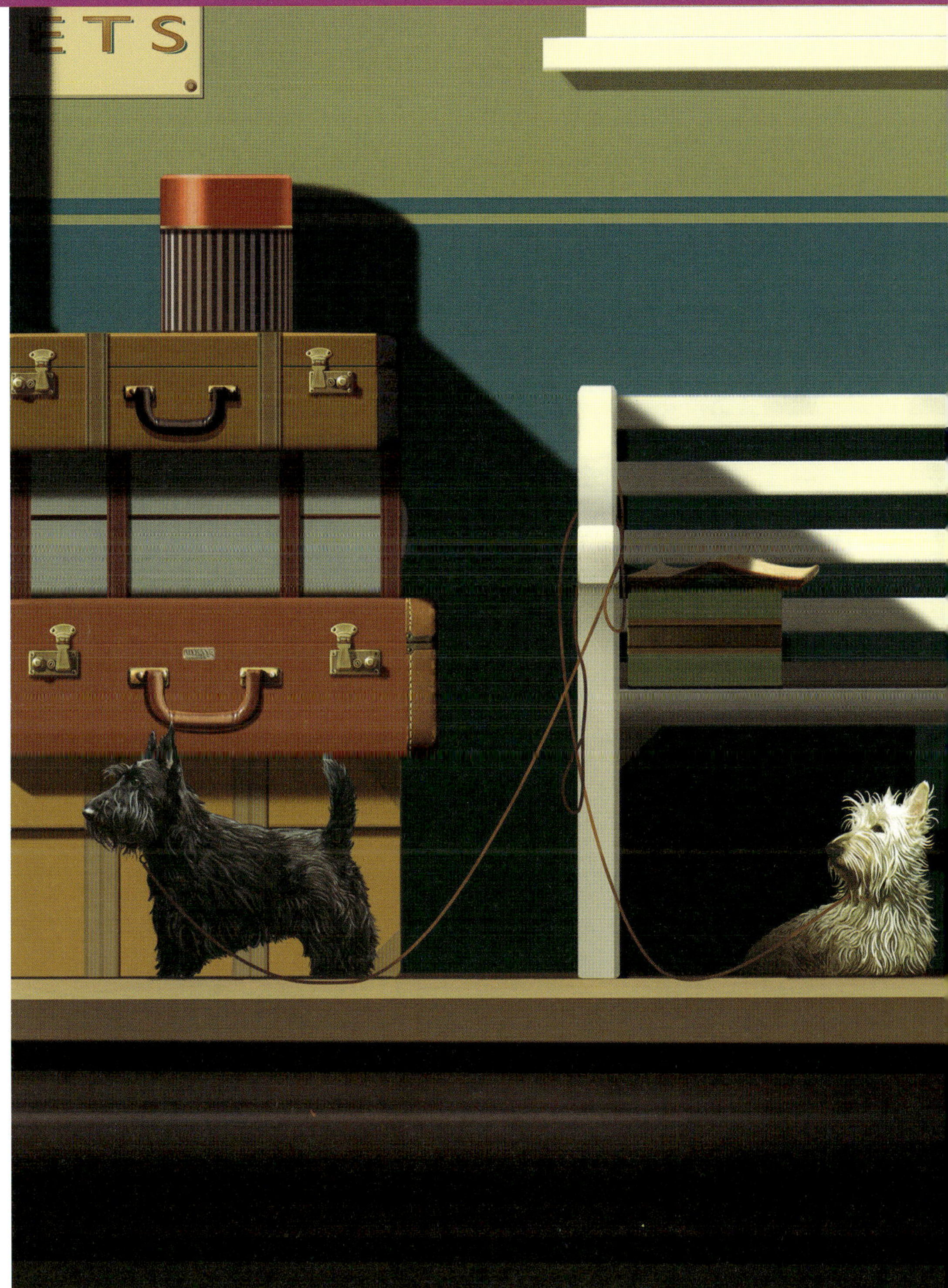
ETS

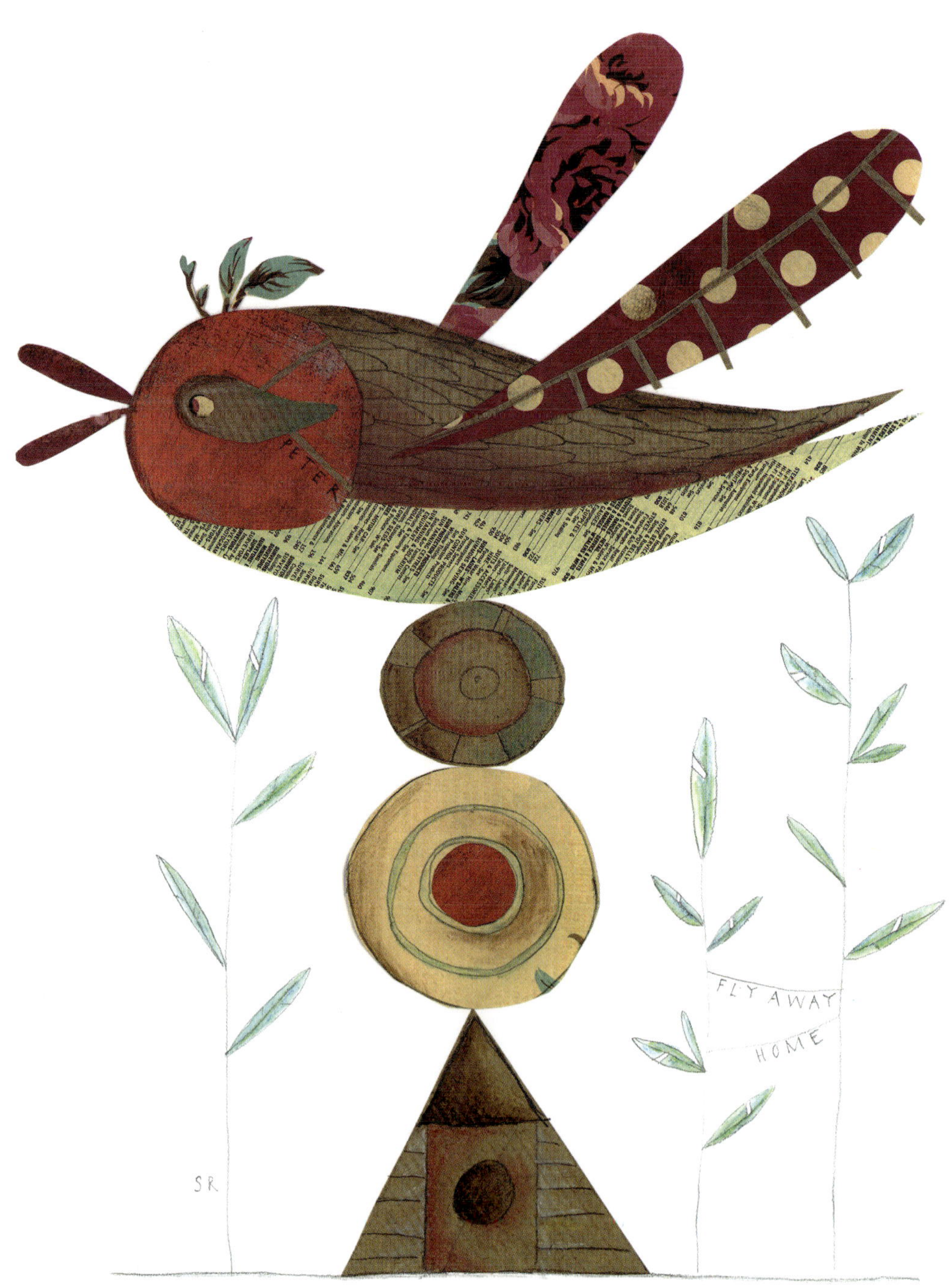
PETER
FLY AWAY
HOME
SR

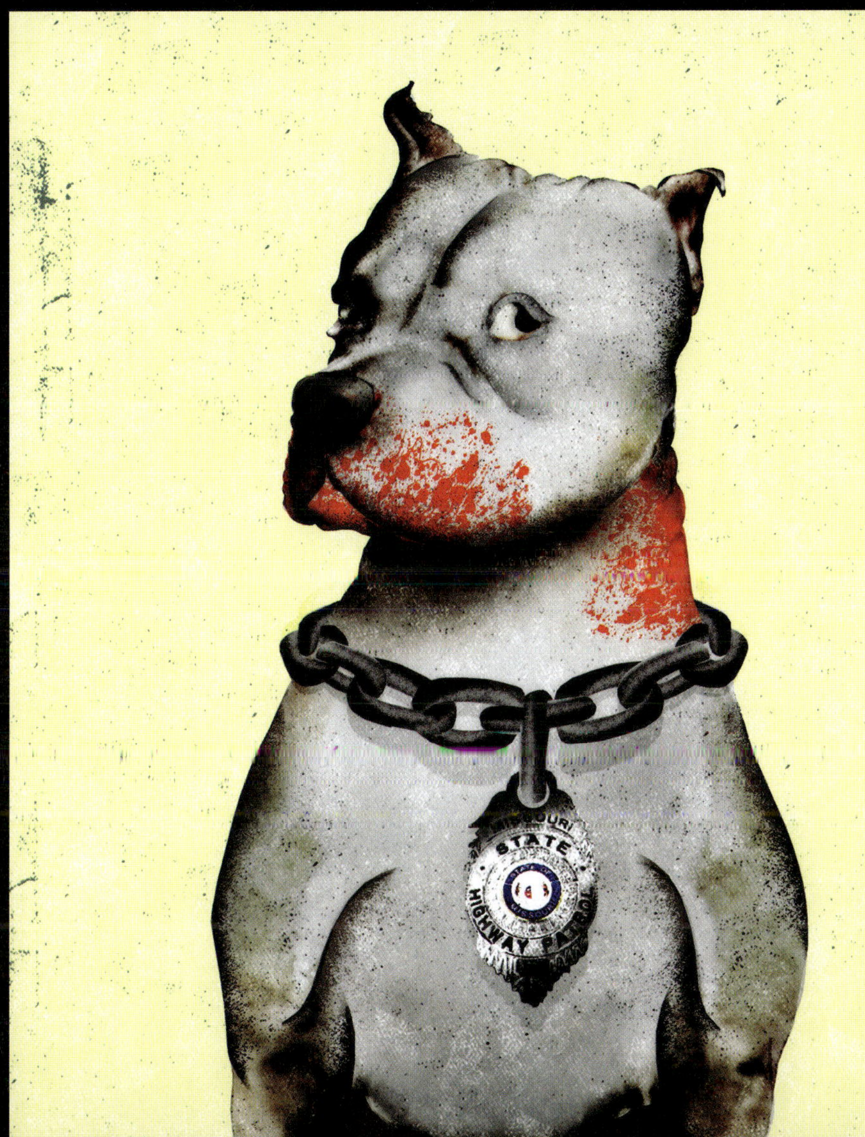
MISSOURI
STATE
HIGHWAY PATROL

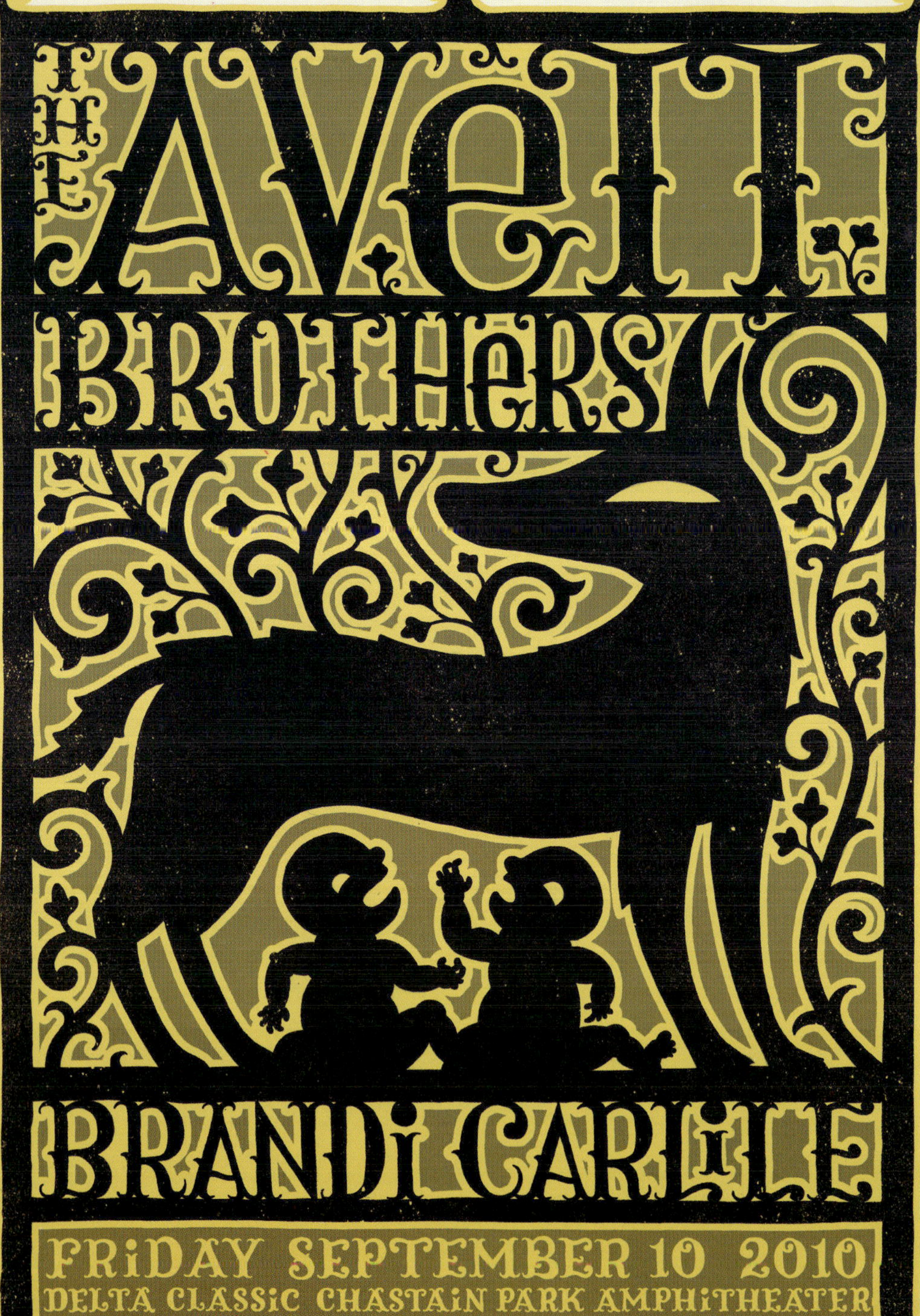
THE AVETT BROTHERS
BRANDI CARLILE
FRIDAY SEPTEMBER 10 2010
DELTA CLASSIC CHASTAIN PARK AMPHITHEATER
ATLANTA GA

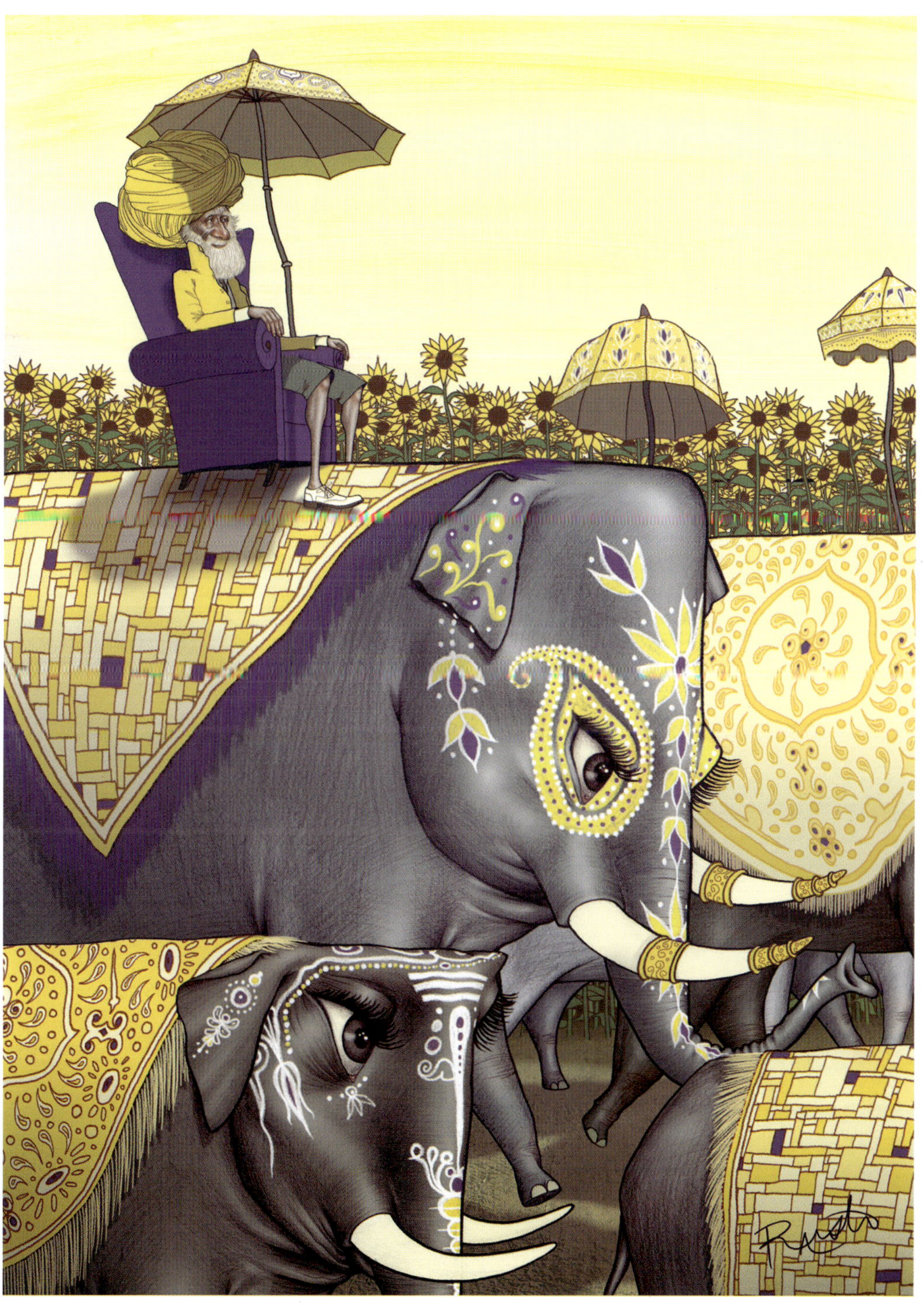

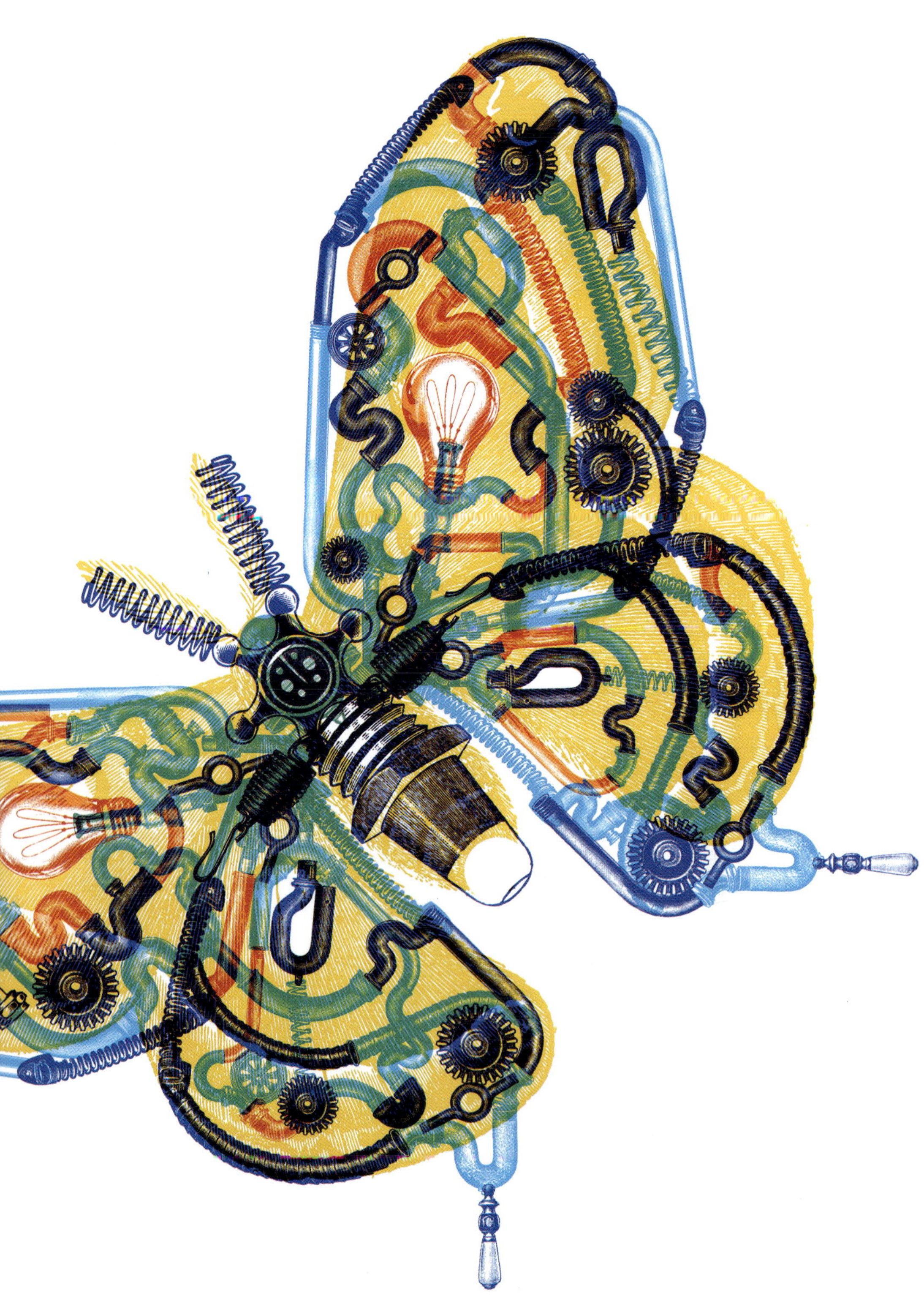

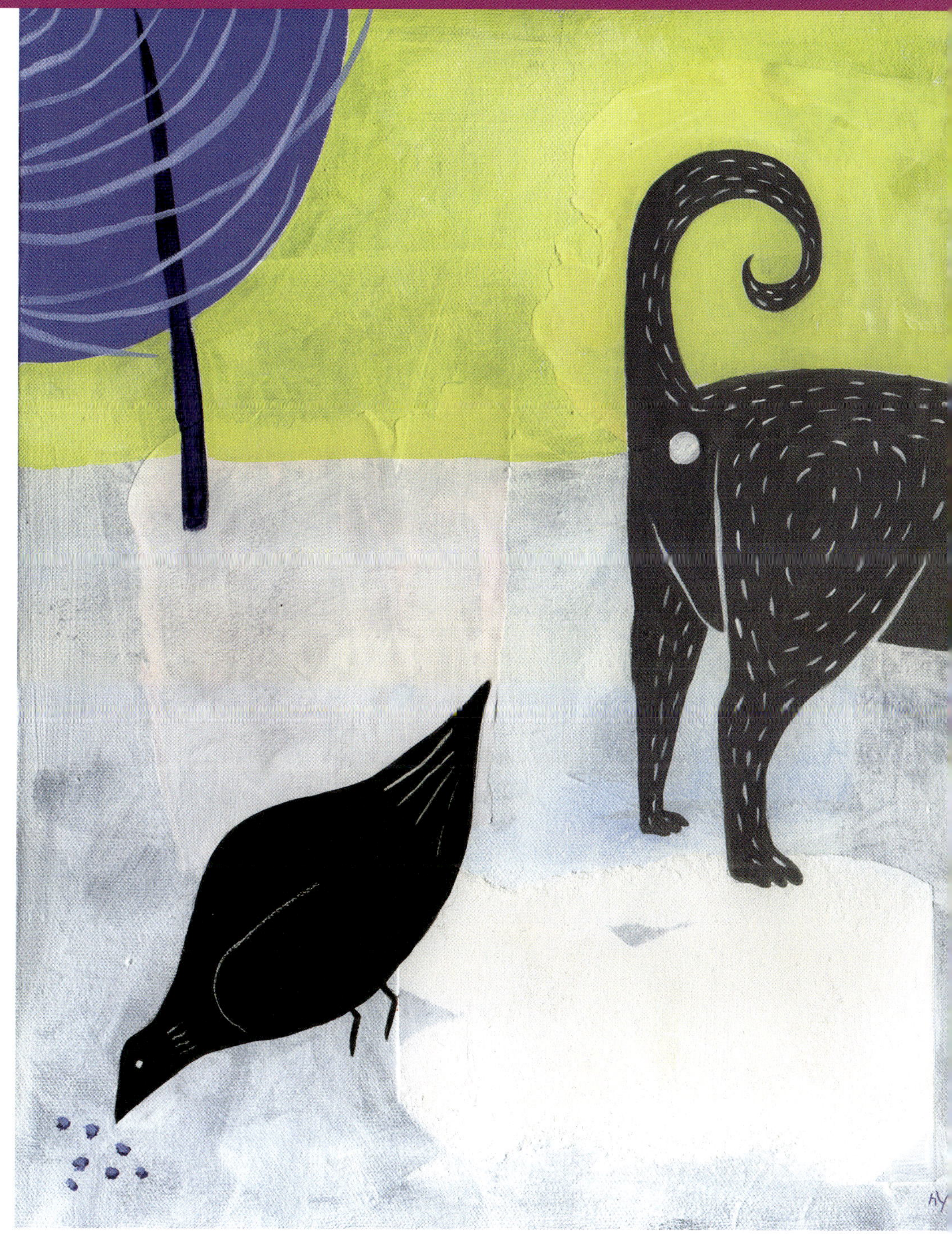

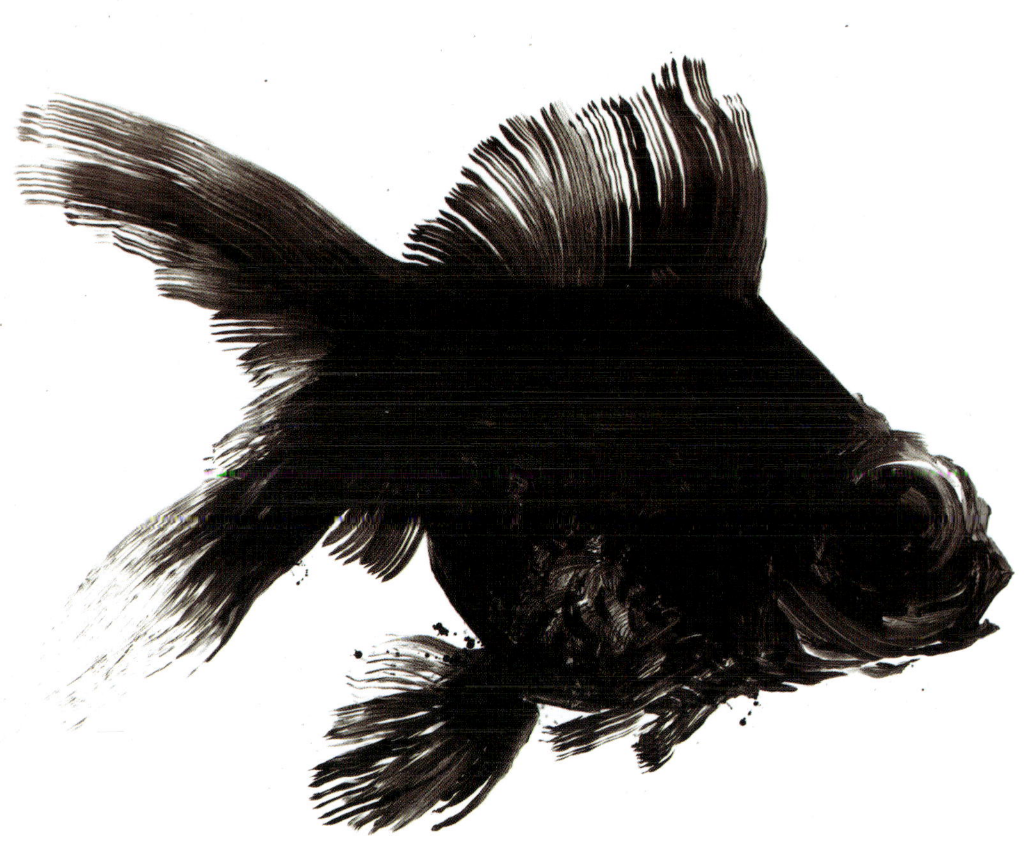

Bill Mayer THEBILLMAYER.COM

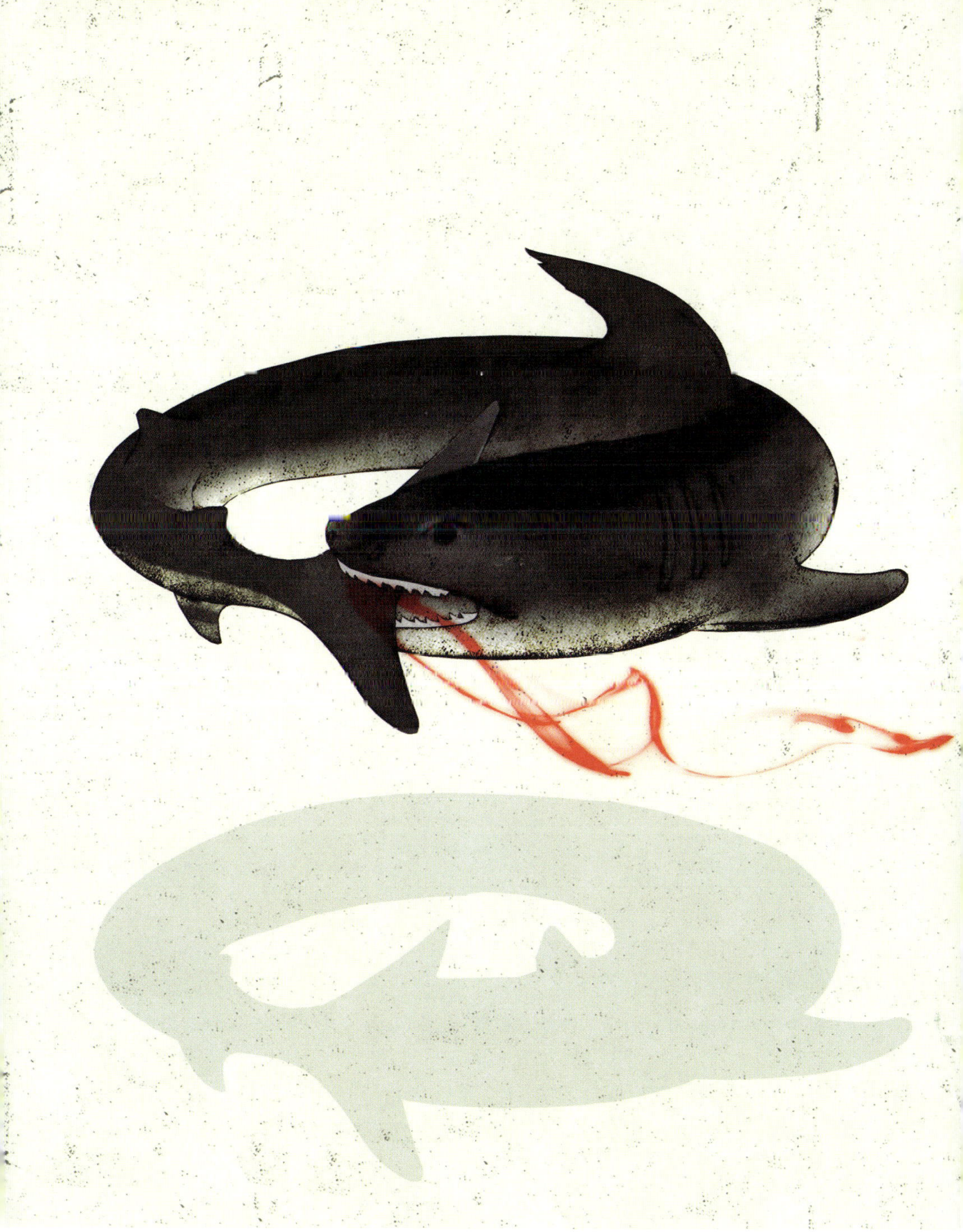

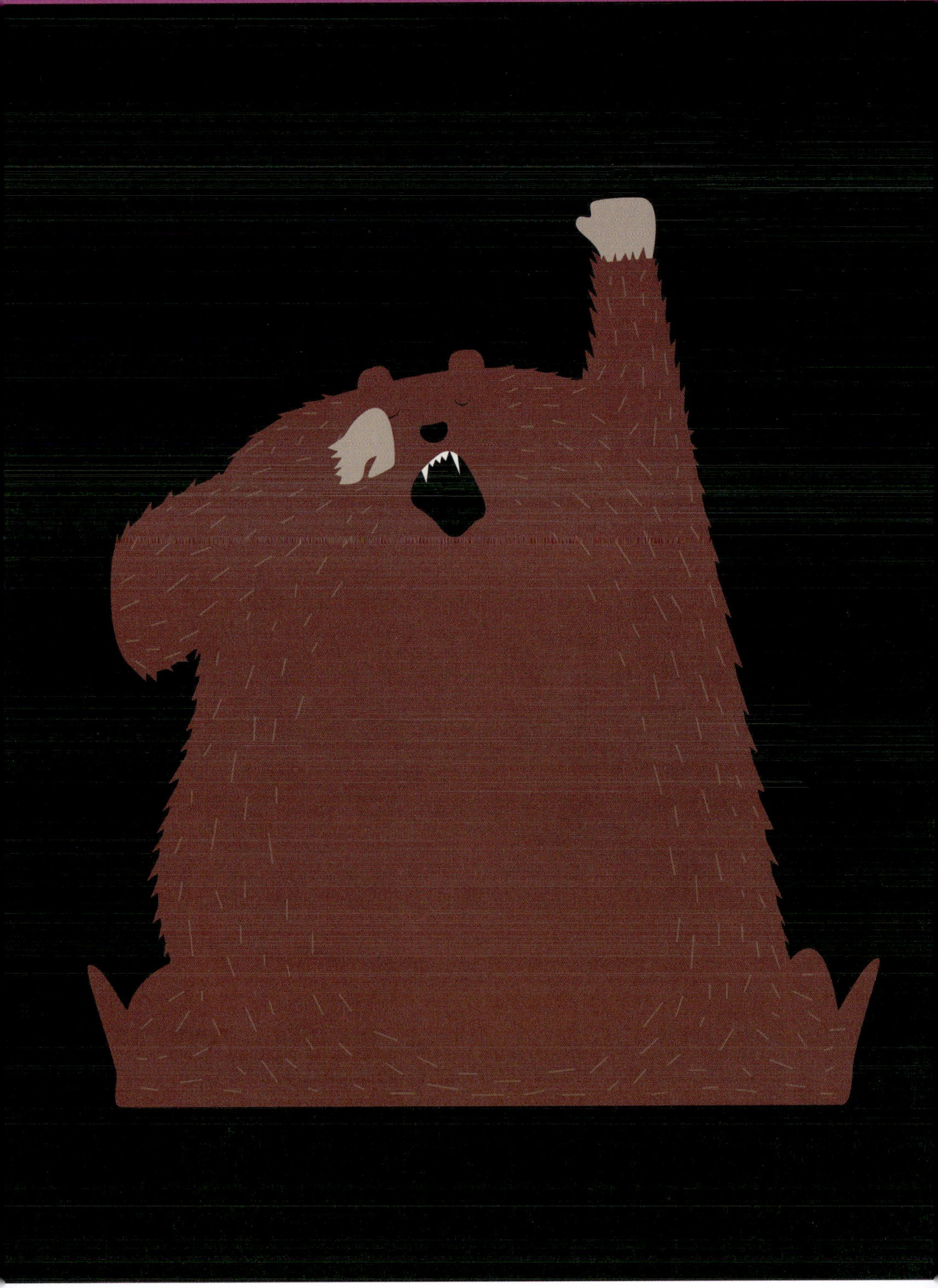

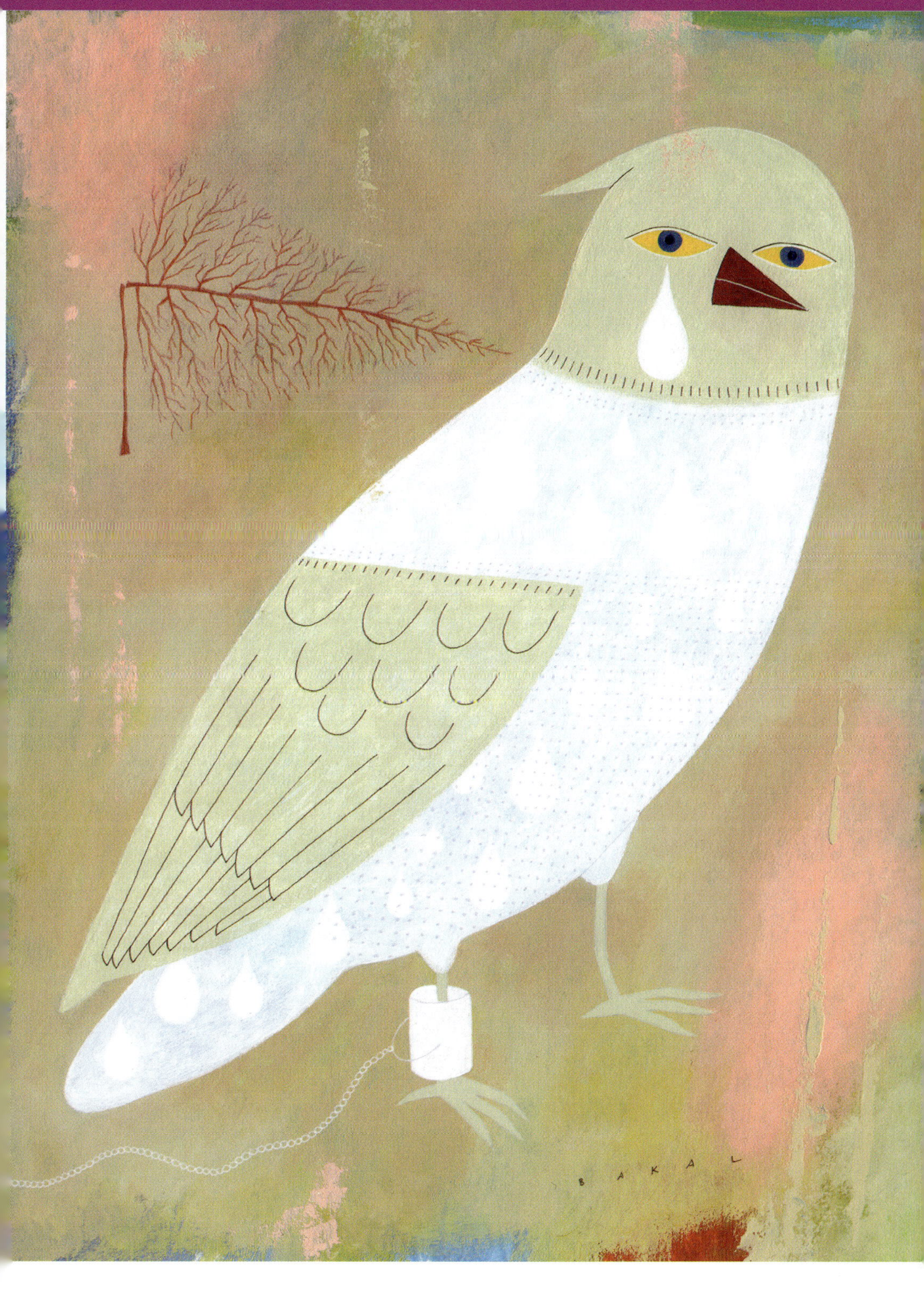
BAKAL

Anja Nolte ANJANOLTE.DE

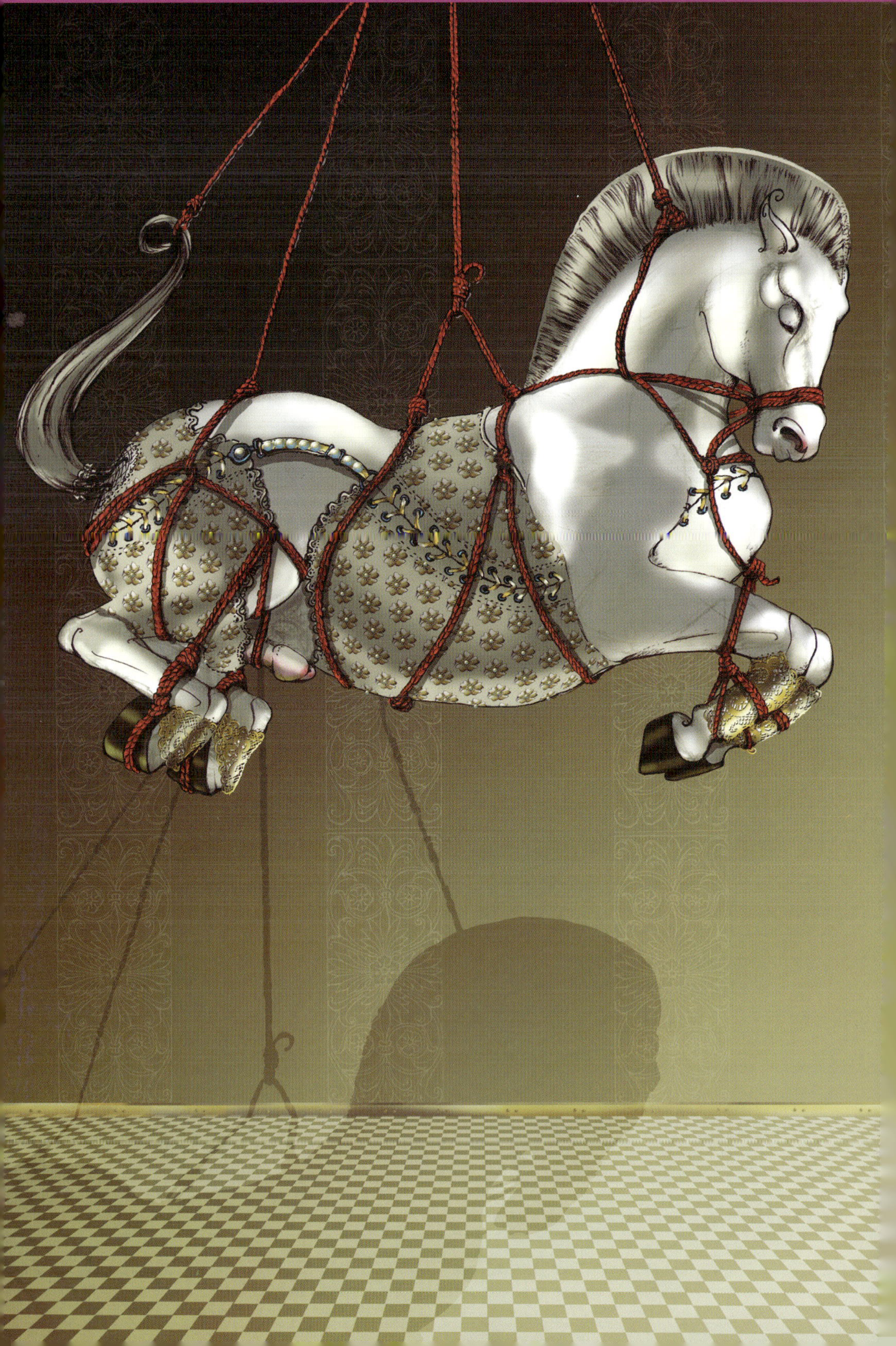

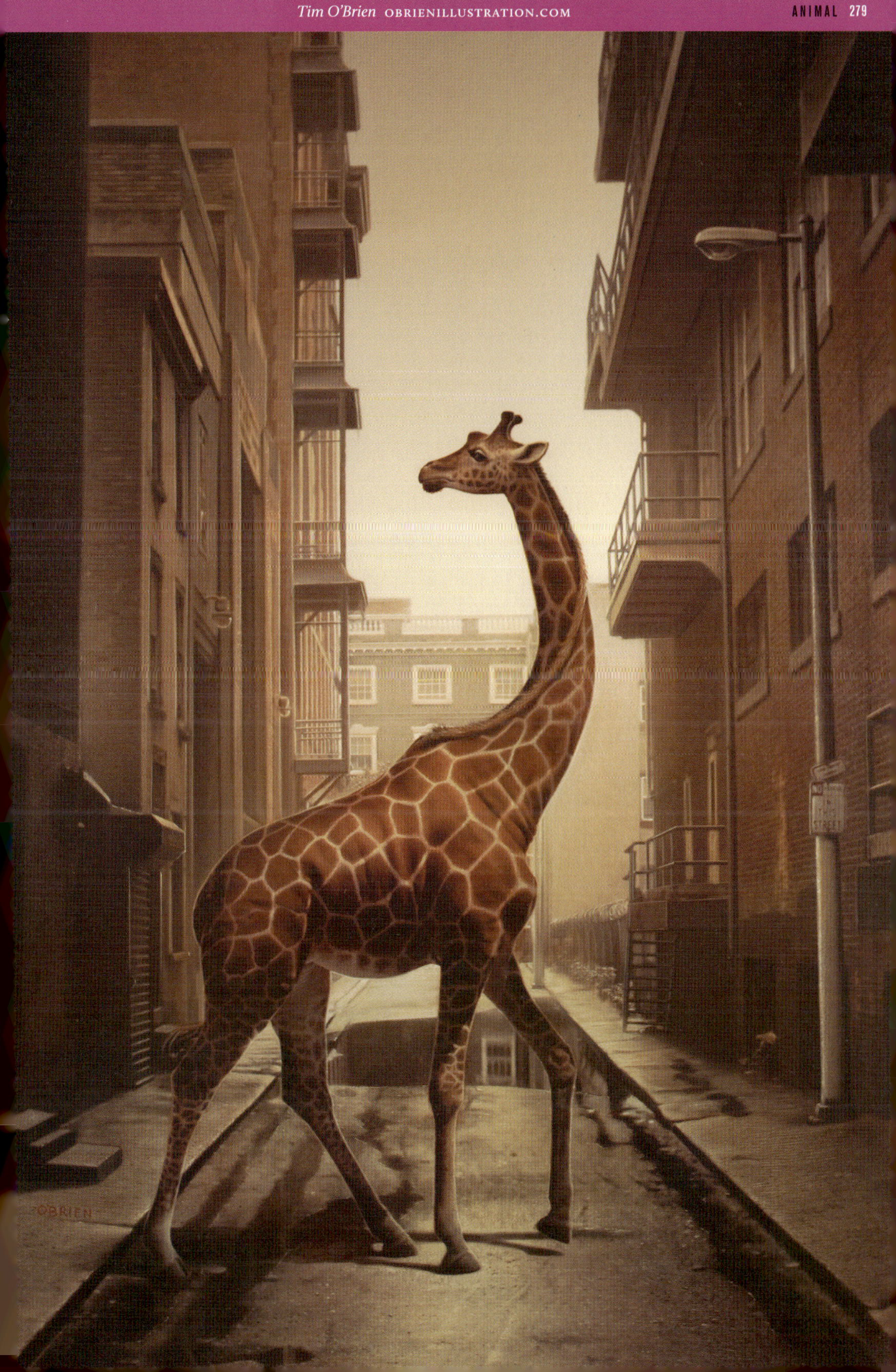

Steven Tabbutt STEVENTABBUTT.COM

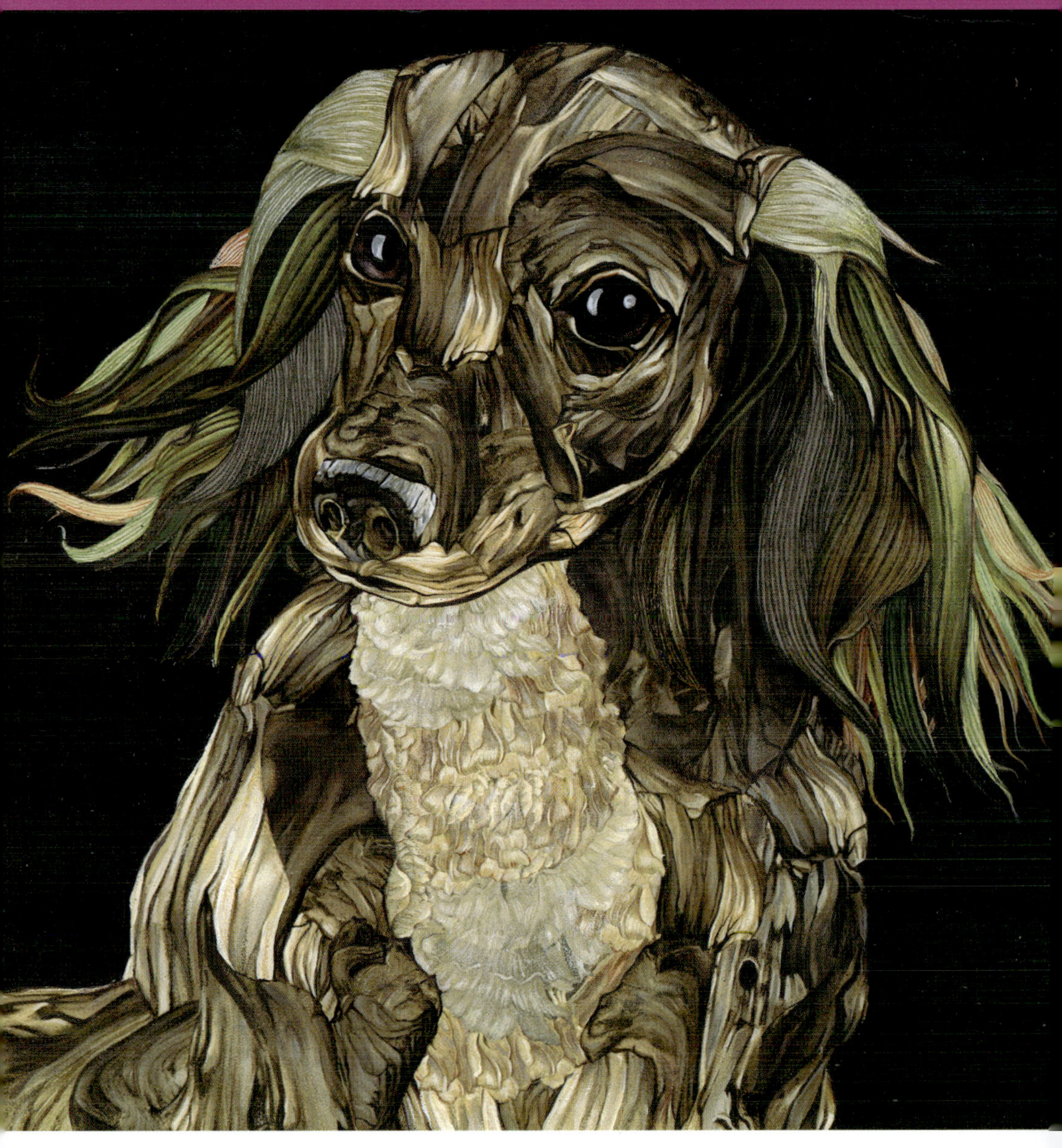

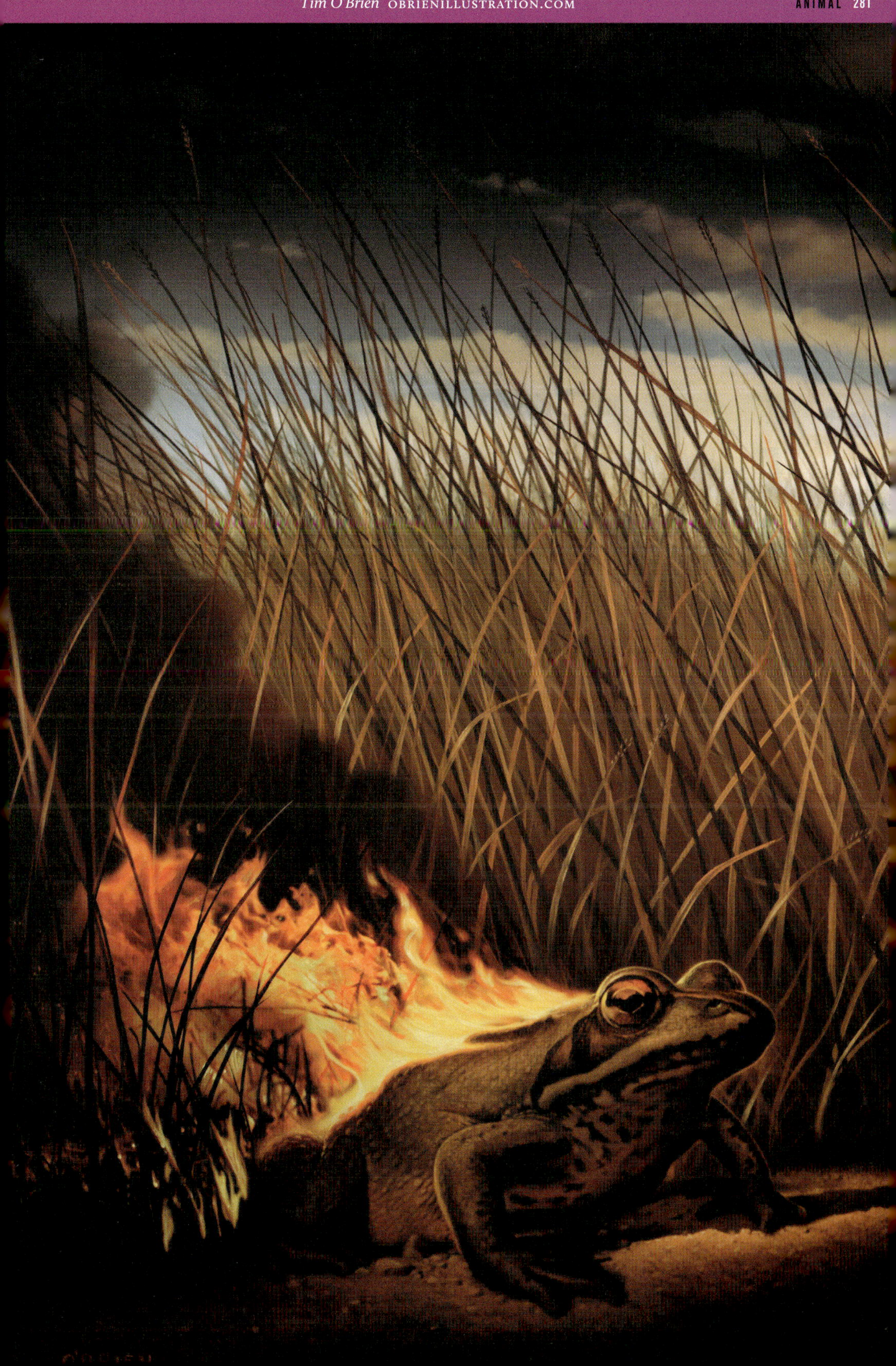

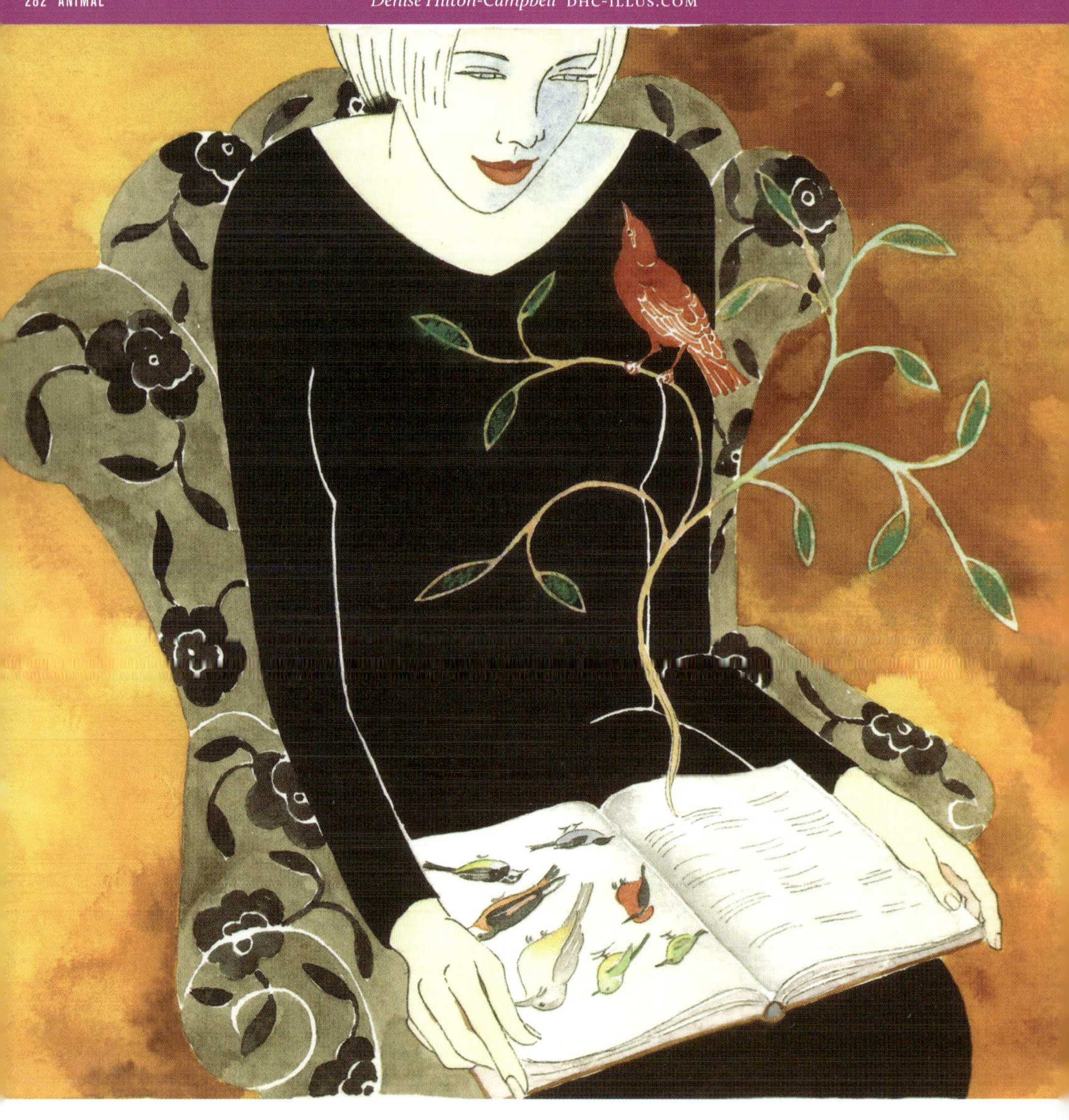

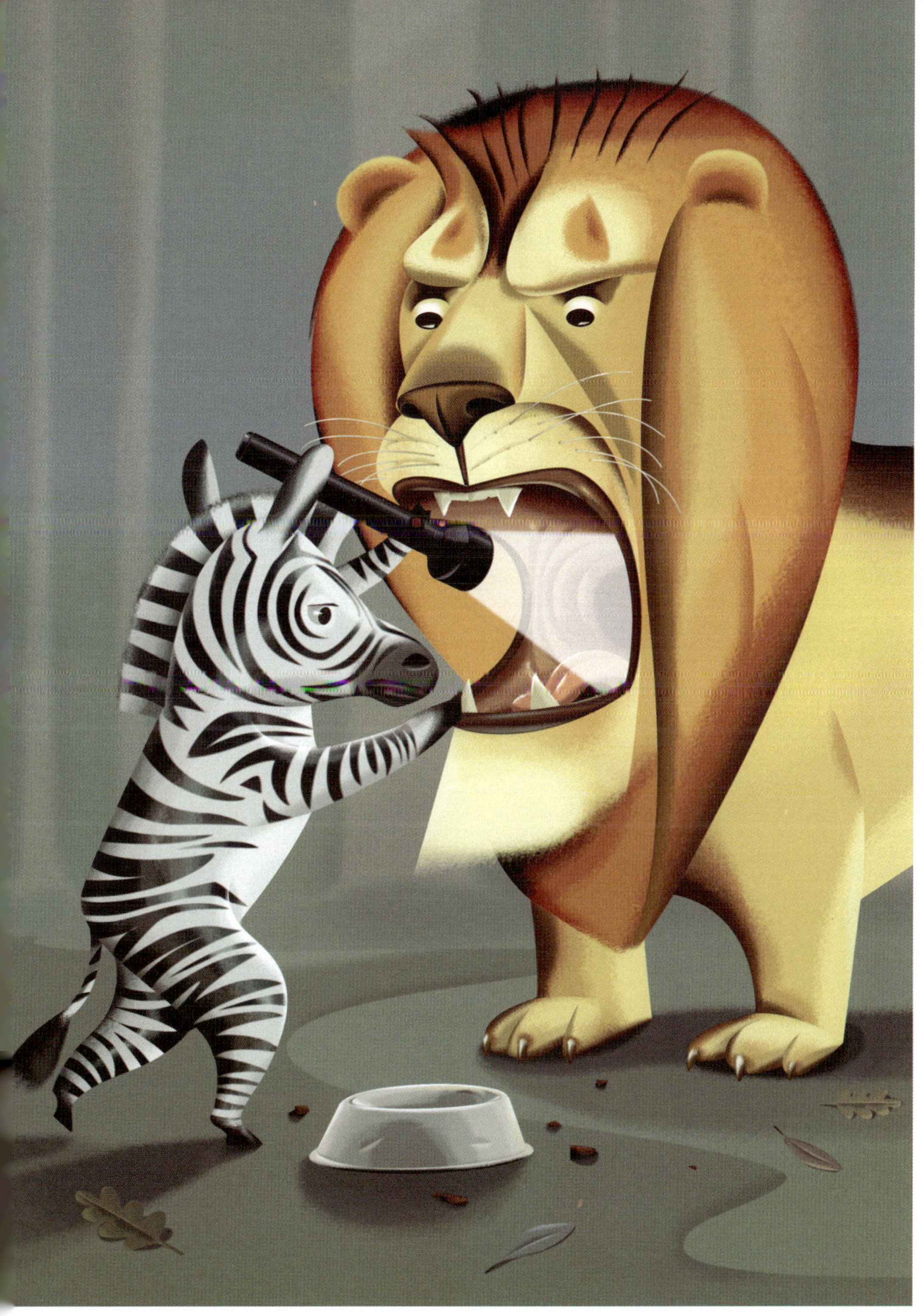

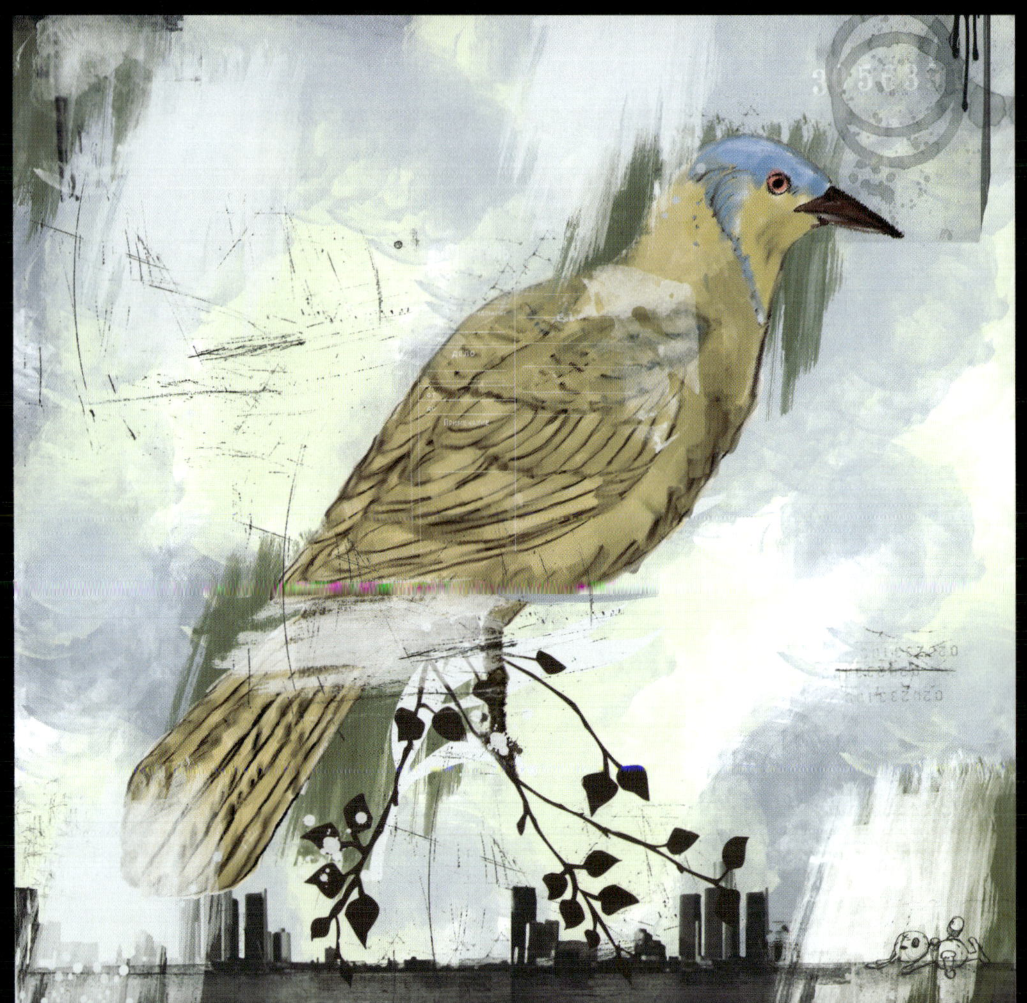

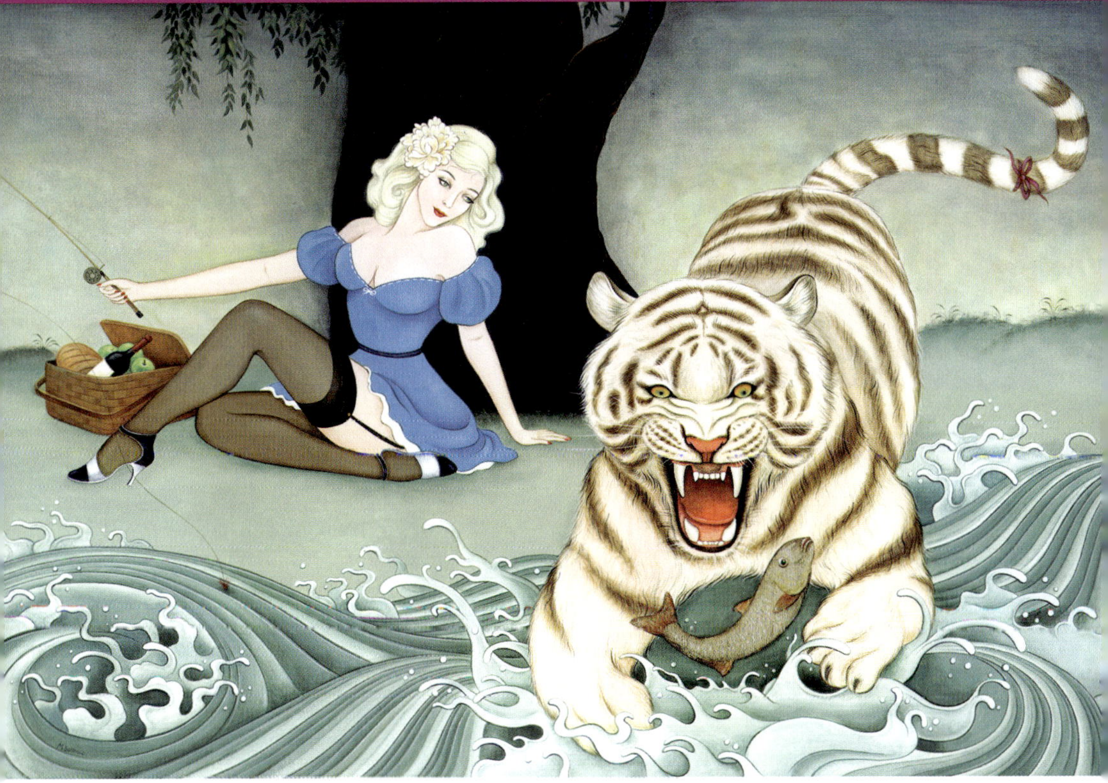

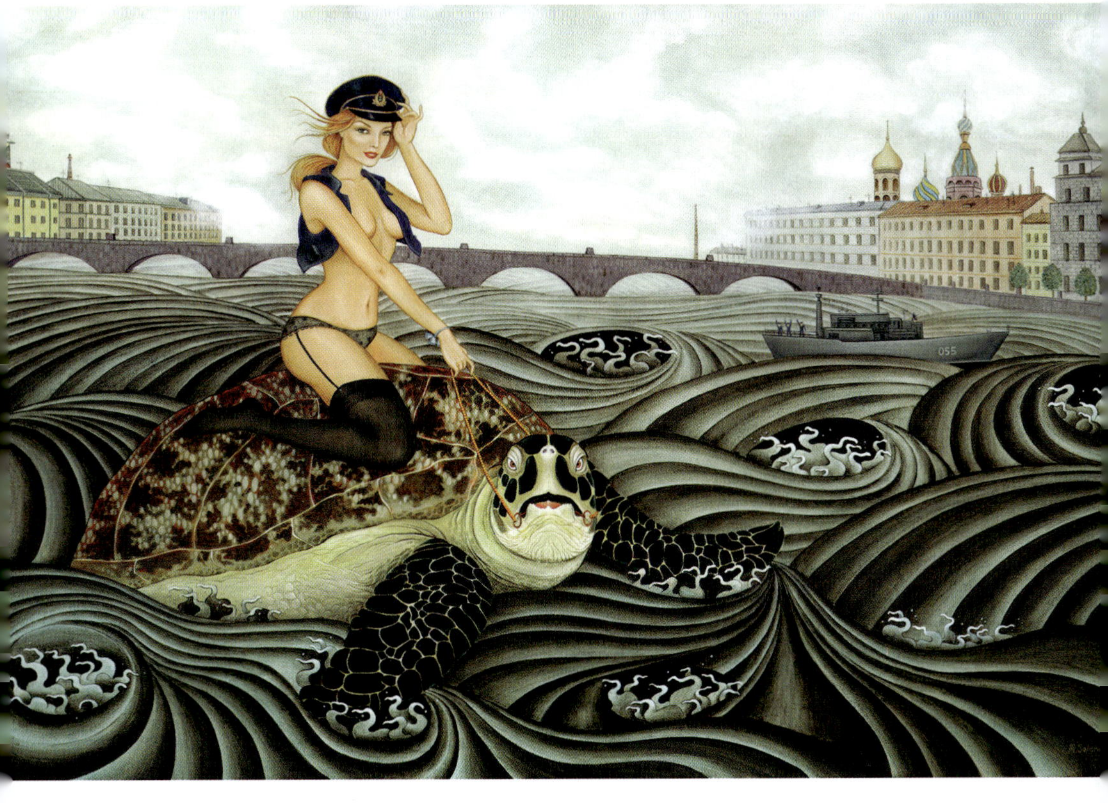

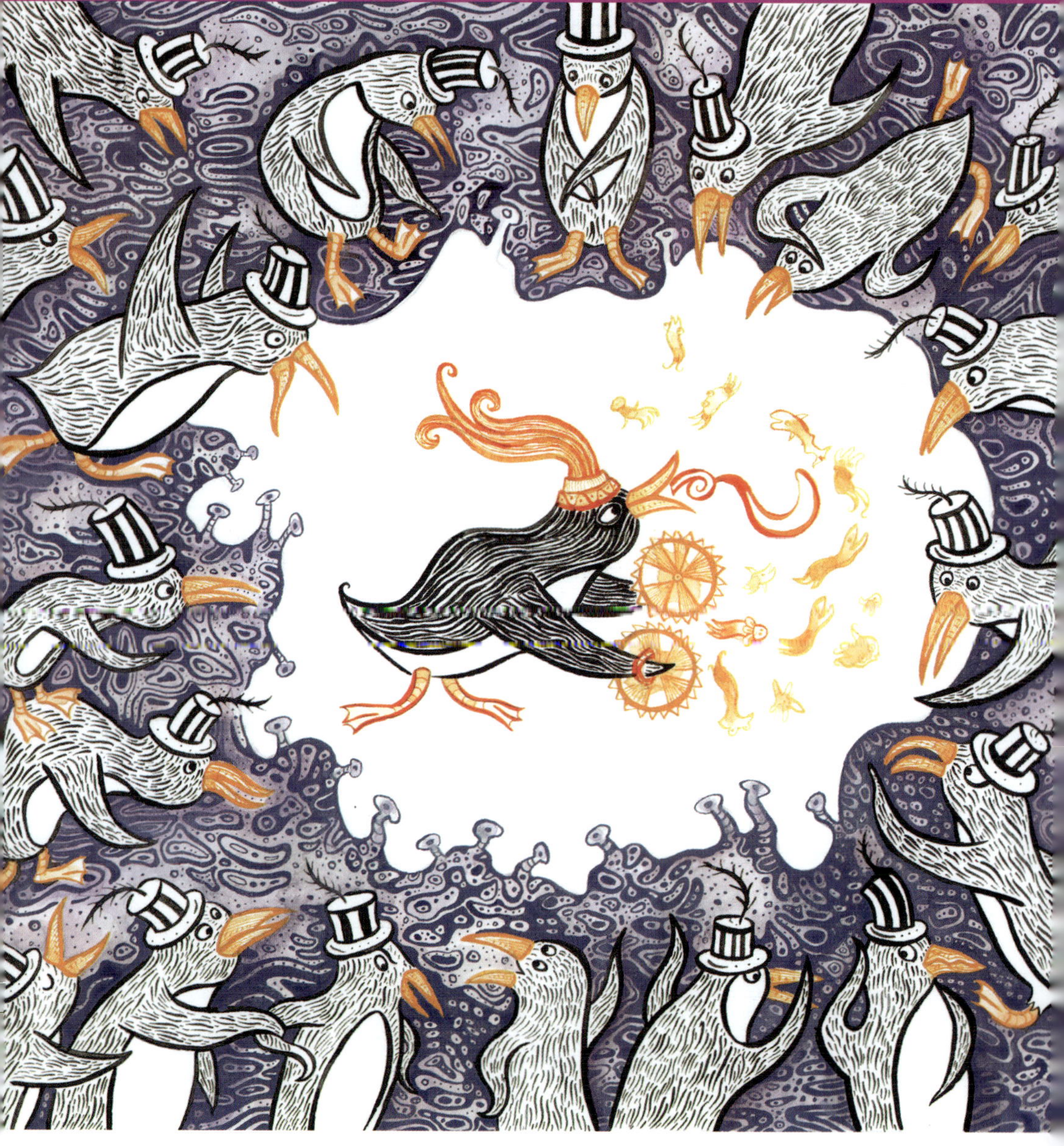

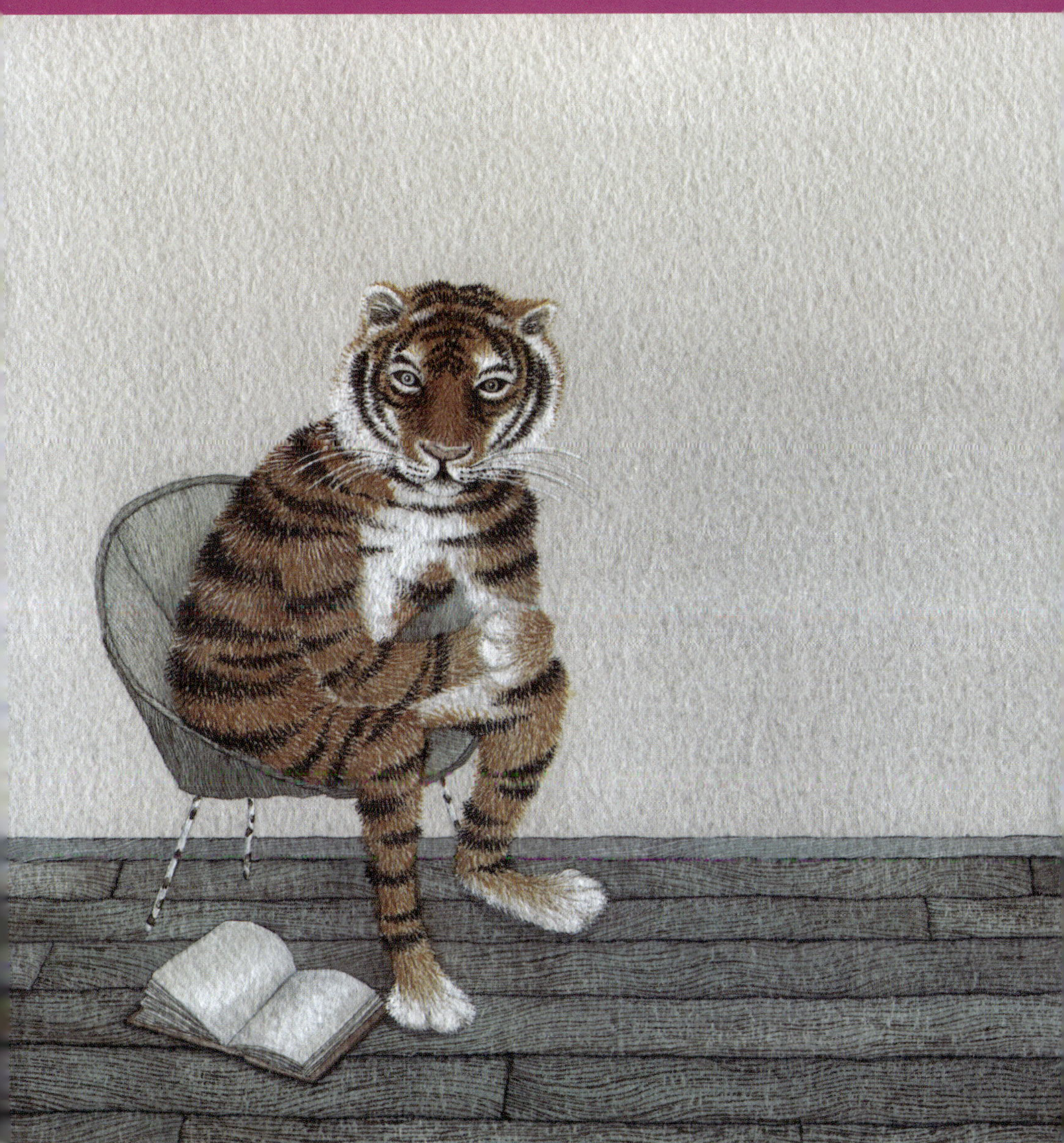

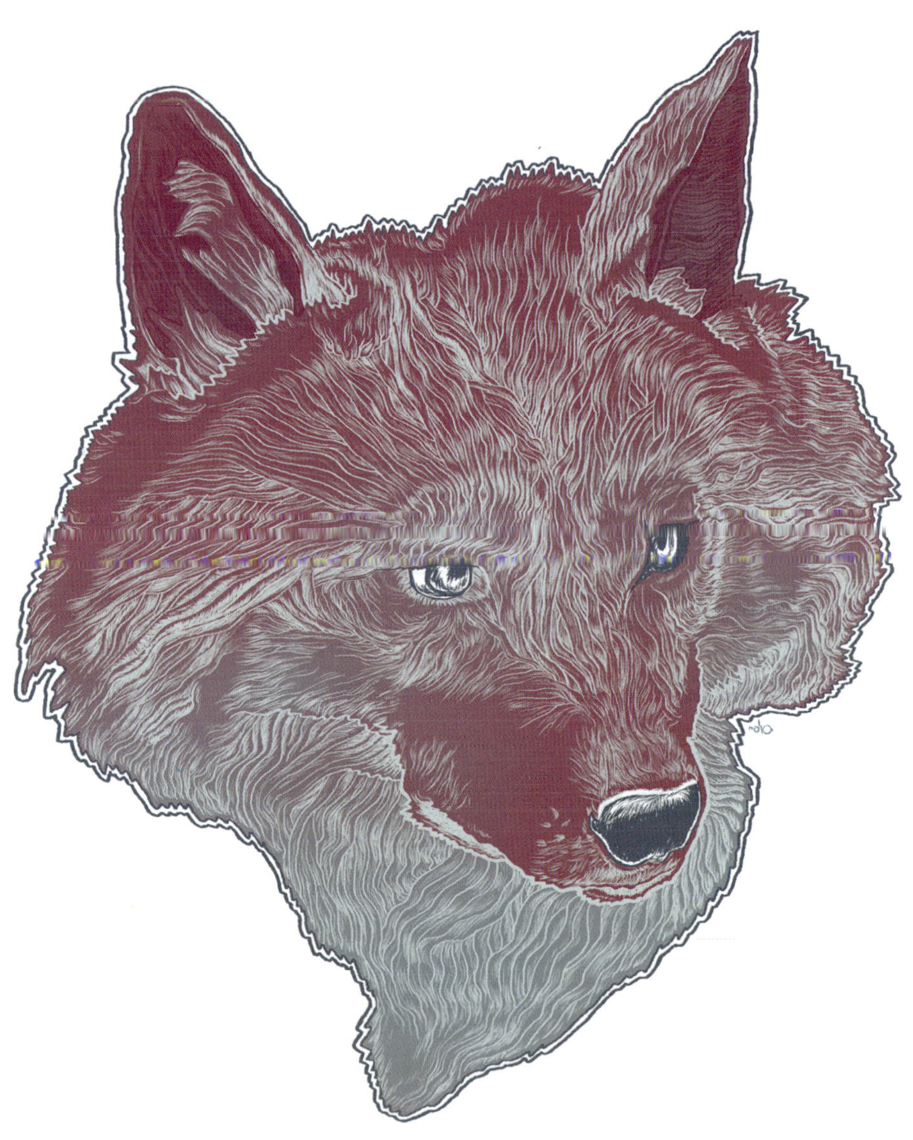

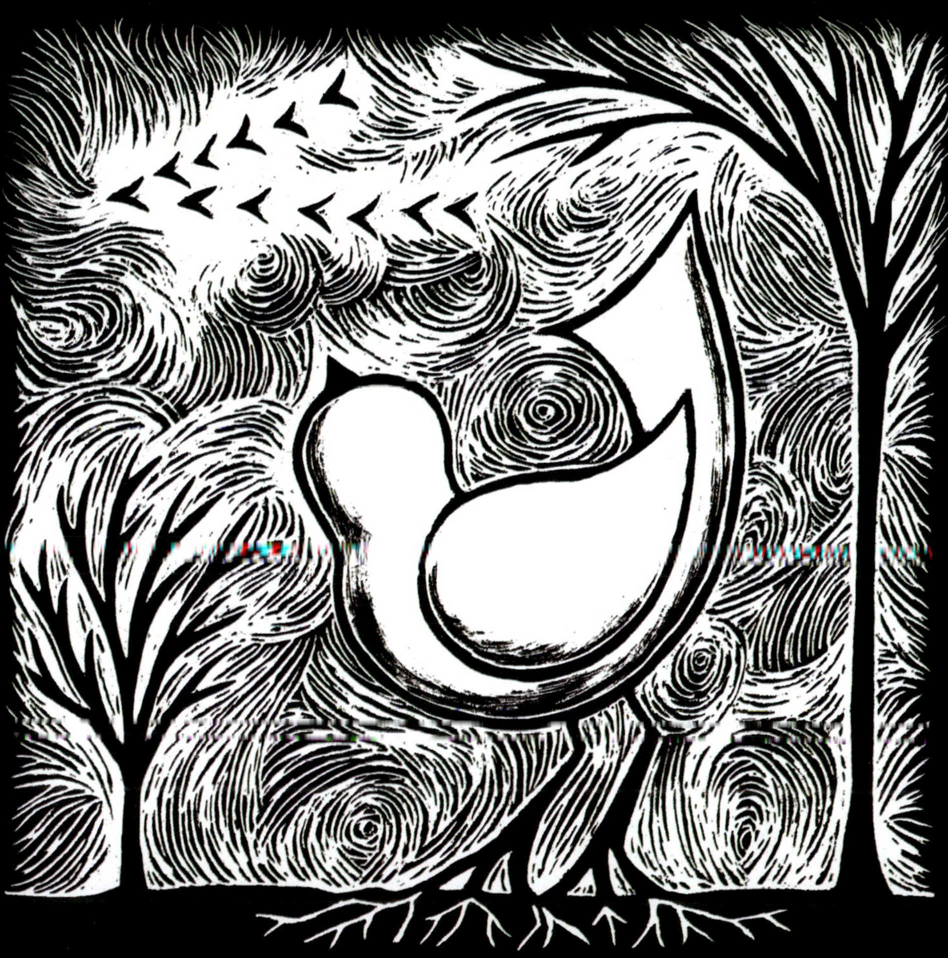

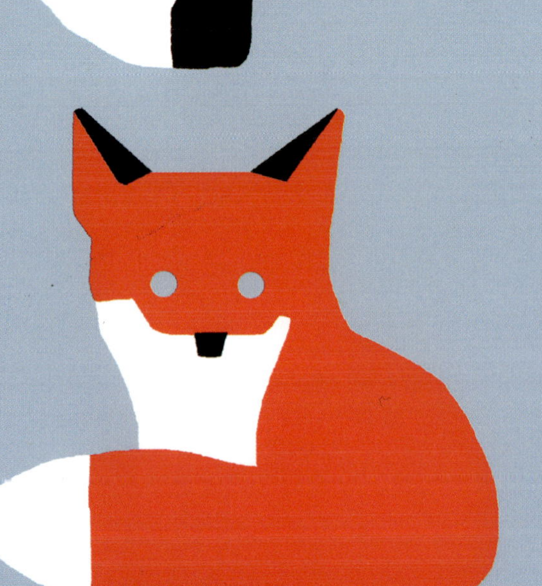

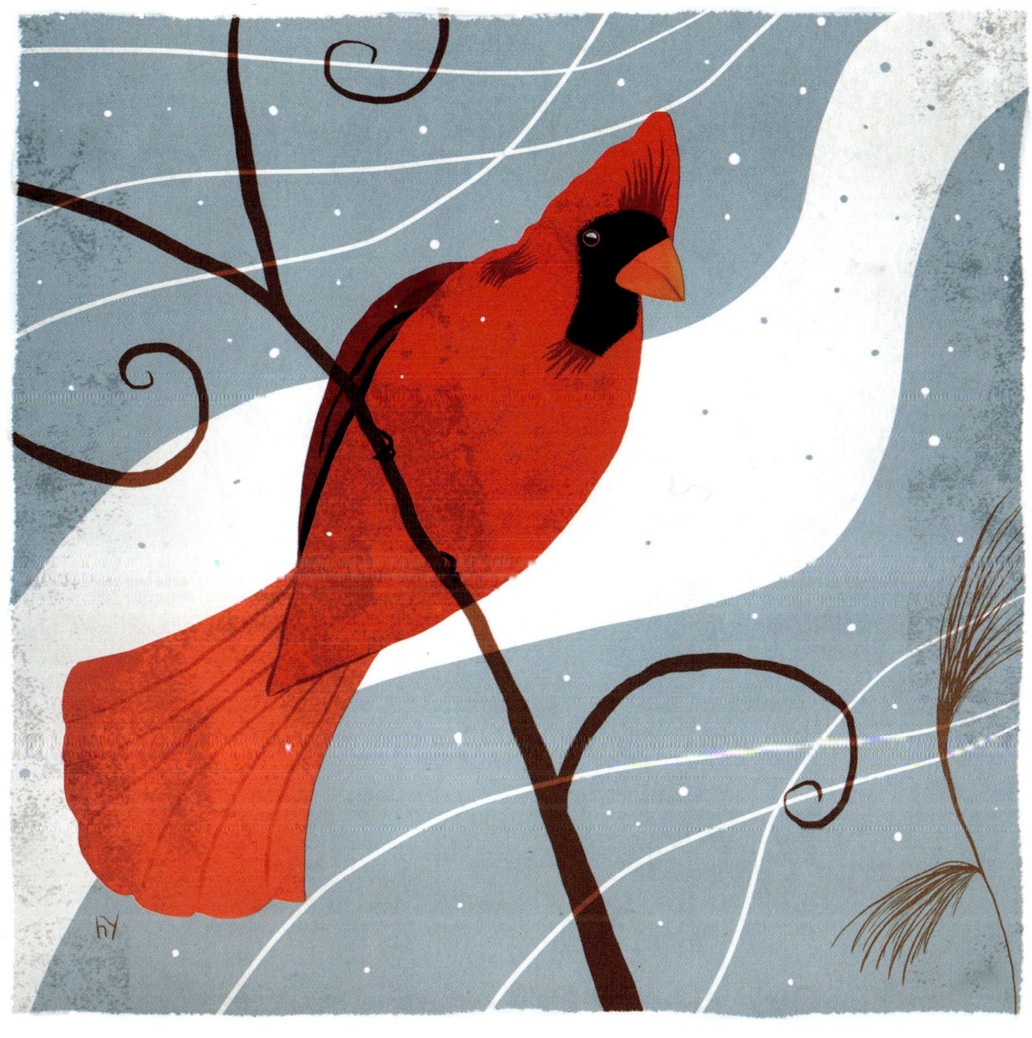

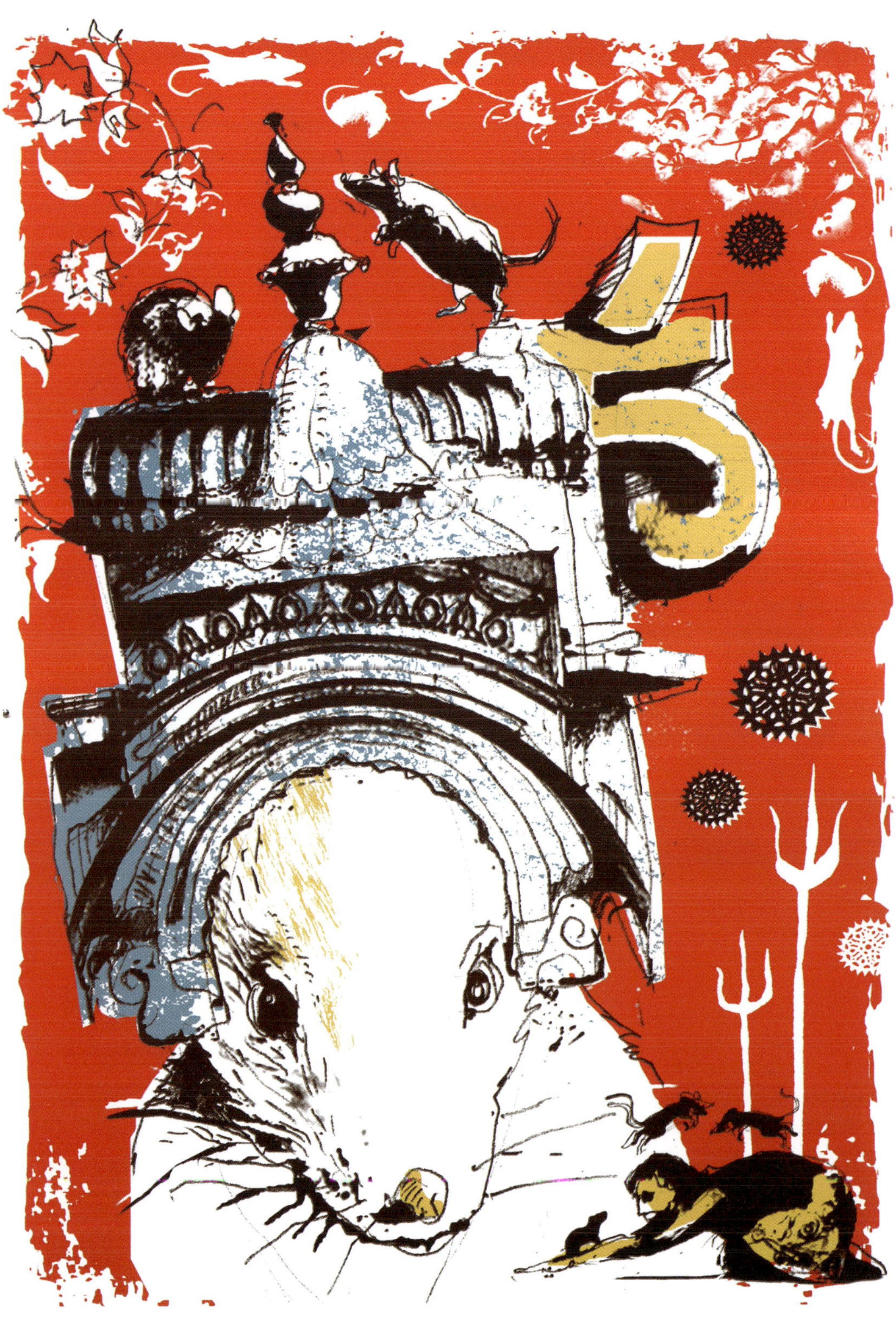

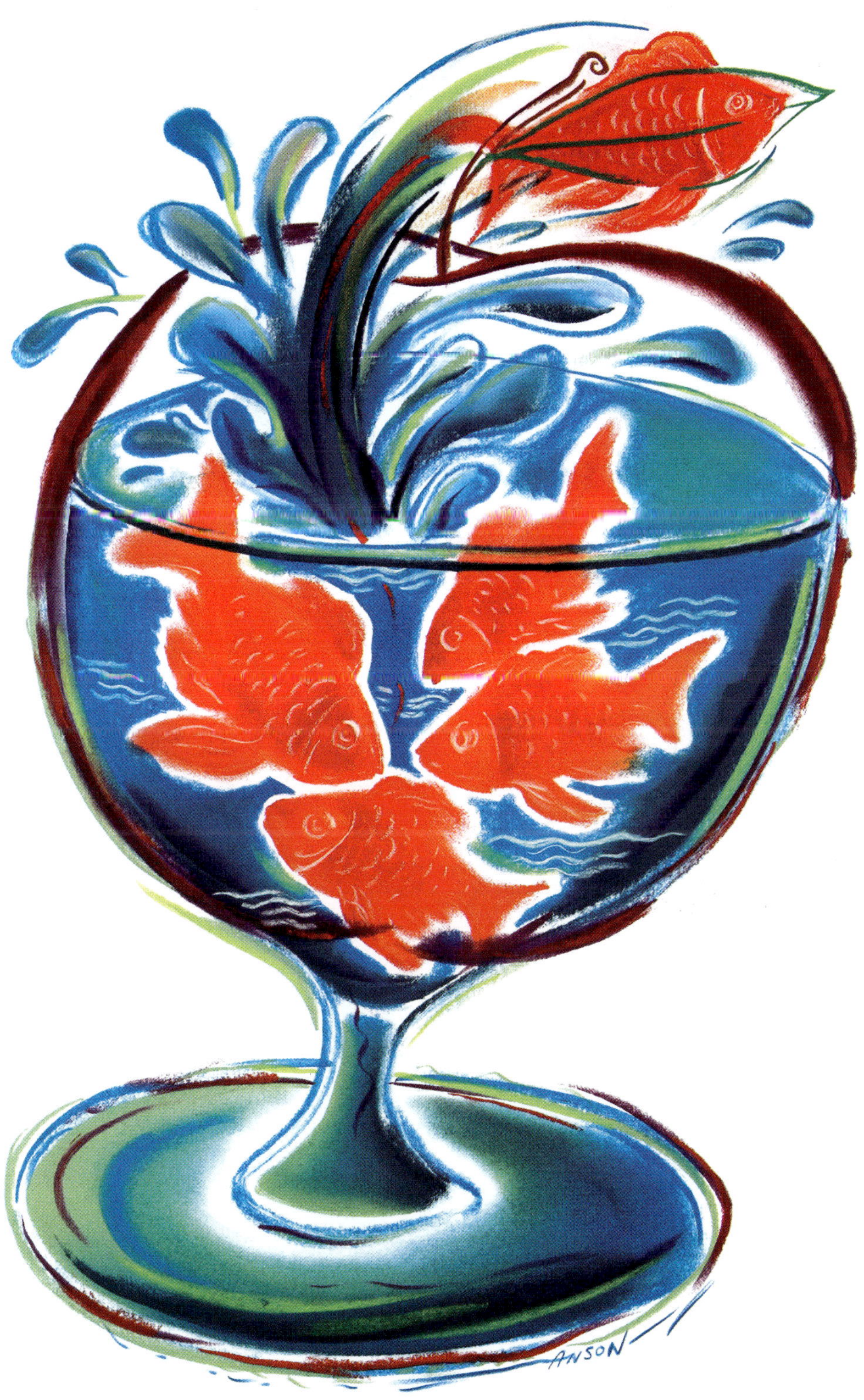

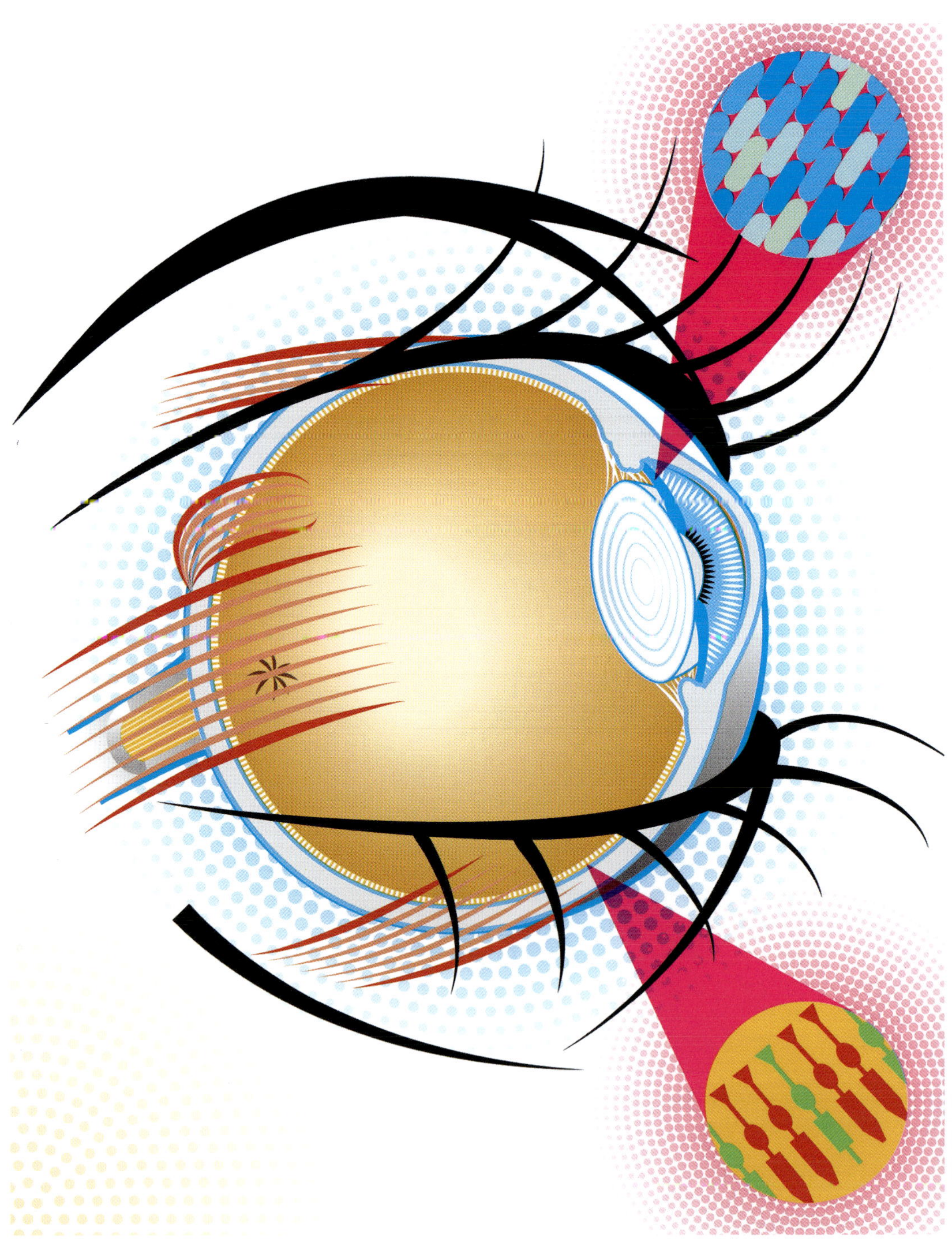

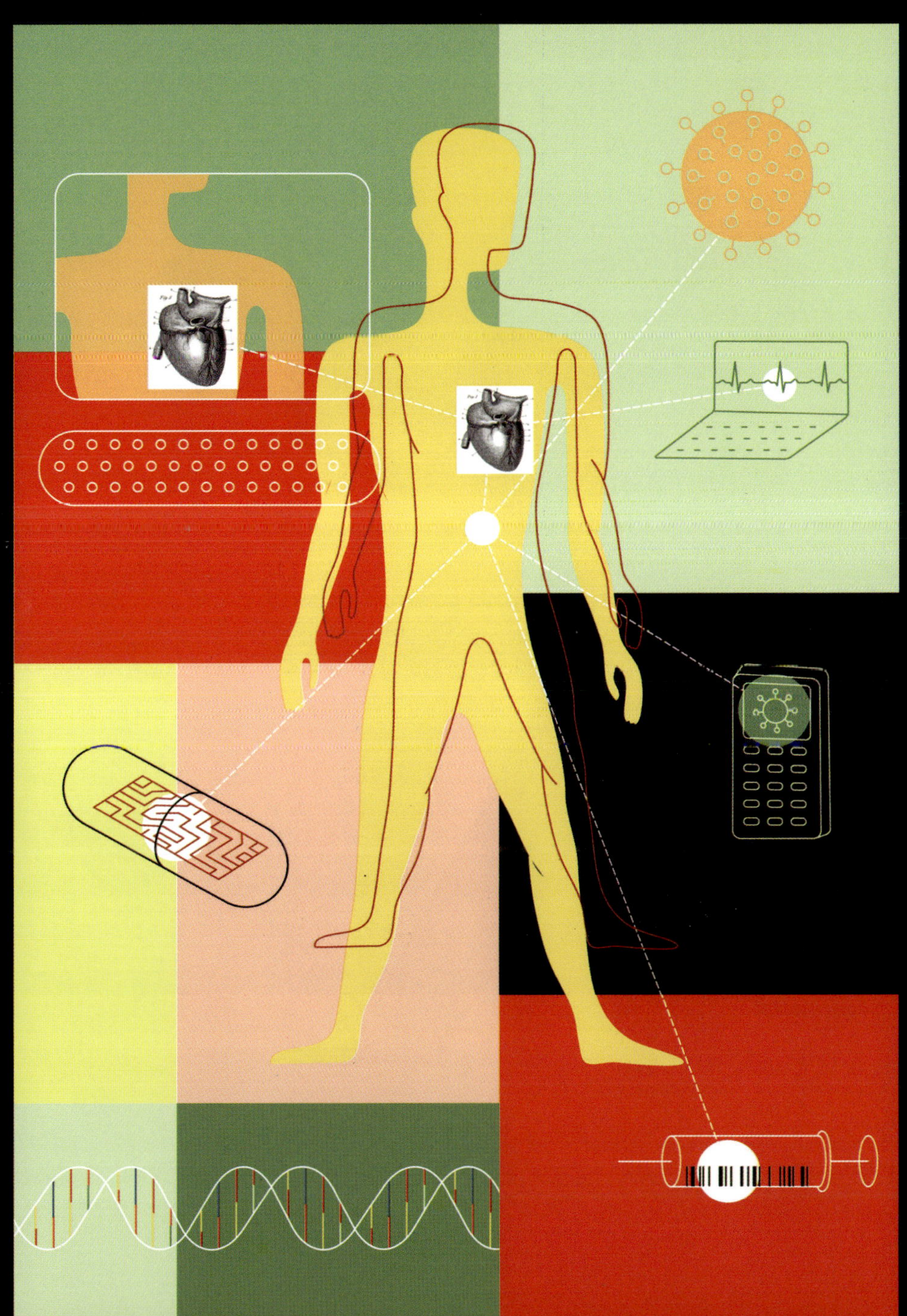

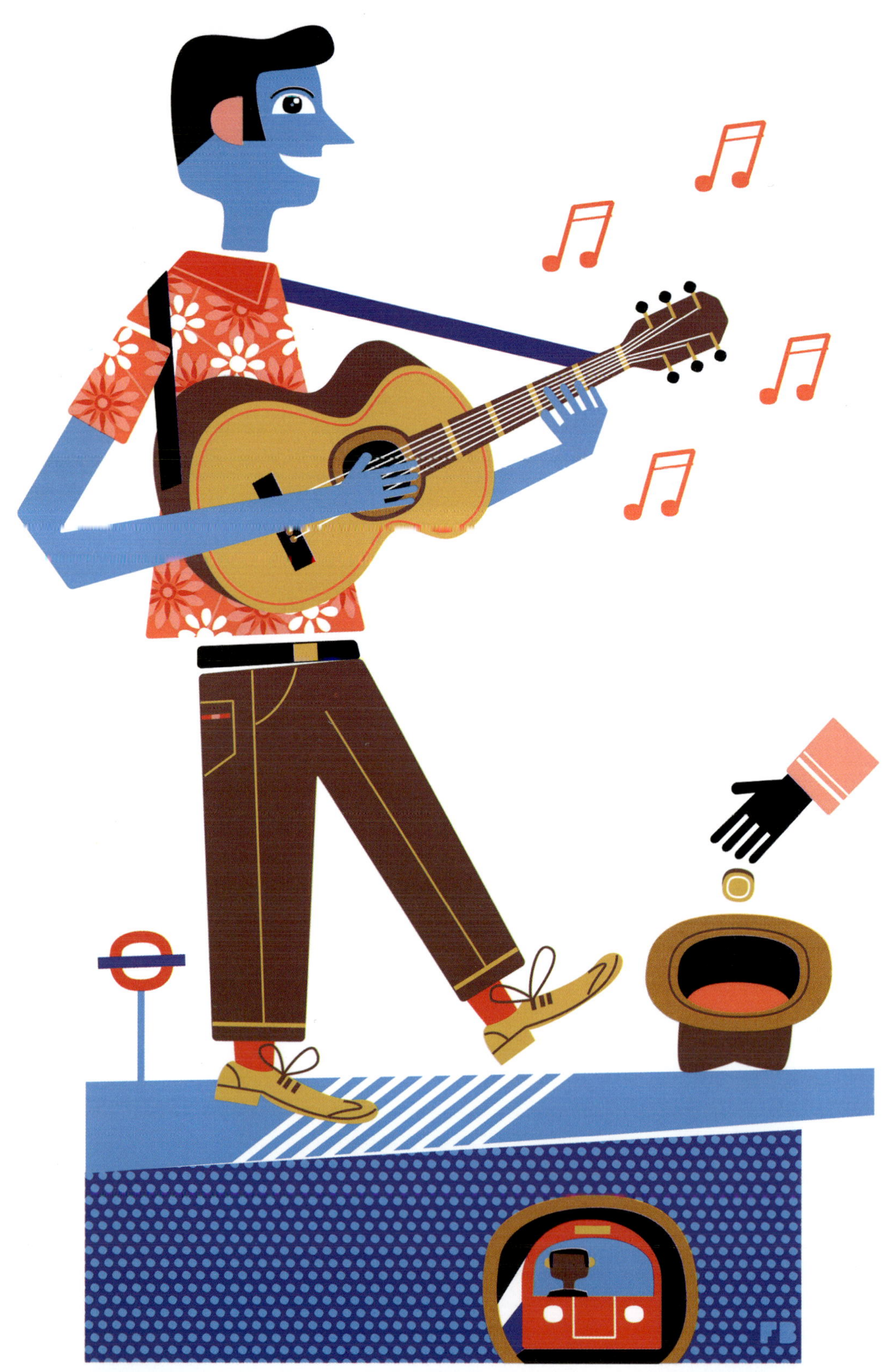

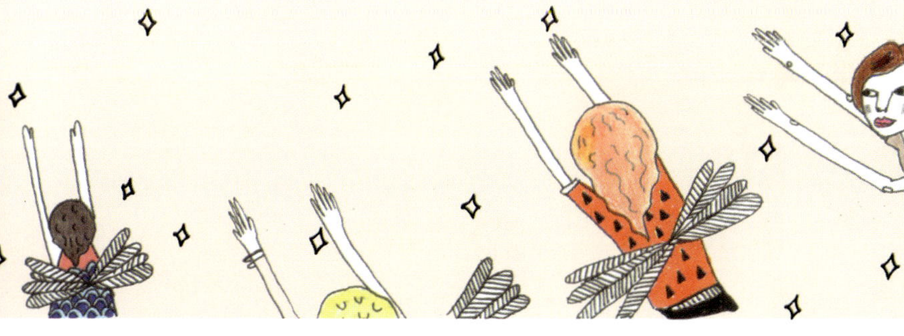

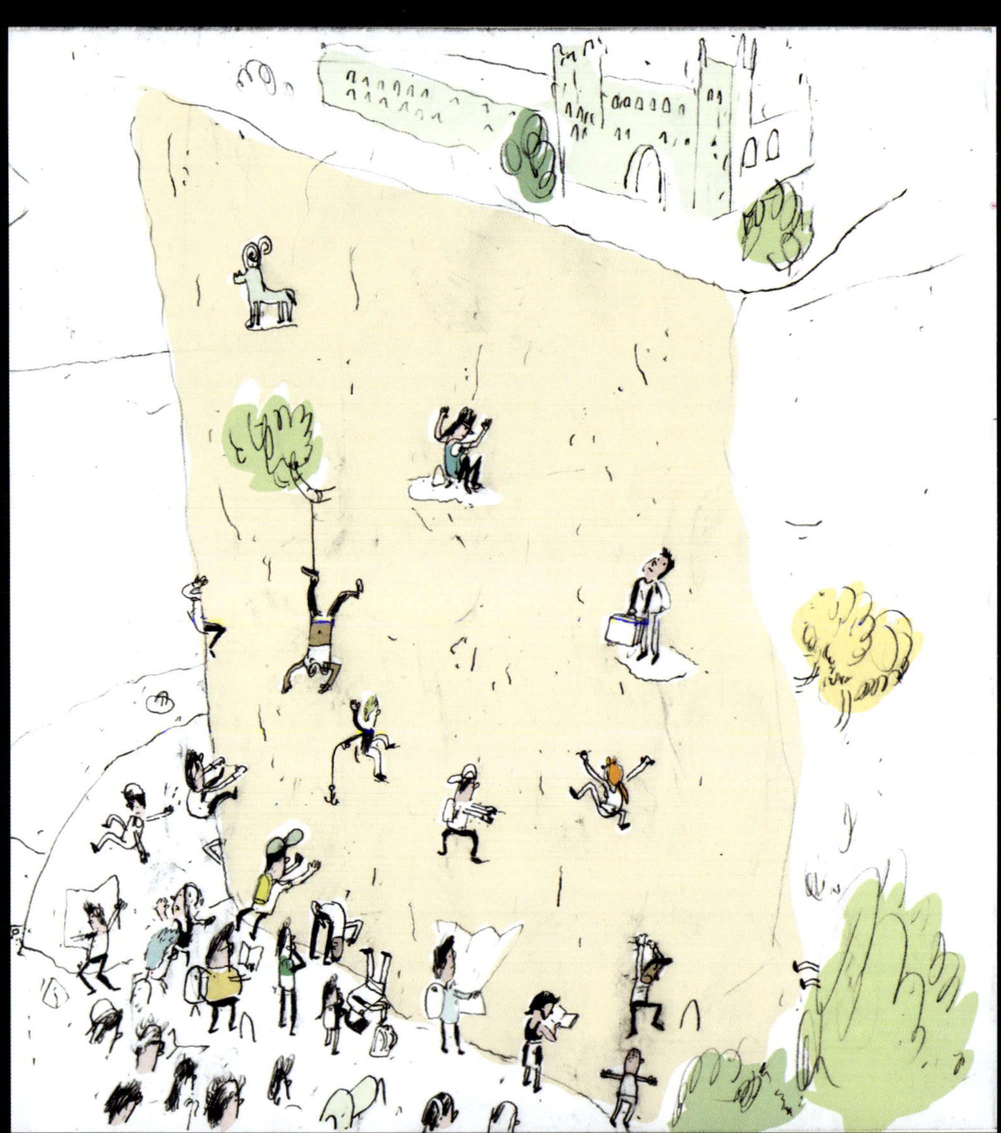

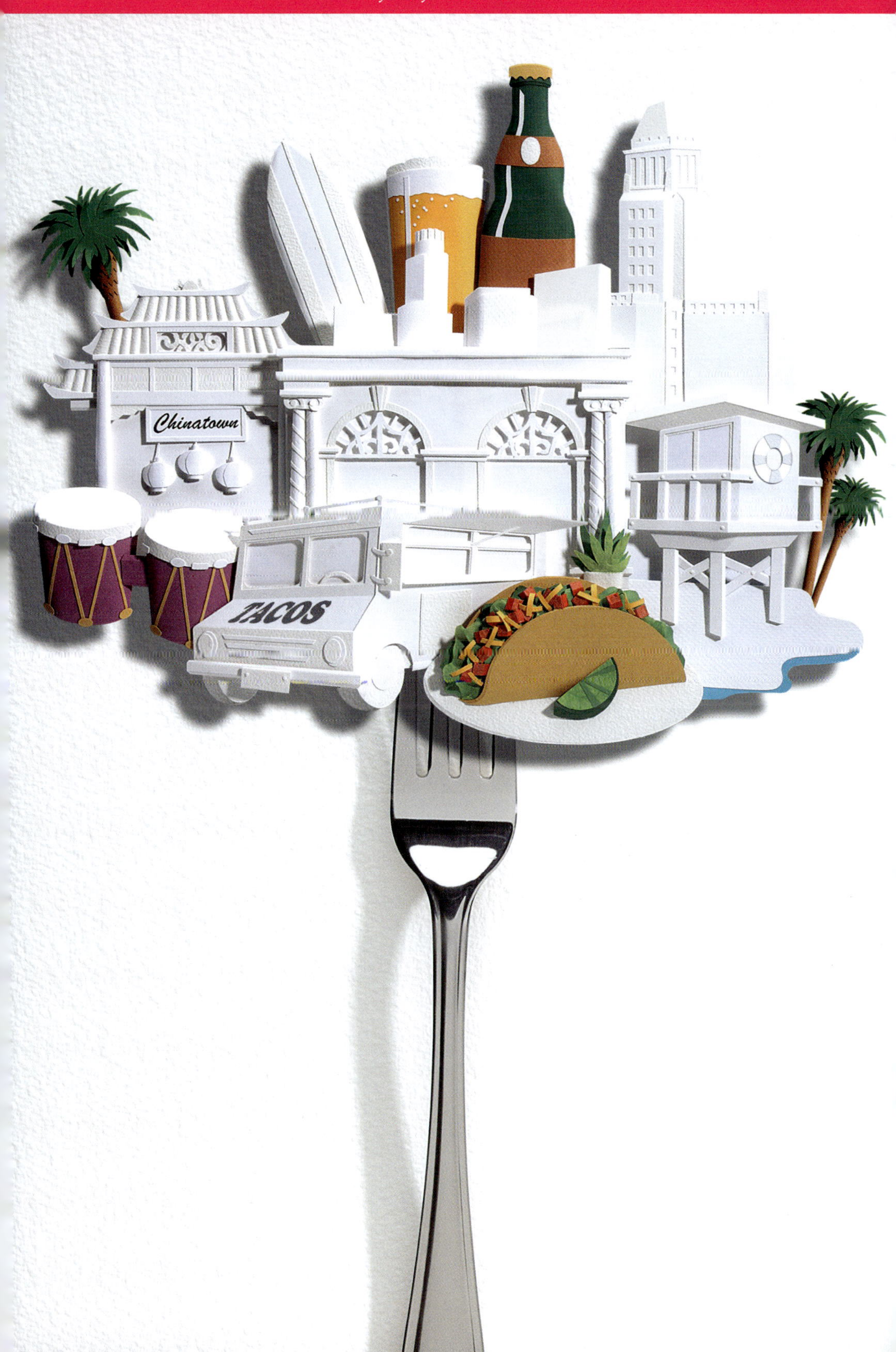
Chinatown
TACOS

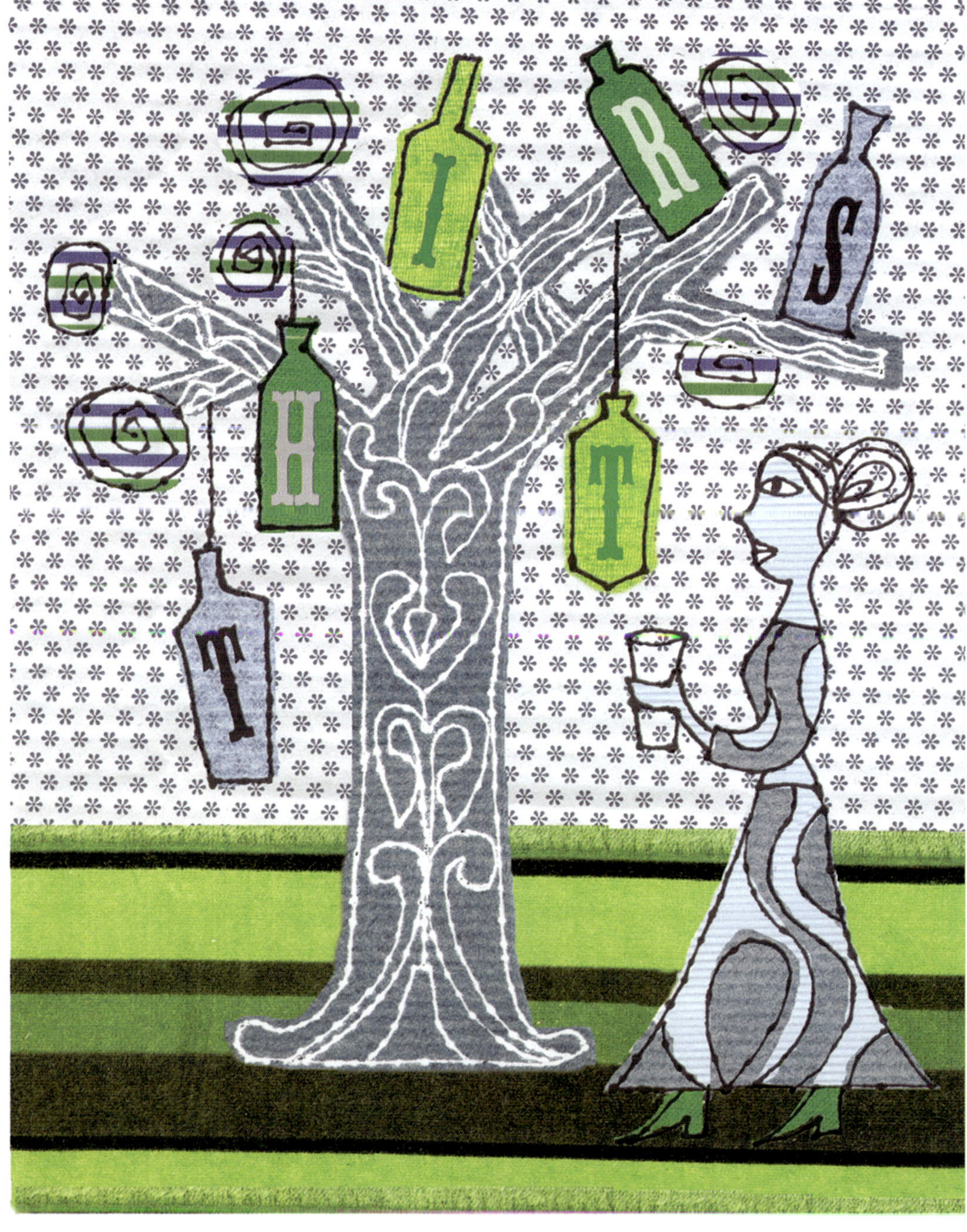

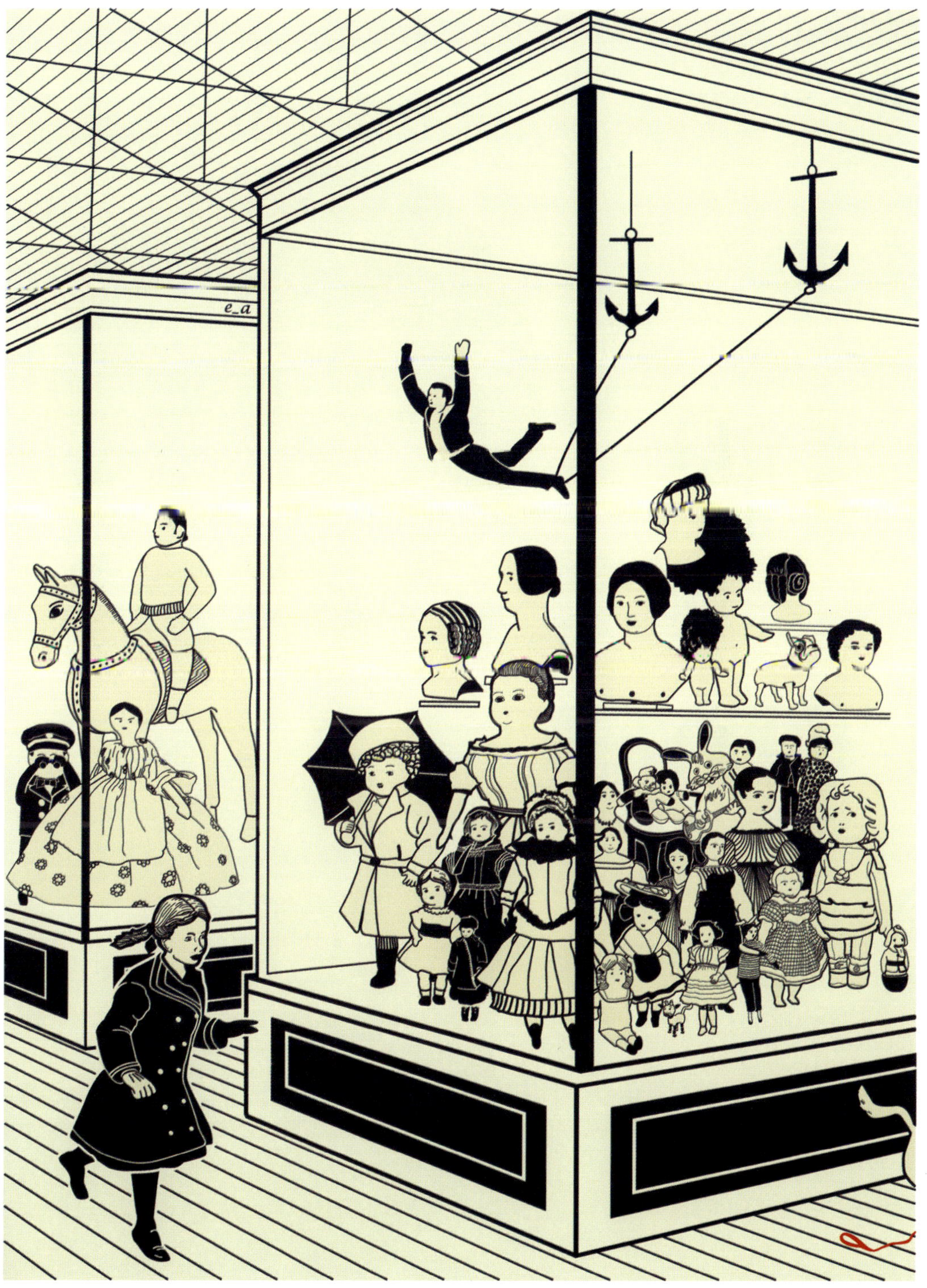

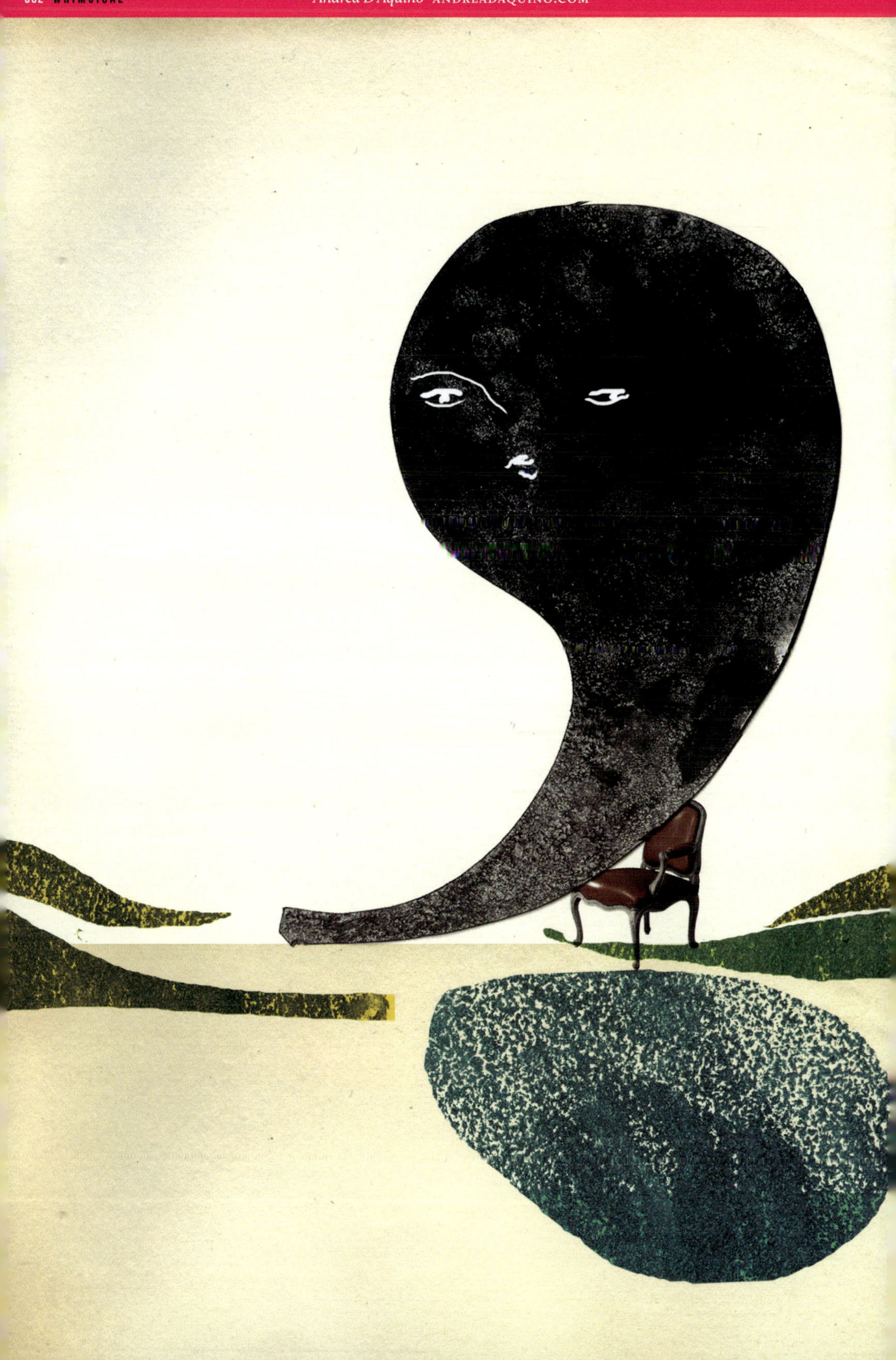

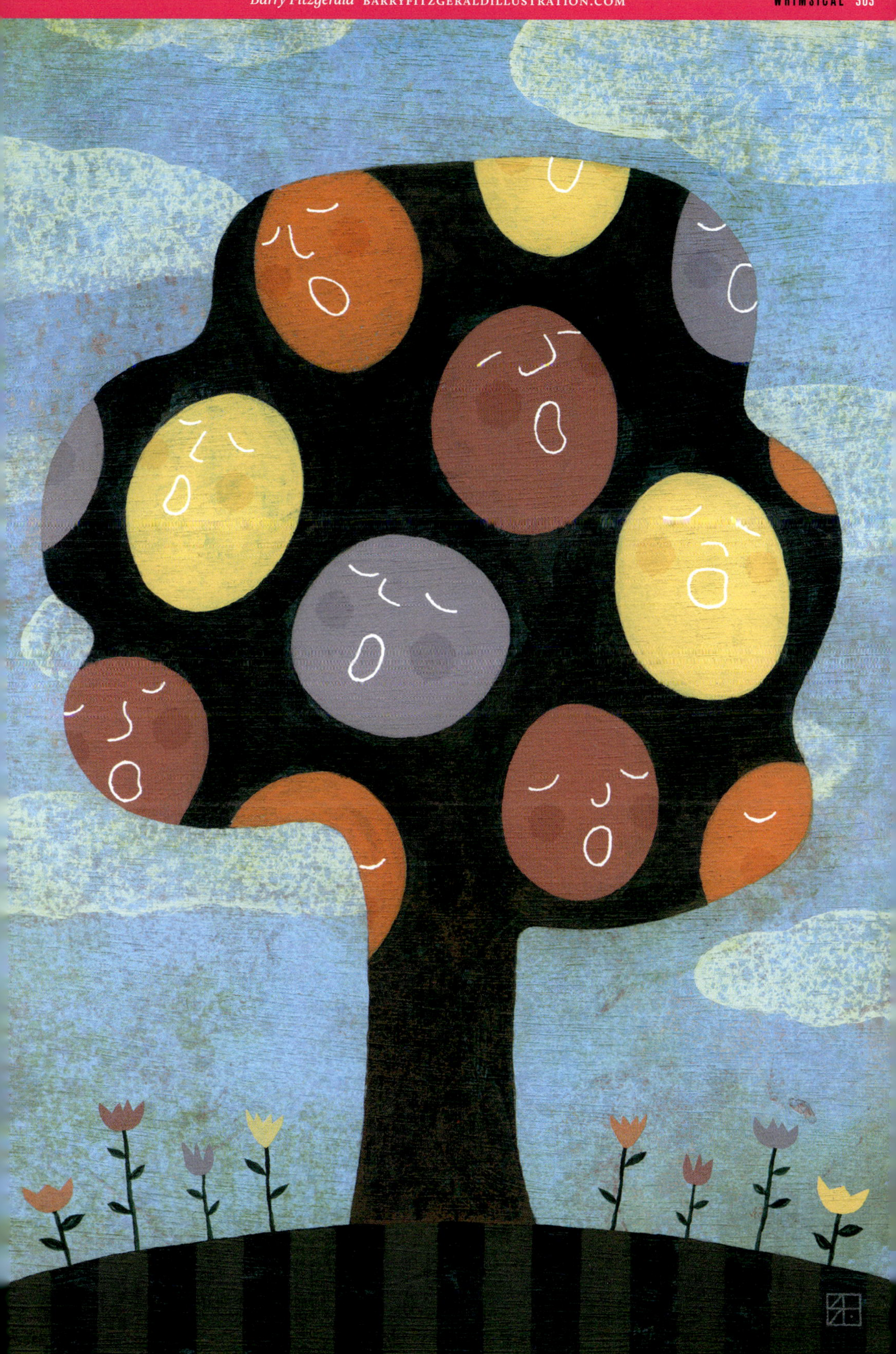

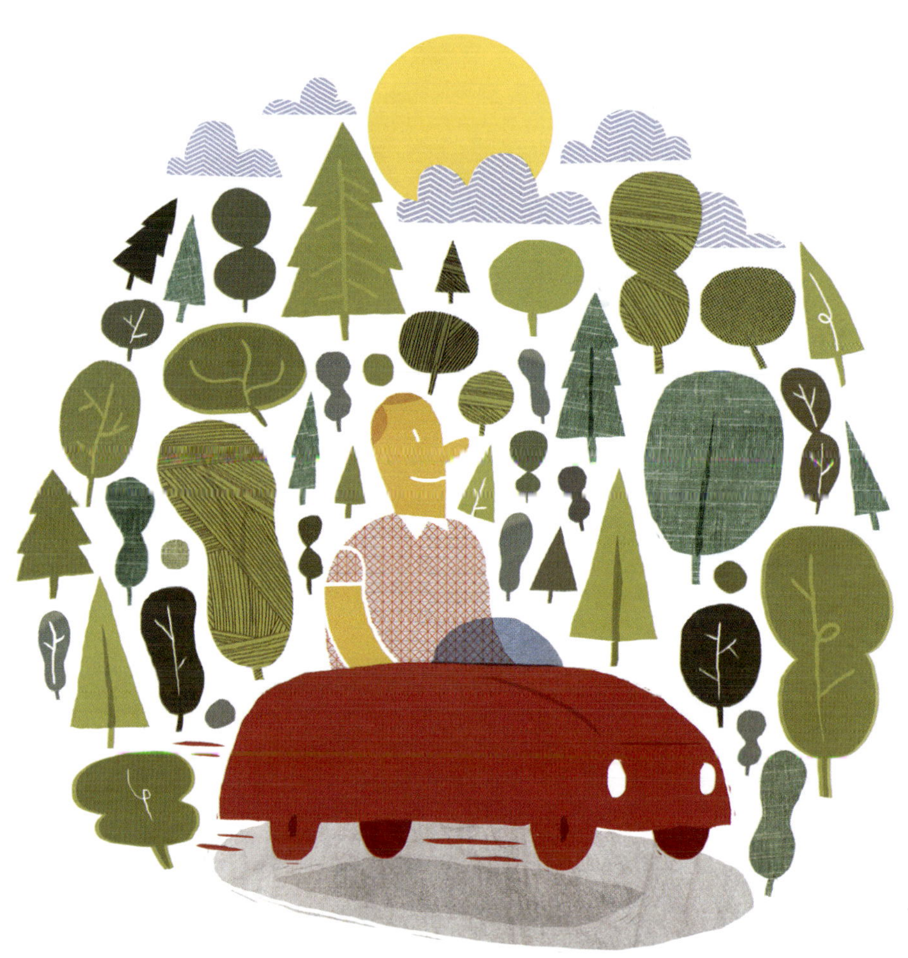
ENJOY SUMMER!

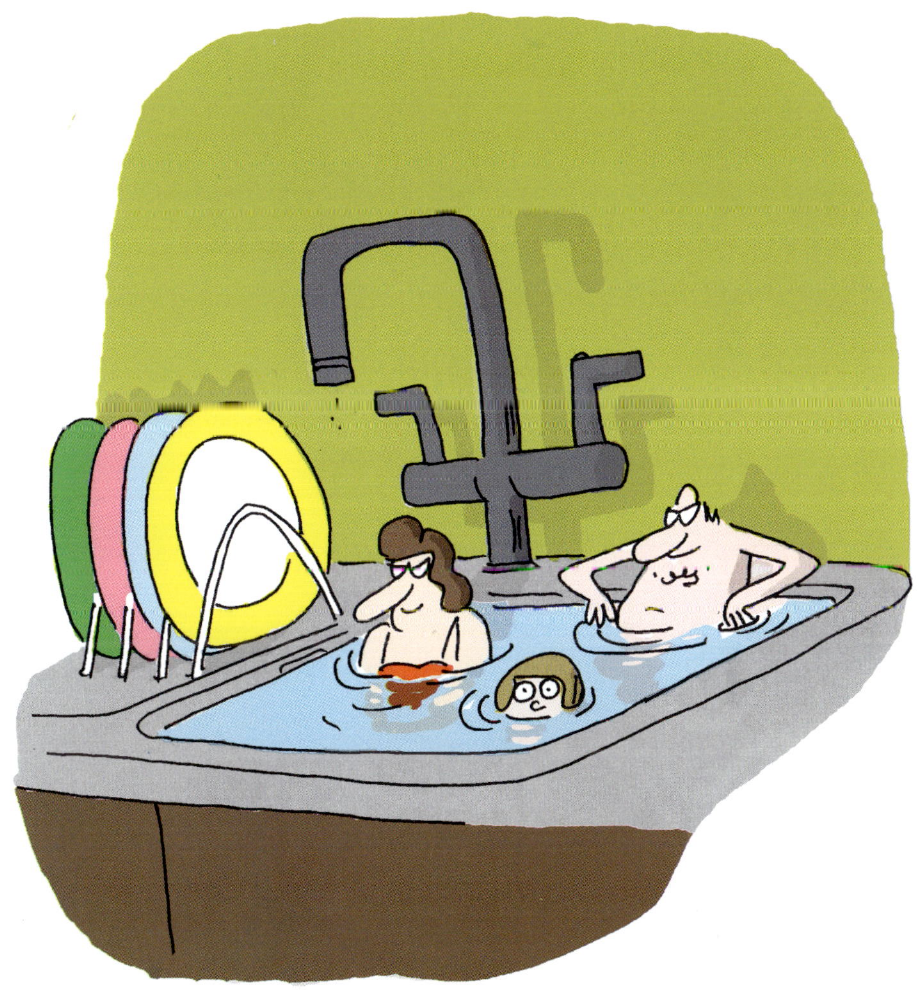

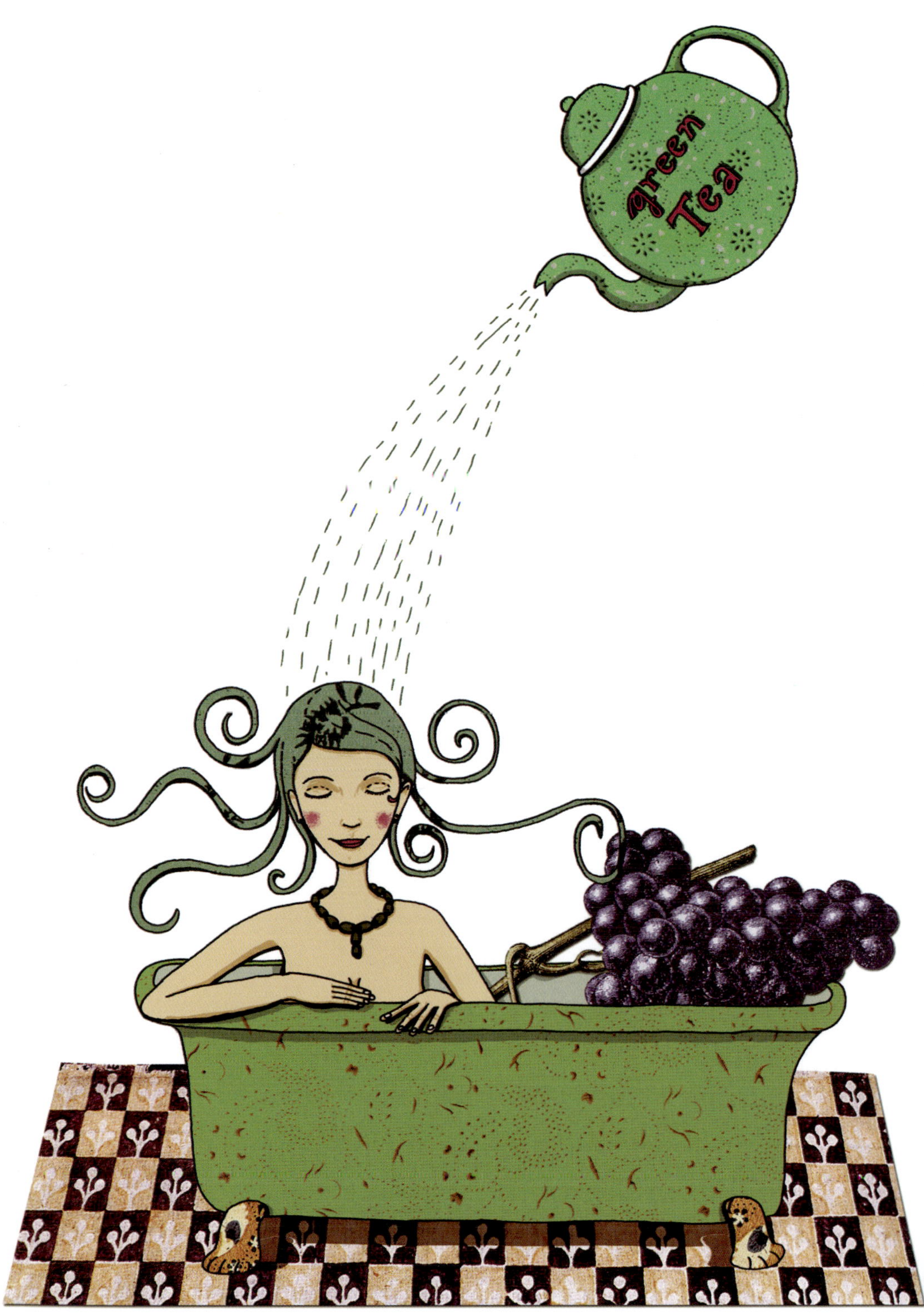
green
Tea

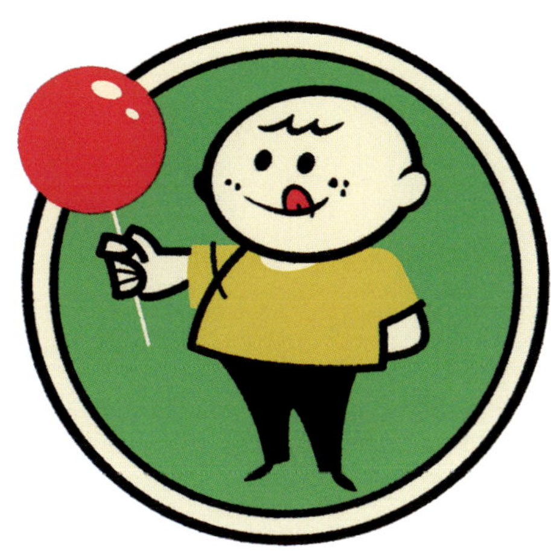

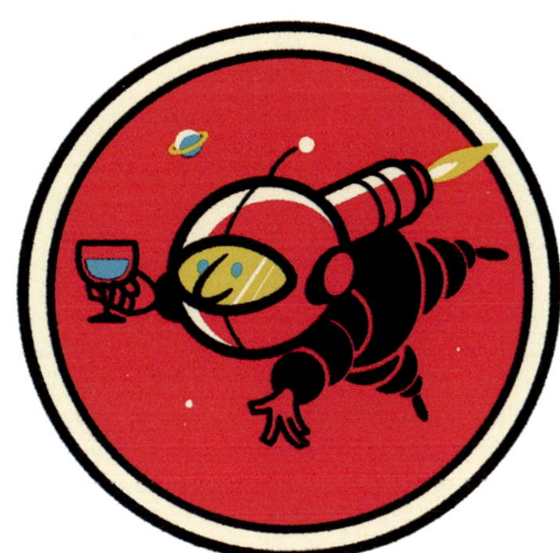

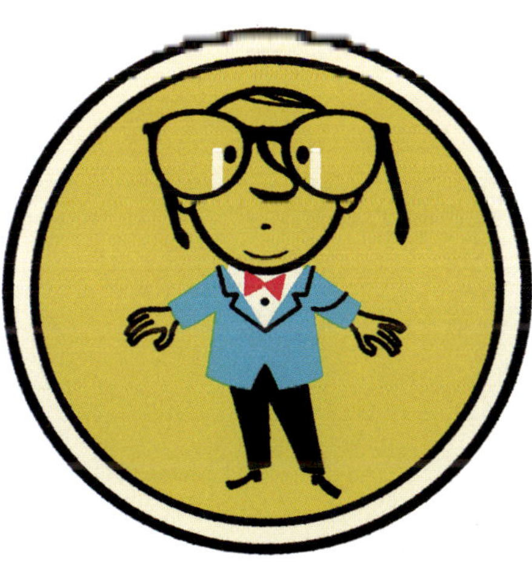

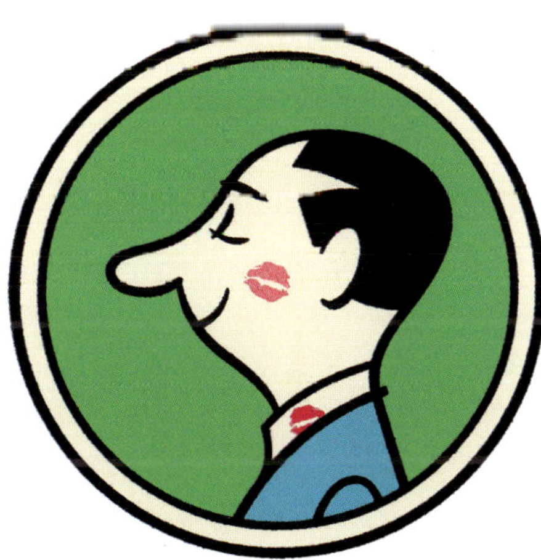

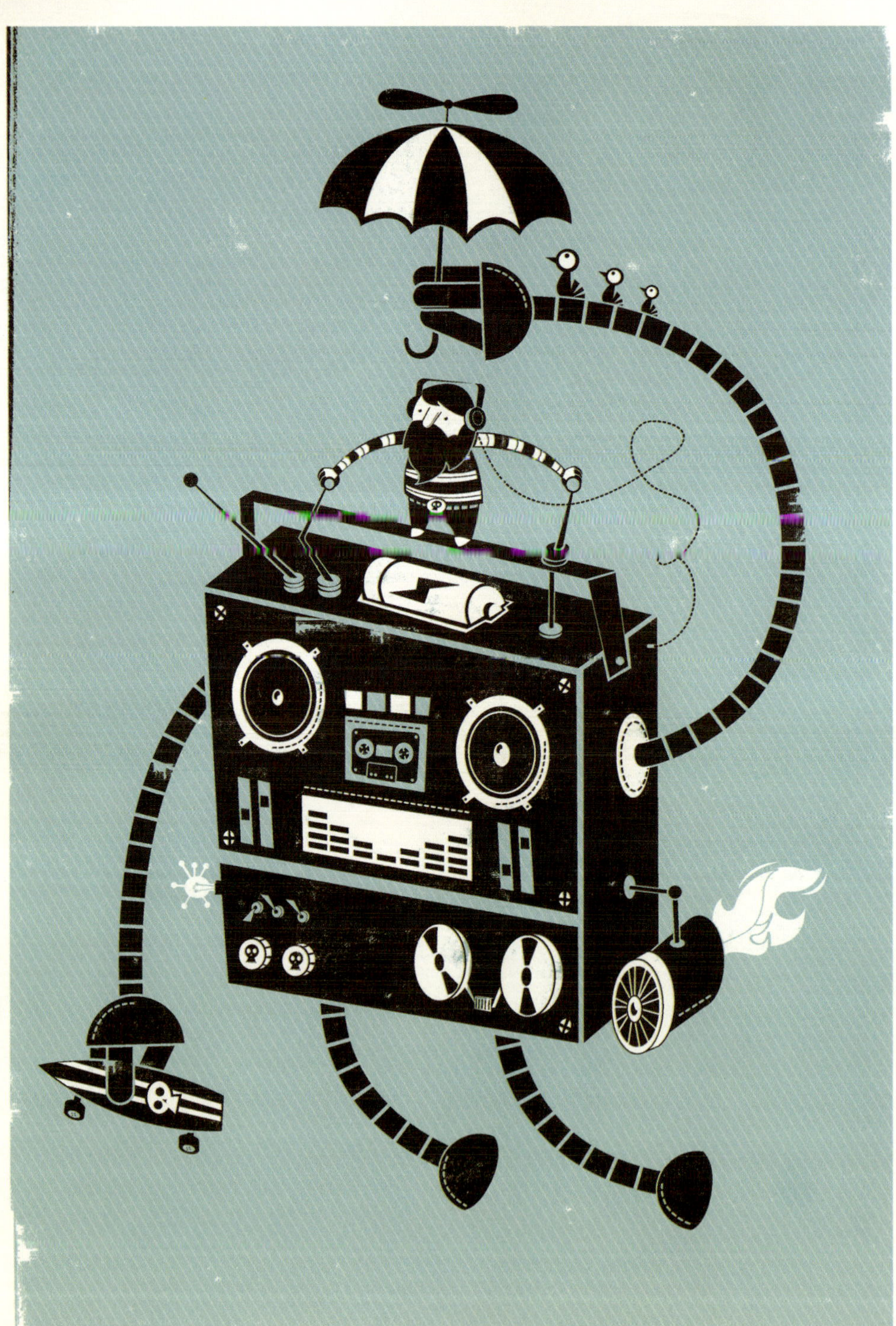

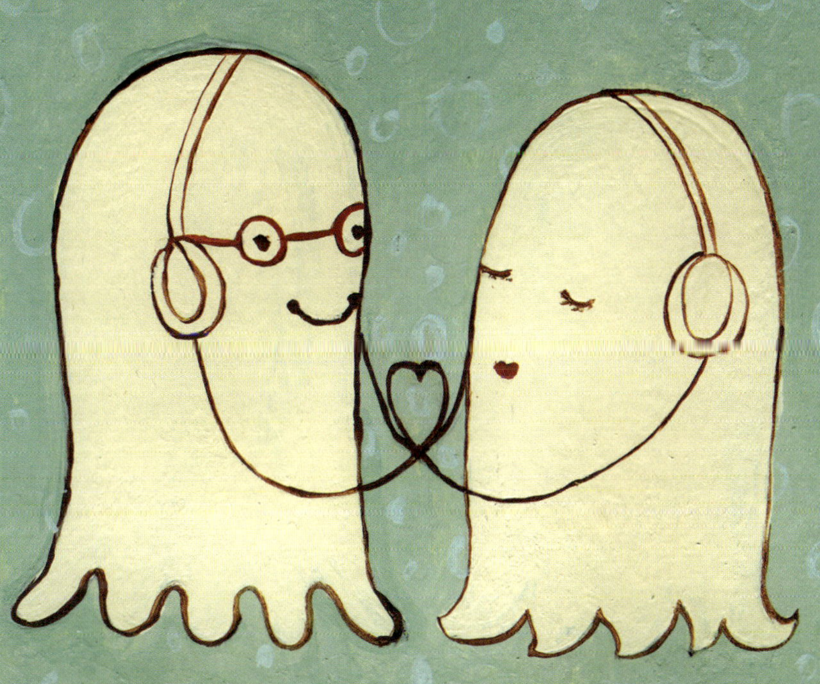

Terri FryKasuba

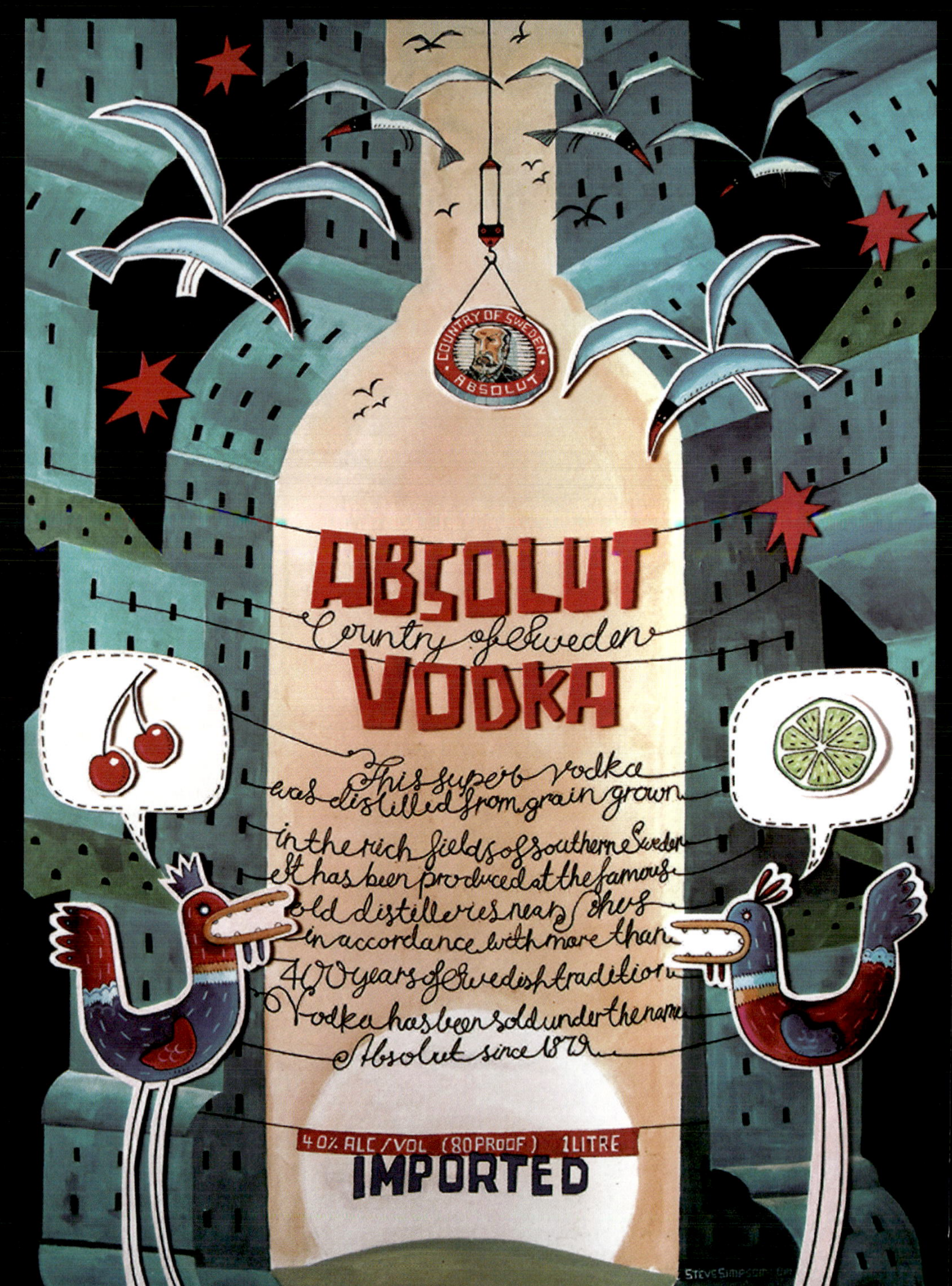
COUNTRY OF SWEDEN
ABSOLUT
ABSOLUT
Country of Sweden
VODKA
This superb vodka was distilled from grain grown in the rich fields of southern Sweden. It has been produced at the famous old distilleries near Ahus in accordance with more than 400 years of Swedish tradition. Vodka has been sold under the name Absolut since 1879.
40% ALC/VOL (80 PROOF) 1 LITRE
IMPORTED
STEVE SIMPSON

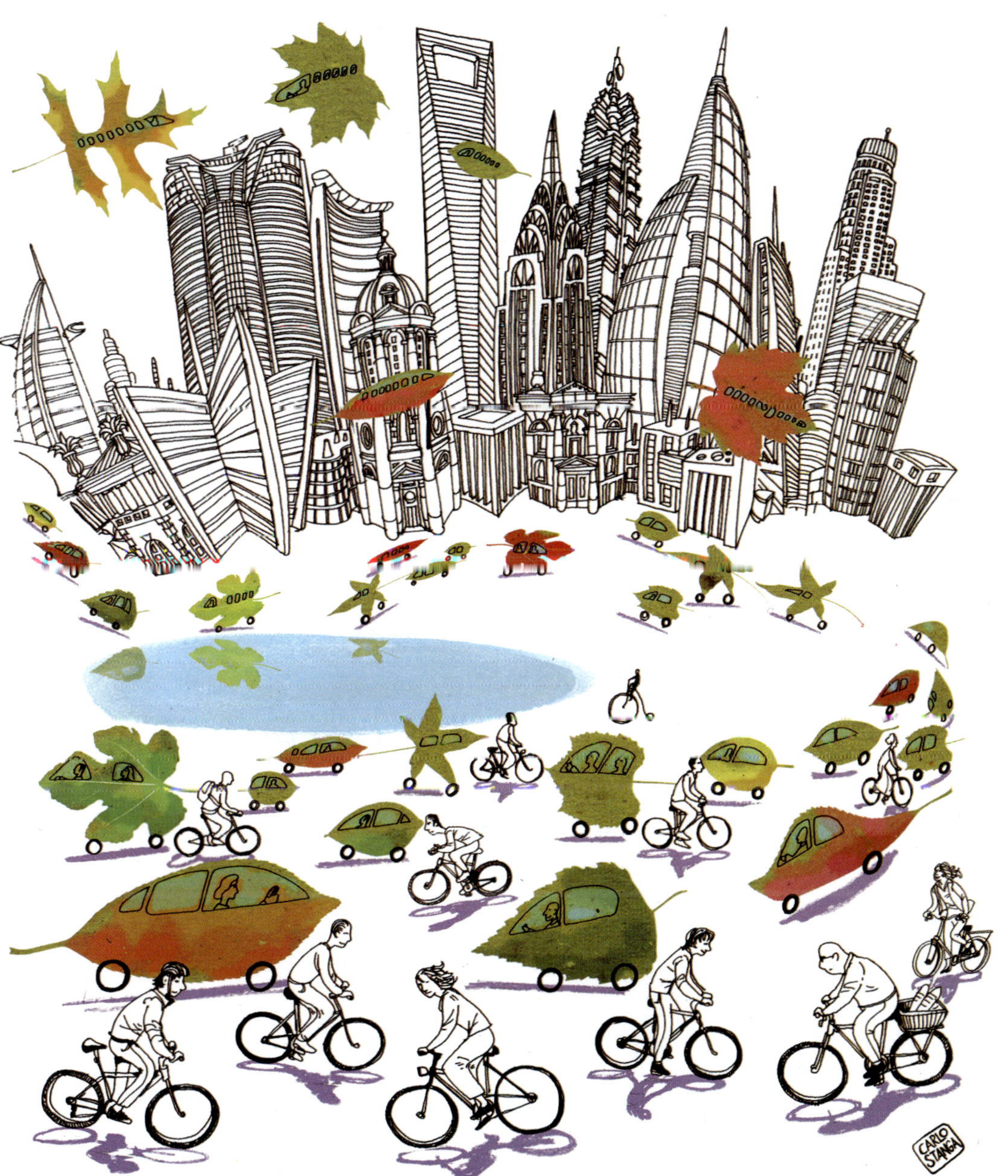

Susan Farrington SUSANFARRINGTON.COM

RoBots AND Friends

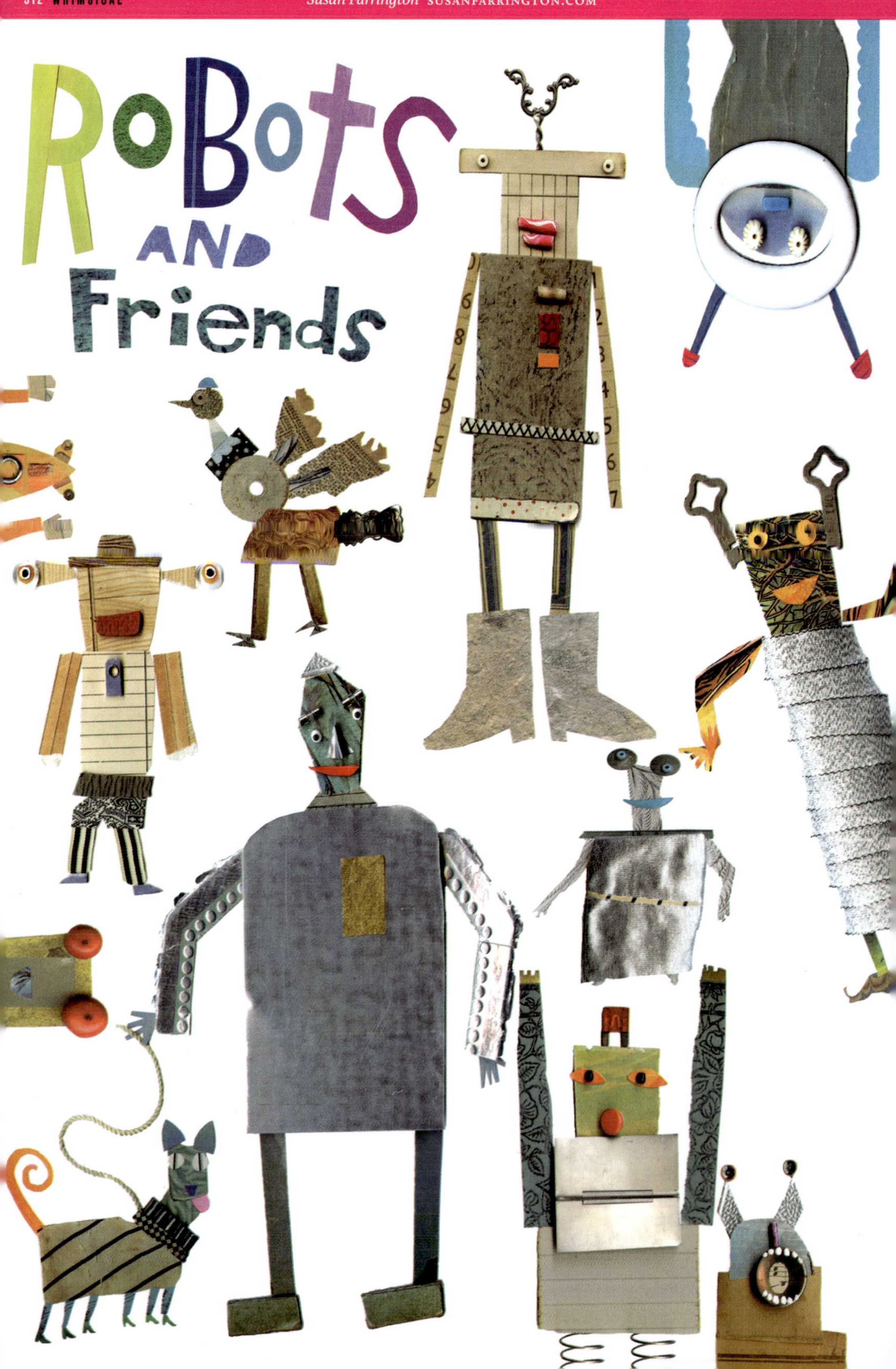

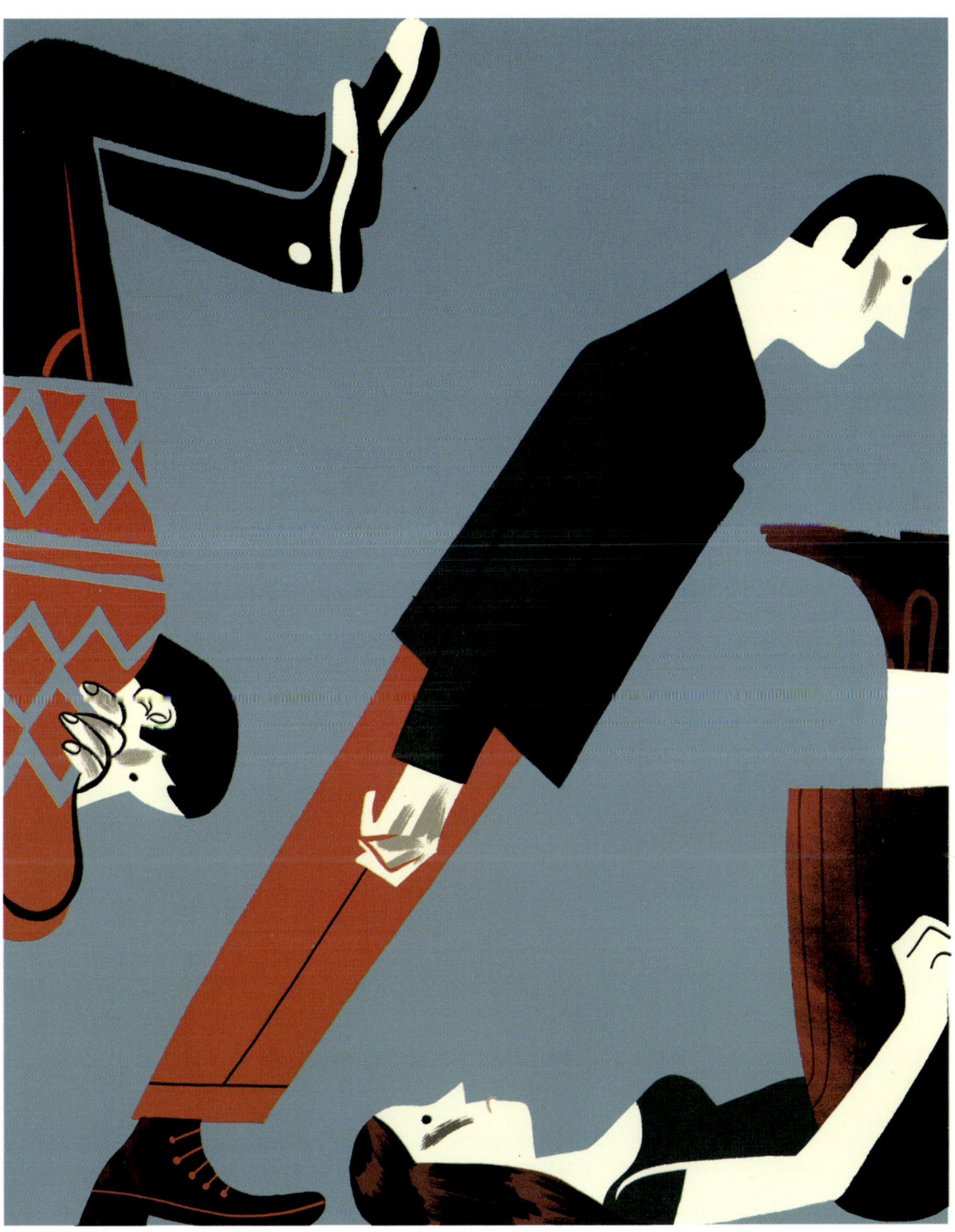

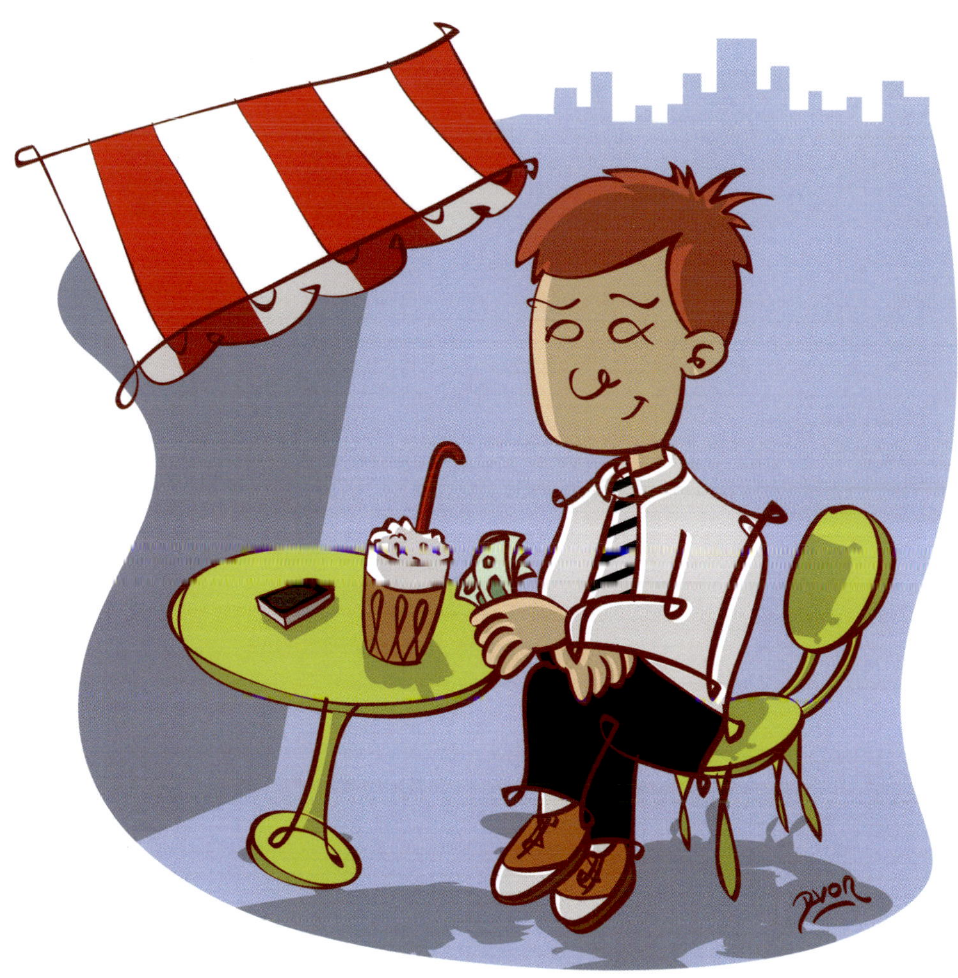

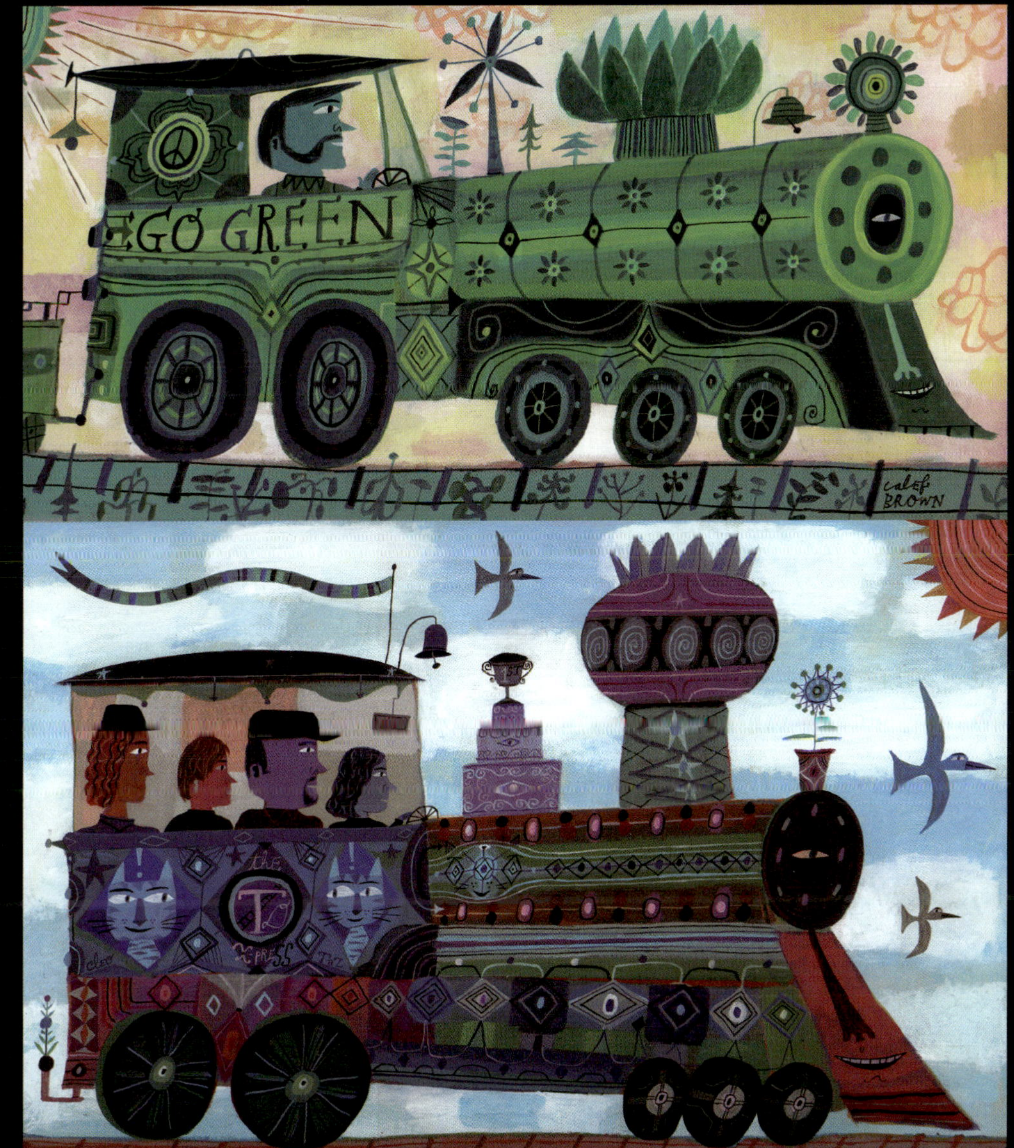
GO GREEN
CALEF BROWN

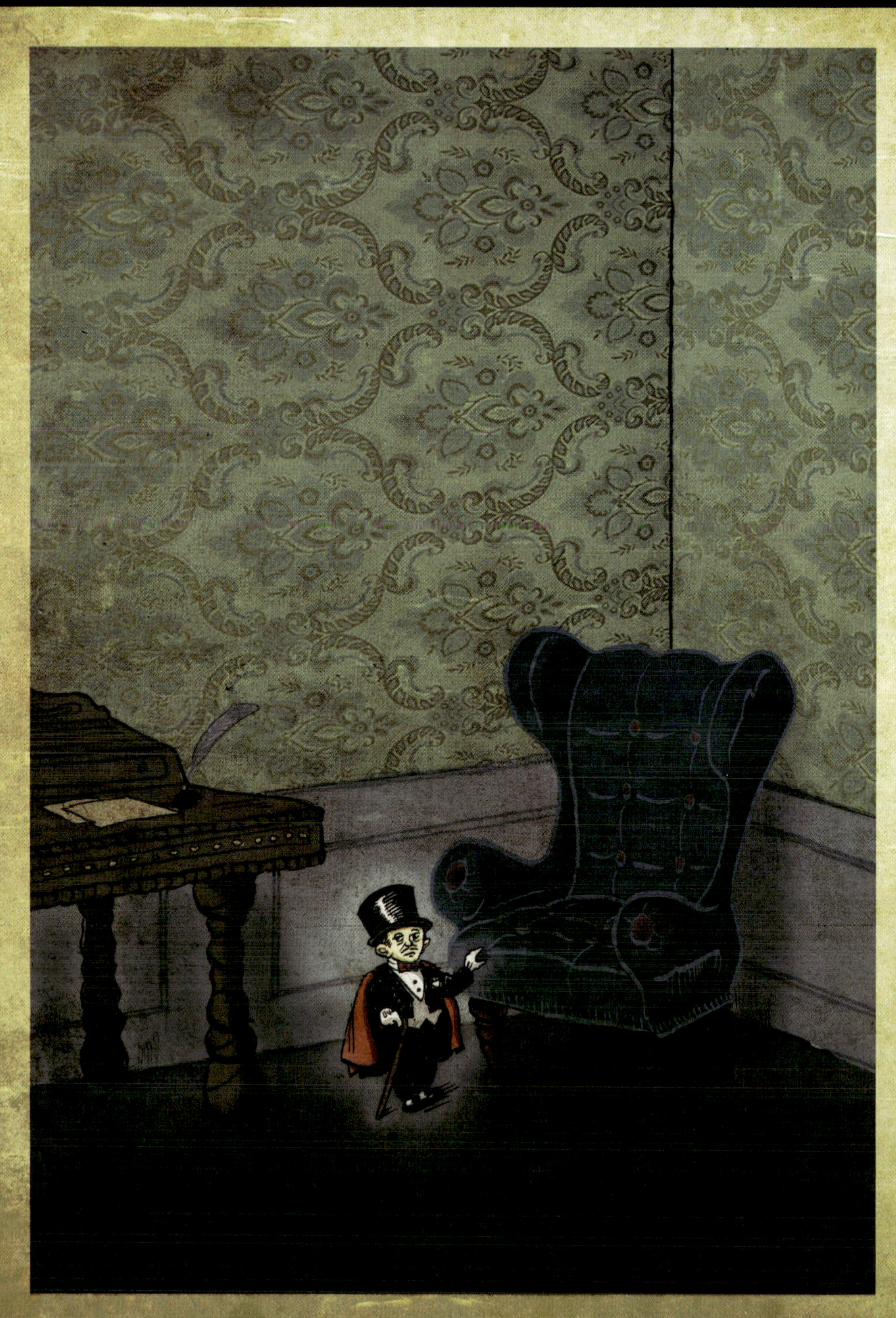

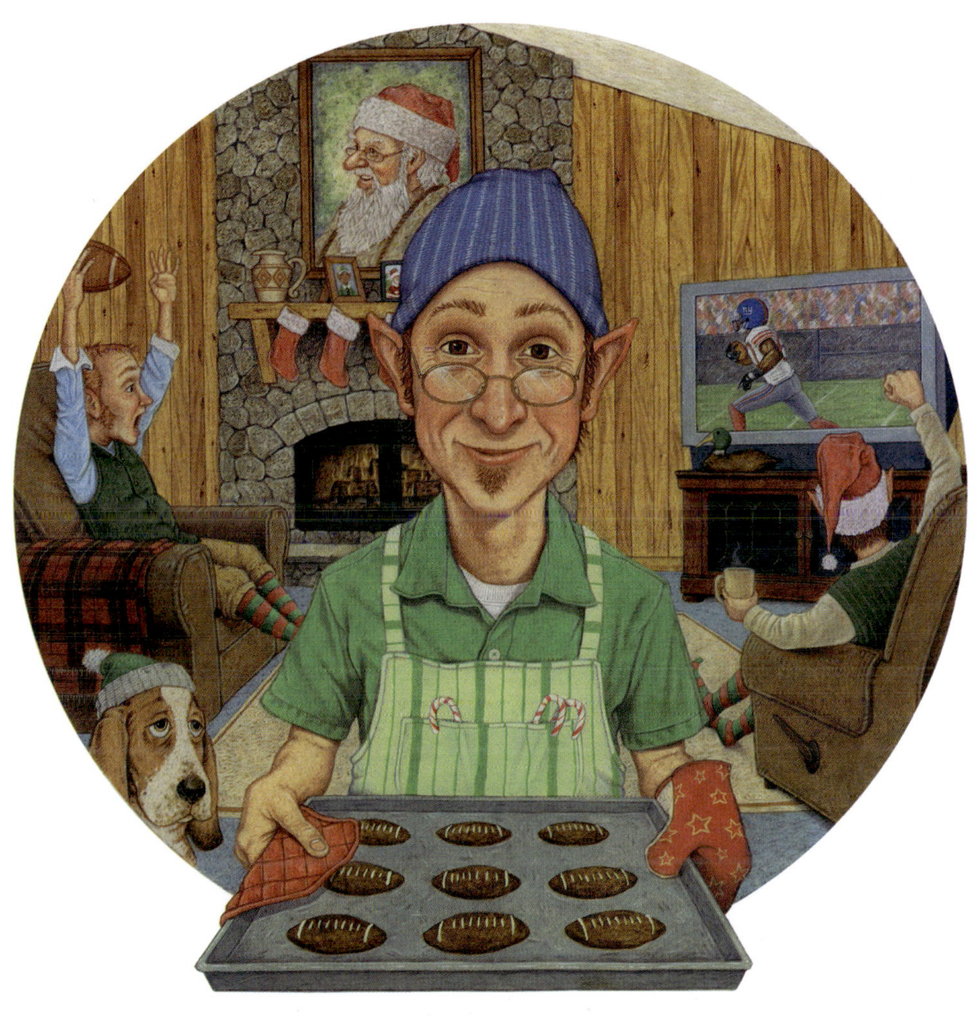

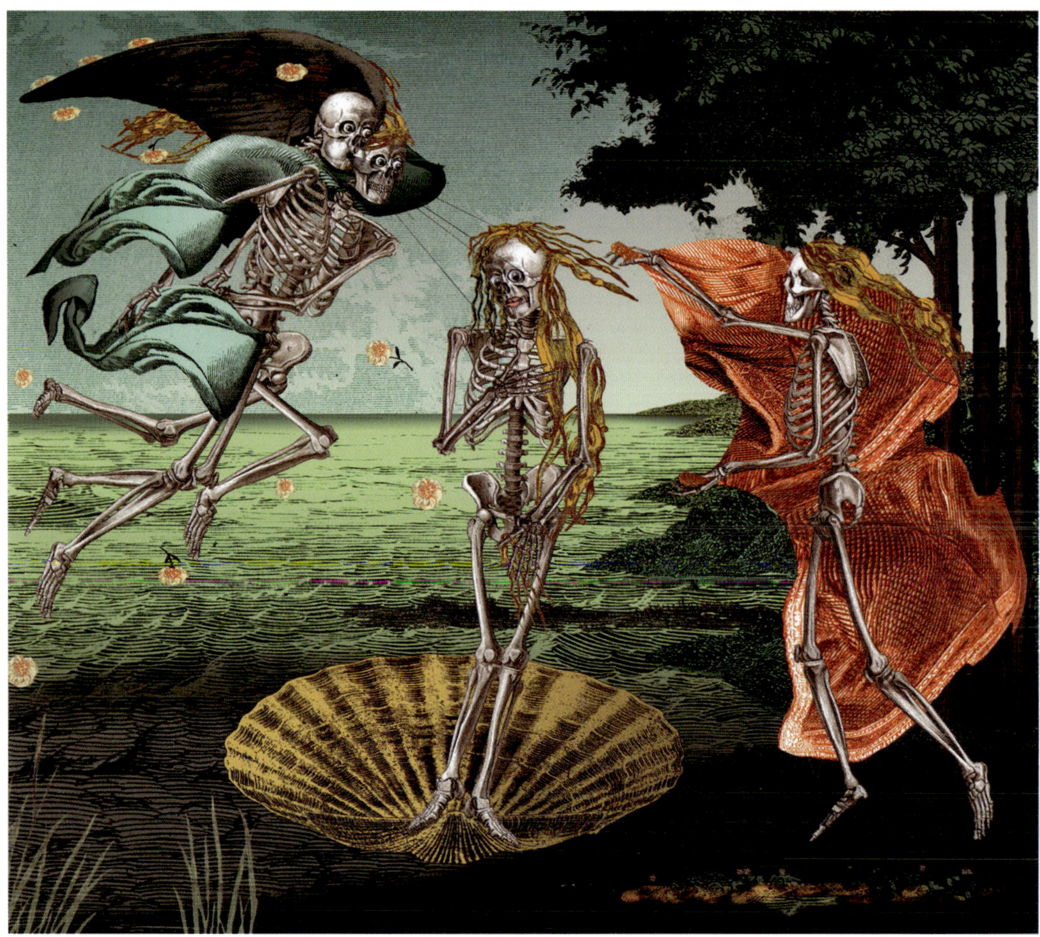

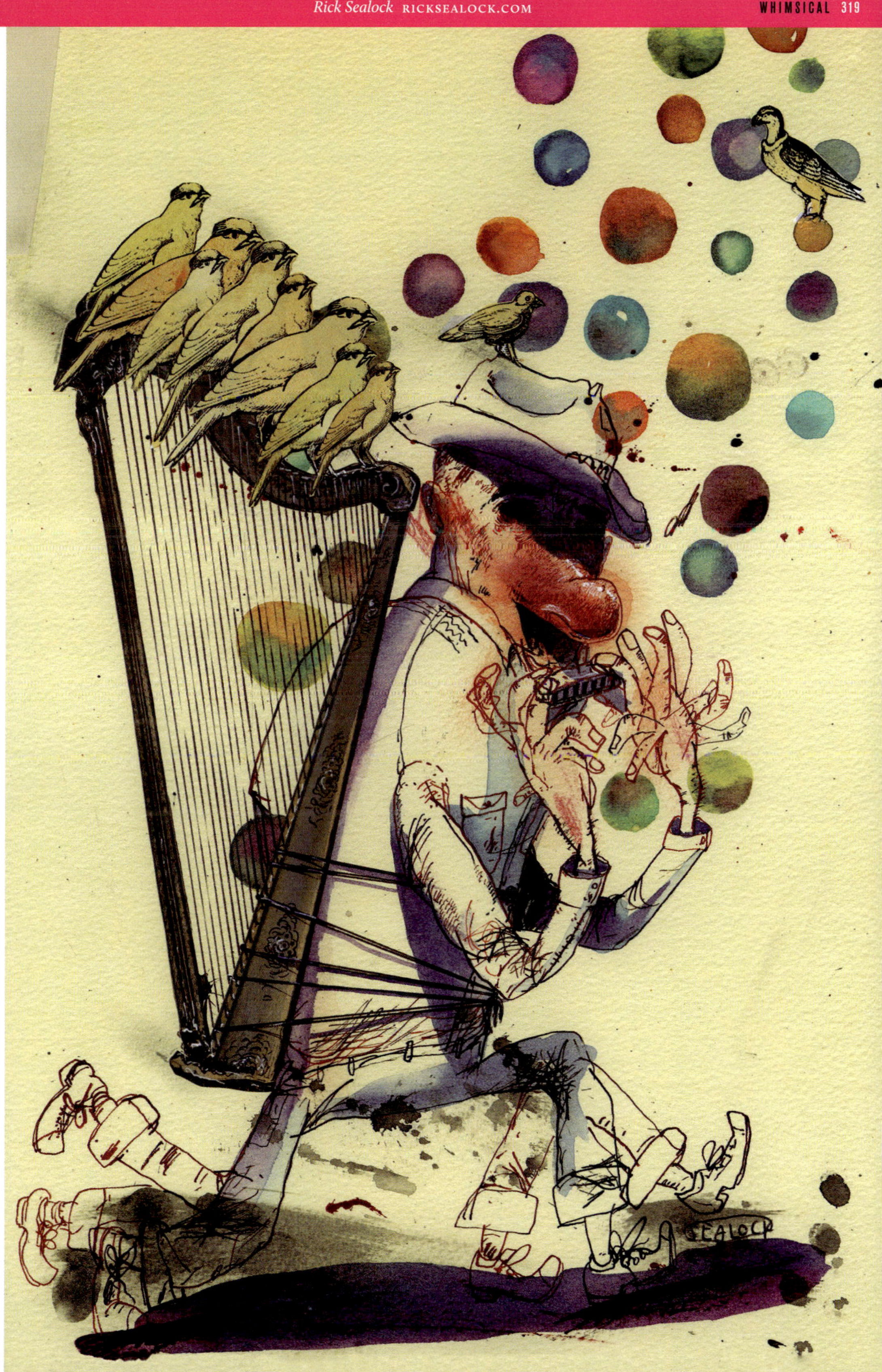
SEALOCK

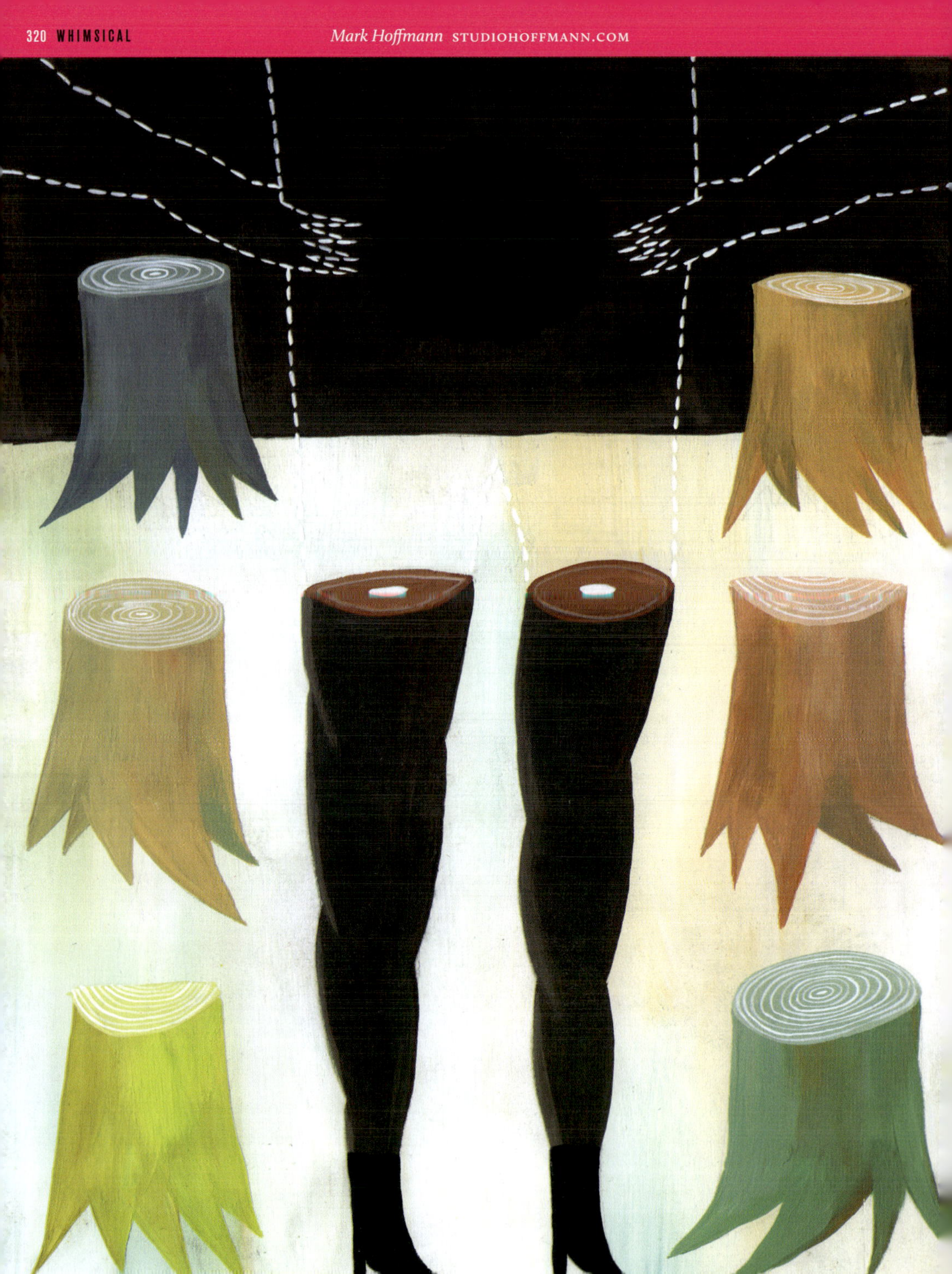

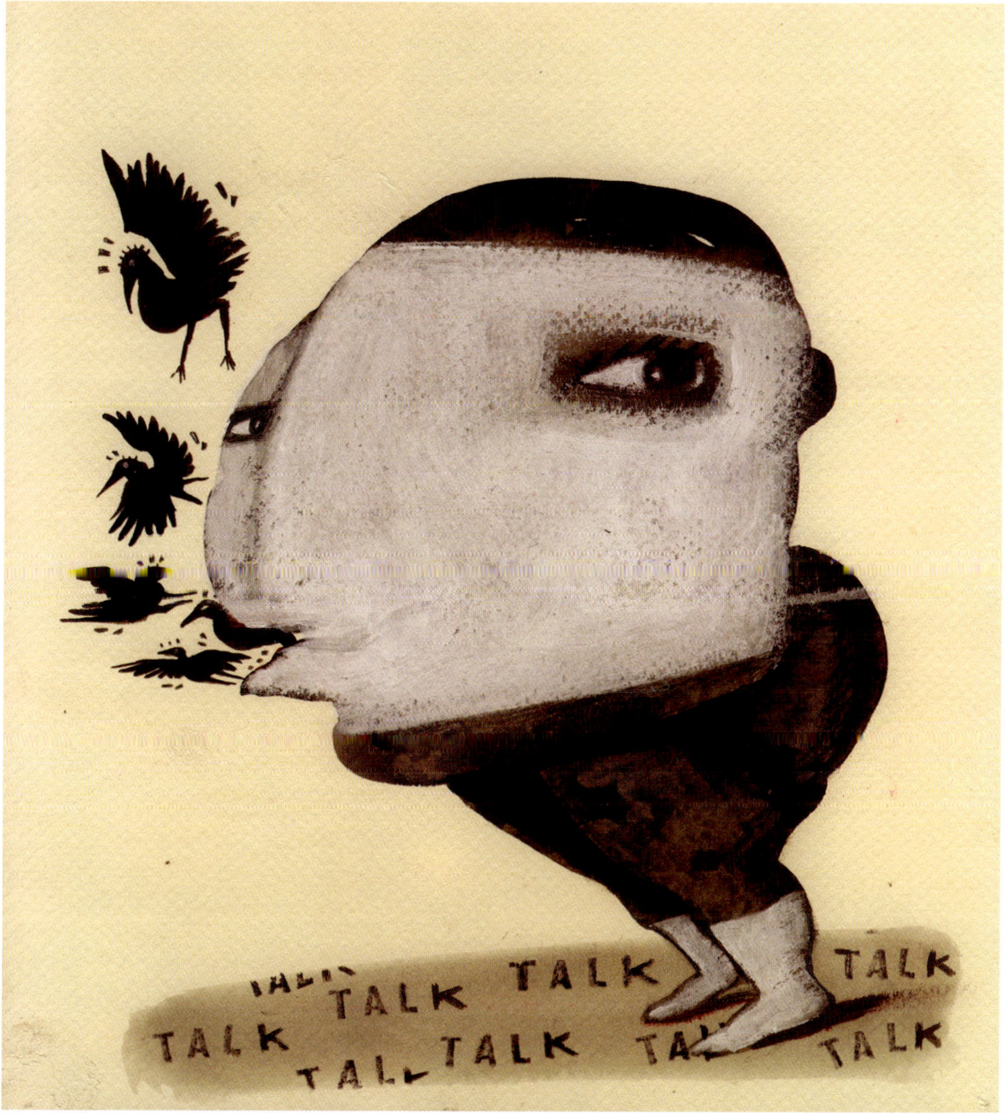

TALK TALK TALK
TALK TALK
TALK TALK TALK TALK

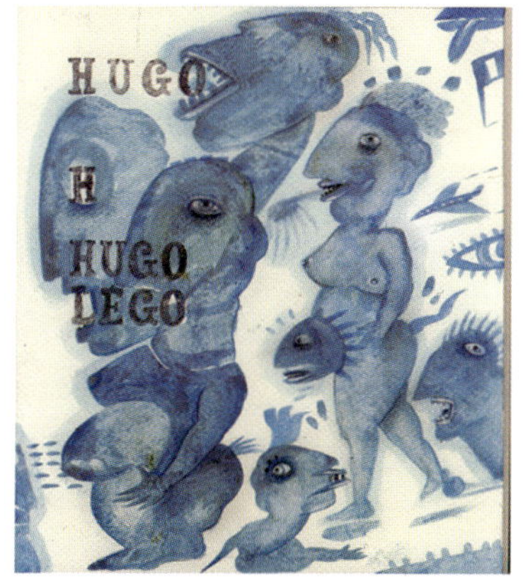

HUGO
H
HUGO
LEGO

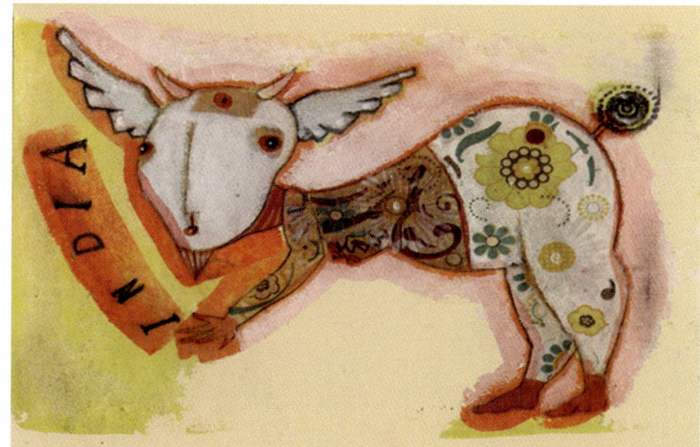

INDIA

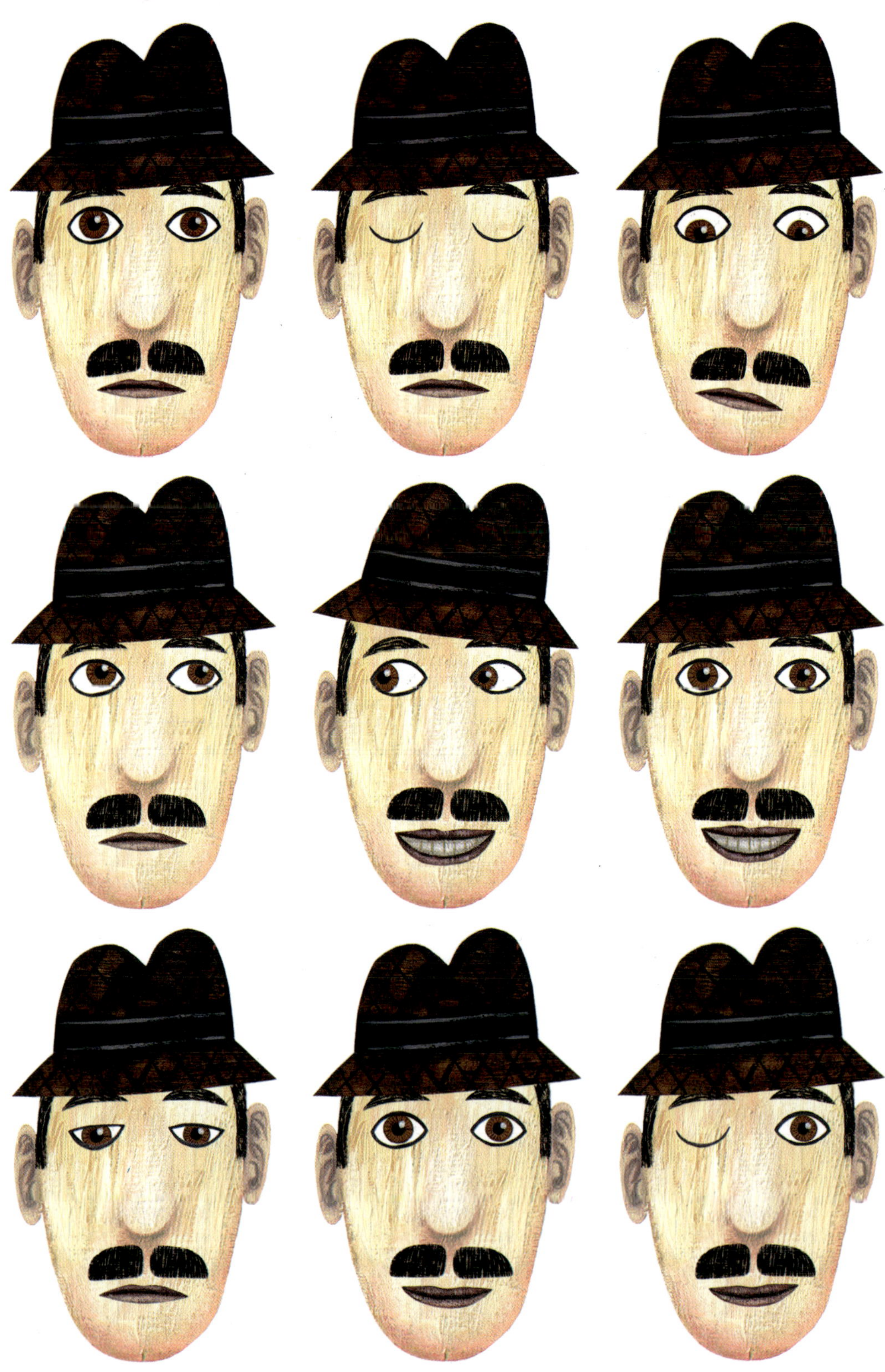

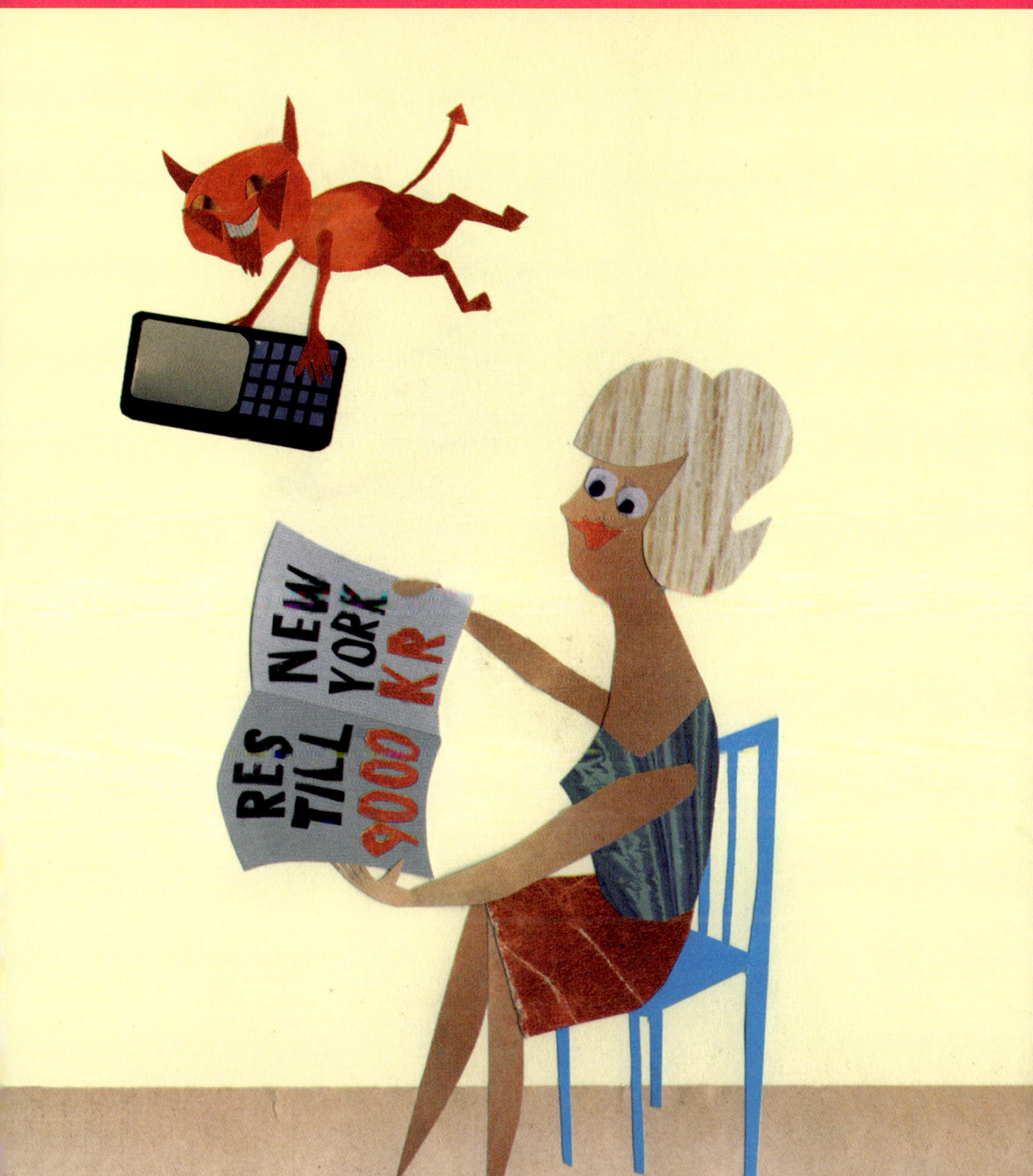
NEW YORK
RES TILL
9000 KR

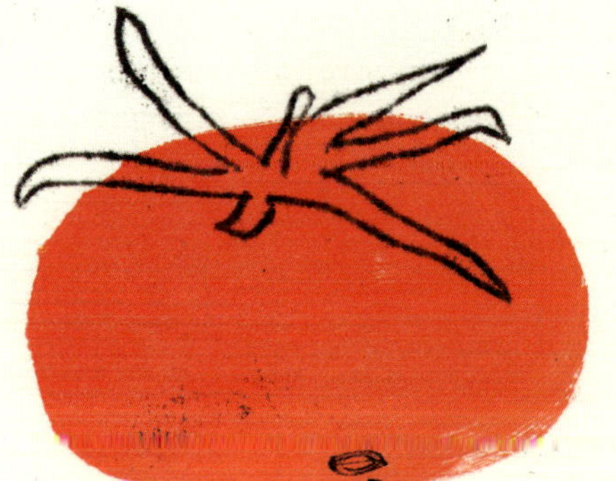
SMALL WORM HOLE.

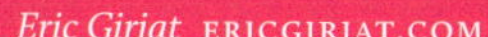

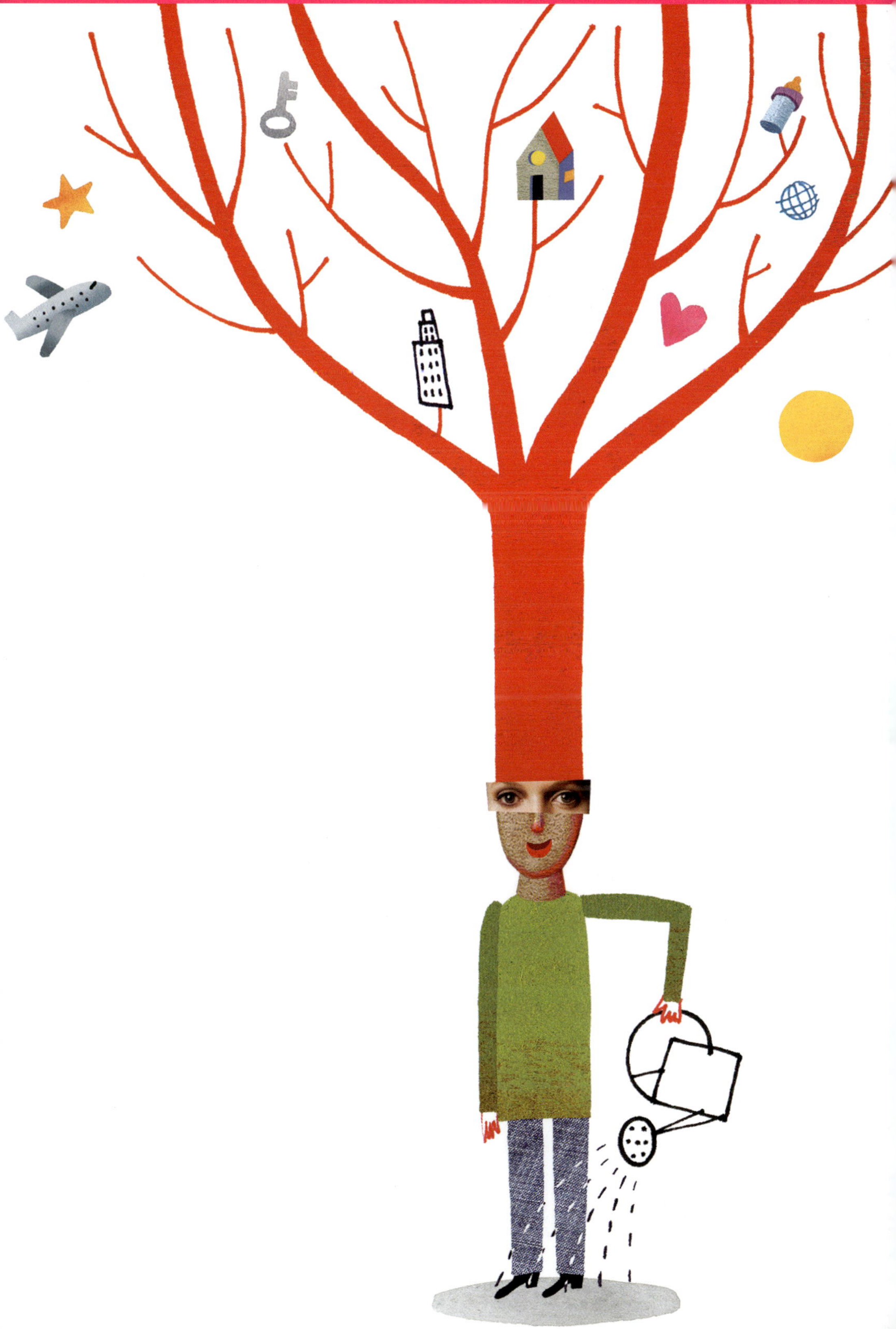

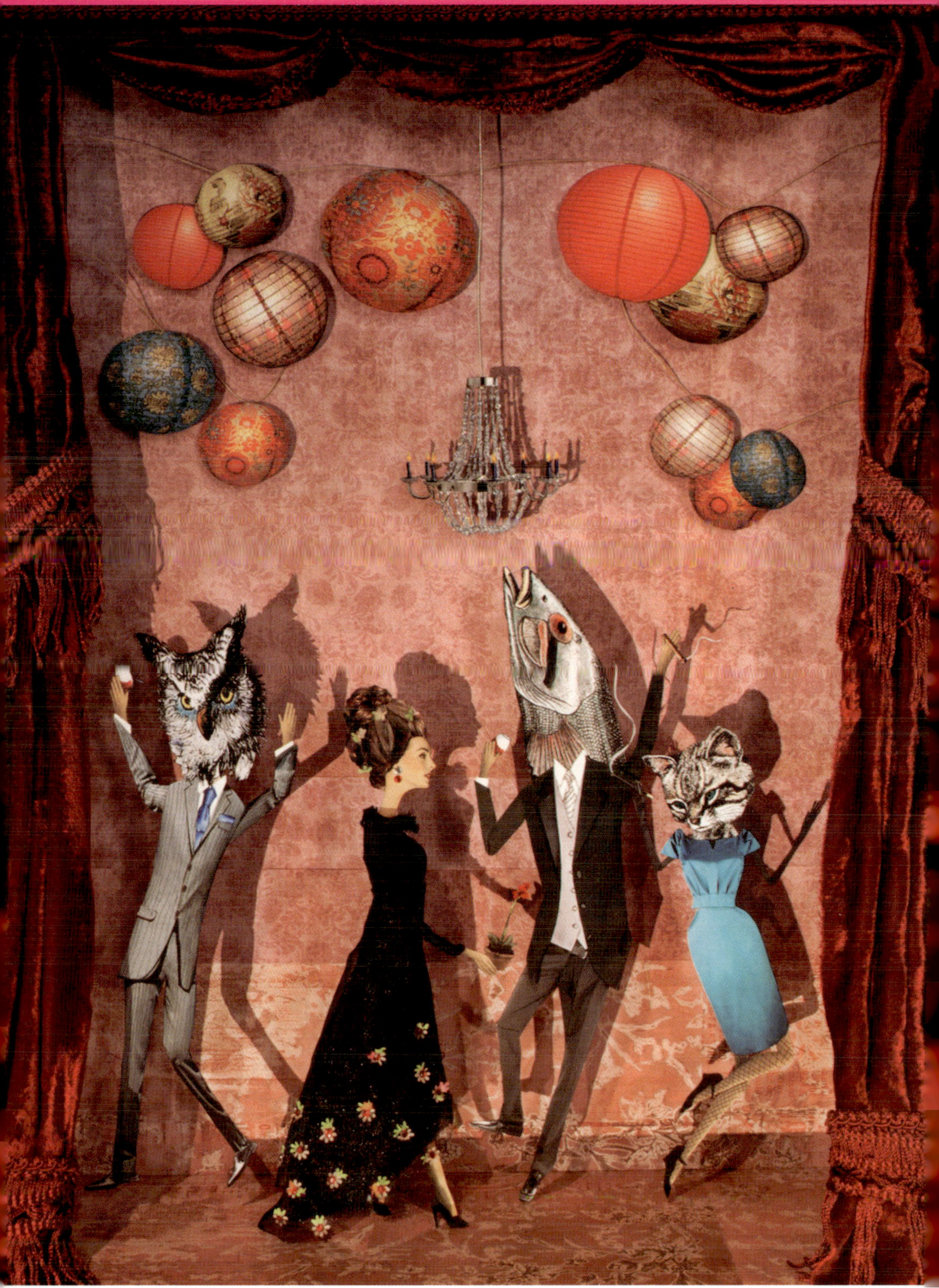

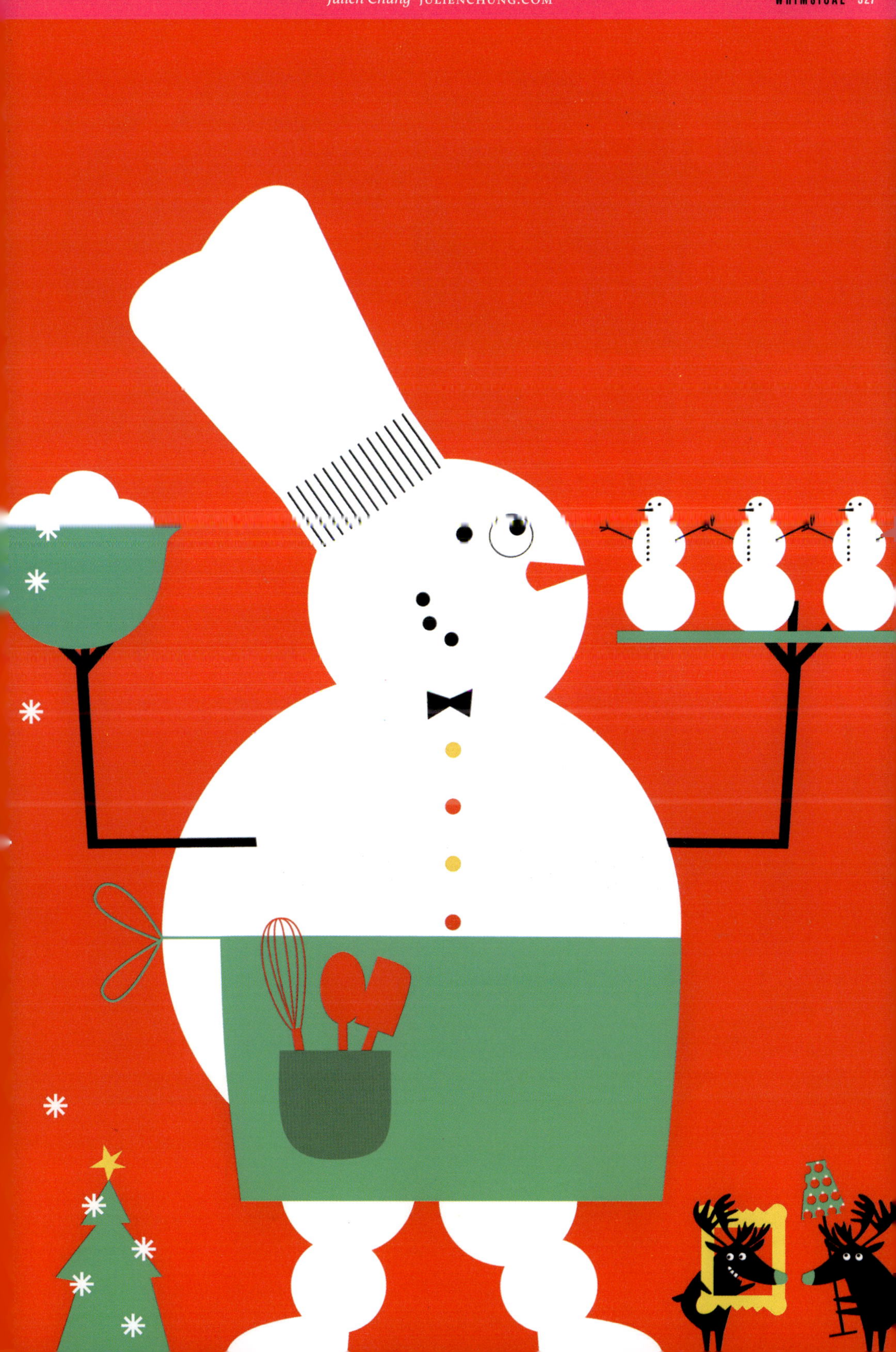

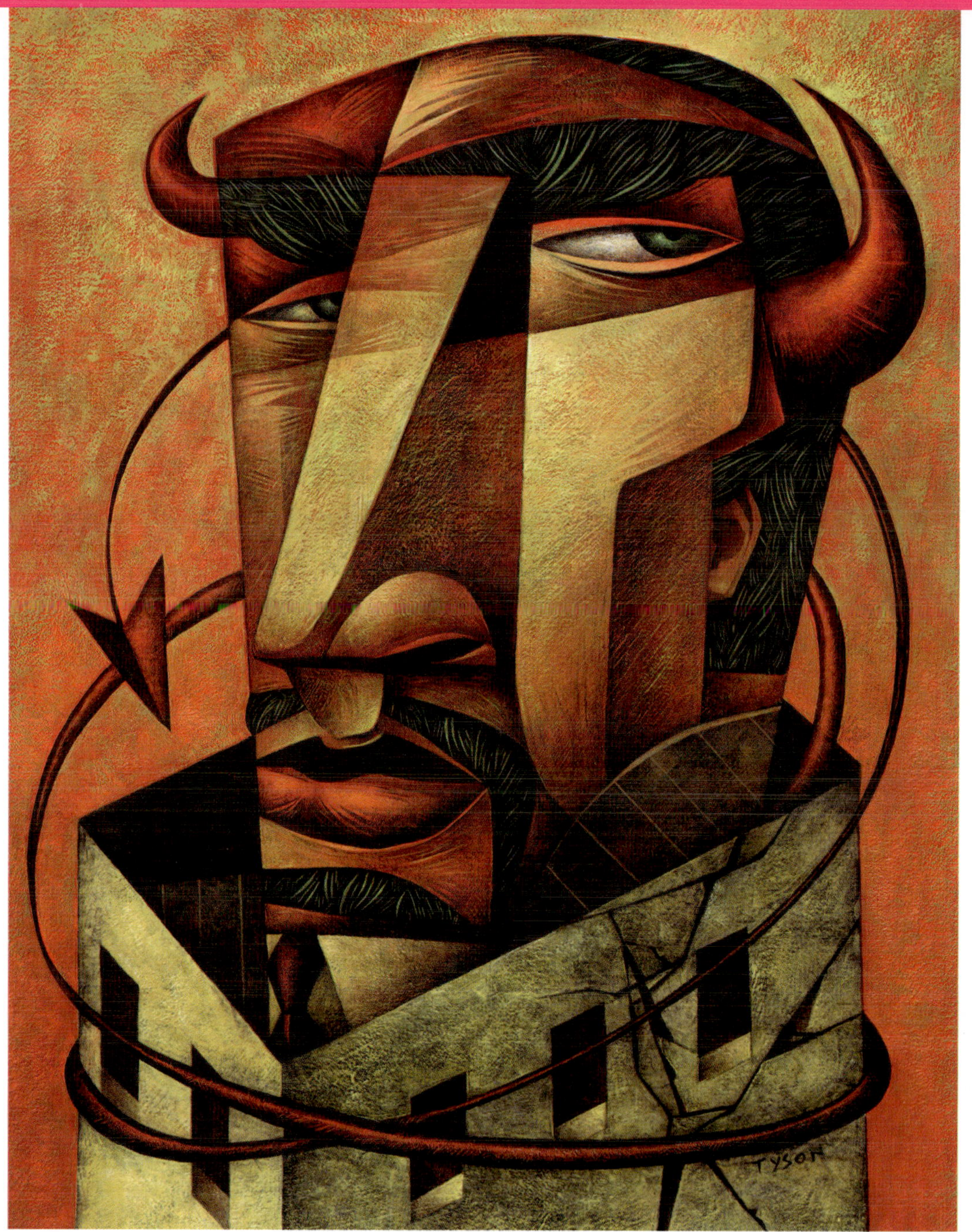

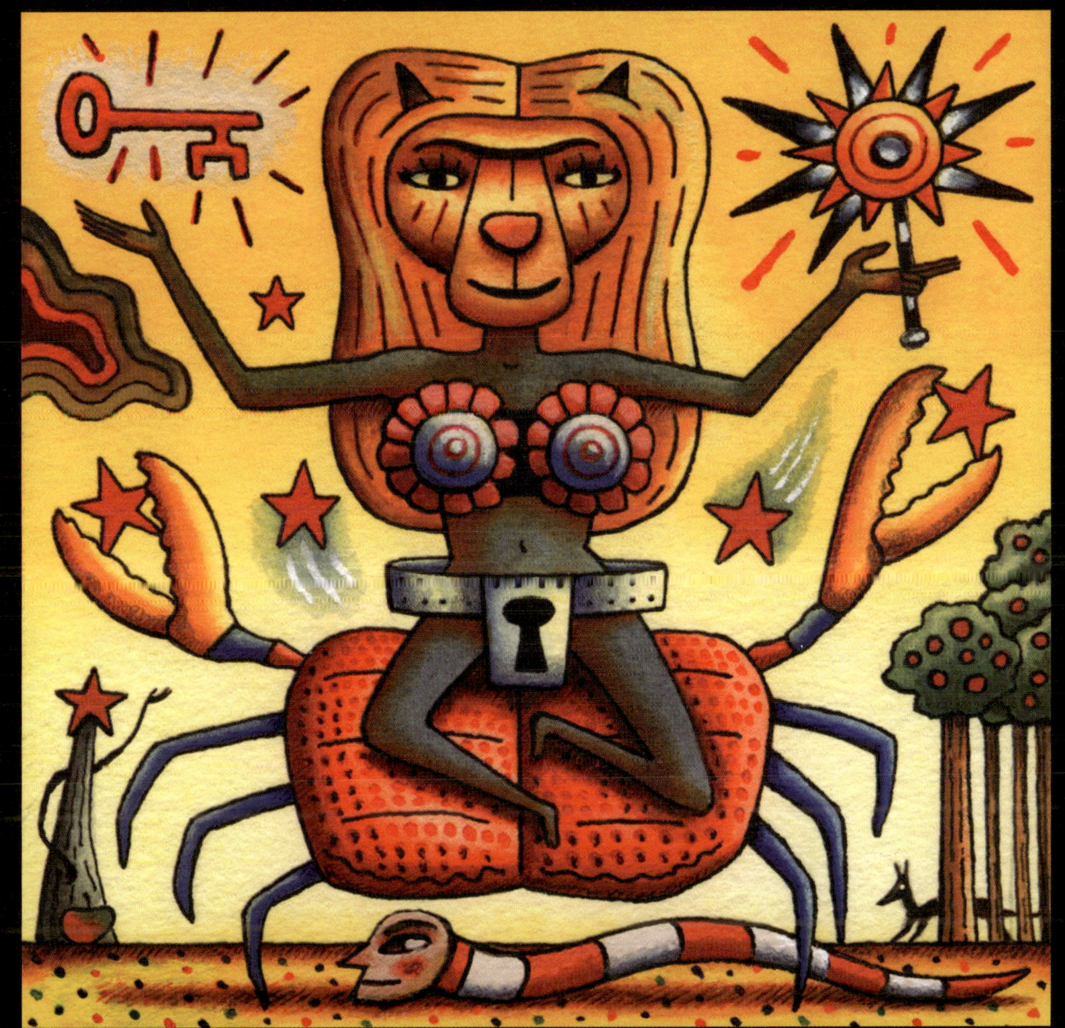

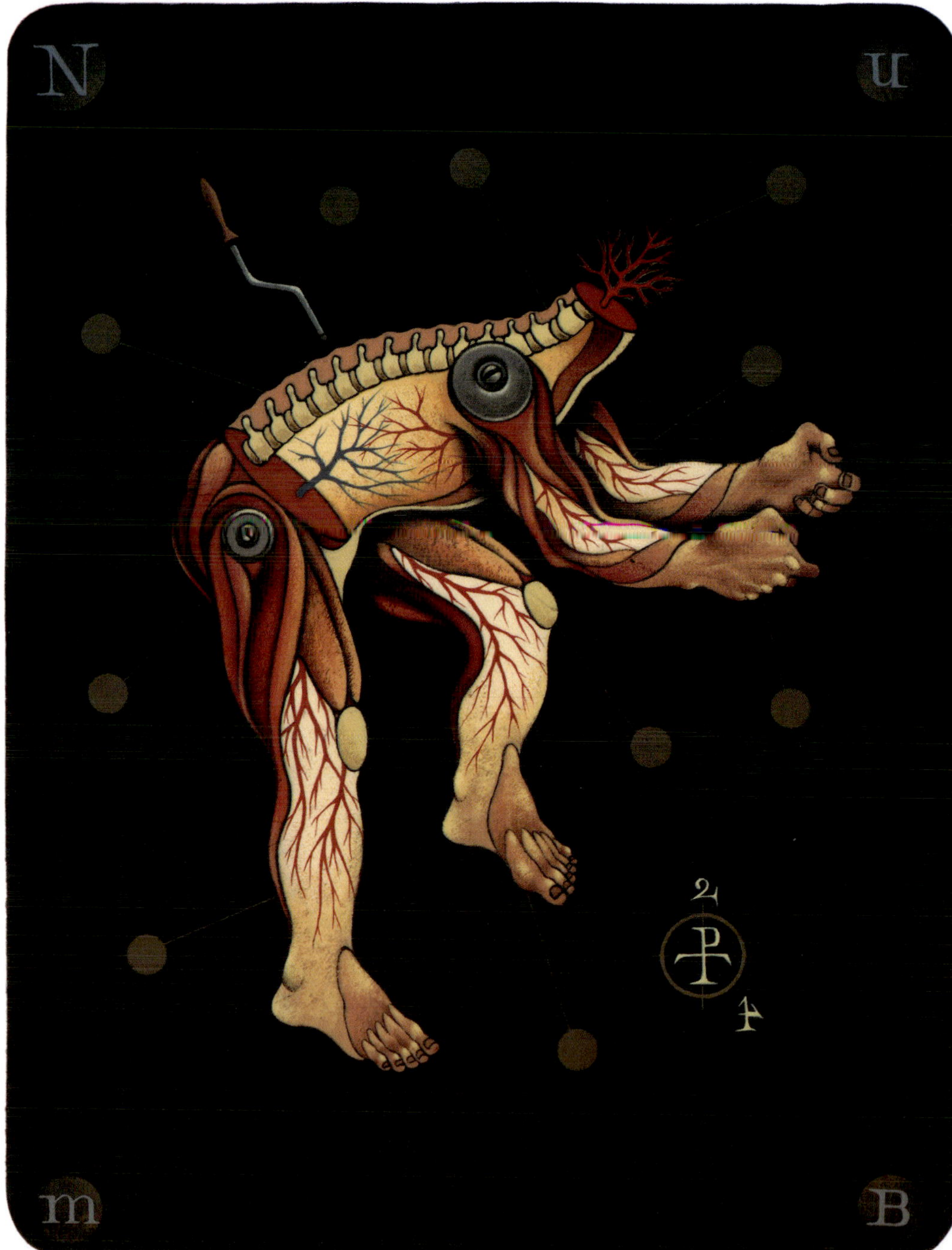

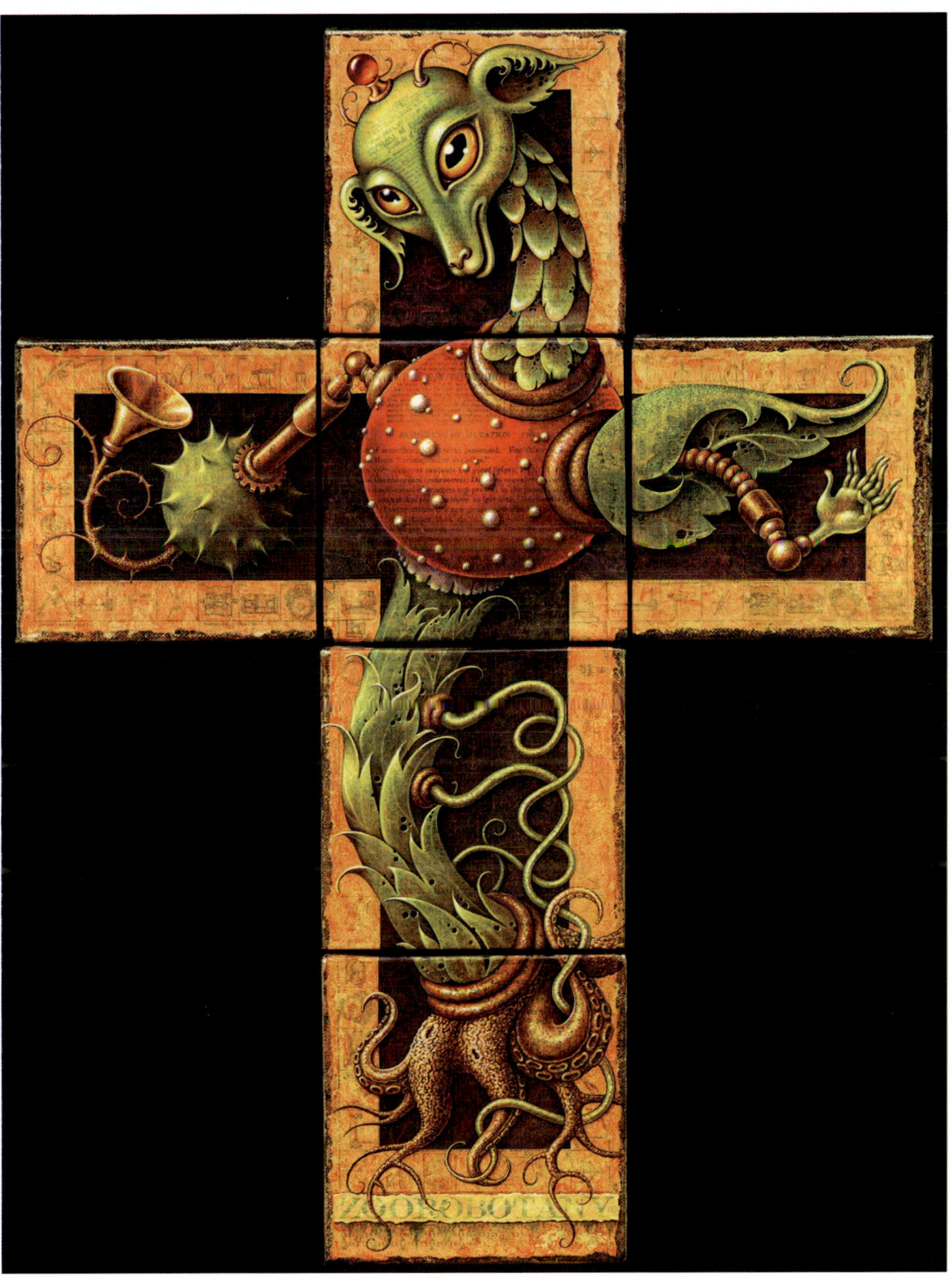

Toby Thane Neighbors HEPCATINK.COM

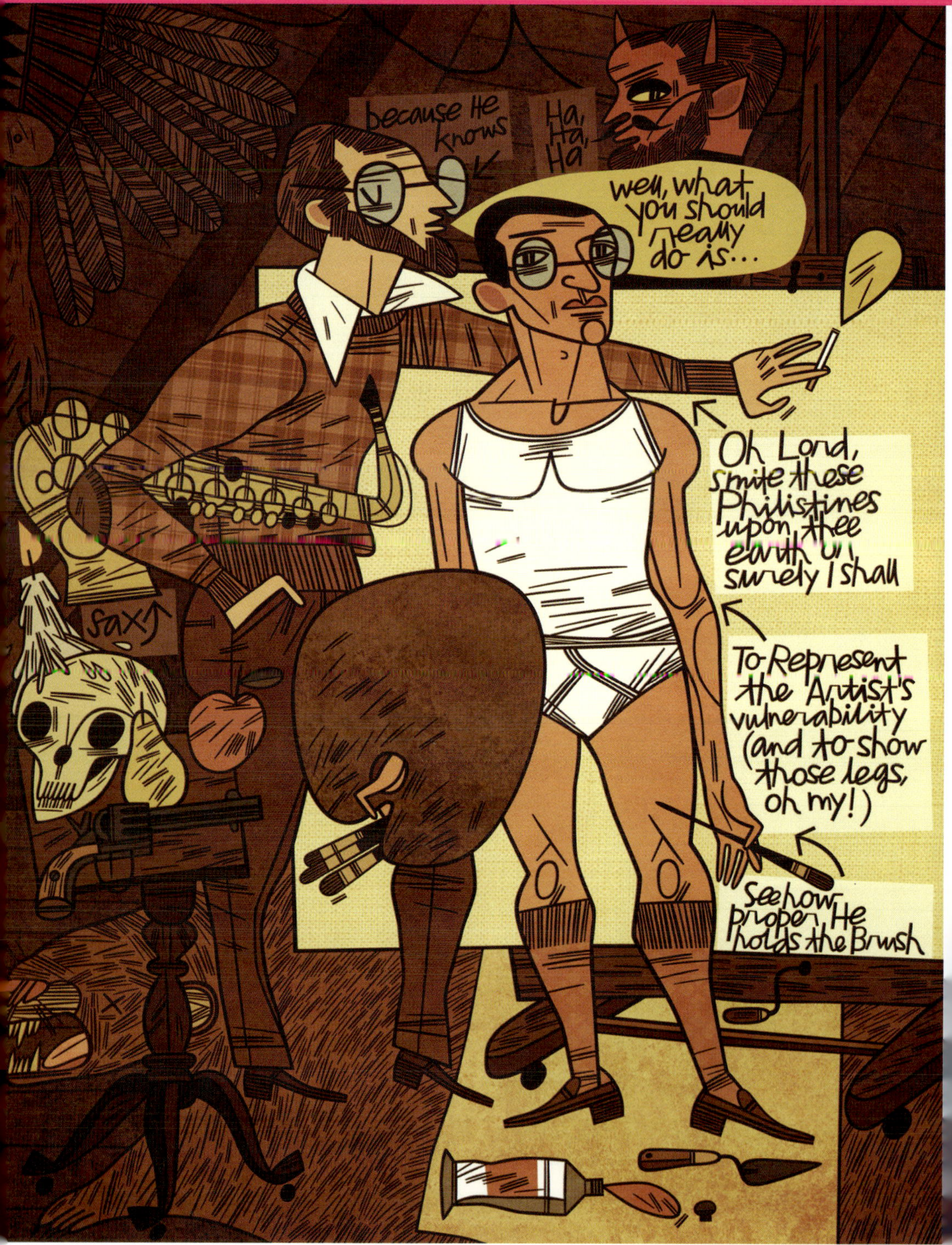

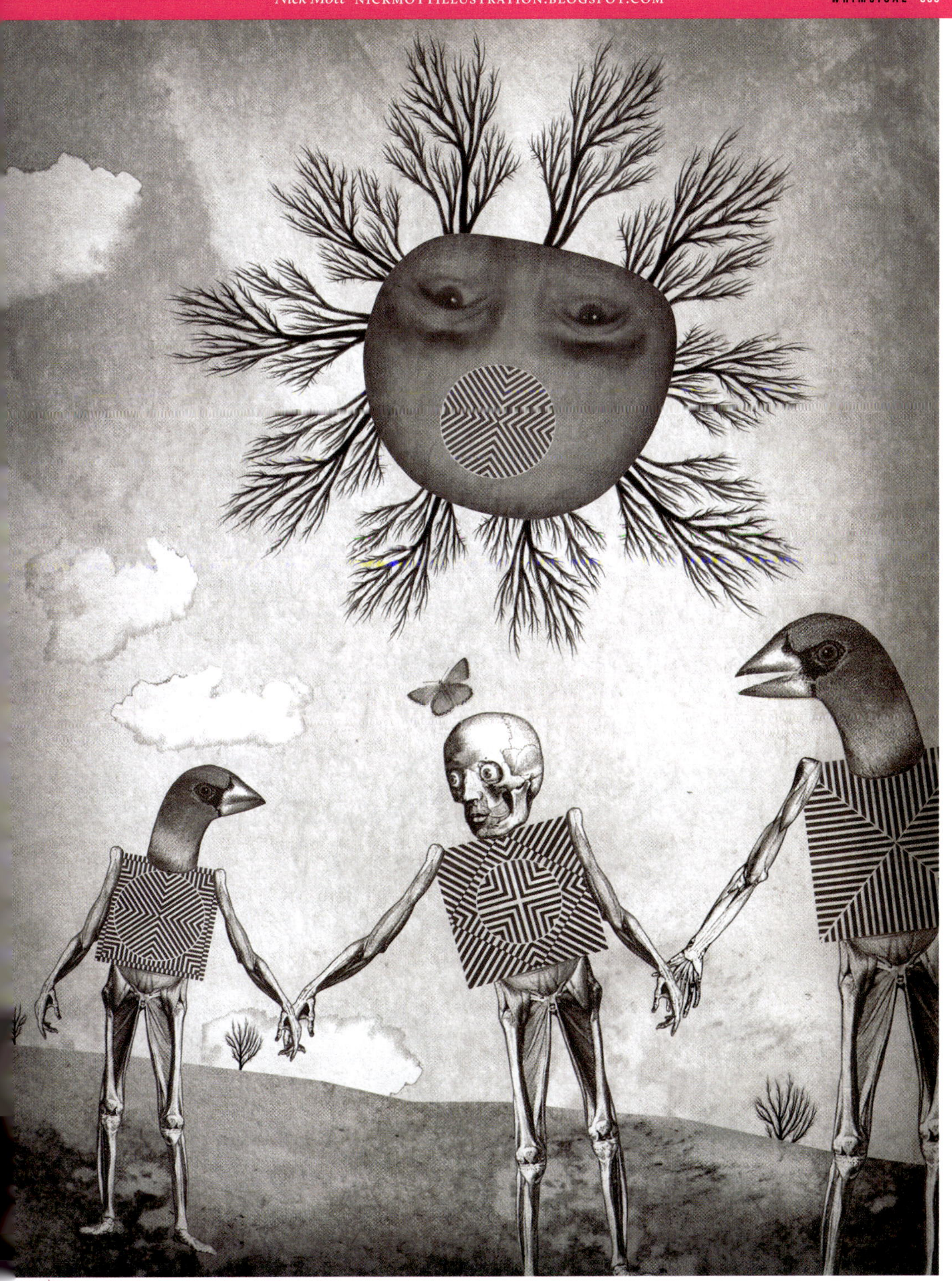

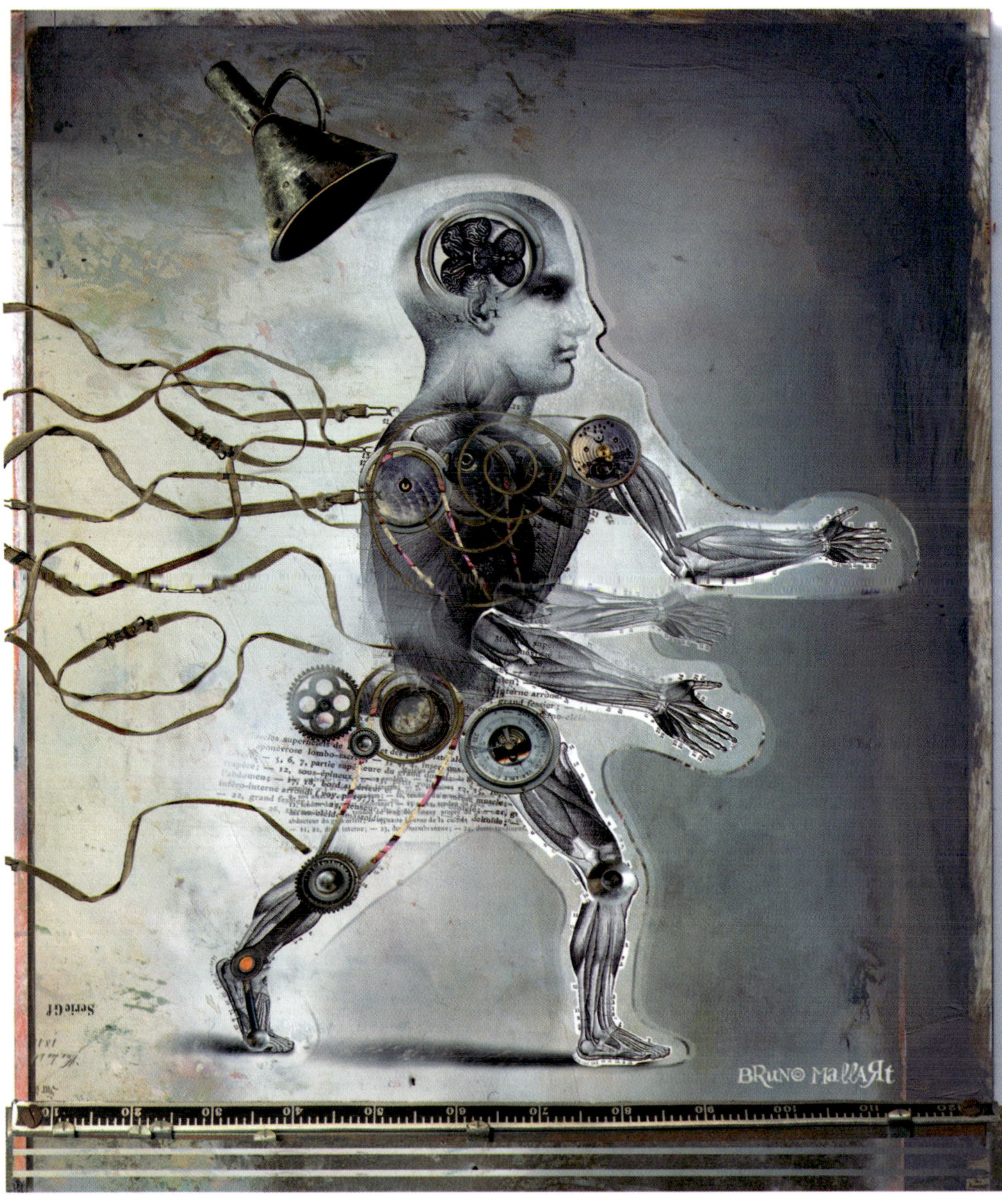

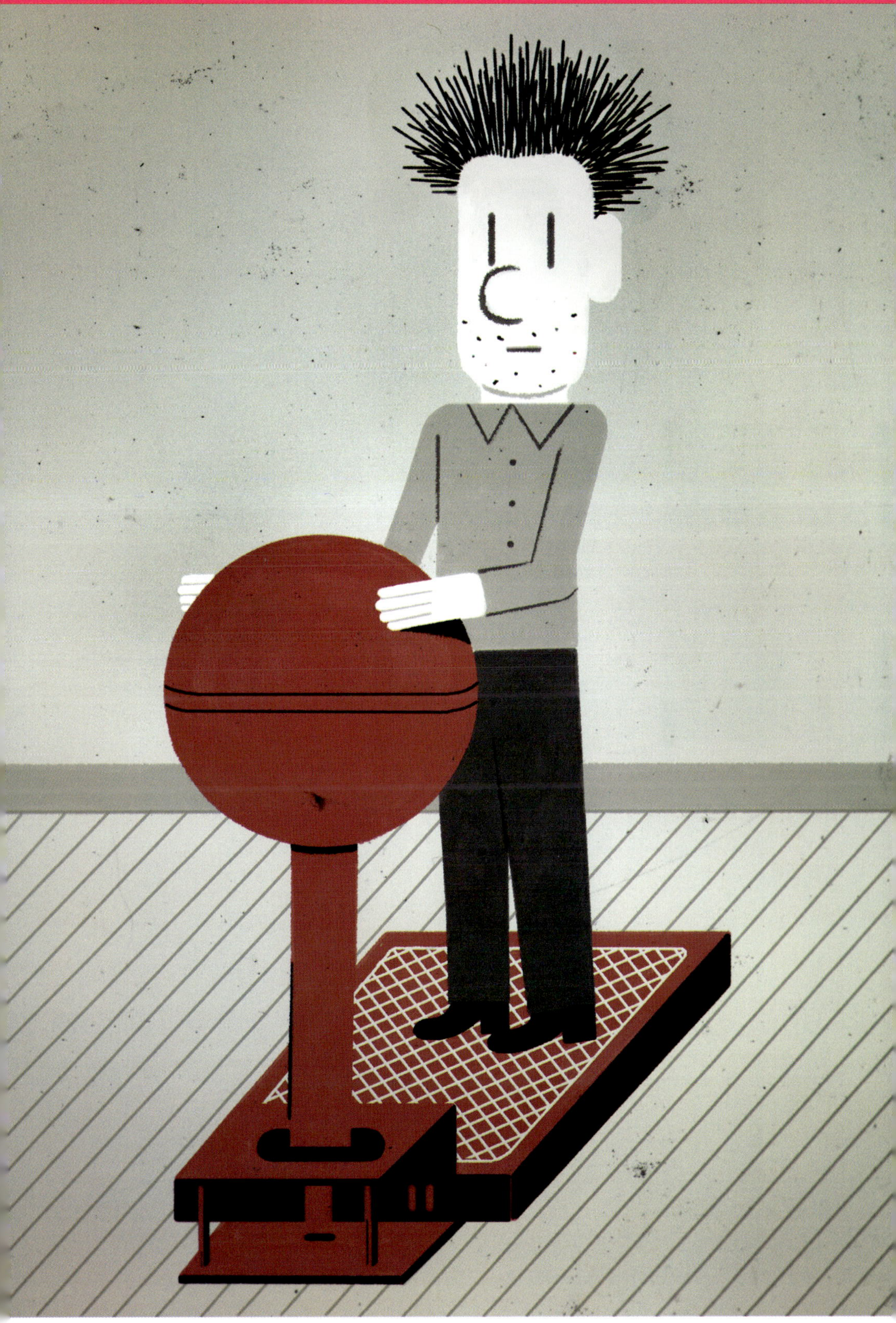

Jose Fragoso FRAGOSOART.COM

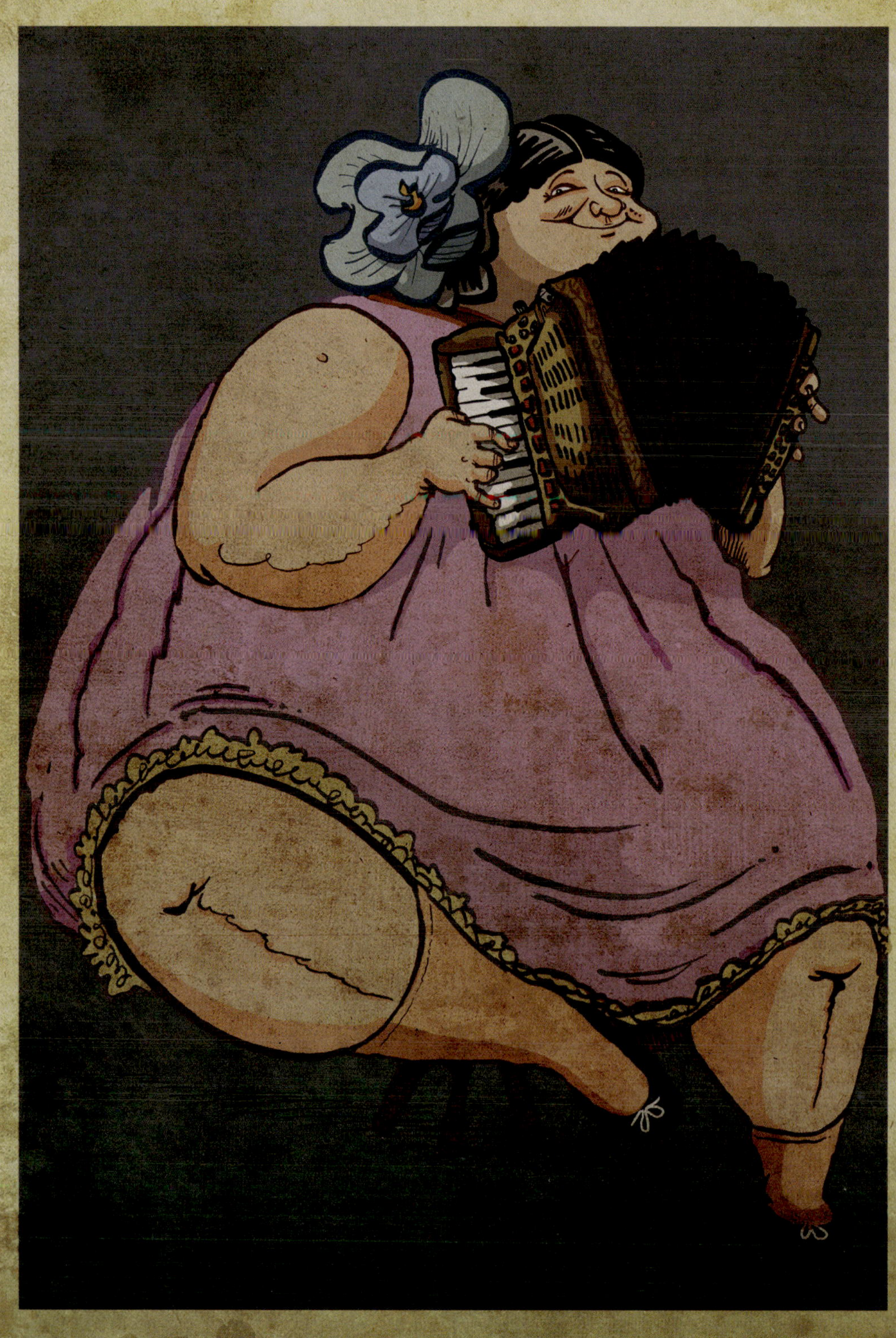

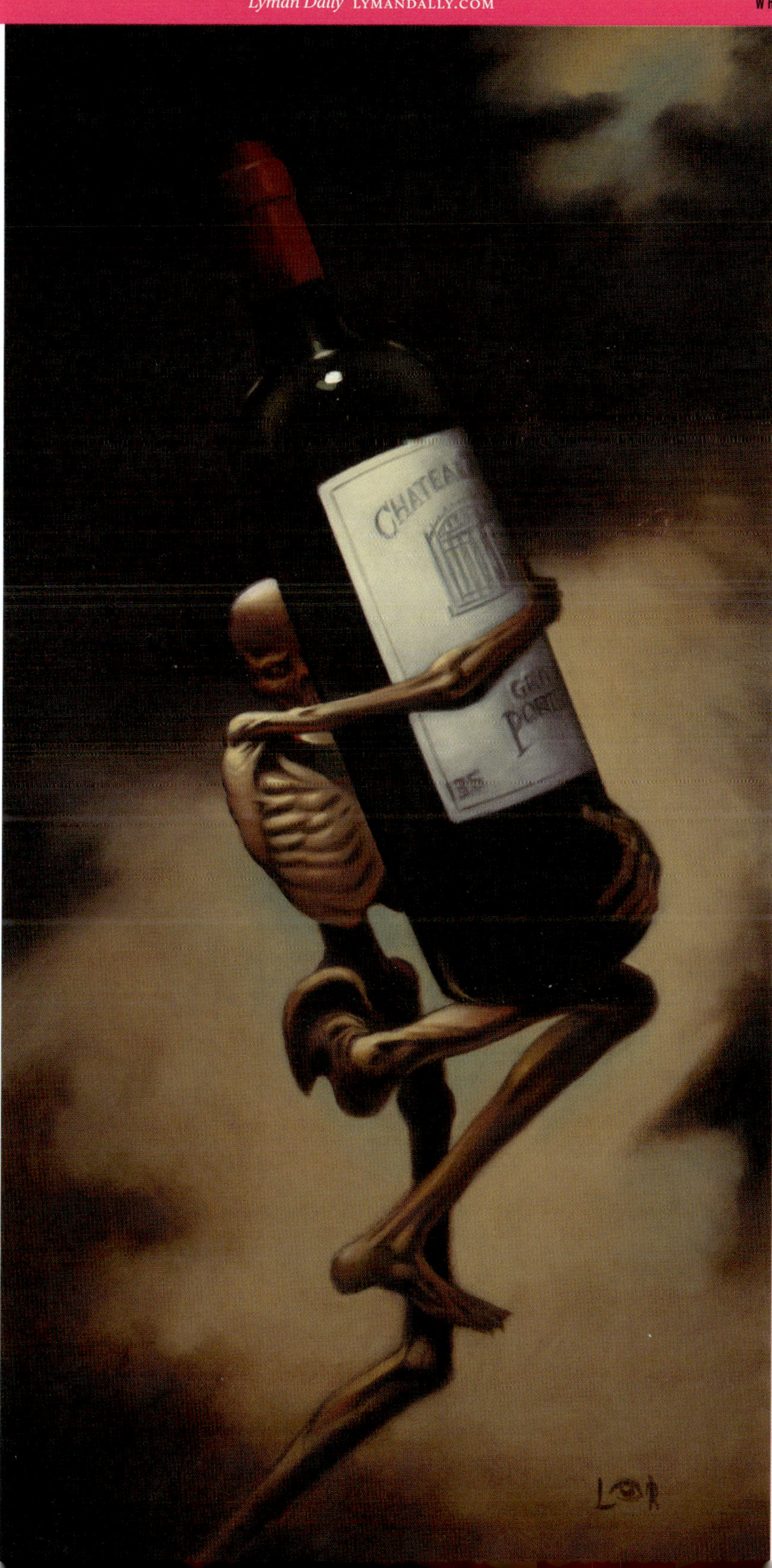

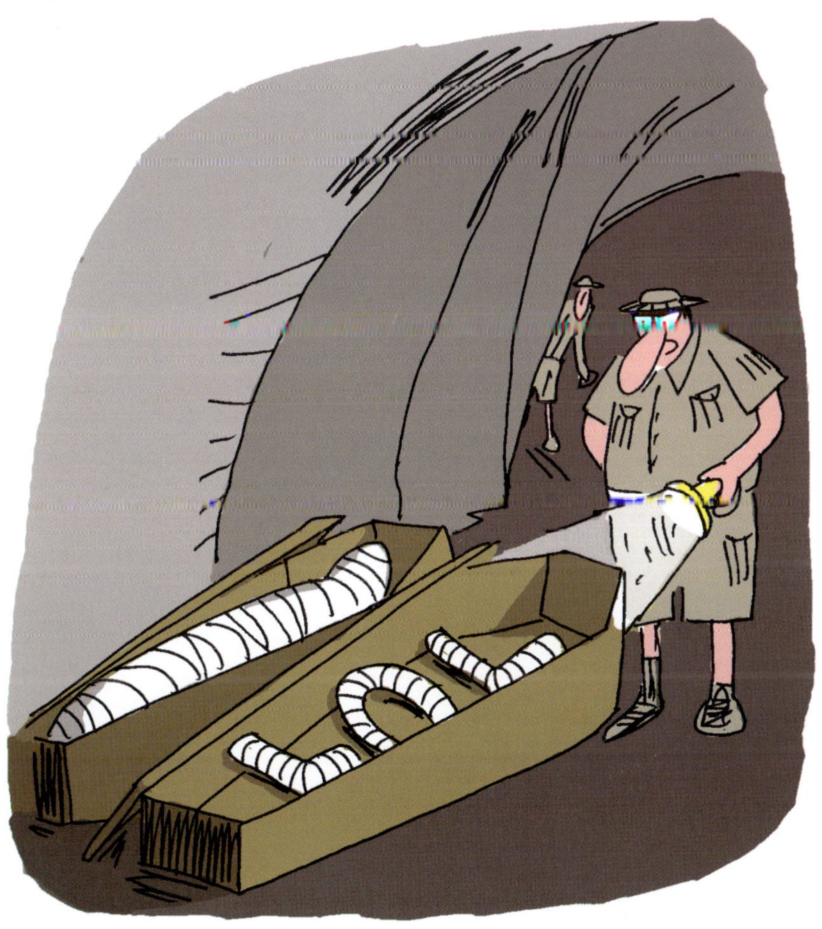
LOL

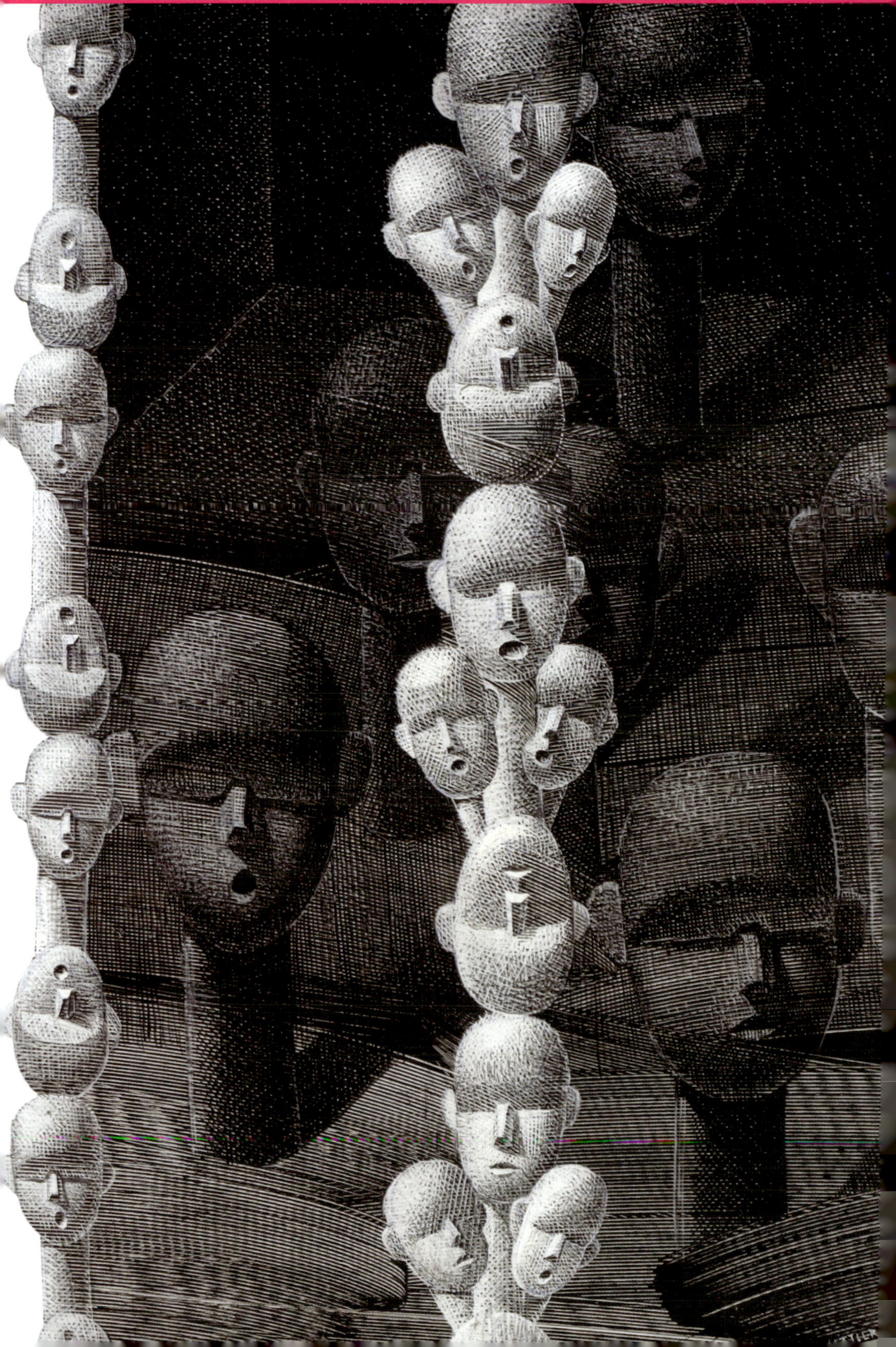

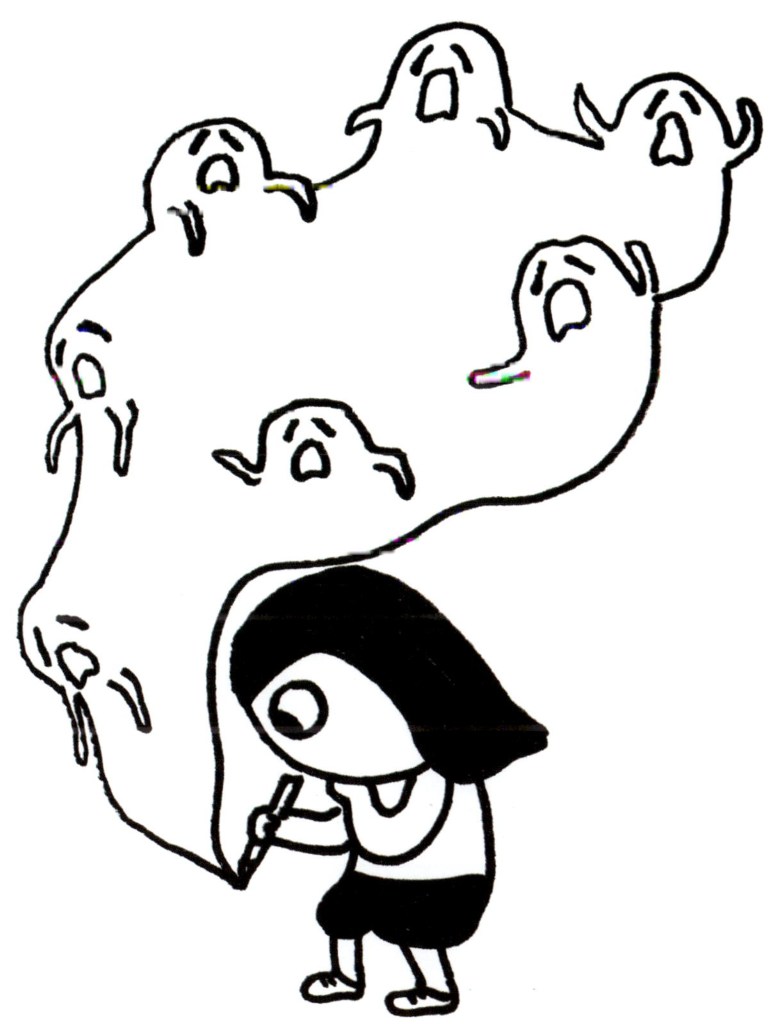

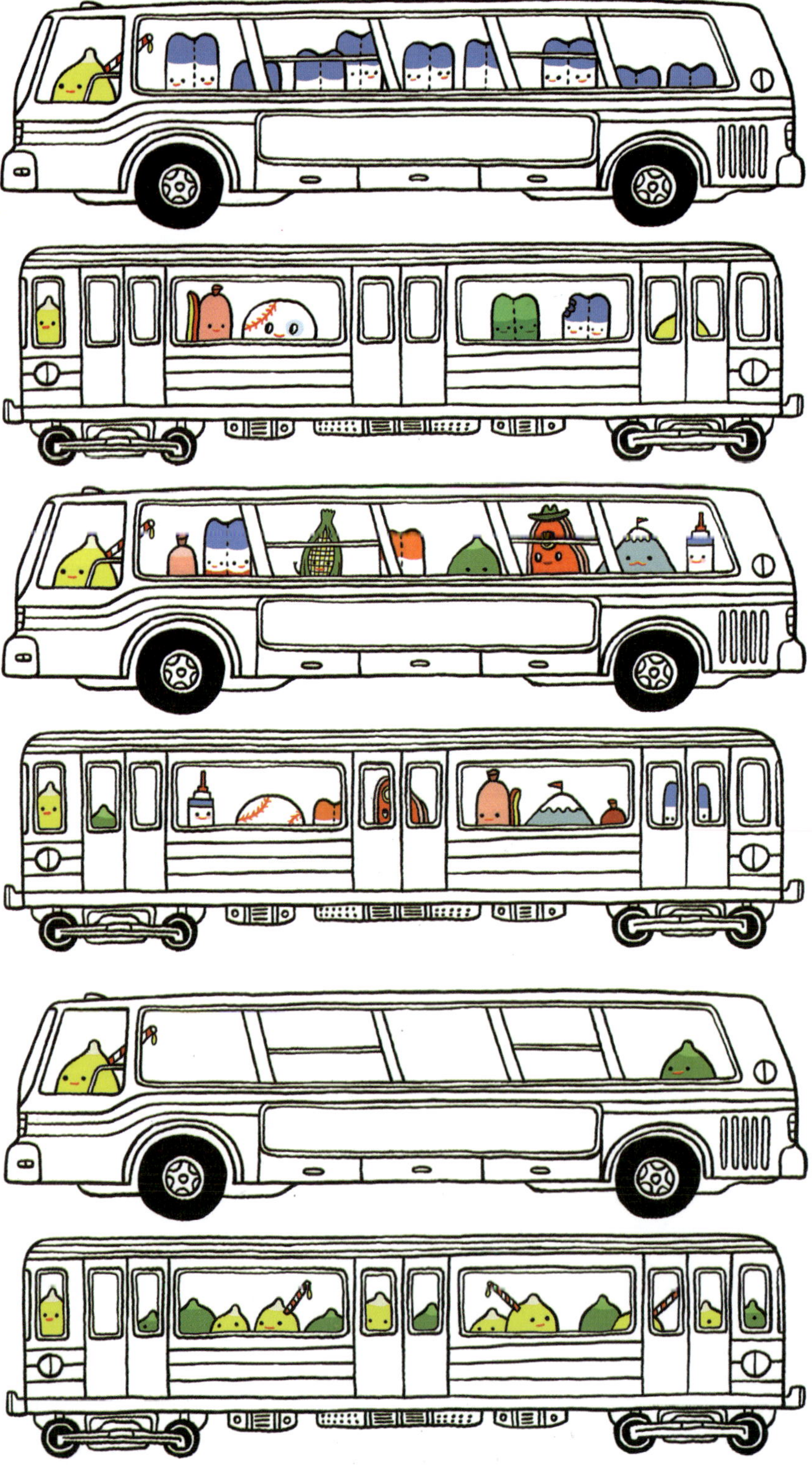

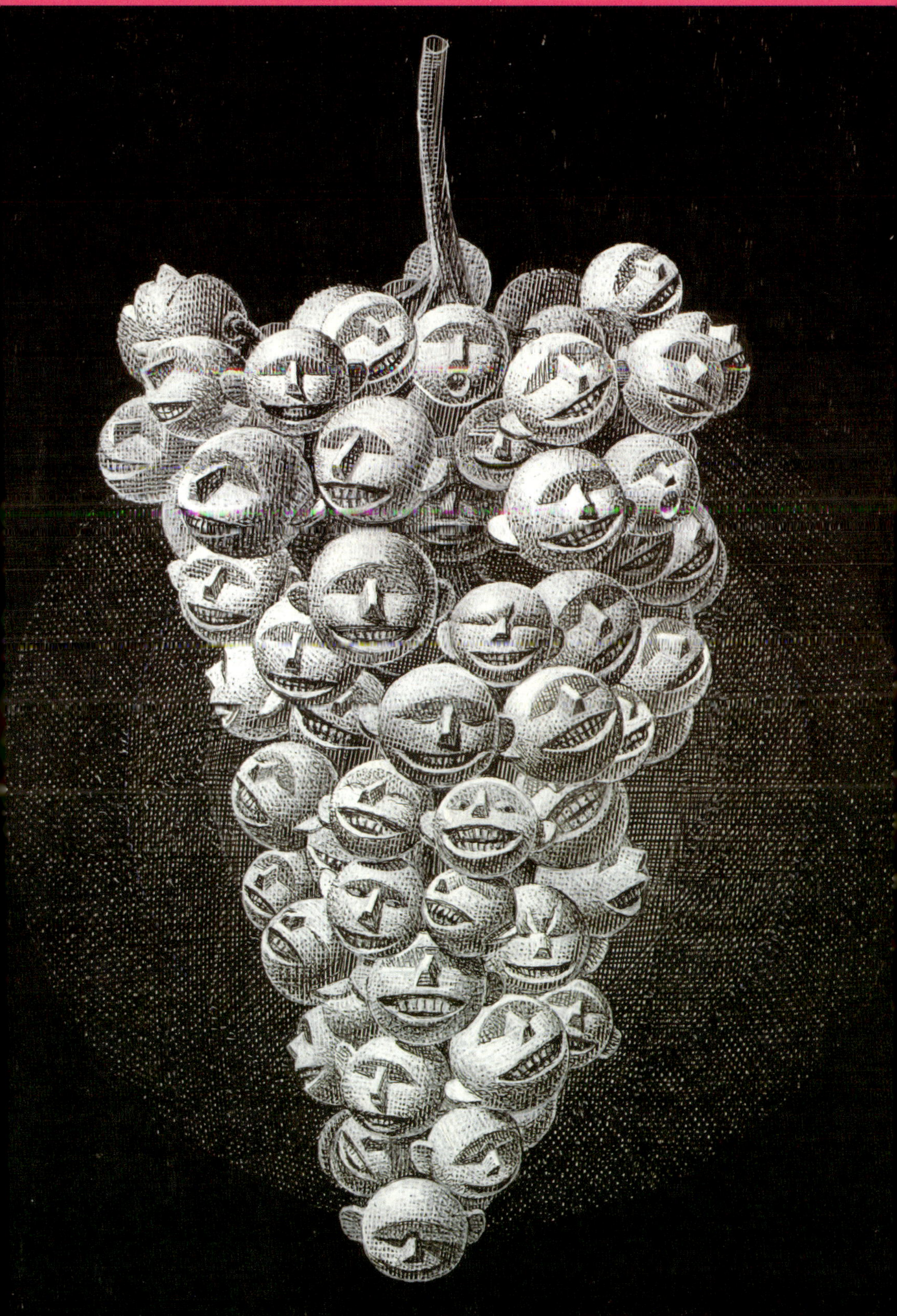

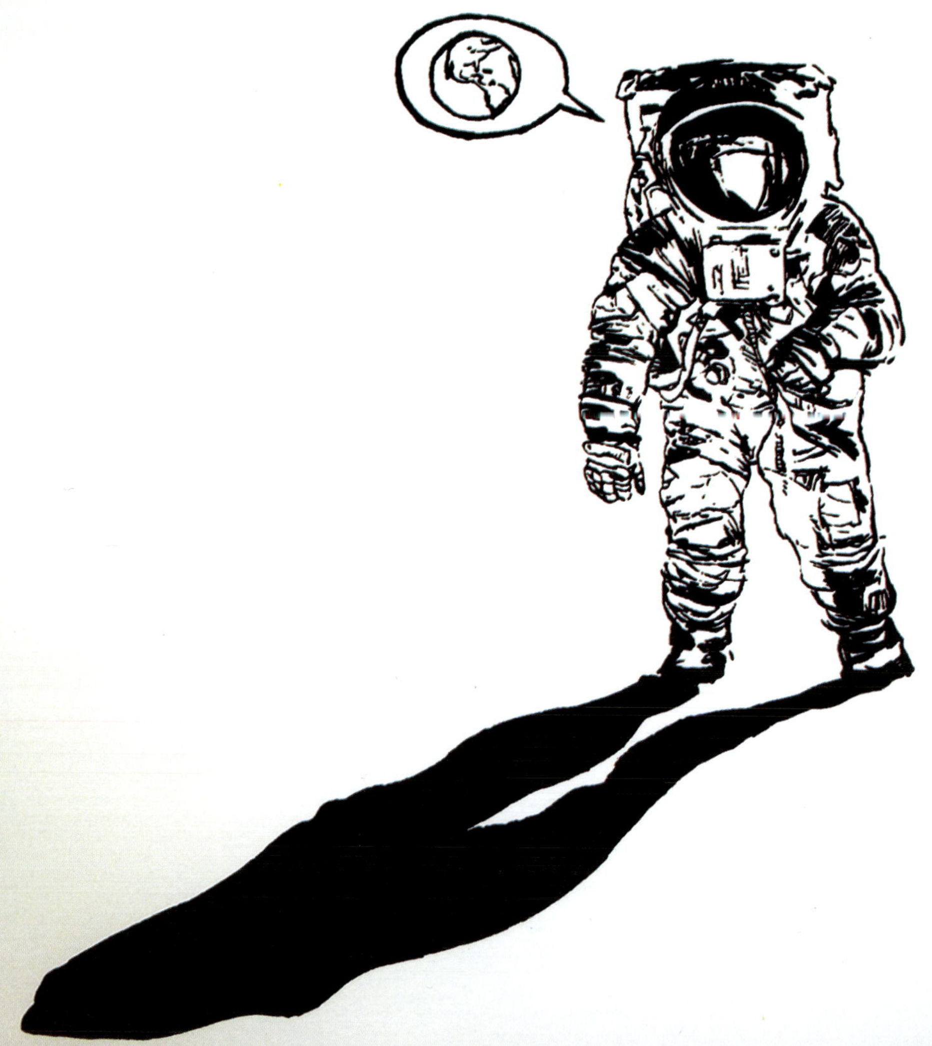
JEREMYSCHILLING.CARBONMADE.COM

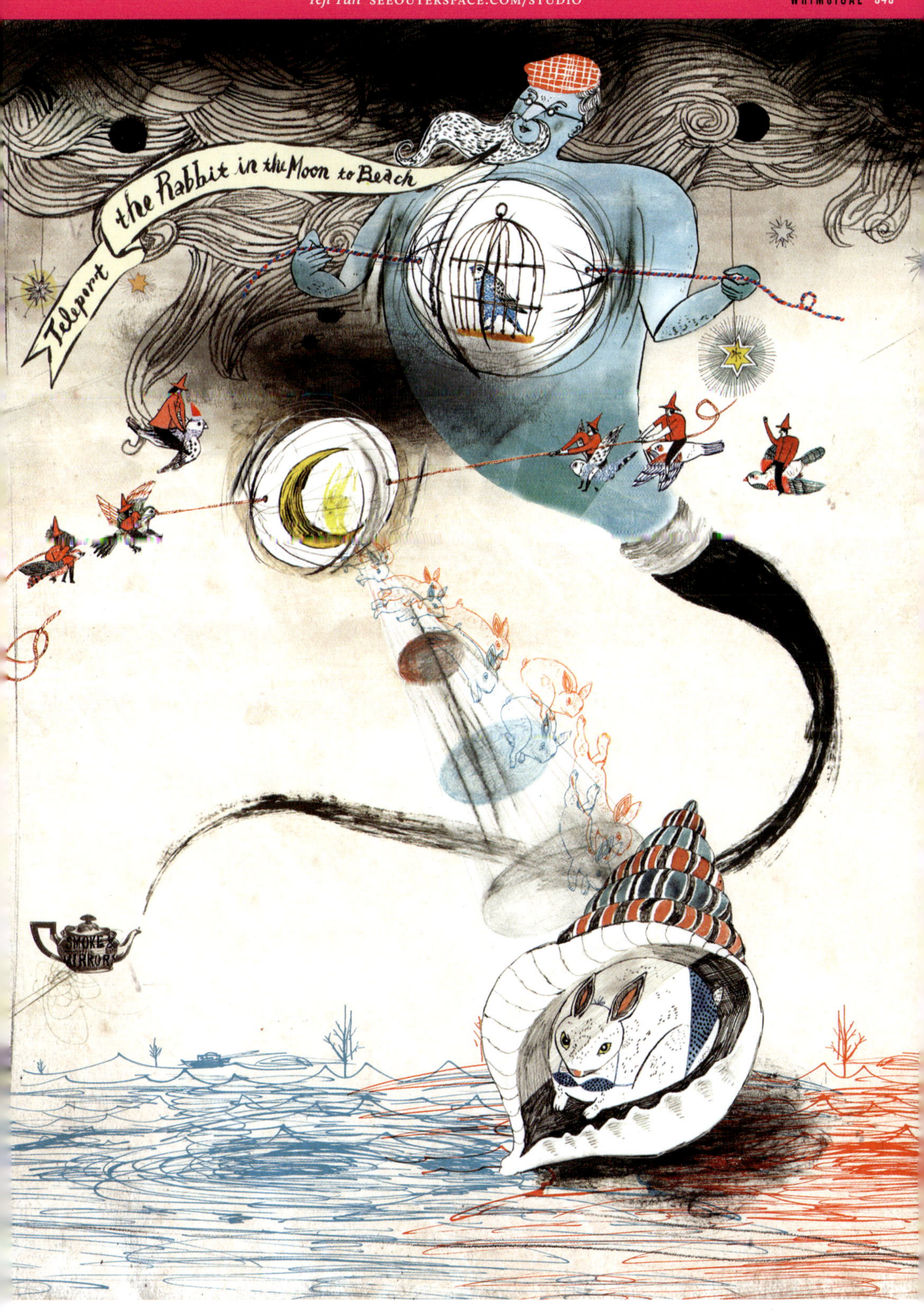
Teleport the Rabbit in the Moon to Beach
SMOKE & MIRROR

Walking around in Tokyo?

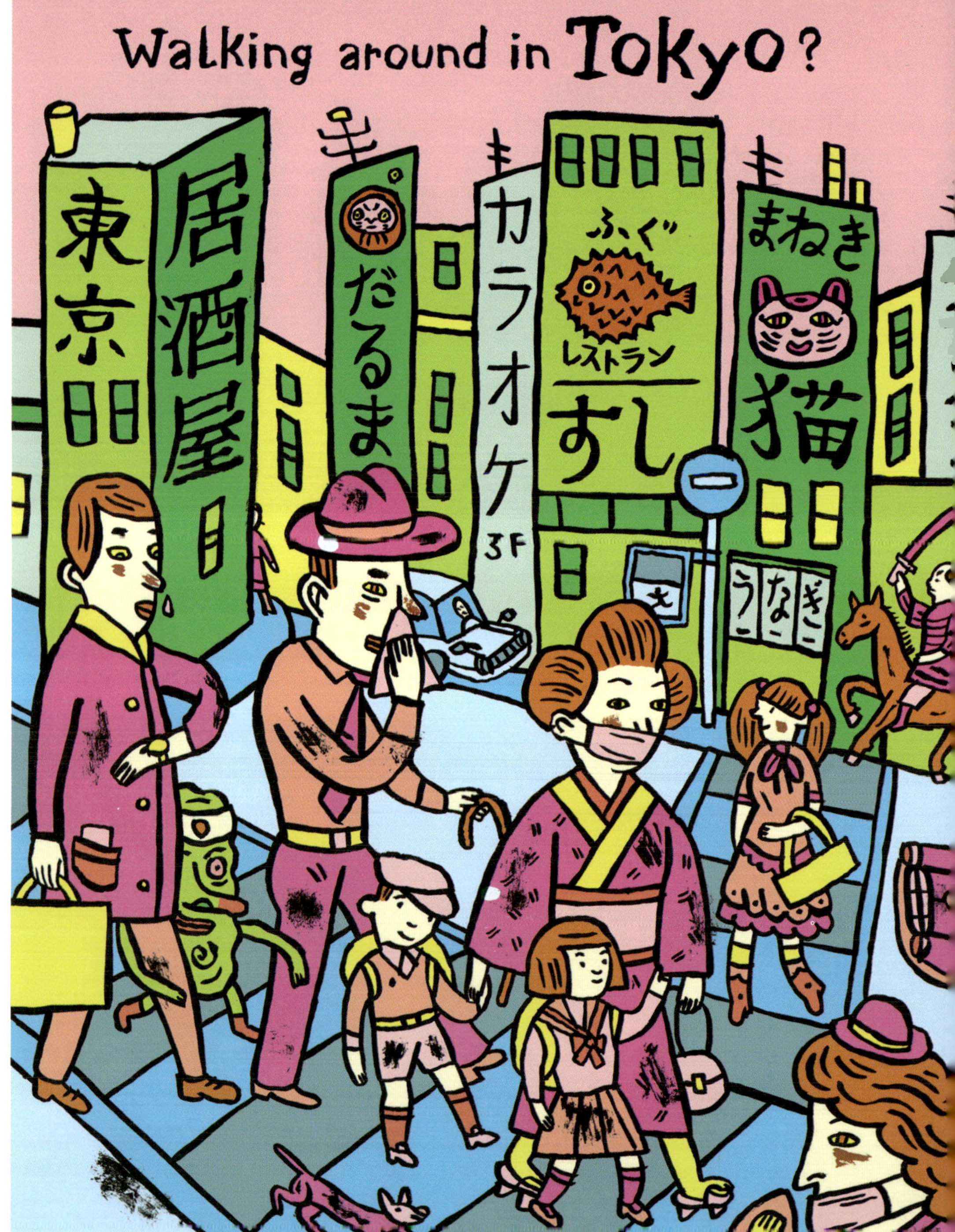

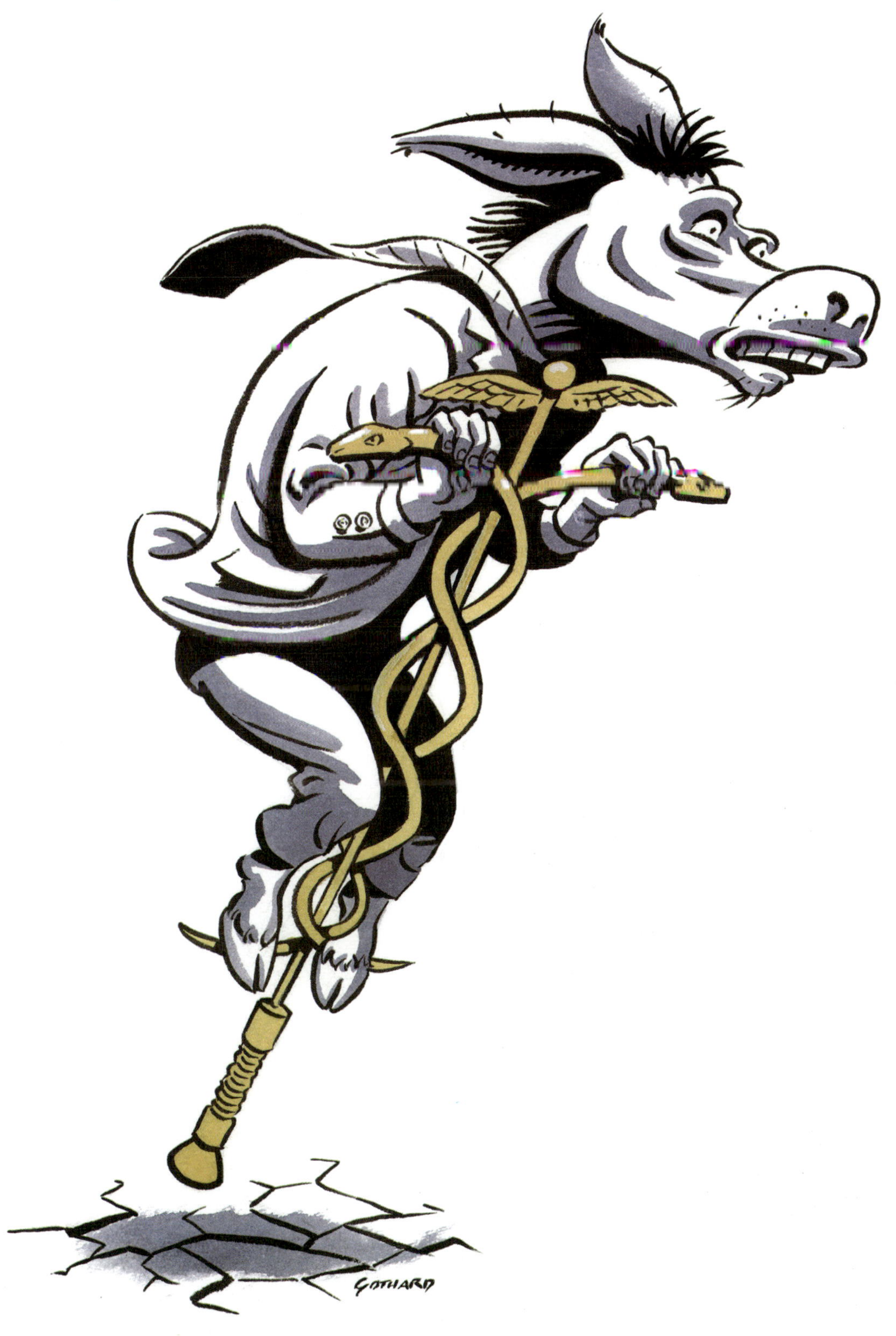
GOTHARD

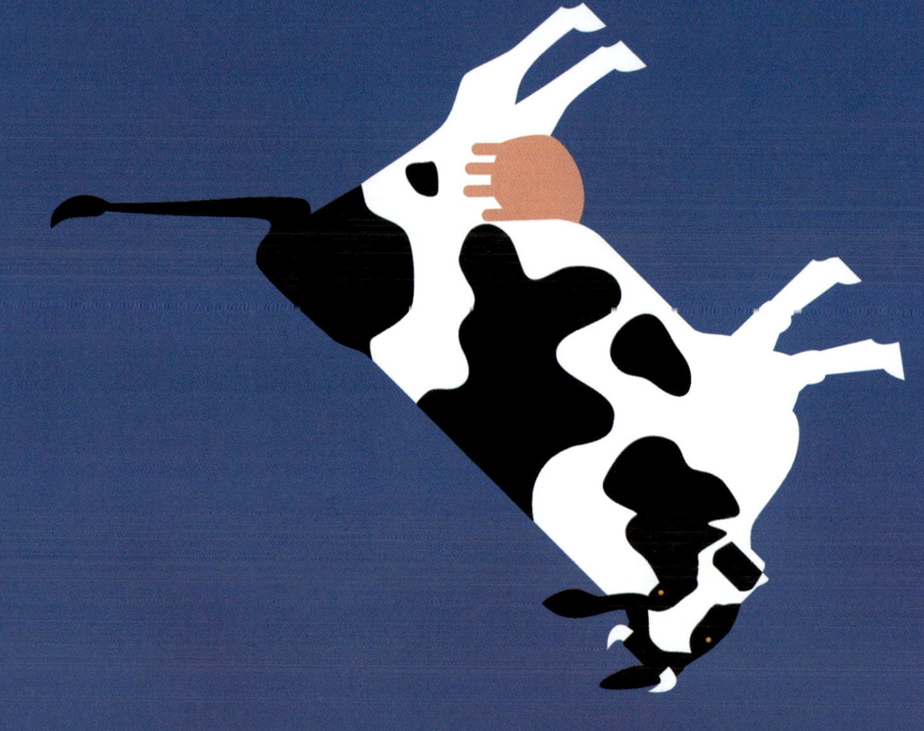

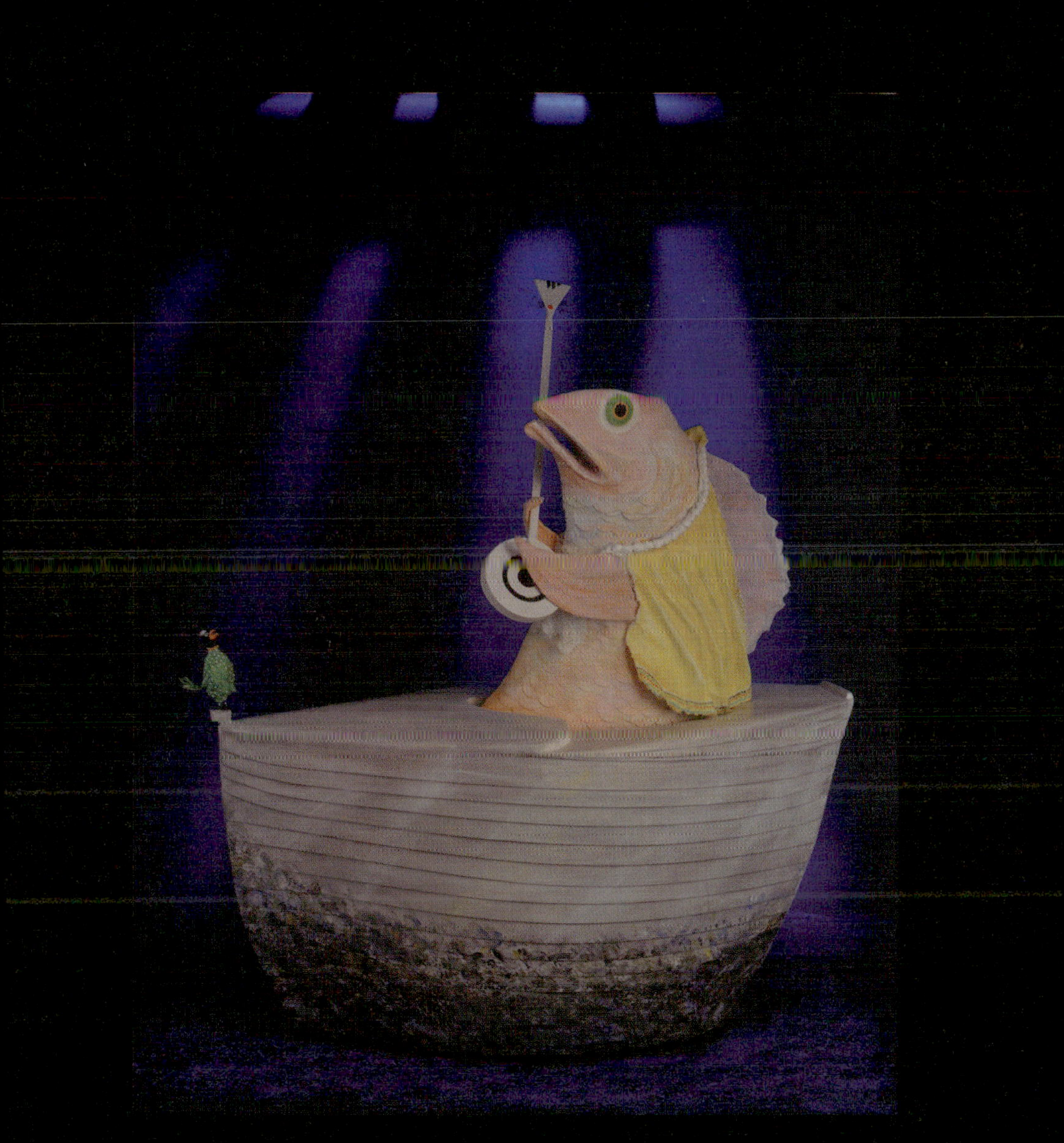

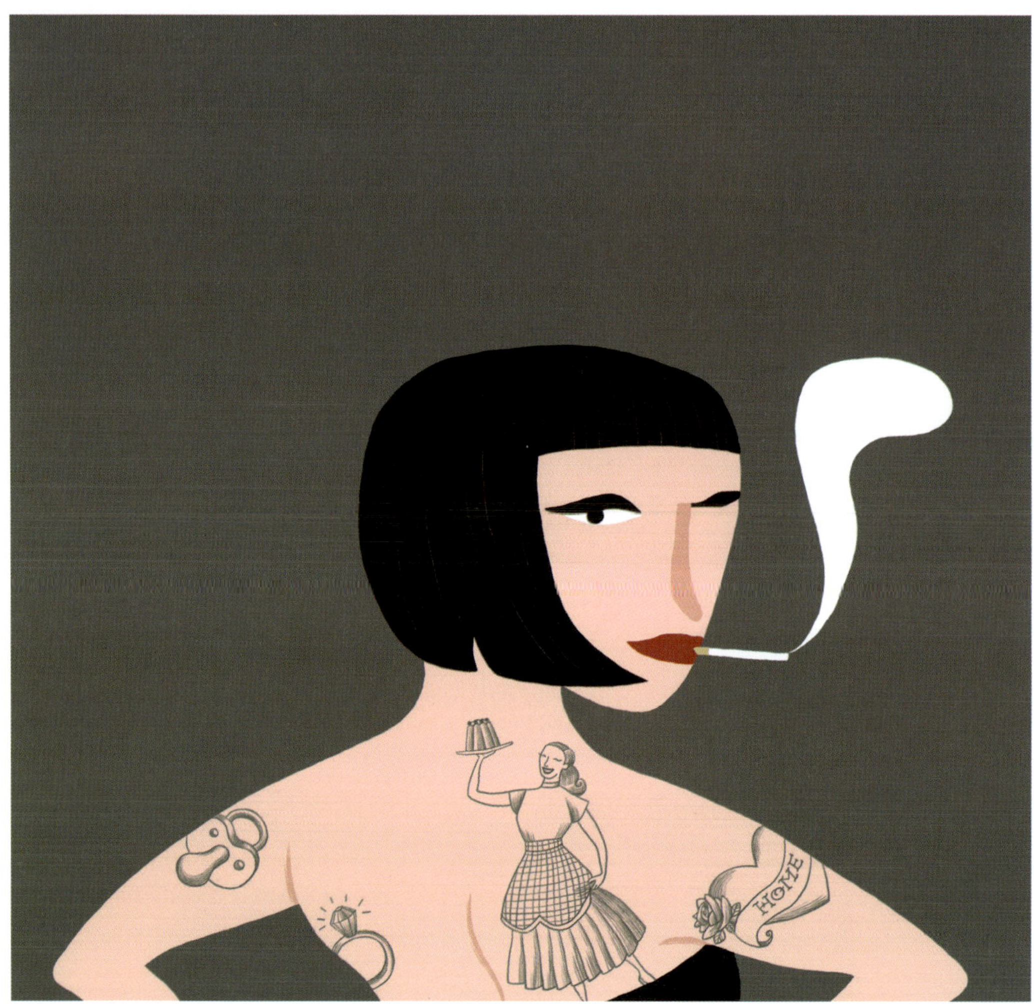

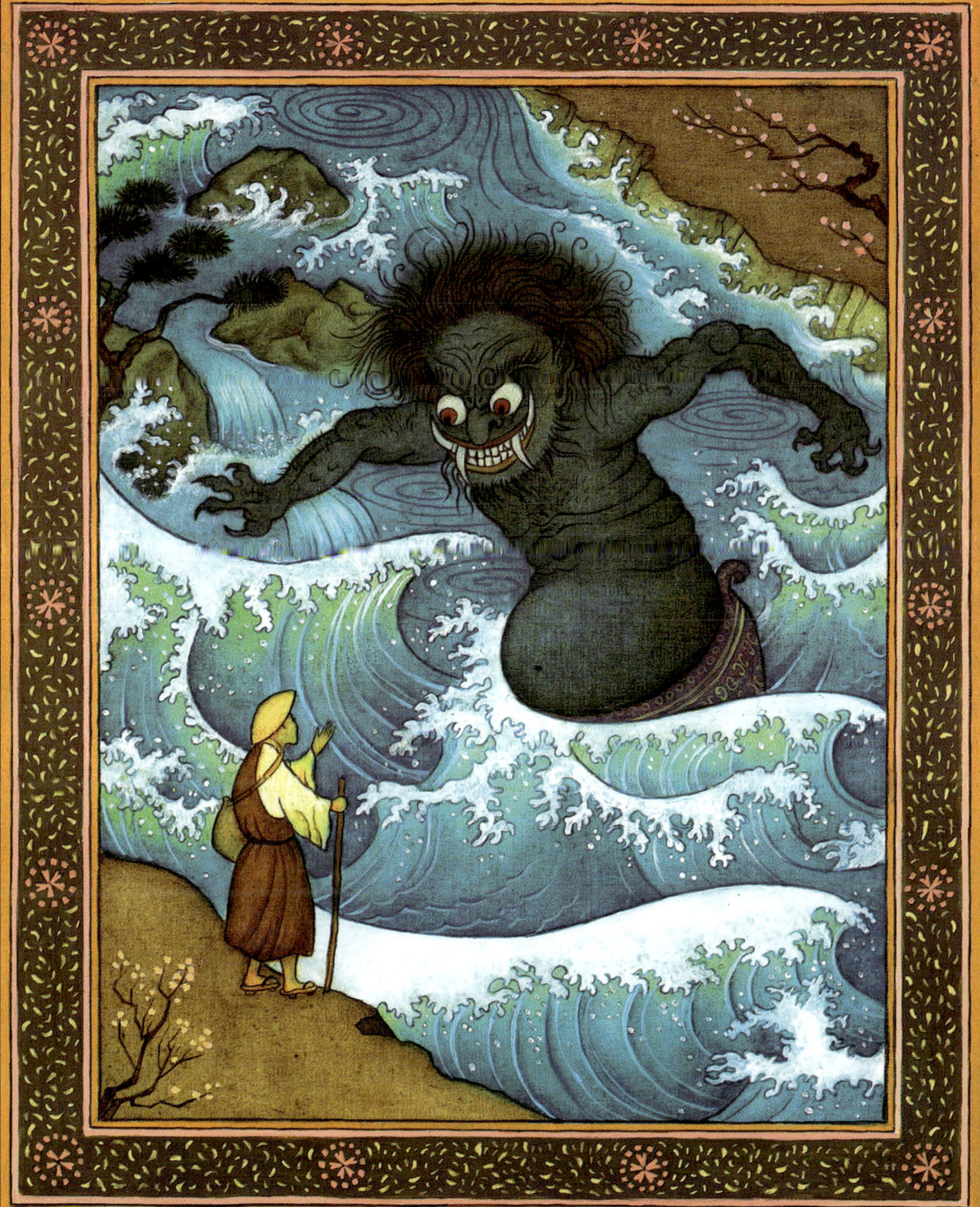

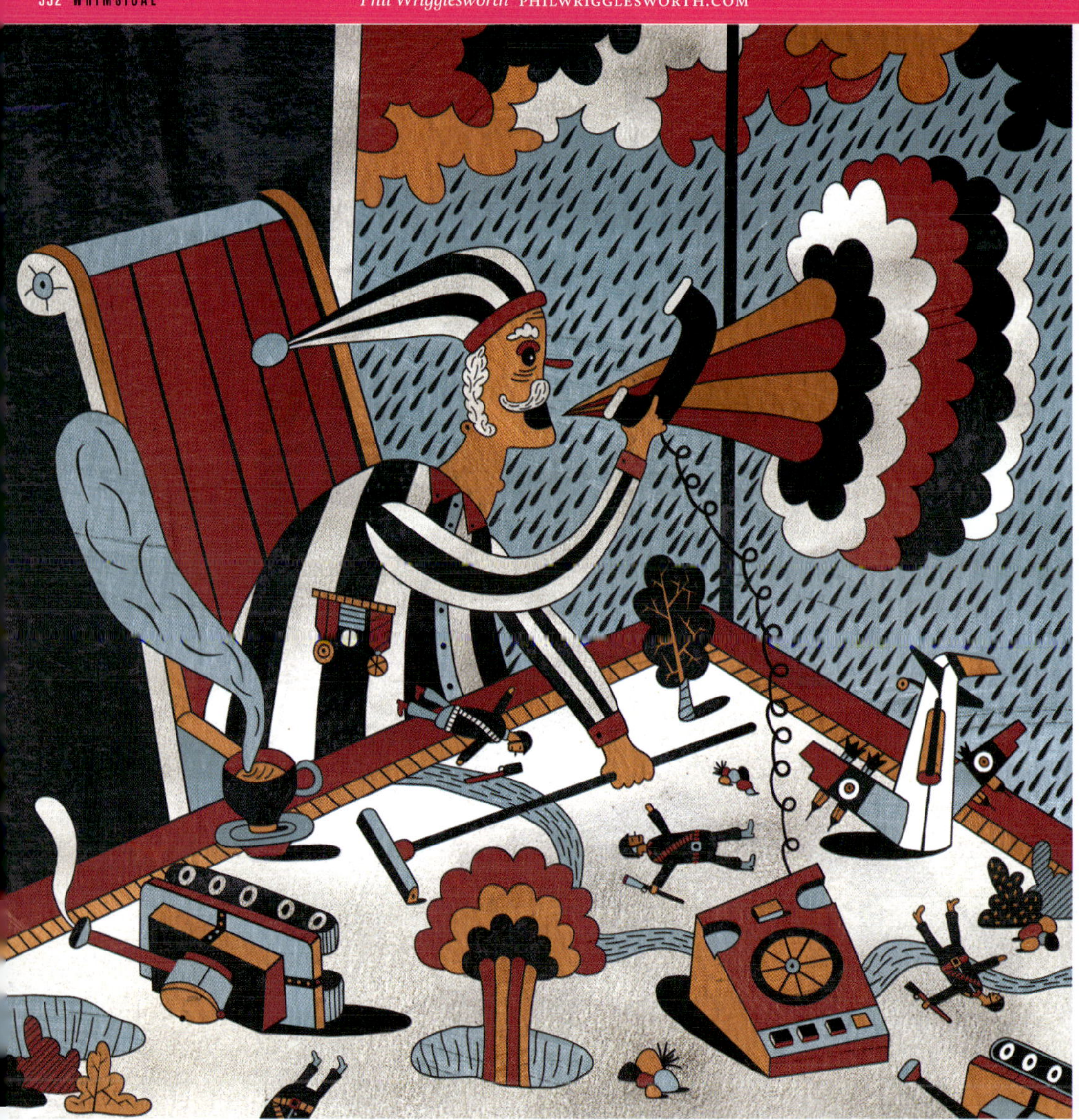

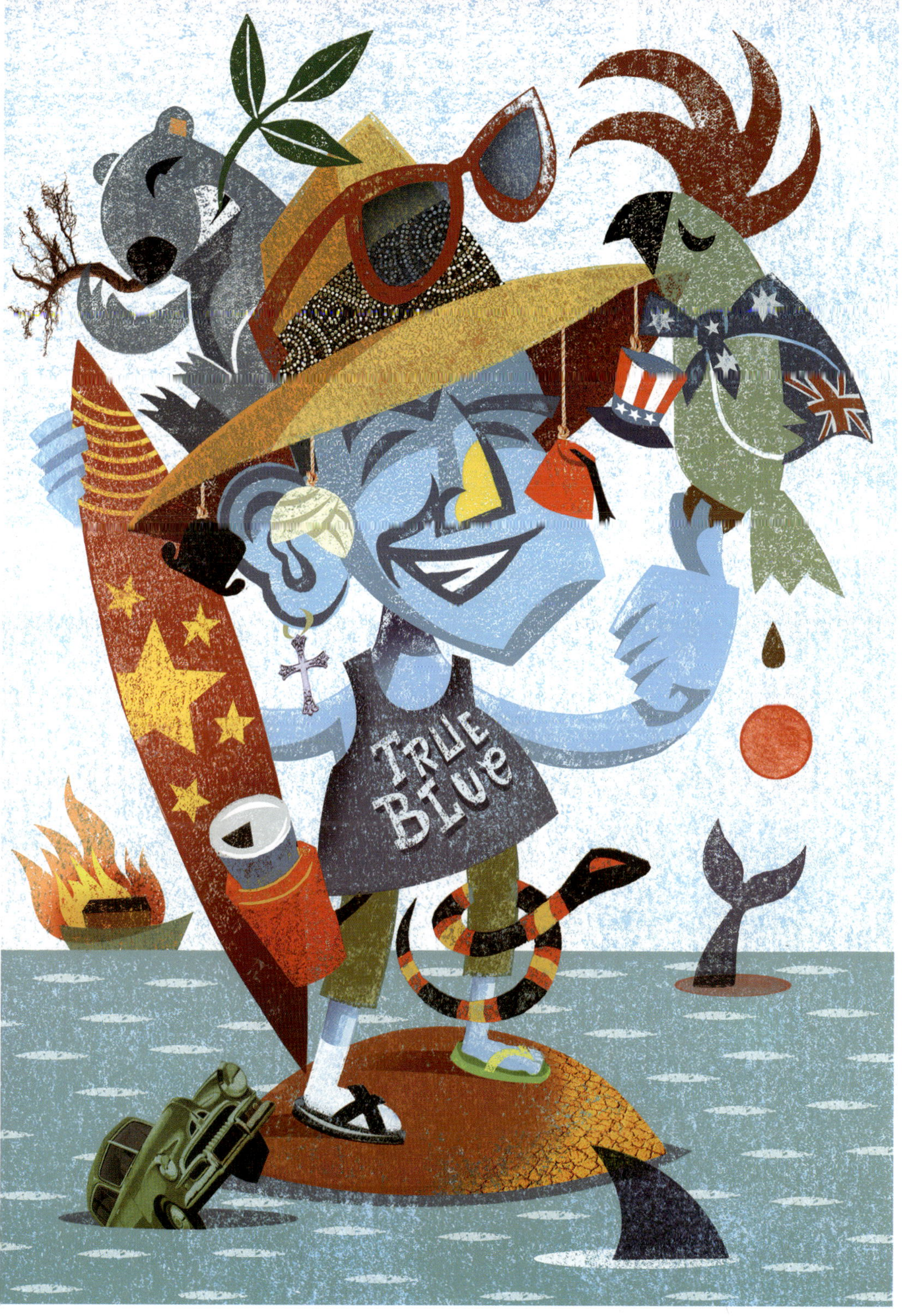
TRUE
BLUE

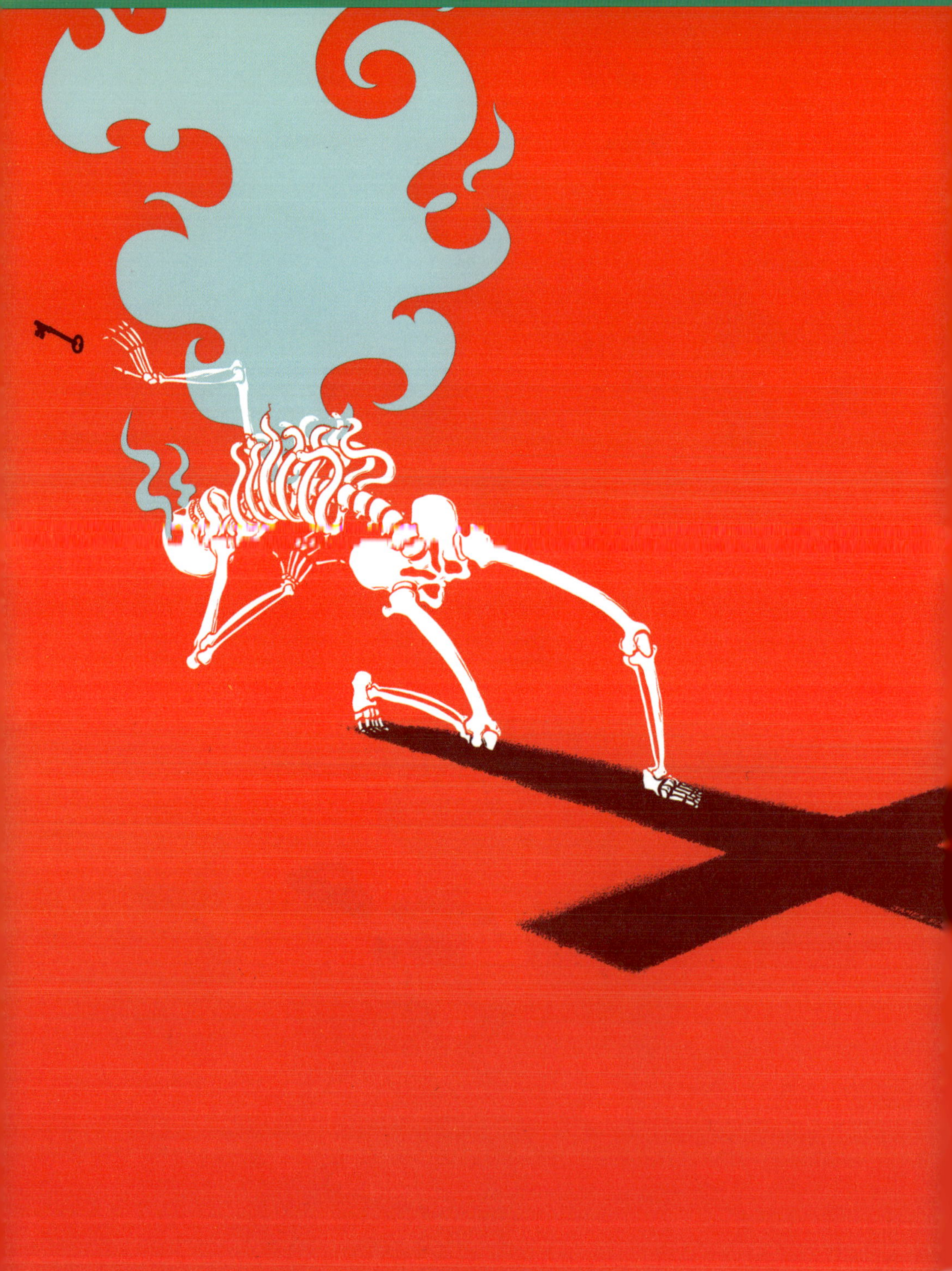

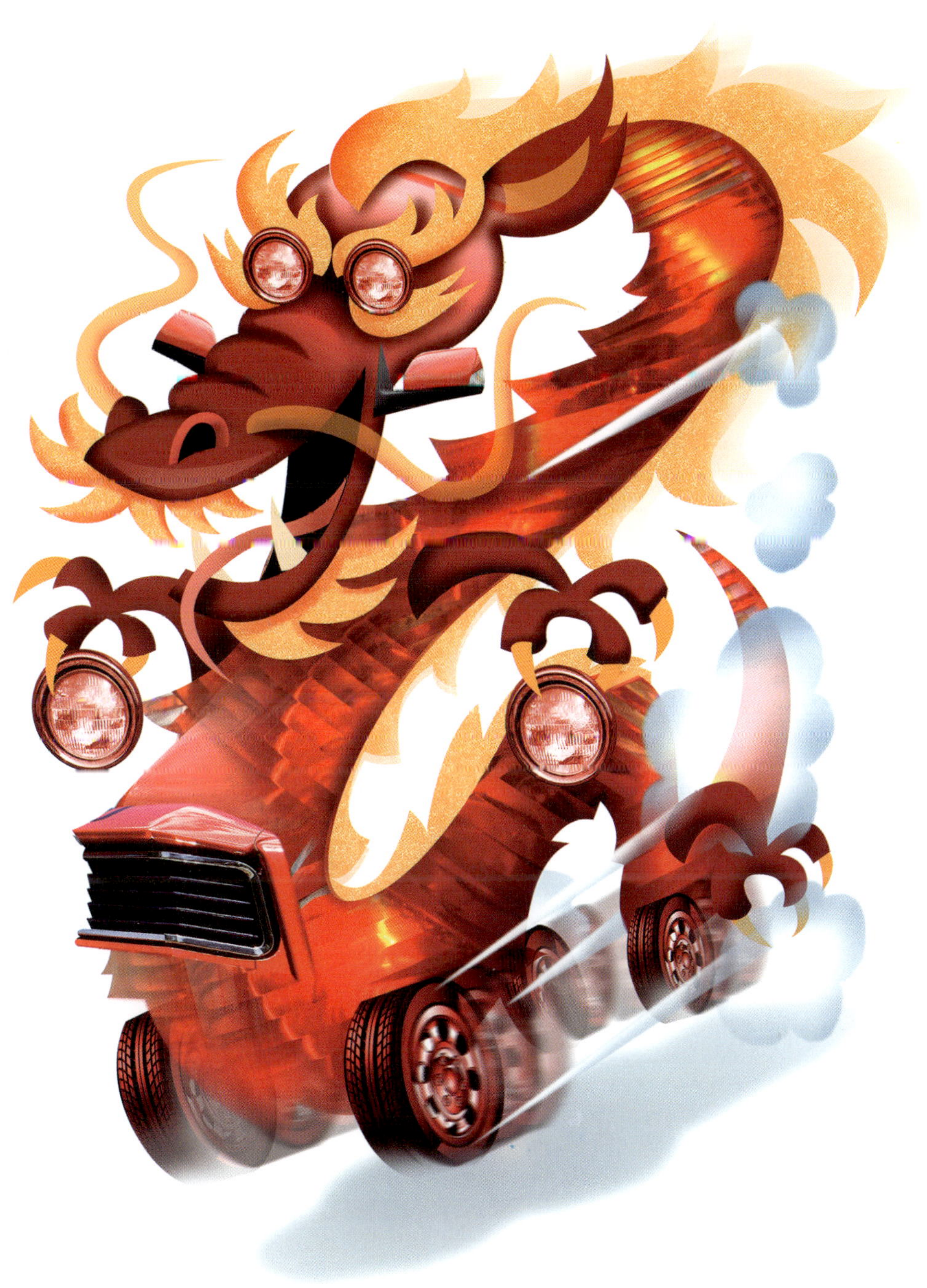

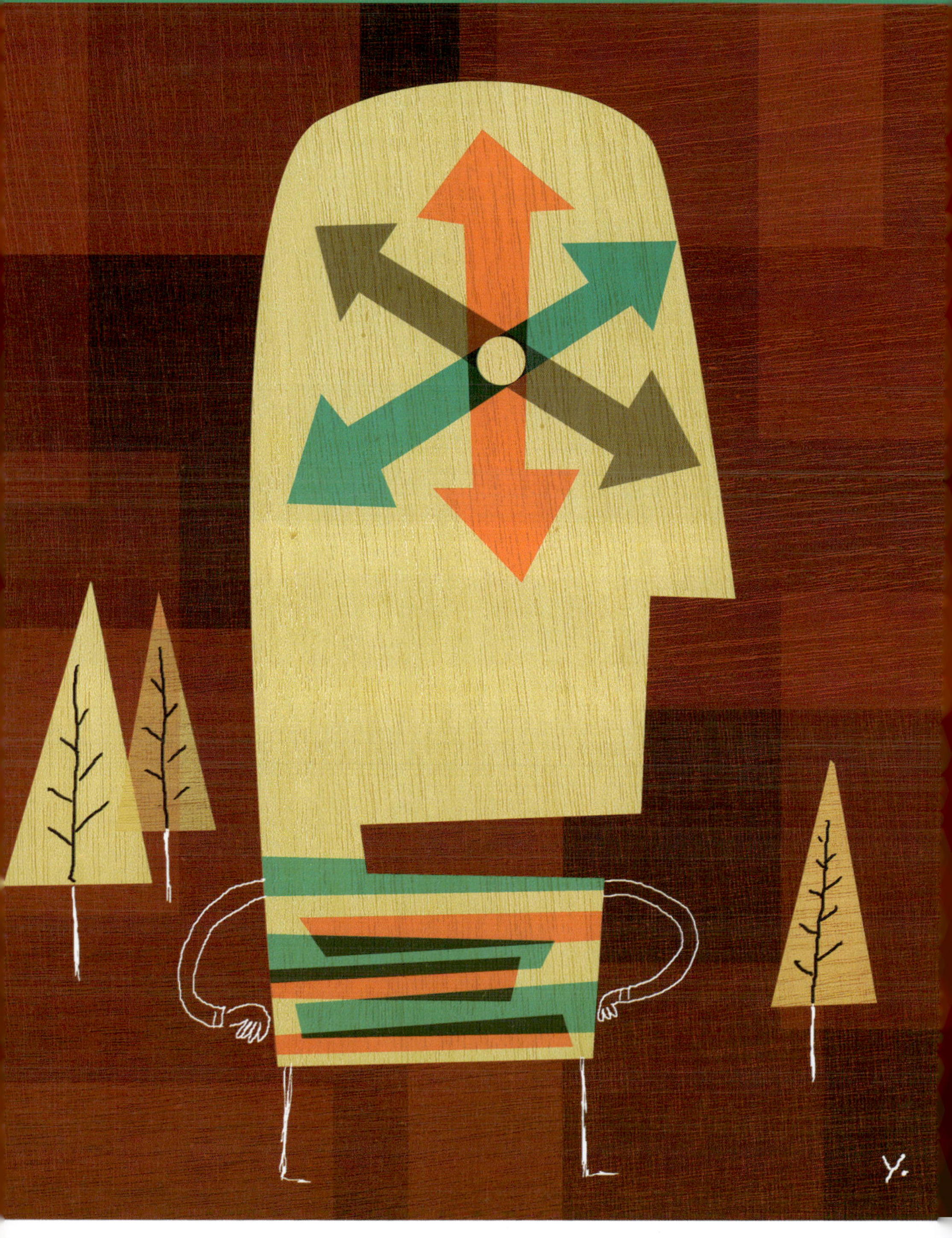

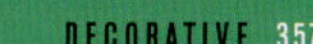

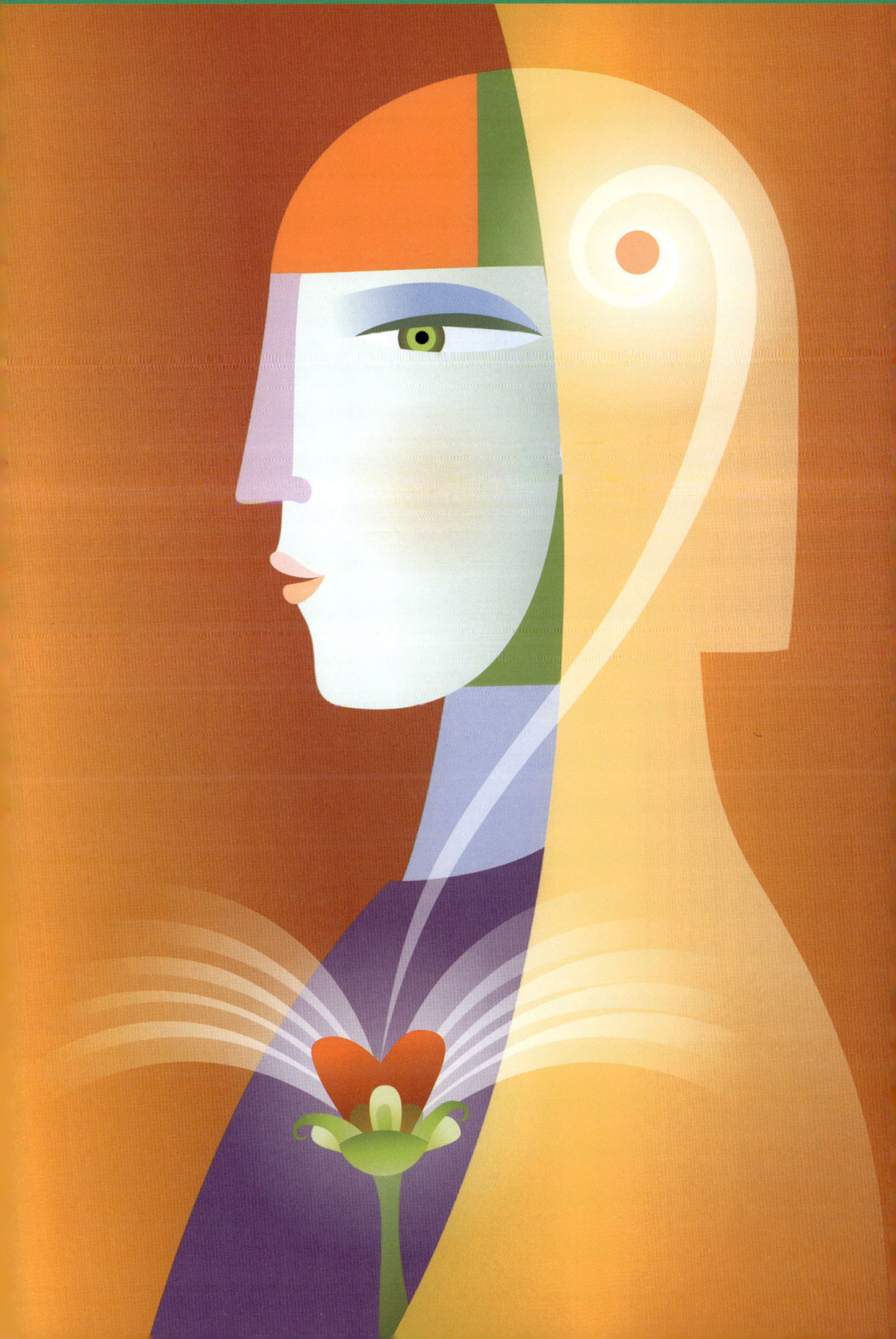

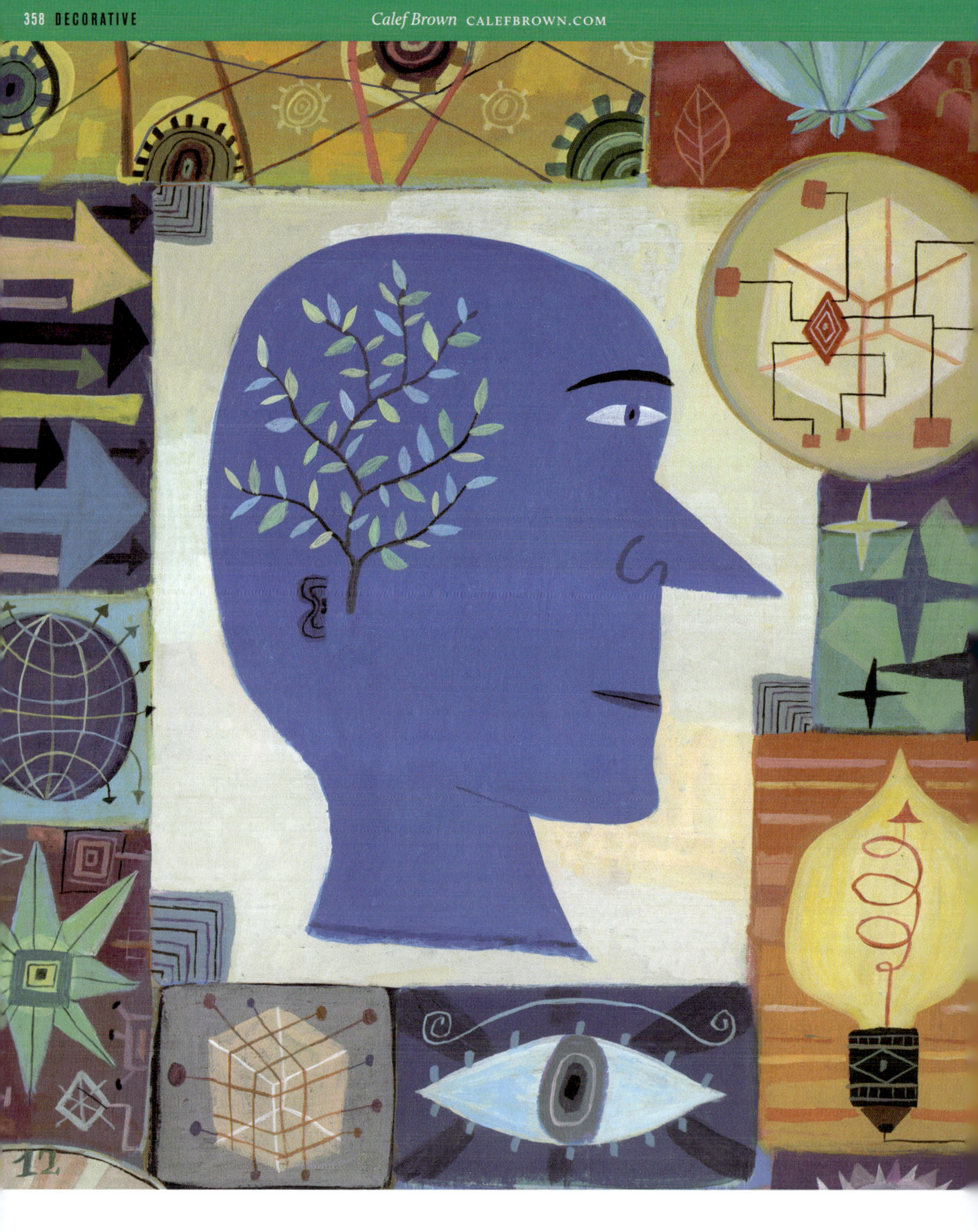

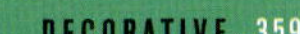

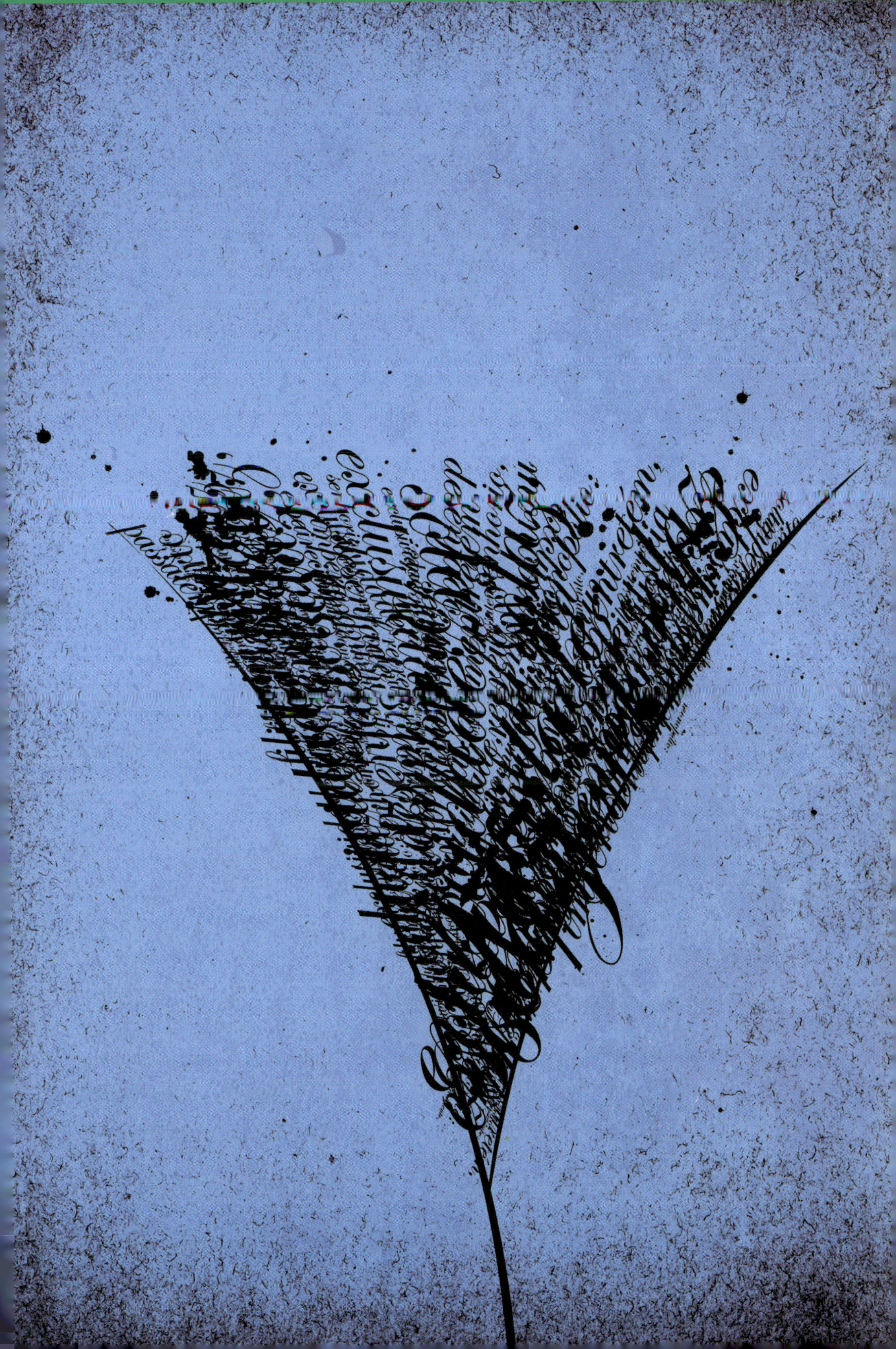

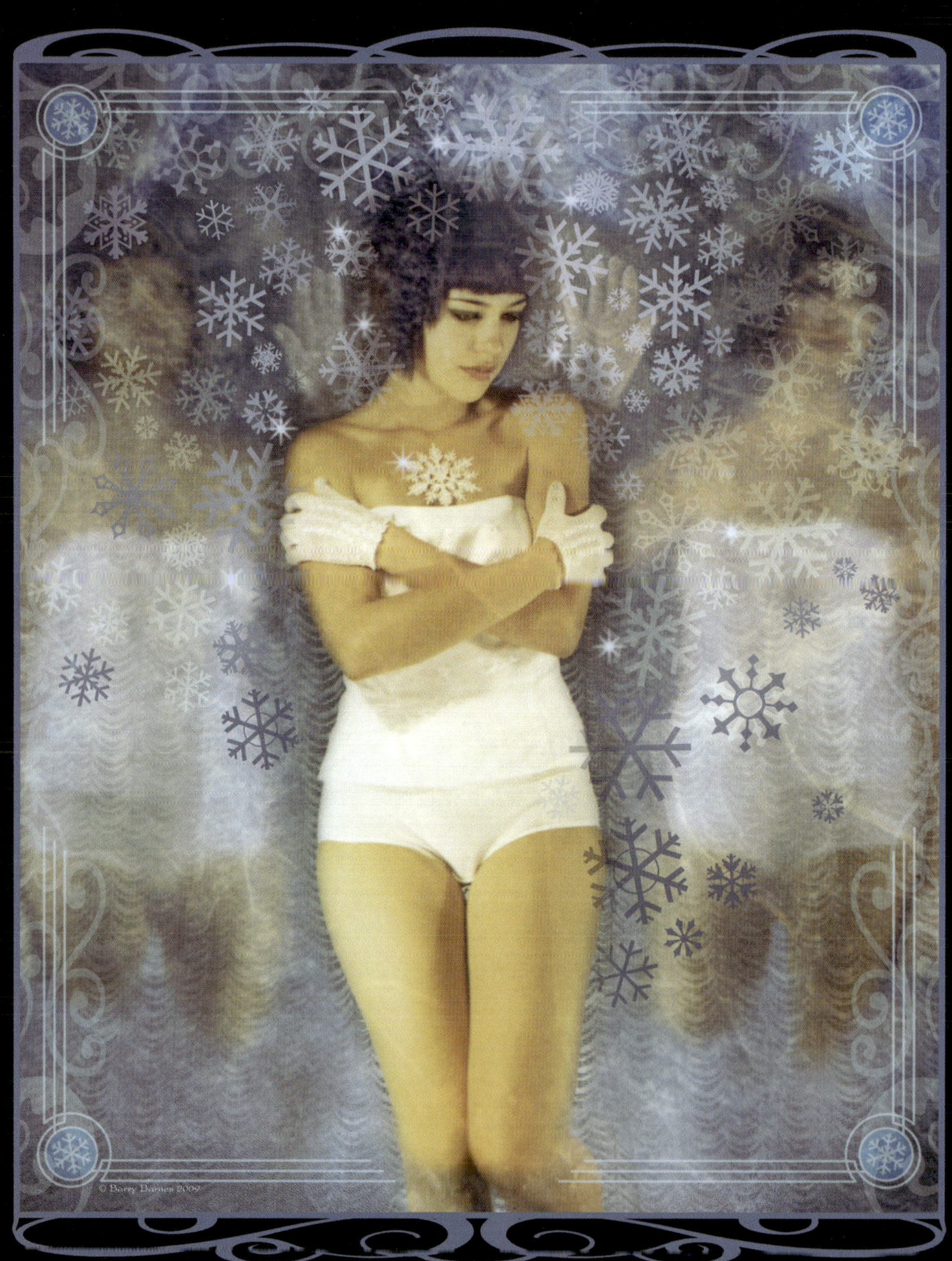
© Barry Barnes 2009

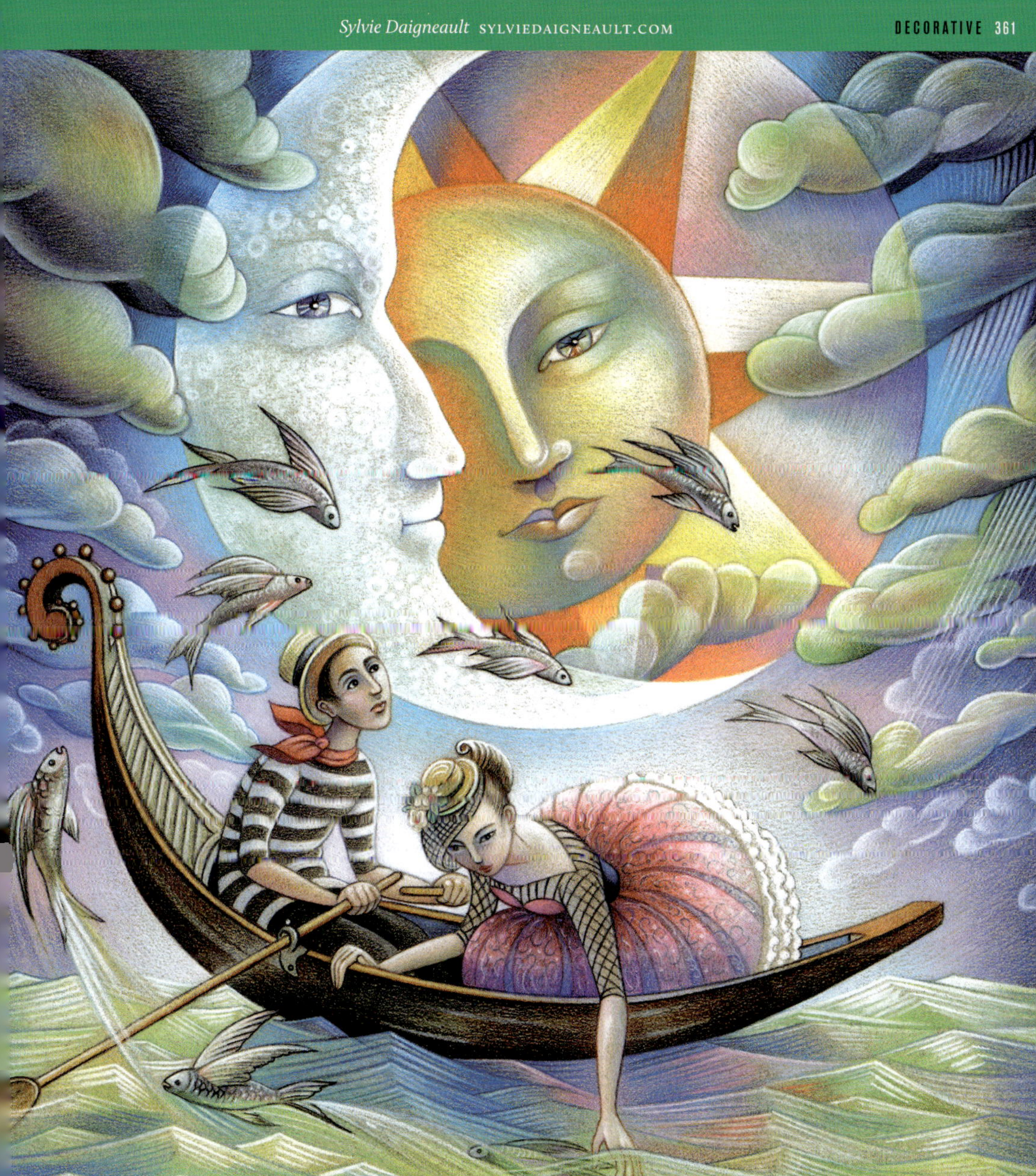

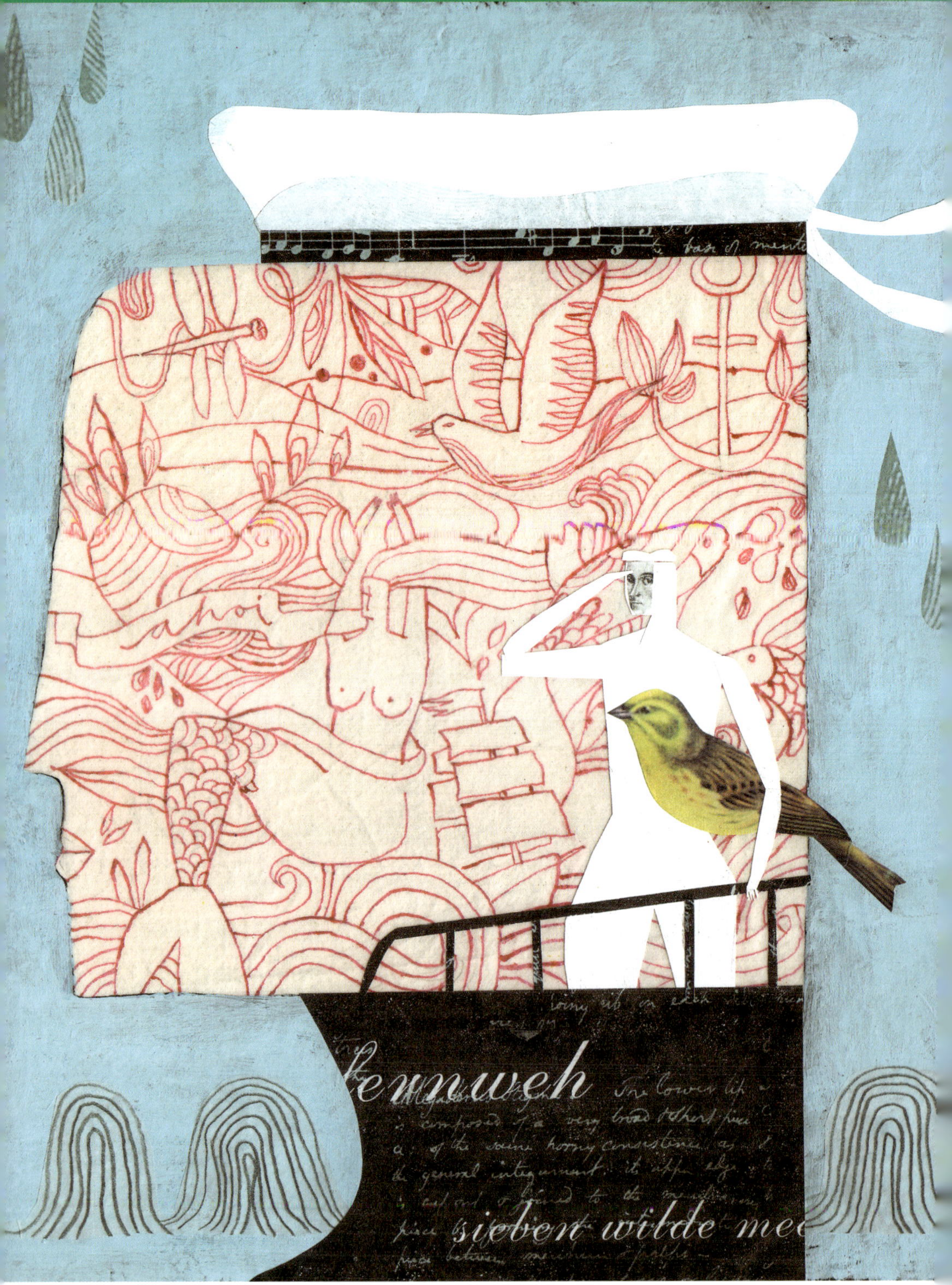

ahoi

ennweh

sieben wilde mee

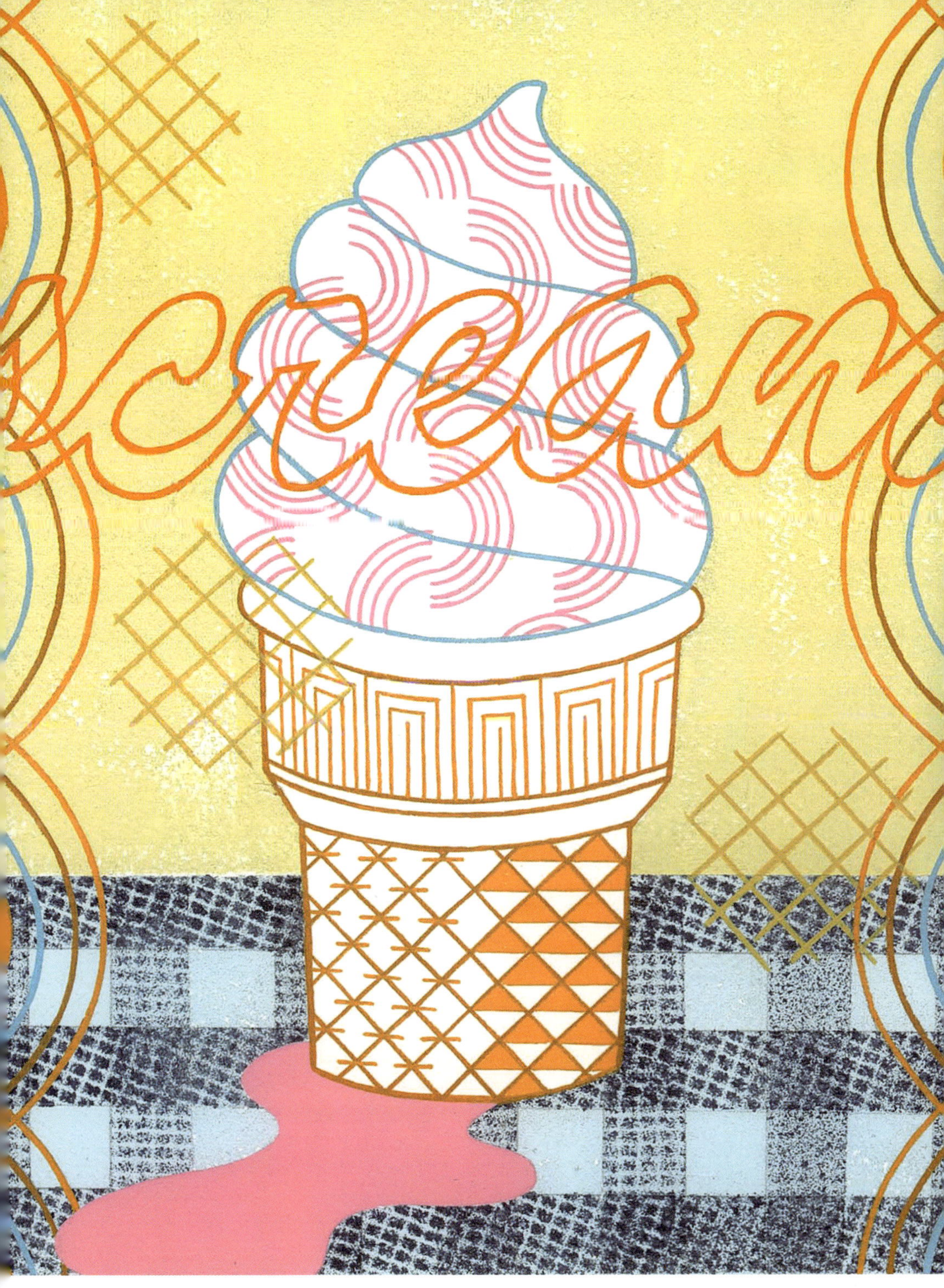
cream

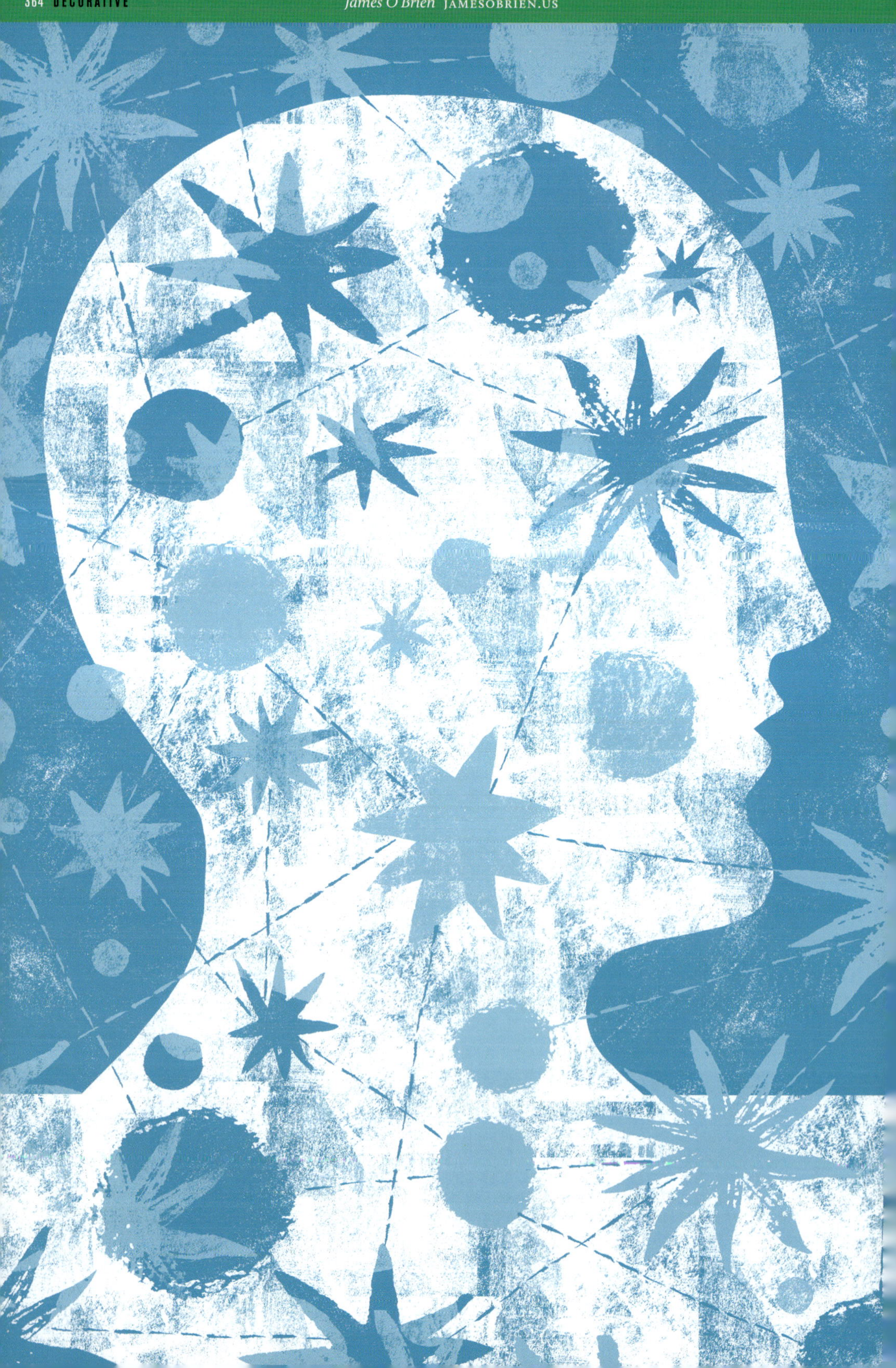

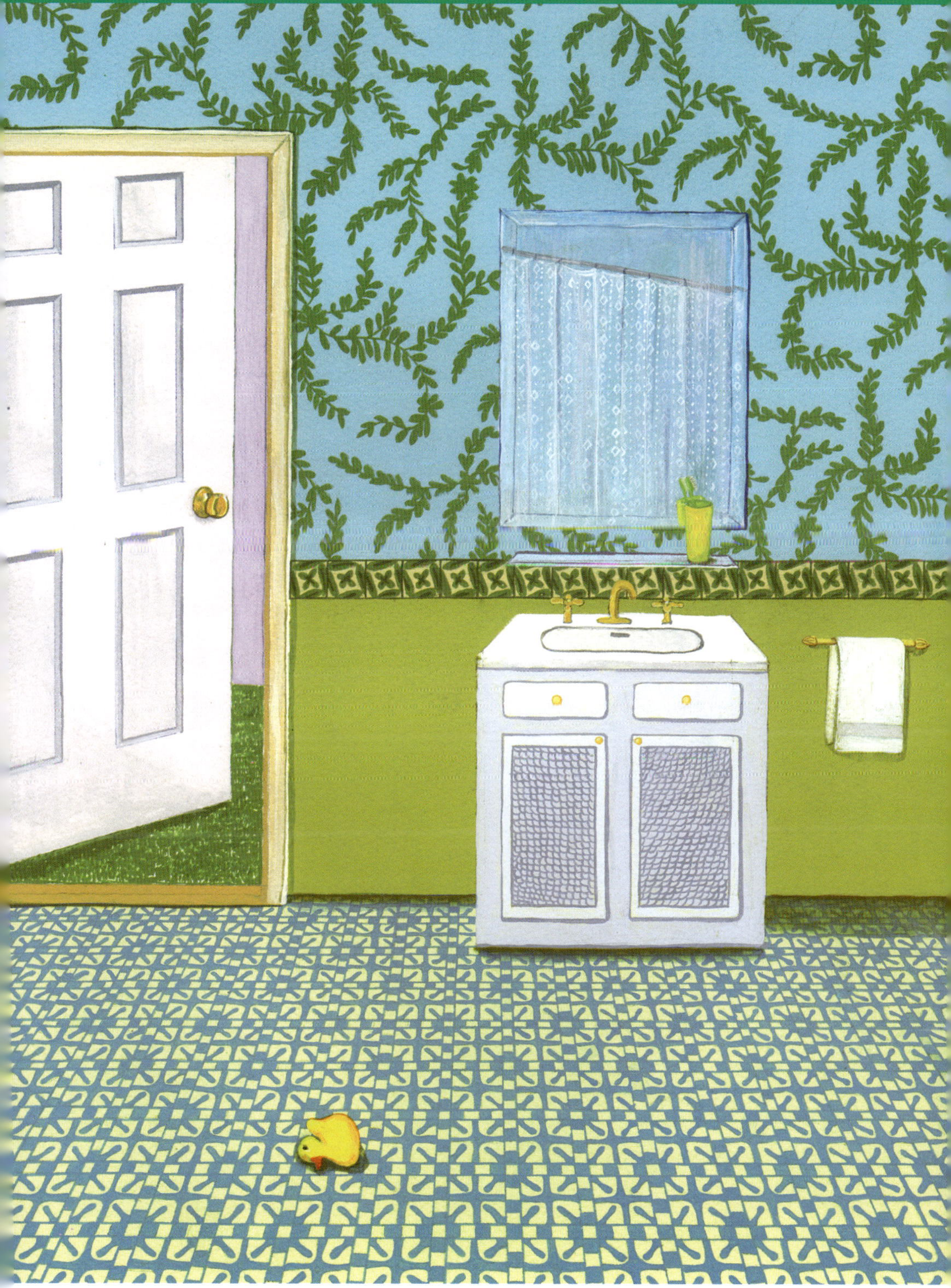

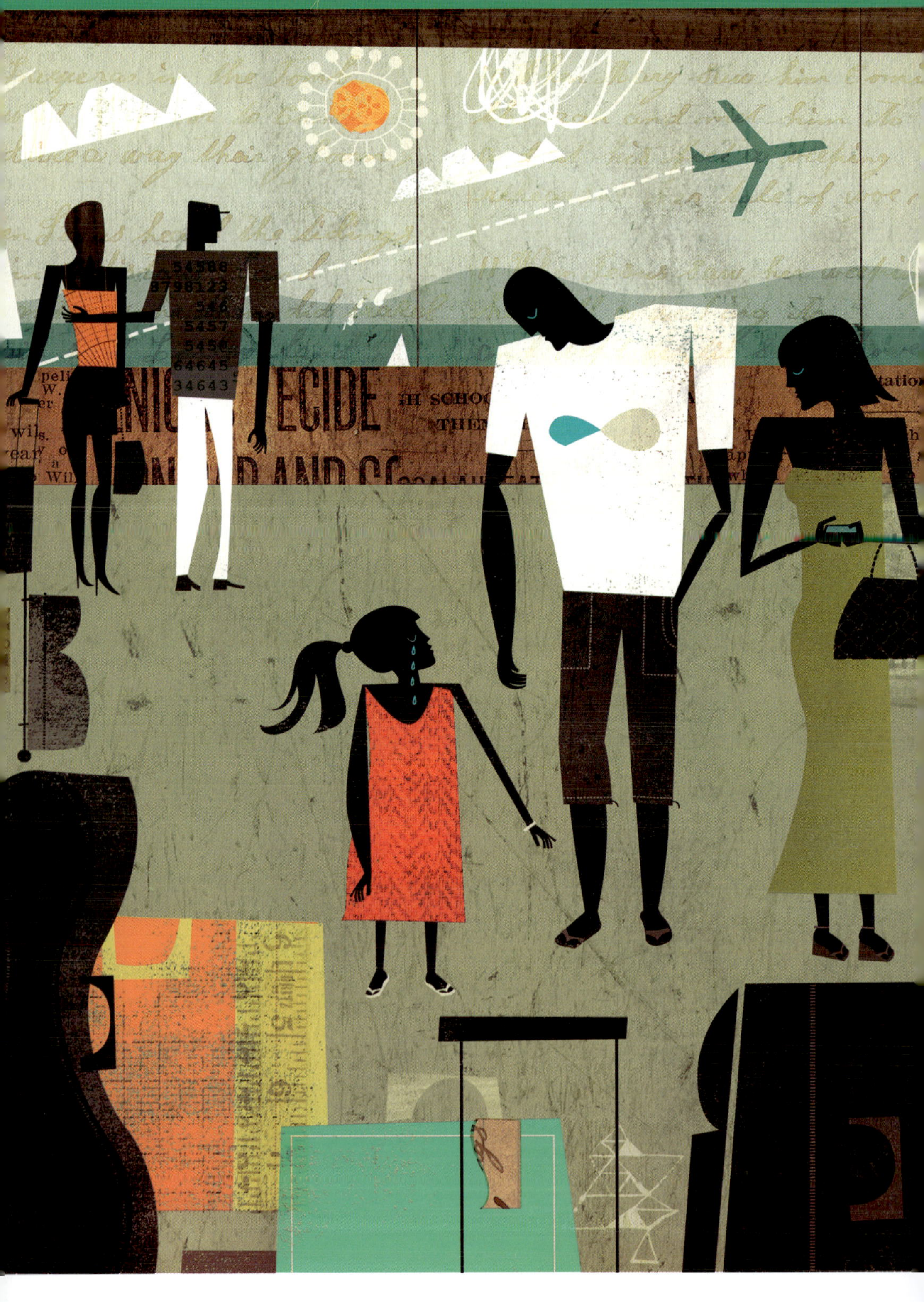

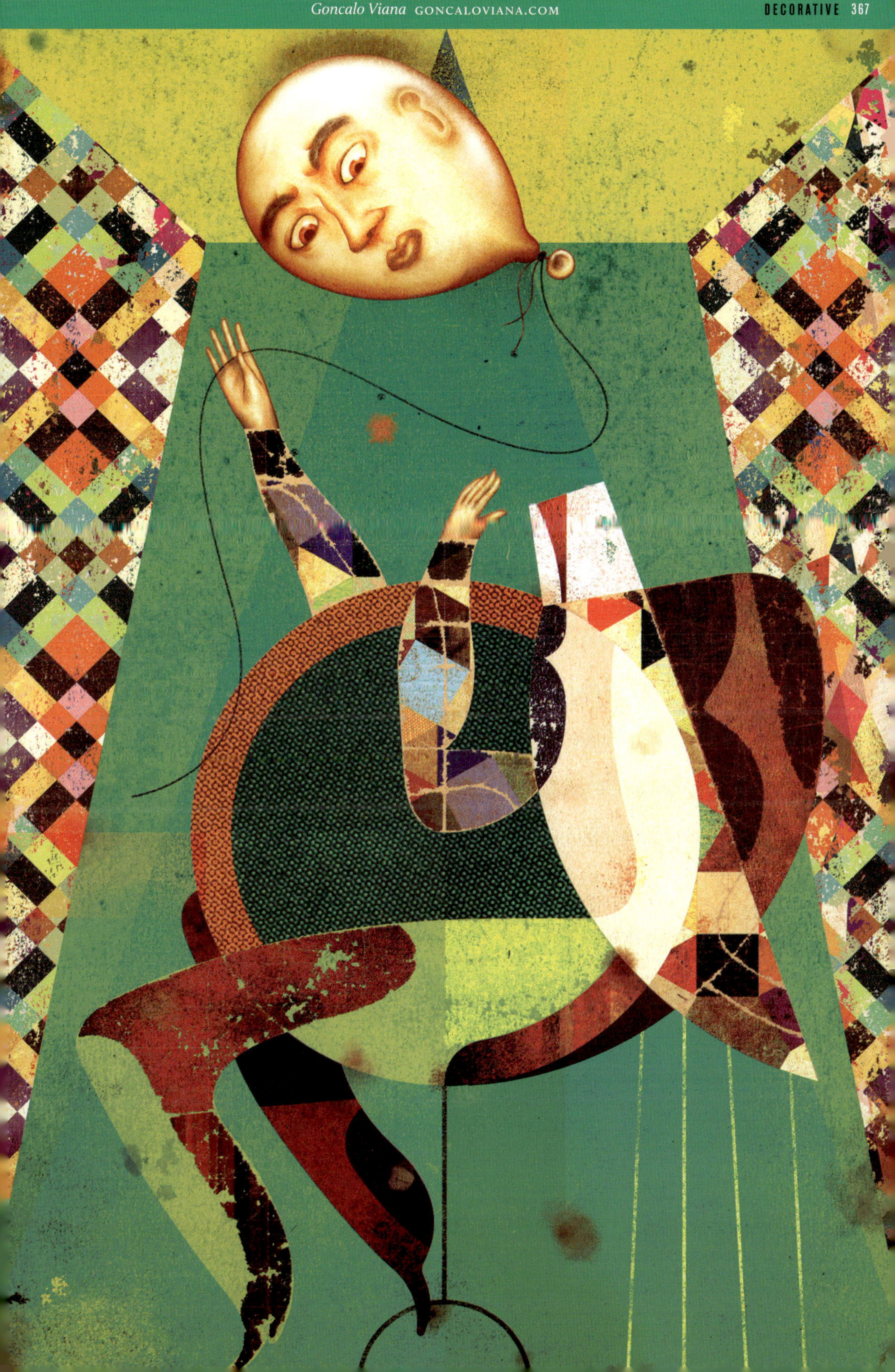

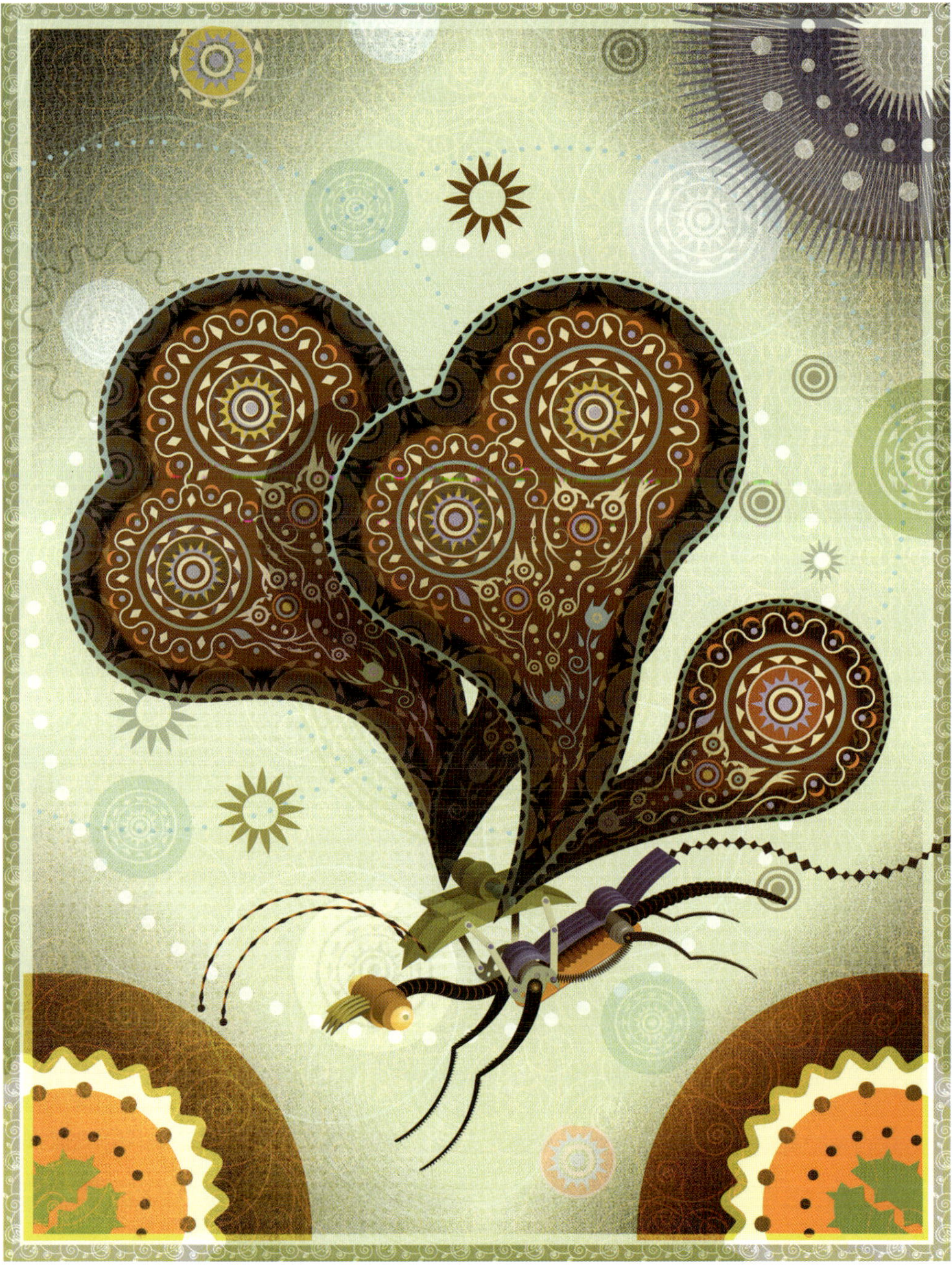

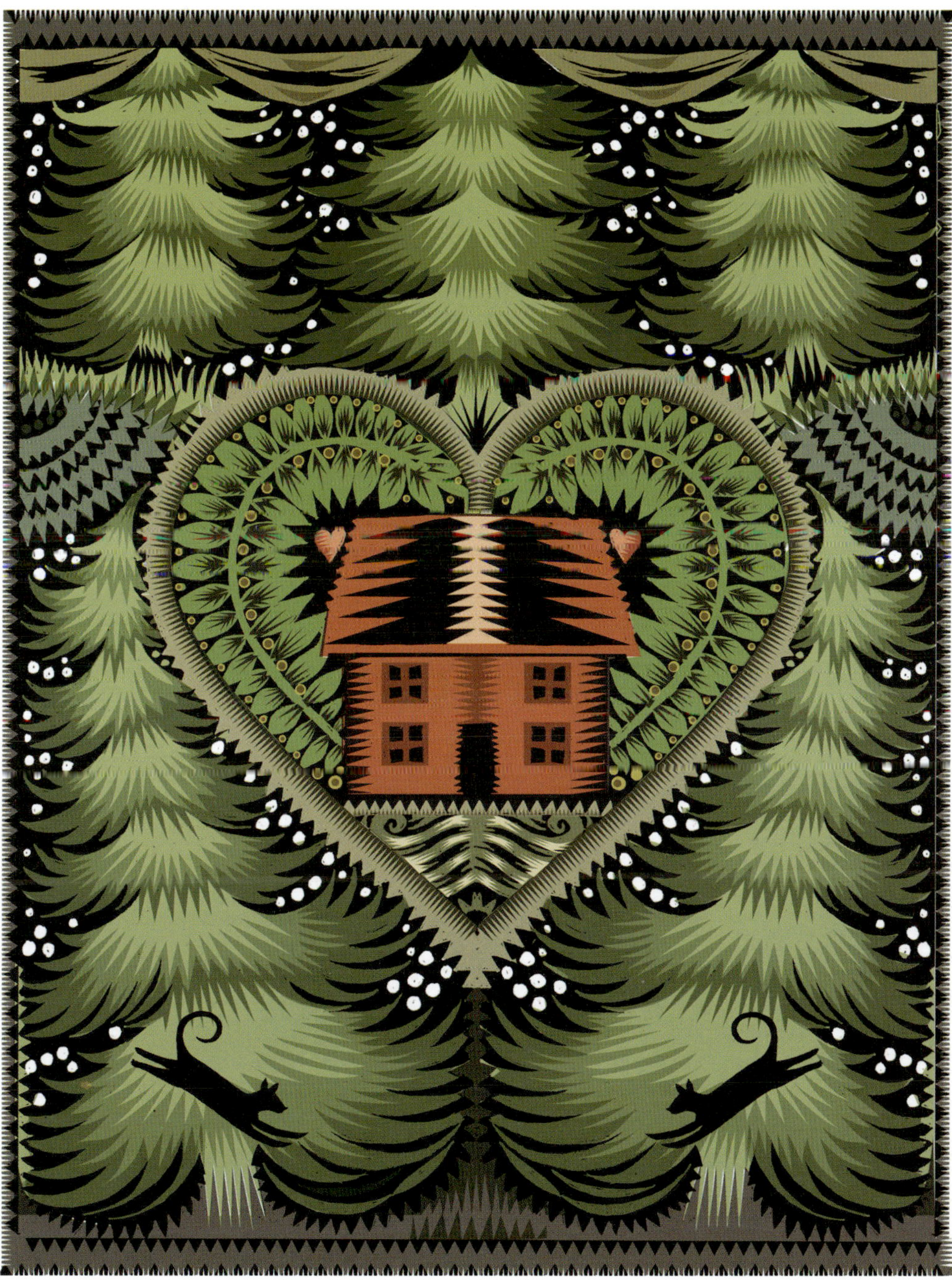

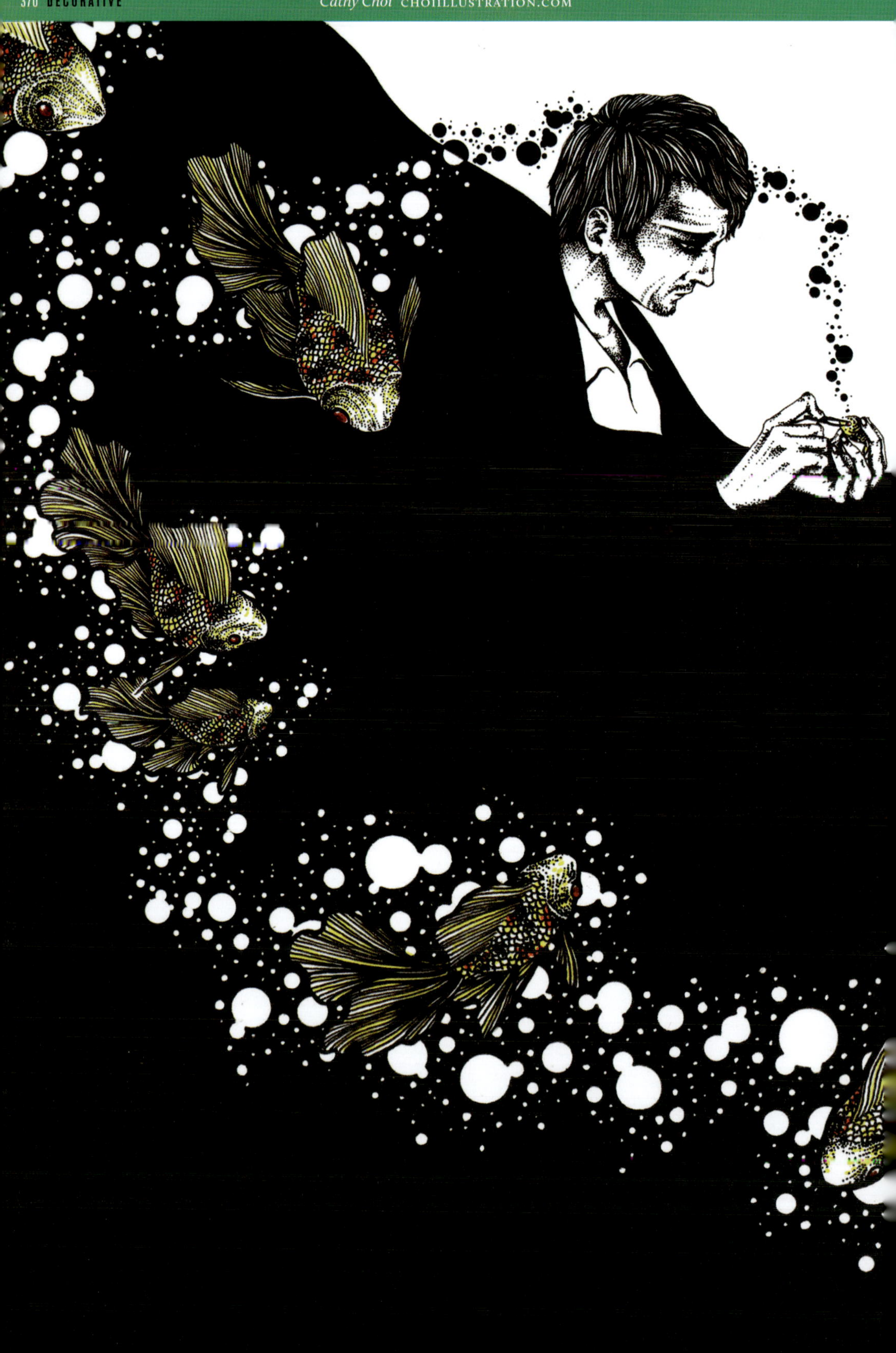

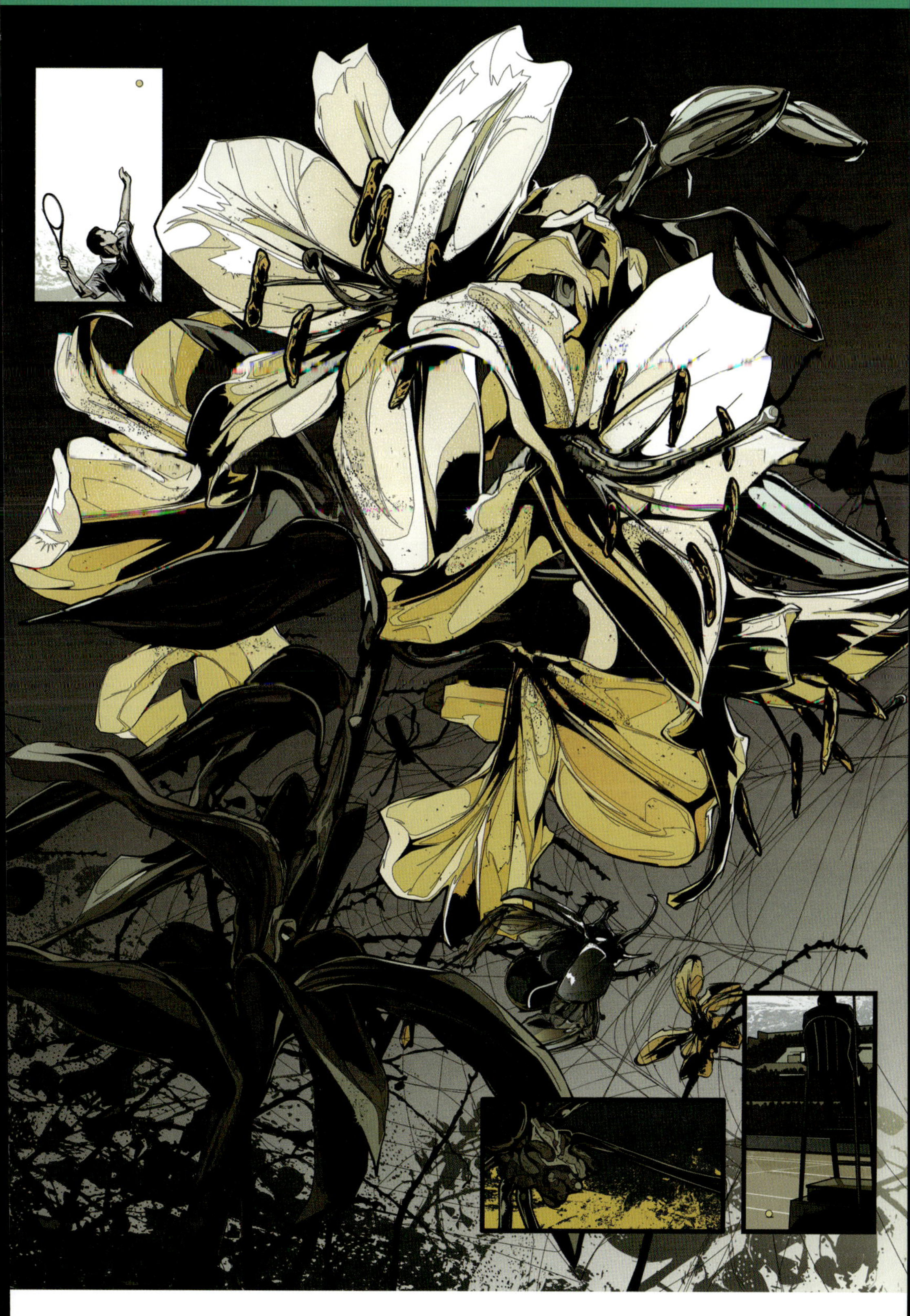

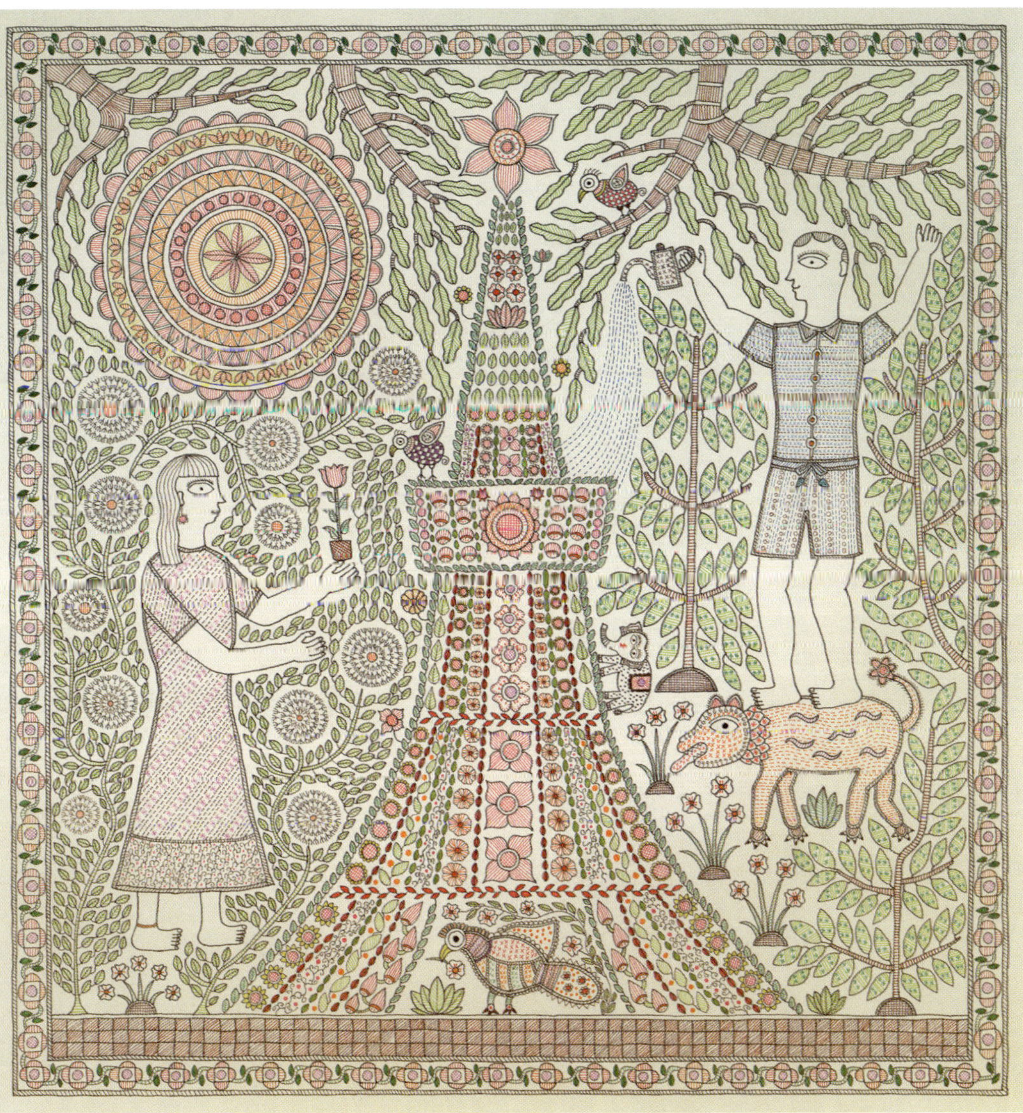

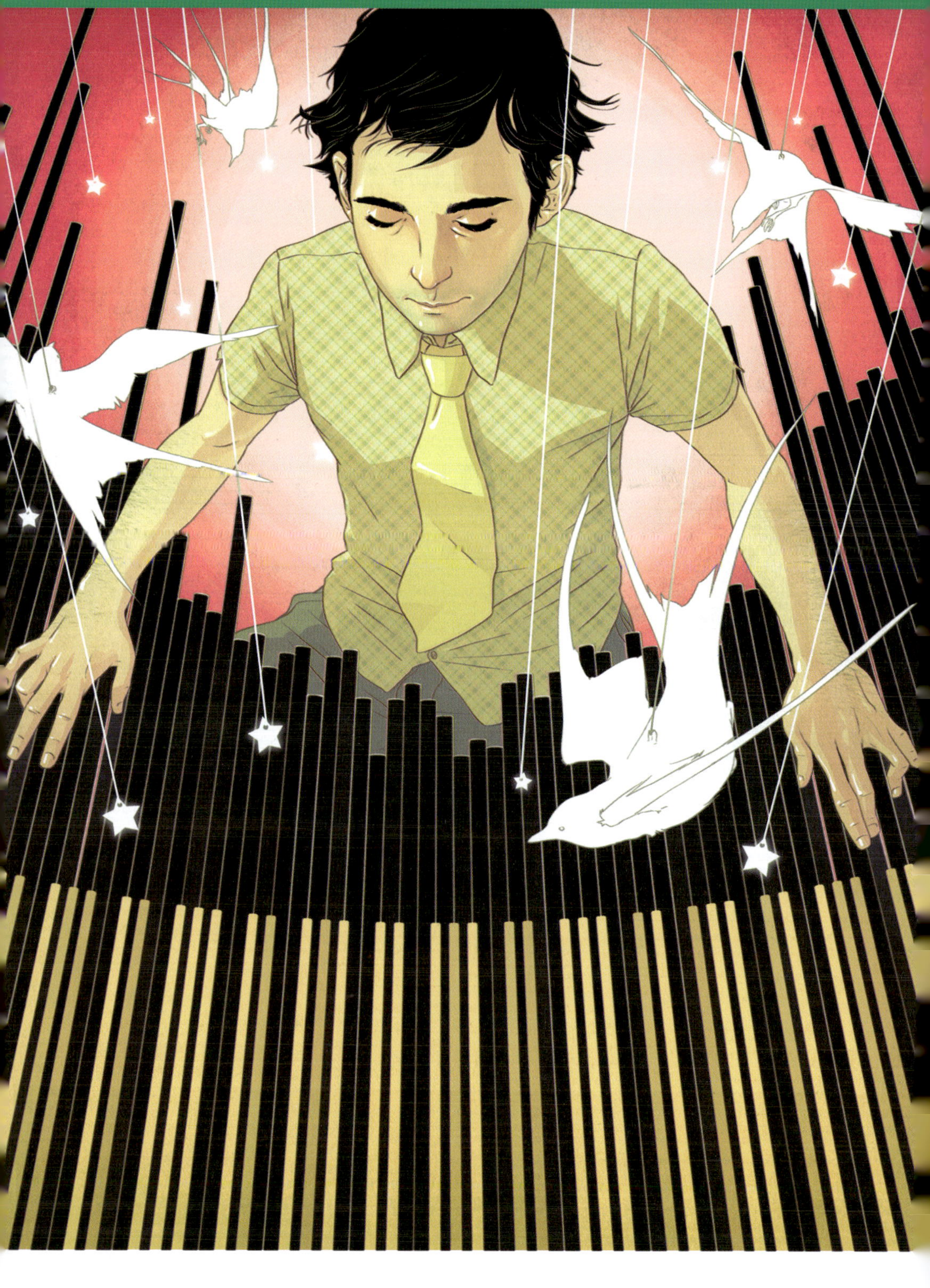

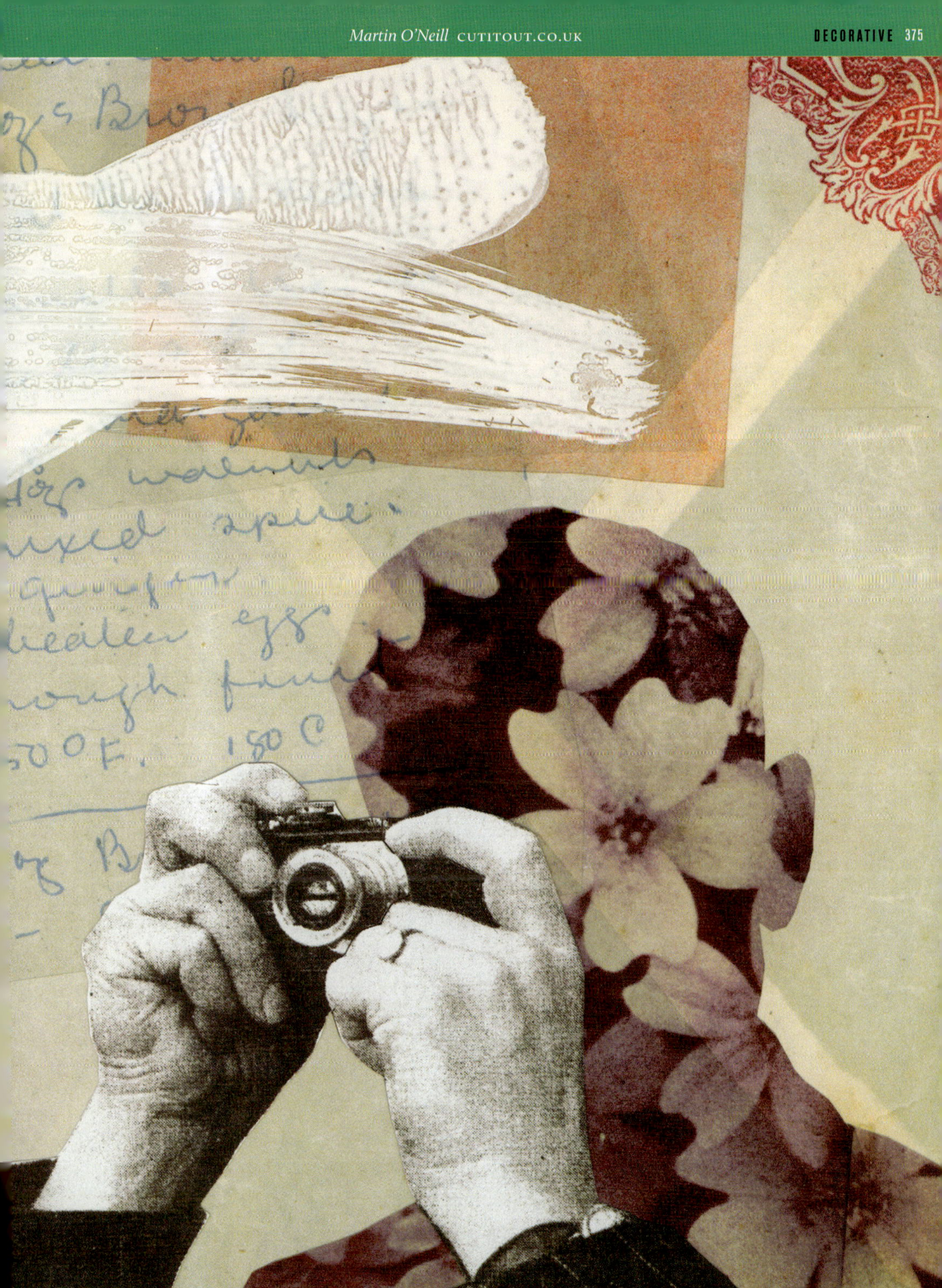

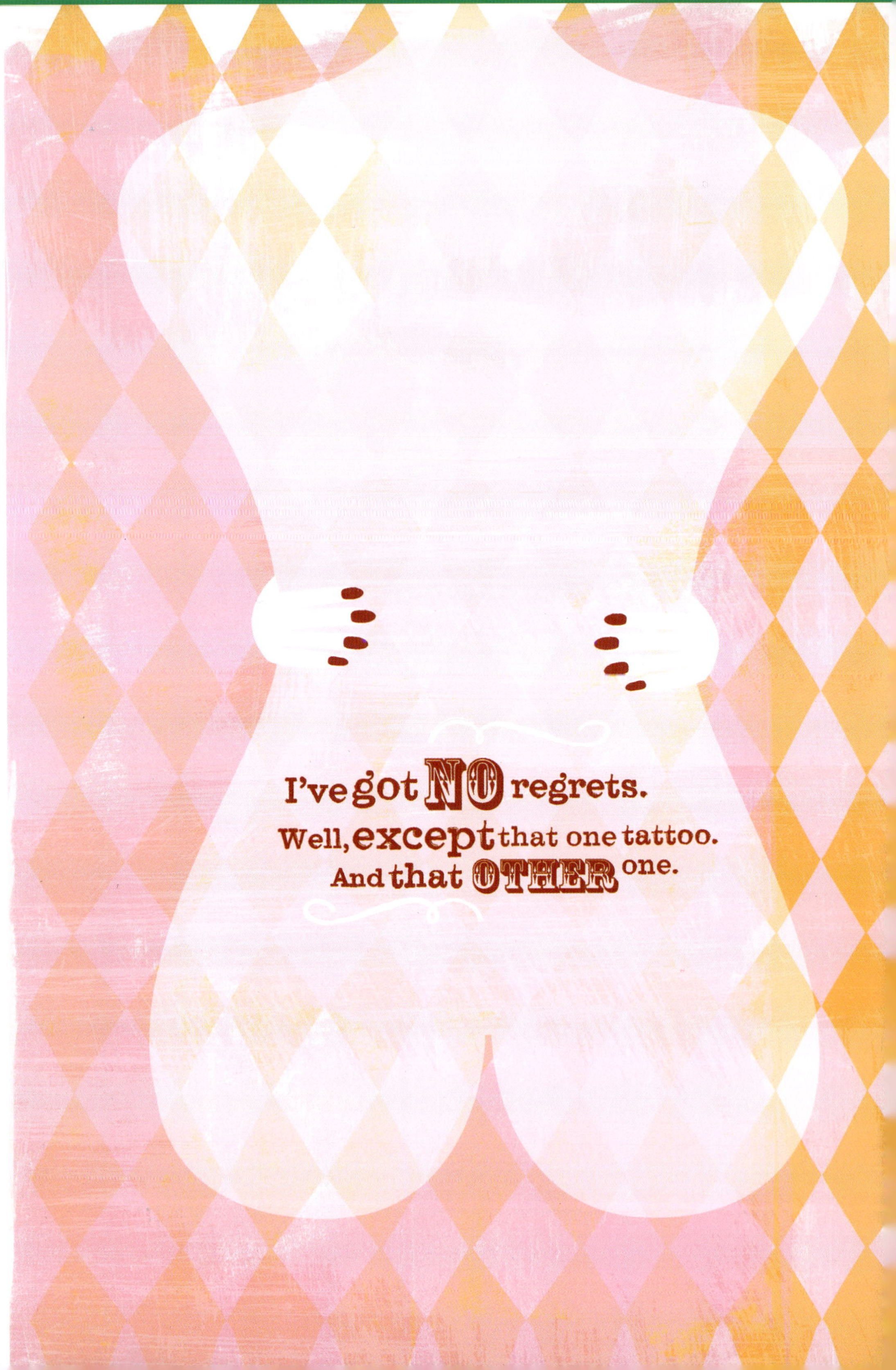

I've got NO regrets.
Well, except that one tattoo.
And that OTHER one.

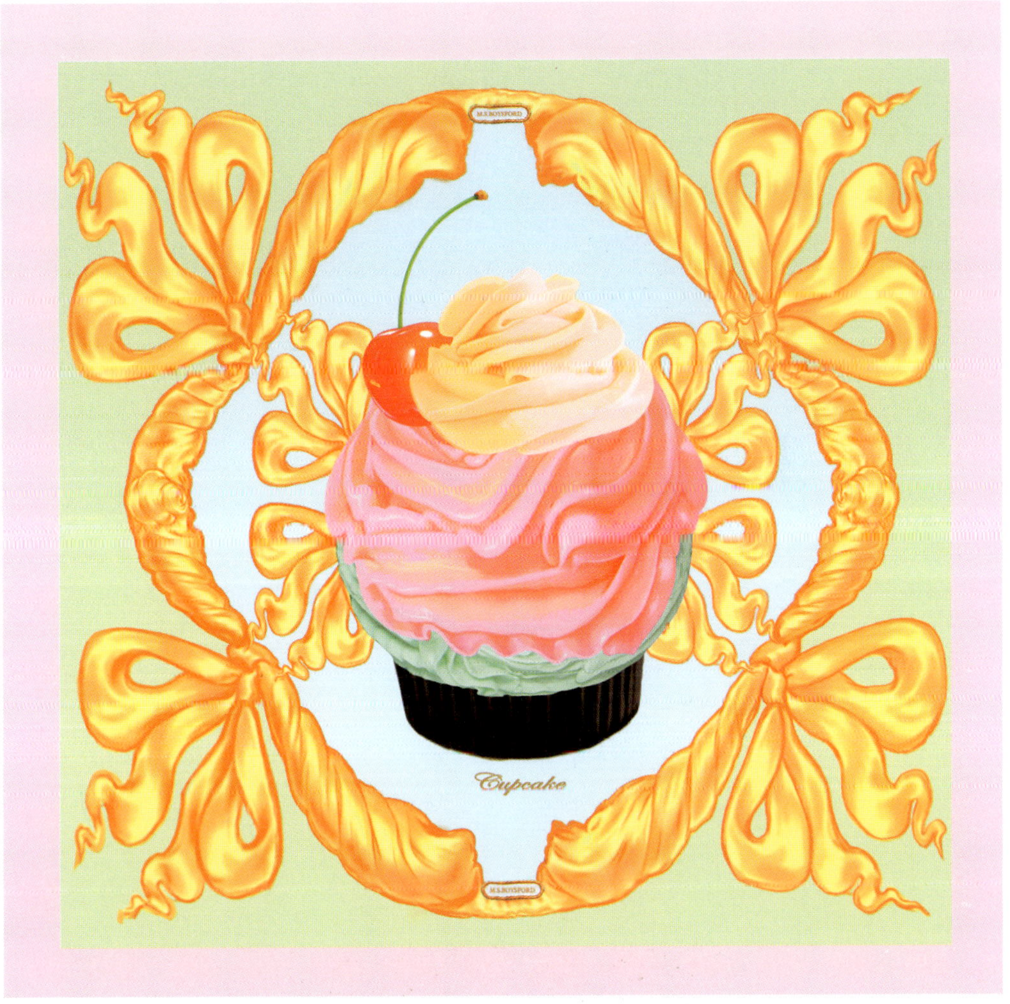
M.S.BOTSFORD
Cupcake
M.S.BOTSFORD

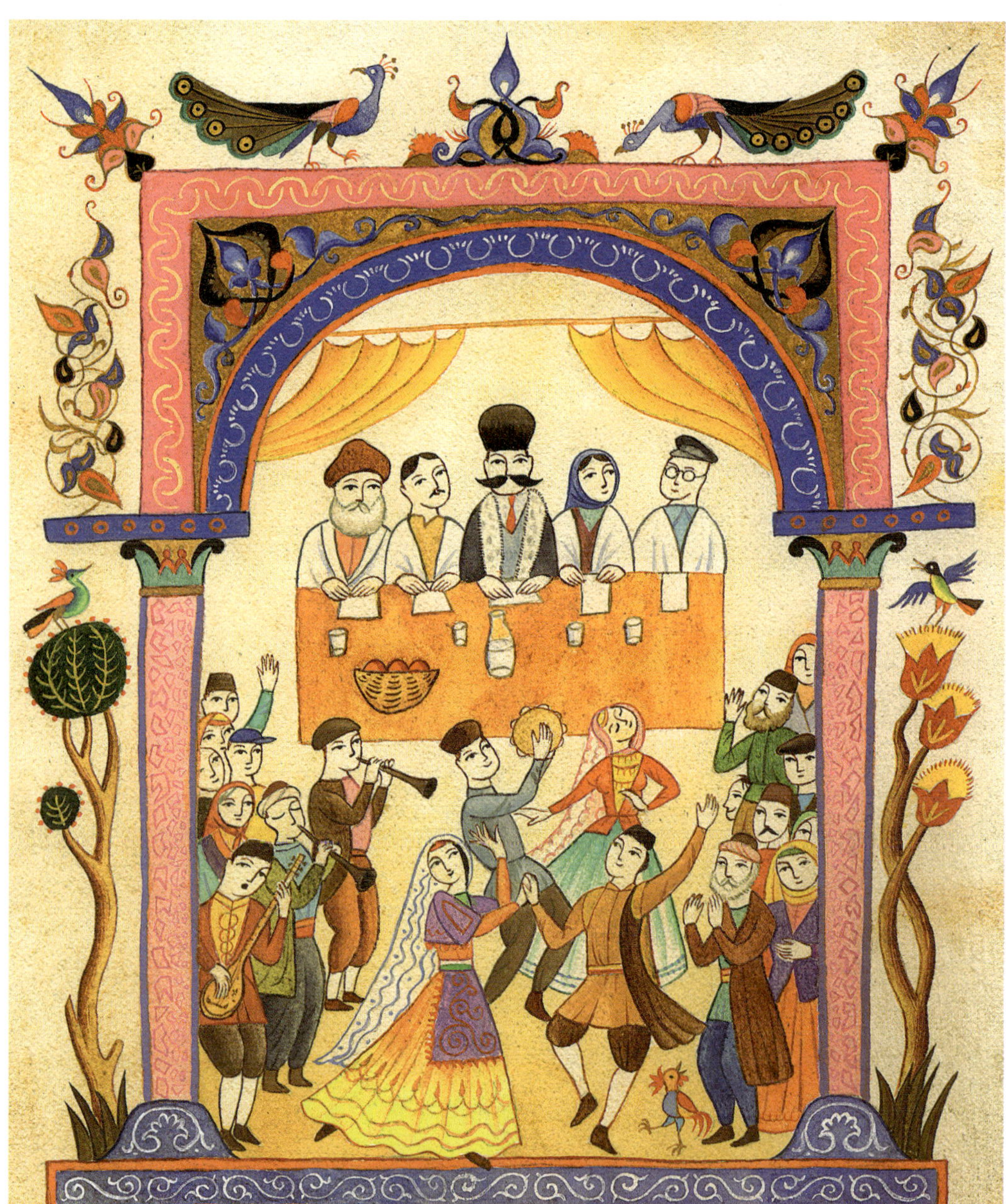

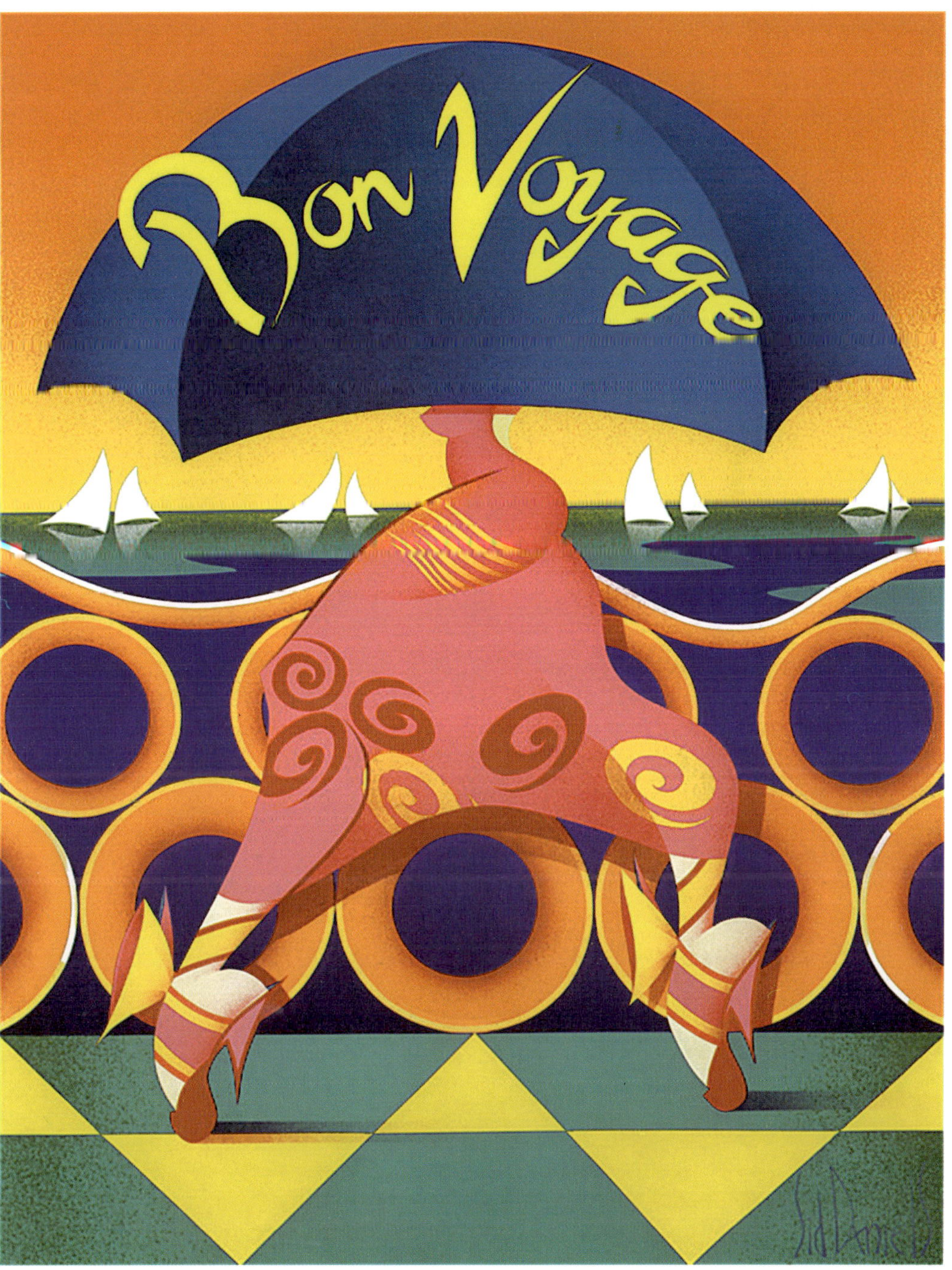
Bon Voyage

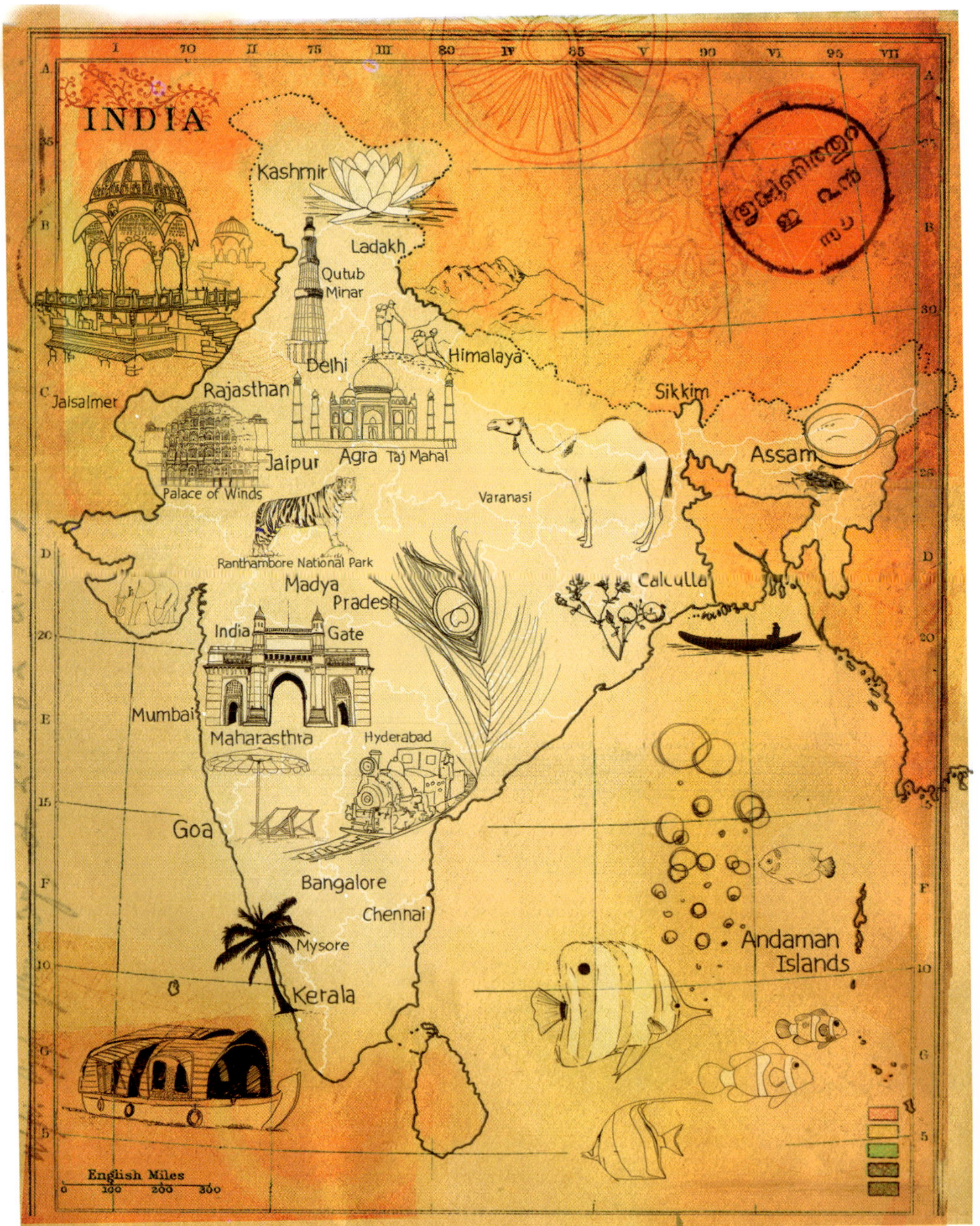
INDIA
Kashmir
Ladakh
Qutub Minar
Delhi
Himalaya
Sikkim
Jaisalmer
Rajasthan
Agra
Taj Mahal
Assam
Jaipur
Palace of Winds
Varanasi
Calcutta
Ranthambore National Park
Madya Pradesh
India Gate
Mumbai
Maharasthra
Hyderabad
Goa
Bangalore
Chennai
Mysore
Kerala
Andaman Islands
English Miles
0   100   200   300

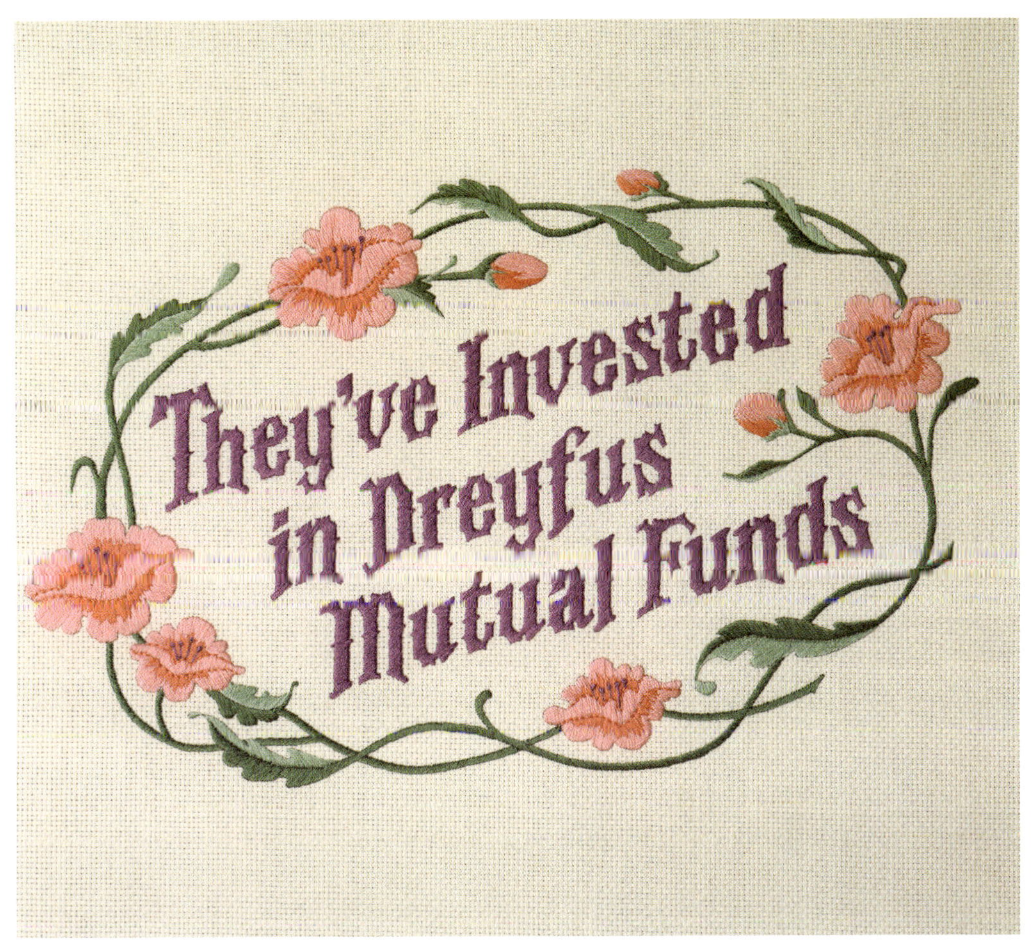
They've Invested
in Dreyfus
Mutual Funds

   Josh McKible MCKIBILLO.COM

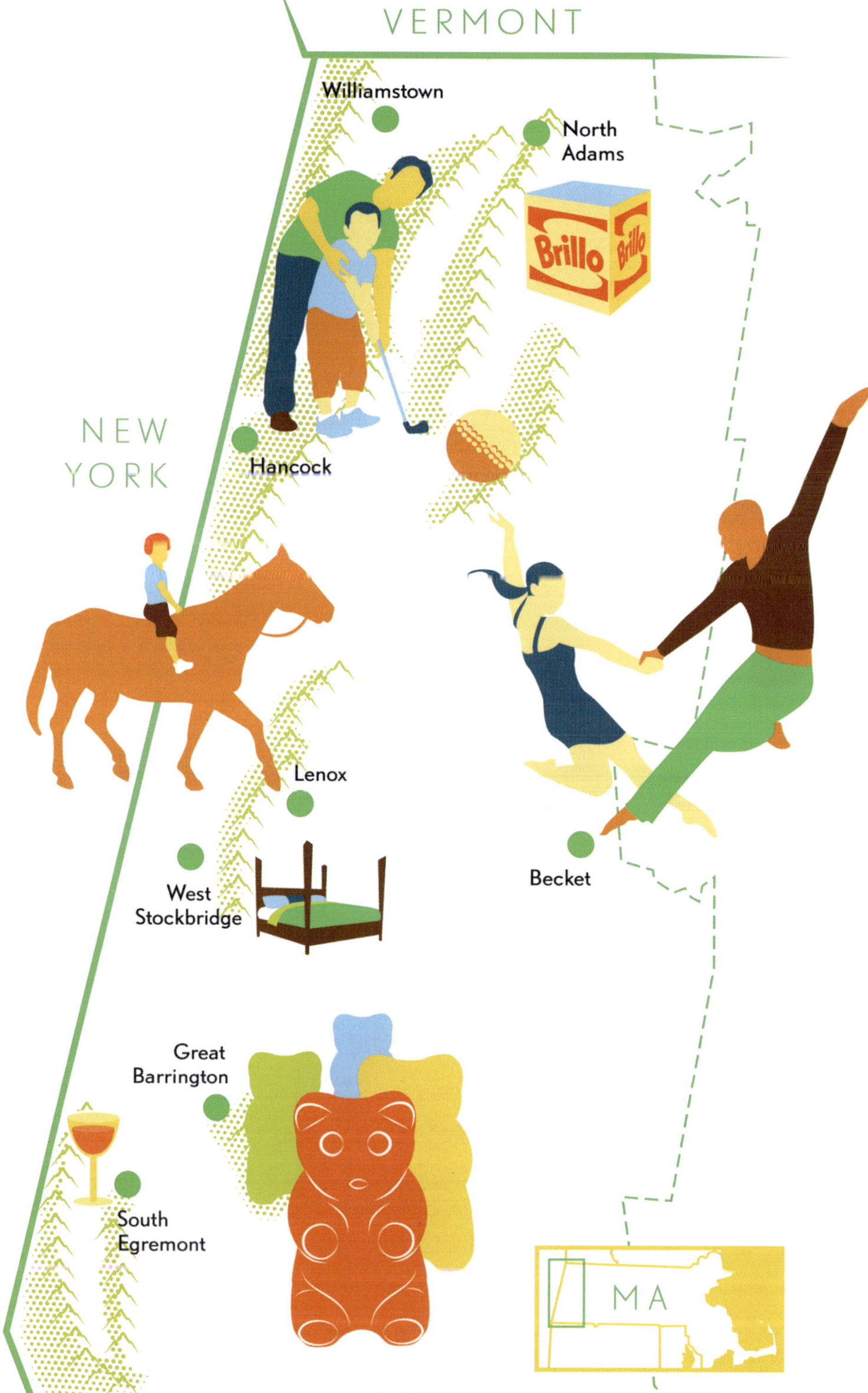

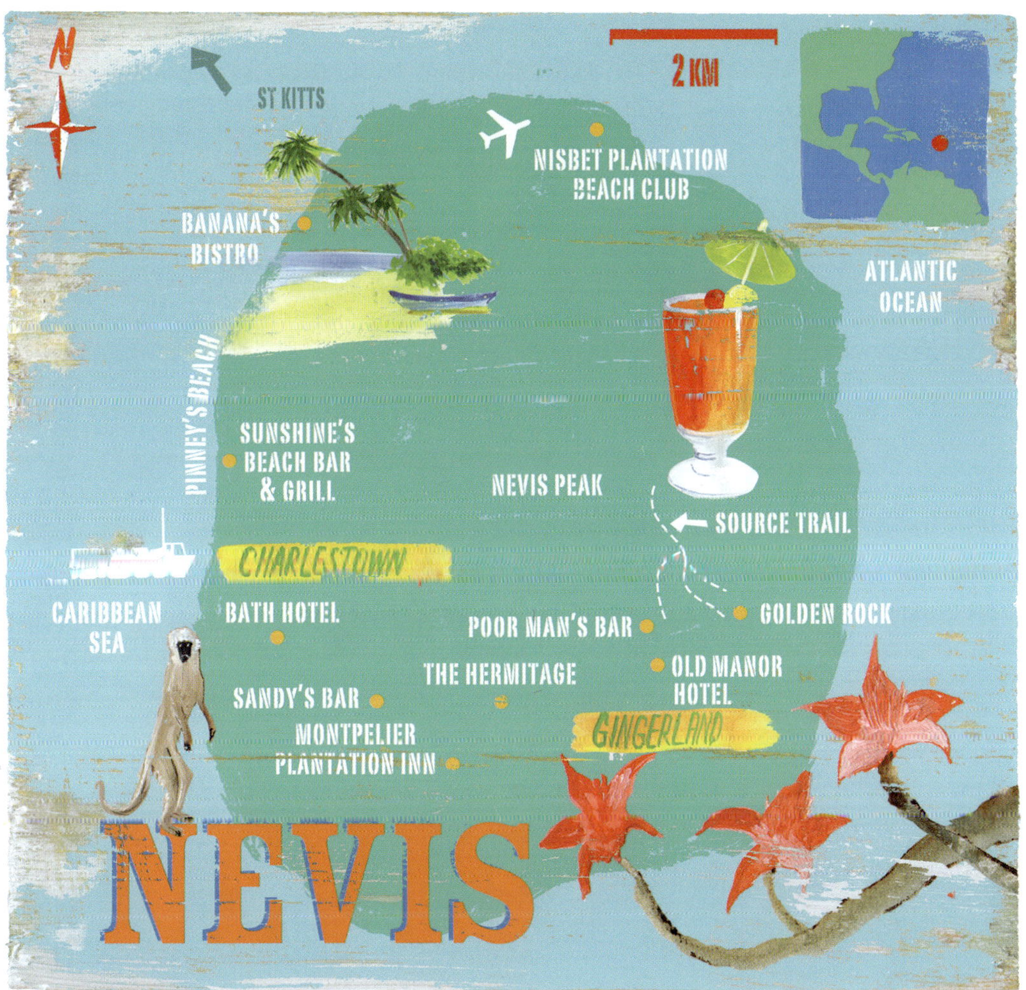
N
2 KM
ST KITTS
NISBET PLANTATION
BEACH CLUB
BANANA'S
BISTRO
ATLANTIC
OCEAN
PINNEY'S BEACH
SUNSHINE'S
BEACH BAR
& GRILL
NEVIS PEAK
SOURCE TRAIL
CHARLESTOWN
CARIBBEAN
SEA
BATH HOTEL
POOR MAN'S BAR
GOLDEN ROCK
THE HERMITAGE
OLD MANOR
HOTEL
SANDY'S BAR
GINGERLAND
MONTPELIER
PLANTATION INN
NEVIS

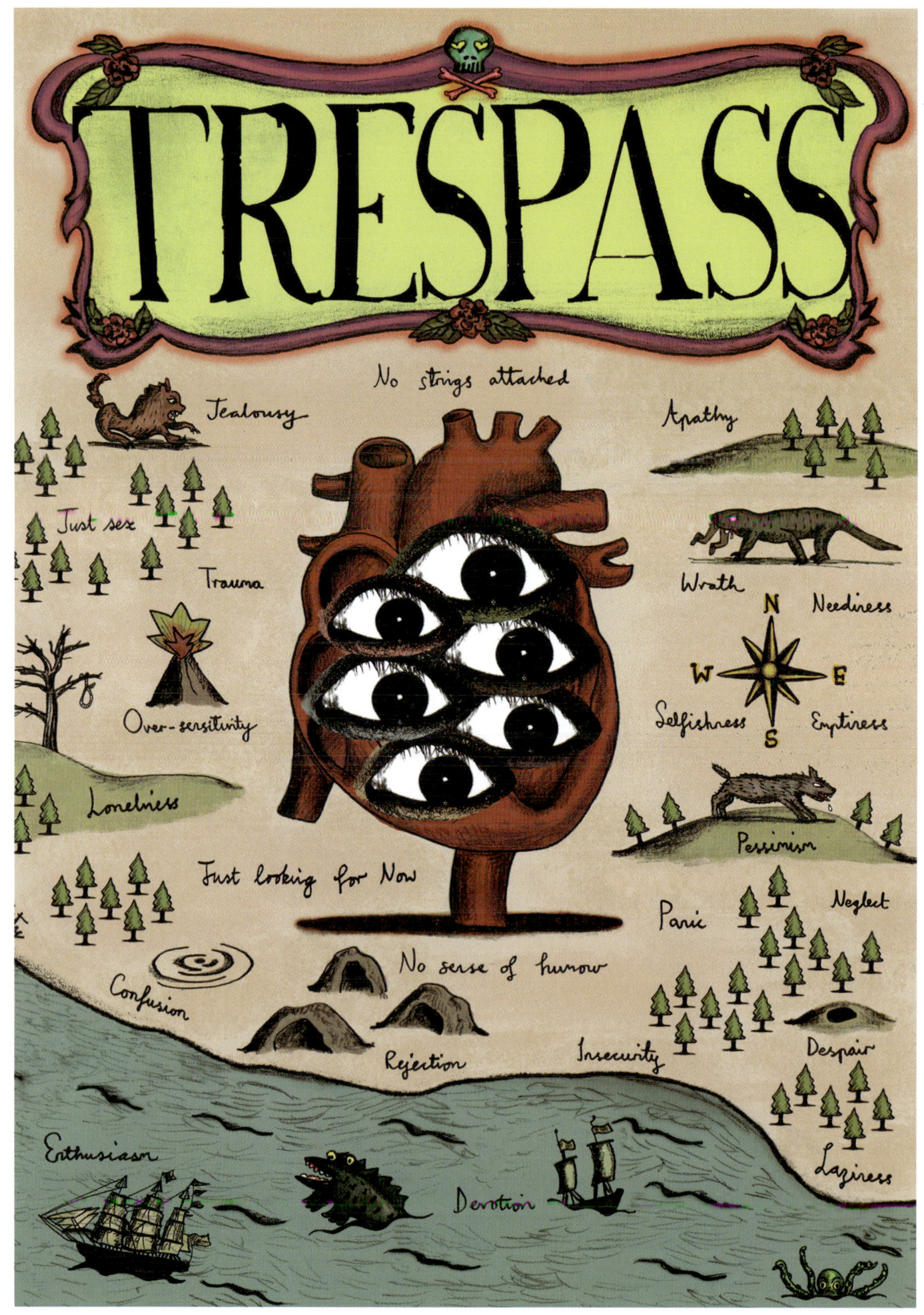
TRESPASS
No strings attached
Jealousy
Apathy
Just sex
Trauma
Wrath
Neediness
Over-sensitivity
N
W E
S
Selfishness
Emptiness
Loneliness
Just looking for Now
Pessimism
Panic
Neglect
Confusion
No sense of humour
Rejection
Insecurity
Despair
Enthusiasm
Devotion
Laziness

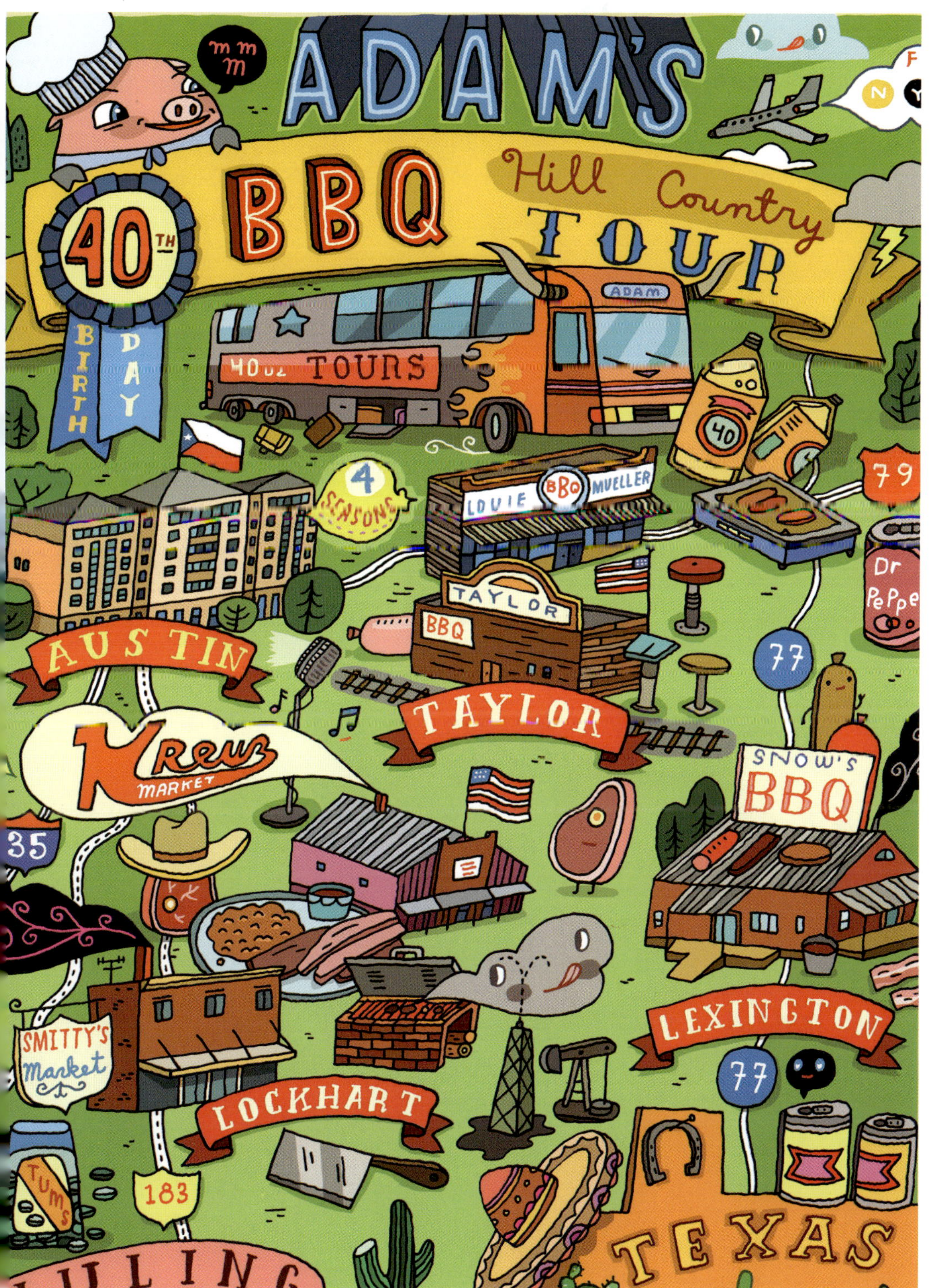
ADAM'S
BBQ
Hill Country
TOUR
40TH
BIRTH DAY
4002 TOURS
ADAM
40
4 SEASONS
LOUIE MUELLER BBQ
TAYLOR BBQ
79
Dr PePPeR
AUSTIN
TAYLOR
77
Krew MARKET
SNOW'S BBQ
35
LEXINGTON
77
SMITTY'S Market
LOCKHART
TUMS
183
LULING
TEXAS

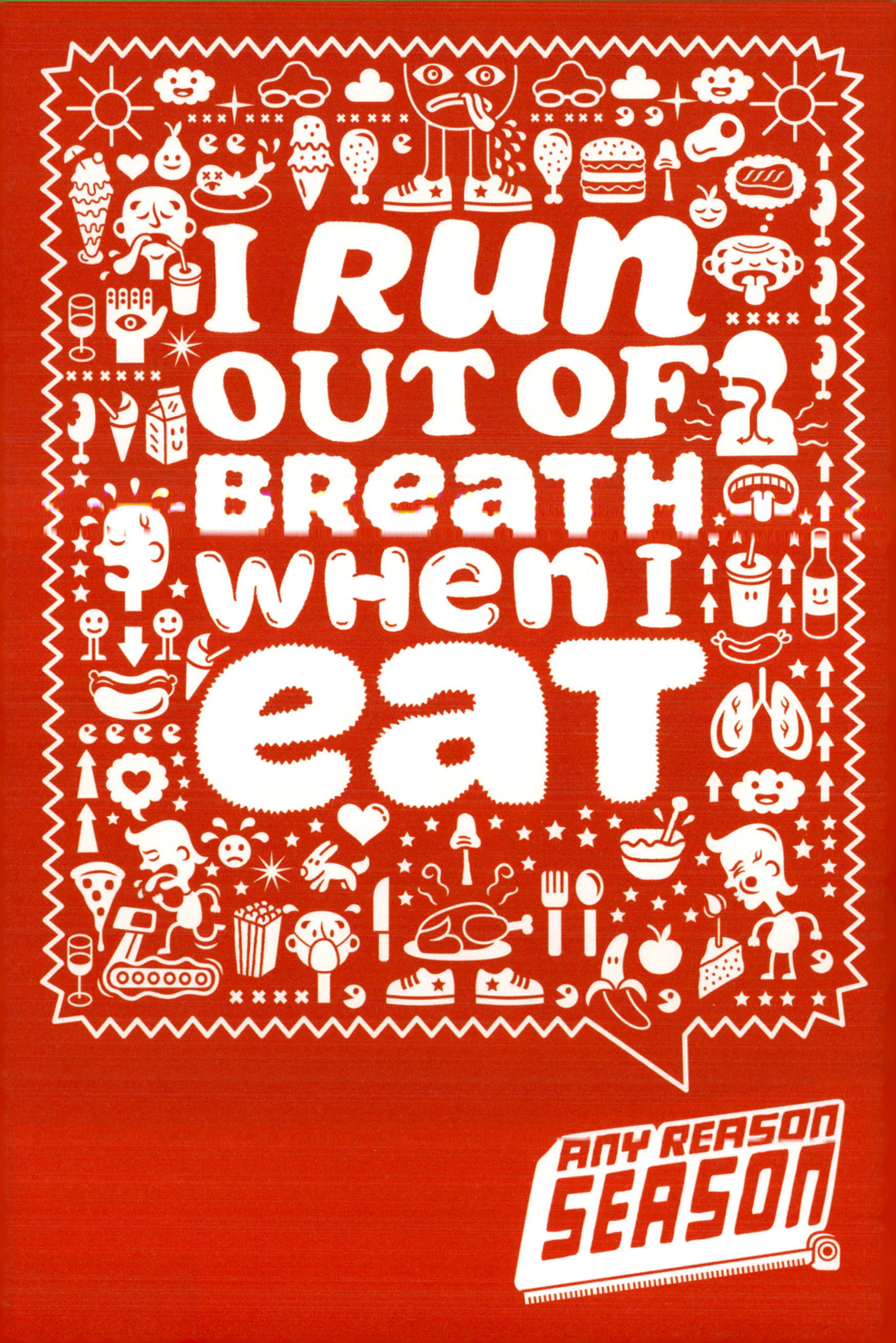

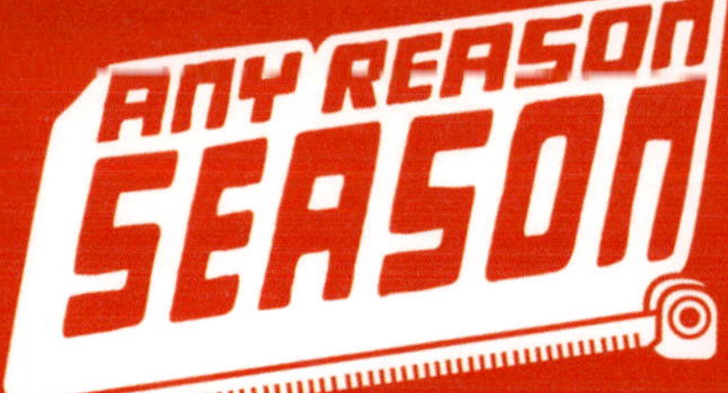
I RUN OUT OF BREATH WHEN I EAT
ANY REASON SEASON

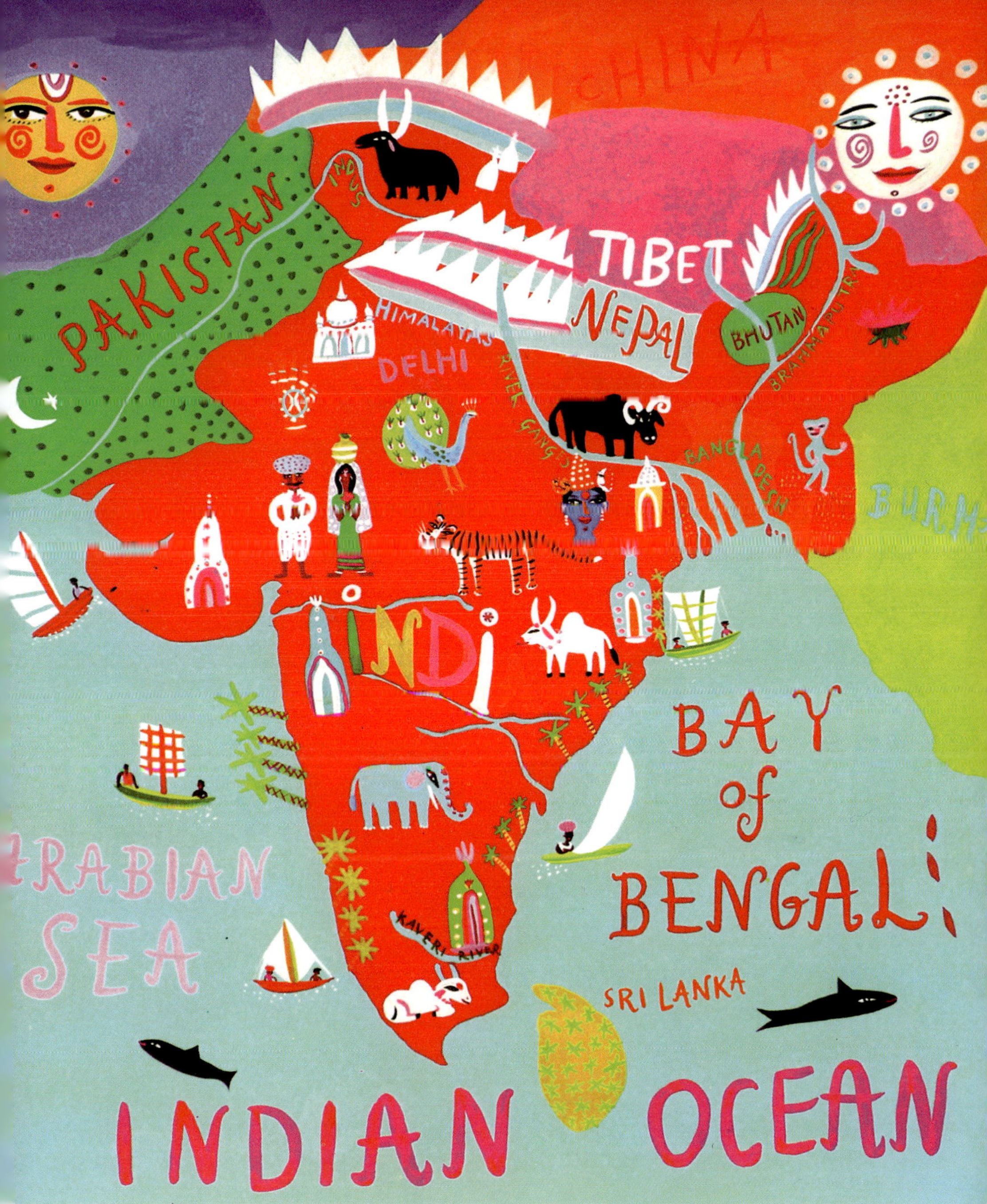
CHINA
PAKISTAN
INDUS
TIBET
NEPAL
BHUTAN
BRAHMAPUTRA
HIMALAYAS
DELHI
RIVER GANGES
BANGLA DESH
BURMA
INDIA
KAVERI RIVER
ARABIAN SEA
BAY of BENGAL
SRI LANKA
INDIAN OCEAN

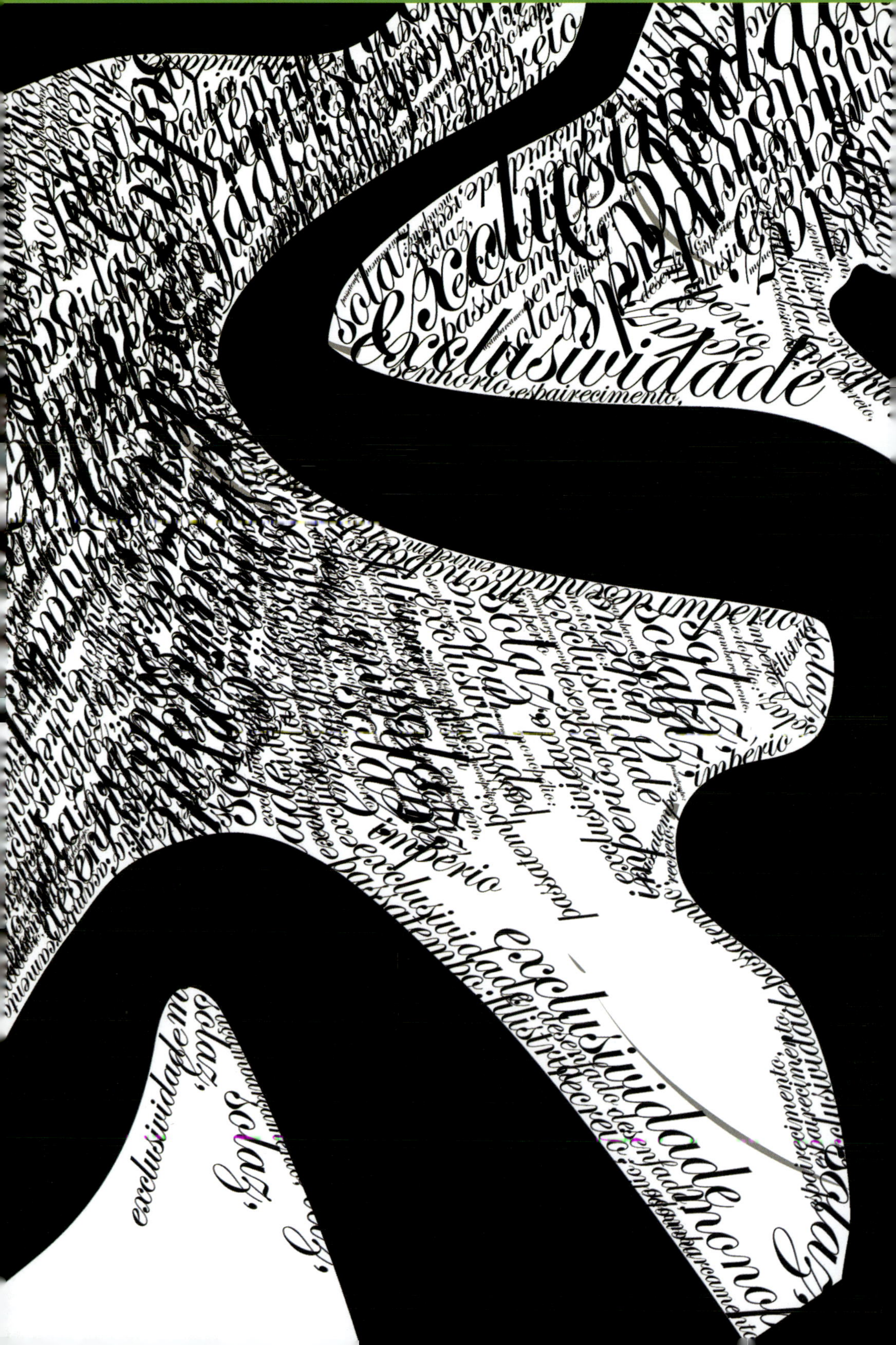

ILLO 11 INDEX

390 INDEX

RICHARD M ABARNO 349
401 364 9408
richard@abarnoillustration.com
www.abarnoillustration.com

ELEFTHERIA ALEXANDRI 301
+30 694 469 2650
e_a@ilikeyellow.com
www.ilikeyellow.com

A. RICHARD ALLEN 92
+44 120 252 5181
info@arichardallen.com
www.arichardallen.com
www.morgangaynin.com

TORIL BÆKMARK 185
+45 232 094 02
mail@torilbaekmark.dk
www.torilbaekmark.dk

SCOTT BAKAL 46, 104, 277
631 525 2309
info@scottbakal.com
www.scottbakal.com

DAVOR BAKARA 314
+49 711 408 4854
illustration@davorbakara.com
www.davorbakara.com

ANNA & ELENA BALBUSSO 44
+39 027 010 8739
apiue@balbusso.com
www.balbusso.com

BARRY BARNES 105, 360
510 223 6114
trainedeye@earthlink.net
www.trainedeyegraphics.com

CHRISTIANE BEAUREGARD 357
514 935 6794
c.beauregard@videotron.ca
www.lindrensmith.com
www.christianebeauregard.com

BECK 70, 90, 305, 339
+49 3414 783 9195
beckszwm@gmail.com
www.newtoonsontheblog.info

NAAMA BENZIMAN 147
+97 23 527 8872
naamaben@netvision.net.il
www.naamabenziman.com

KAKO BERGAMINI 371
212 687 6463
kako@kakofonia.com
www.kakofonia.com
www.levycreative.com

MEGAN BERKHEISER & MIKE
CALDWELL 326
212 615 6707
meganberkheiser@pushart.com
www.pushart.com

GUY BILLOUT 61, 91
917 691 9672
guy@guybillout.com
www.guybillout.com

JOSÉE BISAILLON 188
450 904 2563
info@joseebisaillon.com
www.joseebisaillon.com
www.morgangaynin.com

PHIL BLISS 40, 73
585 732 5087
pbliss@rochester.rr.com
www.philbliss.com

FREDDY BOO 166, 296
+44 778 900 4174
boo@freddyboo.com
www.freddyboo.com

RICHARD BORGE 34
917 494 4567
contact@richardborge.com
www.richardborge.com

JACQUELINE KARI BOS 297
917 975 3278
bos.jacqueline@gmail.com
www.jacquelinekari.com

MINAKO SAITOH BOTSFORD 377
+81 467 24 6497
minakos@minakos.com
www.minakos.com

SHANNON ROBERT BRADY 133, 292
612 386 7288
shannon@shannonbrady.com
www.shannonbrady.com

CALEF BROWN 315, 358
207 373 0300
calef@calefbrown.com
www.calefbrown.com

NIGEL BUCHANAN 80, 283
+61 29 699 3694
nigel@nigelbuchanan.com
www.nigelbuchanan.com
www.rappart.com

MARC BURCKHARDT 115
512 458 1690
marc@marcart.net
www.marcart.net

CHRISTINA DALLORSO BUSH
505 699 7004
cdbstudio@msn.com
www.wooloo.org/dallorsobush

CHRIS BUZELLI 83
212 614 8111
cb@chrisbuzelli.com
www.chrisbuzelli.com

PATRICIA CANTOR 208
714 558 0725
pat@patriciacantor.com
www.patriciacantor.com
www.andreabrownlit.com

STEVEN CARROLL 157
+44 173 862 2083
email@stevecarroll.co.uk
www.stevecarroll.co.uk

ELIZABETH CASSETTI 369
607 387 5424
q@theluckystone.com
www.qcassetti.com

KAT CHADWICK 178, 198
+63 19 415 6222
kat@katchadwick.com
www.katchadwick.com
www.jackywinter.com

JOOHONG CHAE 227
718 644 5223
contact@joohongch.com
www.joohongch.com

LINA CHEN 158, 172
917 647 9698
lina@lina-chen.com
www.lina-chen.com

CHIE CHIE 146
+61 7 430 037 632
changchie@yahoo.com.au
www.chiechie.com.au

MARCOS CHIN 142
646 416 0936
marcos@marcoschin.com
www.marcoschin.com

CATHY CHOI 370
858 926 9001
cathychoi@choiillustration.com
www.choiillustration.com

NISHANT CHOKSI 222, 307
+44 785 536 2694
nish@nishantchoksi.com
www.nishantchoksi.com

JAMEY CHRISTOPH 203
216 255 7338
christoph.jamey@gmail.com
www.workbook.com/portfolios/
christoph
www.redpaintbox.com

JULIEN CHUNG 202, 327
450 679 0240
julienchung@hotmail.com
www.julienchung.com
www.bradfordlicensing.com

JIM COHEN 65, 215, 221
847 726 8979
jim@jimcohenillustration.com
www.jimcohenillustration.com

TIMOTHY COOK 41, 42
301 949 5002
tim@timothycook.com
www.timothycook.com

DAVID COPESTAKES 191
215 264 9953
dcopestakes@verizon.net
www.stakecreativedesign.com

CHRISTOPHER CORR 258, 387
+44 207 600 7958
chriscorr@yahoo.com
www.christophercorr.com

MARTIN CÔTÉ 249
514 521 1253
martinco@videotron.ca
www.lisemadore.com

NED CULIC 353, 355
6139 502 3733
ned@nedculic.com
www.nedculic.com

MARGARET CUSACK 139, 381
718 237 0145
cusackart@aol.com
www.margaretcusack.com

PETER CUSACK 125
646 842 2683
peter@petercusack.com
petercusack.com
www.morgangaynin.com

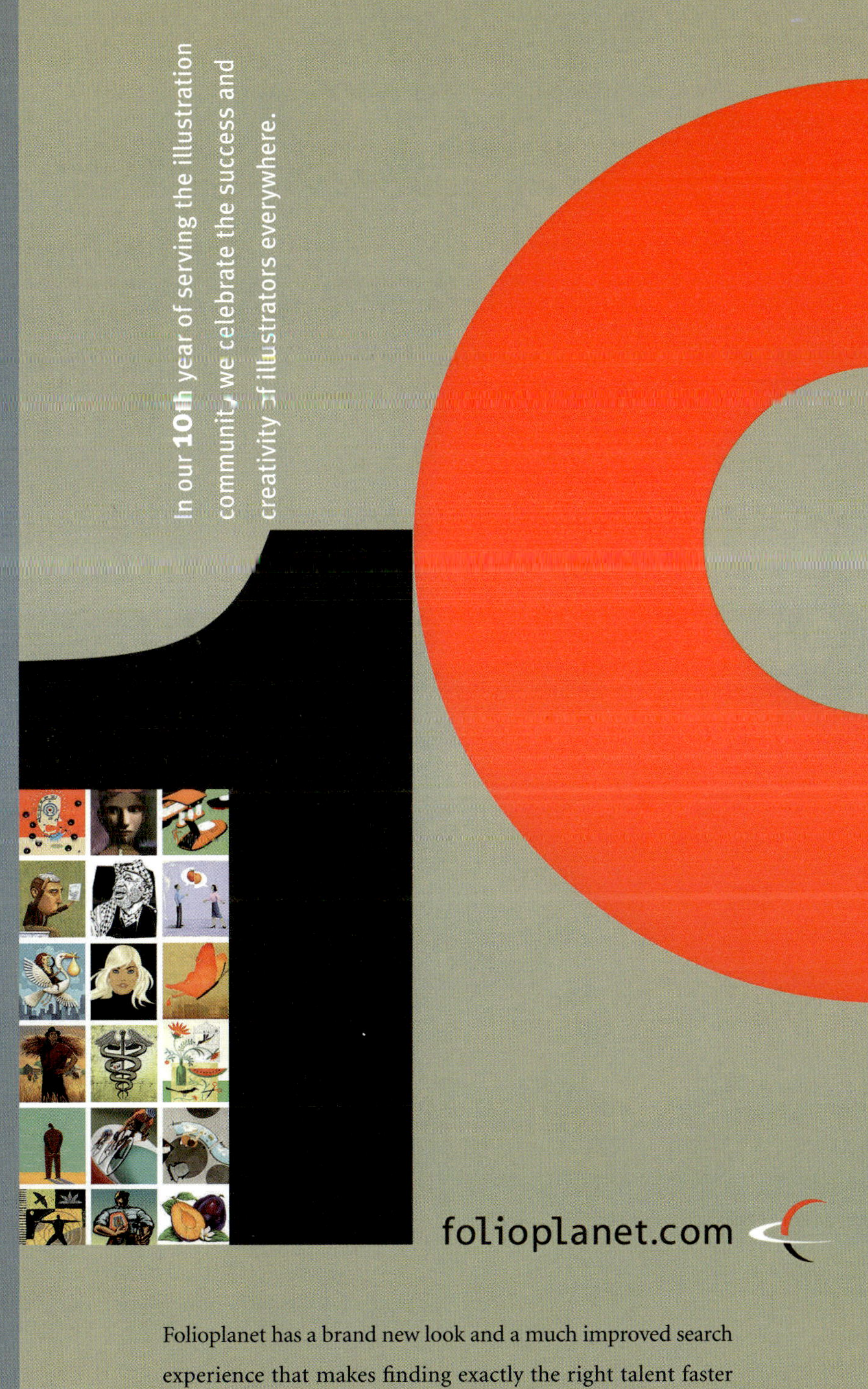

In our 10th year of serving the illustration community, we celebrate the success and creativity of illustrators everywhere.

folioplanet.com

Folioplanet has a brand new look and a much improved search experience that makes finding exactly the right talent faster and more intuitive than ever before. We have also made our portfolio images larger while maintaining the user interface speed that Folioplanet has always been known for.

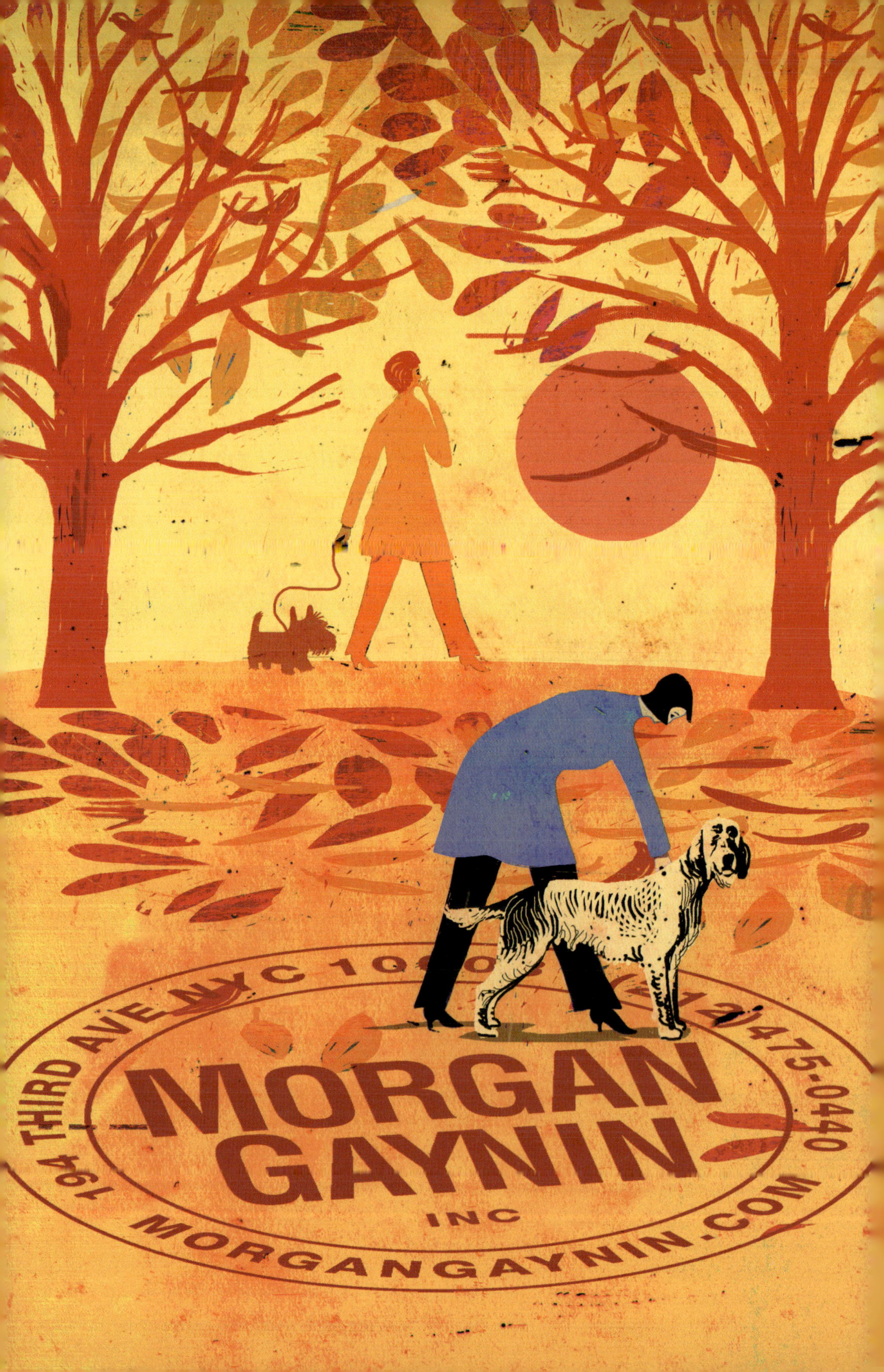
MORGAN
GAYNIN
INC
194 THIRD AVE NYC 10003
(212)475-0440
MORGANGAYNIN.COM

DAVE CUTLER 53
203 938 7067
dcutler@optonline.net
www.illoz.com/davecutler

SYLVIE DAIGNEAULT 361
416 961 0681
sylvie@sylviedaigneault.com
sylviedaigneault.com
www.morgangaynin.com

PAUL DALLAS 60
416 977 6000
paul@pauldallas.com
www.pauldallas.com

LYMAN DALLY 337
973 763 6910
lymandally@mac.com
www.lymandally.com

TONI DAMKOEHLER 45, 242
920 465 5147
damkoeht@uwgb.edu
www.tonidamkoehler.com

HUGH D'ANDRADE 270
415 513 3444
hugh@hughillustration.com
www.hughillustration.com

SID DANIELS 379
305 673 4329
sid@siddaniels.com
www.siddaniels.com

SONJA DANOWSKI 175
+49 307 552 7810
mail@sonjadanowski.de
www.sonjadanowski.de

ANDREA D'AQUINO 302
212 741 7487
andreadaquino@mac.com
www.andreadaquino.com

VICTORIA DAVIS 194, 200
415 694 2365
victoriadavis.illustrations@gmail.com
www.victoriadavisart.com

LIAM DERBYSHIRE 54
+44 751 463 5996
liamderbyshire@hotmail.co.uk
www.liamderbyshire-illustrations.com

AMY DEVOOGD 182
608 692 3386
amy@devoogd.com
www.devoogd.com

TIM DINTER 253
+49 30 281 4856
post@timdinter.de
www.timdinter.de

DRZ 113
312 576 1211
james@drzis.in
www.drzisill.in

PENELOPE DULLAGHAN 141, 324
317 363 6060
penny@penelopeillustration.com
www.penelopeillustration.com
www.scotthull.com

JEAN-MANUEL DUVIVIER 25
+322 648 0512
jmduvivier@skynet.be
www.jmduvivier.com
www.munrocampagna.com

MARK EBERHARDT 219
716 207 3903
mark@markeberhardt.com
www.markeberhardt.com

ELKE EHNINGER 362
+49 404 325 3550
mail@ehninger-illustration.de
www.ehninger-illustration.de

PETER ELLIS 102
+44 208 690 5013
pete@drawgood.com
www.drawgood.com

MAX ESTES 304
479 403 9943
max@maxestes.com
www.maxestes.com

SUSAN FARRINGTON 265, 312
508 380 2737
crickettieldowen@gmail.com
www.susanfarrington.com
www.lillarogers.com

JOÃO FAZENDA 313
+44 780 766 1685
info@joaofazenda.com
www.joaofazenda.com

BARRY FITZGERALD 303
785 841 2983
bfitz@ku.edu
www.barryfitzgeraldillustration.com

BRIAN FITZGERALD 67
+353 1 284 6373
brian@brianfitzer.ie
www.brianfitzer.ie

JAMES FLAMES 354
718 790 7363
contact@jamesflames.com
www.jamesflames.com

JESSICA FORTNER 266
416 367 2482
info@jessicafortner.com
www.jessicafortner.com

JOSE FRAGOSO 316, 336
+34 69 640 6034
josefragoso@fragosoart.com
www.fragosoart.com

CHRIS FRENCH 234
250 419 2666
studio@graficpacific.com
www.graficpacific.com

MARTIN FRENCH 103, 108
503 926 2809
studio@martinfrench.com
www.martinfrench.com

SARAJO FRIEDEN 196
323 462 5045
sarajo@sarajofrieden.com
www.sarajofrieden.com
www.lillarogers.com

JAMES FRYER 21
+44 125 267 1377
james_fryer72@ntlworld.com
www.jamesfryer.co.uk

DAVID FULLARTON 75
415 254 4297
david.fullarton@gmail.com
www.davidfullarton.com
www.joaniebrep.com

YOKO FURUSHO 144
917 501 1247
info@yokofurusho.com
www.yokofurusho.com

TOM GARRETT 27
612 827 2897
tom_garrett@comcast.net
www.tomgarrett.us

BEPPE GIACOBBE 36, 37
212 475 0440
b.giacobbe@beppegiacobbe.com
beppegiacobbe.com
www.morgangaynin.com

MICHAEL GIBBS 52
703 502 3400
mike@michaelgibbs.com
www.michaelgibbs.com

ERIC GIRIAT 325
+33 66 198 3609
e.giriat@wanadoo.fr
www.ericgiriat.com

MICHAEL GLENWOOD 64, 163
888 818 9811
michael@mglenwood.com
www.mglenwood.com

JOHANNA GOODMAN 112
917 327 5339
johanna@johannagoodman.com
www.johannagoodman.com

DAVID GOTHARD 347
610 417 4941
dg@davidgothard.com
www.davidgothard.com

AAD GOUDAPPEL 72, 276, 348
+31 10 414 7493
aad@aadgoudappel.com
www.aadgoudappel.com

KAREN GREENBERG 183, 376
646 894 5796
karen@karengreenberg.com
www.karengreenberg.com

MOLLY GRUNDY 149
647 215 5704
molly.grundy@gmail.com
www.gogogrundy.wordpress.com

CONSTANZE GUHR 306
+49 304 849 4647
birkenstaub@gmx.de
www.constanzeguhr.de

OLAF HAJEK 119
+49 1512 124 8546
mail@olafhajek.com
www.olafhajek.com
www.ba-reps.com

ANTONY HARE 156
226 688 6082
ant@siteway.com
www.siteway.com

JANNE HARJU 214
+35 840 522 3353
janne@janneharju.com
www.janneharju.com

TAKAHISA HASHIMOTO 373
+81 805 642 3914
contact@takahisahashimoto.com
www.takahisahashimoto.com

LARS HENKEL 252
+49 2212 988 3400
lars@reflektorium.de
www.reflektorium.de

KIM HERBST 95
732 718 6874
kmh@kimherbst.com
www.kimherbst.com

DENISE HILTON-CAMPBELL 282
760 644 5671
d.hilton.campbell.illus@gmail.com
www.dhc-illus.com
www.salzint.com

JAKOB HINRICHS 20
+49 1769 636 5532
mail@jakobhinrichs.com
www.jakobhinrichs.com

AGNIESZKA HOBBS 164
+44 124 357 2558
agnieszka_hobbs@hotmail.com
www.hobbsillustration.com

MARK HOFFMANN 320
781 771 5733
mh@studiohoffmann.com
www.studiohoffmann.com

SARA HOFMANN 130
323 899 2543
sara@saratheresiahofmann.com
www.saratheresiahofmann.blogspot.com

DAVID HOHN 209, 213
503 848 9412
david@davidhohn.com
www.davidhohn.com

PAUL HOPPE 50
917 774 5455
info@paulhoppe.com
www.paulhoppe.com

MAYUMIN HOSOYA 187
+81 333 411 0907
mayumin@pop07.odn.ne.jp
www.mayumin.net

ROBIN HURSTHOUSE 94
+44 794 191 5571
robin@robinhursthouse.co.uk
www.robinhursthouse.co.uk

IC4DESIGN 250
+81 082 243 1999
info@ic4design.com
www.ic4design.com
www.pocko.com

ILLWORX 226
609 332 6241
ryanfriant@gmail.com
www.illworx.com

HIROMICHI ITO 114
+81 33 710 5634
hello@hiromichiito.com
www.hiromichiito.com

LANCE JACKSON 132
925 253 3131
lancejjackson@earthlink.net
www.lancejackson.net

MARILYN JANOVITZ 31
212 727 8330
mjanovitz@earthlink.net
www.marilynjanovitz.com

SCOTT JESSOP 383
751 928 9170
scott_jessop@btinternet.com
www.jessopart.com

HAYATO JOME 171, 174
8133 405 8816
jome@j.email.ne.jp
www.peacecard.com/jome

ROSS JONES 267
215 232 6666
ross@9600limited.com
www.illustrationonline.com

KATHI KAEPPEL 235
+49 179 510 8993
kathi@monogatari.de
www.kathikaeppel.de

TIBOR KÁRPÁTI 24, 88
+36 30 282 9868
karpatitibor@yahoo.com
www.tiborkarpati.com

TERRI FRY KASUBA 309
610 202 2905
terri@kasubadesign.com
www.kasubadesign.com
www.jenvaughnart.com

MIDORI KOBORO 262
+81 33 382 7858
mail@kessoku.net
www.kessoku.net

DON KILPATRICK III 58, 124
212 475 0440
don@donkilpatrick.com
www.donkilpatrick.com
www.morgangaynin.com

TATSURO KIUCHI 77
201 944 6058
info@tatsurokiuchi.com
www.tatsurokiuchi.com
www.heflinreps.com

JEAN-CHRISTIAN KNAFF 321
416 686 7030
knaffmiceli@sympatico.ca
www.mikka.ca

URS J. KNOBEL 153, 154
+41 41 781 2550
info@ursjknobel-art.ch
www.ursjknobel-art.ch

ULI KNÖRZER 151, 173
+49 302 243 0236
info@uliknoerzer.com
www.uliknoerzer.com

KATRINA KOPELOFF 286
720 352 3791
katrina@katrinakopeloff.com
www.katrinakopeloff.com

TAKASHI KOSHII 240
+81 35 317 1040
ko4an@wa2.so-net.ne.jp
www.takashikoshii.com

JON KRAUSE 33, 89
215 338 1531
jk@jonkrause.com
www.jonkrause.com

NORA KRUG 346
862 219 1127
info@nora-krug.com
www.nora-krug.com
www.rileyillustration.com

THOMAS KUHLENBECK 32, 135
+49 251 131 2516
info@thomas-kuhlenbeck.com
www.thomas-kuhlenbeck.com
www.larkworthy.com

ANITA KUNZ 122, 131
416 364 3846
akunz@anitakunz.com
www.anitakunz.com

DAVID LABROZZI 256
571 228 0491
david@labrozziillustration.com
www.labrozziillustration.com

ANNA EMILIA LAITINEN 287
+35 840 592 6602
annaemilial@gmail.com
www.annaemilia.com

HUGH LANGIS 79
416 923 7111
hugh@hughlangis.com
www.hughlangis.com

MATHIEU LAVOIE 290
514 777 1884
mlavoa@gmail.com
www.mlavoa.com

CATHERINE LAZURE 300
212 690 1867
catherine@catherinelazure.com
www.catherinelazure.com

DONGJUN LEE 216
416 854 3892
illudj@gmail.com
www.dongjunlee.com

ANDRÉ LETRIA 204, 322
+35 196 663 2210
andreletria@andreletria.pt
www.andreletria.com

ANSON LIAW 76, 293
416 466 3345
ansonliawillustration@rogers.com
www.illoz.com/liaw
www.morgangaynin.com

ANDERS LINDHOLM 205, 230
+70 835 6250
anders@alprod.se
www.alprod.se

CAROLINE LIST 145
+44 753 247 1066
carolinelist@googlemail.com
www.collagecomposer.com

BRIGITTA GARCIA LOPEZ 101
+41 044 381 5301
bgl@hispeed.ch
www.brigitta-garcia-lopez.com

AMALIA LOW 201
+57 1 614 6921
amalialow@amalialow.com
www.amalialow.com

ANNE LÜCK 372
+49 304 098 7577
welcome@annelueck.com
www.annelueck.com

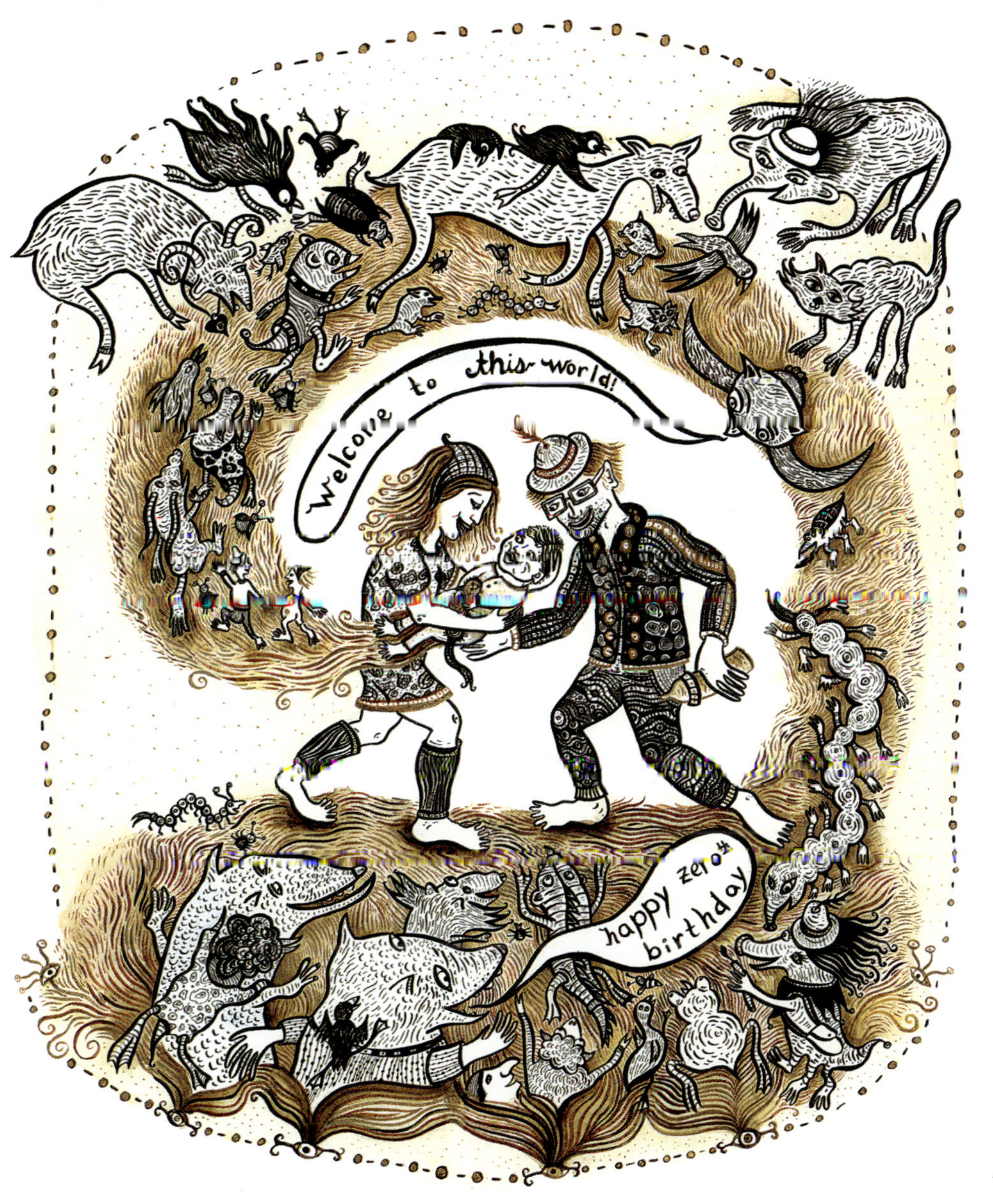

ARTIST: *Katrina Kopeloff,* NEW YORK

JOHN MACCONNELL 162
717 571 1588
john@johnmacconnell.com
www.johnmacconnell.com

KEITH MACLELLAND 55
802 558 7399
keith@yourillustrator.com
www.yourillustrator.com

JENS MAGNUSSON 152, 323
+46 870 918 2672
jens@jensjens.com
www.jensjens.com

BRUNO MALLART 334
212 807 6627
bruno.mallart@orange.fr
www.brunomallart.com
www.davidgoldmanagency.com

JOHN MALLOY 288
443 682 0055
hello@johnmalloy.com
www.johnmalloy.com

CHRISTA MARQUEZ 289
757 561 3083
christamarquez@ymail.com
www.christamarquez.com

TIM MARRS 111
+44 771 400 2447
tim@timmarrs.co.uk
www.timmarrs.co.uk
www.ba-reps.com

JORGE MASCARENHAS 148
510 301 2934
jorge@jorgemstudio.com
www.jorgemstudio.com
www.levycreative.com

BILL MAYER 97, 195, 217, 274, 359, 388
404 378 0686
bill@thebillmayer.com
www.thebillmayer.com

MELISSA MCGILL 284
702 875 1675
melissa@melissamcgill.com
www.melissamcgill.com

JONATHAN MCHUGH 86
+44 289 147 2503
jonathan.mchugh@beepencil.com
www.beepencil.com

JOSH MCKIBLE 28, 294, 382
+81 901 105 7575
josh@mckibillo.com
www.mckibillo.com

KAGAN MCLEOD 179
416 461 0993
k@kaganmcleod.com
www.kaganmcleod.com

LUC MELANSON 335
450 975 7836
luc@lucmelanson.com
www.lucmelanson.com

SOLONGO MELLECKER 228, 285
706 399 2374
msolongo@gmail.com
www.msolongo.com

AARON MESHON 342, 385
718 858 8485
hello@aaronmeshon.com
www.aaronmeshon.com

KATE MILLER 260
+0795 899 8078
kate@kate-miller.com
www.kate-miller.com
www.ba-reps.com

ANDREW MITCHELL 223, 232
949 387 7696
andy@ajmitchellart.com
www.ajmitchellart.com

PETER MITCHELL 298
416 578 6685
peter@petermitchell.net
www.petermitchell.net

KELLY FREDERICK MIZER 192, 211
414 839 3736
kelly@loloink.com
www.loloink.com

GERALD MOLL 99
+49 177 704 0175
post@geraldmoll.de
www.geraldmoll.de

CHRISTIAN MONTENEGRO 118
+54 114 658 5015
christian@christianmontenegro.
com.ar
www.christianmontenegro.com.ar

GONI MONTES 374
678 860 6934
goni@goniart.com
www.goniart.com

LESLIE MOORE 206
416 702 4889
leslie@illustrationbyleslie.com
www.illustrationbyleslie.com

JOE MORSE 121
416 769 5301
joe@joemorse.com
www.joemorse.com
www.heflinreps.com

NICK MOTT 333
+44 782 154 0803
nicholasmott@hotmail.co.uk
www.nickmottillustration.blogspot.
com

SHAWN MURENBEELD 30, 170
519 942 2552
shawn@touchwooddesign.com
www.touchwooddesign.com

CHRIS B. MURRAY 138
215 756 3226
contact@chrisbmurray.com
www.chrisbmurray.com

ALEX NABAUM 117
435 654 8501
alex@alexnabaum.com
www.alexnabaum.com

TOBY THANE NEIGHBORS 332
903 815 1972
hepcatink@gmail.com
www.hepcatink.com

GARY NEILL 49, 84
+44 797 386 6739
gary@garyneill.com
www.garyneill.com
www.ba-reps.com

MEREDITH NELSON 263
217 390 6977
mail@meredith-nelson.com
www.meredith-nelson.com

ROBERT NEUBECKER 93, 96
435 729 0049
robert@neubecker.com
www.neubecker.com

SHAW NIELSEN 308
303 517 8065
sn@shawnielsen.com
www.shawnielsen.com
www.rappart.com

CHRISTOPHER NIELSEN 338
212 687 6463
chris@chrisillo.com
www.chrisillo.com
www.levycreative.com

PEG NOCCIOLINO 71
607 759 9039
info@grafikmuse.com
www.pegnocciolino.com

ANJA NOLTE 199, 278
+49 1768 107 3516
mail@anjanolte.de
www.anjanolte.de

JAMES O'BRIEN 68, 364
612 819 2837
info@jamesobrien.us
www.jamesobrien.us

TIM O'BRIEN 279, 281
718 282 2821
tonka1964@aol.com
www.obrienillustration.com

KATE O'LEARY 220
773 865 4467
kate@kateoleary.com
www.kateoleary.com

DONOUGH O'MALLEY 22
+35 387 689 8295
pencilrobot@yahoo.ie
www.pencilrobot.net

MARTIN O'NEILL 176, 375
212 643 0896
oneill@dircon.co.uk
www.cutitout.co.uk
www.threeinabox.com

JIM PAILLOT 229, 231
480 633 2485
jim@jimpaillot.com
www.jimpaillot.com

CAP PANNELL 318
214 343 2189
cap@psgdesign.com
www.cappanell.com

DOUG PANTON 368
416 920 5612
studio@dougpanton.com
www.dougpanton.com

PAPRIKO 107
+41 79 632 6889
hello@papriko.com
www.papriko.com

SOYOON PARK 184
917 733 7078
soyoonpark911@gmail.com
www.soyoonpark.com

NISHAN PATEL 233
609 610 0732
nishanarts@gmail.com
www.nishanpatel.com

VALERIA PETRONE 350
+39 345 618 7878
valeria@valeriapetrone.com
www.valeriapetrone.com
www.morgangaynin.com

NOAH PATRICK PFARR 165
503 866 2623
noah@noahillustration.com
www.noahillustration.com

LEAH PALMER PREISS 331
919 833 8443
curiouser@mindspring.com
www.leahpalmerpreiss.com

ELENA PRETTE 159, 189
+39 339 833 2099
Info@elenaprette.com
www.elenaprette.com

SEAN G. QUALLS 128
718 768 8133
seanqualls@hotmail.com
www.seanqualls.com

MAURIZIO QUARELLO 212
+39 333 543 5049
maurizio@quarello.com
www.quarello.com
www.morgangaynin.com

JASON RAISH 271
917 690 2251
jason@jasonraish.com
www.jasonraish.com

CLAUDE RAMEY 26
512 992 3851
claude.ramey@gmail.com
www.claudcramey.com

STEPH RANSOM 268
+61 39 384 6786
steph@stephransom.com
www.stephransom.com

MARIA RENDON 210
626 695 7123
maria@mariarendon.com
www.mariarendon.com

MARCELA RESTREPO 29, 238
+61 43 145 3065
lefthandside@gmail.com
www.marcelarestrepo.com
www.jackywinter.com

MARIAN HEIBEL RICHARDSON 168
239 403 4393
marianhr@comcast.net
www.marianrichardson.com
www.joaniebrep.com

CAROLYN RIDSDALE 82
+61 29 705 0498
carolyn@carolynridsdale.nl
www.carolynridsdale.com

JOHN RIORDAN 127
+44 781 513 4473
john@johnriordan.co.uk
www.johnriordan.co.uk

LIZZIE ROBERTS 244
+49 179 793 9187
mail@illugrafique.com
www.illugrafique.com

PAUL ROGERS 100, 239
626 564 8728
paulrogers@attglobal.net
www.paulrogersstudio.com
www.heflinreps.com

KIM ROSEN 140
845 591 0682
kim@kimrosen.com
www.kimrosen.com
www.jenvaughnart.com

MATT ROTA 63
410 493 0521
mattrota@mattrotasart.com
www.mattrotasart.com

TAKAYUKI RYUJIN 248
+33 360 6965
ryujing@yb3.so-net.ne.jp
www.tap-room.net

JOSEPH SALINA 126
416 367 8421
j.salina@sympatico.ca
www.josephsalina.ca

SHELLEY SAVOR 160
905 508 6172
shsavor@me.com
www.shelleysavor.com

JEREMY SCHILLING 344
860 908 0606
jeremyschil@gmail.com
www.jeremyschilling.carbonmade.com

FLORIAN SCHMITT 62, 85
+49 1766 216 3033
Info@florianart.com
www.florianart.de

RICK SEALOCK 319
519 744 2412
sealock@rogers.com
www.ricksealock.com

SERGE SEIDLITZ 56, 386
+44 771 890 2506
mail@sergeseidlitz.com
www.sergeseidlitz.com
www.debutart.com

JASON SEILER 109
212 223 9545
seilerillustration@gmail.com
www.jasonseiler.com

ANDREW SELBY 259
+44 797 327 1449
andrew.selby1@virgin.net
www.andrew-selby.com

THOM SEVALRUD 363
416 922 9303
thom@thomsevalrud.com
www.thomsevalrud.com
www.i2iart.com

MICHAEL SHEEHY 329
+44 137 989 0917
michael.sheehy@btinternet.com
www.michaelsheehy.co.uk

STEVE SIMPSON 310
+35 387 265 9641
mail@stevesimpson.com
www.stevesimpson.com

LAURA SMITH 181, 186
323 467 1700
laura@laurasmithart.com
www.laurasmithart.com

ALENKA SOTTLER 59, 150, 155, 340, 343
+38 64 138 4750
alenka.sottler@guest.arnes.si
www.sottler.si

SQUID 341, 384
+44 774 609 9737
squidishere@gmail.com
www.squidishere.com

CARLO STANGA 237, 311
+20 336 604 4002
carlo@carlostanga.com
www.carlostanga.com
www.morgangaynin.com

BRIAN STAUFFER 47, 74, 98, 161, 269, 275
866 220 3142
brian@brianstauffer.com
www.brianstauffer.com

JUDY STEAD 110
704 877 5988
judy@judystead.com
www.judystead.com
www.morgangaynin.com

OTTO STEININGER 245, 246, 295
646 706 6229
ottosteininger@gmail.com
www.ottosteininger.com
www.threeinabox.com

ERIKA STEISKAL 134
330 718 1283
erikasteiskal@yahoo.com
www.erikasteiskal.com

DANIEL STOLLE 43
+35 8045 232 2600
daniel@d-stolle.de
www.d-stolle.de
www.agoodson.com

STEVEN STREISGUTH 255
862 432 5637
steve.streisguth@gmail.com
www.streisguth.com

STEVEN TABBUTT 130, 241, 280
917 207 9706
stovetabbutt@nyc.rr.com
www.steventabbutt.com

BINNY TALIB 197
212 663 2311
binny@binny.com.au
www.binny.com.au
www.painted-words.com

AI TATEBAYASHI 66
917 821 4329
ai@miniai.com
www.miniai.com

DANTE TERZIGNI 366
216 832 9495
dterzigni@yahoo.com
www.danteterzigni.com

JACOB THOMAS 81, 106
718 795 7447
jthomasillustration@gmail.com
www.jthomasillustration.com

DAVEY THOMPSON 207
780 668 2330
daveythompson@mac.com
www.daveythompsonillustration.com

ANGELINE THONG 218
415 613 1176
kisengure@gmail.com
www.fng.carbonmade.com

SUE TODD 243
416 784 5313
sustodd@rogers.com
www.suetodd.com

KEIKO TOKUSHIMA 247, 365
646 248 9443
keiko@keikotokushima.com
www.keikotokushima.com

TIM TOMKINSON 35
917 952 1549
timtomkinson@mac.com
www.timtomkinson.com

ANTHONY TREMMAGLIA 57
613 255 4972
anthony@tremmaglia.ca
www.tremmaglia.ca

JIM TSINGANOS 48, 87
+61 42 526 3926
jim@tsinganos.com
www.tsinganos.com

POL TURGEON 330
514 273 8329
pol@polturgeon.com
www.polturgeon.com
www.lindgrensmith.com

RICHARD TUSCHMAN 51, 180
216 702 3088
rt@richardtuschman.com
www.richardtuschman.com

SARA TYSON 328
705 378 0893
sara@saratyson.com
www.saratyson.com

KURT VARGO 137
912 897 9595
kvargo@scad.edu
www.vargoart.com

RICCARDO VECCHIO 129
917 291 7618
vecchio.riccardo@gmail.com
www.riccardovecchio.com

GARY VENN 143
+64 21 124 1759
gvenn.illustration@gmail.com
www.garyvennillustration.com

MARCO VENTURA 120, 123
+39 02 832 1374
marcoventura@tiscali.it
www.venturamarco.com

GONCALO VIANA 367
+35 191 632 2606
mail@goncaloviana.com
www.goncaloviana.com

STEFANO VITALE 351, 378
+39 04 171 9273
stefanovitale@hotmail.com
www.stefanovitale.com
www.lindgrensmith.com

SALLY VITSKY 299
804 355 3815
svitsky@comcast.net
www.vitsky.com

CONSTANZE VON KITZING 224
+49 178 31 3351
info@constanzevonkitzing.de
www.constanzevonkitzing.de

ANDREA WAN 38, 251
778 883 8585
andrea@andreawan.com
www.andreawan.com

ELLEN WEINSTEIN 264
917 653 4097
ellen@ellenweinstein.com
www.ellenweinstein.com

JAKOB WESTMAN 23
+46 70 545 4940
me@jakobwestman.com
www.jakobwestman.com

ELYSE WHITTAKER-PAEK 190
626 215 3248
elyseaussie@gmail.com
www.elyse.biz

CARL WIENS 78, 272
613 476 2500
wiens@kos.net
www.carlwiens.com

MICK WIGGINS 39
510 524 3076
mick@mickwiggins.com
www.mickwiggins.com

JONATHAN WILLIAMS 177
+44 5600 479 886*
contact@jonathanwilliams.co.uk
www.jonathanwilliams.co.uk

TANIA WILLIS 236
+85 29 641 9600
taniawillis@hkstar.com
www.taniawillis.com

KATIA WISH 225
978 857 2390
katia@katiawish.com
www.katiawish.com

PHIL WRIGGLESWORTH 352
+44 793 979 4267
phil@philwrigglesworth.com
www.philwrigglesworth.com

STEPHANIE WUNDERLICH 69
+43 40 4325 0200
info@wunderlich-illustration.de
www.wunderlich-illustration.de
www.threeinabox.com

AYAKO YAMAZAKI 234
+44 888 9470
info@aymzk.jp
www.ayakoym.exblog.jp

JAMES YANG 356
212 807 6627
james@jamesyang.com
www.jamesyang.com
www.davidgoldmanagency.com

HEIDI YOUNGER 167, 273, 291
631 356 5176
heidi@heidiyounger.com
www.heidiyounger.com

YEJI YUN 345
+44 786 815 3062
seeouterspace@gmail.com
www.seeouterspace.com/studio

VINCENT ZAWADA 116, 317
970 424 0342
vzawada@yahoo.com
www.vincentzawada.com

TINA ZELLMER 380
+49 17 7779 5921
info@tinazellmer.com
www.tinazellmer.com
www.agoodson.com

HENNING ZIEGLER 169
+49 30 4737 2302
buero@henningziegler.de
www.henningziegler.de

Remember you'll also find direct links
to their site and/or their reps site at
3x3directory.com